HARCOURT
Science

Harcourt School Publishers

Orlando • Boston • Dallas • Chicago • San D

www.harcourtschool.com

Cover Image

The saw-whet owl (*Aegolius acadicus*) is 17–19 cm (about 6.5–7.0 in.) tall. It lives in Canada, the United States, and Mexico. It eats small birds, mammals, and frogs. Sometimes it eats birds and mammals as large as itself!

Printed in the United States of America

ISBN 0-15-311209-3

11 12 13 14 15 16 17 18 19 20 032 10 09 08 07 06 05

Authors

Marjorie Slavick Frank
Former Adjunct Faculty Member at
    Hunter, Brooklyn, and Manhattan
    Colleges
New York, New York

Robert M. Jones
Professor of Education
University of Houston-Clear Lake
Houston, Texas

Gerald H. Krockover
Professor of Earth and Atmospheric
    Science Education
School Mathematics and Science
    Center
Purdue University
West Lafayette, Indiana

Mozell P. Lang
Science Education Consultant
Michigan Department of Education
Lansing, Michigan

Joyce C. McLeod
Visiting Professor
Rollins College
Winter Park, Florida

Carol J. Valenta
Vice President—Education, Exhibits,
    and Programs
St. Louis Science Center
St. Louis, Missouri

Barry A. Van Deman
Science Program Director
Arlington, Virginia

iv

UNIT B

LIFE SCIENCE

Living Things Grow and Respond

UNIT C

EARTH SCIENCE
The Living Planet

PHYSICAL SCIENCE

Matter and Energy

UNIT F

PHYSICAL SCIENCE

Forces and Machines

Using Science Process Skills

When scientists try to find an answer to a question or do an experiment, they use thinking tools called process skills. You use many of the process skills whenever you think, listen, read, and write. Think about how these students used process skills to help them answer questions and do experiments.

Eileen is finding feathers to add to her feather collection. She **observes** them carefully. She **compares** them to see how they are alike and how they are different. Then she **classifies** them into groups by their colors.

Try This Use the process skills of observing, comparing, and classifying to organize your own collection of nature objects.

Talk About It By what other characteristics could Eileen classify her feather collection?

Process Skills

Observe — use the senses to learn about objects and events

Compare — to observe characteristics of things or events and observe how they are alike or different

Classify — to organize objects or events into groups based on certain characteristics

Brett wants to plant a vegetable garden. He observes that plants seem to grow strong and healthy on the left side of his backyard. On the right side, the plants are small and thin. He wonders if the soil on the left side of the garden will be better for growing his vegetables. He decides to **gather, record,** and **display data** about the soil. He takes a liter of soil from the left side of the backyard, places it in a jar, and adds a liter of water. He screws the top on the jar, shakes it, and lets the soil settle. He does the same thing with soil from the right side of the back yard. He makes notes and draws pictures about his investigation.

When the soil has settled, Brett observes the jars. He sees that the soil in the jar has settled in layers. In the jar from the left side of the yard, he observes a thin layer of pebbles, a thin layer of sand, and a thick layer of black dirt. In the jar from the right side, he observes a thick layer of pebbles and a thick layer of sand. He doesn't see any black dirt. He **predicts** that if he plants in the soil with the black dirt, his vegetables will grow better.

Try This Gather, record, and display data about a topic that interests you. Make a prediction based on your observations.

Talk About It How did gathering and recording data help Brett make his prediction?

Process Skills

Gather data — to make observations to use to make inferences

Record data — to write down observations

Display data — to show data in tables, charts, or graphs

Predict — to form an idea of an expected outcome based on observations or experience

Tamara needs a jacket. The one she likes comes in either black or white. Tamara wonders which jacket would be warmer. She **hypothesizes** that the black jacket will be warmer than the white one. She **plans and conducts a simple investigation** to find out if her hypothesis is correct.

Tamara places a black sheet of paper and a white sheet of paper in the sun. She lays a thermometer in the center of each piece so she can measure the temperature of the paper. She sets a stopwatch for 30 minutes.

When the stopwatch signals, Tamara checks the thermometers. The thermometer on the black paper shows 28°C, the white paper shows 23°C. Tamara **infers** that black objects absorb more light than white objects, so the black jacket will be warmer.

Try This Make a hypothesis about something you are interested in. Plan and conduct an investigation to test your hypothesis.

Talk About It Would Tamara's hypothesis be correct if the jackets were made of two different materials? Why or why not?

Process Skills

Hypothesize — to make a statement about an expected outcome based on observation, knowledge, and experience

Plan and conduct simple investigations — to identify and perform the steps necessary to find the answer to a question, using appropriate tools and recording and analyzing the data collected

Infer — use logical reasoning to explain events and make conclusions based on observations

Jake is packaging a glass vase to mail to his grandmother. He wants to package it in a way that will prevent damage to it in the mail. He read an ad that said bubbled plastic wrap would protect it best. He plans an experiment to test the bubbled wrap against other protective padding.

First Jake **identifies and controls the variables** that will affect his experiment. He finds three boxes that are exactly the same. He gets bubbled plastic wrap, a bag of foam peanuts, some newspapers, and three eggs. He wraps one egg in bubbled plastic wrap and places it in a box, making sure the egg and wrap fill the box. He pours foam peanuts into the second box, filling it half full. He places an egg in the middle of that box, and then fills it the rest of the way with foam peanuts. He half-fills the third box with crumpled newspapers, adds the egg, and then fills the box with the newspaper. He tapes all three boxes closed.

Jake places the three boxes near the edge of a table. He gently pushes the boxes over the edge. Then he opens the boxes to see if any eggs are broken. He finds that the egg padded by newspaper is the only one broken. He infers that the bubbled plastic wrap is more protective than newspaper. He will **experiment** to further test the bubbled plastic wrap against the foam peanuts.

Try This Plan an experiment to test different brands of a product your family uses. Identify the variables that you will control.

Talk About It Did Jake's experiment help him find the answer to his question? What could he do for a second experiment?

Process Skills

Identify and Control Variables — identify and control factors that affect the outcome of an experiment

Experiment — design ways to collect data under controlled conditions to test a hypothesis

You will have many opportunities to practice and apply these and other process skills in *Harcourt Science.* An exciting year of science discoveries lies ahead!

LIQUID STARCH
32 fl. oz. (1 QT) 946mL

Safety in Science

Doing investigations in science can be fun, but you need to be sure you do them safely. Here are some rules to follow.

1 **Think ahead.** Study the steps of the investigation so you know what to expect. If you have any questions, ask your teacher. Be sure you understand any safety symbols that are shown.

2 **Be neat.** Keep your work area clean. If you have long hair, pull it back so it doesn't get in the way. Roll or push up long sleeves to keep them away from your experiment.

3 **Oops!** If you should spill or break something, or get cut, tell your teacher right away.

4 **Watch your eyes.** Wear safety goggles anytime you are directed to do so. If you get anything in your eyes, tell your teacher right away.

5 **Yuck!** Never eat or drink anything during a science activity unless you are told to do so by your teacher.

6 **Don't get shocked.** Be especially careful if an electric appliance is used. Be sure that electric cords are in a safe place where you can't trip over them. Don't ever pull a plug out of an outlet by pulling on the cord.

7 **Keep it clean.** Always clean up when you have finished. Put everything away and wipe your work area. Wash your hands.

In some activities you will see these symbols. They are signs for what you need to be safe.

Be especially careful.

Wear safety goggles.

Be careful with sharp objects.

Don't get burned.

Protect your clothes.

Protect your hands with mitts.

Be careful with electricity.

Understanding Living Things

LIFE SCIENCE

Understanding Living Things

Unit Project

Cell Model

Use clay to make a model of an animal cell. Label the parts of the cell by placing labels on toothpicks and sticking the toothpicks in the clay. Write a report in which you compare an animal cell to a plant cell. Describe how they are different from each other.

Chapter 1

Cells, Genetics, and Heredity

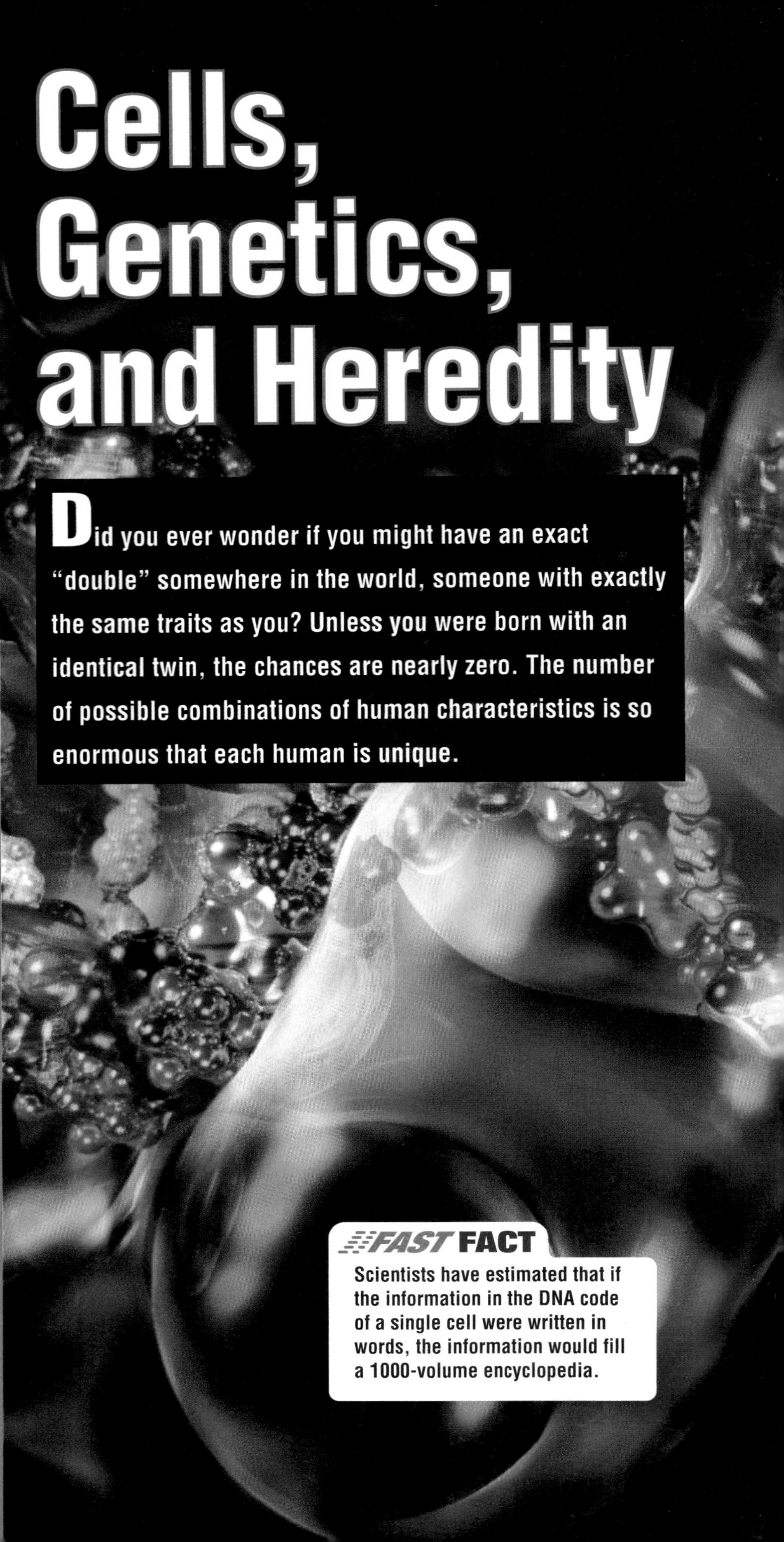

Did you ever wonder if you might have an exact "double" somewhere in the world, someone with exactly the same traits as you? Unless you were born with an identical twin, the chances are nearly zero. The number of possible combinations of human characteristics is so enormous that each human is unique.

Vocabulary Preview

cell membrane
cell wall
cytoplasm
mitochondria
chloroplast
vacuole
nucleus
chromosome
nuclear membrane
DNA
genes
mitosis
meiosis
sexual reproduction
dominant
recessive
Punnett square

FAST FACT

Scientists have estimated that if the information in the DNA code of a single cell were written in words, the information would fill a 1000-volume encyclopedia.

Gregor Mendel studied the inherited traits of pea plants for a period of eight years. During this time he grew over 30,000 plants.

It's impossible to guess from an organism's size the number of chromosomes its cells have. A goldfish has 94 chromosomes, while humans have only 46.

Amoeba

Chromosomes per Cell in Various Organisms

Organism	Chromosomes
mosquito	6
housefly	12
pea	14
onion	16
carrot	18
starfish	36
human	46
amoeba	50
dog	78
goldfish	94

An artist's idea of what DNA looks like

How Do Plant and Animal Cells Differ?

In this lesson, you can . . .

INVESTIGATE the parts that make up a plant cell.

LEARN ABOUT the parts of plant and animal cells and how the cell parts work.

LINK to math, writing, technology, and other areas.

INVESTIGATE

The Structure of Cells

Activity Purpose The parts of a cell are much too small to see without magnification. In this investigation you will **observe** photographs of plant cells as seen through a microscope. Then you will use your observations to **make a model** of a typical plant cell.

Materials

- plastic jar
- water
- 2 balloons
- index cards
- plastic bag
- sand
- red and green clay

Activity Procedure

1 **Observe** the pictures of the magnified plant cells. Find the parts that all the cells have in common.

2 Now use your observations to write a plan for how you will **make a model** of a typical plant cell. Decide how you can best show the cell, using the materials you have.

3 Show your plan to your teacher. When your teacher approves, make your model. (Picture A)

4 **Observe** your model. Write a description of each cell part you have modeled, and tell what you think the part's function might be. Use a separate index card for each cell part.

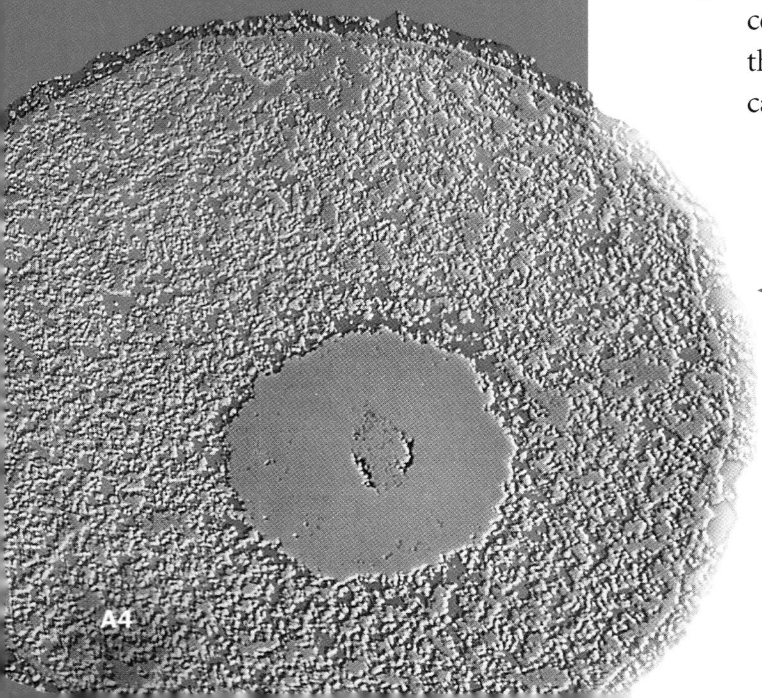

◀ All living things are made up of cells similar to the one shown here.

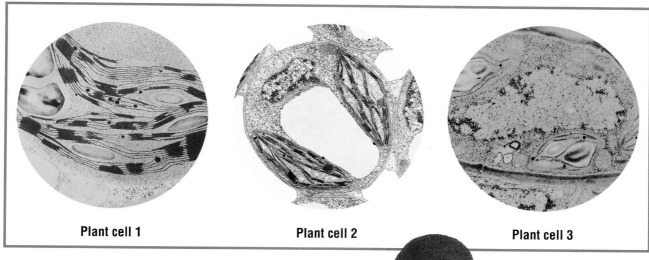

Plant cell 1   Plant cell 2   Plant cell 3

Draw Conclusions

1. Why was it useful to **observe** several plant cells before making your model?

2. What can you **infer** about the function of the thick layer that surrounds the cell?

3. What can you **infer** about the function of the thin layer that lines the cell?

4. **Scientists at Work** Scientists often **make models** to help them make inferences. How did making a model help you make inferences about the parts of a cell?

Picture A

Investigate Further Use a Microslide viewer or microscope with prepared slides and look at three more plant cells. What differences do you see? How would you use these observations to change the model you made in this activity?

Process Skill Tip

Cells and their parts are too small to handle. When you **use a model,** you can handle the parts, move them around, and **infer** how they might work together.

How Plant and Animal Cells Differ

The Discovery of Cells

- what the cell theory is
- the similarities and differences between plant and animal cells

VOCABULARY

cell membrane
cell wall
cytoplasm
mitochondria
chloroplast
vacuole
nucleus
chromosome
nuclear
    membrane
DNA

Take a close look at a living thing, such as a plant leaf. No matter how hard you try, you won't be able to see its cells. Most cells are so small that thousands could fit on the period at the end of this sentence. Nobody even knew about cells until they could be magnified enough to be seen.

People built the first microscopes about 350 years ago. Microscopes magnified tiny things, opening up a whole new world to the scientists of the time. One of the first people to study the tiny building blocks that make up all living things was an English scientist named Robert Hooke. People still call these structures *cells*, the name that Hooke gave them more than 300 years ago.

✔ **Before the invention of the microscope, why couldn't scientists learn what living things were made of?**

In 1665, using a microscope he built himself, Robert Hooke observed a thin slice of cork. He saw something never seen before. Hooke drew a picture of the hundreds of "tiny boxes" that he saw through his microscope. The boxes reminded him of the rooms in a monastery. Hooke gave them the same name—*cells*. ▶

▼ **Hooke's drawing of the cork cells he saw through the microscope**

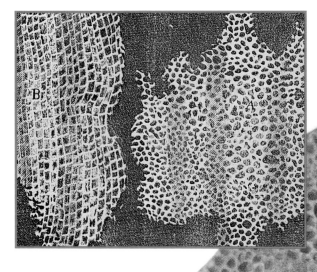

The Cell Theory

Since microscopes were invented in the 1600s, they have become much more powerful. As a result, scientists have discovered a lot about what cells are made of and what they do. By the end of the 1800s, scientists had a theory—the cell theory—that summarized much of what they had learned. The cell theory has three main parts:

Cells are the basic building blocks of all living things. All living things are made up of cells. Larger organisms most often have more cells and more kinds of cells than smaller organisms do. A human being, for example, has about 50 billion cells of more than 200 kinds. The photographs on this page show some of the kinds of cells in plants and animals.

All life activities take place in cells. Each kind of cell carries out the activities for which it is adapted. Movement, for example, happens because muscle cells contract, or shorten.

New cells are produced by existing cells. New cells come from other cells, not from anything else. Because organisms are made up of cells, the only way an organism can grow larger is by producing new cells. Your body grows because new cells are produced by existing cells. New cells also replace damaged or worn-out cells. Millions of the cells in your body die every second, but new cells are produced to take their place. Your skin, for example, is continuously producing new cells as old skin cells die and fall away.

✔ **What are the three parts of the cell theory?**

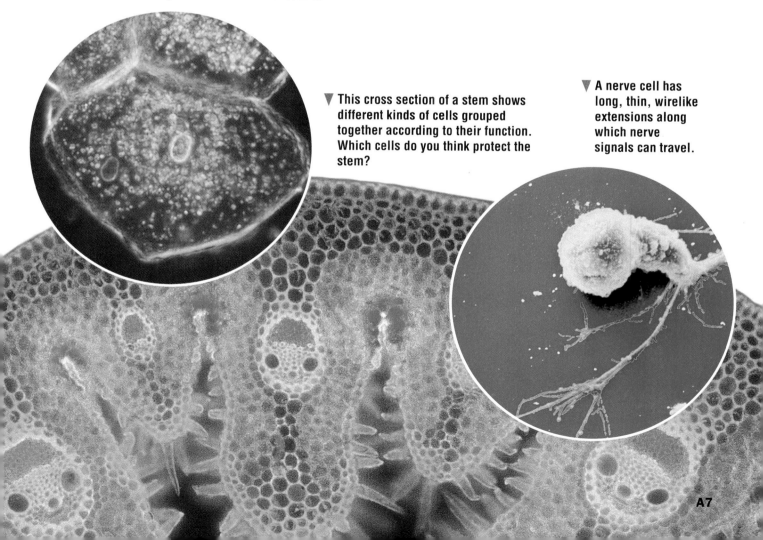

▼ **A cheek cell is flat and tough to protect the tissue beneath it.**

▼ **This cross section of a stem shows different kinds of cells grouped together according to their function. Which cells do you think protect the stem?**

▼ **A nerve cell has long, thin, wirelike extensions along which nerve signals can travel.**

The Parts of a Cell

You learned that cells have different functions and different shapes and sizes. However, all cells in all living things are alike in some ways.

All cells are covered with a thin layer called the **cell membrane**. This membrane holds the cell material inside and controls what enters and leaves the cell. The membrane lets food, oxygen, and water flow into the cell when they are needed, and it lets the cell's wastes flow out.

Plant cells have a **cell wall**—a stiff outer layer that protects the cell and gives it shape.

Cell walls remain long after the rest of the cell dies. Cell walls are what Hooke saw when he observed cork through a microscope. Animal cells do not have cell walls.

Inside the cell membrane in both plant and animal cells is a colorless, jellylike substance called **cytoplasm** (SYT•oh•plaz•uhm). The cytoplasm holds the cell's *organelles*, tiny structures that carry out cell activities.

Each kind of organelle has a specific function. Bean-shaped organelles called **mitochondria** (myt•oh•KAHN•dree•uh) release the energy

THE INSIDE STORY

Comparing Animal and Plant Cells

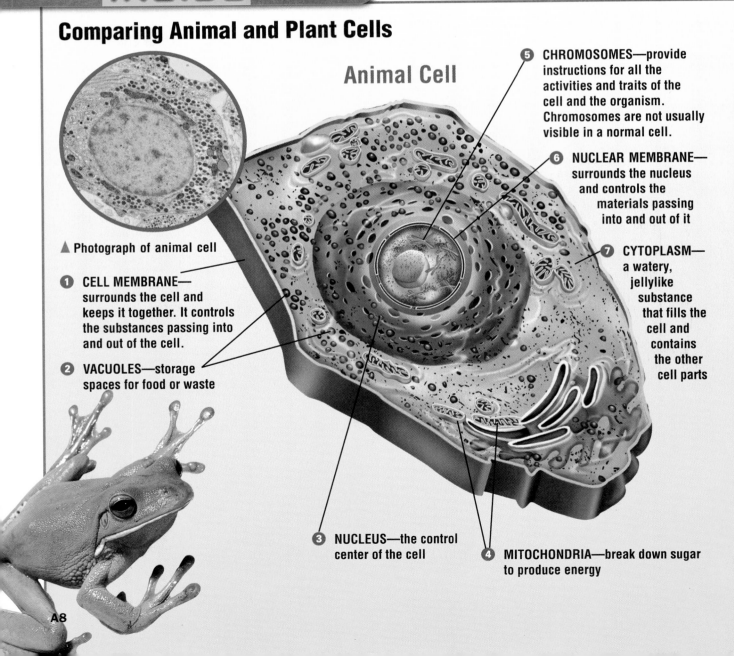

Animal Cell

▲ Photograph of animal cell

5 CHROMOSOMES—provide instructions for all the activities and traits of the cell and the organism. Chromosomes are not usually visible in a normal cell.

6 NUCLEAR MEMBRANE—surrounds the nucleus and controls the materials passing into and out of it

7 CYTOPLASM—a watery, jellylike substance that fills the cell and contains the other cell parts

1 CELL MEMBRANE—surrounds the cell and keeps it together. It controls the substances passing into and out of the cell.

2 VACUOLES—storage spaces for food or waste

3 NUCLEUS—the control center of the cell

4 MITOCHONDRIA—break down sugar to produce energy

stored in sugars to carry out the cell's activities. Each cell in your body contains between ten and several hundred mitochondria.

Plant cells contain a kind of organelle called a **chloroplast** (KLAUR•oh•plast) that enables the plant to make its own food. (Animals cannot make their own food. Their cells do not contain chloroplasts.) A **vacuole** (VAK•yoo•ohl) is a space in a cell enclosed by a membrane. Food, water, and wastes are stored in vacuoles.

Most cells have an organelle called the **nucleus**. The nucleus is the control center of the cell and directs all the cell's activities. It contains chromosomes. A **chromosome** (KROH•muh•sohm) is a structure that contains the information necessary to determine characteristics of the organism. The **nuclear membrane** surrounds the nucleus and holds it together.

✔ **What structures do plant cells have that animal cells do not have?**

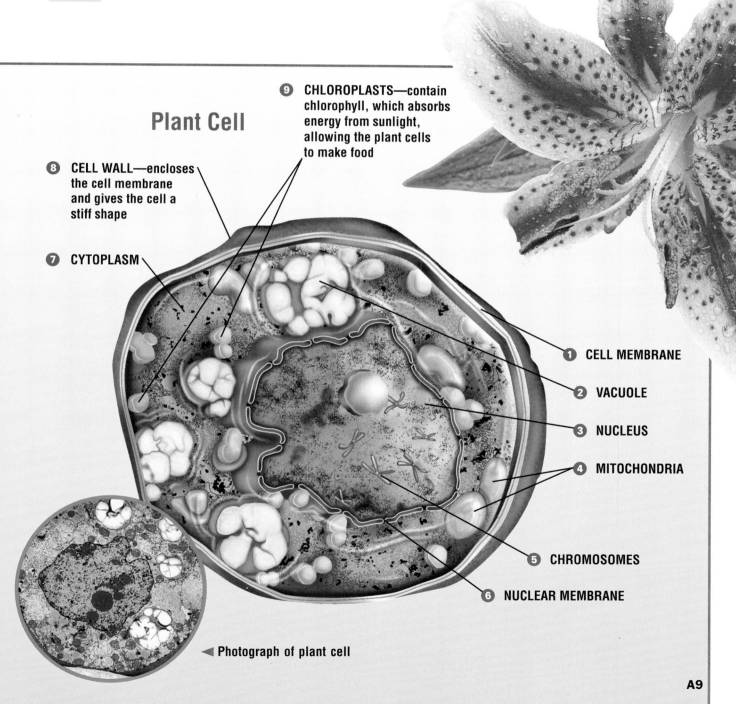

Plant Cell

9 CHLOROPLASTS—contain chlorophyll, which absorbs energy from sunlight, allowing the plant cells to make food

8 CELL WALL—encloses the cell membrane and gives the cell a stiff shape

7 CYTOPLASM

1 CELL MEMBRANE

2 VACUOLE

3 NUCLEUS

4 MITOCHONDRIA

5 CHROMOSOMES

6 NUCLEAR MEMBRANE

◀ Photograph of plant cell

The Nucleus of a Cell

When you read about the cell theory, you learned that cells perform all the activities of a living organism. Just as a car needs a driver to control it, a cell needs instructions to work properly.

The nucleus is the control center of the cell. It contains chromosomes, tiny structures that look like rods. Chromosomes are made of proteins and **DNA**, a complex chemical that contains information about every part of an organism. DNA directs the life activities of the cell.

Some people call DNA "the blueprint of life." A blueprint for a house contains the information and instructions about how the house is built. In a similar way, the DNA in a cell contains the information and instructions about how the cell is built.

The photograph below shows the nucleus of a cell magnified many thousands of times. The nuclear membrane surrounds the nucleus and separates it from the rest of the cell. The nucleus sends out its instructions—in the form of chemicals—through tiny openings in the nuclear membrane. The chemicals are instructions for specific functions of the cell.

✔ **Why is the nucleus considered the control center of the cell?**

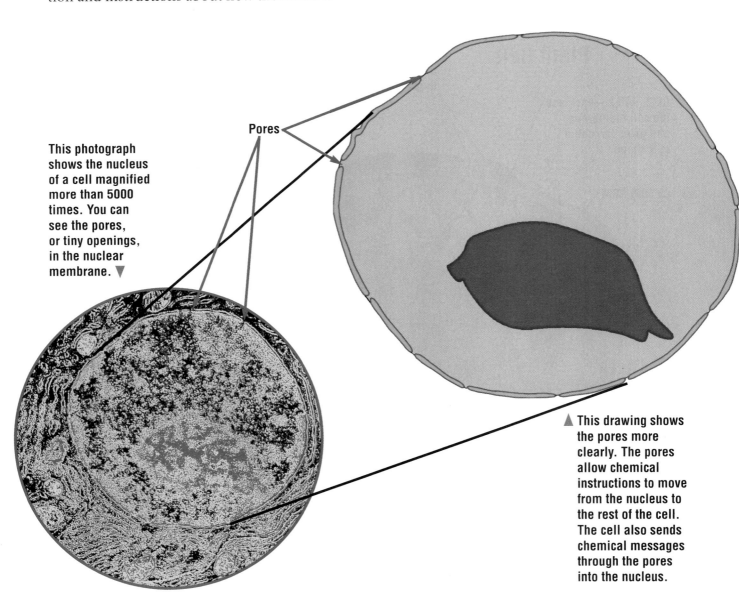

Pores

This photograph shows the nucleus of a cell magnified more than 5000 times. You can see the pores, or tiny openings, in the nuclear membrane. ▼

▲ This drawing shows the pores more clearly. The pores allow chemical instructions to move from the nucleus to the rest of the cell. The cell also sends chemical messages through the pores into the nucleus.

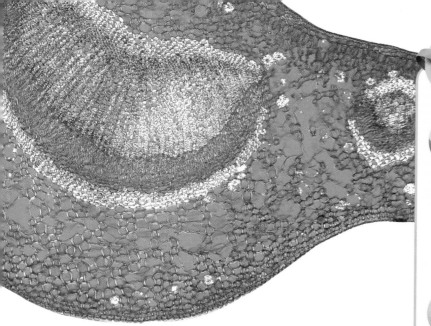

▲ A magnification of a plant cross-section shows the many different kinds of cells that help the plant survive.

Summary

According to the cell theory, all living things are made up of cells. All activities of living things take place in cells. All new cells come from existing cells. Plant and animal cells both have a cell membrane, cytoplasm, a nucleus, mitochondria, and vacuoles. Plant cells also have a cell wall and chloroplasts. The nucleus of a cell controls the cell's activities.

Review

1. How did cells get their name?
2. How does an organism grow larger?
3. What are the three parts of the cell theory?
4. **Critical Thinking** Which of your cells would you expect to have more mitochondria: your muscle cells or your bone cells? Explain your answer.
5. **Test Prep** Which of the following has a cell wall?
   A a nerve cell
   B a leaf cell
   C a cheek cell
   D a bone cell

LINKS

MATH LINK

How Small? A stack of 10 sheets of paper is about 1 mm thick. The thickness of a red blood cell is about $\frac{1}{20}$ the thickness of a single sheet of paper. A micron is 0.001 mm, so there are 1000 microns in a millimeter. How thick is a red blood cell in microns?

WRITING LINK

Informative Writing—Compare and Contrast Write an explanation that would help a fourth-grade student compare and contrast animal and plant cells.

SOCIAL STUDIES LINK

History of Science The cell theory resulted from the work of many scientists over a period of 200 years. Find out about the contributions of Matthias Schleiden, Antoni van Leeuwenhoek, Theodor Schwann, and Rudolf Virchow to the cell theory.

ART LINK

A Very Small City Think of ways to compare a cell and its parts with a small factory or a village. Imagine how you could represent each cell part. Mitochondria, for example, could be electric generators. Make a drawing or painting of your version of a cell.

TECHNOLOGY LINK

Learn more about plant and animal cells by visiting this Internet site.
www.scilinks.org/harcourt

SCI**LINKS**™
THE WORLD'S A CLICK AWAY

LESSON 2

How Do Cells Reproduce?

In this lesson, you can . . .

INVESTIGATE how exact copies are made of cells.

LEARN ABOUT two different ways in which cells reproduce.

LINK to math, writing, technology, and other areas.

A cell splitting to form two new cells ▽

INVESTIGATE

How New Cells Are Made

Activity Purpose According to the cell theory, new cells can come only from existing cells. In this investigation you will **observe** the growth of cells in an onion root tip. You will use your observations to **infer** how cells produce exact copies of themselves.

Materials
- Microslide viewer
- Microslide of onion root tip

Activity Procedure

1 You will **observe** one instant in the life of the onion root tip. At that instant, different cells were preserved at different stages of cell division. Place the slide on the microviewer. Adjust the focus so that you can **observe** the cells. (Picture A)

2 **Record** your observations of cell division by drawing at least four stages of division. (Picture B)

This is a slice of the root tip of an onion. What you see is a single layer of cells that are no longer alive. A dye has been added so the structures inside the cells can be seen. Find the areas where new cells are being produced. ▼

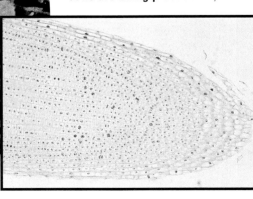

Picture A

Picture B

3 **Show the sequence** of the process of cell division by numbering your drawings from 1 to 4.

Draw Conclusions

1. How could you tell that the cells you observed were dividing?

2. In what order do the stages of cell division occur? Describe each of the cells you drew.

3. **Scientists at Work** Scientists sometimes need to find the sequence of events to better understand a process. What clues might a scientist studying the division of onion cells look for in order to figure out the sequence?

Investigate Further Look at other slides of plant cells. Try to find any areas other than the root tip where plant cells are dividing. If you have access to a microscope, use one to observe prepared slides of an onion root tip. See page R5 for tips on using a microscope.

Process Skill Tip

To **show the sequence** of a group of events or items, first **compare** them carefully. Their differences should give you clues to the correct order.

How Cells Reproduce

How Do Plants and Animals Grow?

In the investigation, you observed onion cells producing new cells. Each dividing cell is too small to have a large effect on the onion plant. But many cells in the onion root divide at the same time. The cells they produce also divide, producing still more cells. Together, all of this activity has a large effect on the onion plant—it grows.

Most living things begin life as a single cell. The series of photographs below shows how a single cell can grow and multiply until it has produced a fully formed frog. Frogs' eggs are easy to see because they are large. As you can see in the photographs, the single egg cell splits into two cells. Those two cells then split, producing a total of four cells and then eight cells. The cells keep dividing this way, and by the time a tadpole hatches, it is made up of millions of cells.

You began life as a single cell, which divided to form new cells. As your cells divided, you grew inside your mother's body. By the time you were born, you were made up of billions of cells. They were not all the same. Some were bone cells, some were muscle cells, and some were skin cells.

◀ One cell

The small pictures show three stages in the reproduction of cells in a frog embryo. The embryo starts as a single cell. The cell divides and forms new cells until a tadpole hatches. The tadpole can eventually grow to become a frog. (Eggs magnified about 50 times)

▲ Two cells

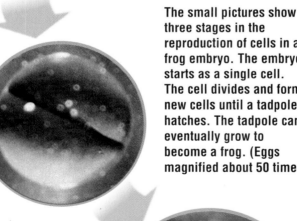

Eight cells ▶

After you were born, you kept growing because your cells continued to divide. You'll keep growing bigger and taller as your cells keep dividing. But will you grow bigger and bigger every year of your life?

Most living things do not grow at the same rate throughout their lives. Growth often starts slowly, gets faster, and then slows down or stops. The graph shows the typical growth rate of a plant. Many living things have a similar pattern of growth.

Throughout your life your body cells continue to divide and replace cells that are damaged or worn out. However, you will probably stop growing larger sometime before you are 21 years old. The rate of cell division in your body will change, according to the instructions sent by your DNA.

✔ **When do plants grow fast, and when do they grow slowly?**

▼ **The chromosomes in the nucleus of a cell carry genes, which are made up of DNA.**

DNA, the Blueprint of Life

The DNA in each cell controls the entire development of an organism. It is the "master plan" for every one of the organism's cells.

In the last lesson, you learned that the nucleus of both plant and animal cells contains chromosomes. Chromosomes contain sections of DNA called **genes**. Genes control specific cell activities and characteristics of every organism.

A human has 46 chromosomes and about 50,000 genes. Some genes control eye color. Others control height.

When body cells divide, the new cells have the same DNA as the original cell. Every one of an organism's body cells contains the same complete DNA. The DNA code that instructs the human brain to develop is also found in the cells of a person's liver. However, DNA codes are used only when they are needed. The DNA that instructs brain cells to grow is switched off in every cell except brain cells.

✔ **Where is an organism's DNA located?**

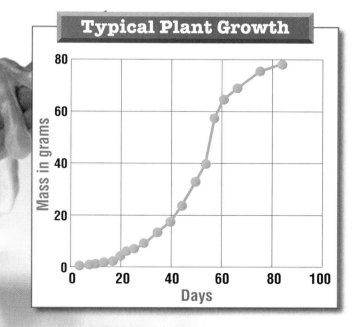

Typical Plant Growth

▲ This graph shows the typical growth rate of a plant.

Mitosis

Take a look at your hand. Knowing how small each cell is, you can't even imagine how many cells are in just one fingertip. You began life as a single cell, so the cells in your body must have divided millions and millions of times.

When a cell divides, some parts simply split into two. But the nucleus of the dividing cell cannot simply split into two parts, because all of the chromosomes from the original cell are needed in each new cell. If the chromosomes were simply divided into two groups, each new cell would have only half of the DNA. If cells continued to divide, the amount of DNA would keep decreasing. But a complete set of chromosomes is needed for every body cell.

The diagram shows what happens to a cell's chromosomes during cell division. Each of the chromosomes is copied exactly. The two identical sets of chromosomes are sorted out so that each new cell gets a complete set. The process of cell division that produces new body cells with complete sets of chromosomes is called **mitosis** (my•TOH•sis).

The cell in the diagram is from an organism that has two pairs of chromosomes, or four in all. Before mitosis, the chromosomes are copied so the cell has eight chromosomes. The chromosomes and their copies are joined at their centers and line up along the middle of the cell. They then split apart. One set of chromosomes goes to each side of the cell. Two new cells form.

Each new cell is an exact copy of the original cell. On page A18 you can observe photographs of the stages of mitosis.

✓ **If a cell that has 20 chromosomes undergoes mitosis, how many chromosomes will each of the new cells have? Explain.**

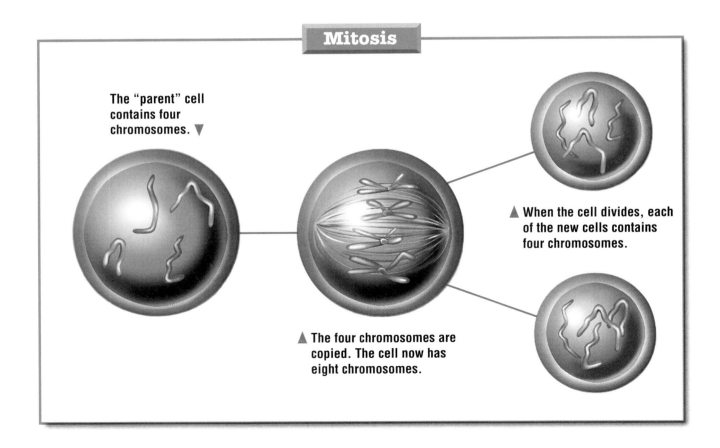

Mitosis

The "parent" cell contains four chromosomes. ▼

▲ When the cell divides, each of the new cells contains four chromosomes.

▲ The four chromosomes are copied. The cell now has eight chromosomes.

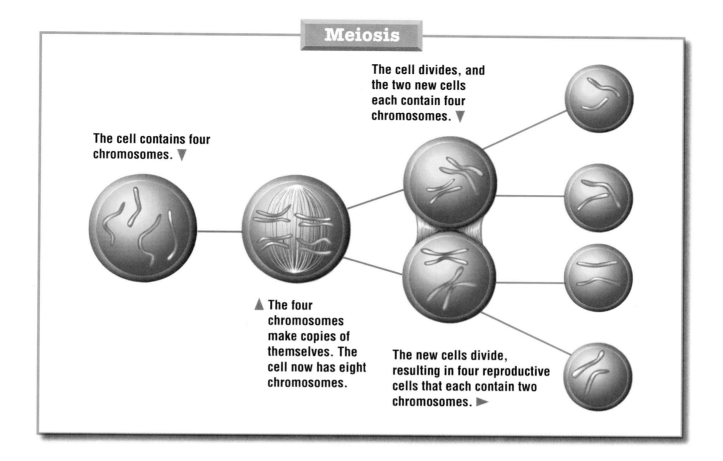

The cell divides, and the two new cells each contain four chromosomes. ▼

The cell contains four chromosomes. ▼

▲ The four chromosomes make copies of themselves. The cell now has eight chromosomes.

The new cells divide, resulting in four reproductive cells that each contain two chromosomes. ▶

Meiosis

In mitosis exact copies of cells are made. This is how you grow and how dead cells in your body are replaced. Another kind of cell division takes place to form reproductive cells such as eggs and sperm.

The process that forms reproductive cells is called **meiosis** (my•OH•sis). In meiosis each new cell contains only half the number of an organism's chromosomes. As a result, when two reproductive cells join, they form a cell with the correct total number of chromosomes. If sperm and egg cells were formed by mitosis instead, each would have a complete set of chromosomes. When two reproductive cells joined, the resulting cell would have twice as many chromosomes as it should.

The diagram shows what happens to the chromosomes in a cell during meiosis. The cell in the diagram is from an organism that has two pairs of chromosomes, or four in all.

Meiosis actually includes two cell divisions. Before the first, each of the chromosomes in the original cell is copied. The cell then has eight chromosomes. The new copies of the chromosomes remain attached to the originals. With their copies attached, chromosomes from the cell's original pairs separate and move to opposite ends of the cell. Then the cell divides. Each new cell has half the chromosomes from the original cell, plus their copies.

The two cells then start a new division. In each cell, each chromosome and its copy split apart. Each of the four new cells that are produced has just two chromosomes—half the original number.

On page A19 you can observe photographs of an actual cell going through meiosis.

✔ **In what way does a cell formed by meiosis differ from a cell formed by mitosis?**

Stages in Cell Division

The photographs on these pages show cells dividing.

The cell on the left is from the tip of an onion root. It is the same kind of cell that you observed in the investigation in this lesson. The root tip and the tip of the stalk are where most of the growth of an onion occurs.

The cell on the right is a male reproductive cell from a lily.

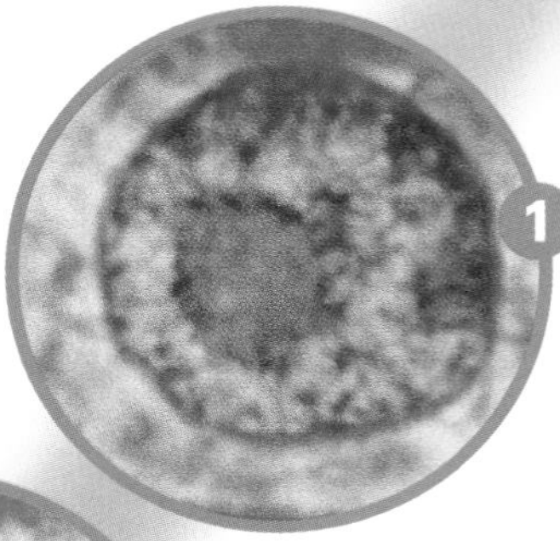

1 Before the cell divides, the chromosomes are copied. At this point, the chromosomes are long and thin and difficult to see.

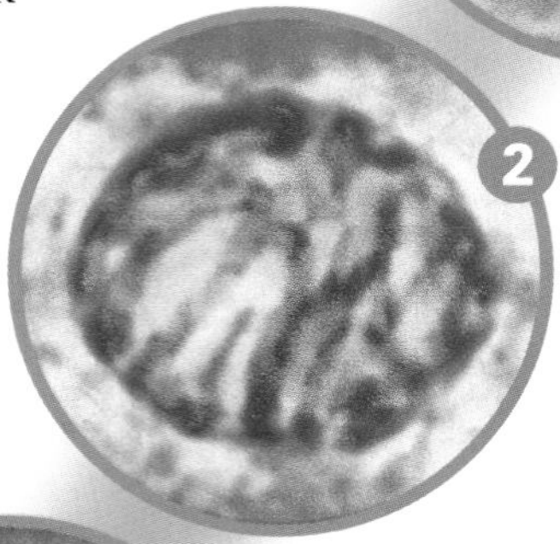

2 The double-stranded chromosomes begin to shorten and thicken. They become visible as rods. Each double strand is held together at the center. The nuclear membrane disappears.

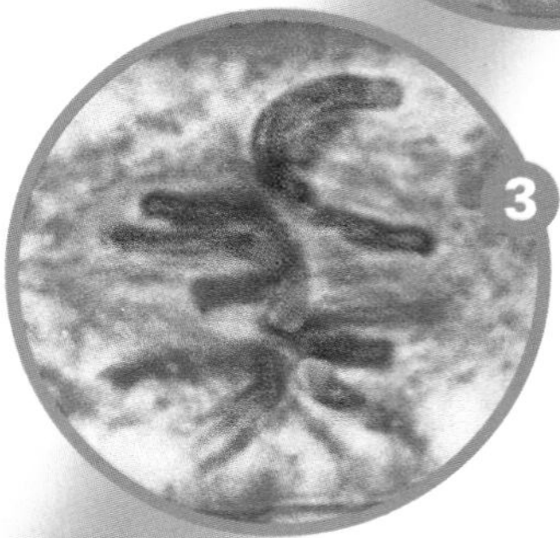

3 Fibers, called spindles, form across the cell. The middle of each double-stranded chromosome lines up with the others along the center of the spindle.

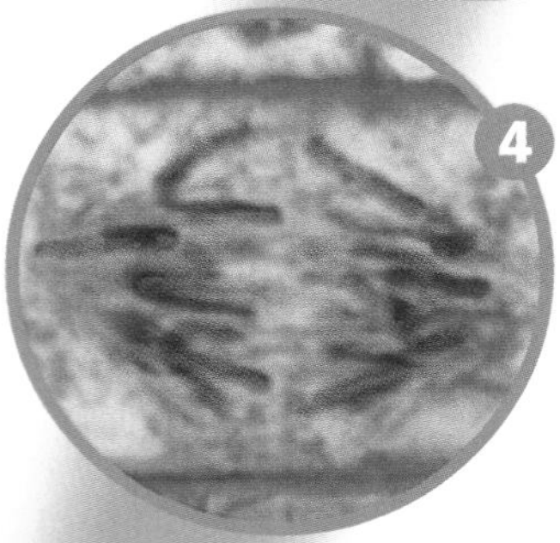

4 The two strands of each chromosome separate. The chromosomes move along the spindle to opposite ends of the cell.

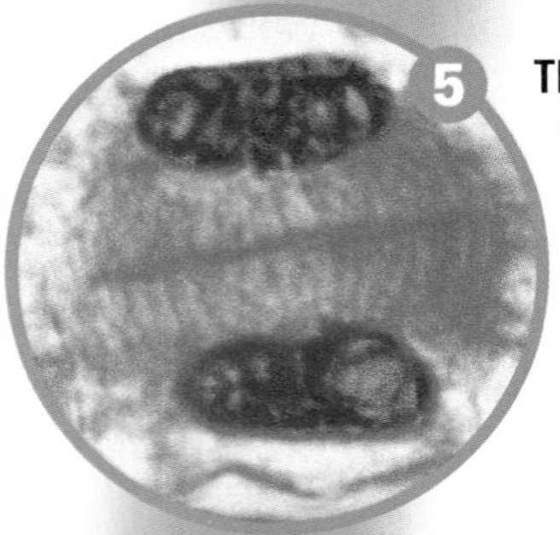

5 The chromosomes become long and difficult to see again. The cell splits and new nuclear membranes form.

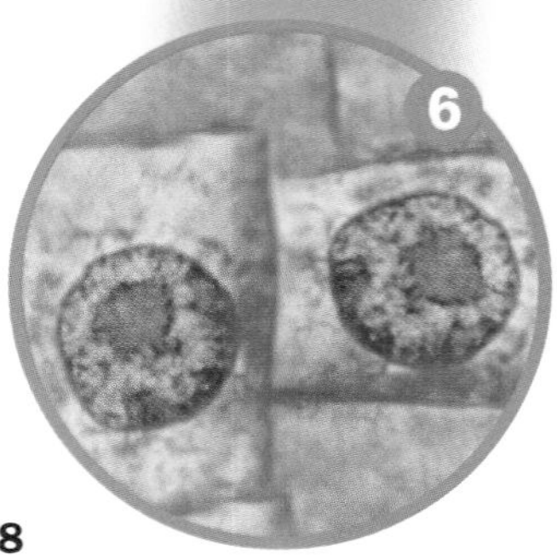

6 New cells can undergo mitosis and split again.

◄ Onion root tip

Meiosis

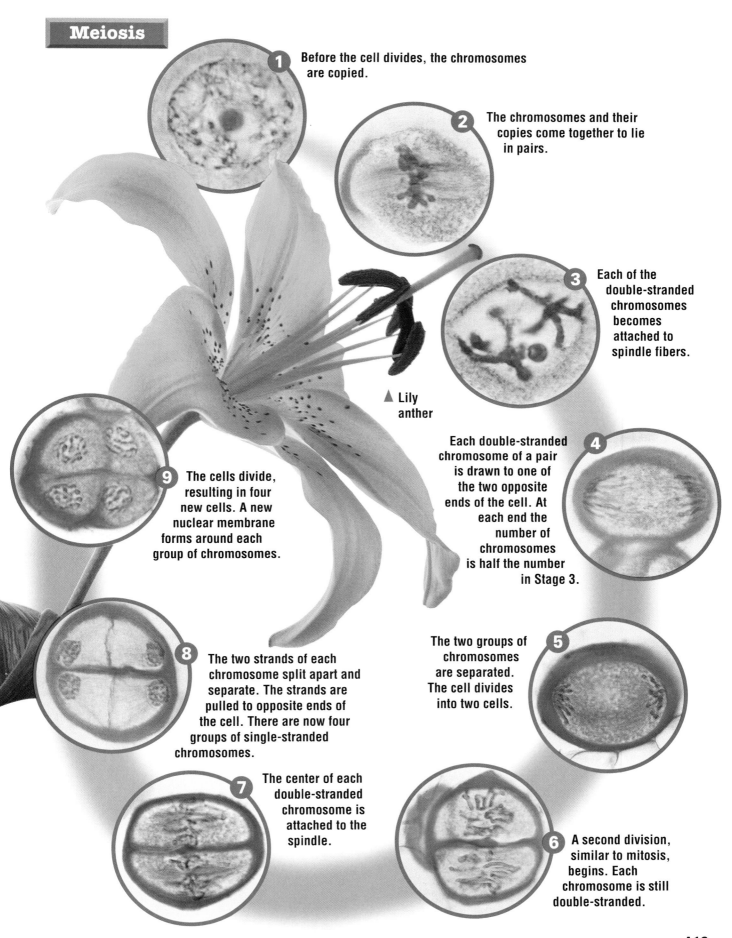

1 Before the cell divides, the chromosomes are copied.

2 The chromosomes and their copies come together to lie in pairs.

3 Each of the double-stranded chromosomes becomes attached to spindle fibers.

▲ Lily anther

4 Each double-stranded chromosome of a pair is drawn to one of the two opposite ends of the cell. At each end the number of chromosomes is half the number in Stage 3.

9 The cells divide, resulting in four new cells. A new nuclear membrane forms around each group of chromosomes.

8 The two strands of each chromosome split apart and separate. The strands are pulled to opposite ends of the cell. There are now four groups of single-stranded chromosomes.

7 The center of each double-stranded chromosome is attached to the spindle.

5 The two groups of chromosomes are separated. The cell divides into two cells.

6 A second division, similar to mitosis, begins. Each chromosome is still double-stranded.

Variation in Organisms

As a result of meiosis, sperm and egg cells each have half the number of chromosomes of an organism's body cells. The cell that is formed when female and male reproductive cells join has a complete set of chromosomes. Half are from the mother, and half are from the father. As a result, a new organism receives half its genes from its mother and half from its father.

Since the new organism has genes from both parents, it will have a new combination of traits, or characteristics—some from its mother and some from its father. The variation, or difference, in traits among members of plant or animal species is mostly due to the combining of cells that have gone through meiosis.

When you observe members of your own species, you can see a large variation in traits. Because people have 46 chromosomes and about 50,000 genes, there is an enormous number of possible combinations. The color of

▲ Offspring often resemble the parents. But they are often quite different.

◄ Which of the puppies' traits were inherited from the mother dog (black and white), and which were inherited from the father dog (mostly white)?

people's hair and eyes, their height and shape, whether they are right-handed or left-handed—all of these traits result from the combination of genes that a person has inherited. In the next lesson, you will find out that children can even inherit traits that are not seen in either of their parents.

✓ **How does meiosis produce variation?**

Summary

When an organism grows, its cells divide over and over again through mitosis. Before mitosis, a cell's chromosomes are copied. During mitosis two new cells are formed, each identical to the original cell. Meiosis forms reproductive cells that each have half as many chromosomes as the original cell. When two reproductive cells join, the resulting cells have a complete set of chromosomes—half from the mother and half from the father.

Review

1. Why are chromosomes copied before mitosis?

2. How does a new cell formed by mitosis compare with the original cell?

3. Why is there variation in new organisms formed from the joining of two reproductive cells?

4. **Critical Thinking** In which cells would you expect mitosis to occur more often—the cells of an adult person's skin or the cells of an adult person's teeth? Explain.

5. **Test Prep** Suppose an organism has 16 chromosomes in each of its body cells. How many chromosomes are there in one of its reproductive cells formed by meiosis?

   A 4
   B 8
   C 16
   D 32

LINKS

MATH LINK

Sequences Some cells divide once every 20 minutes. At this rate, how many cells would there be 1 hour, 2 hours, and 3 hours after a single cell began mitosis?

WRITING LINK

Informative Writing—Description Suppose that you could shrink to the size of a cell and observe mitosis. Write a story for a classmate to describe what you would observe during the process, and what you might see as the result of mitosis.

HEALTH LINK

Genes and Disease Some diseases are caused by faulty genes. Sickle cell anemia, hemophilia, and cystic fibrosis, for example, are each caused by a single gene. Find out how these diseases are inherited and how they are treated.

LANGUAGE ARTS LINK

Word Origins Both *mitosis* and *meiosis* are words that came from the Greek language. Find out what the Greek words mean, and write a paragraph to explain how they relate to these two processes.

TECHNOLOGY LINK

To learn more about how genes and heredity lead to variation, watch *Bioengineered Plants* on the **Harcourt Science Newsroom Video.**

LESSON 3

How Are Traits Inherited?

In this lesson, you can . . .

INVESTIGATE how the color of corn kernels is inherited.

LEARN ABOUT how traits are passed from parents to offspring.

LINK to math, writing, social studies, and technology.

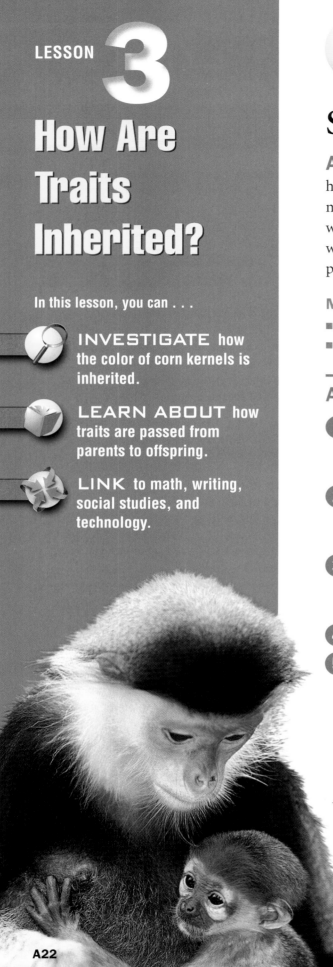

◀ Offspring resemble their parents in many ways. This is because of the way meiosis allows for both parents to contribute to the genes of the offspring.

Seed Color in Corn

Activity Purpose Have you ever seen ears of corn hanging on doors in the fall? Why does the corn have kernels that are different colors? In this investigation you will **observe** an ear of corn produced when a corn plant with white kernels was crossed with a corn plant with purple kernels.

Materials
- purple-and-white corn
- paper and pencil

Activity Procedure

1 Take one ear of purple-and-white corn. **Observe** the corn, and **estimate** the number of purple kernels and the number of white kernels.

2 Copy the chart form on the next page. **Count** the purple kernels and white kernels. **Record** the two numbers. (Picture A)

3 **Find the ratio** of purple kernels to white kernels. How many purple kernels are there for every white kernel?

4 Share your results with the class.

5 **Find the class totals** for purple kernels and white kernels.

Picture A

Number of Kernels of Corn

Purple	White
|||	

6 Now **find the class ratio** of purple kernels to white kernels.

Draw Conclusions

1. What **ratio** of colors did you find for your ear of corn?

2. How did your results compare with the results of the whole class?

3. **Scientists at Work** Scientists make **inferences** from their **observations**. They often **use numbers** to support their inferences. The larger the number of observations they study, the more likely their inferences are to be correct. What might you infer about the ratio of purple kernels to white kernels? Should it change for each ear of corn? How could you **use numbers** from your class and other classes to support your **inference**?

Investigate Further Get an ear of yellow-and-white corn. Find the ratio of yellow to white kernels. Is it the same as or different from the ratio of purple to white kernels?

A23

How Traits Are Inherited

Mendel's Pea Plants

FIND OUT

• how living things inherit traits from both parents

• what controls the traits that organisms show

• how organisms can carry traits that they do not show

VOCABULARY

sexual reproduction
dominant
recessive
Punnett square

When a baby is born, family friends may point out how the baby looks like its parents. They might say, "She has her father's eyes and her mother's nose" or "He looks just like his grandfather." Offspring often look like their parents—and sometimes their grandparents. Tall parents often have children who will become tall, for example, and plants with red flowers usually produce other red-flowered plants.

An Austrian monk named Gregor Mendel was the first person to show how traits are passed from parents to offspring. In the mid-1800s, Mendel carefully observed the pea plants he grew in his garden. Pea plants have many different traits. For example, some are tall and others are short; some have green seeds and others have yellow seeds. Mendel found that pea plants usually produced offspring like themselves. Tall plants produced tall plants, and short plants produced short plants. But what would happen if tall and short plants were crossbred, or bred with each other? Mendel chose seven traits that were easy to tell apart. After his experiments, he was able to describe how inheritance works.

In many species of plants, pollen from one plant is carried to another plant. Pollen contains male reproductive cells. When the reproductive cells of the plants join, they form a seed that will produce a new plant. Reproduction by the joining of a male and a female reproductive cell is called **sexual reproduction**. The pea plant reproduces by sexual reproduction, but its male and female parts are completely enclosed by the petals of its flowers. The male and female reproductive cells that join to form a seed come from the same plant.

◄ Mendel experimented with pea plants for eight years. He studied the results of crossbreeding plants that had different traits. Mendel published the results of his experiments in 1865, but they were ignored for a long time.

Mendel took pollen from a plant that had purple flowers and pollinated a plant that had white flowers. All the offspring had purple flowers. When he bred tall and short plants with each other, all the offspring were tall. The offspring of plants with opposite traits showed only one of the traits. It seemed that the other trait had disappeared.

The offspring self-pollinated. The male and female reproductive cells of the same plant joined to produce a seed. Mendel planted the seeds they produced. The traits that had disappeared now returned. Some new plants had purple flowers and others had white flowers. Some new plants were tall and others were short.

Mendel kept careful counts of his results. When he counted the new generation from self-pollinated plants, Mendel found that there were about three plants with purple flowers for every plant with white flowers, a ratio of 3 to 1. And there were about three tall plants for every short plant. In each case, the ratio was about the same—3 to 1.

Mendel repeated his experiment with other traits. The results were always the same—the new plants showed only one trait. But in the second generation, the missing trait returned in about one of every four offspring. Mendel realized that the missing trait had been present all along, even though it did not show.

✔ **Why did Mendel choose pairs of traits that were easy to tell apart?**

Mendel chose to experiment with the pea plant for several reasons. Pea plants were easy to get. They grow rapidly and show traits that are easy to tell apart. It is easy to cross different pea plants. But left to themselves, they self-pollinate with little chance of any accidental pollination between plants. ▶

▲ When pea plants that have purple flowers are crossed with pea plants that have white flowers, all the offspring have purple flowers.

◀ The seeds of the pea plant also show traits. They can be green or yellow, round or wrinkled.

▲ The pods of pea plants are either yellow or green. When Mendel crossed plants that had different colored pods, all the offspring had green pods.

Dominant and Recessive

When Mendel did his experiments, little was known about how traits are inherited. The most common belief of the time was that a cross of two different traits would result in a blend. If a tall plant was crossed with a short plant, for example, people expected the result to be a plant of medium height. Mendel proved that idea to be wrong.

Mendel suggested that each plant carries two factors for each trait that it shows. When a parent plant makes reproductive cells, only one factor is passed on to the offspring. Because the offspring receives a factor from each parent, it carries two factors for the trait. In a pea plant the factors for height are a factor for tallness and a factor for shortness.

Each of the two factors that a plant carries can be the same, or they can differ. If a pea plant has two factors for tallness, it will be tall. But if the factors are different, one factor may be **dominant** (DAHM•uh•nuhnt)—it will determine the trait that is shown. A trait that is caused by the presence of a dominant factor is a

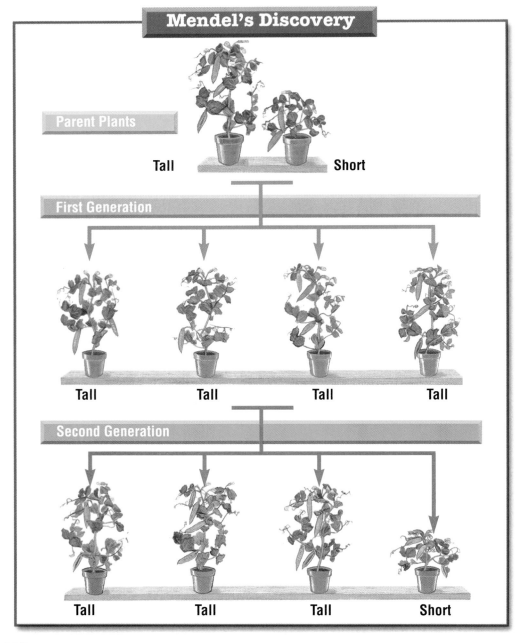

Mendel's Discovery

Parent Plants

Tall   Short

First Generation

Tall   Tall   Tall   Tall

Second Generation

Tall   Tall   Tall   Short

◄ When Mendel crossed a tall pea plant with a short pea plant, all the offspring were tall. The factor for tallness in the plant is dominant. In the second generation, one-fourth of the offspring showed the recessive factor for shortness.

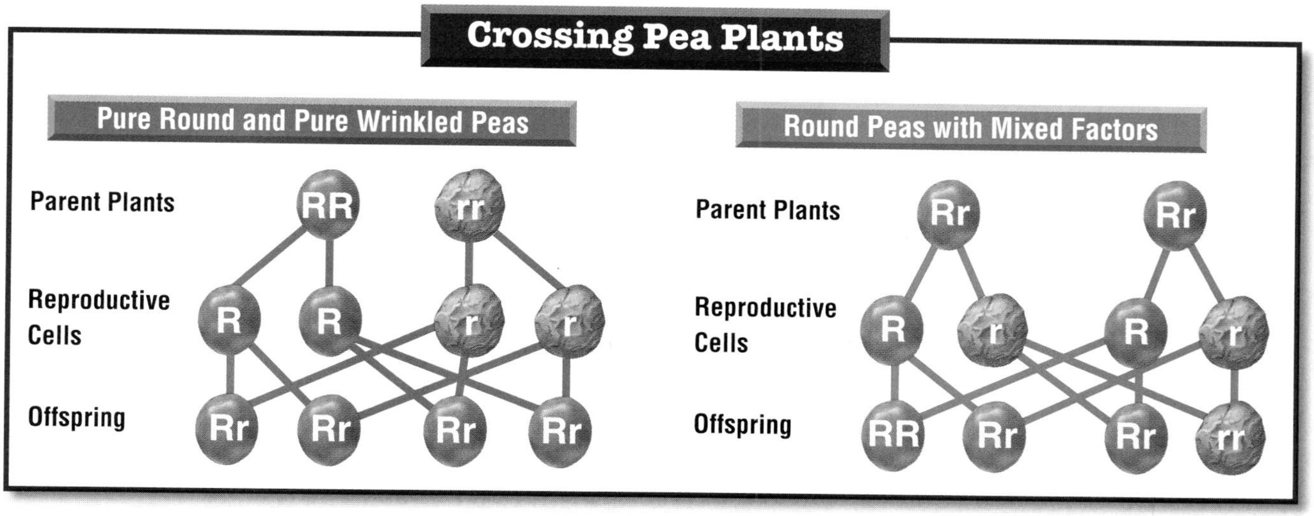

Crossing Pea Plants

Pure Round and Pure Wrinkled Peas

Parent Plants — RR — rr

Reproductive Cells — R — R — r — r

Offspring — Rr — Rr — Rr — Rr

▲ This diagram shows how factors are inherited when a pea plant that has round seeds is crossed with a pea plant that has wrinkled seeds. One plant has two factors for round seeds (R), and the other plant has two factors for wrinkled seeds (r). The factors separate when reproductive cells are formed. The bottom row shows the possible combinations of factors in the offspring.

Round Peas with Mixed Factors

Parent Plants — Rr — Rr

Reproductive Cells — R — r — R — r

Offspring — RR — Rr — Rr — rr

▲ This diagram shows the results of crossing two of the first generation plants from the diagram shown at the left. How many of the offspring have the factor for wrinkled seeds? How many of the offspring have wrinkled seeds?

dominant trait. One dominant trait in pea plants is tallness.

When the factors of a pair are different and one is dominant, the other is **recessive** [rih•SES•iv]. The trait that results from the combination of two recessive factors is a recessive trait. A plant will show a recessive trait only if both of its factors for that trait are recessive. For example, a short pea plant must have two factors for shortness. A pea plant with one factor for tallness and one factor for shortness will be tall, because the factor for tallness is dominant.

Using the idea of dominant and recessive factors, Mendel could explain why a recessive trait showed in one-fourth of the offspring of the second generation. Mendel began his experiments with what he called truebreeding seeds. The seeds for tall plants would always produce tall plants, and the seeds for short plants would always produce short plants. Truebreeding tall plants have two factors for tallness. Truebreeding short plants have two factors for shortness.

The diagram above on the left shows what happens when a plant that has truebreeding round seeds is crossbred with a plant that has truebreeding wrinkled seeds. A capital letter

stands for a dominant factor, in this case an *R* for *round seeds*. The matching lowercase letter stands for the recessive factor, in this case, for wrinkled seeds. All of the possible combinations of factors in the offspring are the same. Each plant has a factor for round seeds and a factor for wrinkled seeds. All the plants' seeds are round because the factor for round seeds is dominant.

The diagram on the right shows what happens when two of the offspring plants are crossed. This time, there are three possible combinations, shown in the third row. The first plant has two factors for round seeds, so it has round seeds. The next two plants have factors for both round and wrinkled seeds. They have round seeds because round seeds are dominant. The final plant has two factors for wrinkled seeds, so it has wrinkled seeds. One-fourth of the plants show the recessive factor. Mendel's explanation supports the results he obtained in his experiments.

✓ **If the offspring of two short pea plants are crossed, will they produce any tall pea plants? Explain.**

Inheritance of Traits

Mendel's explanation of inheritance doesn't apply only to pea plants. Most plants and animals have two parents and inherit some traits according to the principles that Mendel discovered.

You can see on the faces of your friends some traits that are passed from parents to offspring. Having dimples, for example, is an inherited trait. When such traits are dominant, they are likely to appear in many generations of a family.

You can often see dominant traits in the parents, children, and grandchildren of the same family.

The illustration shows some of the inherited traits that can be found on a person's face. There are other traits that show on a person's face as well. Eye color is not the result of a single dominant trait. But brown eyes are generally dominant and blue eyes are generally recessive.

✔ **Name three dominant traits and three recessive traits in humans.**

This face shows some of the traits that people inherit from their parents. Detached earlobes, dimples, and cleft chins are dominant traits. A widow's peak and attached earlobes are recessive traits. ▼

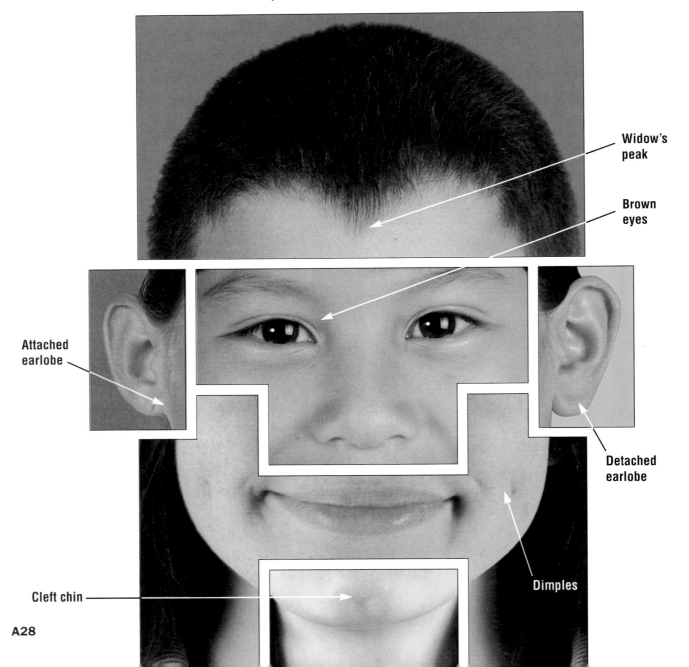

Widow's peak

Brown eyes

Attached earlobe

Detached earlobe

Dimples

Cleft chin

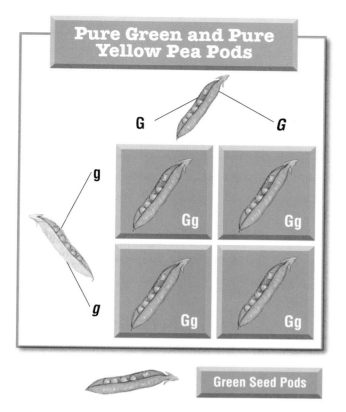

Pure Green and Pure Yellow Pea Pods

G   G

g
g

Green Seed Pods

▲ When Mendel crossed plants that had green pods with plants that had yellow pods, all of the offspring had green pods.

Mixed Green and Pure Yellow Pea Pods

G   g

g

g

Gg   gg

Gg   gg

Yellow Seed Pods

▲ The results are very different if one of the green-pod plants that were offspring from the Punnett square at the left is crossed with a yellow-pod plant.

Punnett Squares

An easy way to find all the possible combinations of factors in the offspring of two parents is to use a checkerboard-type diagram called a **Punnett square**. The Punnett squares on this page show combinations of factors for the color of pea pods. Pea pods can be either green or yellow. The capital letter *G* stands for the dominant color, green. The small letter *g* stands for the recessive color, yellow.

The factors present in the parent plants are shown at the top and on the left side of a Punnett square. The factors in each parent are separated so that each factor has a single column or row of the square. The possible combination of factors in each box of the square is found simply by placing the column factor next to the row factor. Both Punnett squares on this page show the possible results of crossing a plant that has

green pods with a plant that has yellow pods. Why are the results different?

The Punnett square at the top left of the page shows a cross between a plant with two factors for green pods and a plant with two factors for yellow pods. All the offspring have one factor for green pods and one factor for yellow pods. Yet they all have green pods because green is the dominant color for pods.

Suppose one of these offspring plants is crossed with a plant that has yellow pods. The plant with green pods has one green and one yellow factor. The plant with yellow pods must have two yellow factors, since yellow is recessive. The Punnett square at the top right shows the possible results.

✔ **If you had a pea plant that has green pods, how could you find out if it has a hidden factor for yellow pods?**

The Role of Genes

Mendel discovered the importance of factors in inheritance. At the time, however, nobody knew exactly what Mendel's factors were. In fact, Mendel's work was ignored until about 1900.

After the discovery of the process of mitosis, scientists hypothesized that chromosomes were responsible for heredity. In the early 1900s scientists observed that the behavior of chromosomes during meiosis seemed to be similar to the action of Mendel's factors. This led to the development of the chromosome theory, which states that factors, which we now know are genes, are located on the chromosomes. Because each organism has pairs of chromosomes, with one chromosome coming from each parent, genes also occur in pairs. As you learned, the number of chromosomes in a reproductive cell is halved during meiosis. In this way, the genes in a pair are separated, and each reproductive cell that is formed receives one of the genes.

Mendel was able to discover how heredity works in pea plants because the traits he studied were easy to tell apart. Not all traits are so distinct, however, and heredity does not always follow Mendel's laws. Many traits are controlled by more than one gene pair. Skin color and height in humans, for example, result from several different genes.

✔ **What are Mendel's factors and where are they located?**

These chromosomes carry the dominant gene that allows people to roll their tongues. ▶

Does the person on the right have these genes?

◀ Having color is a dominant trait.

Summary

Gregor Mendel discovered that traits are inherited through factors from each parent. These factors were later found to be genes. Genes occur in pairs. When a reproductive cell is formed, it has a single gene from the pair, so offspring receive one gene from each parent. Traits of dominant genes are shown, and these hide recessive gene traits. Punnett squares can be used to see all possible ways genes from two parents can combine in the offspring.

Review

1. Why didn't Mendel have to pollinate the first generation pea plants in order to produce the second generation?

2. Having round seeds is a dominant trait, and having wrinkled seeds is a recessive trait. What genes does a pea plant with wrinkled seeds have?

3. How many genes out of a gene pair does a plant get from each of its parents?

4. **Critical Thinking** Suppose that when two tall pea plants are crossed, all the offspring are tall. Could any of the offspring have a gene for shortness? Explain.

5. **Test Prep** A Punnett square is used to find —
   A gene combinations of offspring
   B the number of genes in offspring
   C the genes in true-breeding pea plants
   D the dominance of genes

LINKS

MATH LINK

Probability When Mendel crossed pea plants that each had a tallness and a short-ness gene, one-fourth of the offspring would have two genes for shortness. Write *T* (for the tallness gene) on one side of two differ-ent counters and *t* (for the shortness gene) on the other side. How could you model Mendel's results by tossing the counters? Why would your results become closer to Mendel's the more times you tossed the counters?

WRITING LINK

Informative Writing—Explanation Sup-pose Mendel did the investigation at the beginning of this lesson. Write a paragraph for your teacher telling how Mendel would explain the results.

SOCIAL STUDIES LINK

Traits in History Choose two figures in American history who were part of the same family—the family of President John Adams for example. Find portraits or photographs of family members in books. See if you can observe any traits they had in common.

TECHNOLOGY LINK

Find out more about genes and heredity by experimenting with *Traits—Now You See Them, Now You Don't* on the **Harcourt Science Explorations CD-ROM.**

Understanding Genetics

Mendel's Factors

The father of genetics was Gregor Mendel, an Austrian monk and scientist who spent much of his life studying pea plants. Mendel realized that parents passed on what he called "factors" to their offspring. Although Mendel published his results on laws of heredity in 1865, it wasn't until the early 1900s that scientists began to understand his research and recognize genetics as a science.

A New Century, a New Science

In the early 1900s, scientists renamed Mendel's factors "genes." Slowly, a number of scientists in different fields began to make discoveries. Geneticists identified chromosomes and determined that genes were located on chromosomes. Meanwhile, chemists made discoveries about the nature of DNA.

Linking It All Together

In the 1940s scientists discovered the link between DNA and genes. In 1953 the combined research of Rosalind Franklin, Maurice Wilkins, James Watson, and Francis Crick led to the discovery of the structure of DNA—the double helix.

Mapping

Using their new knowledge of DNA, scientists set to work to identify the precise sites on chromosomes where specific genes occur. This process is called gene mapping. The Human Genome Project, established in 1988, is a cooperative scientific effort to map all the genes on a human chromosome. In 1995 scientists completed an entire genetic blueprint for a bacterium. The blueprint contains 1.8 million genetic instructions and would, in theory, enable scientists to make the bacterium from scratch.

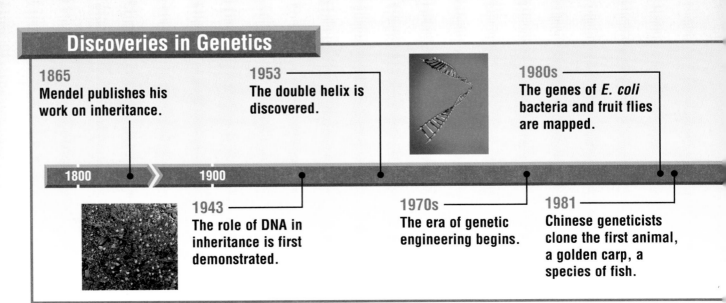

Discoveries in Genetics

1865
Mendel publishes his work on inheritance.

1953
The double helix is discovered.

1980s
The genes of *E. coli* bacteria and fruit flies are mapped.

1943
The role of DNA in inheritance is first demonstrated.

1970s
The era of genetic engineering begins.

1981
Chinese geneticists clone the first animal, a golden carp, a species of fish.

1800   1900

Engineering

The discovery of plasmids—free-floating DNA molecules in bacteria—eventually enabled scientists to alter, or engineer, genes. In 1973 scientists isolated a bacterial gene for metabolizing sugar and put this gene into a plasmid. When they inserted the plasmid into an *E. coli* bacterium, its offspring carried the new gene. By the 1980s scientists were using plasmids to get bacteria to produce useful products, such as vaccines and insulin, as well as crops that are resistant to disease and that produce more food.

A Controversial Frontier

Genetic engineering led to the development of cloning—a process in which an offspring has the genes of only one parent. In February 1996 Scottish scientists successfully cloned a sheep by using the genetic material from the cell of one parent sheep. This advance, however, is as controversial as it is amazing. Some people, including scientists, worry that in the wrong hands, cloning could become a dangerous tool.

Dolly was the first mammal to be reproduced by cloning.

THINK ABOUT IT

1. Why was discovering the structure of DNA so important in the study of genetics?
2. Why are people concerned about the use of cloning?

1985
A gene that leads to human cancer is discovered.

2000

1990
A four-year-old girl with a rare medical disorder becomes the first to benefit from gene therapy.

1996
Dolly the cloned sheep is born and continues to develop normally.

A33

Barbara McClintock

GENETICIST

Dr. Barbara McClintock is considered one of the greatest geneticists of the twentieth century. She made her mark by doing research that has helped us better understand heredity. Dr. McClintock earned many important honors for her work. She was elected to the National Academy of Sciences in 1944, and she received the Nobel Prize for her work in genetics in 1983.

Dr. McClintock earned a Ph.D. in botany (BAHT•uhn•ee)—the study of plants—at Cornell University in 1927. For the next 14 years, she stayed there doing genetic research on corn. After 1941, she worked alone at a lab on New York's Long Island, doing genetic research. At the time, scientists were just beginning to understand the connection between heredity and the cell structures that control it. From her research Dr. McClintock concluded that chromosomes can "cross over." That means pieces of chromosomes that are next to each other can break off and mix to make new genetic combinations. This important idea was unusual and was not well received at the time. Much later, however, the work of other geneticists supported this idea.

Dr. McClintock's work was even more remarkable because it was done at a time when Mendel's work

had just been rediscovered. For a long time Mendel's discoveries had been largely unknown and at the time Dr. McClintock was working, they had not yet been widely accepted. Yet Dr. McClintock had based much of her work on Mendel's ideas. As a result, many of her ideas were too far ahead of their time to be accepted by other scientists. As Mendel's work was studied, understood, and confirmed, however, Dr. McClintock's work also became more widely accepted. Even though her ideas were not accepted at first, she continued to do her research and to support her hypotheses with additional evidence. Now her work is an important part of our understanding of genetics.

THINK ABOUT IT

1. What important discovery did Dr. McClintock make?
2. Why were Dr. McClintock's ideas not accepted at first?

Some of the corn Dr. McClintock studied

Collapsing an Egg

How does a cell membrane work?

Materials

- raw, uncracked egg
- wide-mouthed jar of vinegar with a lid
- wide-mouthed jar of corn syrup

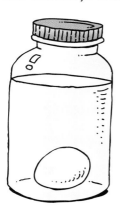

Procedure

1 Gently place the egg in the jar of vinegar, and close the lid.

2 Let the jar sit for three days.

3 Take the egg out of the vinegar, and put it in the corn syrup.

4 Let the jar sit three more days.

Draw Conclusions

While in the vinegar, the egg grew larger. What substance passed into the egg through the membrane surrounding the egg? While the egg was in the syrup, what substance passed out of it? Did the yolk pass through the membrane? What does this tell you about the egg membrane? How is it like a cell membrane?

Breeding Manx Cats

How do cats pass genes to their offspring?

Materials

- 2 small cards marked *N* for *no tail*
- 2 small cards marked *n* for *tail*

Procedure

1 Among Manx cats, the lack of a tail is a dominant trait. NN is one possible gene combination for a Manx cat with no tail. Use the cards to show another possible combination.

2 Show the gene combinations of two tailless Manx cats that had a kitten with a tail. Draw a Punnett square, if necessary. What gene combination does the kitten have?

3 Suppose a tailless Manx cat and a Manx cat with a tail had one kitten. Could you predict definitely whether the kitten would have a tail? Why or why not?

4 If the cats from Step 3 had four kittens, how many would you expect to be tailless? Why?

Draw Conclusions

What do you need to know in order to determine the probability that a gene will be passed on from parents to offspring?

Chapter 1 Review and Test Preparation

Vocabulary Review

Match the terms in List B with the definitions in List A. The page numbers in ( ) tell you where to look in the chapter if you need help.

List A

1. Rodlike structures in the nucleus
2. Stiff layer that surrounds a plant cell but not an animal cell
3. Layer that surrounds the nucleus and controls what enters and leaves it
4. Structure that contains chlorophyll
5. Thin layer that surrounds a cell and controls what enters and leaves it
6. Control center of the cell
7. "Blueprint of life"
8. Jellylike substance that fills a cell
9. Structures that release energy in a cell
10. Storage spaces in a cell
11. The joining of egg and sperm cells
12. Chart that shows possible outcomes of a genetic cross

List B

A. cell membrane (A8)

B. sexual reproduction (A24)

C. DNA (A10)

D. mitochondria (A8)

E. chloroplast (A9)

F. nucleus (A9)

G. chromosomes (A9)

H. nuclear membrane (A9)

I. Punnett square (A29)

J. cytoplasm (A8)

K. cell wall (A8)

L. vacuoles (A9)

Connect Concepts

Use the terms in the Word Bank to complete the concept map.

meiosis	body	offspring	eggs
recessive	cells	dominant	genes
mitosis	traits	sperm	

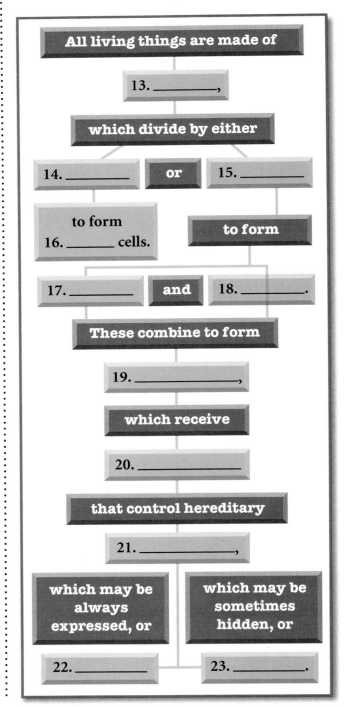

All living things are made of

13. _____,

which divide by either

14. _____   or   15. _____

to form
16. _____ cells.

to form

17. _____   and   18. _____.

These combine to form

19. _____,

which receive

20. _____

that control hereditary

21. _____,

which may be always expressed, or   which may be sometimes hidden, or

22. _____   23. _____.

Check Understanding

Write the letter of the best choice.

24. Which statement is **NOT** part of the cell theory?
    A All living things are made of cells.
    B All life activities take place in cells.
    C Cells are microscopic.
    D New cells are produced by existing cells.

25. Plant cells differ from animal cells by —
    F having vacuoles
    G having no DNA
    H having a nuclear membrane
    J having cell walls

26. The control center of the cell is the —
    A nucleus
    B mitochondrion
    C cell membrane
    D cytoplasm

27. Mitosis is cell division in which the chromosomes —
    F are halved
    G are duplicated
    H are dominant
    J are recessive

28. Meiosis is cell division in which the number of chromosomes —
    A is halved   C remains the same
    B is doubled   D is reduced by two

Critical Thinking

29. Would you expect to find chloroplasts in the cells of a root? Explain.

30. Why can't reproductive cells be formed by the process of mitosis?

31. Suppose green pods are dominant and yellow pods are recessive. Two yellow-podded plants are crossed. What can you tell about the color of the pods of their offspring?

Process Skills Review

32. How might you **use a model** to describe the structures and functions of a plant cell to a younger brother or sister?

33. Make a diagram or a poster **showing the sequence** of the stages of mitosis in an animal cell. Why is it important for this process to take place in a certain sequence?

34. Suppose that in a certain kind of mouse, black fur is dominant over red fur. **Use numbers** to describe the ratio of the expected offspring of a cross between two mice that each have one recessive gene for fur color.

Performance Assessment

Dominant and Recessive

Suppose that in a certain kind of plant, red flowers are dominant and yellow flowers are recessive. A plant that has two genes for red flowers is crossed with a plant that has yellow flowers. Use a Punnett square to show the possible offspring of this cross. State the possible offspring as percentages of plants with red flowers and with yellow flowers. Also show the possible offspring of a cross that forms the second generation. Give the percentages of the possible offspring.

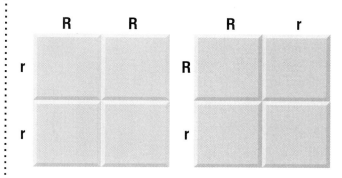

Classification

The human species has increased so greatly in population in the twentieth century that it sometimes seems as if humans outnumber every other creature. However, the world is home to millions of different species and the members of many groups are far more numerous than humans. Many small animals, such as ants, not only outnumber humans but they also—as a group—outweigh us.

Vocabulary Preview

classification
Linnaean system
Animalia
Plantae
Fungi
Protista
Monera
adaptation
genus
species
dichotomous key

FAST FACT

Insects make up the largest group of known species. Of the insects, about 120,000 species are butterflies or moths; 100,000 species are ants, bees, or wasps; and at least 300,000 species are beetles. Beetles make up more than one-fourth of all animal species.

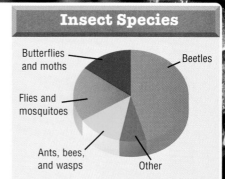

Insect Species

Butterflies and moths

Beetles

Flies and mosquitoes

Ants, bees, and wasps

Other

Some fungi are predators. The fungus *Arthrobotrys dactyloides* uses loops of threads to trap roundworms. The fungus then digests the roundworm.

Bacteria are the hardiest of all living things. Some survive temperatures below freezing for years. Others can live in the boiling water of hot springs. Still others can survive in very hot acid. Bacteria have been found inside granite rocks, in the depths of the ocean, and in the stratosphere.

What Are the Kingdoms of Organisms?

In this lesson, you can . . .

 INVESTIGATE how to classify objects.

 LEARN ABOUT the kingdoms into which scientists classify living things.

 LINK to math, writing, health, and technology.

 **INVESTIGATE**

Classifying Beans

Activity Purpose To talk to one another and be understood, we need to agree on the meanings of words. To talk about living things, we need to know that everyone is talking about the same organism. Classifying gives people who understand the classification system a way to define organisms. In this activity you will **classify** beans and share your classification system.

Materials
- 1 bag of beans
- poster board
- clear adhesive tape or glue

Activity Procedure

1 Pour out the beans from your bag, and **observe** them carefully. Imagine that the beans represent newly discovered organisms. (Picture A)

2 **Classify** or sort the beans into separate groups of similar beans. Use all the characteristics you can observe, and place all beans with the same characteristics in the same group. (Picture B)

3 Draw a picture of one bean from each of your groups, give it an identifying name, and write a short description of it.

4 Make a poster showing how you grouped the beans, the names you gave them, and a description of each bean type. Tape or glue a few beans of each type next to your descriptions.

Draw Conclusions

1. **Compare** your results with the results of other members of the class. How many different ways did all of you find to classify the beans?

2. What characteristics did you use to **classify** the beans? What characteristics did some of your classmates use?

3. Now that you have seen other classification systems, how might you change your own? Explain your answer.

4. **Scientists at Work** Scientists **classify** living things to show how they are similar and how they are different. Why do you think it's important for scientists to agree on a set of characteristics for classifying living things?

Investigate Further Choose a different set of objects such as marbles, buttons, or rocks. Make up a classification system for the objects. What similarities does this system have to the system you found for the beans? What differences are there?

Picture A

Picture B

Process Skill Tip

To **classify** objects, you first need to observe and describe them carefully. By doing this, you can identify similarities and differences between the objects. Then you can tell which ones belong in the same group.

Classification of Living Things

FIND OUT

- why living things are classified
- how living things are classified into kingdoms

VOCABULARY

classification
Linnaean system
Animalia
Plantae
Fungi
Protista
Monera
adaptation

Why Living Things Are Classified

If you go to a grocery store to buy apples, you can find them by remembering that apples are fruits and looking for them where fruits are displayed. The store arranges items in groups so that customers know where to find them. The arrangement of things in groups of similar items is called **classification**.

Scientists classify living things to describe what they are like and how they relate to other organisms. So far, between 1 and 2 million kinds of living things have been discovered and named. However, scientists estimate that there may be more than 10 million different kinds of living things. Without a system of classifying, scientists could not share information about all these organisms.

There is no one correct classification system for living things. A system is correct as long as it is useful. For scientists the best classification system is one that allows them to identify organisms correctly and to interpret how living things are related. However, even a good

The History of Classification

This time line describes some of the ways in which people have classified living things over the last 2,500 years.

Aristotle   350 B.C.

Aristotle's classification system groups organisms first as plants or animals. It then groups animals by how they move—fliers, swimmers, or walkers. It groups plants by size—as herbs, shrubs, or trees.

A system used by herbalists classifies plants by how they are used medically and whether or not they are poisonous.

B.C. | A.D.

A.D. 300 – A.D. 1500s

system may need to be improved. Scientists sometimes need to change their classification systems because of new information they have learned. The time line on these pages summarizes the history of changes in classification systems.

One of the first systems for classifying living things was developed about 350 B.C. by the Greek philosopher Aristotle. At the time, people recognized only about 1000 different kinds of living things.

As scientists learned more, Aristotle's system became less useful. World explorers returned from their travels with thousands of plants and animals Europeans had never seen before. The invention of the microscope led to the discovery of tiny forms of life. The number of known living things increased greatly, and the newly discovered ones did not all fit well into Aristotle's system.

In the 1700s, the Swedish scientist Carl von Linné developed a new classification system for living things. First, he grouped all living things into two major groups that he called kingdoms —the plant kingdom and the animal kingdom. Next, he organized the members of each kingdom into smaller groups based on their features. Then, he divided these groups into smaller groups. This system, called the **Linnaean system**, was useful for storing and finding information about living things. It became the basis for our present system of classification.

Von Linné also invented a system for naming living things. Scholars of the 1700s communicated in Latin, and von Linné gave every organism that was known at the time a Latin name that consisted of two words. He gave himself a Latin name as well. He has become known as Carolus Linnaeus.

✓ **Why do scientists classify living things?**

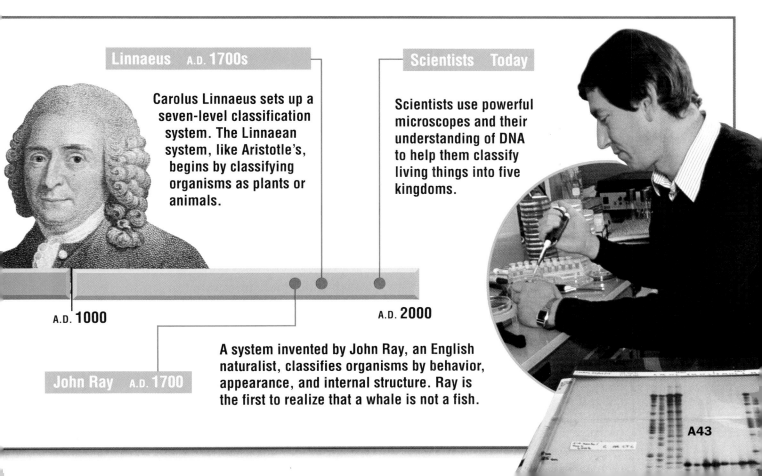

Linnaeus A.D. **1700s**

Carolus Linnaeus sets up a seven-level classification system. The Linnaean system, like Aristotle's, begins by classifying organisms as plants or animals.

Scientists Today

Scientists use powerful microscopes and their understanding of DNA to help them classify living things into five kingdoms.

A.D. **1000**

A.D. **2000**

John Ray A.D. **1700**

A system invented by John Ray, an English naturalist, classifies organisms by behavior, appearance, and internal structure. Ray is the first to realize that a whale is not a fish.

A43

How Living Things Are Classified

Although we still use the Linnaean system, some of the reasons for placing an organism in a particular group have changed. Also some of the groups themselves have changed. For example, Linnaeus started with only two kingdoms. In the present system of classification, there are five kingdoms. Some scientists have suggested that there are six or seven kingdoms.

An organism's structure and features are important characteristics for classifying. For example, fish are classified by the shape and position of their fins, and mammals are classified by the structure, number, and placement of their teeth. However, modern classification is based on other characteristics as well.

There are differences in the cells of different organisms. There are also differences in the ways organisms get their food. Scientists use these two characteristics—cell structure and ways of getting food—to place organisms in kingdoms. Scientists have discovered that many organisms are very different from most animals and plants. They do not, therefore, belong in either the kingdom **Animalia** (an•uh•MAYL•yuh) or the kingdom **Plantae** (PLAN•tee). These organisms have been placed in one of three other kingdoms.

The members of the kingdom **Fungi** (FUHN•jy) have cells similar to those of plants and often look like plants. However fungi do not make their own food. They take the nutrients that they need from the environment.

The members of the kingdom **Protista** (proh•TEES•tuh) often have traits of both plants and animals. Most protists are one-celled. Their cell contains one or more nuclei and most of the structures found in plant and animal cells. Some protists make their own food. Others take in food from the environment, as animals do. Still others get food in both ways.

▲ Scientists use DNA analysis to help them classify organisms. The patterns produced by the DNA of organisms are compared. Similarities and differences are noted and the relationship of the organisms is inferred from the comparison.

◄ *Euglena* is a type of protist. It has chloroplasts and can make its own food, as plants do. It can also take in nutrients from its surroundings, as fungi do. *Euglena* can even move, as animals do, by lashing a whiplike structure back and forth.

When scientists first examined bacteria, they found cells unlike those of members of any of the other kingdoms. Bacteria have cell walls as plant cells do, but the structure of the walls is different. The cells of bacteria do not have a nucleus. These organisms either make their own food or take in nutrients from their environment. As a result of their differences from other organisms, bacteria are placed in kingdom **Monera** (moh•NAIR•uh).

✔ **What traits do scientists use to classify living things into kingdoms?**

Plants

The kingdom Plantae includes a great variety of organisms, from tiny mosses to giant redwood trees. How do scientists separate plants into related groups?

Scientists look at the different adaptations of plants to group them. An **adaptation** is a structure or feature of an organism that helps it meet a particular need in its natural habitat.

One adaptation of some plants is the presence of tissue that moves water and nutrients from roots to leaves. The presence or absence of this tissue is used to divide plants into two major groups. The stems of lilies, for example, can transport water. Mosses have no system to transport water. Because of this difference, lilies and mosses are placed in separate groups.

The way plants reproduce is also used to place them in groups. Some plants, such as ferns, produce spores to reproduce, while others produce seeds. Some plants, such as pine trees, produce seeds that have no outer covering. Others, such as apple trees, produce seeds that are covered by a fruit. Some plants, such as orchids, have flowers that contain the reproductive organs of the plant. Others have no

such structure. Scientists use all of these features to help them classify plants.

Scientists also look at the structures of the roots, stems, and leaves of plants. They look at the size, shape, and division of the leaves of plants. They may look at the bark of a tree or the shape of a flower to help determine how the plant is related to others.

Scientists have classified all the kinds of living plants into 12 groups called divisions. These large divisions are divided into smaller groups to help scientists organize and understand the organisms that make up the kingdom Plantae.

✔ **What characteristics do scientists use to classify plants?**

Equisetum is a plant commonly called a horsetail or scouring rush. These tough, strong plants got their name because they were used in frontier times to scour, or scrub, pots and pans. ▶

◀ Orchids are one of many different groups of flowering plants. Worldwide, there are about 24,000 different kinds of orchids. Many of them grow in rain forests.

◀ The sundew plant is one of about 350 kinds of plants that trap small animals such as insects. These insect-eating plants usually grow in poor soil. They make their own food but need nutrients that they get from their prey.

A45

▲ A Spanish dancer is a kind of mollusk. Mollusks also include oysters, squid, and garden snails.

▲ A sea urchin has an internal skeleton but no backbone. Most sea urchins have a body covered with sharp spines that protect them from animals that would eat them.

▲ This animal, called a water bear, lives between the grains of sand on a wet beach or shoreline. It is one of many animals that have been discovered because of the microscope. The animal pictured here has been magnified more than 1000 times.

Animals

If you ask a friend to name an animal, you're likely to get a correct answer. Your friend might name a pet, such as a cat or a dog; a farm animal, such as a cow or a pig; or a "zoo animal" such as a giraffe or a bear. Yet all of these animals are members of just one group— mammals. There are about 4500 different kinds of mammals in the world. But there are more than a million different kinds of animals.

Scientists classify animals into two large groups based on whether the animal has a backbone or not. For the group of animals without a backbone, scientists look at what the skeleton is made of, how it is shaped, and whether it is inside the body or outside the body tissue. For example, sea urchins and clams both have skeletons made of limestone. However, the clam's skeleton, or shell, is on the outside of its body and the sea urchin's skeleton is on the inside of its body. There are many more animals without a backbone than there are animals with a backbone.

Animals with a backbone are organized into groups based on their body coverings, how they reproduce, how they breathe, and other characteristics. There are five large groups of animals with a backbone.

✓ **What characteristics are used to classify an animal?**

◄ Meerkats are one example of animals with a backbone. The meerkat is a mammal, one of the five large groups of animals with a backbone.

Fungi and Protists

Organisms in the kingdom Fungi are all around you. Yeast—which makes bread rise—and bread mold are two types of fungus.

Scientists classify fungi by their shape, size, way of reproducing, whether they are one cell or many, how and where they live, and other similar characteristics. One-celled fungi like yeast are unusual. Most fungi, like the mushroom and the bracket fungi common in forests, are made up of more than one cell.

Many organisms that make up the kingdom Protista have characteristics of both plants and animals. Most of these organisms are single-celled.

Scientists classify protists by whether they are more animal-like or plantlike. They group the plantlike protists by their color, whether the cell is surrounded by a shell or not, and whether the protist takes in nutrients from the environment. Scientists group animal-like protists by shape, size, what the organism uses to move around, and other characteristics.

Protists may be unfamiliar to you because you can't see them without magnification. But protists are all around you. One gram of soil—much less than a teaspoonful—can contain more than 150,000 protists.

✔ **What characteristics do scientists use to classify protists?**

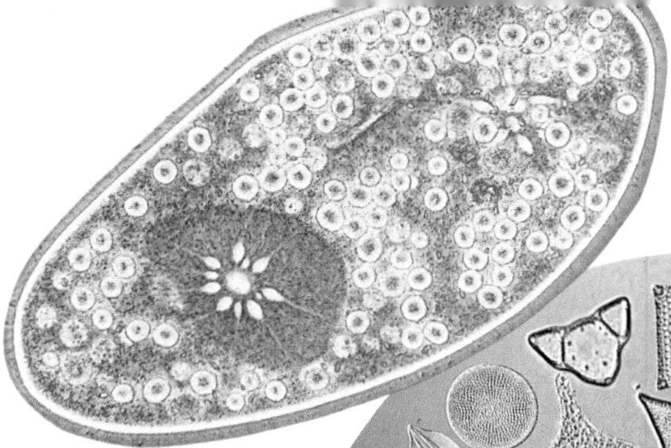

▲ The protist *Paramecium* swims by moving the tiny hairs on its surface.

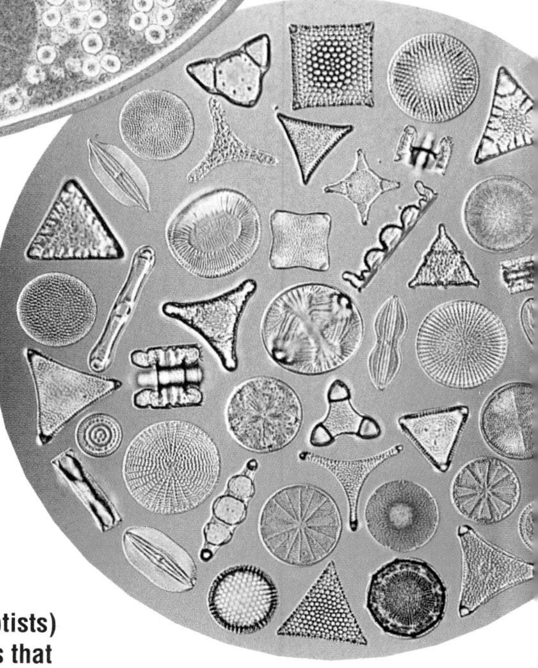

Diatoms (plantlike protists) and foraminifera (animal-like protists) both have shells that support and protect the cells. Under magnification you can see the beautiful shapes and colors of the diatom shells. ▲

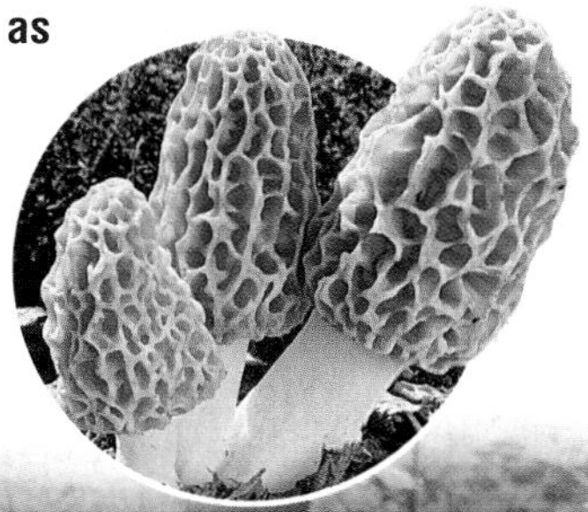

Many kinds of fungi live in the forest. Some of the mushrooms, such as the morel shown here, are considered tasty treats. However, many of the mushrooms that grow in the wild are extremely poisonous. ▶

When bracket fungi grow on dead trees like this one, they take in nutrients from the tree. ▶

A47

The Kingdoms of Living Things

Kingdom	Description	Kinds Known
Plantae	multicelled, cell walls, nucleus, make their own food, cannot move	about 265,000
Animalia	multicelled, no cell walls, nucleus, eat food, most can move	more than 1,500,000
Fungi	mostly multicelled, cell walls, nucleus, take in food, cannot move	about 100,000
Protista	mostly single-celled, some have cell walls, nucleus, take in food or make their own food, many can move	about 60,000
Monera	single-celled, cell wall, no nucleus, take in food or make their own food, some can move	about 2700

Bacteria are classified according to shape. They can be spirals, spheres, or rods. Their cell walls give different kinds of bacteria their particular shapes.

Monerans

The kingdom Monera consists of bacteria. It includes both bacteria that cause disease and bacteria that do not cause disease, including cyanobacteria. Cyanobacteria, or blue-green bacteria, make up the green scum that you can often see on the surface of ponds.

Monerans are the most numerous organisms on Earth. A gram of soil that might contain 150,000 protists could hold over 2 billion monerans. Bacteria exist in almost every environment, from the depths of the oceans to the upper atmosphere.

Scientists classify bacteria by the size and shape of the cell. They also consider how the cells are arranged in relation to each other.

All of life on Earth belongs to one of the five kingdoms—Plantae, Animalia, Protista, Fungi, and Monera. The chart on this page defines each of the kingdoms by its most important features.

✓ **How do monerans differ from all other organisms?**

Summary

Scientists classify living things to organize information about them and to show relationships between them. The characteristics they use to classify organisms include the structure and number of their cells; the ways they get food; and their color, shape, size, mobility, and DNA. All living things are placed in one of five kingdoms—Plantae, Animalia, Protista, Fungi, or Monera.

Review

1. What is the purpose of classification?

2. Which two characteristics are the most important for classifying organisms into kingdoms?

3. What characteristics does an organism that belongs to the kingdom Plantae have?

4. If you discovered a new multicelled organism that could move, in which kingdom might you place it? Explain your answer.

5. **Critical Thinking** What scientific invention caused scientists to decide that there should be more than two kingdoms? Explain your answer.

6. **Test Prep** Which kingdom is made up of organisms that have cells without cell walls?

   A Plantae

   B Fungi

   C Animalia

   D Monera

LINKS

MATH LINK

Oodles of Organisms A gram of soil can hold 150,000 protists or 2,000,000,000 monerans. About how many times as great as the number of protists is the number of monerans?

WRITING LINK

Informative Writing—Description Suppose that you could tour the microscopic world of organisms. Write a journal entry for your teacher to describe the kinds of things you might see on your journey. Be sure to tell which kingdom each of the living things you see belongs to.

HEALTH LINK

Organisms and Disease Some protists, fungi, and monerans cause human diseases. Malaria, for example, is caused by a protist. Find out about one organism that causes a disease. Research the disease and how modern medicine treats it.

TECHNOLOGY LINK

Visit the Harcourt Learning site for related links, activities, and resources.
www.harcourtschool.com

WELCOME TO
THE
LEARNING
SITE

LESSON 2

How Are Kingdoms Subdivided?

In this lesson, you can . . .

INVESTIGATE how to develop a system for identifying beans.

LEARN ABOUT the seven levels of classification and how to use a dichotomous key.

LINK to math, writing, language arts, and technology.

How to Develop a Key

Activity Purpose In Lesson 1 you developed a classification system for beans. In this investigation you will develop a key to help others identify their beans by the same names you used.

Materials
- bean classifications from the investigation in Lesson 1
- paper and pencil

Activity Procedure

1. Use your classification system from the investigation on pages A40–A41. (Picture A)

2. Make a simple flowchart or other diagram that would allow others to correctly identify their beans by the same name you gave to yours. Don't rely on pictures only! (Picture B)

3. Test your identification key by asking another student to use it to identify one or more beans.

◀ Shells on a beach show the diversity of living things.

Picture A

Picture B

Draw Conclusions

1. **Compare** your key with those of classmates. How many kinds of keys were made? Are some keys easier to use than others? Explain your answer.

2. Why might a key be a more useful tool than a set of pictures of organisms?

3. **Scientists at Work** When scientists classify items or make keys for identification, they **gather** and **record data** carefully and precisely. Why might scientists want to avoid using imprecise terms such as *small, big, heavy,* and *light* in a key?

Investigate Further Choose another group of objects or organisms. Write a key to help people identify the objects or organisms.

Process Skill Tip

To **gather** and **record data,** you first need a set of careful observations. Then determine which of your observations are the most important for someone who is doing the same kind of work.

This is one way to make a key to help people identify animals. ▶

A51

How Kingdoms Are Subdivided

Grouping Living Things

FIND OUT

- how kingdoms are subdivided into phylum, class, order, family, genus, and species
- how organisms are named
- how to use a dichotomous key

VOCABULARY

genus
species
dichotomous key

When you mail a letter to a friend, you can be pretty sure that it will be delivered to the right person. The mail carrier won't just ask around to find out if anyone knows where your friend might be. Instead, the postal service will use the same classification system you used when you wrote your friend's name and address on the envelope. The categories included in an address are the name of the person to whom the envelope is addressed, apartment number, building (or house number), street, city, state, and sometimes country.

A member of one category of the postal classification system must be part of the next larger category. For example, a street is in a city, and a city is in a state. An address in Canada, for example, must not include a street in the United States.

The Linnaean classification system groups living things in a similar way. Linnaeus described seven levels of classification. He called the largest group a kingdom. The other levels, in order from largest to smallest, are phylum, class, order, family, genus, and species. A group on one level is made up of smaller, related groups on the level below it. A kingdom is made up of several related phyla, and each phylum is made up of several related classes. The species in one genus are more closely related to each other than they are to species of any other genus. Families in one order are more closely related to each other than they are to families in other orders. You'll find out more on pages A54 and A55.

Just as an apartment in San Francisco is also in California, an organism that belongs to an order also belongs to the class that contains that order. And just as a resident of the United States cannot live on a street in Mexico, a member of one kingdom cannot belong to a family that is part of another kingdom.

Each part of the postal classification system—building number, street, city, state, and country—is a part of all of the levels above it. ▼

world
continent
country
state
city
street
house

✔ **In which of Linnaeus's levels would you expect all the members to be the most similar to each other? Why?**

These two animals show why scientists need a single system for naming organisms. In different parts of the country, each animal is called a gopher.

Number of Species in Some Phyla of the Animal Kingdom		
Number	**Phylum**	**Includes**
1,000,000	Arthropoda	insects, spiders, crabs
50,000	Mollusca	oysters, snails, squid
43,000	Chordata	fish, mammals, birds
9000	Annelida	earthworms, leeches
6000	Echinodermata	sea stars, sea urchins

▲ Keeping track of all the species in the animal kingdom would be impossible without a naming system. The scientific names of the animals provide information about how animals are related between various species.

Naming Living Things

What is a gopher? The answer depends on the person you ask. In the Midwest, people call a striped ground squirrel a gopher; in the Southeast, people know a burrowing tortoise as a gopher. Two different organisms may be called by the same name, or one organism may be called by different names. For example, the animal called a mountain lion in some parts of the country is called a puma, cougar, or panther in other parts of the country.

Identifying an organism can be difficult when several organisms are called by the same name, or when one organism is called by several names. To avoid this confusion, scientists use a system of scientific names for living things. The system was set up by Linnaeus, who gave each organism a two-part name.

The first part of an organism's name is its genus name. A **genus** (JEE•nuhs) is a group of organisms that share major characteristics and are therefore closely related. For example, cats that purr are part of the genus *Felis*, which is Latin for "cat." A genus name always begins with a capital letter and is either underlined or in italics.

The second part of a scientific name identifies one specific organism in the genus. For example, the house cat is *Felis domesticus*, and the mountain lion is *Felis concolor*. Each different kind of organism is a **species** (SPEE•sheez). A species name always begins with a lowercase letter and is also underlined or in italics.

If all scientists use an organism's scientific name, they can be sure they are all referring to the same organism when they talk or write about it. The scientific name also contains information about how the organism is related to other organisms.

✓ **Why do scientists use scientific names for organisms?**

A53

The Seven Levels of Classification

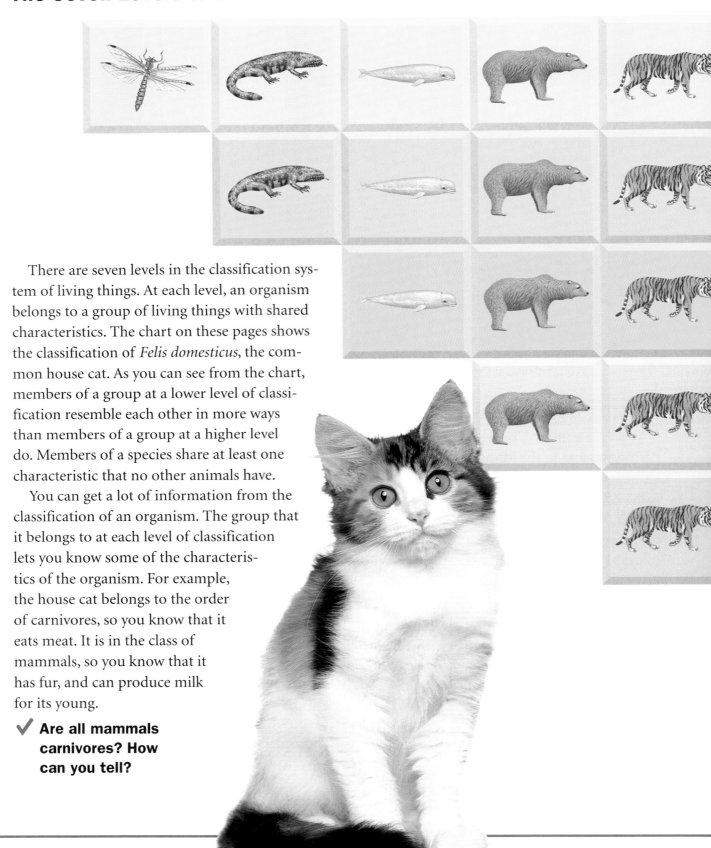

There are seven levels in the classification system of living things. At each level, an organism belongs to a group of living things with shared characteristics. The chart on these pages shows the classification of *Felis domesticus*, the common house cat. As you can see from the chart, members of a group at a lower level of classification resemble each other in more ways than members of a group at a higher level do. Members of a species share at least one characteristic that no other animals have.

You can get a lot of information from the classification of an organism. The group that it belongs to at each level of classification lets you know some of the characteristics of the organism. For example, the house cat belongs to the order of carnivores, so you know that it eats meat. It is in the class of mammals, so you know that it has fur, and can produce milk for its young.

✔ **Are all mammals carnivores? How can you tell?**

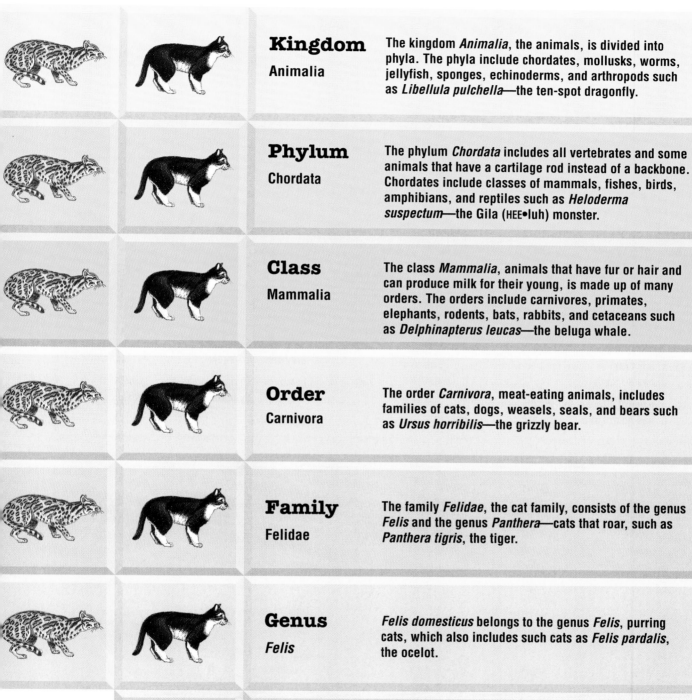

Kingdom
Animalia

The kingdom *Animalia*, the animals, is divided into phyla. The phyla include chordates, mollusks, worms, jellyfish, sponges, echinoderms, and arthropods such as *Libellula pulchella*—the ten-spot dragonfly.

Phylum
Chordata

The phylum *Chordata* includes all vertebrates and some animals that have a cartilage rod instead of a backbone. Chordates include classes of mammals, fishes, birds, amphibians, and reptiles such as *Heloderma suspectum*—the Gila (HEE•luh) monster.

Class
Mammalia

The class *Mammalia*, animals that have fur or hair and can produce milk for their young, is made up of many orders. The orders include carnivores, primates, elephants, rodents, bats, rabbits, and cetaceans such as *Delphinapterus leucas*—the beluga whale.

Order
Carnivora

The order *Carnivora*, meat-eating animals, includes families of cats, dogs, weasels, seals, and bears such as *Ursus horribilis*—the grizzly bear.

Family
Felidae

The family *Felidae*, the cat family, consists of the genus *Felis* and the genus *Panthera*—cats that roar, such as *Panthera tigris*, the tiger.

Genus
Felis

Felis domesticus belongs to the genus *Felis*, purring cats, which also includes such cats as *Felis pardalis*, the ocelot.

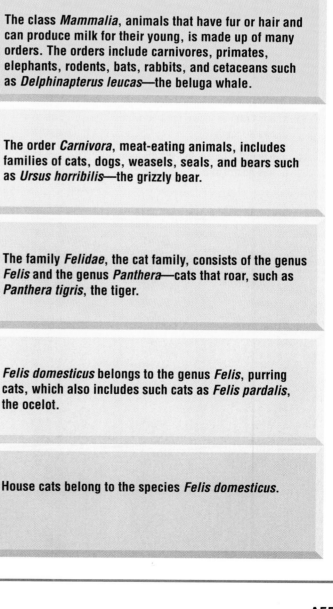

Species
Felis domesticus

House cats belong to the species *Felis domesticus*.

Using a Key

Have you ever hiked through the woods and noticed an animal that you had never seen before? Even people who study nature cannot recognize every living thing they encounter. When bird-watchers and others interested in nature go hiking or camping, they often carry guides that help them identify species of living things they observe. One type of guide is a field guide—a book with pictures or photographs of local animals or plants.

Another guide that can be used to identify an organism based on its characteristics is a **dichotomous key** (dy•KAHT•uh•muhs kee). It consists of a series of choices that lead to the correct name of the organism you want to identify. *Dichotomous* means "divided into two parts." Each step of the key presents a pair of phrases describing an organism's characteristics. Only one of the phrases applies to the organism you are identifying, and that choice directs you to another pair of phrases and another choice. The process continues until you reach the name of the organism.

The dichotomous key on this page can be used to identify certain species of animals. Follow the steps in the key.

✔ **What are the names of the animals in the photographs labeled *A*, *B*, and *C*?**

Dichotomous Key

❶ a. tail fins are horizontal—whale . . . . go to 2
b. tail fins are vertical—fish . . . . go to 3

❷ a. has teeth or tusk—toothed whale . . . . . . go to 4
b. has no teeth . . . . baleen whale

❸ a. has gill slits behind mouth—shark . . . . . . go to 5
b. has no gill slits . . . . nonshark fish

❹ a. black with white underside . . . . killer whale
b. tusk, gray with dark spots . . . . narwhal

❺ a. head is hammer shaped . . . . . hammerhead shark
b. tail is half the body length . . . . thresher shark

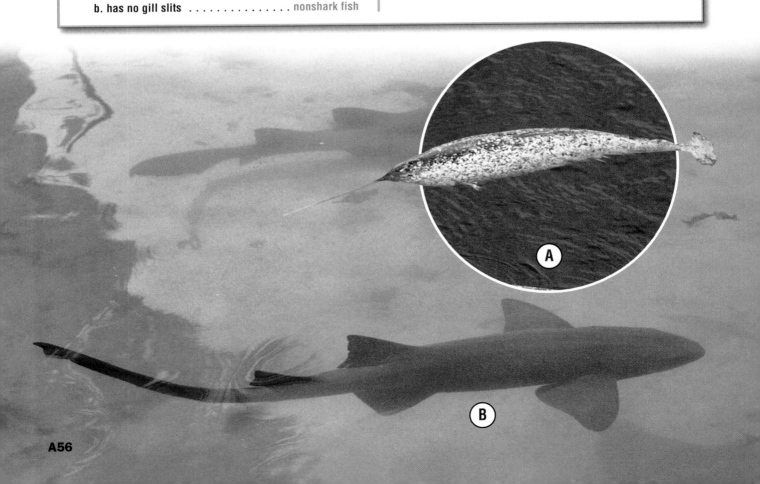

A56

C

Summary

There are seven levels of classification. A kingdom is divided into smaller groups: phylum, class, order, family, genus, and species. The scientific name of an organism has two parts—its genus and species names. A dichotomous key is one type of guide used to identify living things. It presents a series of choices that lead the user to the correct identification of a living thing.

Review

1. What two parts make up an organism's scientific name?

2. What are the advantages of using an organism's scientific name?

3. Which organisms share more characteristics, the members of a species or the members of an order? Explain your answer.

4. **Critical Thinking** Can two species be members of the same family but not the same genus? Can they be members of the same genus but not the same family?

5. **Test Prep** The scientific name of a red maple tree is correctly written as —

    A *Acer rubrum*

    B Acer Rubrum

    C *Acer Rubrum*

    D *Acer* rubrum

MATH LINK

Lots of Bugs Of an estimated 1,400,000 described species, about 62% are arthropods. Of the arthropods, about 86% are insects. About how many species of insects are there?

WRITING LINK

Expressive Writing—Poem or Song Lyrics Write a poem or song that would help your classmates remember the seven divisions of classification and their proper order from kingdom down to species.

LANGUAGE ARTS LINK

Naming a Species The first person to describe a new species has the privilege of naming it. People often name species after themselves or their friends. For example, *Rhea darwinii* is a bird named after Charles Darwin. Some names are expressive: *horrida*, *tormentor*, and *abominator* are each a kind of mosquito. Some groups have been given funny names: a genus of squash bug is named *Polychisme* (pronounced "Polly kiss me"). Invent a new organism, draw or describe it, and make up a scientific name for it.

TECHNOLOGY LINK

To learn more about classification, watch *Dinosaur Rock* on the **Harcourt Science Newsroom Video**.

MICROSCOPE TECHNOLOGY

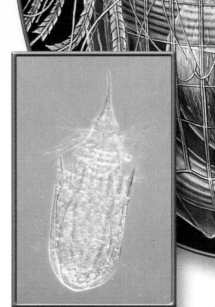

Scientists are developing microscopes that allow them to look clearly at smaller and smaller objects.

How does a microscope work?

All microscopes need some form of light or energy to light up an object to be viewed. Another device in the microscope magnifies and focuses an image formed by the light. Most of the microscopes you may be familiar with are optical microscopes. They use visible light to light up objects. A glass lens or series of lenses focuses the light and magnifies the object.

How small an object can microscopes make visible?

All microscopes are limited by the type of light or energy they use to allow scientists to view things. In theory, a microscope can show details in objects that are as small as the wavelength of the type of light or energy it uses. So, in theory, optical microscopes can show detail in objects that are as small as a single wavelength of visible light. But in reality, a microscope is limited by the lenses that are used in it. Because of this limitation, optical microscopes

can't show very clearly anything that has been magnified more than about 1000 times. That can make a very tiny object appear large. But there are even smaller objects that an optical microscope can't help us see.

How do scientists see even smaller objects?

Improved microscopes use forms of light and energy such as electrons, X rays, ultraviolet light, and ions to allow scientists to view tiny objects. Electron microscopes use beams of electrons to light up objects. The wavelength of an electron is much smaller than the wavelength of visible light. So, a beam of electrons (rather than a beam of light) can produce images of much smaller objects. An electron microscope can show objects that measure less than 2 angstroms. One angstrom is one-billionth of a centimeter (about 4 ten-billionths of an inch).

The atomic force microscope produces images by dragging a tiny needle across an object. The needle bumps up and down as the atoms on the tip of the needle are repelled by the atoms on the object. A computer then turns these movements into a three-dimensional color image. This microscope allows scientists to see the outlines of atoms.

Why is developing new types of microscopes important?

The microscope is one of the most important scientific tools. In medicine, microscopes are used to examine blood and tissue samples for

◄ Loriciferans (lor•ih•SIF•uh•rens) are a new phylum of animals that have been studied by using a scanning electron microscope. The small image on the left is a scanning electron micrograph. The large image is a drawing made from a scanning electron microscope image.

diseases. Engineers use microscopes to examine and develop tiny computer chips and electronic devices. In the future, new microscopes could help scientists map genes and discover more about the structure of viruses. New treatments for diseases, smaller and faster computer chips, and new types of materials could result from the ability to see and work with smaller objects.

THINK ABOUT IT

1. Why do scientists use microscopes?
2. In what way have microscopes been improved over time?

WEB LINK:
For Science and Technology updates, visit The Learning Site.
www.harcourtschool.com

Careers | Microscope Technician

What They Do
Microscope technicians can help doctors determine the state of a patient's health by using microscopes to examine samples of the patient's blood and tissue. The cause of a specific disease can often be determined only by examining a patient's blood or tissue under a microscope.

Education and Training Microscope technicians need a background in physics and optics. They also should be familiar with using computers. Microscope technicians first earn a high school diploma and then must take technical courses to qualify for a license.

Geerat Vermeij

BIOLOGIST

"My fourth-grade teacher aroused in me a lasting curiosity about things unknown. She created a freedom for me to observe, an encouragement to wonder, and an environment in which to ask questions."

Dr. Geerat Vermeij (GIR•aht ver•MAY) is an expert on how mollusks develop. Mollusks include animals that have shells (such as clams and snails) as well as animals that do not (such as squid and octopods). Some mollusks live on land, but many live in water. Dr. Vermeij's detailed descriptions of every ridge, twist, and turn in the shells of certain mollusks have helped us understand how these animals change as they mature.

Dr. Vermeij has been blind since he was four years old. As a result, he has always relied on sounds, odors, shapes, and textures to observe and study the

world around him. He says his fourth-grade teacher sparked his interest in science with her shell collection. He spent hours exploring the shells with his fingers. He observed them through their shapes and textures. Soon he imagined himself exploring the places where they were found and learning about the creatures that once lived inside them.

Geerat Vermeij decided he would go to college and become a scientist. However, he did not plan to stay indoors in a laboratory. "There is no substitute for making one's own observations in the wild," he says. That's what he has done. Braving venomous snakes, dangerous crocodiles, rough seas, and the edges of high cliffs, he has traveled around the world to observe the creatures he studies.

Dr. Vermeij's work has helped explain how a mollusk's shell protects its soft body and how these animals compete for survival. He continues to explore the world through touch and his other senses and to encourage others to do the same.

THINK ABOUT IT

1. What is Dr. Vermeij's area of study?
2. How might the fact that Dr. Vermeij is blind have resulted in his unique contribution to our knowledge of certain mollusks?

Sorting Pasta

How can you use a dichotomous key to categorize different kinds of pasta?

Materials
- 5 or 6 kinds of uncooked pasta
- transparent tape

Procedure

1. Begin the key by writing these statements:
   1a. The pasta is tube-shaped.   Go to 2.
   1b. The pasta is not tube-shaped.   Go to 3

2. Sort your pasta into a pile that is tube-shaped and a pile that is not tube-shaped.

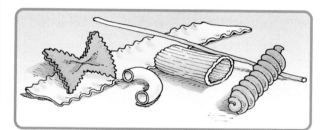

3. Add this pair of statements to your key:
   2a. The tube is straight.
   2b. The tube is curved.

4. If only one kind of tube-shaped pasta is straight, tape an example opposite Statement 2a. If only one kind of tube-shaped pasta is curved, tape an example opposite 2b.

5. Think of statements for 3a and 3b to divide the pasta that is not tube-shaped into two groups. Continue to divide the pasta into pairs of groups to complete your key.

Draw Conclusions

If two kinds of tube-shaped pasta are straight, how could you divide them into two groups? What would you write beside statement 2a? What pair of statements would divide the straight, tube-shaped pasta into two groups?

Sorting Fungi

How can you identify types of mold?

Materials
- several kinds of moldy food (such as bread, citrus fruit, cheese) in tightly sealed, clear, plastic bags
- hand lens

Procedure

1. Examine each kind of mold with the hand lens.
   CAUTION **Do not open bags to make your observations.** Mold is part of the Kingdom Fungi and includes many species. Use this dichotomous key to identify the kinds of mold.
   1a. Black, white, or gray fuzz   Go to 2.
   1b. Yellow or blue-green fuzz   Go to 3.
   2a. No rootlike threads and many dark balls (spores)   *Aspergillus flavus*
   2b. Many white or gray rootlike threads   Go to 4.
   3a. Yellow rootlike threads and many dark balls   *Aspergillus niger*
   3b. Blue-green or gray rootlike threads and few dark balls   *Penicillium*
   4a. Beige or white rootlike threads and few dark balls   *Mucor*
   4b. Gray or white rootlike threads and many dark balls   *Rhizopus*

Draw Conclusions

How did you differentiate among the types of mold? Why do you think mold grows on food?

Chapter 2 Review and Test Preparation

Vocabulary Review

Write the correct term to complete the sentences. The page numbers in ( ) tell you where to look in the chapter if you need help.

classification (A42)   **Monera** (A44)

Linnaean system (A43)   **adaptation** (A45)

Animalia (A44)   **genus** (A53)

Plantae (A44)   **species** (A53)

Fungi (A44)   **dichotomous key** (A56)

Protista (A44)

1. One-celled organisms that have one or more nuclei and are similar in structure to plant and animal cells are in the kingdom ____.

2. The first part of a scientific name is the ____ name, and the second part is the ____ name.

3. A ____ is a group of organisms that share major characteristics.

4. Animals belong to the kingdom ____, and plants belong to the kingdom ____.

5. An ____ is a trait that better suits an organism to its environment.

6. Organisms that have cells similar to plants but do not make their own food belong to the kingdom ____.

7. A series of choices that leads to the correct identification of an organism is called a ____.

8. The ____ is a classification system in which living things are divided into smaller and smaller groups.

9. The kingdom ____ includes bacteria and blue-green bacteria.

Connect Concepts

Complete the chart.

The five kingdoms are —

10. _____   11. _____   12. _____   13. _____   14. _____

The seven levels of the Linnaean system, in order from largest to smallest, are —

15. _____   19. _____

16. _____   20. _____

17. _____   21. _____

18. _____

Check Understanding

Write the letter of the best choice.

22. A certain one-celled organism has chloroplasts, a nucleus, and a whiplike flagellum. It is classified as —

    A a plant

    B an animal

    C a protist

    D a moneran

23. A characteristic that separates monerans from all other organisms is that —

    F they have a cell wall

    G they have no nucleus

    H they are single-celled

    J they cannot move

24. Scientists discussing a particular organism use its scientific name —

    A to establish how it is related to other organisms

    B to impress other scientists

    C to avoid confusion about the identity of the organism

    D to place it in a dichotomous key

25. Organisms that are members of the same order are not necessarily members of the same —

    F phylum

    G class

    H family

    J kingdom

26. An organism's scientific name is made up of the names of its —

    A genus and species

    B kingdom and species

    C kingdom, family, and species

    D family, genus, and species

Critical Thinking

27. Describe classifications you use in your everyday life.

28. A scientist believes she has discovered a new species. How can she check to make sure that her species has not been described before?

29. Not all scientists classify organisms in exactly the same way. In fact, some scientists use a seven-kingdom classification system rather than a five-kingdom system. Are they wrong? Explain.

Process Skills Review

30. What characteristics could you use to **classify** a group of buttons?

31. Under the classification system currently in use, how do scientists **organize data** about living things?

Performance Assessment

A Key for Diatoms

Study the photograph of diatoms on page A47. Choose one diatom to classify. Make a list of the characteristics of your diatom, based on what you observe in the photograph. Design a dichotomous key with at least four steps to identify the diatom you have selected.

Unit Project Wrap Up

Here are some ideas for wrapping up your unit project or doing other projects.

Display at a Science Fair

Display your cell model and report in a school science fair. Be prepared to answer questions people may have about cells.

Make a Diagram

Use a computer software program to make a diagram showing how organisms are classified.

Draw a Chart

Draw a chart that explains how traits are inherited. Choose a plant or animal, and explain its inherited characteristics.

Investigate Further

How can you make your project better? What other questions do you have about living things? Plan ways to find answers to your questions. Use the Science Handbook on pages R2–R9 for help.

Living Things Grow and Respond

UNIT
B

LIFE SCIENCE

Living Things Grow and Respond

Unit Project

Botanical Garden

Design a botanical garden. Organize the garden so that plants of the same type are together. Plan for ways to meet the needs of the plants. Also plan places for insects, mammals, birds, and other animals to live. Draw a map of your garden and label all its features.

Plant Growth and Responses

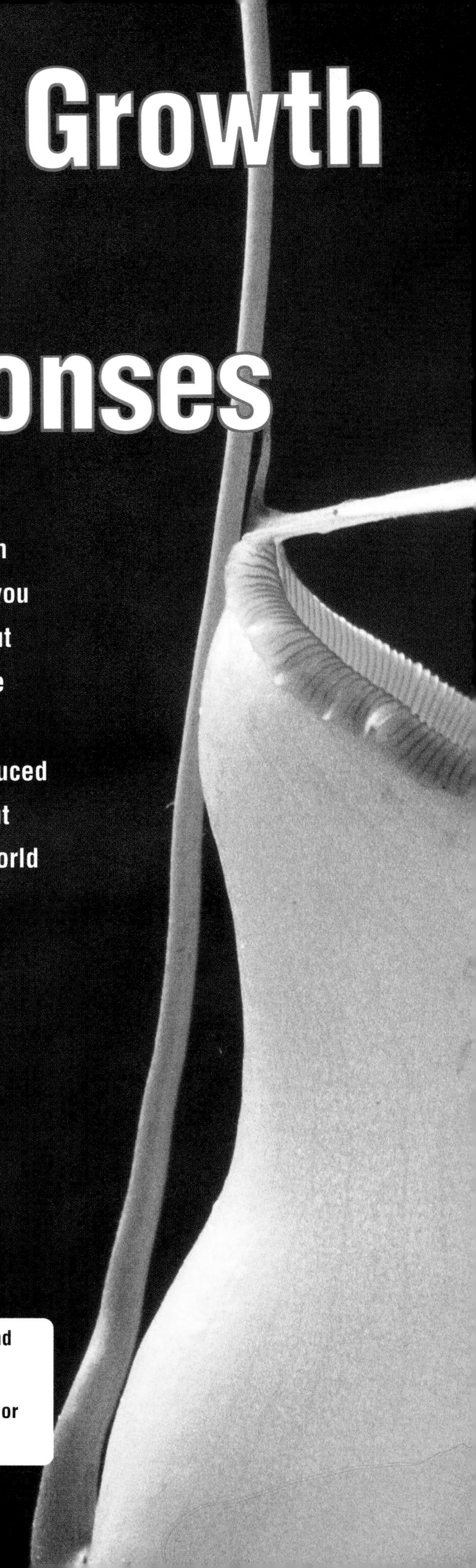

You might not pay much
attention to plants—but you
couldn't stay alive without
them. You eat plants, use
furniture made of plants,
and breathe oxygen produced
by plants. A world without
plants would also be a world
without people.

Vocabulary Preview

vascular plant
xylem
phloem
nonvascular plant
tropism
phototropism
gravitropism
long-day plant
short-day plant

FAST FACT

Several types of plants trap and
"eat" insects. The pitcher
plants of Malaysia, however,
are large enough to trap birds or
small mammals.

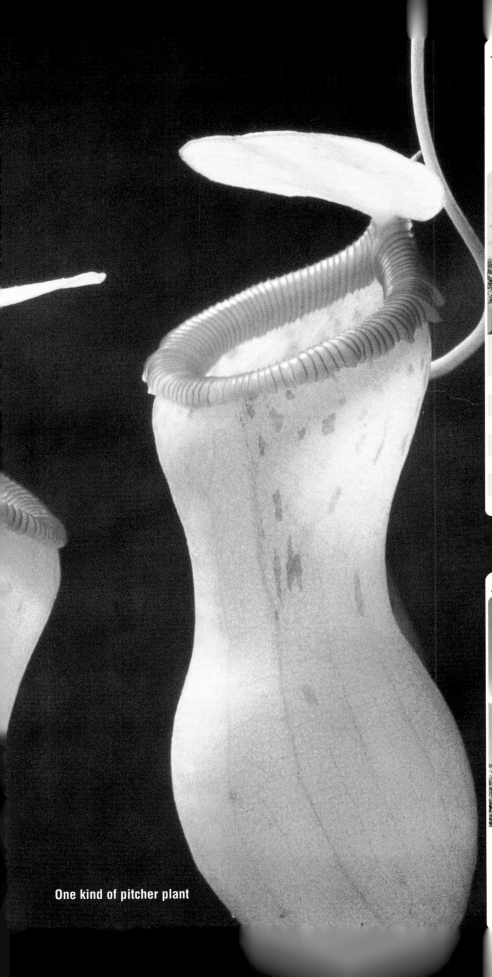

One kind of pitcher plant

Tall Trees		
Tree	Height	
	feet	meters
Apple	20–30	(6–9)
Live oak	40–50	(12–15)
Paper birch	50–70	(15–21)
Elm	80–100	(24–30)
Ponderosa pine	100–180	(30–55)
Douglas fir	180–250	(55–76)
Redwood	200–275	(61–84)

1

How Do Plants Meet Their Needs?

In this lesson, you can . . .

INVESTIGATE seed germination and seedling growth.

LEARN ABOUT plant growth, plant structures, and how plants meet their needs.

LINK to math, writing, art, and technology.

Banana leaves have slits that let water run through. ▽

INVESTIGATE

Germinating Seeds

Activity Purpose Most plants grow from seeds. Some seeds germinate—or sprout—quickly. Other seeds take years to germinate. No matter how long they take, seeds germinate only under certain conditions. In this investigation you will **control variables** in an experiment to find out what those conditions are.

Materials

- paper towels
- 5 clear plastic cups
- 20 bean seeds
- masking tape
- permanent marker
- water
- graduate or measuring cup
- shoe box with lid

Activity Procedure

1 Fold a paper towel so that its width is the height of one of the cups. Use it to line the sides of the cup. Then fill the cup carefully with crumpled paper towels. Repeat this step for each cup. (Picture A)

2 Between the paper lining and the side of each cup, place four bean seeds. You should be able to see the beans through the plastic.

3 Using masking tape and a marker, label the cups *A, B, C, D,* and *E.* Follow the directions next to the letter for each cup: (Picture B)

A Slowly drip water into the cup until the paper towels are moist. Place the cup in the shoe box. Close the lid. Add water each day to keep the towels moist.

B Fill the cup with water.

C Add *no* water.

Picture A

Picture B

D Moisten the paper towels as for A, and keep them moist each day.

E Moisten the paper towels as for A, and keep them moist each day.

4 Place Cups A, B, C, and D in a warm place, but not directly over a heater and not in direct sunlight. Place Cup E in a refrigerator. **Observe** the cups daily to see how many beans are sprouting. **Record** your observations. **Compare** your results with those of your classmates.

Draw Conclusions

1. In which cups did you **observe** the seeds sprouting?

2. Based on the results of your experiment, what **conclusions can you draw** about what seeds need in order to germinate?

3. **Scientists at Work** Scientists often **control variables** in an experiment to make sure their conclusions are accurate. Sometimes they need to refine an experiment to make sure they are testing only one variable at a time. What variables did you test in this experiment? How could you change the experiment to test only a single variable?

Investigate Further Suppose you were planting a garden. How could you use the results of this experiment to decide when, where, and how to plant seeds?

Process Skill Tip

A *variable* is a factor that could affect the results of an experiment. To make sure that their conclusions are accurate, scientists need to **identify and control variables**. To control variables, you need to set up experimental conditions to test only one thing at a time.

Adaptations of Plants

Most Plants Grow from Seeds

FIND OUT

- how plants grow from seeds
- what plants need in order to grow and how they meet their needs
- the differences between vascular and nonvascular plants

VOCABULARY

vascular plant
xylem
phloem
nonvascular plant

Most plants produce new plants from seeds. Walk through an overgrown field or an empty lot, or even down a city street, and you'll find seeds of many sizes, colors, and shapes. Some, such as the seeds of the dandelion, are like parachutes. Others are burs that stick to clothing and fur like Velcro. Look on trees, and you'll find many other kinds of seeds. Maybe you've seen the winged seeds on maples, the acorns on oaks, and the seeds in the cones on pine trees.

But how do seeds germinate? When conditions are right, seeds absorb water. The seeds swell. If there is not enough water in the soil, the seeds won't sprout. If there is too much, the seeds will not get enough oxygen, and they will rot.

Seeds also need warmth to germinate. In regions where winters are cold, seeds do not begin to sprout and grow until spring arrives. Some will sprout in the colder ground of early spring. Others need the sun-warmed ground of late spring or early summer.

When a seed germinates, it splits open and a small seedling appears. A tiny root begins to grow downward. Then a tiny shoot begins to grow upward. Soon leaves form at the tip of the shoot. In some plants, branches may grow from lateral, or side, buds. The tips of the side branches grow, and they, too, form leaves and more lateral buds. In this way, branches produce more branches.

✔ **What happens first when a seed germinates?**

A shoot grows longer as the cells at its tip divide and grow longer. ▼

Growth also occurs at the very tip of a root. The root pushes deeper into the soil as the cells at the root tip divide and grow longer. ▼

A tree seedling grows only where plant cells are dividing rapidly. This is most often at the tip of the root and the tip of the shoot. ▶

Plant Needs

After a seed has germinated and begun to grow, the new plant needs certain materials to stay healthy.

All plants need water. In fact, water makes up as much as 95 percent of some plants. All life processes inside plant cells take place in a watery solution. Also, all of the materials carried through a plant are transported in water.

Plants also need sunlight. The process of photosynthesis, in which plants make food, requires sunlight, water, and carbon dioxide. Plants have chloroplasts, which are full of the green coloring chlorophyll. Chlorophyll captures the energy from sunlight. The energy is used to combine carbon dioxide and water to produce sugar and oxygen.

Plants also use oxygen to release the energy from food for life processes. When oxygen combines with the sugar, the process produces energy, carbon dioxide, and water.

Plants also need nutrients such as nitrogen, phosphorus, and sulfur, which serve a variety of purposes. They are used to make important parts of plant cells. They also help carry out some of the processes of the cells. The nutrients, which are dissolved in water, are transported throughout the plant. Plants will not grow well if they do not have enough of these nutrients.

✔ **What five essential materials do plants need?**

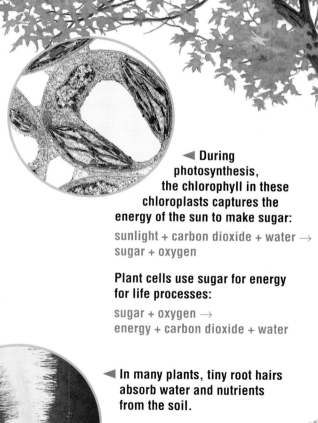

◀ Oxygen and carbon dioxide pass into and out of the leaves through *stomata* (stoh•MAH•tuh), tiny pores on the surface of the leaves. Much of the water is reused within the plant cell.

◀ **During photosynthesis, the chlorophyll in these chloroplasts captures the energy of the sun to make sugar:**

sunlight + carbon dioxide + water →
sugar + oxygen

Plant cells use sugar for energy for life processes:

sugar + oxygen →
energy + carbon dioxide + water

◀ In many plants, tiny root hairs absorb water and nutrients from the soil.

Vascular Plants

The water and nutrients absorbed by a plant's roots travel throughout the plant. The food made in the leaves also travels through the plant to the places where energy is needed. Many kinds of plants have tissues, or specialized groups of cells, that carry water and dissolved materials. Plants that have these tissues are called **vascular plants**. The oak tree shown on these pages is a vascular plant.

The tissues that carry water form a system of vessels that reach all parts of the plant. The vessels are made of two kinds of tissue: xylem and phloem. **Xylem** (ZY•luhm) carries water and

THE INSIDE STORY

Inside an Oak Tree

Some plants, like this oak tree, have woody stems. Their stems get thicker each year. Bark forms around stems, branches, and parts of the roots. As the tree grows thicker, new xylem and phloem form. ▶

old xylem

new xylem

The xylem tissue forms continuous, hollow tubes. These tubes reach from the roots all the way up the trunk and through the branches to the leaves. Xylem cells have very thick walls, which provide support for vascular plants.

Water and nutrients are absorbed through the root hairs. They move into the xylem. Phloem carries food to the roots, where much of it is stored, and to all other parts of the plant, where it is used in life processes. ▶

nutrients from the roots to the leaves. **Phloem** (FLOH•uhm) carries food from the leaves to the other parts of the plant for use and storage.

Some of the food is carried to the roots, where it is stored for the winter. In the spring this food moves through the phloem to the buds, where new stems and leaves are about to grow.

One reason vascular plants can grow very large is that they have xylem and phloem to carry water, nutrients, and food to all their parts.

✔ **Why does a vascular plant need both xylem and phloem?**

Inside a leaf, larger veins branch into smaller and smaller veins. In these veins, xylem carries water and nutrients to the leaf cells. Phloem carries food from the leaf cells. The carbon dioxide used in photosynthesis enters the leaf through stomata. So does the oxygen that is used to release energy.

xylem

phloem

Nonvascular Plants

Not all plants have xylem and phloem. Some plants, such as mosses and liverworts, are called **nonvascular plants**. They do not have true roots. They also do not have tissues through which water, nutrients, and food can be transported.

Because nonvascular plants lack xylem and phloem, each cell must absorb water and nutrients directly from the soil or air. Water passes from cell to cell. Some nonvascular plants need a lot of water to stay alive. They live in moist places. They are often found in shady places in woods and swamps. Some nonvascular plants grow close together. This gives them some support, as xylem does for vascular plants.

Because they do not have tissues to transport food and water, nonvascular plants cannot grow very large. However, like all plants, nonvascular plants make food through photosynthesis. They have parts that resemble leaves, stems, and roots. These are less-complex structures than

◀ The ground in woodlands and near streams and waterfalls is moist and shady, and is often covered with mosses.

A bed of moss is actually made up of hundreds of tiny individual moss plants. The plants grow very close together to form a thick, spongy, bright-green mat. ▼

similar parts of vascular plants. The leaflike parts of mosses and liverworts contain chlorophyll, but these parts have only one or two layers of cells. Each plant is attached to the soil by long, hairlike cells called *rhizoids* (RY•zoydz).

✓ **Why are nonvascular plants small?**

Summary

Seeds germinate when they have the right amounts of oxygen, water, and warmth. Growth occurs at the tips of the roots and shoots and at the lateral buds. Plants need water, sun, and carbon dioxide to carry on photosynthesis. They need oxygen and sugar to produce energy for life processes. They also need nutrients, which they absorb from the soil through root hairs. Vascular plants have xylem, which transports water and nutrients from the roots throughout the plant. They also have phloem, which transports food from the leaves to all other parts of the plant. Nonvascular plants do not have tissues to transport materials.

Review

1. Under what conditions do seeds germinate?
2. How can you make sure that a houseplant stays healthy?
3. Why can most vascular plants grow much taller than nonvascular plants?
4. **Critical Thinking** Suppose you pound a nail into a tree trunk. Will the nail stay at the same height each year? Explain.
5. **Test Prep** Nutrients are carried through a vascular plant by —
   A seedlings
   B bark
   C xylem
   D phloem

LINKS

MATH LINK

Calculating Germination Rates A germination rate is given on the back of every package of seeds. The seed companies have tested their seeds to determine the rate. If, for example, 75 out of 100 seeds sprout, then the germination rate is 75 percent. Calculate the following germination rates as percents: 10 out of 25 seeds, 28 out of 50 seeds, 36 out of 50 seeds.

WRITING LINK

Informative Writing—Compare and Contrast Write a paragraph for your classmates in which you compare xylem and phloem tissues with the delivery systems at a factory.

ART LINK

Seed Crafts Seeds show a great variety of sizes, shapes, and colors. They can be used for decoration in countless ways. People use them for jewelry, collages, sculptures, mobiles, and more. Make your own art project using seeds.

TECHNOLOGY LINK

To learn more about plant adaptations and growth, watch *Giant Plant Gene* on the **Harcourt Science Newsroom Video.**

How Do Plants Respond to Their Environments?

In this lesson, you can . . .

INVESTIGATE how roots respond to the environment.

LEARN ABOUT how plants respond to light, gravity, touch, and length of the day.

LINK to math, writing, social studies, and technology.

INVESTIGATE

Do All Roots Grow Down?

Activity Purpose When a seed is planted, it may be upside down in the ground. If it is, will the root still grow downward and the shoot still grow upward? In this investigation you'll **experiment** to find out.

Materials

- clear plastic cup
- paper towels
- water
- sprouted bean seed (from previous investigation)

Activity Procedure

1 Line the inside of a plastic cup with several layers of paper towels. Moisten the paper towels.

2 Carefully place the sprouted bean seed between the paper towels and the side of the cup. Position it so that its root is pointing downward. (Picture A)

3 Place the cup in a cabinet or a room that is dark all the time.

4 After a day or two, turn the cup on its side. Keep the paper towels moist, and **observe** the results after another day or two. (Picture B)

◀ Desert plants can live well in places with little rainfall. They lose little moisture, and they have large shallow root systems to take in as much water as possible.

Picture A

Picture B

Draw Conclusions

1. What happened to the seed's root after you turned the cup on its side?

2. What **hypothesis** might explain your **observations**?

3. **Scientists at Work** Scientists have **experimented** to **observe** the different effect of gravity in outer space on germinating seeds. When wheat seeds germinated in an orbiting space shuttle, the roots and shoots grew in every direction. What can you **conclude** from this experiment?

Investigate Further Try an **experiment** like the one above. Place four sprouted lima beans with roots pointing in different directions in a plastic cup lined with moist paper towels. Put the cup in a dark place. Keep the paper towels moist, but don't turn the cup. What do you **predict** will happen to each of the roots?

Process Skill Tip

To **draw conclusions**, you need to carefully think about all of the information you have. You need to think about what you already know and what you found out in your experiment.

How Plants Respond to Their Environments

Tropisms

Suppose you turn a potted flowering plant on your windowsill so that the flowers face the room. Before long the plant stems will bend so that the flowers again face the light from the window.

The response of a plant to turn toward or away from anything in its environment is called a **tropism** (TROH•piz•uhm). The word *tropism* comes from a Greek word that means "to turn." A response to light, like the one shown by flowers on the windowsill, is called **phototropism**. Plants are said to show *positive phototropism* because they turn toward light.

In the investigation, you saw another kind of tropism. The root of a plant grows downward, in the direction of gravity. This is **gravitropism**. Roots show *positive gravitropism*—they bend in the same direction as the pull of gravity. The shoot of a seed shows *negative gravitropism*—it bends away from the pull of gravity.

Some plants respond to touch. For example, squash, pumpkins, and cucumbers have threadlike tendrils that are sensitive to touch. The tendrils grow toward the side that is touched. In this way, they can grow around objects they touch to gain support from them.

✔ **In what ways do some plants respond to light, gravity, and touch?**

FIND OUT

- **how plants respond to their environments**
- **why different plants flower at different times of the year**

VOCABULARY

tropism
phototropism
gravitropism
long-day plant
short-day plant

Examples of Tropisms

◀ The shoots of a plant grow upward. This helps plant seedlings break through soil to reach sunlight.

Plants need light, and they are able to respond to get the most available. ▶

Mimosa pudica is a tree or shrub with delicate green leaves. ▶

If you touch its leaves, they immediately close up. People call the mimosa the "sensitive plant." ▶

How Tropisms Affect Plants

Plants can't move around as most animals do, so plants can't respond to their environments in the same way. However, tropisms help plants get the things they need to survive.

Plant stems as well as leaves show positive phototropism—they grow toward light. The leaves of plants turn so that they get the largest amount of sunlight possible.

Because of positive gravitropism, the roots of a plant grow down into the soil, where they can take in water and minerals. The shoots show negative gravitropism—they grow upward, against the direction of the force of gravity. When they break through the surface of the ground, they get the light they need.

The tropism for touch can also help plants get light. Plants such as cucumbers have tendrils that respond to touch, allowing them to climb up supports and get more sunlight.

In about 1880 the British scientist Charles Darwin and his son Francis did experiments on tropisms in plants. They grew grass seedlings and noticed that the shoots bent toward the light just below the tips of the seedlings. This is the part of the plant where the seedlings are growing fastest. The Darwins did experiments in which they changed the seedling tips.

They cut the tips off the shoots of some seedlings and left the shoots of other seedlings whole. Then they put all the seedlings in the light. Only the shoots that were whole bent toward the light. The shoots without tips no longer bent toward the light. This happened even though the part of the shoot that usually bent toward the light was still there.

They also covered the tips of some shoots so that light could not reach them. These shoots failed to bend toward the light. Shoots that were covered with transparent caps, on the other hand, did bend toward the light.

Finally, they covered the part of the seedling just below the tip. This was the part that usually bent toward the light. However, even when this part of the seedling received no light, it still bent toward the light. The Darwins concluded that the tip of the shoot is the part that senses light and that it passes this information to the growth zone, just below the tip. Later experiments confirmed what the Darwins discovered.

✔ **How do tropisms help plants survive?**

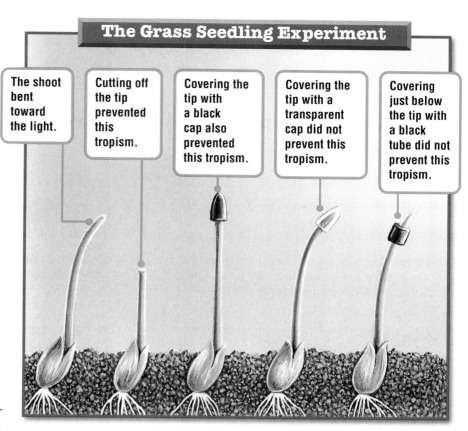

The Grass Seedling Experiment

The shoot bent toward the light.

Cutting off the tip prevented this tropism.

Covering the tip with a black cap also prevented this tropism.

Covering the tip with a transparent cap did not prevent this tropism.

Covering just below the tip with a black tube did not prevent this tropism.

▲ The Darwins' experiments showed these results.

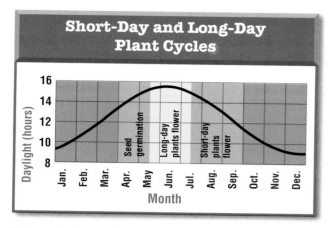

Short-Day and Long-Day Plant Cycles

This graph shows the yearly change in day length for 43° north latitude. When do long-day plants flower at this location? When do short-day plants flower?

Strawberries are short-day plants that produce fruit in the late spring and early summer.

Some plants show daily rhythms. These Livingstone daisies open their petals in the morning and close them at night.

Plant Rhythms

As the seasons change, the temperature changes. The number of hours of daylight, or the length of the day, also changes. When it is colder, days are shorter. When it is warmer, days are longer. In many parts of the world, there are extreme changes in the number of hours of daylight.

To survive, plants must be able to change with the seasons. They have to adapt to the temperature, and they must grow when it's warm and rest when it's cold. Many plants change with the seasons by responding to changes in the length of the day.

Different plants respond in different ways. **Long-day plants** flower when there is more than a certain number of daylight hours—generally between 14 and 16 hours. The nights are short. Even though they are called long-day plants, it is the amount of darkness that determines when the plants bloom. Spinach, potatoes, clover, and lettuce are long-day plants—they bloom when nights are short. They begin to flower in late spring or early summer. This allows them enough time to make seeds before the first frost.

Short-day plants flower when there is less than a certain number of daylight hours—generally between 11 and 15 hours. They need long periods of darkness before they can bloom. Poinsettias, strawberries, and ragweed are short-day plants. There are also plants that flower regardless of the length of the day. They begin to flower from midsummer to autumn. These plants take less time to make seeds than long-day plants. So, like long-day plants, they produce seeds before the first frost.

✔ **What is the difference between short-day plants and long-day plants?**

Summary

A tropism is a plant's turning toward or away from something in the environment. Roots show gravitropism by growing downward. Plants show phototropism by growing toward light. Some plants are sensitive to touch. Plants also adapt to the seasons. Long-day plants flower when the number of daylight hours is more than a certain number. Short-day plants flower when the number of daylight hours is less than a certain number. These adaptations help plants survive.

Review

1. How does gravitropism help plants survive?
2. Which plants' flowers produce seeds faster, short-day plants or long-day plants?
3. Why do plants need to produce seeds before the first frost?
4. **Critical Thinking** If a potted plant is turned on its side, how will its growth change?
5. **Test Prep** If a plant's roots grow toward leaking underground pipes, what might the plant be showing a tropism toward?

   A touch

   B the length of the day

   C gravity

   D water

LINKS

MATH LINK

Cocklebur Blooms A cocklebur flowers when there are at least 16 hours of daylight. What is the ratio of day to night, expressed in lowest terms, that the cocklebur needs to bloom?

WRITING LINK

Informative Writing—Description Choose a single plant that you see each day. Write journal entries for your classmates describing how the plant changes during two weeks.

SOCIAL STUDIES LINK

Calendars Some ancient peoples, such as the Celts, the Egyptians, and the Mayas, developed calendars for the year. These helped them know when to plant their crops. Find out about these or other ancient ways of measuring time and how they helped agriculture.

TECHNOLOGY LINK

Learn more about plant responses to the environment by visiting this Internet Site.
www.scilinks.org/harcourt

GENETIC ENGINEERING
RISKS

Can genetically altered, or changed, plants cause unexpected problems when they are released into the natural environment?

What is genetic engineering?

Genes are the "blueprints" that determine the characteristics of living things. Using the technology known as genetic engineering, scientists can make copies of genes from one organism and place them in another. This process produces combinations of genes that don't occur in nature. It also gives organisms new characteristics or abilities they wouldn't normally have. Genes can be designed in the lab to give a plant or animal a desired trait.

Genetic engineering has been helpful. For example, it has allowed manufacturers to increase the amounts of important medicines they make. One such medicine is insulin, which some people who have diabetes must use regularly. Researchers insert into bacteria the human gene that allows human bodies to make insulin. The bacteria then make the insulin.

Genetic engineering can make plants resistant to herbicides.

How can genetic engineering help farmers?

Genetic engineering is an important tool for farmers. Scientists can alter plants grown as crops to increase the plants' resistance to chemicals called herbicides that are used to kill weeds. The herbicides can be used to kill the weeds without killing the crop. Scientists have developed genetically engineered soybean and cotton plants that are resistant to herbicides.

How might the transfer of genes cause problems?

Scientists have found that when a genetically engineered crop grows near a weed, it can transfer the altered trait to the weed. The genetically altered weeds pass on the trait to their offspring. Some scientists fear that this could result in species of superweeds that even the most powerful herbicides could not kill. In that case, stronger herbicides would be needed to kill the weeds. These could cause greater harm to the environment than the herbicides now do.

Some scientists also think it is possible for the genes to spread, or migrate, from plants into microorganisms in the wild. Unlike higher animals, bacteria and viruses can accept genes from different species and pass along genes. In this way, the pests and diseases could also become resistant to pesticides and herbicides.

What should be done about stopping the migration of genes?

Although many environmentalists are concerned, some companies that develop genetically engineered plants are not. The companies say that government controls on the release of genetically altered plants into the environment are strict enough to prevent any problems. Other scientists support greater controls on the release of genetically altered plants, animals, and microorganisms. They point to other scientific advances that were thought at first to be safe but were later found to harm the environment. For example, chemicals called chlorofluorocarbons (CFCs) were once widely used in such products as aerosol spray cans and food packaging. But scientists discovered that CFCs were destroying the ozone layer in the atmosphere, so now it is against the law to use them in aerosols. People who have concerns about migrating genes don't want to have another situation in which scientists must find a solution after damage has already been done.

THINK ABOUT IT

1. How can genetic engineering be helpful to farmers?
2. How might genetically engineered crops cause problems?

WEB LINK:
For Science and Technology updates, visit The Learning Site.
www.harcourtschool.com

Careers Tree Surgeon

What They Do Tree surgeons plant, feed, prune, and provide pest control for trees. They must know about various tree species and diseases that can affect them. Tree surgeons then must know what to do to save or get rid of diseased trees.

Education and Training Tree surgeons must know a lot about trees and gardening and should also enjoy working outdoors. Tree surgeons should have at least a high school education.

Elma Gonzalez

BIOLOGIST

"The courses you take and the books you read are like place markers along the road. But they are not the vehicle. You are. . . ."

Dr. Elma Gonzalez is a respected professor and researcher in the field of botany. Her research could one day help scientists better understand how plant cells store energy and how seeds germinate. Her research involves advanced theoretical knowledge of how a cell takes on and uses energy. It also requires great skill in specialized laboratory techniques.

Dr. Gonzalez worked hard to get to where she is today. When she was a child in Mexico, she had to leave school each day, from spring through fall, to pick crops with her family. Going to school and finding time to study were difficult. But with great determination, she graduated from high school and went on to college. After earning a degree in biology and chemistry, she went on to earn a Ph.D. in cellular biology.

For many years, Dr. Gonzalez has taught cellular biology at the University of California at Los Angeles, where she specializes in plant research. Her research focuses on the function of different parts of plant cells and on the structures of different plant cells. But teaching young people, and getting them excited about careers in science will always be important to her.

THINK ABOUT IT

1. What might Dr. Gonzalez's research one day teach scientists?
2. What evidence is there that Dr. Gonzalez values education?

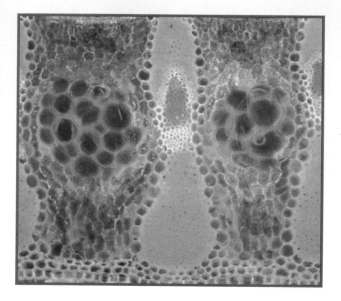

◀ How plant cells function and how they store energy are important parts of Dr. Gonzalez's research.

Traveling Water

How does water move through moss and other nonvascular plants?

Materials

- small plate of dry sphagnum moss
- shallow container of water
- green food coloring
- hand lens

Procedure

1. Color the water by adding green food coloring.

2. Gently pull out a strand of moss. Make sure one end remains attached to the rest of the moss.

3. Put the end of the strand in the container of water, as shown.

4. Using the hand lens, observe what happens.

Draw Conclusions

How do you know the water has entered the moss? How did the water enter and spread through the moss? How is this movement different from water movement in vascular plants? Why does the moss feel damp?

Growth and Touch

How do vines wrap around supports?

Materials

- clear plastic cup lined with a paper towel
- water
- 4 morning glory or moonflower seeds
- 4 pencils
- masking tape

Procedure

1. Wet the paper towel, and slip the seeds between the towel and the cup.

2. Put the cup in a warm, lighted place, and keep the towel moist.

3. Wait two to three weeks, until the seeds sprout and the stems reach the top edge of the cup.

4. Tape the pencils to the outside of the cup, as shown.

Draw Conclusions

When a stem reached a pencil, which side grew faster—the inside part touching the pencil or the outside part not touching the pencil? How does this behavior help the seedlings survive? In what direction are the seed roots growing? How does this help the seedling survive?

Chapter 1 Review and Test Preparation

Vocabulary Review

Use the terms below to complete the sentences. The page numbers in ( ) tell you where to look in the chapter if you need help.

xylem (B8)
vascular plant (B8)
phloem (B9)
nonvascular plant (B10)
tropism (B14)
phototropism (B14)
gravitropism (B14)
long-day plants (B16)
short-day plants (B16)

1. When the length of daylight is greater than a certain amount, ____ flower. When daylight length is less than a certain amount, ____ flower.

2. The tissue that carries water from the roots of a plant to its leaves is called ____.

3. ____ causes the roots of a plant to grow downward.

4. An oak tree is an example of a ____, which has xylem and phloem.

5. A response that causes a plant to turn toward light, or ____, can cause houseplant stems and leaves to turn toward windows.

6. A plant that does not have xylem or phloem is called a ____.

7. A plant shows a ____ any time it turns toward or away from something in the environment.

8. The tissue that carries food to all parts of the plant is ____.

Connect Concepts

Use the words in the word bank to complete the chart.

lateral buds   **carbon dioxide**   **minerals**
gravity   **oxygen**   **sunlight**
water   **roots**

What Seeds Need to Sprout	What Plants Need to Grow	The Parts of Plants That Grow	How Plants Respond
the right temperature	sunlight, oxygen, water	the tips of the shoots	Roots grow in the direction of the force of
9. _____	11. _____	13. _____	15. _____
10. _____	12. _____	14. _____	shoots grow toward
			16. _____

Check Understanding

Write the letter of the best choice.

17. When plant cells use food, which substance do they produce?
    A oxygen
    B carbon dioxide
    C sugar
    D seeds

18. Examples of vascular plants are —
    F mosses
    G liverworts
    H ferns
    J diatoms

19. What parts of a tree make food for the whole plant?
    A roots   C xylem
    B leaves   D phloem

20. The Darwins found that grass seedlings bent toward light if —
    F the tips of the seedlings were cut off
    G black caps were placed over the tips
    H the roots were cut
    J transparent caps were placed over the tips

21. Plants that flower when day length is less than a certain amount are —
    A long-day plants
    B short-day plants
    C tropical herbs
    D tropisms

Critical Thinking

22. When a white carnation is placed in water with red food coloring in it, its petals soon turn red. Explain why this happens.

23. If you had a bag of a plant's seeds, how could you find out whether the plant is a long-day or a short-day plant?

Process Skills Review

24. If you wanted to do an experiment on phototropism, what **variables** would you need to **control**? What variables would you need to test?

25. Suppose you tried to germinate some seeds in the refrigerator and some at room temperature. What **conclusion can you draw** if the seeds fail to germinate?

Performance Assessment

Responding to Color

Write a plan for an experiment to find out what effects the color of light has on the growth of seedlings. List the variables for the seedlings in the experiment. Indicate which of the variables you need to test by writing a *T* next to them in your list. Decide what observations you would make to conclude what effect the color of light has on plant growth. Present your plan to the class.

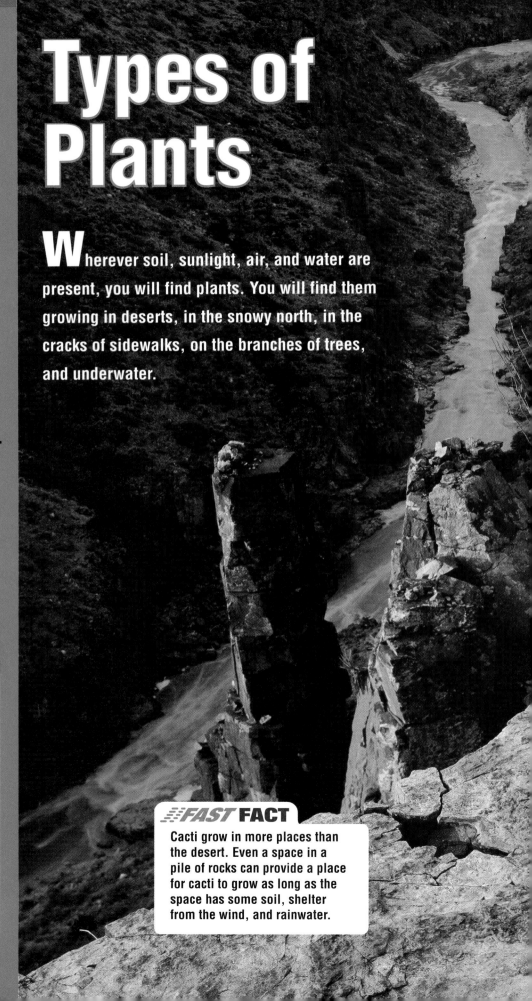

Chapter 2

Vocabulary Preview

moss	pistil
spore	stigma
fern	style
conifer	ovary
pollen	embryo
petal	runner
stamen	grafting
anther	
asexual reproduction	
gymnosperm	
angiosperm	
pollination	
dicotyledon	
monocotyledon	
fertilization	

Types of Plants

Wherever soil, sunlight, air, and water are present, you will find plants. You will find them growing in deserts, in the snowy north, in the cracks of sidewalks, on the branches of trees, and underwater.

FAST FACT

Cacti grow in more places than the desert. Even a space in a pile of rocks can provide a place for cacti to grow as long as the space has some soil, shelter from the wind, and rainwater.

The navel orange is an unusual fruit because it has no seeds. The first navel orange tree was a genetic accident. Ever since, navel oranges have grown on branches that have been grafted onto normal orange trees.

The oldest seed to be grown successfully came from a 10,000-year-old Arctic lupine plant. Most seeds, however, remain able to produce a plant for only a few years.

Seed Life	
Plant	Years
Cucumber	5
Turnip	5
Lettuce	4
Pumpkin	4
Tomato	3
Beet	3
Pepper	2
Sweet corn	2
Carrot	1
Pea	1

LESSON 1

What Are Mosses?

In this lesson, you can . . .

 INVESTIGATE where mosses grow.

 LEARN ABOUT the structures of mosses and how they reproduce.

 LINK to math, writing, social studies, and technology.

Mosses play an important part in the lives of many small animals. This beetle makes its home in mosses. ▽

Where Mosses Grow

Activity Purpose When you walk through a park or a forest, you may first notice the large living things, such as trees. Then you might look down and see small wildflowers and ferns. If you look down even lower, you can see mosses, which often grow almost flat on the ground. In this investigation you'll find out where mosses grow and the conditions they need in order to live.

Materials
- photographs of mosses

Picture A
Picture B

Picture C
Picture D

Picture E
Picture F

Activity Procedure

1 **Observe** the mosses in Pictures A–F.

2 **Record** your **observations** in a chart like the one shown here. Draw a picture of each moss, and describe it. Pay close attention to the surroundings of each moss. Describe the environment in which the moss is growing. Remember to include details such as the place where the moss grows, the surrounding living things, and the amounts of sunlight and moisture in the environment. If you can **infer** the approximate temperature from the picture, include that information in your description, too.

Observations of Mosses

Picture	Description	Environment

Draw Conclusions

1. By **observing**, what did you **infer** about the surroundings in which mosses can live?

2. What can you **hypothesize** about what mosses need in order to grow?

3. Where might you expect to find mosses growing? List at least three places not shown in the photographs on page B26.

4. **Scientists at Work** Scientists can test a **hypothesis** by **observing** further. How could making observations help you test your hypothesis about what mosses need in order to grow?

Investigate Further Look for mosses by using what you have found out. Check your own ideas about the places where mosses grow.

Process Skill Tip

If you **observe** carefully and often, you're more likely to be correct when you **hypothesize**. Observations also provide evidence to support your hypothesis.

Nonvascular Plants

FIND OUT

• about the structures of mosses and how mosses meet their needs

• about how mosses reproduce

• about other nonvascular plants

VOCABULARY

moss
asexual reproduction
spore

Mosses

A **moss** is a very short green plant that does not have true leaves, stems, and roots. It's a nonvascular plant, so it does not have xylem or phloem to carry water, nutrients, and food.

Mosses have structures that look like leaves, stems, and roots. The leaflike structures of mosses are green. The moss makes food within these structures. Unlike true leaves, however, these structures do not have veins, and they are only one or two cells thick. The stemlike structures of mosses have cells for carrying water and food. The water and food move through them slowly. They are not like the complex tissue in vascular plants. The rootlike structures of mosses

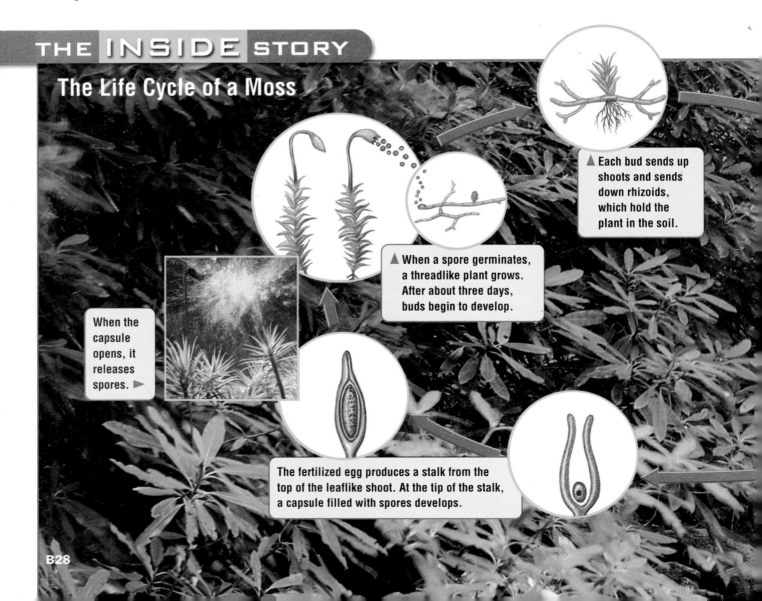

THE INSIDE STORY

The Life Cycle of a Moss

▲ Each bud sends up shoots and sends down rhizoids, which hold the plant in the soil.

▲ When a spore germinates, a threadlike plant grows. After about three days, buds begin to develop.

When the capsule opens, it releases spores. ▶

The fertilized egg produces a stalk from the top of the leaflike shoot. At the tip of the stalk, a capsule filled with spores develops.

B28

◀ The heavy-walled cells in the center of a moss stem are specialized for moving water. The cells just outside those cells are specialized for food transport. Both are much simpler than the xylem and phloem tissues in vascular plants.

hold the plant in the soil. Unlike the roots of vascular plants, they do not absorb much water or many nutrients.

As you observed in the investigation, mosses grow best in moist, shady places. Mosses often grow on a shady forest floor or beside pools or streams. Some mosses, such as peat moss, grow in bogs or swamps and can hold quite a lot of water.

Mosses have a life cycle with two very different stages. One generation looks plantlike. The plantlike generation carries out sexual reproduction. It makes egg and sperm cells that join to produce a new moss plant.

Then the other generation begins. This generation looks like a stalk that grows out of the leaflike part of the moss. This generation carries out **asexual reproduction**, in which a new plant is produced without the joining of a sperm and an egg cell. The stalk produces spores. A **spore** is a structure that contains cells that can grow into a new plant without joining with other cells.

✔ **How do mosses differ from vascular plants?**

Mosses Help the Environment

Mosses often grow in dense layers and cover very large areas. They are attached to the soil, so they help keep it from being eroded by the wind or rain. Mosses also store nutrients. When they die, the mosses decompose, and their matter returns to the environment. The nutrients and other matter from the mosses greatly improve the soil for other plants.

Many species of mosses are sensitive to polluted air. When the air where they live becomes polluted, many mosses die. Then they are no longer seen growing in their usual surroundings. In this way mosses can show where there is pollution.

✔ **How do mosses help the environment?**

▲ Some shoots grow a structure that produces eggs, and some grow a structure that produces sperm.

After rain or a heavy dew, the sperm swim through the standing water and fertilize the eggs. ▼

◀ In Japan, where there is little space for gardens, moss gardens are popular. Mosses in different shades of green are planted around carefully arranged rocks.

B29

Other Nonvascular Plants

Mosses are not the only nonvascular plants. Others are liverworts and hornworts. They grow in the same kinds of surroundings as mosses, sometimes among them. But liverworts and hornworts are even smaller than mosses, and they don't grow in such large clumps. Only the most careful observers notice them. You need a hand lens to see the structures of these tiny plants.

Although nonvascular plants have many things in common, they can have different structures. Mosses have leaflike structures all the way around their stemlike structures. But liverworts have leaflike structures that are flat and scaly. Their stemlike structures lie along the ground. The word *wort* means "herb." Liverworts got their name because some of them are shaped like the human liver.

Hornworts, as you might guess, have structures that look like an animal's horns. The "horns" are reproductive structures that produce spores. The green leaflike part of a hornwort is very small and very simple. It has a flat, rounded shape and no clear stemlike structure.

Like mosses, both liverworts and hornworts have two different generations. At times, you may see the horns of a hornwort. These are on the spore-producing generation. On liverworts, you may see small green structures that look like umbrellas. These carry out sexual reproduction.

✔ **How are liverworts and hornworts similar to mosses?**

The hornlike structures of this hornwort, *Anthoceros*, can continue producing spores over a long period of time. ▼

This liverwort, *Marchantia*, can be found on the banks of cool streams, where it sometimes grows in large mats. Bright yellow spore capsules form on the undersides of the umbrella-like female plants. ▶

Summary

Mosses, liverworts, and hornworts are non-vascular plants. They do not have vascular tissue to transport water or many nutrients. They do not absorb much water and nutrients through their rootlike structures. They usually live in areas that are shady and moist, where they will not dry out. All have a life cycle with two different generations. One generation reproduces sexually when egg and sperm unite. The other generation reproduces asexually by means of spores.

Review

1. In what kinds of places do nonvascular plants grow?
2. What is the difference between the two generations of a moss plant?
3. What are two other kinds of nonvascular plants?
4. **Critical Thinking** Mosses can live only in moist places because they do not have a good transport system for water. What is another reason for their living in moist places?
5. **Test Prep** Which of the following are nonvascular plants?
   - **A** bacteria
   - **B** fungi
   - **C** liverworts
   - **D** elm trees

LINKS

MATH LINK

Ratios A liverwort may reach a height of 2 cm. A redwood tree may reach a height of 100 m. What is the ratio of the height of the liverwort to that of the redwood tree?

WRITING LINK

Informative Writing—Explanation Suppose you live near a volcano that has not erupted in a while. One of the signs that an eruption might occur is that the volcano releases polluting gases. One day you observe that many mosses are dying. You are not aware of any increase in local air pollution because of humans. Write a short letter to a newspaper to explain why you think the nearby volcano may erupt. Use the death of mosses as evidence.

SOCIAL STUDIES LINK

Mosses in History During World War I, soldiers used sphagnum (SFAG•nuhm) moss to cover wounds. Some Native Americans used it for babies' diapers. Today it's used for growing plants. Find out how other mosses have been used in the past and how they are used today.

TECHNOLOGY LINK

Learn more about mosses and other plants by visiting this Internet Site.
www.scilinks.org/harcourt

LESSON 2

What Are Ferns and Gymnosperms?

In this lesson, you can . . .

INVESTIGATE how ferns differ from conifers.

LEARN ABOUT the structures of ferns and gymnosperms and how they reproduce.

LINK to math, writing, social studies, and technology.

Comparing Ferns and Conifers

Activity Purpose You may have seen ferns before. You can tell them from most other plants by their large, feathery leaves, or *fronds*. Ferns often grow on the forest floor and in shady parts of gardens. You may also know about conifers—trees and bushes that have cones and needlelike leaves. Pine trees and fir trees are examples of conifers. In this investigation you'll **observe** various parts of ferns and conifers. You'll find out how they are alike and how they are different.

Materials

- fern frond
- conifer needles
- hand lens
- conifer cone
- safety goggles

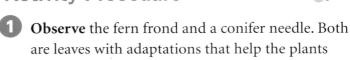

CAUTION

Activity Procedure

1 **Observe** the fern frond and a conifer needle. Both are leaves with adaptations that help the plants survive.

2 **Compare** the leaves, and **record** your observations by drawing the leaves and by describing what you see. Use a hand lens to **observe** the underside of the fern frond and the structure of the conifer needle. (Picture A)

3 Now **observe** and **compare** the conifer cone and the photograph of a conifer cone on page B33. They both came from the same kind of tree. **Record** your observations.

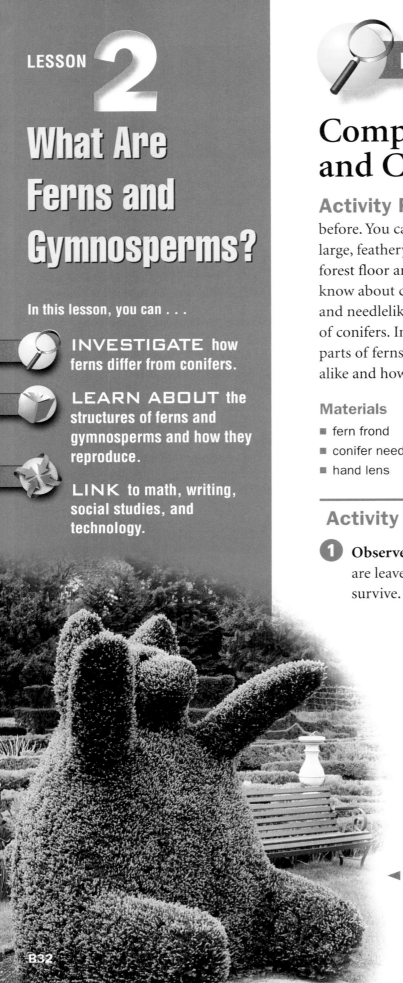

◀ Topiary (TOHP•ee•air•ee) is the art of forming living plants into ornamental shapes. Gymnosperms are often used for topiary.

Picture A

Picture B

4 **CAUTION** **Put on your safety goggles.** Carefully break open the cone, and **observe** it. **Record** your observations. (Picture B)

▲ Conifer cone

Draw Conclusions

1. Are ferns vascular plants? Are conifers? How do you know?

2. Ferns can grow in shady places, and conifers can survive periods when there is little water. **Infer** the leaf adaptations that help the plants survive these conditions.

3. What did you **observe** on the underside of the fern frond? What might you **infer** about the structures you saw there?

4. **Scientists at Work** Scientists **compare** objects to find out how they are alike and how they are different. Compare the cone you **observed** to the photograph of the conifer cone. What differences do you observe between the two cones? What can you **infer** from your observations?

Investigate Further The seeds of conifers are adapted so that they can travel. Examine a conifer seed to find the adaptation that enables it to travel.

> **Process Skill Tip**
>
> If you **compare** the structures of different objects, you can often **infer** how they differ in what they do.

Ferns and Gymnosperms

FIND OUT

- the structures and life cycle of ferns and gymnosperms
- how conifers are adapted to their habitats
- the uses of conifers

VOCABULARY

fern
gymnosperm
conifer
pollen

Ferns

Ferns are vascular plants that first appeared on Earth about 400 million years ago. Like other very ancient groups of vascular plants, ferns reproduce without seeds. Today most fern species live in moist, shady locations. Their feathery fronds spread out and have a large surface area. Because of their shape, fronds can collect a lot of light, so they are able to live on the dimly lit forest floor.

As with mosses, the life cycle of a fern includes two different generations. The asexual generation reproduces by spores that grow on the undersides of some of its fronds. The spores are inside brownish structures called *sori*. On different ferns the sori have different shapes and are arranged in different patterns. The sori may be round or shaped like rods or crescents. They are arranged either on the edges of the fronds or along the middle. The spores in the sori are released when the spores are mature.

Fern spores do not dry out easily. They can survive for a long time before they germinate. The spores are often blown to new locations by the wind.

When a fern spore falls to the ground, it doesn't begin to grow fronds right away. Instead, the spore grows into a tiny heart-shaped plant called a *prothallium*. The prothallium does not look like a fern frond at all. If you observe closely, you may find prothallia growing in

Spores are produced in the brown sori on the undersides of some fern fronds. ▼

Prothallium

Fiddlehead

Sori

◀ The heart-shaped prothallium (proh•THAL•ee•uhm) is the sexual generation in the fern's life cycle. It produces sperm and egg cells. Prothallia don't have vascular tissues.

◀ When fern fronds break through the ground, they are tightly coiled. They are called fiddleheads because they look like the curl at the top of a violin. As they grow, the fiddleheads unroll and spread out.

▲ Staghorn ferns can do well indoors in conditions like those of a rain forest. They need warm, moist air, lots of water, and some light, but not direct sunlight.

damp, shady places where there are ferns. Prothallia are often less than 1 cm (about 0.4 in.) across.

Underneath the prothallium little structures grow that produce sperm and eggs. This is the sexual generation of the fern plant. The sperm must swim through water to the egg cell. When a sperm cell and an egg cell join, a new fern plant with fronds begins to grow. This is the beginning of the other generation of the fern's life cycle.

There are more than 12,000 species of ferns in the world today. Most of the species grow in tropical rain forests, but many live in cooler areas. They are quite different in size and shape. Some are only 2.5 cm (about 1 in.) in length. Others look like trees and grow more than 28 m (about 92 ft) tall!

On ferns that grow in temperate climates, the structures that look like stems are actually parts of the fronds. The stems lie on or under the surface of the soil. On a few ferns, such as the large tree ferns of the tropics, the stem is upright and forms a trunk. Tree ferns like these are the tallest kinds of ferns.

▲ Tree ferns are most common in damp rain forests in mountainous regions in the tropics. *Cyathea australis* is found on Norfolk Island in the South Pacific. It can reach a height of 28 m (about 92 ft).

Some ferns have tropisms for touch. For example, staghorn ferns, which grow in tropical rain forests, cling to trees. A lower frond of the staghorn fern is like a suction cup that holds the plant to a tree's bark. This frond clings tightly to the tree except at the top of the frond, where it opens out. Nutrients that fall into the opened part of this frond supply the fern with materials it needs to make food. The plant's other fronds look like a male deer's (a stag's) horns, from which the plant gets its name.

✓ **What structures are involved in the asexual generation of a fern?**

Gymnosperms

Nonvascular plants reproduce by spores. Ferns, which are vascular plants, also reproduce by spores. The most common plants on Earth are those that reproduce by seeds.

Seeds might be called survival packages for new plants. Inside a seed is a tiny plant, called an embryo, as well as food for the embryo. An outer coating protects the seed. Making seeds is a great advantage for plants that live on land. The seeds can stay as they are for a long time, until conditions are good for growth.

There are two groups of plants that have seeds. A **gymnosperm** (JIM•noh•sperm) is one kind of plant with seeds. This word comes from ancient Greek words meaning "naked" and "seed." Gymnosperm seeds are said to be naked because they are not surrounded by a "container." The other group of plants with seeds are flowering plants. These plants have seeds that are surrounded by a container called an *ovary*. Gymnosperms do not produce flowers and ovaries, so they are called nonflowering plants.

One kind of gymnosperm is a **conifer**. *Conifer* means "cone bearer." These plants grow cones like the ones you observed in the investigation in this lesson. The cones are the reproductive structures that produce seeds. Most trees with needlelike leaves that stay on the tree all year are conifers.

Conifers are the largest of the four groups of gymnosperms. The other groups have far fewer

◄ *Ginkgo biloba* is the only remaining species of the ginkgoes. Ginkgoes are sometimes called living fossils because they are very similar to plants that lived millions of years ago. A ginkgo's leaves are unusual— they grow on the ends of shoots, are fan-shaped, and have parallel veins. Ginkgoes are often planted along city streets because they can survive disease, insects, and pollution.

◄ Cycads grow in warm areas. They look like short palm trees and are sometimes called sago palms. But they are not really palms at all. The seeds are in cones at the top of the stem.

Welwitschia mirabilis grows in the deserts of southern Africa. Many of these plants live for more than 100 years. This gymnosperm produces only two leaves, although there seem to be more because the leaves split as they grow. Every year, stiff, stemlike growths develop where the leaves join the trunk. The growths bear small male cones and bright-red female cones. ▼

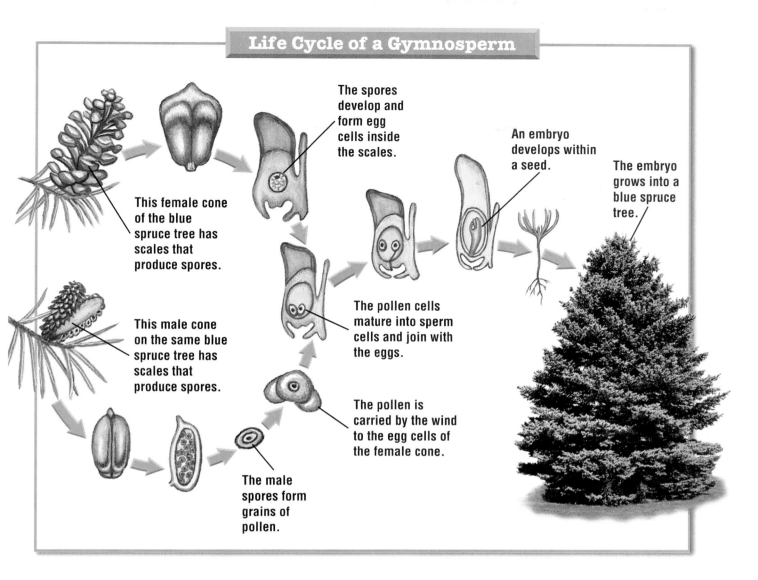

The spores develop and form egg cells inside the scales.

This female cone of the blue spruce tree has scales that produce spores.

This male cone on the same blue spruce tree has scales that produce spores.

An embryo develops within a seed.

The embryo grows into a blue spruce tree.

The pollen cells mature into sperm cells and join with the eggs.

The pollen is carried by the wind to the egg cells of the female cone.

The male spores form grains of pollen.

species than the conifers. Those groups are ginkgoes (GING•kohz), cycads (SY•kadz), and welwitschia (wel•WICH•ee•uh). They are shown in the photographs on page B36.

✓ **How do gymnosperms differ from ferns?**

Life Cycle of Conifers

Conifers have two kinds of cones—small male cones and large female cones. Both kinds form spores. Spores from the male cone develop into **pollen**. Each grain of pollen has two male sex cells. Spores from the female cone develop into egg cells. The egg cells stay inside the cone.

When the egg cells in a female cone are mature, the cone forms a sticky liquid. Grains of

pollen, carried on the wind, are trapped in this liquid. The pollen grains mature into sperm cells and fertilize the female egg cells. Unlike the sperm cells of nonvascular plants or ferns, the sperm cells of conifers do not need water to travel to the egg cells.

The fertilized egg in the female cone slowly forms an embryo within a seed. When the seed is mature, the female cone opens its scales, releasing the seeds. Conifer seeds often have "wings" that help them travel on the wind. When conditions are right, the seeds germinate and a new plant starts to grow.

✓ **How do the two kinds of cones on a conifer differ?**

The leaves of most conifers are very thin and pointed. They are coated with a thick, waxy covering that helps the plant keep its water.

White spruce trees have short leaves and long cones. ▶

Pitch pines have needles in bunches of twos and threes and long, rounded cones. The seeds have "wings" that can be carried by the wind. ▶

Yews can be low shrubs or small trees. Their seeds, unlike those of most other conifers, grow in small cups that are open on one end. These cups look like berries, and they are highly poisonous to humans. ▶

Adaptations

Because of their adaptations, conifers can live in dry environments and in places that are sometimes freezing cold. Their seeds can survive long dry or cold periods and then can germinate and grow when conditions are better.

Many people call conifers evergreens. This is because most conifers have narrow, hard, green leaves, most of which stay on the tree all year. Pines and firs have needlelike leaves. Cedars have scalelike leaves. The small surface area of conifer leaves and their thick, waxy coating help prevent loss of water. These adaptations help the tree survive when water is not available.

Conifers that grow in cold climates also produce a chemical that prevents the water in the tree from freezing. This is like adding antifreeze to the water so that it can flow even when the temperatures are below freezing.

Many conifers are also adapted to heavy snow. The snow falls off their sloping branches and smooth, flexible leaves. That way, the branches don't break under the weight of the snow.

✓ **How are conifers adapted to dry conditions?**

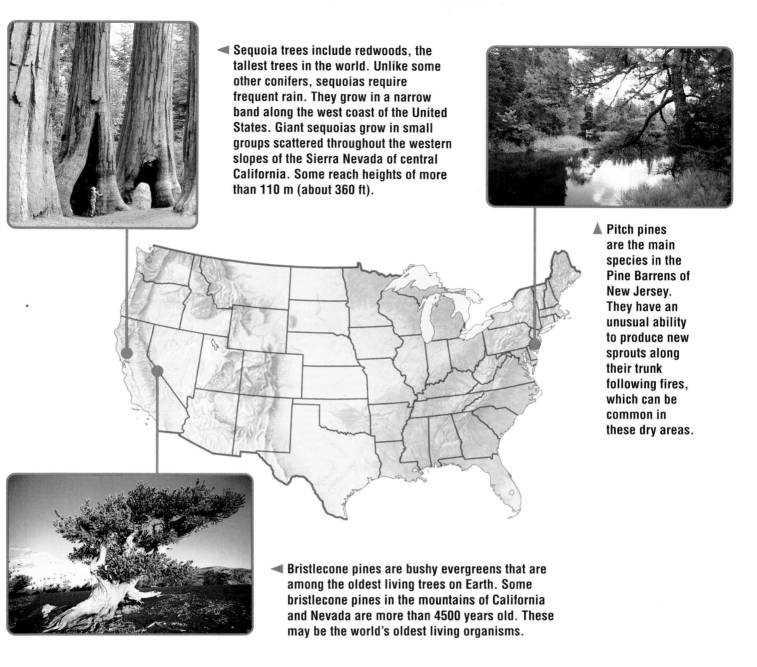

Sequoia trees include redwoods, the tallest trees in the world. Unlike some other conifers, sequoias require frequent rain. They grow in a narrow band along the west coast of the United States. Giant sequoias grow in small groups scattered throughout the western slopes of the Sierra Nevada of central California. Some reach heights of more than 110 m (about 360 ft).

Pitch pines are the main species in the Pine Barrens of New Jersey. They have an unusual ability to produce new sprouts along their trunk following fires, which can be common in these dry areas.

Bristlecone pines are bushy evergreens that are among the oldest living trees on Earth. Some bristlecone pines in the mountains of California and Nevada are more than 4500 years old. These may be the world's oldest living organisms.

Where Conifers Grow

Conifers grow all around the world, but especially in cold regions. They encircle the far north in a solid band of forest that stretches across North America, Scandinavia, and Siberia. These northern forests of conifers, called the taiga (TY•guh), have long, hard winters with lots of snow. And in places where high mountains reach southward, conifers can be found on the steepest slopes.

Conditions in the taiga make it ideal for conifers. However, these forests are not good for many other kinds of plants. The soil is not very rich, because the cold temperatures slow down the decay of materials. As a result, fewer nutrients enter the soil. Also, the shade from the conifers prevents many other vascular plants from growing on the forest floor.

Not all conifers grow in cold regions. Many can be found in warmer areas that have dry, sandy soil in which other trees can't grow. The pitch pines shown on this page, for example, grow in the Pine Barrens of New Jersey.

✓ **Where are most conifers found, and why?**

How People Use Conifers

People have found many uses for conifers, and in many places these trees are farmed. The wood from conifers is called softwood because it is usually much softer than wood from trees such as oak, maple, and hickory. Conifer wood isn't as strong as hardwood. But it is the most common wood used to build houses and other buildings in North America. Two of the conifers most often used in building are the Douglas fir and the loblolly pine. These trees grow tall and straight. They grow fast, so they are often planted for lumber.

Conifer wood is also used for plywood, which is made by gluing together several thin layers of wood with their grains in opposite directions. Plywood is strong, stiff, and inexpensive to make. It is often used for cabinets and as parts of floors and walls.

Most of the paper made in North America is also made from conifer softwood. The wood is ground into a fine pulp, mixed with water, and then spread evenly over a screen. After the water drains off, the pulp is pressed into sheets of paper. Spruces are especially good for producing paper pulp because they have very strong, long fibers.

Chemists have developed many useful items from the chemicals in conifers. Some products, such as alcohols, are used in manufacturing, medicines, and explosives. Acetylene is used as a fuel. Another product made from conifers is the fabric called rayon. Rayon is used to make clothing. It's also used in automobile tires and even bowling balls.

Conifers are often planted in rows on the edges of fields to block the wind. Around homes they give year-round shade. Conifers such as hemlocks, yews, pines, junipers, and cedars are often planted because they are beautiful and stay green in cold climates all year.

This circle graph shows how conifer wood is used in the United States. ▼

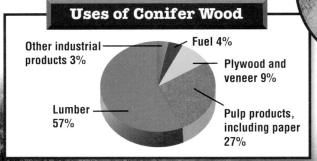

Uses of Conifer Wood

Other industrial products 3%
Fuel 4%
Plywood and veneer 9%
Lumber 57%
Pulp products, including paper 27%

◄ Piñon (PEEN•yahn) pines are small pine trees that grow in dry areas. Their small cones contain seeds called pine nuts, or pignoli (peen•YOHL•ee). These are good to eat and are used in foods such as pesto.

Spruce trees provide much of the material used to make the fabric known as rayon. Material from the tree is treated with chemicals to make a thick liquid. The liquid is pumped through a pinhole into an acid bath, where it forms rayon fibers. The fibers are then drawn together to form yarn. ▼

Conifer forests are peaceful, beautiful places to visit. Because these forests have little growth under the trees, they often have good hiking trails. Thousands of visitors enjoy America's majestic conifer forests every year.

✓ **What are some uses of conifers?**

Summary

Ferns are some of the simplest vascular plants. The large surface area of their fronds allows them to grow well in low light. Ferns produce spores on the undersides of some of their leaves. The sexual generation of a fern is very small. The plants usually identified as ferns are the much larger spore-producing generation.

Gymnosperms are nonflowering plants that produce seeds in cones. They have male cones that produce pollen and female cones that produce egg cells and then seeds. Conifers, the most common gymnosperms, have needlelike leaves and are well adapted for dry or freezing weather. Most are found in northern regions.

Review

1. Why do ferns need a damp environment to reproduce?

2. Why do ferns grow well in environments with little light?

3. Why are conifers found mostly in northern regions?

4. **Critical Thinking** Conifers produce large amounts of pollen—many more grains than are used to fertilize the conifer egg cells. Why is this necessary?

5. **Test Prep** Which is **NOT** a major use of conifers?

   A lumber

   B food

   C chemicals

   D fibers

LINKS

MATH LINK

Geometry The diameter of General Sherman, a giant sequoia in California, is about 10 m. What length of rope would you need to completely encircle the trunk of the tree? Remember that the perimeter of a circle is found by multiplying the diameter by pi. Use 3.14 for pi.

WRITING LINK

Informative Writing—How-to Paper-making is an important industry in the United States. Find out how paper is manufactured. Then write a short report for your classmates telling how paper is made from trees.

SOCIAL STUDIES LINK

How Native Americans Used Conifers Native Americans once used lodgepole pines for lodge and tepee supports. Find out about these and other uses of conifers among different Native American tribes. Write a paragraph to describe your findings.

TECHNOLOGY LINK

Visit the Harcourt Learning Site for related links, activities, and resources. **www.harcourtschool.com**

WELCOME TO THE LEARNING SITE

How Are Angiosperms Different from Other Plants?

In this lesson, you can . . .

INVESTIGATE the parts of a flower.

LEARN ABOUT the functions of the parts of angiosperms.

LINK to math, writing, technology, and other areas.

INVESTIGATE

The Parts of a Flower

Activity Purpose When you think about flowers, you probably think about the shape and color of their petals and maybe their scent. The most noticeable part of most flowers is the petals, but there are other flower parts that are very important. In this investigation you will **observe** some parts of a flower.

Materials
- flower
- paper towel
- hand lens

Activity Procedure

1 Lay the flower on the paper towel.

2 Handle the flower gently while you **observe** its parts. Be sure to look at the center between the petals. (Picture A)

3 Now use the hand lens to examine the parts of the flower. Draw what you **observe**. (Picture B)

4 The flower includes at least three different structures. Are there at least three different structures in your sketch? If not, **observe** the flower again and revise your sketch.

◄ Gladioluses (glad•ee•OH•luhs•uhz) have tall, slender stems with large, silky flowers and long, sword-shaped leaves. They reproduce in two ways. The flowers make seeds that develop into new plants. Underground stems also produce new shoots.

Picture A

Picture B

Draw Conclusions

1. Describe the structures you **observed** in the flower.

2. What do you **infer** are the functions of these structures?

3. **Scientists at Work** Scientists **communicate** information in many ways. They use drawings, diagrams, words, and measurements. **Compare** these methods. Choose one of the flower structures you drew. Which method or combination of methods do you think would be the most helpful for communicating information about the structure? Explain.

Investigate Further The next time you see someone throwing away wilted or dead flowers, ask if you may have one. Examine it to see if its structures are different from those of a fresh flower.

Angiosperms

Angiosperms Are Flowering Plants

FIND OUT

- the features of angiosperms

- the structures of flowers and their function in reproduction

- the ways in which pollination occurs

VOCABULARY

angiosperm
stamen
anther
pistil
stigma
petal
style
ovary
pollination

An **angiosperm** (AN•jee•oh•sperm) is a vascular plant that produces flowers. Wherever you go, you are likely to see angiosperms. The grasses in lawns, the vegetables and flowers in gardens, the trees in orchards, and the crops in fields are all angiosperms.

Grasses, vegetables, flowers, and trees may seem to have little in common. But all angiosperms have basic similarities. Their name comes from Greek words that together mean "seeds in a vessel." Unlike gymnosperm seeds, which are not contained in a structure, the seeds of angiosperms are contained in fruit. Tomatoes, acorns, and bean pods are all fruit. So are the foods that we usually call fruit, such as apples, pears, and oranges. In biology, a structure that encloses seeds is a fruit.

Angiosperms produce fruit from their flowers, which are the reproductive structures of the plants. After the egg cell in a flower has been fertilized, it develops into the fruit that contains the plant's seeds. Many angiosperms produce flowers that are so small you might not notice them. The grass in a lawn, for example, produces tiny flowers whose petals are not colorful. The flowers on some trees, such as cherry trees, dogwoods, and magnolias, are brilliant and obvious. The flowers on many other trees, however, are hard to see. On the angiosperms that we call "flowers"—roses, daffodils, and pansies, for example—the flowers usually have the most noticeable parts.

Angiosperms and gymnosperms also have different kinds of leaves. Most angiosperms have flat, wide leaves. Most gymnosperms have needlelike leaves.

The variety of sizes and shapes of angiosperm leaves is huge. Some leaves measure 1 m (about 3 ft) from stalk to tip. Others, like the leaves of the duckweed that floats on ponds, are tiny. Whatever their shape, most angiosperm leaves have a network of veins through which food and water are transported.

◄ Many of the foods that people eat are produced by angiosperms. We eat angiosperms' roots (carrots and parsnips), stems (celery), and leaves (lettuce and cabbage). We eat their flower buds (broccoli), seeds (peas), and fruit (tomatoes and apples).

◄ Spanish moss isn't a moss at all. It's an angiosperm that produces tiny flowers.

In angiosperms the xylem and phloem that transport materials are made up of highly specialized cells. The cells function like tubes. They transport materials better than the xylem and phloem in ferns and gymnosperms.

The adaptations that allow angiosperms to survive from year to year are different from those of gymnosperms. For example, *annual* plants are angiosperms that go through their entire life cycle, from seed to flower to seed, in less than a year. Annuals usually have soft stems. Although annuals die when winter comes, they have produced seeds that will sprout the following year.

Other soft-stemmed angiosperms, including many spring flowers, do not die in winter, although they appear to. The parts of the plant above the ground wither and die. Underground, the plants are alive as bulbs or fleshy roots. When the warm weather returns, they send up shoots and they flower again. These angiosperms are called *perennials* (puhr•EN•ee•uhlz).

Many angiosperms have woody stems. These plants include broadleaved trees such as oaks, maples, and beeches, as

well as shrubs such as roses. They are perennials, but they do not die back to the ground. Their tough stems protect both their aboveground growth and their roots. As colder weather approaches, most of these plants drop their leaves. The plants become dormant during the winter. They grow new shoots and leaves when warm weather returns.

With about 235,000 known species, angiosperms are the most successful plants on Earth. They have both the greatest number of species and the greatest number of individual plants. The adaptations of their xylem and phloem make their transport systems the most efficient of any plants. They are well adapted for many kinds of environments. The fruit they produce not only protect the seeds but also help spread them. The fruit attract animals, which eat them. The seeds pass through the animals' digestive systems. The animals deposit the seeds far from the parent plants. All of these adaptations have resulted in the success of angiosperms.

✓ **What are the two main characteristics of all angiosperms?**

◄ The genus *Magnolia* includes trees and shrubs that have large, sweet-smelling flowers.

◄ This barrel cactus makes food and stores water in its stem. Its leaves have adapted by becoming spines, which don't perform photosynthesis. The cactus flowers for a short time after a brief rainy season.

Flower Parts

You observed some of the parts of a flower in the investigation. You may recognize them in the diagram. It is of a lily that has been cut to show its parts.

Clustered around the center of a flower are several stemlike structures called stamens. Each **stamen** (STAY•muhn) is one of the flower's male reproductive organs. A stamen has two parts.

The **anther** (AN•thuhr) produces pollen grains. The *filament* (FIL•uh•muhnt) connects the anther to the plant.

At the center of a flower is a structure called the **pistil** (PIS•tuhl). This is the female reproductive organ. It consists of three main parts. At its tip is the **stigma** (STIG•muh). The stigma

THE INSIDE STORY

The Anatomy of a Flower

The largest and most visible parts of a flower are usually its petals. Each **petal** helps protect the other parts of the flower. Petals are often colorful. The colors help attract the insects and other animals that are important to the plant's reproduction. Below the petals are *sepals* (SEE•puhlz). They are usually smaller than the petals and resemble green leaves. Before a flower blooms, the sepals completely enclose the bud. They protect the inner parts of the flower. After the flower blooms, the sepals spread apart and may drop off.

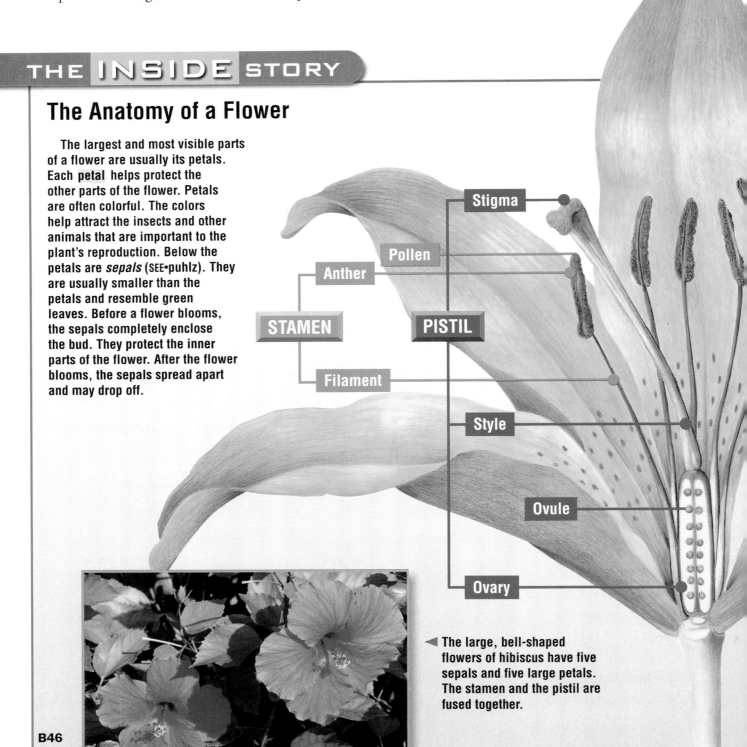

◄ The large, bell-shaped flowers of hibiscus have five sepals and five large petals. The stamen and the pistil are fused together.

is sticky, so when pollen grains land there, they stick.

Below the stigma is the stemlike part of the pistil called the **style**. It connects the stigma to the **ovary** below. Inside the ovary are *ovules* (AHV•yoolz), in which the flower's egg cells develop.

Pollination occurs when pollen from the anthers lands on the stigma. The pollen grains grow tubes that stretch through the style to the ovary. When the pollen tubes reach the ovary, sperm cells from the pollen grains enter the ovules. The fertilized egg cells develop into seeds.

✔ **What are the functions of a flower's pistil and stamens?**

Angiosperms vary in the number, shape, and color of their flower parts. Some flowers don't have one or more of the parts shown in the large diagram. Sometimes many flowers grow together but look like only one flower. For example, a dandelion is made up of hundreds of tiny flowers pressed closely together.

The petals of different flowers give them a unique shape and appearance. The bearded iris and the lily of the valley are two examples of the way petals can make flowers look quite different.

Dandelion

Bearded iris

Lily of the valley

◀ The beautiful flowers of waterlilies have four sepals and many petals. In the center of a waterlily, a group of pistils is fused together in a saucerlike shape, surrounded by many stamens.

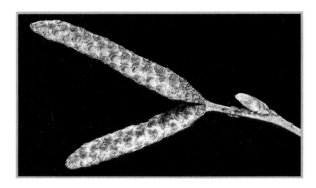

▲ Many trees, including oaks, birches, and maples, have very small flowers that grow in tight bunches called *catkins*. The male and female parts are in separate catkins. The wind carries pollen from the male catkins to the female catkins.

Flowers and Pollination

For pollination to take place, pollen grains must reach the stigma of a flower. Flowers have various adaptations to help pollination occur.

Flowers that are pollinated by insects often have brightly colored petals and strong scents. They produce a sweet liquid called *nectar* that some animals use as food. The bright colors and scents of the flowers are signs to the insects that the flowers have nectar. Some flowers pollinated by bees have markings that aren't visible to most other animals.

Flowers pollinated by insects have heavy, sticky pollen that gets caught on an insect's body. The pollen rubs off on the stigma of the next flower the insect visits.

Insects aren't the only animals that pollinate flowers. Birds as well as bats and other small mammals also carry pollen from one flower to another. Many of the flowers pollinated by birds are red, a color to which birds are attracted. In many cases one species of animal pollinates only one species of flower. The plant and the animal depend on each other.

Flowers not pollinated by animals usually rely on the wind to carry pollen from their anthers to their stigmas. These include the flowers of birches, oaks, corn, and grasses. The flowers are usually small, unscented, and barely noticeable. They don't need to attract animals. A wind-pollinated flower often produces a lot of light, dry pollen that the wind can carry to the stigmas of other flowers.

✔ **How do wind-pollinated flowers and insect-pollinated flowers differ?**

Insects are not the only animals that pollinate flowers. This bat eats the sweet nectar of the cactus flower. As it pushes its face into the flower to get food, grains of pollen from a previous flower rub off and pollinate the cactus flower.

▲ The honeycreeper lives in tropical America and Hawai'i. It pokes its bill into flowers to get nectar. As it does, it also pollinates the flower.

Summary

Angiosperms produce flowers. They have efficient vascular systems and broad leaves. Their seeds are enclosed in fruit. These adaptations have resulted in their being the most successful plants on land today. All parts of a flower contribute to the plant's sexual reproduction. Some flowers are pollinated by insects or other animals. Others depend on the wind to carry pollen from one flower to another.

Review

1. What are three adaptations that help angiosperms live on land?

2. What parts of a flower produce pollen?

3. How do insects pollinate flowers?

4. **Critical Thinking** Some hummingbirds that eat nectar have very long, thin beaks. What can you tell about the flowers that provide them with nectar?

5. **Test Prep** The parts of a flower that enclose a bud before it blooms are the —

   A filaments

   B stamens

   C pollen grains

   D sepals

LINKS

MATH LINK

Fractions Suppose a flowering plant produces 120 seeds, but only 16 of the seeds sprout and grow. What fraction of the plant's seeds become new plants? Express your answer in lowest terms.

WRITING LINK

Expressive Writing—Poem Many poets have written famous poems about flowers. Write a poem for your classmates that tells what flowers in general, or a favorite flower, means to you.

SOCIAL STUDIES LINK

Flowers as Emblems Since earliest times, nations and states have used flowers as their emblems, or symbols. The official flower of the United States is the rose. Find out what your state flower is and why it was chosen.

ART LINK

Flowers in Art Most cultures have used flowers as subjects of paintings or designs. Study paintings of flowers. Draw or paint a flower in the style of your favorite flower painting.

TECHNOLOGY LINK

Learn more about plants and their uses by watching *Rain Forest to Shuttle* on the **Harcourt Science Newsroom Video.**

How Do Angiosperms Reproduce?

In this lesson, you can . . .

INVESTIGATE the structures of seeds.

LEARN ABOUT how angiosperms reproduce.

LINK to math, writing, art, and technology.

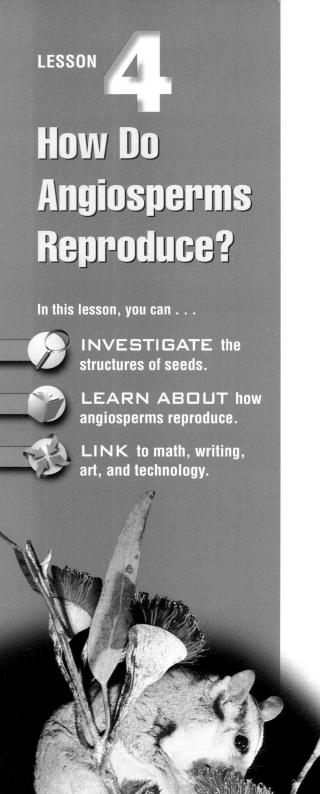

Inside Seeds

Activity Purpose The pollination of an angiosperm flower results in a fruit that contains seeds. Under the right conditions, a tiny seed can grow into a much larger plant. An acorn is a seed that is about the size of one of your fingertips. Yet it may grow into a towering oak tree. In this investigation you'll **observe** the insides of some seeds. You'll find out about the beginning of life for two different kinds of angiosperms.

Materials

- paper towels
- lima beans
- corn kernels
- hand lens
- plastic knife

Activity Procedure

1 Cover your desk with paper towels. Lima beans and corn kernels are seeds. Use the hand lens to **observe** the two kinds of seeds. Make a sketch of each. (Picture A)

2 Carefully peel the outside covering from each seed. Then open the seeds. You may need to cut open the corn seed.

3 Use the hand lens to **observe** each seed's structures. **Record** your observations by drawing what you see. (Picture B)

4 **Compare** the structures inside the two seeds. Look for similarities and differences. From your **observations**, **infer** what the function of each part of the seeds might be.

◀ The mouse-sized honey possum of Australia eats nectar, thereby playing an important part in the way this flowering plant reproduces.

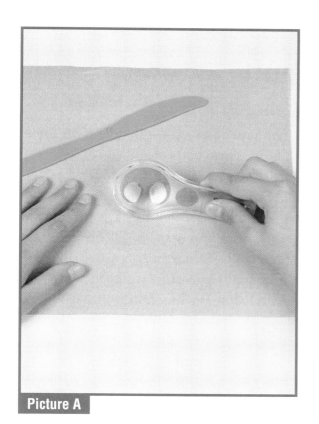

Picture A

Picture B

Draw Conclusions

1. What can you **infer** about the outside covering of the seeds? Is the function the same for both seeds?

2. Were you able to identify a tiny plant in each seed? Which part of the seed was it?

3. What did you **infer** about the function of the other parts of the two seeds? Is the function the same for both seeds?

4. **Scientists at Work** To **classify** organisms, scientists **observe** and **compare** their characteristics. The seeds you observed belong to two different groups of angiosperms. What differences in the seeds did you observe?

Investigate Further Look again at the two seeds. Find the tiny plant in each, and try to figure out which part of it will become the root and which part will become the shoot. Plant similar seeds and observe them to see if you are correct.

Seeds and Fruit

Two Kinds of Flowering Plants

VOCABULARY

dicotyledon
monocotyledon
fertilization
embryo
runner
grafting

In the investigation, you may have observed two similar parts under the outer coating of the lima bean. These parts are called *cotyledons* (kaht•uh•LEED•uhnz). They are seed leaves that store food for the young plant within the seed. The lima bean is a **dicotyledon** (dy•kaht•uh•LEED•uhn), because it has two seed leaves. Dicotyledons are often called dicots. Oak trees, roses, and beans are dicots.

A corn kernel, like the one you observed, does not have two similar parts. It has only one cotyledon, a leaflike structure wrapped around the young plant. Corn is a **monocotyledon** (mahn•oh•kaht•uh•LEED•uhn), because it has only one seed leaf. Monocotyledons are often called monocots. Grasses, corn, and palm trees are monocots.

The flower parts of monocots occur in multiples of three. For example, a monocot flower may have six petals, three sepals, and nine stamens. The flower parts of dicots occur in multiples of four or five.

The leaves of the two groups also show differences. Monocot leaves have veins that run side by side without crossing each other. Dicot leaves have netlike veins that branch out in many directions and cross each other. The vascular tissues in a monocot are scattered throughout the stem. In a dicot they are arranged in a ring going up the stem. Monocots have slender roots that spread out in all directions. Some dicots, such as carrots, have one main root, called a *taproot.*

✔ **What characteristics of monocots and dicots differ?**

Differences Between Monocots and Dicots

Monocots				
one cotyledon	flower parts in threes	parallel leaf veins	scattered vascular tissue	spread-out roots

Dicots				
two cotyledons	flower parts in fours or fives	netlike leaf veins	vascular tissue in a ring	many have taproots

From Flower to Fruit

Pollination is the first step in angiosperm reproduction. The reproductive process is complete when a seed sprouts into a new plant.

Pollination occurs when pollen grains from a flower are deposited on the stigma of a flower of the same species. Then the pollen grains grow tubes. These go through the style and reach the ovules in the flower's ovary. There are usually many pollen grains on a stigma, and each one grows its own tube.

Each pollen grain contains two sperm cells. When the tube from a pollen grain reaches an ovule, the sperm cells travel down the tube. One sperm cell joins with an egg cell in the ovule. This process is called **fertilization**. The fertilized egg develops one or two cotyledons and an **embryo**, the tiny plant that forms in the seed. The other sperm cell joins with a different cell in the ovule to form a food source. This nourishes the embryo as it germinates. Angiosperms are the only living things in which sperm cells function in these different ways.

The flower's fertilized egg cells develop into seeds. As this happens, the ovary swells and grows into a fruit. A fruit is a structure that surrounds and protects the seeds. Some fruit serve as food for animals that eat the fruit and spread the seeds. Other fruit are adapted to travel on the wind. When winter is over, seeds that have reached areas with the right conditions germinate and grow into new plants.

✔ **What is the function of the tubes that grow from pollen grains?**

Egg cells

Ovules

Pollen tube

Once a flower has been pollinated, tubes begin to grow down the style to the ovary.

When the cells inside the ovules have been fertilized, the flower begins the process of becoming a fruit. The petals are no longer needed, and they fall off the plant.

As the seeds develop, the ovary develops into a fruit.

Fruit

The fertilized ovules develop into seeds, each with an embryo, a source of food, and a seed coat.

Each seed contains a tiny embryo, which will grow into a new plant when conditions are right.

Seeds

New plant

A berry has seeds throughout its flesh. That's why a tomato is classified as a berry.

A drupe, such as this peach, has a single seed with a hard shell. ▼

Fruit

If you asked for some fruit, you might be surprised if you got pea pods, cucumbers, or walnuts. But each of these items really is a fruit. So are apples and oranges and most of the other sweet, juicy plant foods that people usually call fruit.

In science the word *fruit* is used for the part of an angiosperm that contains seeds. Tomatoes are fruit, and so are peanuts and raspberries. They all contain seeds. *Dry fruit* include peas, beans, and other seeds in pods, as well as nuts. *Fleshy fruit* include apples, cucumbers, and other fruit with pulp.

Scientists classify fleshy fruit by their structure. Different kinds of fruit have different structures because they develop from different flower parts. Some even develop from several flowers.

A fleshy fruit that has a single seed in a hard covering is classified as a drupe. The seed developed from a single pistil, and the fleshy pulp came from a single ovary. Plums, cherries, and peaches are drupes.

Some fleshy fruit have cores that contain several seeds with leathery seed cases. These fruit are classified as pomes. They include apples and pears. A pome's core developed from a flower's ovary. The fleshy part around the core developed from parts of the flower that surrounded the ovary.

A berry also contains many seeds. But they aren't grouped together in a core. The seeds are scattered throughout the flesh of a single enlarged ovary. Blueberries, tomatoes, and watermelons are berries. But strawberries, blackberries, and raspberries are not berries. They are aggregate fruit. Each fruit is made up of groups of smaller fruitlets. Each fruitlet developed from a pistil of one flower that has many pistils.

Sometimes groups of fruitlets that form a single fruit develop from the pistils of several flowers of the same species. The results are classified as multiple fruit. These include pineapples and figs.

✔ **Why isn't a raspberry a true berry?**

The seeds in an apple are all in its core, so it is a pome. ▼

▲ Blackberries are groups of tiny fruitlets that formed from a single flower. They are classified as an aggregate fruit.

◄ Many different pineapple flowers combined their fruit to form this pineapple. It is classified as a multiple fruit.

Spreading of Seeds

Suppose seeds just fell to the ground under their parent plants. If they did, they might not get enough light, water, and nutrients to survive. But plants have adaptations for reaching other places.

Fleshy fruit are often brightly colored. These colors attract animals that eat the fruit. The soft part of the fruit is digested. The seeds in the fruit pass through the animals' digestive systems unharmed. The seeds are carried to wherever the animals' droppings fall.

Animals also help spread burs. Burs are seeds with hooks that catch on the animals' fur. Later the burs are rubbed or scratched off.

Plants such as grasses have seeds that are light enough to be carried by the wind. Other plants scatter their seeds themselves. As their seed cases grow, tension is built up that finally causes the seed cases to burst and to throw the seeds through the air. Sometimes the bursting is set off by the wind or by an animal touching the seed cases.

✔ **How does the spreading of seeds help them germinate?**

Squirrels don't always eat the nuts and other seeds they buried to store for the winter. In the spring these seeds may germinate and grow. ▼

A thick, hard shell protects the seed of a coconut. Coconuts often fall into the ocean. Then they wash ashore at other locations, where they can germinate and grow. ▶

Strawberry plants produce long runners that spread out over the ground. New plants grow from buds on the runners and send roots into the soil. ▶

Asexual Reproduction

Some plants reproduce without using seeds, a process called asexual reproduction. Asexual reproduction produces new plants that have exactly the same genes as the parent plant.

Many plants can grow from leaf cuttings. Leaves from the parent plant that are placed in water or in rich soil can develop into new plants.

Plants like strawberries and spider plants reproduce by **runners**. These are long, slender stems that grow close to the ground and put out roots and shoots. The new plants can grow to live without the parent plant. Some garden plants, such as irises, produce underground stems that divide. Each stem grows into a new plant.

Tubers are plants with swollen underground stems that store food. Potatoes are tubers. Their sprouting "eyes" grow into new plants.

Farmers grow certain plants by a form of asexual reproduction called **grafting**. They join parts of two plants together to make a single plant. The new plant has some characteristics of both of the parent plants. By grafting, farmers can grow plants faster and change the time of year that they bear fruit. Grafting can also produce plants with stems and roots that grow in poor soil but with fruit that would normally require rich soil.

✔ **What are three different kinds of asexual reproduction?**

Uses of Angiosperms

WOOD

Broad-leaved trees such as oak, maple, and walnut are sometimes called hardwoods. Hardwoods are used to make furniture and flooring that needs to be strong and long-lasting.

FOOD

People depend on flowering plants for food, including almost all grains, fruits, and vegetables. Many of the animals that we use for food also live on flowering plants.

CLOTHING

Cotton, a fabric often used for clothing, is made from the fruit of cotton plants. Linen is a fabric made from the fibers of flax plants.

MEDICINES

Since ancient times, people have known that some flowering plants are useful for medicines. For example, the juice of aloe plants has been used to treat burns. The plant in the picture is a rosy periwinkle, from which two cancer-fighting medicines are made.

DECORATION

Many decorative trees and shrubs are angiosperms, and most gardens are planted with flowers. People use cut flowers in their homes, for celebrations, and as gifts.

SCENTS

Oils from flowers such as roses and lilies are used in perfumes. Dried flowers are sometimes used to freshen rooms, drawers, and closets.

Summary

Angiosperms are divided into two groups—monocots and dicots. Monocots have one cotyledon, flower parts in threes, parallel veins in their leaves, scattered vascular bundles in their stems, and spreading root systems. Dicots have two seed leaves, flower parts in fours or fives, netlike veins, vascular bundles arranged in a ring in their stems, and often one main taproot. The ovules in a pollinated flower are fertilized and become seeds encased in fruit. Fleshy fruit include drupes, pomes, berries, aggregate fruit, and multiple fruit. Seeds can be spread by wind, animals, or water. Many plants can reproduce asexually from cuttings, underground stems, runners, and grafting.

Review

1. How do monocot and dicot seeds differ?
2. Where are the egg cells in a flower located?
3. How does the bright color of some fruit help spread their seeds?
4. **Critical Thinking** Suppose some farmers wanted to produce new apple trees just like the ones already in their orchard. What method of reproduction would be best?
5. **Test Prep** Which of these is **NOT** a fruit?
   A a raspberry
   B a tomato
   C a potato
   D an apple

LINKS

MATH LINK

Multiples Flowers may be monocots or dicots. The number of petals on a monocot is a multiple of 3. The number of petals on a dicot is a multiple of 4 or 5. If you counted 12 petals on a flower, could you tell whether it was a monocot or a dicot? Explain your answer.

WRITING LINK

Informative Writing—Description Write a paragraph for a friend, describing a plant you would like to invent by grafting two other plants together.

ART LINK

Dried Flowers Many cut flowers stay beautiful indefinitely if you hang them upside down until they are completely dry. Then you can use them in arrangements. You can also press flowers between sheets of paper that absorb the moisture. Put some flowers and absorbent paper between two heavy books for a couple of weeks. Then use them to make an arrangement or picture.

TECHNOLOGY LINK

Learn more about plant reproduction by visiting the Smithsonian Institution Internet Site.
www.si.edu/harcourt/science

Smithsonian Institution®

Advances in Agriculture

Prehistoric Farming

It's hard to think of a time when people did not practice agriculture—the planting, tending, and harvesting of plants for food. In fact, archaeologists agree that agriculture may have had its beginnings as early as 10,000 B.C., when prehistoric people began destroying plants they could not eat that competed with plants they could eat. A thousand years later (about 9000 B.C.), people realized that some of the wild plants they ate could be grown from seeds. Grains such as wheat and barley were most likely the first crops. The earliest farming tools included hand-pulled plows, curved knives called sickles, and grinding stones. These inventions, as simple as they may seem, were important for the development of agriculture.

Farming in Early Civilizations

The next two great agricultural advances were made between 5,000 and 3,000 B.C. in Egypt and Mesopotamia. The first was the invention of a wooden plow that could be pulled by an ox. With an ox instead of the farmer pulling the plow, a much greater area could be plowed in less time. The second was the development of irrigation, or watering, systems that could be used on large areas of land. Irrigation made it possible for people to grow crops in regions with little rainfall.

The Spread of Advanced Agriculture

During the time of the Roman Empire, the Romans took new methods of farming to every land they conquered. They may have been the first to realize the importance of rotating crops and of leaving a field unplanted, or fallow, for a period of time. Different crops use different amounts of nutrients, and some crops add nutrients to the soil, so crop rotation keeps nutrients in the soil from being used up.

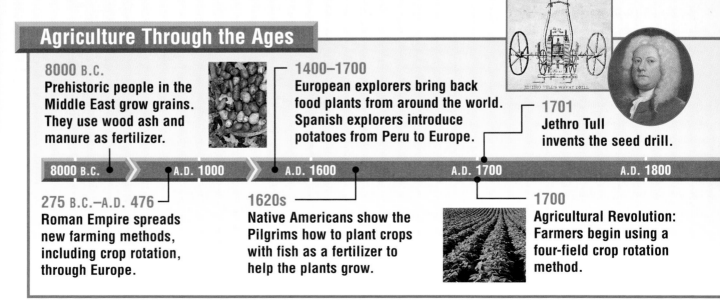

Agriculture Through the Ages

8000 B.C.
Prehistoric people in the Middle East grow grains. They use wood ash and manure as fertilizer.

1400–1700
European explorers bring back food plants from around the world. Spanish explorers introduce potatoes from Peru to Europe.

JETHRO TULL'S WHEAT DRILL

1701
Jethro Tull invents the seed drill.

8000 B.C.   A.D. 1000   A.D. 1600   A.D. 1700   A.D. 1800

275 B.C.–A.D. 476
Roman Empire spreads new farming methods, including crop rotation, through Europe.

1620s
Native Americans show the Pilgrims how to plant crops with fish as a fertilizer to help the plants grow.

1700
Agricultural Revolution: Farmers begin using a four-field crop rotation method.

Advances in agriculture continued through the Middle Ages, each leading to the production of larger crops with less work. For example, in the 900s, a harness was invented that allowed horses to pull plows. The faster horse soon replaced the slow-moving ox in the field.

The Agricultural Revolution

The agricultural revolution began in Great Britain in the 1700s, thanks to an Englishman named Jethro Tull. Tull invented the horse-drawn hoe and the seed drill. The seed drill was the first machine that could drill even rows of holes in a field and drop seeds into them. Farmers also improved their methods of crop rotation. Since larger crops meant fewer farms were needed, many farmers left the countryside and moved to cities to find work.

The Machinery of Modern Agriculture

In 1892 American farmers began to use steam-powered tractors. By the 1920s, however, gasoline-powered tractors had begun to replace steam-powered tractors and animals for pulling equipment. Today, farmers use a variety of powerful machines such as combines (KAHM•bynz) that do several jobs and seed drills that can drill up to 12 rows at a time.

High-Tech Plants

Over the centuries farmers have done many things to change crop plants. People have grafted trees to get better fruit. They have also crossbred different varieties of the same plant. The hybrid plants that result have better taste, produce larger crops, and resist insects and diseases. Today many crops, including most types of corn, are hybrids.

For centuries farmers have tried putting different materials on the soil to improve their crops and on the plants to kill pests. Today farmers have a great variety of products, both natural and human-made, that they can use. There are pesticides to kill insects, herbicides to kill weeds, and fertilizers to help plants grow.

Since the 1970s scientists have worked to change the genes of crop plants. With the new genes they are given, plants are better able to resist insect pests and plant diseases. In the future, this genetic engineering may allow farmers to raise crops without the use of chemicals, making it cheaper to farm.

THINK ABOUT IT

1. Why would pulling nonedible weeds be considered the beginning of agriculture?
2. Why was the seed drill such an important part of the agricultural revolution?

1945
The first chemical herbicide is patented in the United States.

1900	2000

Today
Scientists study the genes of plants to find ways to make them better able to resist pests, diseases, and drought. They also look for ways to increase crop yield.

A combine does several jobs—it cuts a plant stalk, separates the seed from the straw and other waste materials, collects the seeds in a bin, and returns the waste to the ground.

Marion Myles

PLANT PHYSIOLOGIST

Dr. Marion Myles has always loved plants, so it's no surprise that she became a botanist. As a specialist in an area of botany called plant physiology, Dr. Myles studies the functions and chemistry of the parts of plant cells. Some of the chemicals she has discovered in plants have become important ingredients in medicines.

When she was very young, Marion Myles decided that she wanted to go to college and study plants. After studying botany at the University of Pennsylvania and then earning a master's degree, she taught college biology. Then, because she wanted to study plants in a laboratory, she went to Iowa State University to complete her Ph.D. and continue her research.

Dr. Myles has always been fascinated by the many chemicals that plants produce, and she studies them in her work. She has researched many types of plant chemicals, such as the poisons plants produce to protect themselves. She is interested in the relationship between the structure of plant substances and what they do in the plant cell. Dr. Myles is also interested in the effects that plant chemicals can have on people. For example, plants produce many chemicals that we use in medicines, such as the chemical from willow bark that was the original active ingredient in

aspirin. Dr. Myles hopes that her work will one day produce additional useful products.

When she is not teaching or working in the laboratory, Dr. Myles spends her time in other useful ways. She has worked for organizations, such as the American Association for the Advancement of Science, that promote science and try to interest young people in science careers.

THINK ABOUT IT

1. How might Marion Myles's work have helped people with illnesses?

2. Identify one type of medicine that uses a chemical substance from plants.

◀ Plant growth and development are important areas of research for Dr. Myles.

Growing Plants from Spores

How does a fern reproduce from spores?

Materials

- fern with spores that have turned dry and brown
- pot of potting soil with peat moss
- plastic wrap
- saucer of water

Procedure

1. Sprinkle the spores over the soil, and cover the pot with plastic wrap.

2. Move the pot to a light but not sunny location. Place the pot in the saucer.

3. Keep water in the saucer.

4. When the ferns are 2.5–4 cm tall, move clumps of them to their own pots.

Draw Conclusions

How does fern reproduction differ from reproduction in other plants with which you may be familiar? In what ways do you think that spores have helped ferns survive?

Growing Plants from Seeds

Which parts of seeds are essential for growth?

Materials

- 10 lima bean seeds, soaked overnight
- knife and cutting board
- 3 plastic pots filled with potting soil
- saucers for the pots
- pot labels and a marker
- water

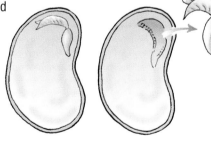

Procedure

1. Have an adult help you split all but two of the seeds in half. Keep the two best cotyledons (halves), with embryos (tiny plants). Throw the rest away.

2. Use your fingernail to remove the embryos from two cotyledons.

3. Label the pots *Complete seeds*, *No embryos* and *No cotyledons*.

4. Plant the two complete seeds in one pot, the two cotyledons with no embryos in another, and the two embryos in the third pot. Water the pots and place them in a warm, sunny spot. Observe their growth.

Draw Conclusions

Which pot of seeds grew best? Why did the cotyledons without embryos fail to grow? Why did the embryos without cotyledons grow less well than the complete seeds?

Chapter ② Review and Test Preparation

Vocabulary Review

Use the terms below to answer questions 1 through 15. The page numbers in ( ) tell you where to look in the chapter if you need help.

moss (B28)	**pistil** (B46–B47)
asexual reproduction (B29)	**stigma** (B46–B47)
spores (B29)	**style** (B46–B47)
fern (B34)	**ovary** (B46–B47)
gymnosperms (B36)	**pollination** (B48)
conifers (B36)	**fertilization** (B53)
pollen (B37)	**embryo** (B53)
angiosperms (B44)	**monocotyledon** (B52)
stamen (B46–B47)	**dicotyledon** (B52)
anther (B46–B47)	**grafting** (B55)
	runners (B55)

1. ____ have seeds enclosed in fruits.

2. An angiosperm can be either a ____ or a ____.

3. ____ are cone-bearing trees that are ____, producing naked seeds.

4. A ____ is a vascular plant that produces ____ rather than seeds.

5. Pollen forms on the ____ at the top of the ____ of a flower.

6. ____ occurs when pollen lands on a sticky ____.

7. ____ is a kind of plant reproduction without sex cells.

8. Trailing stems that form new plants are called ____.

9. A flower's ____ consists of the stigma, ____, and ovary.

10. ____ occurs when sperm cells and egg cells unite.

11. A ____ is a plant without true stems, leaves or roots.

12. When two different plants are joined, it is called ____.

13. The tiny plant inside a seed is an ____.

14. Ovules are located within the ____.

15. Animals or the wind can carry ____ to another location.

Connect Concepts

Use the terms from the word bank to complete the concept map below.

seeds	**spores**	**liverworts**
vascular	**gymnosperms**	

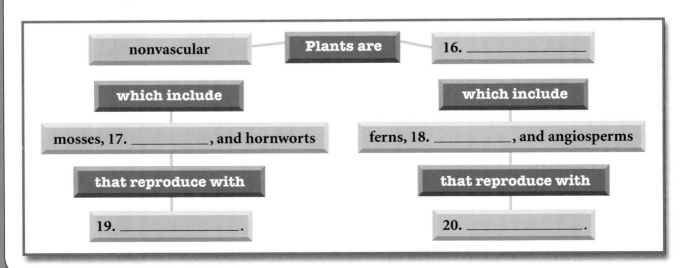

Check Understanding

Write the letter of the best choice.

21. What is the name of the tissue that plants have to transport water from roots to leaves?

    A spore   **C** pollen

    B phloem   **D** xylem

22. Where do the seeds of a conifer develop?

    F in the male cone

    G in the female cone

    H in the pollen

    J in the xylem

23. Examples of gymnosperms include —

    A conifers   **C** ferns

    B cycads   **D** both **A** and **B**

24. Monocots have —

    F netlike veins

    G two cotyledons

    H vascular tissue in rings

    J spread-out roots

25. Grafting is a method of —

    A using runners

    B leaf cutting

    C asexual reproduction

    D sexual reproduction

26. The female parts of the flower include —

    F stigmas   **H** petals

    G anthers   **J** sepals

Critical Thinking

27. How would you try to cross a hibiscus that has purple flowers with a hibiscus that has red flowers?

28. Why do fruit farmers often keep beehives in their orchards?

29. Suppose you had a damp, shady spot in your yard. What kinds of plants would do best there? Explain.

Process Skills Review

30. If a tree has needlelike leaves, what kind of plant would you **hypothesize** it is? What other characteristics would you look for to support your hypothesis?

31. **Compare** monocots and dicots in regard to cotyledons, leaf veins, roots, and flower parts.

32. If a plant has bright flowers, what can you **infer** about its pollination?

33. Suppose you have discovered a new plant near your home. How would you **communicate** information about your discovery?

Performance Assessment

Designing a Plant

If you had a fern, a gymnosperm, a monocot, and a dicot that each measured 0.5 meters (1.5 ft) tall, what procedures would you follow to identify which plant was which? List the methods you would use, and the characteristics of each kind of plant you would compare.

Chapter 3

Invertebrates

Being vertebrates ourselves, we might think that a backbone is essential to all animals. The truth, however, is that animals in more than nine out of ten species do *not* have a backbone. Crabs, spiders, butterflies, and bees—to name only a few animals—are invertebrates.

Vocabulary Preview

vertebrate
invertebrate
endoskeleton
exoskeleton
sponge
cnidarian
flatworm
roundworm
parasite
segmented worm
mollusk
arthropod
arachnid
insect
echinoderm

≡FAST FACT

There are more species of beetles than of any other animal. But if you could weigh all the animals on Earth, ants would account for 10 percent of the weight.

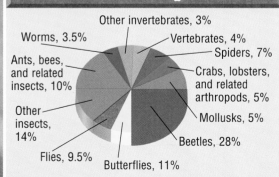

Number of Species

Other invertebrates, 3%
Worms, 3.5%
Vertebrates, 4%
Spiders, 7%
Ants, bees, and related insects, 10%
Crabs, lobsters, and related arthropods, 5%
Other insects, 14%
Mollusks, 5%
Flies, 9.5%
Beetles, 28%
Butterflies, 11%

A strand of spider silk is five times as strong as a strand of steel of the same weight and thickness.

Can something without a backbone grow to be very large? The truth is that some invertebrates grow to a remarkable size.

Big Invertebrates

Animal	Size
Goliath spider	11 in.
Starfish	38 in. 11lb
Giant spider crab	body 12–14 in., claw span 8–9 ft
Lobster	42 lb 11 oz
Clam	49 in. 579.5 lb
Jellyfish	diameter 7.5 ft, tentacle 120 ft
Sponge	diameter 3 ft, height 3.5 ft

1

What Are Vertebrates and Invertebrates?

In this lesson, you can . . .

INVESTIGATE how to design an environment for an animal.

LEARN ABOUT how animals meet their needs and how animals are classified.

LINK to math, writing, physical education, and technology.

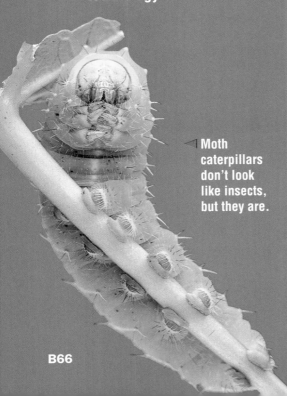

Moth caterpillars don't look like insects, but they are.

INVESTIGATE

Designing Habitats

Activity Purpose   Each environment on Earth has its own conditions. The animals in each environment may have different adaptations that enable them to meet their needs in the environment. However, all animals have some basic needs in common.

   In this investigation you will find out how one animal is adapted to meet its basic needs in its environment. Then you'll design a terrarium (tuh•RAIR•ee•uhm) that could also enable the animal to live and grow.

Materials
- cardboard box
- art supplies and natural materials for a diorama

Activity Procedure

1 Choose one of the following animals: the Chilean rose tarantula, the giant green iguana, or the green tree frog.

2 Read in the appropriate chart about the animal's natural environment and about its habits. **Infer** what the animal needs to survive and how its environment meets these needs.

3 Draw a terrarium that would provide the animal with what it needs to survive. Make sure that you consider all the animal's needs.

4 Build a diorama that shows your animal in the terrarium. (Picture A)

Chilean Rose Tarantula

- lives in semidry environments
- temperature of environment is 21°–24°C
- lives in burrow during day
- eats at night
- eats insects
- eats only once a week

Giant Green Iguana

- lives in humid environments
- can survive temperatures as low as 27°C
- often basks in direct sunlight when the temperature is above 32°C
- lives in trees
- eats in the daytime
- eats leaves and flowers
- eats daily

Picture A

Green Tree Frog

- lives in rain-forest environments
- temperature of environment about 29°C all the time
- lives in trees
- eats during the day
- eats insects
- needs one or two insects each day to survive

Draw Conclusions

1. **Compare** your diorama to those of other students. How are they alike and how are they different? How do these similarities and differences reflect the needs of the animals?

2. From what you have learned in this activity, what can you **infer** about the needs of all animals?

3. **Scientists at Work** Scientists **plan and conduct simple investigations** to test hypotheses and inferences they have made. Write a plan for a simple investigation you might be able to do to find out if your terrarium would be a suitable habitat for your animal. Make certain that your investigation would not harm the animal.

Investigate Further Find out more about the animal you chose for this investigation. Use reference books or encyclopedias. Change your diorama if you need to, based on what you find out.

Process Skill Tip

Scientists **plan and conduct simple investigations** to test ideas they have about how things relate or work. A simple investigation should focus on only one question.

Two Types of Animals

All Animals Have the Same Basic Needs

FIND OUT

- about animal needs and how animals meet them
- how animals can be classified in two groups

VOCABULARY

vertebrate
invertebrate
endoskeleton
exoskeleton

An adult giant green iguana may grow to be almost 1.5 m (about 5 ft) long. A young tarantula grows until it is about the size of your hand. Animals grow larger as they mature. Some change shape as they grow. Frogs start life as eggs and hatch into tadpoles that do not look much like adult frogs. As a tadpole grows, it loses its tail and develops legs. It finally becomes an adult frog. Animals can reach adulthood only if all their basic needs are met. These needs include food, oxygen, water, and protection from predators and other dangers in the environment.

Animals need food so they can have the energy to grow and to perform all life processes. Unlike plants, which make their own food, animals must find and eat food to survive. Some animals eat only plants. Others eat animals. And many animals eat both plants and animals. You can infer an animal's diet by observing its teeth. Teeth with broad surfaces can grind up plants. Long and sharp teeth can tear meat.

Sharks depend on their strength and speed as they hunt for food. Many other ocean animals strain tiny plants and animals from the water around them. Sponges pull water into their pores and strain bacteria, algae, or decaying plant or animal matter from the water. The largest animal on Earth, the blue whale, eats some of the smallest animals and plants. Blue whales strain ocean water through sievelike structures called baleen. In this way, a blue whale can consume as much as 3500 kg (about 7700 lb) of food in a single day.

Adult foxes care for their young and teach them how to protect themselves. ▼

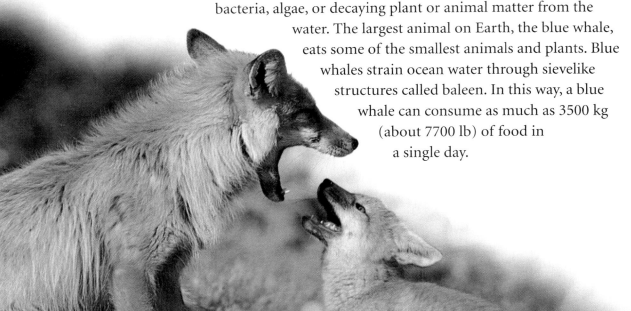

Australian termites build mounds from bits of soil mixed with saliva. A mound can be 6 m (about 20 ft) tall and is divided into many chambers. It protects the termites from the weather and from predators. It is also a safe place in which young termites can hatch and grow.

Water is a basic need of all animals, not just those that live in water. All animals are made up of cells, which are mostly water. Most life processes take place in a watery solution inside the cells. Animals that live in water can take it in directly from their surroundings. Land animals must find water in order to stay alive.

Even animals that have enough food, oxygen, and water need one other thing. They need protection from the weather and from predators. Many animals build shelters or use naturally formed shelters. Some animals, such as armadillos and turtles, have armorlike shells for shelter and protection. Scorpions and wasps protect themselves by stinging their attackers. Some animals are protected because they look like their surroundings, which keeps predators from finding them. Other animals defend themselves by traveling in large groups or by running to escape danger.

✔ **What do all animals need to survive?**

Animals eat food for energy, but they can't use the energy unless they also have oxygen. Animals that live on land get oxygen from the air. Animals such as worms absorb the oxygen they need through the surface of their bodies. Most animals have more complex adaptations for getting oxygen. Insects have air tubes that extend to the body organs from openings on the insects' sides. Frogs and snakes have small, simple lungs. Birds and mammals, which are more active, have larger, more specialized lungs. These lungs enable them to take in the amount of oxygen they need.

Animals that live in water take in oxygen directly from the water. Many of these animals have gills, thin tissues that absorb oxygen from the water that passes over them.

The axolotl (AKS•uh•laht•uhl) is an amphibian. Unlike many other amphibians, it lives almost all of its life in the water. It gets oxygen from the water through its gills. ▶

Vertebrates

Scientists divide the animal kingdom into two major groups—vertebrates and invertebrates. A **vertebrate** (VER•tuh•brit) is an animal that has a backbone. An **invertebrate** (in•VER•tuh•brit) is an animal that does not have a backbone.

Vertebrates are part of the animal phylum known as chordates. At some stage of their development, all chordates have four characteristics. First, every chordate has a *notochord*—a long, flexible rod of specialized cells that runs along much of the body. Second, beside the notochord is a nerve cord that connects the animal's brain with the other parts of its body. Third, a chordate has gill slits. Finally, a chordate has a tail. Although some mature

vertebrates do not have some of these characteristics, they all begin their lives as embryos that do have them. For example, cows do not have gill slits, but cow embryos do.

Among the chordates, the vertebrates are the largest group. Vertebrates include fish, amphibians, reptiles, birds, and mammals.

Vertebrates differ from other chordates because their notochord develops into a backbone. A mammal, for example, begins life as an embryo with a notochord. But soon bones develop around the notochord and replace it. The bones are *vertebrae* (VER•tuh•bray), individual parts of a backbone. They surround and protect the nerve cord.

The backbone is the core of a vertebrate's skeleton. It supports the other bones that form the animal's skeleton. A vertebrate has an **endoskeleton**—a system of connecting bones that lie within the animal's body. (The prefix *endo-* means "inside.") The skeleton supports the body and protects its most important organs. It also provides a system of levers, operated by muscles, that enables the body to move.

✔ **What is a vertebrate, and what are some examples of vertebrates?**

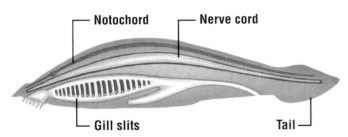

Notochord — Nerve cord
Gill slits — Tail

A lancelet is a chordate that lives in the water. It has a notochord, a nerve cord, gill slits, and a tail. But its notochord doesn't develop into a backbone. So a lancelet is not a vertebrate.

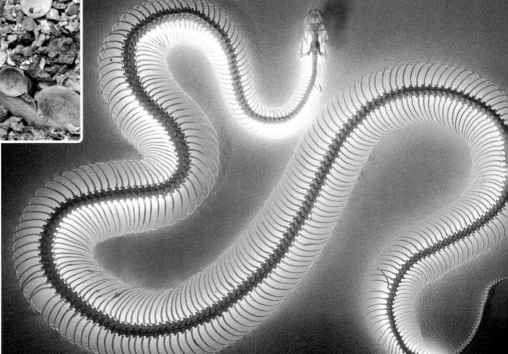

With its long string of vertebrae, a snake can bend, crawl, climb, and swim. Its backbone is made up of as many as 300 vertebrae. Humans have 33 vertebrae. ▶

◀ Dragonflies are insects that are often found near water. Dragonflies might be called living fossils because fossils of dragonflies look like the living animals. A dragonfly has four wings.

Invertebrates

Vertebrates make up about 4 percent of the animal kingdom. The other 96 percent of animal species are invertebrates.

Sponges, worms, centipedes, mollusks, and insects are just some of the animals that are invertebrates. Invertebrates have many adaptations that enable them to survive without a backbone.

Some invertebrates, such as sponges, have no head, mouth, or internal organs. Their body walls are only a few cells thick. However, the adaptations of sponges enable them to survive in their environments.

Some invertebrates, such as starfish, sea urchins, and sand dollars, have an unusual body arrangement. Their bodies are like the spokes of a wheel around a hub. This is called *radial symmetry*. They are not like most other animals, which have right and left sides that mirror each other. Among the animals with sides that mirror each other, the largest group is the arthropods, which include lobsters, crabs, spiders, and insects.

Most arthropods have an exoskeleton. An **exoskeleton** is a skeleton that is outside of an animal's body. (*Exo-* means "outside.") An exoskeleton protects the tissues and organs of an arthropod's body and gives it support. The skeleton is jointed, allowing arthropods a greater variety of movements than many other invertebrates.

✔ **How do vertebrates and invertebrates differ?**

The Portuguese man-of-war looks like a jellyfish, but it is not. It floats on the surface of the sea. Its mouth is at the center of its hollow body, surrounded by stinging tentacles that capture prey.

Diversity in the Animal Kingdom

Flatworms and roundworms, 2%
Jellyfish and related animals, 1%
Mollusks (clams and snails), 5%
Earthworms, 1%
Vertebrates, 4%
Other invertebrates, 2%
Arthropods, 85%

▼ The queen conch is a sea snail with a spiral shell. Conchs are mollusks, as are clams, snails, octopods, and squid. Most of these invertebrates have soft bodies that are protected by hard outer shells.

Invertebrate Environments

Almost any environment that supports vertebrates also supports invertebrates. In fact, there are far more invertebrate habitats than vertebrate habitats.

Invertebrates are Earth's most common animals both in numbers of species and in numbers of individuals. Look almost anywhere and you will find invertebrates such as insects, worms, and sow bugs. You may not see them at first, because many of them are well hidden. They may be under rocks or in the soil. Some live in moist, shady places, and others can be found in rotting logs.

Some invertebrates survive best in dry air and bright sunshine. They can be found above the ground. They feed on plants, other invertebrates, or small vertebrates. Many fly through the air, landing to eat or to rest. The leaves and stems of weeds, flowers, bushes, and trees are also environments in which many invertebrates live. Even when these animals are hard to find, you may see signs of them, such as spider webs, chewed leaves, or tiny mounds of dirt.

Invertebrates don't live just on land. Millions of these animals live in the oceans. At low tide, holes and trails show where they've been. Invertebrates such as marine worms and clams bury themselves in the wet sand. In deeper water, horseshoe crabs, starfish, and lobsters move across the ocean floor.

Tropical seas provide habitats for invertebrates such as corals and sponges. Freshwater environments also supply the needs of invertebrates. Lakes and ponds, and the mud at the bottom of them, provide many habitats for invertebrates.

✔ **Where would you look for invertebrates in your area?**

▲ An orb weaver spider makes complicated webs between tree branches or flower stems. Threads of dry silk extend from the center of the web, like spokes of a wheel. Coiling lines of sticky silk connect the spokes. The web is the spider's habitat and a trap for its prey.

A water spider lives most of its life under water. It breathes air from bubbles that it holds close to its body. Its underwater nest is a bell-shaped silk web that it fills with air bubbles.

▲ A trapdoor spider digs a burrow in the ground and covers the entrance with a lid, or trapdoor. It uses the burrow as protection and as a nest for its young. The trapdoor is made of silk and is attached to the lining of the burrow by silk hinges.

Summary

All animals have the same basic needs, which include food, water, oxygen, and protection. Animals can be divided into two groups—vertebrates and invertebrates. Vertebrates include all animals with a backbone. They have an endoskeleton. Invertebrates include all animals without a backbone. Many of these animals have an exoskeleton. Ninety-six percent of all animal species are invertebrates.

Review

1. Why is water a basic need of all animals?
2. How does an insect get the oxygen it needs?
3. What do all vertebrates have?
4. **Critical Thinking** A chameleon is a lizard that can change its color. When it's surrounded by leaves, the chameleon is green, and when it's on bark, it is brown. What basic need does this adaptation meet?
5. **Test Prep** Which animal has an exoskeleton?
   A a dragonfly
   B a snake
   C a cheetah
   D a shark

LINKS

MATH LINK

Graphing Different kinds of graphs can show the same data. Draw a bar graph or a pictograph for the data in the circle graph on page B71. Which graph better helps you compare the percentages?

WRITING LINK

Informative Writing—How-to Go to a pet store and interview a salesperson about the care a particular invertebrate needs. Use the information to write a pamphlet for pet owners about taking care of that animal.

PHYSICAL EDUCATION LINK

Exercise for Your Pet One of the things people need for good health is exercise. Find out what sort of exercise your favorite pet animal needs. Make a plan that would help the pet get the right exercise.

TECHNOLOGY LINK

Visit the Harcourt Learning Site for related links, activities, and resources.
www.harcourtschool.com

WELCOME TO
THE
LEARNING
SITE

What Are Sponges, Cnidarians, and Worms?

In this lesson, you can . . .

INVESTIGATE sponges, planarians, and hydras.

LEARN ABOUT the body structures and life cycles of sponges, cnidarians, and worms.

LINK to math, writing, social studies, and technology.

INVESTIGATE

Three Groups of Invertebrates

Activity Purpose Sponges, planarians, and hydras are three kinds of invertebrates that live in water. As invertebrates, these share some characteristics, but they also differ greatly. In this investigation you will **compare** these animals to discover their similarities and differences.

Materials
- hand lens
- sponge
- living planarian
- Microslide Viewer and slides of hydras

Activity Procedure

1 Use your hand lens to **observe** the sponge and the planarian. Draw a picture of each. Include all of the structures you see. (Picture A)

2 **Observe** the hydra by using the Microslide Viewer and slides. (Picture B)

3 **Compare** the three animals, and **record** your **observations** by writing a description of each one. Describe the structures you observe.

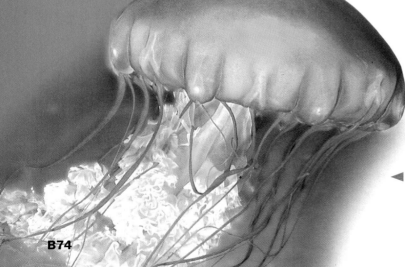

◄ The sea nettle has tentacles with stinging cells to trap and sting small ocean organisms.

Picture A

Picture B

Sponge

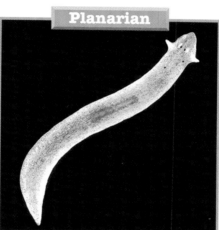

Planarian

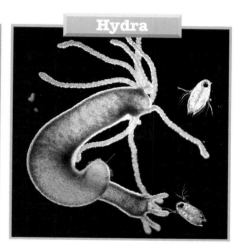

Hydra

Draw Conclusions

1. What similarities and differences among the animals did you **record** in your descriptions?

2. As you **compared** the animals, which animal seemed to have the simplest body structure? Explain.

3. **Scientists at Work** When scientists discover information through their investigations, they **communicate** their findings to others who study the same things. One way to communicate **observations** is to write a description. How else might scientists communicate their observations?

Investigate Further If you have access to a microscope, use it to **observe** animals you can find in a drop of pond water.

Process Skill Tip

To **communicate** your observations and conclusions so that others can understand them, include as much detail as possible in your descriptions. Use correct spelling and clear language.

Sponges, Cnidarians, and Worms

Sponges

A **sponge** is one type of animal that filters the water it lives in to get food. Unless you observe a sponge under very high magnification, it seems to be inactive and to have no animal-like characteristics at all. In fact, biologists 200 years ago thought that sponges were plants.

A sponge has only two layers of cells. The outer surface of a sponge's body is dotted with tiny openings. These openings lead to canals, which are made up of specialized cells with whiplike structures that beat rapidly. This motion helps pump water into the canals. These cells also have tiny threadlike structures that remove small food particles from the water. The water leaves the sponge's body through an opening called a vent.

Between the outer layer of a sponge and the inner layer is a jellylike layer that contains cells that have different functions. They carry food from the collecting cells to the other cells in the sponge. They also make materials that form a kind of skeleton for the sponge. The skeleton is made up of tiny rodlike structures of tough protein called *spicules* (SPIK•yools). It takes thousands of connected spicules, or pieces of protein, to form a sponge's skeleton.

Scientists know of about 5000 species of sponges. Most of these live in shallow ocean waters where they attach themselves to hard underwater surfaces, such as the ocean floor, rocks, other animals, and human-made structures. Different species of sponges have

FIND OUT

- about sponges, cnidarians, and worms
- how each of these animals has adaptations that enable it to survive

VOCABULARY

sponge
cnidarian
flatworm
roundworm
parasite
segmented worm

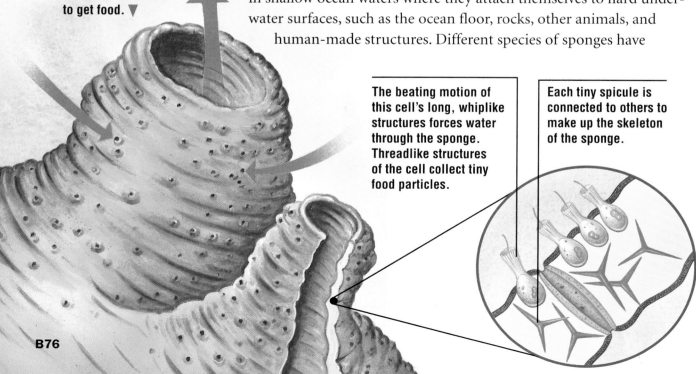

A living sponge filters the water it lives in to get food. ▼

The beating motion of this cell's long, whiplike structures forces water through the sponge. Threadlike structures of the cell collect tiny food particles.

Each tiny spicule is connected to others to make up the skeleton of the sponge.

B76

different colors, shapes, and sizes. Some are black, brown, or gray, and others are bright shades of red, blue, purple, and yellow. Some sponges are shaped like fingers, some look like the branches of a tree, and others are round. The smallest sponges are about 1 cm (about $\frac{1}{2}$ in.) across, and the largest are 2 m (about 6 ft) across.

Some of the smaller species of sponges live in fresh water. They can be found in lakes, ponds, and streams, growing on rocks or sticks under water. Because they are usually covered with algae, they are hard to see.

Most often sponges reproduce asexually. Buds and branches grow from a parent sponge. These

People use the word *sponge* to name the soft plastic material used for cleaning. Sponges that are sold as "natural" or "real" sponges, however, are sponge skeletons made of protein. In this country, the natural-sponge industry is centered in Tarpon Springs, Florida. Divers collect the sponges from underwater beds growing on the ocean floor. The sponges are then left to dry until only their protein skeletons remain.

buds break off and grow into new sponges. Some sponges also reproduce sexually, forming egg and sperm cells. A fertilized egg cell forms a larva that leaves the parent sponge and travels through the water to another part of the ocean floor. There it attaches itself to a hard surface, where it develops into an adult sponge.

✓ **Why is a sponge classified as an animal?**

This is the skeleton of a Venus's-flower-basket sponge. Its spicules are made of silica, or glass. These sponges grow at great depths, where ocean currents move slowly.

Sponges in tropical waters can be brightly colored. They are often found growing on or near coral reefs. ▼

B77

Cnidarians

When you observed a hydra, you may have seen tentacles extending from the large part of its body. Even though it is small, a hydra can sting its prey or predators with poison found in some of its tentacle cells. This ability to sting is a characteristic of all the animals called **cnidarians** (ny•DAIR•ee•uhnz).

Cnidarians are carnivorous, or meat-eating, invertebrates. They have tentacles all around the mouth. After the prey is stung and stunned, the tentacles pull the prey toward the mouth. The mouth is connected directly to the middle of the body, where the food is digested. Once the food is digested, wastes leave through the mouth.

A cnidarian does not have organs in its body. Instead, cnidarians have cells that are organized into tissues—groups of cells that work together. Many of their body functions are carried out by tissues or cells. For example, the outer layer of tissue of a cnidarian protects the organism. The inner layer of tissue digests its food. In addition to their stinging cells, cnidarians also have other specialized sensory cells.

All cnidarians live in water. Most live in sea water, as do most species of sponges. Hydras belong to the only class of freshwater cnidarians.

Cnidarians have radial symmetry. Their body parts are arranged around a center, like spokes around the hub of a wheel. Even so, different cnidarians have different forms. Jellyfish shaped like umbrellas, sea anemones (uh•NEM•uh•neez)

The largest structure built by organisms on Earth isn't the Superdome in New Orleans or the Great Wall of China—it's Australia's Great Barrier Reef. The reef, which is about 2000 km (about 1250 mi) long, was formed by corals. ▼

Coral is a cnidarian that lives in groups called colonies. A coral produces a skeleton to protect its soft body. New coral polyps grow on top of the skeletons of dead corals. ▶

As a colony of corals grows, it forms a coral reef. Coral reefs are the habitats of many kinds of other animals, both vertebrates and invertebrates.

that look like flowers, and corals shaped like vases are all cnidarians. They all have a hollow pouch with a single opening—the mouth—and a circle of tentacles around it.

A cnidarian that has a vase-shaped form like the hydra is called a polyp (PAHL•ip). Sea anemones and corals are also polyps. The other form of cnidarian is called a medusa. A medusa has a bowl-shaped body from which its tentacles hang down.

A medusa is the adult stage in the life cycle of some cnidarians. Adult jellyfish are medusas that develop from polyps as they mature. Not all cnidarians develop into medusas. Sea anemones and hydras, for example, remain as polyps when they are mature.

Cnidarians reproduce both sexually and asexually. In jellyfish the medusa releases sperm and egg cells into the water, where fertilization takes place. Fertilized egg cells develop into larvae that can move through the water. The larvae settle on the ocean floor and develop into polyps. In its polyp form, the jellyfish reproduces asexually. It forms medusas that break off from the parent and swim away.

✔ **What characteristics do all cnidarians have in common?**

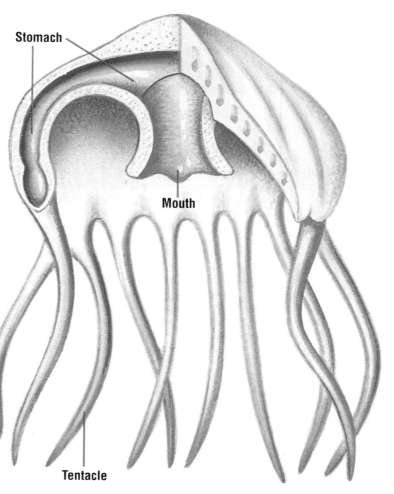

▲ An adult jellyfish, or medusa, is bowl-shaped. Some of the cells of its tentacles contain a coiled thread that has tiny hooks, or barbs, on it. The barbs can inject a poison that can paralyze a small fish.

A comb jelly belongs to a phylum related to the cnidarians. Comb jellies have eight bands of comblike organs on the sides of their bodies. The combs are rows of tiny hairs that move the animal through the water. Like fireflies and glowworms, some comb jellies can produce light. They may or may not have tentacles, and they don't have stinging cells. ▼

▲ Sea nettles are a common jellyfish often seen in the water or washed up on shore. They swim by expanding and contracting their bodies. The word *cnidarian* comes from a Greek word that means "sting." Like all cnidarians, sea nettles can sting.

Worms

There are many phyla of worms. Some types of worms, such as segmented worms, have complex body systems. But some, such as flatworms and roundworms, have a simpler body organization. These organisms differ from sponges and cnidarians in the shape of their bodies. While sponges may have no symmetry and cnidarians have radial symmetry, flatworms and roundworms have *bilateral* (by•LAT•er•uhl) *symmetry*. Each side of the body of one of these worms is a mirror image of the other side.

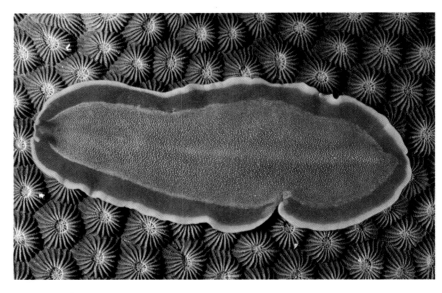

▲ This is another example of a flatworm. It lives in ocean environments. Often it is part of coral reef ecosystems.

Flatworms

A **flatworm** has a flattened body, a digestive system with only one opening, and a simple nervous system. A planarian is one kind of flatworm.

Planarians live in freshwater streams, lakes, and ponds. They are usually small. Most are less than 30 mm (about 1 in.) long. Planarians stay out of the light. During daylight they can be found under rocks or in the mud at the bottom of their freshwater environments.

Planarians are not familiar to most people. However, as you saw in the investigation, you can easily identify them by their triangle-shaped heads and their eyespots. When seen under a microscope, planarians look cross-eyed.

A planarian has body organs made up of tissues. It also has sense organs in its head. Two nerve cords run down the length of its body. A planarian has a mouth at the end of a long tube. The tube is near the middle of the underside of the planarian's body. It is used to take in food and to push out wastes.

Unlike cnidarians, planarians have reproductive systems with sex organs and can reproduce by mating and laying eggs. They also can regenerate body parts that have been cut off. If a planarian is cut in two, the part with the head will grow a new tail and the part with the tail will grow a new head.

✔ **What characteristics do all flatworms share?**

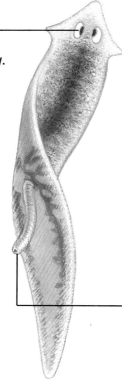

A planarian's eyespots are on the top of its body. They sense light and darkness but can't see actual images. Nerve cords extend the length of a planarian's body. The planarian's mouth is on its underside.

To eat, a planarian extends a tube from its mouth. The tube works like a straw, sucking small particles and liquids into the animal's stomach.

Roundworms

A **roundworm** has a round, tubelike body. Most roundworms are too small to be seen without a microscope. Roundworms are very numerous and live in many types of environments. It has been estimated that a shovelful of soil can contain about 1 million roundworms!

Unlike flatworms, roundworms have a digestive system with two openings. At one end is a mouth where food is taken in. At the other end is an opening through which the worm gets rid of wastes.

The muscles in a roundworm run lengthwise through the worm's body. Roundworms are the only group of worms with this arrangement of muscles. The contraction of these muscles results in the whiplike motion of roundworms.

A roundworm has a nervous system with a brain and other simple sense organs. It also has sex organs that enable it to reproduce sexually. Many roundworms harm other organisms in which they live and feed.

✔ How do roundworms and flatworms differ?

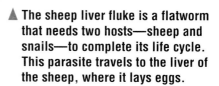

▲ The sheep liver fluke is a flatworm that needs two hosts—sheep and snails—to complete its life cycle. This parasite travels to the liver of the sheep, where it lays eggs.

Parasite Worms

Some worms survive by living on or in another animal and feeding on that animal. An organism that lives this way is called a **parasite** (PAR•uh•syt). It harms the host animal, or the animal that it is feeding on, while it benefits itself.

Flatworm parasites include tapeworms and flukes, both of which harm mammals, including humans. Roundworm parasites include hookworms and *Trichinella*, which are roundworms that live in pigs. They can pass into people who eat undercooked pork.

Many parasite worms have a life cycle that needs two species of host animals. The fluke *Schistosoma*, for example, begins life in a freshwater snail. Many of these parasites then reach human hosts, where they mature within the humans' bodies. The serious disease caused by these parasites affects more than 200 million people in tropical parts of the world.

✔ Why do parasites need a host animal?

◀ The roundworm *Ascaris* is a parasite that harms people. It is estimated that about 650 million people worldwide have the disease caused by this roundworm.

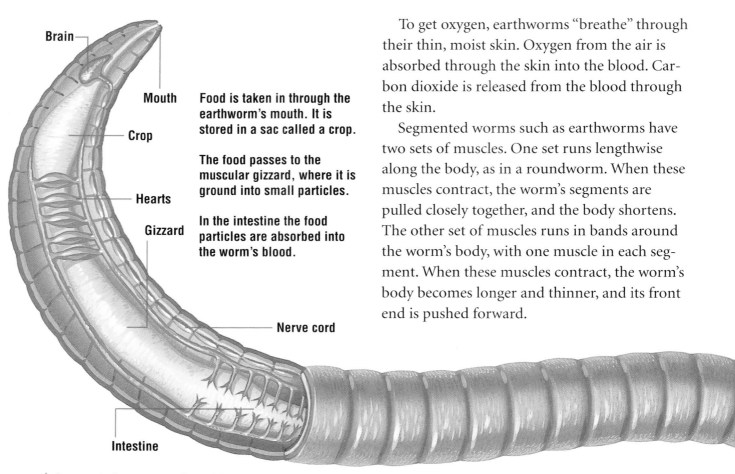

Brain

Mouth — Food is taken in through the earthworm's mouth. It is stored in a sac called a crop.

Crop

The food passes to the muscular gizzard, where it is ground into small particles.

Hearts

Gizzard

In the intestine the food particles are absorbed into the worm's blood.

Nerve cord

Intestine

▲ Segmented worms, such as this earthworm, have bodies formed of connected segments. Some of the worm's body systems are shown in this picture.

Segmented Worms

Earthworms are very different from all the other worms you have learned about. They are part of a group of animals called **segmented worms**. These are worms whose bodies are made up of connected sections, or segments.

An earthworm's body systems are more complex than those of other worms. For example, earthworms have a circulatory system. Five enlarged tubes act as hearts. The tubes pump blood through the major vessels of the worm's body. These major vessels branch into smaller and smaller vessels, supplying blood to every part of the worm's body. An earthworm also has a nerve center, or brain, in its head. This brain is connected to a main nerve that runs the length of the worm's body.

To get oxygen, earthworms "breathe" through their thin, moist skin. Oxygen from the air is absorbed through the skin into the blood. Carbon dioxide is released from the blood through the skin.

Segmented worms such as earthworms have two sets of muscles. One set runs lengthwise along the body, as in a roundworm. When these muscles contract, the worm's segments are pulled closely together, and the body shortens. The other set of muscles runs in bands around the worm's body, with one muscle in each segment. When these muscles contract, the worm's body becomes longer and thinner, and its front end is pushed forward.

The two sets of muscles enable the earthworm to move through the soil, where it takes in food through its mouth. This burrowing not only enables the worm to get food, but it also lets air into the spaces where the worm has traveled. The wastes of the earthworm enrich the soil.

Every earthworm has both male and female sex organs. After worms mate, both partners lay eggs and produce a slimy covering that forms a cocoon protecting the eggs. Fertilized eggs develop, and soon worms hatch from them.

✔ **What is the major difference between an earthworm and other worms?**

Summary

Sponges have just two layers of cells separated with a jellylike layer. Cnidarians, which include sea anemones, corals, and jellyfish, all have simple tissues and bodies that are hollow containers with venomous tentacles circling a mouth. Flatworms have tissues and sense organs and a digestive system with only one opening. Roundworms have a digestive system with two body openings. Many roundworms and flatworms are parasites. Segmented worms, such as the earthworm, have body systems that are more complex than those of other worms, including a circulatory system with five hearts.

Review

1. How do sponges get food?

2. Do cnidarians eat plants, other animals, or both?

3. How does an earthworm differ from a roundworm?

4. **Critical Thinking** A tapeworm is a kind of parasite that has no mouth. It takes in food directly through its body walls. How might these adaptations help a tapeworm survive?

5. **Test Prep** Roundworms have —
   A a digestive system with one opening
   B a circulatory system
   C a digestive system with two openings
   D tentacles

LINKS

MATH LINK

Multiplication A pork tapeworm can grow to be 7 m long inside its host. The tapeworm has as many as 1500 segments, each containing about 80,000 eggs. How many eggs can one tapeworm contain?

WRITING LINK

Informative Writing—Explanation Find out where the word *medusa* comes from, and write a paragraph for your teacher to explain why it is a good name for an adult jellyfish.

SOCIAL STUDIES LINK

Dams and Reservoirs To meet their needs, people have built lakes and reservoirs that hold huge amounts of fresh water. However, this progress has led to unexpected effects. Find out how the Aswan Dam in Egypt or Lake Volta in Ghana has caused an increase in dangerous diseases among the people who live nearby.

TECHNOLOGY LINK

Learn more about coral reefs by visiting the Smithsonian Institution Internet Site.
www.si.edu/harcourt/science

 Smithsonian Institution®

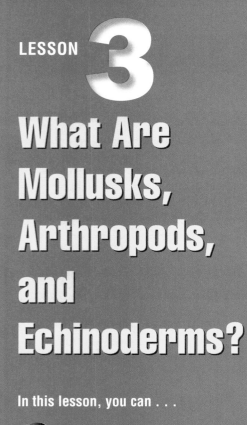
What Are Mollusks, Arthropods, and Echinoderms?

In this lesson, you can . . .

INVESTIGATE the structure of some mollusks, arthropods, and echinoderms.

LEARN ABOUT the adaptations of mollusks, arthropods, and echinoderms.

LINK to math, writing, art, and technology.

Compare Three Groups of Animals

Activity Purpose Some of the invertebrates that you've studied so far may not have been familiar to you. But almost all of the other invertebrates belong to just three groups. You've probably seen examples of them. In this investigation you will compare the characteristics of animals from these groups—mollusks, arthropods, and echinoderms.

Materials

- clam shell
- spirula shell
- snail shell
- grasshopper study sheet
- sea urchin shell
- starfish

Activity Procedure

1 **Observe** the animal samples. Use the pictures on page B85 to add to your observations. The cuttlefish is similar to the animal that contains the coiled spirula shell. (Picture A)

2 **Compare** the characteristics of the animals, and **record** your findings. Note any similarities and differences that you see among the animals.

3 Use your observations to **classify** the animals into three groups. (Hint: One group will have three animals, one group will have two, and one group will have one.)

4 Describe the characteristics that the animals within each group share. For the group that has only one animal, describe or name another animal that belongs in the group.

◄ **This scallop is an invertebrate that has two matching hinged shells. Along the tissue that lines the edges of the shells are two rows of tiny blue eyes.**

Snail

Cuttlefish

Picture A

Clam

Starfish

Draw Conclusions

1. What shared characteristics did you **observe** among the clam, the grasshopper, and the starfish? In what ways was each animal unlike the others?

2. Which of these characteristics did you use to **classify** the animals?

3. Name one more animal that might belong in each of your three groups.

4. **Scientists at Work** Scientists **classify** animals in the same group if those animals have important characteristics in common. How are the **inferences** you made to answer Questions 2 and 3 similar to a scientist's method of classification?

Process Skill Tip

Sharing several characteristics does not always place animals in the same group. For animals to be **classified** in the same group, they must share unique similarities that they—and no other group of animals—have.

LEARN ABOUT

Mollusks, Arthropods, and Echinoderms

FIND OUT

- the characteristics of mollusks, arthropods, and echinoderms
- how mollusks, arthropods, and echinoderms reproduce
- how these animals are important to people

VOCABULARY

mollusk
arthropod
arachnid
insect
echinoderm

Giant clams live on the coral reefs of the southern Pacific Ocean. They can weigh up to 300 kg (about 660 lb). The algae that live in their tissues often give the soft part of the clam a green or blue color. ▼

Mollusks

The groups of invertebrates you looked at in the investigation have a larger number of complex body systems than sponges, cnidarians, and most worms. For example, like the earthworms, the three groups you looked at have circulatory systems—sponges, cnidarians, and other worms do not. The animals in each group have a number of characteristics in common. However, each group also has within it a great variety of forms and adaptations.

A **mollusk** is an animal with a soft body and no bones. The name comes from the Latin word *mollus*, meaning "soft." Mollusks include clams, oysters, slugs, snails, squid, and octopods. Most have hard shells that protect their bodies. But some, such as squid, have no outer shell. Their shells grow within their bodies, providing support. Some mollusks, such as octopods and slugs, have no shell at all, inside or out.

The shell of a mollusk is formed by an organ called the mantle, which lies between the animal's body and its shell. The mantle produces materials that harden into the shell. The shell can grow as the mollusk grows. Mollusks that have no external shells also have mantles.

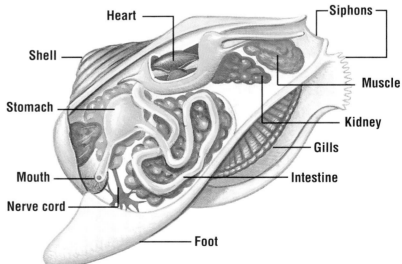

▲ The clam is a mollusk with a hard shell outside its soft body. Clams are filter feeders. They take in and push out water through organs called siphons. Food particles are caught in the gills and are passed to the clam's mouth.

This sea snail has gills that absorb oxygen from sea water. Other marine snails have lungs rather than gills and must bob up to the surface every once in a while to collect air in cavities in their shells. ▶

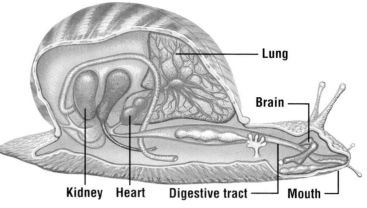

▼ The common garden snail, like all other snails, has a spiral shell protecting the main organs of its body.

Lung

Brain

Kidney   Heart   Digestive tract   Mouth

On these animals the mantle is a tough layer that forms a covering for the soft body.

A mollusk has a muscular foot. Some mollusks use it to burrow into the sand on the ocean floor. Many mollusks use the foot to move across a surface. In octopods and squid, the foot is in the form of several tentacles. Octopods often use these to crawl across the ocean floor.

Mollusks reproduce sexually. They release eggs and sperm into the water, where the eggs are fertilized. The fertilized eggs develop into larvae. The larvae are covered with hairlike structures and move like spinning tops. Each larva can develop into an adult.

Mollusks such as clams and oysters are bivalves. This means that they have two hinged shells that fit together. When a bivalve senses danger, sometimes it pulls the shells together. At other times, a bivalve may use its foot to burrow into the sand quickly. Some bivalves clap the shells together to produce a push that moves the animal away from danger.

▼ The large brain of an octopus controls the movement of each tentacle and the many suckers on the tentacles. The tentacles capture prey. The brain also controls the eyes, which have adaptations similar to those of human eyes, including eyelids.

Many mollusks, such as snails, have only one shell. Some snails live on land, and some live in salt water or in fresh water. Like many other mollusks, snails have a foot they use for movement. They also have two pairs of tentacles on their heads. One pair senses the snail's surroundings, and the other supports the snail's eyes.

Snails have an organ that is called a radula (RAJ•oo•lah). The radula is shaped like a tongue and is coated with ribbons of teeth. It is used like a drill to cut through hard surfaces such as clamshells so the snail can get food.

Octopods and squid are the most active and most intelligent mollusks. They live in the ocean, where they prey on other marine animals. Their brains and well-developed nervous systems enable them to react quickly. Their well-developed sense of sight helps them locate their prey. The feet of octopods and squid are in the form of tentacles. An octopus has eight tentacles, and a squid has ten. These tentacles catch prey and bring it to the animal's mouth. The mouth has strong, beaklike jaws.

An octopus or a squid has two adaptations to defend itself. It can use its jet motion to get away quickly in any direction. It can also squirt out a dark, inky fluid. This fluid forms a cloud in the water and hides the animal as it gets away.

✔ **Name two characteristics of snails.**

Arthropods

An **arthropod** is an animal that has a jointed exoskeleton. The hard skeleton covers an arthropod's body, protects it, and gives it support. Like a coat of armor, the jointed exoskeleton allows an arthropod to bend the parts of its body, such as its legs.

Muscles attached to the inside of the exoskeleton contract and relax, which allows for complex movements. These movements are similar in many ways to those of a vertebrate.

The scorpion uses its large claws to seize prey. Its jointed tail can reach over its head and inject its prey with a poison that stuns or kills. ▼

THE INSIDE STORY

Arthropod Adaptations

Arthropods can be found in every environment that supports life. The tremendous variety of adaptations in arthropods has allowed them to survive almost everywhere on Earth.

Crustaceans

Crustaceans (kruhs•TAY•shuhnz) are one kind of arthropod. Lobsters are crustaceans that live in the water. They show many of the characteristics of crustaceans. Lobsters have three body segments— a head, a thorax, and an abdomen. They have two pairs of antennae that sense their surroundings by feel. The legs around a lobster's head are adapted for capturing prey and carrying it to the animal's mouth. A lobster's claws can crush the shell of an oyster or a clam. The claws are usually not the same size. The larger one is for defense and the capture of food. The smaller claw helps to tear the prey into smaller pieces.

Mouthparts of a lobster ▲

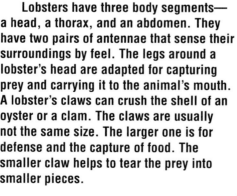

An arthropod's exoskeleton does not grow as the animal gets larger. Several times during its life, an arthropod grows a new, larger exoskeleton. This new exoskeleton remains soft until the animal sheds its old exoskeleton. Then the new one begins to harden. During this process, the animal has little protection against predators. It may conceal itself until its new exoskeleton has hardened.

Every arthropod has legs, a digestive system with two openings, a circulatory system, and a brain. Many arthropods have well-developed organs for sight, sound, and touch. Arthropods reproduce sexually. The female often lays fertilized eggs from which young hatch. Though they have these features in common, arthropods include such different animals as beetles, butterflies, spiders, shrimp, centipedes, and scorpions. Arthropods are by far the largest phylum of animals. Scientists know of more than a million different arthropod species.

✔ **Name two characteristics arthropods share.**

Arachnids

Arthropods also include **arachnids** (uh•RAK•nidz). Spiders, scorpions, ticks, and mites are arachnids. Arachnids have eight legs and no antennae. They breathe through organs called book lungs. Book lungs look like the loosely opened pages of a book. Many arachnids have sharp body parts that inject poison. Most eat other animals, using their pincers or fangs for capturing prey. Almost all arachnids live on land.

Book lungs

▲ The arachnid in these pictures is a tarantula. Tarantulas are sometimes thought of as dangerous animals, but they are actually not as venomous as many other spiders.

The grasshopper has many characteristics in common with all insects. However, its mouthparts are adapted for crushing food. Other insects have mouthparts that pierce, suck, or slice. ▼

Insects

Insects, animals with six jointed legs, are the largest group of arthropods. Many insects have wings. These are the only invertebrates that can fly. Insects get oxygen through air ducts along the sides of their bodies.

Mouthparts of a grasshopper ▲

Helpful and Harmful Arthropods

Insects are the most numerous arthropods and the most numerous animals on Earth. Often, they seem to be pests. But without insects, most plants would not be able to reproduce. Insects pollinate most of the angiosperms that other animals, including humans, use for food. Arthropods such as ladybugs help farmers and gardeners by eating many of the insects that destroy crops or flowers.

Arthropods are a food source for other animals. Much of the seafood that people enjoy comes from the arthropod phylum. Shrimp, lobster, and crab are regarded as treats. Arthropods also produce goods that can be sold. Bees produce honey and the beeswax used in some candles. Bees are also among the most important pollinators of plants.

Fewer than one percent of all arthropod species are harmful, but that's a large number of species. Many insects attack and injure almost all types of plants, including food crops. Some insects destroy corn, some spoil potatoes, and some devour wheat. Other insects are household pests. Moths may ruin clothing. Termites attack the wooden beams and floors of buildings. Ants, cockroaches, and flies infect food with germs.

Some arthropods are venomous to people. Wasps, scorpions, and spiders sometimes inject people with poison that is painful or dangerous. Other insects may carry diseases and infect people.

✔ **How do arthropods help people?**

Beekeepers provide bees with habitats and sell honey and beeswax. The bees in a hive inform each other of the location of a food source, the nectar in flowers. They do this through a "dance" that shows the direction and distance of the food source. ▶

When a starfish finds a mussel, the starfish wraps its arms around the mussel, using suction cups to pull the shells apart. The starfish then extends its stomach into the space between the shells. The starfish's stomach surrounds the mussel's body and digests it. Then it absorbs the digested material. ▶

Echinoderms

Not all invertebrates have exoskeletons. **Echinoderms** (ee•KY•nuh•dermz) are invertebrates that have internal skeletons and spines sticking out from their bodies. Although these spines may seem to be part of an exoskeleton, they are actually part of the skin. The word *echinoderm* comes from the Latin words meaning "spiny" and "skin."

Echinoderms live only in the ocean. They get oxygen from sea water through gills. Examples of echinoderms are starfish, sand dollars, sea urchins, and sea cucumbers.

Although an echinoderm has no brain, it has nerves that enable it to move and feed. Most echinoderms have radial symmetry, with five arms extending from the center of the body. Sea urchins and sand dollars do not have arms like those of starfish. However, they have five paired rows of feet extending symmetrically from the mouth.

The mouth of an echinoderm is at the center of the underside of its body. Many echinoderms have powerful jaws and, hidden among their spines, poison glands. These adaptations enable them to get enough food and to defend themselves.

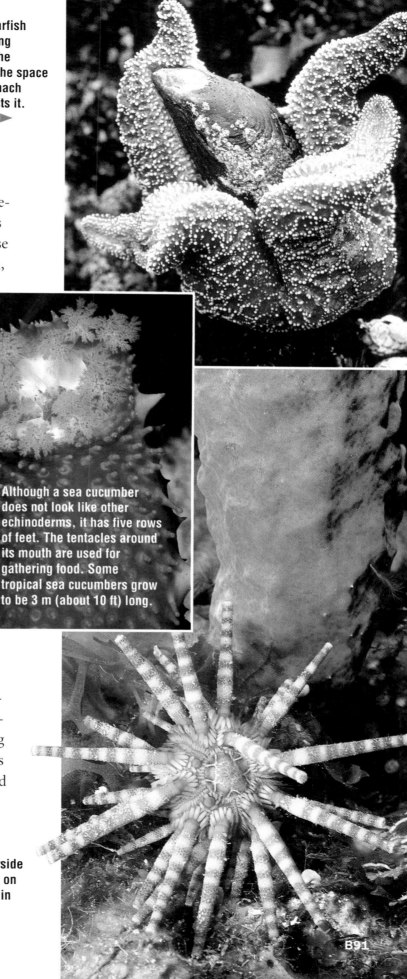

Although a sea cucumber does not look like other echinoderms, it has five rows of feet. The tentacles around its mouth are used for gathering food. Some tropical sea cucumbers grow to be 3 m (about 10 ft) long.

A sea urchin's spines protect it from predators. On this echinoderm's underside are five teeth, which are used to graze on algae. Sea urchins can often be found in tide pools at the seashore. ▶

B91

Echinoderms have an unusual adaptation called tube feet. Most echinoderms have rows of tube feet along the underside of their arms or in rows extending from their mouths. They use these tube feet for moving, feeding, and sensing.

Each foot ends with a sucker. A system of canals within the animal pumps water to each of its feet. When the water is forced into a tube foot, the foot expands and becomes firm enough to walk on. When water is withdrawn from the tube foot, the sucker grasps the surface it is touching. The suckers on a starfish's feet are strong enough to force open the shells of bivalve mollusks, their main food source.

Starfish generally reproduce sexually. Each starfish is either female or male, and each of its arms has sex organs. Females release millions of egg cells, and males release millions of sperm

A brittle star looks like a starfish, but it has thinner arms and no suckers on its tube feet. It moves by waving its arms from side to side. Brittle stars are, in fact, brittle. Their arms can snap off easily.

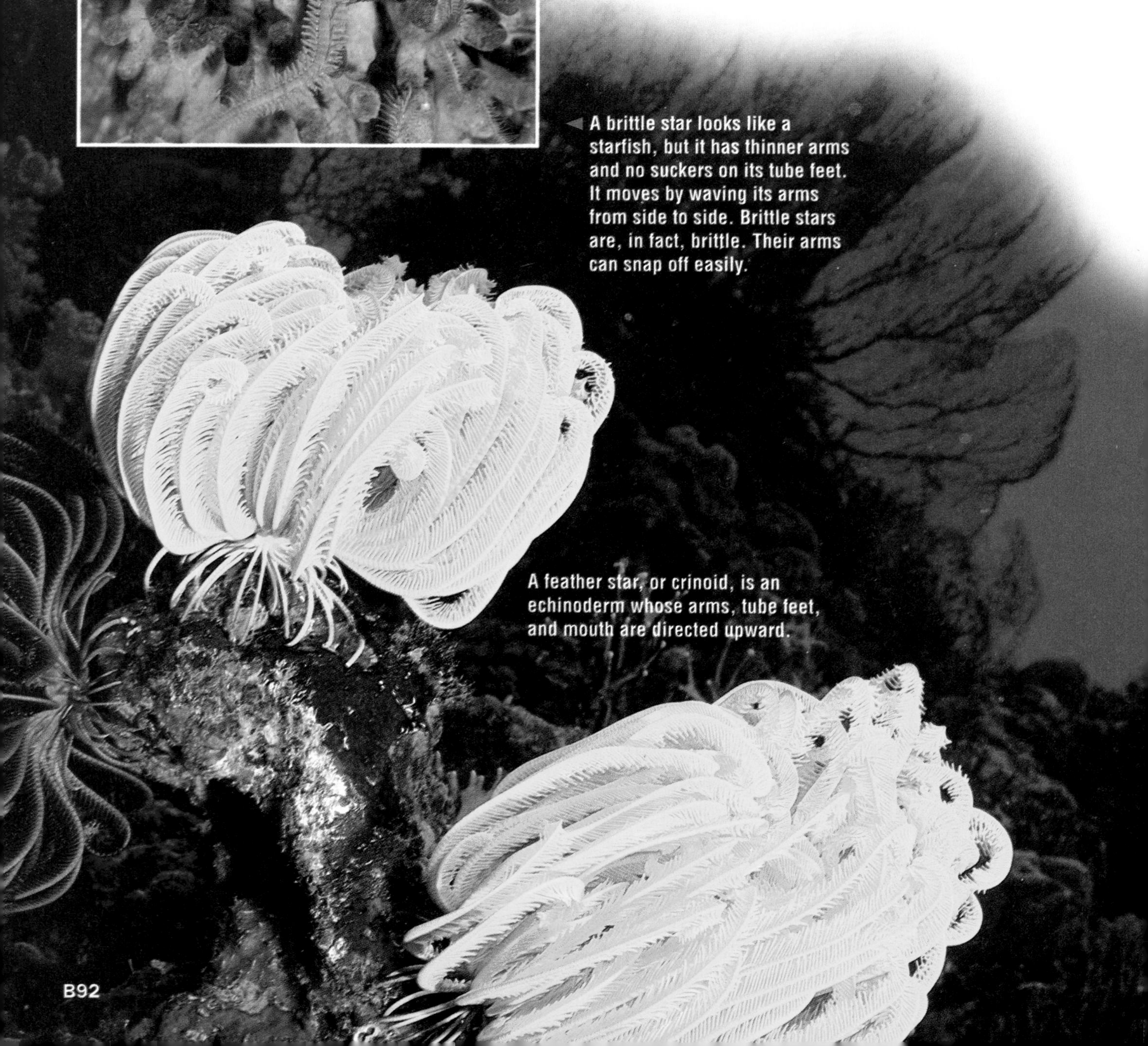

A feather star, or crinoid, is an echinoderm whose arms, tube feet, and mouth are directed upward.

cells into the water. Fertilized eggs hatch into larvae. These drift in the ocean currents for weeks. They then attach themselves to a surface as they mature into adults.

Some echinoderms can also reproduce asexually by regenerating, or forming new parts. Some starfish can regenerate if their bodies are divided in half. Each half grows into a new starfish. A few species of starfish can grow an entire animal from a single arm.

✔ **In what ways are echinoderms different from other invertebrates?**

Summary

Mollusks are soft-bodied invertebrates. They include clams, octopods, oysters, slugs, snails, and squid. Many kinds of mollusks have external protective shells. Arthropods are invertebrates with jointed exoskeletons and legs. They include insects, crustaceans, and arachnids. Spiny-skinned invertebrates, the echinoderms, have tube feet in rows on body parts that surround the animal's center. Echinoderms include starfish, brittle stars, sand dollars, sea urchins, and sea cucumbers.

Review

1. How does an octopus propel itself through the water?

2. What problem does an exoskeleton cause an arthropod?

3. How do the water canals in an echinoderm's body affect the animal's tube feet?

4. **Critical Thinking** What advantages might a winged arthropod have over an arthropod without wings?

5. **Test Prep** An example of an arthropod is —

   A a bivalve

   B an octopus

   C a spider

   D a starfish

LINKS

MATH LINK

Ratios The largest invertebrate is the giant Atlantic squid, which can be up to 20 m long. What is the ratio, in its simplest form, of the height of a 1.5 m-tall student to the squid's length?

WRITING LINK

Narrative Writing—Story Write a short story for a friend in which a knight in armor faces an arthropod that is the same size as the knight.

ART LINK

Sepia Sepia is a brown pigment that originally came from the ink sac of a cuttlefish. Drawings and photographs in this color are sometimes called sepiatones. Find some pictures of sepiatones in reference books, and try drawing one yourself. You can use thinned brown watercolor or a pen with brown ink.

TECHNOLOGY LINK

To learn more about how invertebrates are helping people watch *Predatory Snails* on the **Harcourt Science Newsroom Video.**

CONTROLLING PESTS WITH
PHEROMONES

Scientists are learning to use scents produced by insects to control insect populations.

What are pheromones and how do they work?

Animals use color and sound to attract mates. Some also use smell. Pheromones (FAIR•uh•mohnz) are chemical signals or scents given off by some insects to attract mates so they can reproduce. But scientists have learned to use the insects' own signals to stop them from destroying food crops.

Why are insects a problem for farmers?

Not all insects are pests. Some, such as bees, help farmers by pollinating plants. Many types of insects, however, are destructive. They burrow into fruits or stems to lay eggs, or they eat crops growing in the field. Farmers can lose billions of dollars worth of crops each year because of destruction by insect pests.

How can pheromones be used against pests?

Apple growers in Washington State and peach growers in California use pheromones to control codling moths and oriental fruit moths. These moths produce worms that attack growing fruit.

Because moths are active at night and mate in the dark, they use pheromones to find each other. The female sends out a pheromone scent, which the male follows to her location.

Farmers confuse the insects by putting the pheromone scent on something that looks like a twist tie. They wrap the ties around parts of

◄ Farmers use devices like these to send pheromones through their orchards.

their apple or peach trees. Male insects then pick up the pheromone scent all over the orchard but cannot figure out where to find actual females. The insects can't mate, so females don't produce eggs that become young worms.

Why is using pheromones a good idea?

Using pheromones is a good way to reduce pests because it does not harm the environment. It doesn't work for every pest, but when it does, it helps reduce the use of pesticides that can poison soil and water or harm other organisms.

THINK ABOUT IT

1. How can pheromones help control pests?
2. Why is the use of pheromones good for the environment?

WEB LINK:
For Science and Technology updates, visit The Learning Site.
www.harcourtschool.com

Careers | Pest Control Technician

What They Do Pest control technicians use chemicals and traps to get rid of insects, rodents, and other pests that cause problems for homes and businesses.

Education and Training Pest control technicians should have a background in chemistry, mathematics, and health. They must be good at closely following directions, because mistakes could cause harm to people. Pest control technicians should have a high school education. They must also be licensed.

Ernest Everett Just
ZOOLOGIST/EMBRYOLOGIST

The discoveries in cell biology made by Dr. Ernest Everett Just in the 1920s and 1930s changed the way scientists think about cells and cell parts. He was one of the first biologists to realize the importance of the cytoplasm of a cell. Before his discoveries, many biologists thought that the cell nucleus controlled all cell activities. They thought that the cytoplasm did little and that the outer surface of the cytoplasm did almost nothing. However, after careful observation of the egg cells of certain invertebrates that live in the ocean, Dr. Just discovered that a cell depends on smooth cooperation between the nucleus and the cytoplasm of the cell. He also found that the outer part of the cytoplasm of a cell determines the relationship the cell has with its environment.

Ernest Everett Just was determined to succeed. As a child he worked after school in farm fields near his home in South Carolina to help earn money for his family. His dream was to attend Kimball Academy, an excellent school in New Hampshire. When he was 17, he went to New York City, earned the money he needed, and enrolled at Kimball. He finished its four-year program in just three years. Then he went on to earn a Ph.D. in embryology (em•bree•AHL•uh•jee)—the study of embryos and their development.

For much of his career, Dr. Just taught biology at Howard University in Washington, D.C. During summer breaks, he worked at the Marine Biological Laboratory at Woods Hole, Massachusetts. It was there that he made most of his important discoveries while working with the cells of certain sea animals.

THINK ABOUT IT

1. Identify Dr. Just's main scientific contribution.
2. What research did Dr. Just do that led to his main contribution?

◄ Dr. Just studied cells in the eggs of invertebrates that lived in the sea. These are squid eggs and a young squid.

Seeking Shelter

What kind of environment do sowbugs prefer?

Materials

- wide shoebox with a lid
- sheet of construction paper
- scissors
- dry soil
- tape
- 8–10 sowbugs
- water
- flashlight

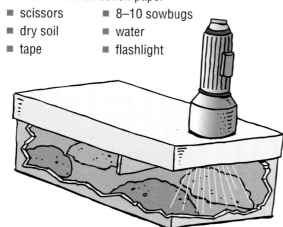

Procedure

1. Tape a paper divider to the top of the box, as shown. Cut it so the sowbugs can crawl under it.

2. Arrange four areas of soil, each covering one-fourth of the bottom of the box. Dampen one area on each side of the divider.

3. Cut a round hole in the center of one end of the lid. Balance the lighted flashlight over the hole.

4. Place the sowbugs on the lighted side of the box. Leave the box and return after 30 minutes.

Draw Conclusions

Which of the four environmental conditions do the sowbugs prefer? Where do you think you would find sowbugs in nature?

Earthworm Movement

How do earthworms move?

Materials

- earthworm
- sandpaper
- square of vinyl tile
- hand lens

Procedure

1. Place the vinyl tile and the sandpaper next to each other.

2. Set the earthworm on the sandpaper. Use the hand lens to watch it move. Sketch what you see.

3. Set the earthworm on the vinyl tile. Use the hand lens to watch it move. If the earthworm is moving differently this time, sketch what you see.

Draw Conclusions

Which body parts do earthworms use to move? Do earthworms move more quickly over a smooth surface or a rough surface? Why do you think that is?

Chapter 3 Review and Test Preparation

Vocabulary Review

Use the terms below to complete the sentences. The page numbers in ( ) tell you where to look in the chapter if you need help.

vertebrate (B70)

invertebrate (B70)

endoskeleton (B70)

exoskeleton (B71)

sponges (B76)

cnidarians (B78)

flatworm (B80)

roundworms (B81)

parasites (B81)

segmented worms (B82)

mollusk (B86)

arthropods (B88)

arachnids (B89)

insects (B89)

echinoderm (B91)

1. Many kinds of ____, the simplest worms that have digestive tracts with two openings, are ____, which harm their hosts.

2. All ____ live in water and have cells that can inject poison into other animals as a form of defense and attack.

3. ____ are filter feeders that live in water and have no tissues or organs.

4. A ____ has a backbone, while an ____ has no backbone.

5. An ____ has spines that project through its skin.

6. The system of connected bones within an animal's body is an ____.

7. Unlike roundworms, ____ have muscles that run in bands around their bodies.

8. Spiders and scorpions are ____.

9. An animal whose hard outer covering, or ____, is jointed is called an ____.

10. A planarian is a ____, and a clam is a ____.

11. The most numerous animals in the world are the ____.

Connect Concepts

Complete the chart by filling in terms from the Word Bank.

insects

body walls

exoskeleton

earthworm

tube feet

cnidarians

parasites

echinoderms

poison

circulatory system

Invertebrate Adaptations

Animals	Adaptations of These Animals
Invertebrates that live only in water and have medusa and polyp forms are known as 12. _____.	These animals have cells that are specialized adaptations for defense and attack and that contain 13. _____.
The only invertebrates that can fly are 14. _____.	Their bodies are supported by a hard 15. _____.
Animals with spiny skins but no exoskeleton are known as 16. _____.	Most of these animals have an unusual adaptation for movement, called 17. _____.
Flatworms and roundworms that feed on and harm other animals are 18. _____.	Some of these animals absorb food through their 19. _____.
An animal with two separate bands of muscles that lives in the soil is an 20. _____.	The characteristic that distinguishes this animal from other worms is its 21. _____.

Check Understanding

Write the letter of the best choice.

22. All animals need food, oxygen, water, and —
    A prey
    B lungs
    C exoskeletons
    D protection

23. Some species of cnidarians exist as both —
    F jellyfish and corals
    G larvae and bivalves
    H polyps and medusas
    J *Hydra* and comb jellies

24. An octopus can hide itself from predators with a cloud of —
    A poison
    B larvae
    C ink
    D parasites

25. An insect has —
    F six legs
    G eight legs
    H ten legs
    J no legs

26. Sand dollars and sea urchins are —
    A arthropods
    B echinoderms
    C mollusks
    D arachnids

Critical Thinking

27. In what way are sponges similar to baleen whales?

28. A praying mantis is an insect that looks like a twig. How does this adaptation help the animal survive?

29. The book lungs of arachnids look like open books with separated pages. Why is this "open-book" structure better than a "closed-book" structure would be?

30. Which is usually the larger animal—a parasite or its host? Explain the reasoning behind your answer.

Process Skills Review

31. If you **observe** that an animal has a jointed exoskeleton, what can you **infer** about the **classification** of the animal?

32. How would you **compare** three unidentified animals—an arthropod, a cnidarian, and a flatworm—to determine which one belongs to each group?

Performance Assessment

Crustacean Behavior

Work with a partner to design an experiment about the behavior of sow bugs. The equipment for your experiment can be everyday household objects such as paper towels, construction paper, a cookie sheet, and tape. Describe how you would find out whether sow bugs are more likely to be found in a dry environment or in a moist environment. Describe how you would find out whether they are more likely to live in light places or in dark places.

Vertebrates

Why do vertebrates make up only about 4 percent of the animal kingdom? Part of the answer is that they are much more complicated creatures that have far fewer offspring than invertebrates. A mosquito may lay 3000 eggs in her short lifetime. An alligator rarely lays more than 60 eggs, once every few years.

Vocabulary Preview

fish
amphibian
cold-blooded
reptile
bird
warm-blooded
mammal
mammary gland

FAST FACT

The fastest human swimmers can move at about 5 mi/hr (8 km/hr)—faster than some fish—but not many people ever reach that speed.

Swift Swimmers	
Fish	Speed (miles per hour)
Sailfish	60
Yellowfin tuna	46
Bluefin tuna	43
Flying fish	40
Dolphin	37
Trout	15

When alligators hatch, many can't escape from their nest until their mother hears them croaking and digs them out.

Electric eels produce a series of very short shocks that last only a few thousandths of a second. Most eels generate around 350 volts—three times the voltage of an electric outlet in your home.

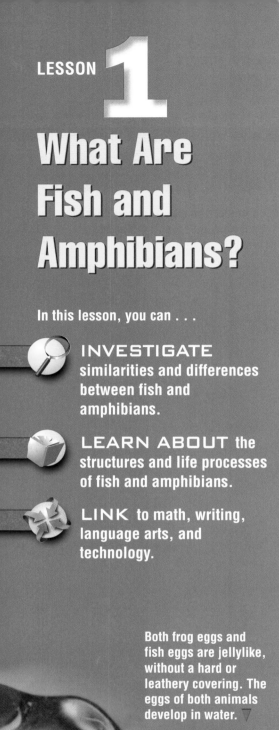

What Are Fish and Amphibians?

In this lesson, you can . . .

INVESTIGATE similarities and differences between fish and amphibians.

LEARN ABOUT the structures and life processes of fish and amphibians.

LINK to math, writing, language arts, and technology.

Both frog eggs and fish eggs are jellylike, without a hard or leathery covering. The eggs of both animals develop in water. ▽

INVESTIGATE

Comparing Fish and Amphibians

Activity Purpose Invertebrates are quite different from each other. But invertebrates have many similarities. Fish and amphibians are also different but similar. In this investigation you'll **observe** and **compare** animals from these two groups of vertebrates to find out their similarities and differences.

Materials
■ diagrams of frog and fish

Activity Procedure

1 **Observe** the diagrams of the fish and the frog. **Compare** the animals' characteristics and behavior. Notice any traits that are unique to either animal. (Picture A)

2 Draw a picture of each animal. Include a size scale on each drawing. Write a brief description of each of the structures in your drawings.

3 Copy the Venn diagram, and **record** how fish and amphibians are alike and how they are different. Add to the diagram any data that you already know about each kind of animal. **Infer** which characteristics are common to all fish and which are common to all amphibians.

Yellow perch

Picture A

Leopard frog

Characteristics of Fish

Shared Characteristics

Characteristics of Amphibians

Draw Conclusions

1. From the information in your Venn diagram, in what ways are fish and amphibians alike?

2. In what ways are they different?

3. **Scientists at Work** *Comparative anatomy* is the study of the structures of different kinds of animals. It involves **observing** and **comparing** structures that may look different but have similar functions. What are two such structures of fish and amphibians?

Investigate Further Study the Venn diagrams made by your classmates. Look for any data that you might add to your own diagram. Working with a partner, use your diagram to write definitions for *fish* and *amphibians*.

Fish and Amphibians

Comparing Fish and Amphibians

FIND OUT

- the differences between fish and amphibians
- the structure of fish and how they meet their needs
- the structure of amphibians and how they meet their needs

VOCABULARY

fish
amphibian
cold-blooded

Of the seven classes of vertebrates, three classes are **fish**, or vertebrates adapted to living their entire lives in water. One class is **amphibians**, or vertebrates that can live in water or on land but must return to the water to reproduce.

As you noticed in the investigation, fish and amphibians differ in important ways, but they share many characteristics. Both fish and amphibians lay their eggs in water. Most fish breathe through gills and spend their entire lives in water. Amphibian young also breathe through gills. But as amphibians mature, most develop lungs. As adults they spend much of their time on land.

Both fish and amphibians are **cold-blooded**. This means that their body temperature changes as the temperature of their surroundings changes. Many cold-blooded animals benefit from living in water because it changes temperature slowly. Some amphibians can control their temperature by lying in the sun or on warm rocks to get warm and returning to the water to cool off.

Fish and amphibians have similar circulatory systems and digestive systems. They also have an internal skeleton, nerves, and muscles that are similar in structure and function to those of all other vertebrates.

✔ **How do the respiratory systems of fish and amphibians differ?**

Comparison of Fish and Amphibians

Characteristics of Fish

Some shared characteristics of amphibians and fish are shown in the overlapping part of this Venn diagram.

Shared Characteristics

Characteristics of Fish
- Gills throughout life
- Scales
- Fins
- Two-chambered heart

Shared Characteristics
- Lay eggs in water
- Jellylike eggs with no hard covering
- Functional gills sometime during life
- Cold-blooded

Characteristics of Amphibians
- Lungs in most adults
- Skin
- Four limbs
- Three-chambered heart

Characteristics of Amphibians

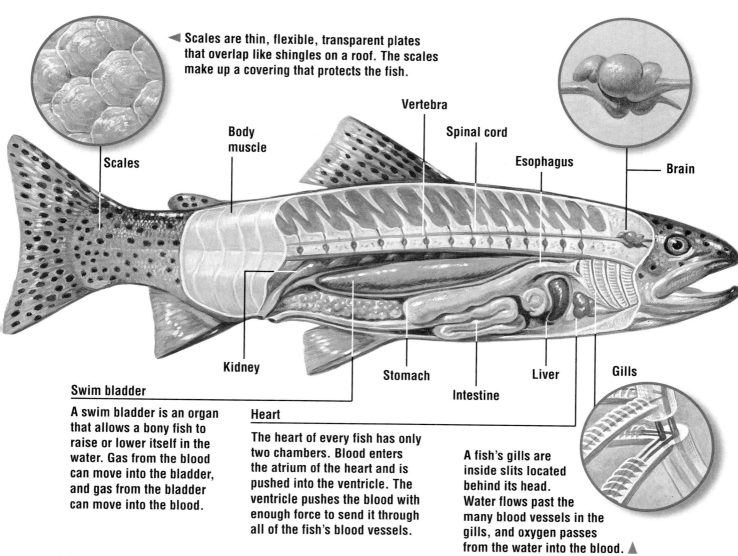

◄ Scales are thin, flexible, transparent plates that overlap like shingles on a roof. The scales make up a covering that protects the fish.

Scales

Body muscle

Vertebra

Spinal cord

Esophagus

Brain

Kidney

Swim bladder

Stomach

Intestine

Liver

Gills

Swim bladder

A swim bladder is an organ that allows a bony fish to raise or lower itself in the water. Gas from the blood can move into the bladder, and gas from the bladder can move into the blood.

Heart

The heart of every fish has only two chambers. Blood enters the atrium of the heart and is pushed into the ventricle. The ventricle pushes the blood with enough force to send it through all of the fish's blood vessels.

A fish's gills are inside slits located behind its head. Water flows past the many blood vessels in the gills, and oxygen passes from the water into the blood. ▲

Fish

A dolphin may look more like a fish than a sea horse does. But a dolphin isn't a fish, and a sea horse is. Dolphins do not have the characteristics of fish, and sea horses do.

The three classes of fish are bony fish, fish with skeletons made of cartilage (KART•uhl•ij)—called cartilaginous fish—and jawless fish. In place of the limbs of many other vertebrates, fish have fins for balance and movement. In a fish, blood is pumped through a network of arteries and veins by a two-chambered heart. The blood gets oxygen when it passes through the gills. Gills absorb oxygen from the water.

Most fish, except for the jawless fish, have hard scales covering their bodies. The scales of bony fish can be smooth, like those on carp and salmon, or rough, like those on bass and perch.

The number of scales doesn't change during a fish's life. The scales that the fish was born with simply grow larger. Sharks and rays, which are cartilaginous fish, have scales that look like small teeth. These scales make the skin as rough as sandpaper.

The internal organs of all fish are similar. A fish has a brain that receives information about the outside world by way of sense organs. It has a digestive system to process food. The digestive systems of bony fish and cartilaginous fish include an esophagus, a stomach, and an intestine. A jawless fish has a simpler digestive system that is little more than a straight tube.

✓ **What can you tell about a sea horse's heart?**

◄ Fish mouths and teeth differ greatly, depending on the kind of food they eat. The barracuda is a predatory fish that has a large mouth and long, sharp teeth.

Bony Fish

Most fish—more than 20,000 different species—are bony fish. Bony fish live in oceans, lakes, and streams from the equator to the polar seas. Because of their greatly different habitats, bony fish have many different forms and behaviors.

Fish that live in the open ocean have stream-lined bodies. They have slim, knifelike side fins and narrow, forked tails. These allow them to swim fast to catch prey or to avoid predators. There is no place to hide in the open ocean, and many of these fish are well camouflaged. The upper parts of their bodies are a metallic blue-green, and their undersides are silvery. This coloring makes them difficult to see from above or below.

Fish that live in coral reefs are often brightly colored. Rather than making them stand out, this helps to hide them among the bright colors of the coral. Spots, stripes, and patches of color break up a fish's outline and confuse predators. Many reef fish have specially shaped fins and tails that help them maneuver around rocks and reefs.

All fish begin life as fertilized eggs. Eggs of most bony fish are fertilized in the water. Females lay thousands or even millions of eggs in the water. Males of the same species shed sperm over the eggs. Most of the eggs end up as food for other water animals, though some fish, such as sea horses, protect their eggs until they hatch.

Bony fish are an important source of food for people all around the world. Every year millions of tons of fish are taken from the ocean. The fishing industry has developed ways of catching large numbers of fish, and the populations of many ocean species have decreased. To stop the decrease, scientists and people who catch fish for a living have been developing ways to raise and farm fish, much as cattle are raised. This can help supply enough fish to eat and may prevent the loss of ocean fish.

✓ **What adaptations help fish survive in their habitats?**

The cleaner wrasse swims right into the jaws of much bigger fish. There it scrapes out parasites and particles of food. As the cleaner wrasse gets fed, the larger fish gets dental care. ▼

The lionfish is one of the most venomous fish in the ocean. Glands in its spiny rays produce a powerful venom that can harm a predator and may even kill a human being. The brightly colored stripes of the lionfish are a warning to predators. ▼

▲ Rays vary in size from this blue spotted ray to manta rays. Manta rays can be up to 6 m (20 ft) across.

▲ Whale sharks are the largest of all sharks, reaching lengths of 8 m (about 26 ft) and weights of more than 17,000 kg (about 37,000 lb). Unlike predatory sharks, whale sharks get their food by sifting plankton from the water.

Fish Without Bones

Cartilaginous fish and jawless fish have no bones. Their skeletons are made of cartilage. Cartilage is a flexible tissue that forms the skeletons of most vertebrate embryos. It is also found as a kind of cushioning material in the adults of many vertebrates. For example, humans have cartilage in their joints, ears, and nose.

The cartilaginous fish include sharks, rays, and skates. Unlike bony fish, these fish have no swim bladders. Many of them cannot stop swimming because the weight of their bodies would pull them down to the bottom. Sharks, rays, and skates have hinged jaws that can open and close. Unlike the eggs of most other fish, the eggs of cartilaginous fish are fertilized within the female body. Many cartilaginous fish bear live young. Skates, however, deposit their fertilized eggs in leathery cases in the water.

More than 350 different kinds of sharks are known. Most have several rows of sharp teeth along their jaws. Although most sharks are fierce predators, they rarely attack humans.

Rays and skates have flattened bodies that allow them to glide along the ocean bottom near the coasts, where most of them live. They eat small fish and mollusks such as clams and oysters. The largest of the rays, the manta ray, lives in the upper waters of the open ocean. Many species of rays have poisonous stingers in their tails. They use the stingers for defense. These rays can be found in fresh water as well as salt water.

The hagfish and the lampreys are the only jawless fish still living. Many lampreys are parasites that attach themselves to their host with their suckerlike mouths. They scrape the host's flesh with their sharp teeth and then suck its blood. Jawless fish have the simplest structure of all fish. They have no jaws, scales, or fins, and their digestive systems are basically straight tubes.

✓ **In what way are jawless fish similar to sharks, rays, and skates?**

Most sharks have powerful jaws packed with many sharp teeth. Some sharks can bite hard enough to cut through a thick piece of steel. The great white shark is one of the ocean's fiercest predators, but usually it is not a danger to humans. ▼

▲ The leopard frog is like most other amphibians without a tail. It has long hind legs and webbed feet adapted for swimming and hopping.

▲ There are about 4400 known species of amphibians. This Chinese salamander is an amphibian with a tail. It started life in the water as a tadpole and then developed into a land animal, which you see here.

▲ The caecilian is an amphibian that has no legs. Most caecilians live underground in the tropics and are almost blind.

Amphibians

Most amphibians spend part of their lives in fresh water and part on land. They are vertebrates that have no covering of scales or hair on their skin. The skin is usually soft, thin, and moist and can absorb water. If they have limbs, amphibians generally have webbed feet with no claws.

Frogs, toads, newts, salamanders, and caecilians (see•SIL•ee•uhnz) are all amphibians. Newts and salamanders have tails throughout their lives. Frogs and toads lose their tails when they reach maturity. Caecilians have no limbs.

The main difference between frogs and toads is in the texture of their skin. Toads have rough, dry skin and frogs have smooth, moist skin. Toads are able to live farther from water than frogs and may visit ponds or lakes only to lay their eggs.

Most frogs, toads, and salamanders hatch in water as tadpoles. Tadpoles swim freely, breathing through gills. They begin to develop lungs at the same time as they grow legs and lose their tails. They also change from having two-chambered hearts to having three-chambered hearts. Tadpoles eat plants, but most adult

An adult amphibian has many of the same organs as other vertebrates that live on land. It has a digestive system and lungs. It also has a three-chambered heart that pumps blood separately to its lungs and to the rest of its body. The amphibian's body is held up by a bony skeleton that has many of the same bones as other vertebrates, but no ribs.

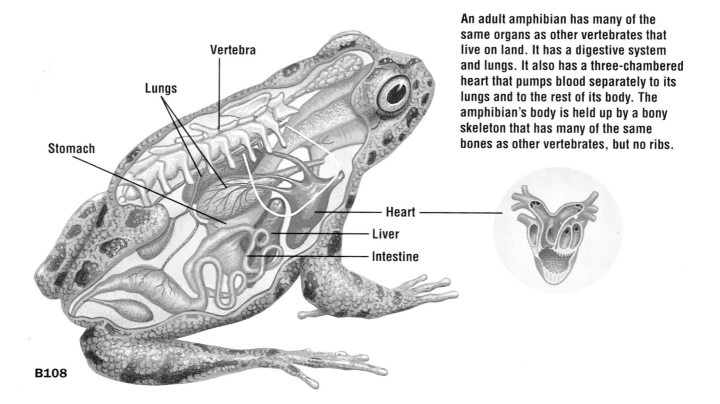

Vertebra

Lungs

Stomach

Heart

Liver

Intestine

amphibians eat other animals, such as insects and worms.

Adult amphibians can breathe in three ways. First, their lungs exchange gases, though not as well as the lungs of many other vertebrates. Second, most amphibians can absorb oxygen through their skin. They get all their oxygen this way while they hibernate in mud during the winter. Third, a network of tiny blood vessels at the roof of an amphibian's mouth absorbs oxygen very well.

✔ **In what three ways can an adult frog breathe?**

Life Cycle of a Salamander

The diagram here shows the stages in the life cycle of a Japanese giant salamander, the largest of the salamanders. It can reach a length of 1.5 m (about 5 ft) and can live up to 50 years. Like other amphibians, the Japanese giant salamander begins life in the water and goes through a series of changes before becoming an adult.

✔ **How are the life cycles of a salamander and a frog similar?**

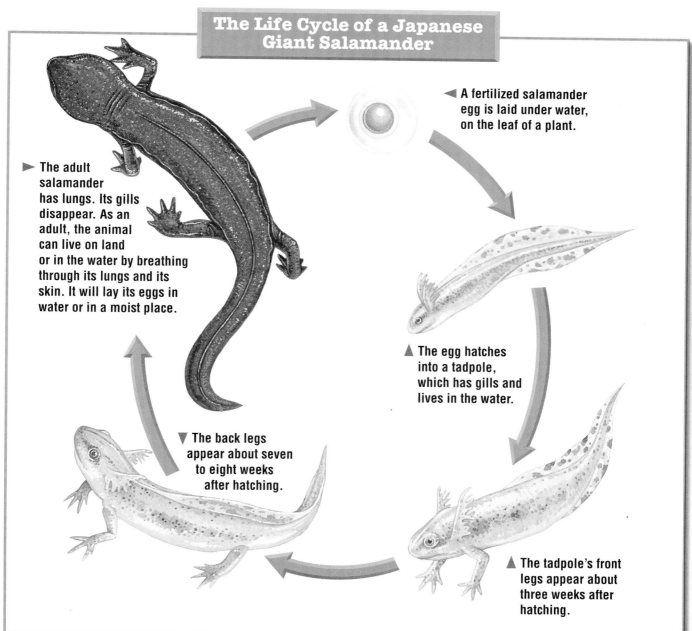

The Life Cycle of a Japanese Giant Salamander

► A fertilized salamander egg is laid under water, on the leaf of a plant.

► The adult salamander has lungs. Its gills disappear. As an adult, the animal can live on land or in the water by breathing through its lungs and its skin. It will lay its eggs in water or in a moist place.

▲ The egg hatches into a tadpole, which has gills and lives in the water.

▼ The back legs appear about seven to eight weeks after hatching.

▲ The tadpole's front legs appear about three weeks after hatching.

Amphibian Adaptations

Amphibians make up the smallest class of vertebrates. But they can be found on every continent except Antarctica, and they live in many different environments. Some frogs and toads, for example, despite their need for moisture, live far from riverbanks and ponds. They live on mountains, high up in rain-forest trees, and even in deserts.

Many amphibians are colored to blend in with their surroundings. Bullfrogs, for example, are green and live in ponds, which are also green. Other adaptations include long, sticky tongues that help frogs and toads catch insects. Their feet are also adapted to their environments. Frogs that swim have webbed feet. Climbing frogs have a suction pad on each toe that allows them to grip branches.

Amphibians are affected by the temperature. In winter, if their surroundings become too cold, frogs and toads dig into the mud and become inactive. They stay still and do nothing except absorb oxygen through their skin. In summer, frogs and toads burrow into the mud if the weather becomes too hot for them.

✔ **What are several amphibian environments?**

◄ This poison arrow frog from the rain forests of South America spends its life in water that collects in the cup of a flower blossom.

The giant toad is a native of the southwestern United States. It can reach a length of 23 cm (about 9 in.). Many toads are protected by a poison that spreads throughout their skin. It is produced in two organs located on the toad's head behind its eyes. These toads often swell up to discourage predators such as snakes. ▼

Summary

Fish and amphibians are cold-blooded vertebrates. Fish live in water and breathe with gills throughout their lives. Most amphibians begin life in water as tadpoles with gills but then develop lungs and legs and live mostly on land.

There are three kinds of fish—bony fish, cartilaginous fish, and jawless fish. Toads, frogs, newts, salamanders, and caecilians are all amphibians.

Review

1. What class of fish has the greatest number of species?
2. How are rays adapted to their environment?
3. In what form do most amphibians begin their lives after hatching from eggs?
4. **Critical Thinking** How do the hind legs of a frog help it survive?
5. **Test Prep** Fish and amphibians both have —
   A gills throughout their lives
   B a three-chambered heart
   C fins throughout their lives
   D a backbone

These long-tailed salamanders spend most of their lives in cool, dark, damp places. Since they have little protection against predators, they hide under logs or rocks. ▼

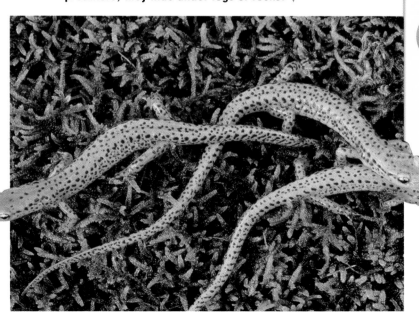

LINKS

MATH LINK

Fish Health A large number of fish species were recently classified by how close to extinction they are. Of these species, 1323 are not threatened with extinction, and 101 are becoming threatened. Another 443 species are vulnerable to extinction, and 291 are in immediate danger of extinction. What percent of all these fish are not threatened?

WRITING LINK

Informative Writing—Explanation Despite an old belief, a toad cannot give a person warts. Write an informative paragraph to some friends in which you explain this fact. Use reference books to find more information about this subject.

LANGUAGE ARTS LINK

Word Meanings Look up the word *salamander* in a dictionary or encyclopedia. You'll discover that one of the word's meanings is "a spirit that lives in fire." Find out what people once believed about salamanders.

TECHNOLOGY LINK

Learn more about types of vertebrates by investigating *Vertebrate Challenge* on **Harcourt Science Explorations CD-ROM.**

What Are Reptiles, Birds, and Mammals?

In this lesson, you can . . .

INVESTIGATE the skeletons of reptiles, birds, and mammals.

LEARN ABOUT how reptiles, birds, and mammals carry out life functions.

LINK to math, writing, art, and technology.

INVESTIGATE

Comparing Skeletons

Activity Purpose Vertebrates can be divided into two groups by comparing the kinds of eggs they have. In one group are the fish and amphibians. In the other group are the reptiles, birds, and mammals. There are clear differences among these last three kinds of animals. But what makes them similar to each other? In this investigation you'll **observe** and **compare** the skeletons of a typical reptile, bird, and mammal.

Materials
- diagrams of reptile, bird, and mammal skeletons
- colored pencils

Activity Procedure

1 **Observe** the diagrams. The skeletons can be divided into two parts. One part consists of the head, neck, and trunk, and the other consists of the limbs. Find these two parts on each diagram. (Picture A)

2 **Compare** the skeletons to find similarities. For example, the different skeletons have the same number of bones in corresponding parts of the limbs. Use the colored pencils to mark the similarities on each diagram.

3 **Observe** and **compare** the pictures of the bone cross sections of birds and mammals. Find similarities and differences among the bones.

◄ The golden lion tamarin is an endangered relative of monkeys and apes. All these types of animals are mammals.

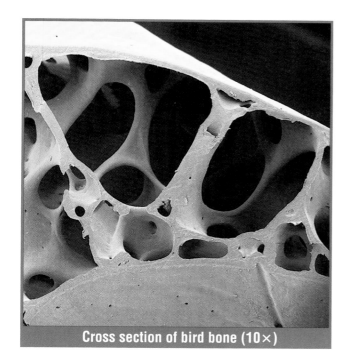
Cross section of bird bone (10×)

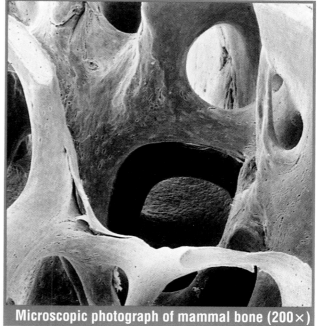
Microscopic photograph of mammal bone (200×)

Draw Conclusions

1. What similarities did you **observe** in the head, neck, and trunk part of the three skeletons?

2. What similarities did you **observe** in the limb part of the skeletons?

3. **Compare** the limbs of the skeletons. **Predict** how many limbs you would find on other animals in these groups.

4. **Scientists at Work** Scientists use microscopes to study the structure of materials. From your **observations** of the bone cross sections, what can you **hypothesize** about the way a bird's bones help it fly?

Investigate Further **Observe** and **compare** the bones at the end of the limbs of the three animals. Discuss with your classmates how the adaptations in each animal are useful to it.

Picture A

Process Skill Tip

When you **hypothesize** about an object or event, you use **observations** to help develop an explanation for it.

B113

Reptiles, Birds, and Mammals

Reproducing and Developing on Land

FIND OUT

- why reptiles, birds, and mammals can live on land, away from water
- the characteristics of reptiles, birds, and mammals
- three different kinds of mammals

VOCABULARY

reptile
bird
warm-blooded
mammal
mammary gland

Fish and amphibians depend on water to reproduce and develop. Their eggs have membranes, but the membranes are thin and the eggs must be laid in water. Reptiles, birds, and mammals, however, can stay on land throughout their lives. They do not have to lay their eggs in water. Each developing embryo is protected by a membrane that encloses it. Within this membrane is the water the embryo needs in order to develop. In addition, the egg has food and nutrients just as fish and amphibian eggs do. The stage in which reptiles, birds, and mammals have gill slits takes place within the membrane.

In birds and most reptiles, the membrane is inside an egg that has a shell. In mammals, the embryo usually develops enclosed within a membrane inside the uterus of the mother. For most reptiles, birds, and mammals, when development inside the membrane is complete, the young hatch or are born having basically the same form as their parents.

✔ **How does the membrane that encloses an embryo allow animal species to survive on land?**

An egg contains its own water supply, allowing the embryo to develop on land. ▼

The embryo is surrounded by fluid within a membrane.

This sac contains water and additional nutrients.

Oxygen and carbon dioxide can pass through the shell of the egg.

The yolk is the embryo's main food supply.

▲ Most reptiles, like this turtle, hatch from eggs.

The Komodo dragon is the largest living lizard, reaching a length of 3 m (about 10 ft). It is found on Komodo and other small islands of Indonesia, where it hunts other animals during the day. ▶

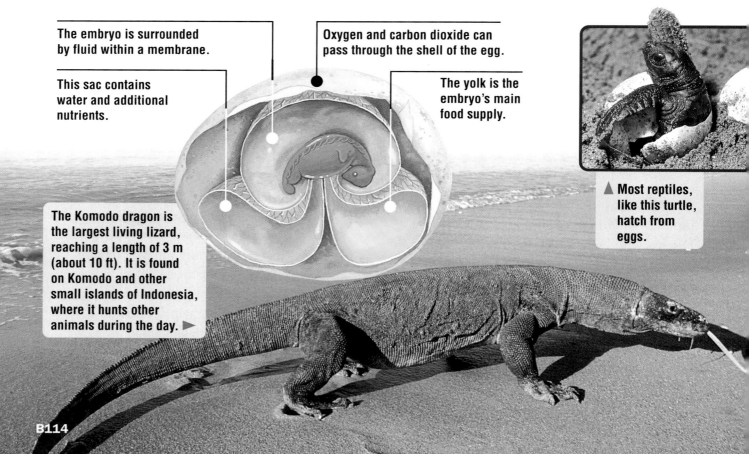

◀ Many snakes are brown, black, or dull-colored. Bright coloring often serves as a warning to other animals that the snake is venomous, although that is not the case with this tree snake.

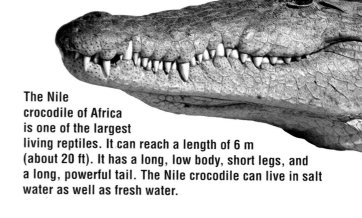

The Nile crocodile of Africa is one of the largest living reptiles. It can reach a length of 6 m (about 20 ft). It has a long, low body, short legs, and a long, powerful tail. The Nile crocodile can live in salt water as well as fresh water.

Reptiles

Reptiles have a dry protective covering of horny scales or plates. They usually have four legs with clawed toes. However, snakes and some lizards don't have any legs. And turtles that live in water have flippers instead of clawed toes. Reptiles have well-developed lungs. Most reptiles are cold-blooded.

There are about 6000 species of reptiles. They belong to four different orders: tuataras (too•uh•TAH•ruhz), turtles, crocodiles and alligators, and lizards and snakes. The tuatara is the only remaining species of its order. Its closest relatives became extinct more than 100 million years ago. Tuataras reach a length of about 60 cm (2 ft) and look like large lizards. They live on islands off the coast of New Zealand.

The largest reptiles are the crocodiles and alligators. Crocodiles have triangular heads with pointed snouts. Alligators have more rounded snouts. Crocodiles and alligators spend much of their lives in water. They use their powerful, flattened tails for swimming. They are covered with horny plates that are strengthened with bone. The eyes and nostrils are raised and stick out above the water while the rest of the animal is under the water. Crocodiles and alligators can stay hidden in the water as they approach prey.

Turtles have a domed upper shell and a flatter lower shell. Some turtles can completely withdraw their tail, legs, and head into the shell. Turtles have a hard, toothless beak and strong jaws. Tortoises, or turtles that live on land, are often plant eaters. Even turtles that live in water, such as the giant sea turtle and the snapping turtle, lay their eggs on land.

Lizards and snakes are members of the same order. Both have scales, and both can unhinge their jaws. This is easier to see in snakes, which can swallow fairly large animals whole. As lizards and snakes grow larger, they shed their skins. Some snakes shed several times a year.

Most lizards eat other animals—usually insects and worms—but some are plant eaters. All snakes are meat eaters. Very few snakes are venomous. Gila (HEE•luh) monsters and bearded lizards are the only venomous lizards. The Gila monster lives in the southwestern United States.

Reptile eggs are always fertilized within the female. Most reptiles lay eggs, which usually have a leathery shell. Hard-shelled eggs are laid by tortoises, crocodiles, and gecko lizards. In some lizards and snakes, the young develop within the female and are born alive.

✓ **How do reptile eggs differ from amphibian eggs?**

A turtle is a reptile that is easy to recognize because of its shell. The top part of the shell contains the backbone and ribs, fused into the horny plates. ▼

Birds

Birds are the only animals that have feathers. Unlike the vertebrates that you've read about so far, birds are **warm-blooded**. Their bodies stay at the same temperature regardless of the temperature of their surroundings. Warm-blooded animals get heat from the energy released in their cells as they burn food. Being warm-blooded allows birds to be active all the time. This is because they can keep warm in cold weather and do not need to stop activity to cool down in warm weather.

A bird's feathers not only allow it to fly but also keep it warm. Down feathers, which are soft and finely divided, are found next to the bird's skin. They trap a layer of air that holds in body heat. The larger contour feathers are used for flying.

Almost all birds can fly. Flight allows them to escape from predators that cannot fly. It helps birds catch insects in the air and search for food over a large area. Flight also allows birds to migrate as the seasons change.

However, flight and maintaining body temperature use up a lot of energy. Many birds eat as much as 30 percent of their body weight in food each day to get the energy they need. They also need a great deal of oxygen to release the energy from the food. Birds have very efficient lungs that are connected to air sacs. These sacs, as well as the lungs, fill with air when a bird breathes, giving the bird more oxygen. The sacs also help keep the bird cool as it flies. Oxygen is carried through a very efficient circulatory system that is powered by a four-chambered heart.

Owls have large, broad heads with feathers around the eyes. They usually live alone and hunt at night. Their soft feathers muffle the swishing sound that most birds make when they fly. So owls can swoop down on their prey without being heard. ▼

▲ Birds' eggs are similar in structure to those of reptiles. But the shells of birds' eggs are brittle rather than leathery.

◀ Not all birds fly. Penguins have wings adapted for swimming. Rheas and ostriches are too heavy to fly, but they can run very fast. The cassowary lives in the forests of Australia and New Guinea. It stands 1.5 m (about 5 ft) tall and can run at speeds of 64 km/hr (about 40 mi/hr).

Many newly hatched birds are helpless. Their eyes are closed, and the few feathers that they have are small down feathers. The parents must keep their young warm, protect them from predators, and bring them food. But young birds grow very fast, and many are ready to leave the nest within a few weeks.

Birds are valuable to humans in several ways. Chickens and other poultry birds provide people with meat and eggs. Birds also help farmers by eating weed seeds and insect pests. Some of the larger birds, such as hawks and owls, kill rats and mice that eat grain crops.

Last but not least, people like birds. Listening to their songs and observing their colors and activities are experiences that many people enjoy.

✔ **What is the difference between birds' eggs and reptiles' eggs?**

A bird's skeleton has adaptations that allow the bird to fly. The wing muscles are attached to the keel, a large extension of the breastbone. Most birds also have a lightweight beak, no teeth, and bones that are light and porous. ▼

Keel

Flying also takes enormous muscle power. The muscles that enable a bird to fly are not in its wings, but in its chest. These muscles are attached to the largest bone in a bird's body, the breastbone. They account for more than one-third of the bird's weight.

To be able to fly, a bird cannot weigh very much. A bird has adaptations that keep it very light for its size. Its bones are not solid but have tiny air spaces in them. The structure of the bones with all these air spaces makes them very strong. The feathers, too, are light and strong. During flight the feathers compress so that the bird's body takes on a more streamlined shape.

A bird also has feet and a beak that are suited for its behavior. A duck, for example, has webbed feet for swimming and a broad, flat bill that it uses to strain water or mud for food. Birds that hunt have long, sharp claws and a hooked beak for tearing.

The arrangement of the toes is different for different birds. Climbing birds such as woodpeckers have two toes in front and two at the back. Perching birds have a single toe at the back. Running birds have all their toes at the front of their feet.

All birds hatch from eggs that have brittle, hard shells. The embryo inside each egg must be kept warm in order to grow and develop. Parent birds sit on their eggs to keep the embryos warm and to protect the eggs from predators.

Mammals

Mammals are warm-blooded vertebrates that have milk-producing glands called **mammary glands**. Because of this adaptation, female mammals can nurse their young without leaving them to find food. Nursing also creates a bond between a mother and her helpless off-spring. It ensures that the mother will take care of them. The pictures on these pages show some of the ways in which mammals bear their young. Generally the young are born alive in a form like that of their parents.

Most mammals have hair and teeth. In fact, mammals are the only animals that have hair. It keeps them warm and helps them save the body heat they produce as warm-blooded animals. Hair can have different forms, such as the quills of a porcupine and the fur of a bear. Some mammals, such as whales and porpoises, have little hair. Armadillos also have little hair and no teeth. They are the only mammals covered with an "armor" of bony plates.

Most types of mammals live on land. Only one type—bats—can fly. They have leathery

THE INSIDE STORY

Mammals are classified into three groups—monotremes (MAHN•uh•treemz), marsupials (mar•SOOP•ee•uhlz), and placentals (pluh•SEN•tuhlz). These groups of mammals differ in how their young develop before and shortly after birth.

Monotremes

There are only three species of monotremes—two species of spiny anteaters and the duckbilled platypus. They lay eggs in burrows in the ground, and the mother keeps the eggs warm until they hatch. After hatching, the young depend on milk from the mother's mammary glands.

A young echidna hatches from its leathery-shelled egg. It will feed on the milk from its mother's mammary glands. ▶

▲ The spiny echidna is a kind of anteater from Australia. It lays eggs but it is a mammal.

Marsupials

Marsupials, or pouched mammals, bear live young, but the newborn is very immature. A newborn marsupial crawls into a pouch on its mother's abdomen, where it nurses on milk from the mammary glands. It stays in the pouch until it has grown and developed more fully. Marsupial mammals are found mainly in Australia. They include kangaroos, koalas, and Tasmanian wolves. The only marsupial that is native to North America is the opossum.

A newborn kangaroo is tiny, blind, and helpless. It crawls to its mother's pouch, where it will stay while it develops. ▶

▲ The kangaroo is a stout marsupial that carries its young in a pouch. Kangaroos are plant eaters that live mostly in Australia.

wings without feathers. Whales and their relatives live in the ocean. Like all mammals, they have mammary glands and feed milk to their young. Rather than hair, whales have thick layers of fat under their skin to protect them from the cold.

The body systems of mammals are highly developed. Their brains and nervous systems are the most developed of all vertebrates. Their circulatory systems are powered by a four-chambered heart. It pumps blood to the lungs to pick up oxygen. Then the oxygen-rich blood returns to the heart and is pumped to the other parts of the body. Mammals are the only animals with a sheet of muscle called a *diaphragm* (DY•uh•fram) within the chest cavity. This muscle is important in allowing them to breathe very efficiently.

Human beings have used other mammals for thousands of years. Animals such as cattle, pigs, and sheep are used as food. Horses and dogs are sometimes used for work. Mammals also provide wool and leather for clothing. And mammals such as cats and dogs are commonly kept as pets.

✔ **What characteristics of mammals make them different from other animals?**

A pig's offspring grow and develop within the mother pig. They are born with the same form as their parents.

Placentals

Placental mammals develop within the female more completely than marsupials do. They are attached by an umbilical cord to a structure called the placenta. Through this organ, nutrients, oxygen, and wastes are exchanged between the developing embryo and the mother.

Placental mammals take a long time to develop before birth. Even after birth they depend on their parents until their nervous systems are fully developed and they have learned to take care of themselves. Some placental mammals, such as horses, can stand and walk minutes after birth. But others, such as cats, are not nearly so mature.

Pigs are placental mammals that have stout, heavy bodies covered with coarse hair. The adult females give birth to large groups of young, which they feed with milk from their bodies.

Placenta

Embryo

Umbilical cord

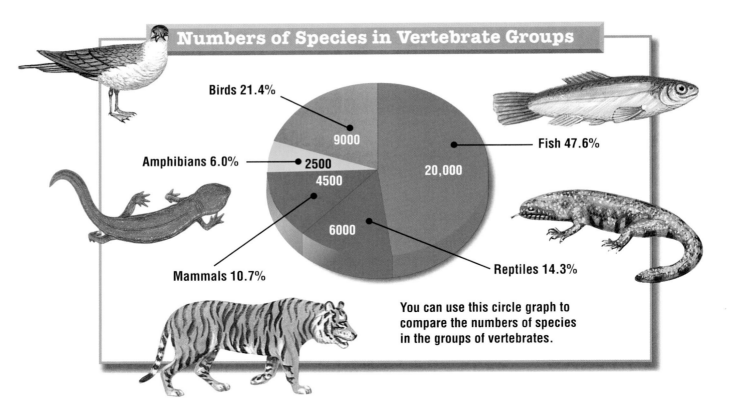

Numbers of Species in Vertebrate Groups

Birds 21.4% — 9000

Amphibians 6.0% — 2500

Mammals 10.7% — 4500

Reptiles 14.3% — 6000

Fish 47.6% — 20,000

You can use this circle graph to compare the numbers of species in the groups of vertebrates.

Review of Vertebrates

Animals as different as fish, frogs, snakes, birds, and cats are all vertebrates. This group of animals is much smaller than the invertebrates, both in number of species and number of individuals.

A vertebrate has a bony or cartilaginous skeleton that includes a jointed backbone. A vertebrate's brain is enclosed in a bony skull. Most vertebrates are large compared to invertebrates and have sharp senses and a large brain. They all have similar body systems that include many of the same organs.

The vertebrates include the classes of fish, amphibians, reptiles, birds, and mammals. The characteristics of each of these groups are summarized in the chart below. The percent of species of each type of vertebrate is shown in the circle graph above.

✔ **Which group of vertebrates shown on the circle graph contains the most species?**

Comparing Vertebrates

	Fish	Amphibians	Reptiles	Birds	Mammals
Chambers of heart	2	3	3 or 4	4	4
Covering on skin	scales	none	scales or plates	feathers	hair
Number of limbs	varies	4 (most common)	4 or none	4	4
Temperature regulation	cold-blooded	cold-blooded	mostly cold-blooded	warm-blooded	warm-blooded
Environment for reproduction	needs water	needs water	doesn't need water	doesn't need water	doesn't need water
Embryo development	mostly in jellylike eggs with no hard covering	mostly in jellylike eggs with no hard covering	mostly in leathery eggs	in hard-shelled eggs	mostly in mother's body

Summary

Reptiles, birds, and mammals are vertebrates. Within the membrane that surrounds their embryos is water needed for development. Because of this, reptiles, birds, and mammals are able to spend their entire lives on land. Most reptile embryos and all bird embryos develop inside eggs. Most mammal embryos develop inside the mother's body. Reptiles are cold-blooded and are covered with scales or plates. Birds are warm-blooded and have feathers. Mammals are warm-blooded and have hair and mammary glands.

Review

1. How can snakes swallow large animals?
2. Which is the largest bone of a bird's body? Why is it so large?
3. What are the three kinds of mammals?
4. **Critical Thinking** In cold climates some mammals and reptiles hibernate during the winter. What can birds do instead of hibernating?
5. **Test Prep** How are birds similar to reptiles?

   A Both lay eggs.

   B Both have membranes that protect the developing embryo.

   C Both are warm-blooded.

   D Both **A** and **B**

LINKS

MATH LINK

Feeding the Shrews The smallest living mammals are shrews, which weigh only about 4 g. They eat as much as two times their own weight in food every day. About how many grams of food can one shrew eat in a growing season that is 4 months long?

WRITING LINK

Persuasive Writing—Opinion Most snakes are harmless to people, and they eat many rodent and insect pests. Write a brief newspaper editorial about how people benefit from wild animals. Use snakes as an example.

ART LINK

Unicorns and Camelopards The Greek historian Herodotus described the strange and wonderful animals that he saw on a trip to Africa. Find out about his observations of the animals he called unicorns and camelopards. Draw pictures of these animals. What are their current names?

TECHNOLOGY LINK

Find out more about one type of vertebrate by watching *Sea Turtles* on the **Harcourt Science Newsroom Video.**

TRACKING ANIMALS BY SATELLITE

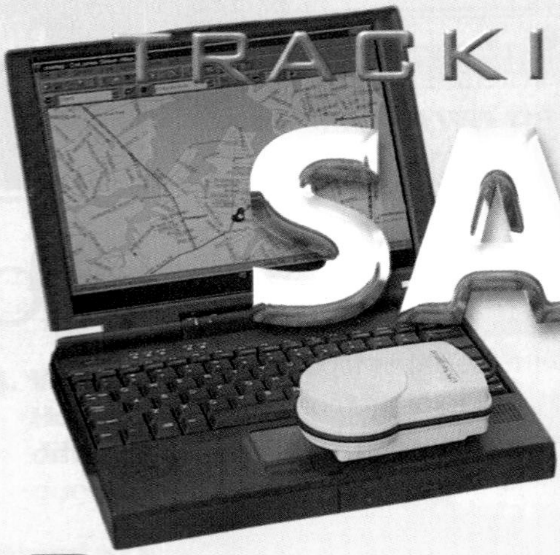

A GPS system

Biologists can use satellite technology to track animals in the wild and help those in danger.

Why do biologists track the locations of manatees?

Years ago, manatees were hunted heavily. As a result, the manatee is now an endangered species. Often biologists capture manatees that are sick or have been injured, get them healthy again, and then release them back into the wild. To follow manatees' movements and to make sure they can survive on their own after living in captivity, biologists place radio tags on some manatees. The radio tags allow biologists to track the manatees by using a satellite system called the Global Positioning System, or GPS.

How does GPS work?

GPS uses 24 car-sized satellites orbiting 19,000 km (about 12,000 mi) above the equator. Each satellite stays above a certain spot on Earth's surface by traveling at the same

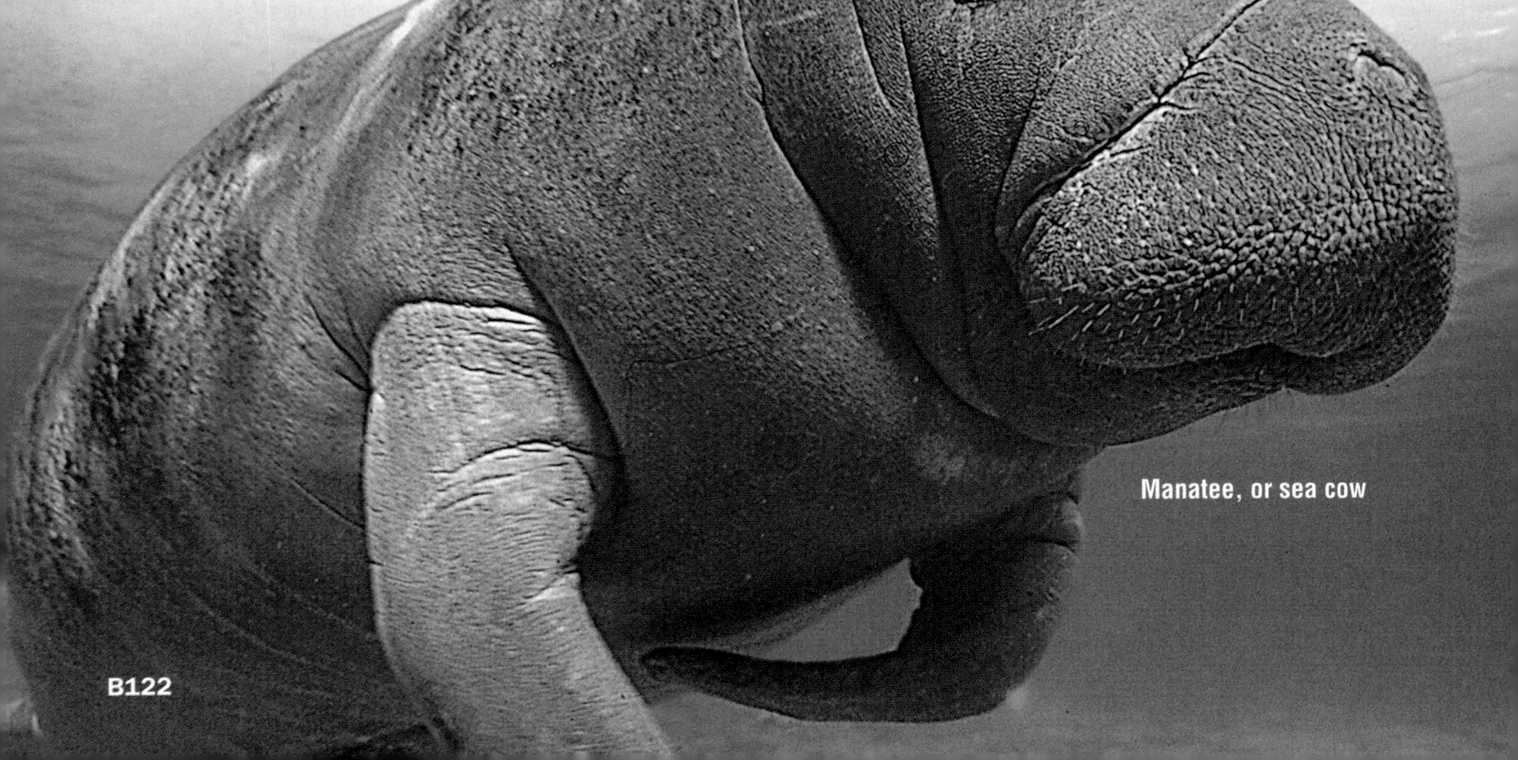

Manatee, or sea cow

speed as Earth's rotation. Each one also sends out a radio signal that identifies it. The location of a GPS receiver on Earth's surface is determined by the length of time it takes radio signals to reach it from four of the satellites. Because each satellite sends out a unique signal and stays above one location, mathematical calculations done by a computer in the receiver can pinpoint the latitude and longitude of any GPS receiver.

How does GPS help biologists track manatees?

In addition to the GPS receiver, the manatee's tag also contains a radio transmitter that continuously sends information about the animal's location to biologists who are tracking it. The position of the animal can be shown on a video map display. If a manatee seems to be in trouble, scientists can go to it and try to help.

How has GPS saved a manatee's life?

Recently GPS was used to save a manatee named Mo. After being raised in captivity, Mo was released off the coast of Florida. Unfortunately, he wandered far offshore and was carried south about 454 km (280 mi) by ocean currents. Biologists checked on Mo's location and found that he was far from areas where he could get food and fresh water. Biologists quickly captured Mo and returned him to Miami for treatment that saved his life.

What are other uses of GPS?

GPS has many other uses. Some of them might even be familiar to you. It is used to help ships, boats, and commercial aircraft to navigate. Some new cars have GPS-run systems that pinpoint a car's location on a computer map and show the driver the best route to a nearby location. One GPS developer thinks that in the future, families could use GPS devices the size of a wristwatch to keep track of their children and pets.

THINK ABOUT IT

1. How is GPS used to identify the location of things on Earth's surface?
2. How has GPS helped biologists save the life of a manatee?

WEB LINK:
For Science and Technology updates, visit The Learning Site.
www.harcourtschool.com

Careers   Marine Biologist

What They Do Marine biologists study ocean species and their environments. They gather specimens from various marine habitats to follow the overall health of ocean organisms and ocean habitats.

Education and Training Marine biologists must have a background in biology, oceanography, chemistry, and environmental studies. They should also have an interest in plants and animals and should enjoy being outdoors and on the ocean. Marine biologists must have at least a bachelor's degree in biology, but many also have a master's degree or doctorate so they can do advanced research.

Archie Carr

CONSERVATION BIOLOGIST/NATURALIST

"Everybody ought to see a sea turtle nesting."

Archie Carr was a writer, teacher, and naturalist who was the world's leading expert on sea turtles. For a long time, Dr. Carr taught students and conducted research at the University of Florida. That was where he started his campaign to preserve nesting grounds for sea turtles. Because of his work, several sea turtle species were saved from extinction.

Dr. Carr grew up with a love of nature. The back yard of his home in Georgia was filled with caged snakes, lizards, and, of course, turtles. It was no surprise when he decided to become a biologist, and in 1937 Carr earned his Ph.D. in zoology, the study of animals. He went on to teach biology, continuing his special interest in sea turtles. When he wasn't teaching, he traveled in Central America and around the world doing research on sea turtles and their place in various ecosystems. His discovery that sea turtles in some places were in danger of extinction led him to his work as a conservationist.

Dr. Carr decided to devote himself to saving endangered sea turtle species. For 20 years he directed the international movement for the conservation of sea turtles. In this role he fought the killing of endangered sea turtles for turtle products. He also campaigned to continue protection of once-endangered species, even when their numbers began to increase. In the 1960s he started and directed the U.S. Navy's Operation Green Turtle. The project distributed green-turtle eggs and young turtles to nesting beaches around the Caribbean and Gulf of Mexico. Biologists wanted to reestablish or increase sea turtle populations at these places.

Scientists who study sea turtles today have concluded that some endangered sea turtle populations are now on the road to recovery. Dr. Carr played a large part in that success.

THINK ABOUT IT

1. Why was it important for Dr. Carr to fight for the protection of sea turtles?
2. What else do conservation biologists such as Dr. Carr do?

Hatching sea turtle

Softening Bones

How can you make bone seem like cartilage?

Materials

- 1 or more uncooked chicken wing bones
- jar with lid, big enough to hold the bones
- white vinegar

Procedure

1. Clean all muscles (meat) and tendons off the bones. **CAUTION** Wash your hands thoroughly after touching raw chicken. It may contain bacteria that could make you sick.

2. Let the bones dry for a day or two.

3. Put the bones in the jar and add enough vinegar to cover them.

4. Close the lid and let the jar sit overnight.

5. Rinse the bones with water and try to bend them.

Draw Conclusions

What does the softened bone look and feel like? The acid in vinegar dissolves some of the minerals in bones. What does this tell you about the difference between bone and cartilage?

Vertebrate Observation Log

How many vertebrates can you spot?

Materials

- calendar
- poster board
- colored pencils

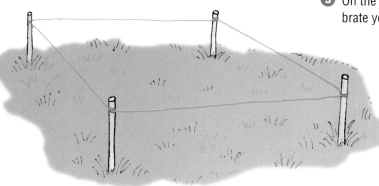

Procedure

1. Choose a time of day and a location that you can watch closely every day for a week.

2. Observe your location each day at the same time for one-half hour. Record all the vertebrates you observe during that time.

3. On the poster board draw a picture of each vertebrate you observe. Classify the vertebrates.

Draw Conclusions

How many different groups of vertebrates did you observe? If you wanted to observe fish and amphibians, what location might you choose?

Chapter (4) Review and Test Preparation

Vocabulary Review

Use the terms below to complete the sentences. The page numbers in ( ) tell you where to look in the chapter if you need help.

cold-blooded (B104)   **warm-blooded** (B116)

fish (B105)   **mammals** (B118)

amphibians (B108)   **mammary**

reptiles (B115)   **glands** (B118)

birds (B116)

1. ___ are cold-blooded vertebrates that lay eggs with leathery coverings.

2. Warm-blooded vertebrates that produce milk are ___.

3. Vertebrates that live their entire lives in the water are ___.

4. The main identifying characteristic of mammals is the presence of ___.

5. ___ are the only animals that have feathers.

6. Animals that take on the temperature of their surroundings are ___. Those that maintain their body temperature despite the temperature of the surroundings are ___.

7. Animals that spend part of their lives in the water and part on land are ___.

Connect Concepts

Complete the chart using terms and phrases from the Word Bank.

in water	eggs with leathery shells	feathers	fish
hair	gills	birds	tadpoles
on land	bear live young	reptiles	

Vertebrates					
Cold-blooded			**Warm-blooded**		
8. _____	Amphibians,	9. _____	10. _____	Mammals	
have 11. _____ all their lives.	such as frogs, have gills as 12. _____	have scales. They lay 13. _____.	have 14. _____. They lay eggs with brittle shells.	have 15. _____. They 16. _____.	
They reproduce 17. _____.		They reproduce 18. _____.			

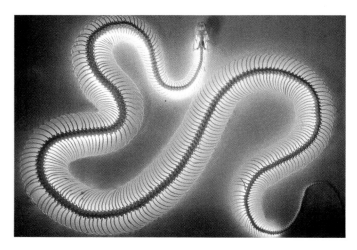

Check Understanding

Write the letter of the best choice.

19. Cartilaginous fish that have jaws include —
  A sharks
  B lampreys
  C whales
  D barracudas

20. An adult frog can breathe with its lungs and through its —
  F gills
  G skin
  H skin and the roof of its mouth
  J skin and gills

21. A cold-blooded vertebrate that lays eggs with leathery shells is —
  A an amphibian
  B a reptile
  C a fish
  D a bird

22. One example of a warm-blooded vertebrate is —
  F an amphibian
  G a bird
  H a reptile
  J a fish

23. A mammal with a pouch is called a —
  A monotreme
  B marsupial
  C whale
  D placental

24. In order to fly, birds need a lot of —
  F weight
  G bone mass
  H oxygen
  J humidity

25. A monotreme is a mammal that —
  A lays eggs
  B has a placenta
  C lives in the water
  D bears live young

Critical Thinking

26. Most birds lay many fewer eggs at one time than reptiles do. Why might this be so?

27. Some animals have feathers or hair as insulation. Why don't reptiles or amphibians have any insulation?

28. How can you use the structure of the skeleton of a vertebrate to infer its habitat?

Process Skills Review

29. What **observations** would you make to **compare** the early development of marsupials and monotremes?

30. If you **observed** an animal that had gills and four limbs, what could you **hypothesize** about the animal?

Performance Assessment

Comparing Animals

Your teacher has photographs of five different animals. Make a chart listing the characteristics of each animal. Circle in red those characteristics that all five animals have in common. Circle in blue a characteristic that is unique to each animal. Describe how each characteristic circled in blue helps the animal that has it.

Unit Project Wrap Up

Here are some ideas for ways to wrap up your unit project.

Develop a Guide

Write a guide that explains the features of your botanical garden. Tell why you located the plants where you did.

Display at a Science Fair

Display your project in a school science fair. Prepare a written report describing the procedure you used and your results.

Classify

Research the classifications for the plants in your botanical garden. Make notes about the classifications on index cards. Display the index cards with your project.

Investigate Further

How can you make your project better? What other questions do you have about living things? Plan ways to find answers to your questions. Use the Science Handbook on pages R2–R9 for help.

The Living Planet

UNIT C

E A R T H   S C I E N C E

The Living Planet

Unit Project

Weather Reports

Develop instruments that will help you measure the weather. Use charts and tables to record changes in the weather. Prepare a weather report each day, and predict weather for the following day. Support your prediction with data you've collected. Then compare your prediction with the actual weather.

Ecosystems— Characteristics and Cycles

Ecosystems are everywhere. Any place where life can occur, it will—on polar ice or in a burning desert, on the ocean floor or the top of a mountain. Some forms of life will be able to adapt to even extreme conditions and to each other.

Vocabulary Preview

environment
biotic
abiotic
habitat
population
community
ecosystem
niche
water cycle
transpiration
evaporation
condensation
precipitation
groundwater
carbon dioxide-oxygen cycle
nitrogen cycle
reusable resources
renewable resources
nonrenewable resources

FAST FACT

Of the 9000 species of birds, about 30 percent live in the Amazon River basin. The number of species decreases from the equator to the poles.

Numbers of Bird Species	
Northern Hemisphere Region	**Number of Bird Species**
Colombia	1525
Guatemala	469
New York State	195
Newfoundland	118
Labrador	81
Greenland	56

Scarlet ibis

1

What Are the Characteristics of an Ecosystem?

In this lesson, you can . . .

INVESTIGATE how climates affect ecosystems.

LEARN ABOUT the ways living and nonliving things interact in an ecosystem.

LINK to math, writing, art, and technology.

Comparing Climates

Activity Purpose If you drive across the country, you'll see a lot of scenery through the car window. The kinds of trees and flowers are different in different places. So are the animals. One factor that is important to organisms living in a place is the climate. In this investigation you will graph the temperatures and rainfall of different regions to compare climates.

Materials

- local weather information
- graph paper
- graphs on pages C4 and C5
- colored pencils

Activity Procedure

1 Find the average rainfall for each month in the area where you live. Record your findings. (Picture A)

2 Find the average temperature for each month in the area where you live. Record your findings.

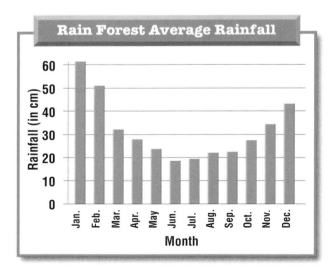

◀ Even tiny animals such as these ladybugs affect their environment. Ladybugs eat smaller insects. How might that affect other organisms in the environment?

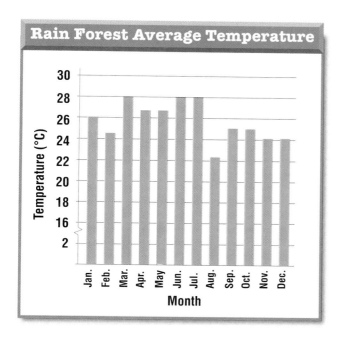

Rain Forest Average Temperature

Picture A

3 On a sheet of graph paper, copy the bar graph showing the rainfall in a tropical rain forest. Use a different color to add bars showing the average rainfall for each month in your area. You will be making a double-bar graph. (Picture B)

4 Repeat the process to make a double-bar graph showing average temperatures for each month in the two regions.

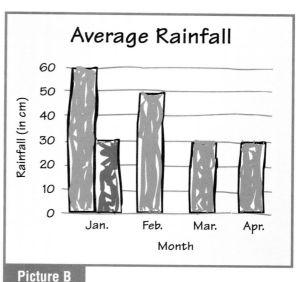

Picture B

Draw Conclusions

1. What can you tell about the rainfall in the tropical rain forest? How does rainfall in your area differ?

2. How is the temperature in your area different from the temperature in the tropical rain forest?

3. Would you expect to find more kinds of plants in your area or in the rain forest? Why? In which area would you expect to find more animals? Why? Would you expect to find in your area any of the plants and animals that live in a tropical rain forest? Explain.

4. **Scientists at Work** Scientists often **use numbers** and graphs to display and **compare** information. How did the graphs you drew help you **compare** the climates of two regions?

Investigate Further Research the climate of a third area—a polar area or a desert, for example. How does climate affect the kinds and numbers of organisms in an environment?

Process Skill Tip

One way to **interpret data** is to **use numbers** and make graphs to find trends or patterns.

The Characteristics of an Ecosystem

Life on Earth

FIND OUT

• how living and nonliving things interact in an ecosystem

• how different factors affect an ecosystem

VOCABULARY

environment
biotic
abiotic
habitat
population
community
ecosystem
niche

Living things inhabit the deepest oceans and the highest mountaintops. However, not every species can live in every place. Palm trees normally don't grow in polar regions. Most fish can't live out of water. Different species have different needs. An organism's **environment** (ehn•VY•ruhn•muhnt)—the surroundings in which it lives—provides it with the specific things it needs.

Every environment is made up of both **biotic** (by•AHT•ihk), or living, and **abiotic** (AY•by•aht•ihk), or nonliving, parts. The biotic parts of an environment include all of its organisms, from the tiniest protist to the tallest tree. Not only do these organisms live in the environment, they help make the environment what it is. Burrowing animals change the shape of the ground. Plant roots anchor the soil and sometimes even split rocks. The organisms interact with each other and with the abiotic parts of the environment.

The abiotic parts of an environment include the physical surroundings—the land, water, and air. They also include the minerals in the soil, the amount of rainfall and sunlight, the temperature, and the humidity. As you discovered in the investigation in this lesson, abiotic factors such as rainfall and temperature vary a great deal. Like every other part of an environment, they help determine what species can live there.

✓ **What is an environment?**

All living things need water. These animals come to a water hole at least once a day. ▶

The land and the oceans provide many different environments for living things.

◀ A region that is near the equator receives more energy from sunlight than one that is distant from it. Plants use the energy to make food.

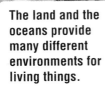

◀ Living things need energy for all of their activities. Mountain gorillas get energy from plants growing in their environment.

Organisms in an Ecosystem

Most environments have many different species living in them. An environment may include land, water, and air, and organisms may live in each of these. The part of an environment in which an organism lives is called its **habitat** (HAB•ih•tat). Within its habitat an organism finds the things it needs, such as food and shelter. Two species with similar needs may have the same habitat. Various species of fish, for example, can share the same lake habitat. If their needs are different, however, species won't share a habitat—a fern and an owl have different habitats in the same forest environment. The size of a habitat depends on the organism. A lion's habitat covers a large area of savanna grassland. Some insects might move only a few meters during their entire lifetime.

Organisms of the same species living together in the same environment make up a **population** (pahp•yoo•LAY•shuhn). The oak trees in a forest make up one population. The leopard frogs in a pond make up a different population. Each population includes only one species. If one lake had seven different species of fish living in it, it would have seven populations of fish.

Populations living in the same environment at the same time make up a **community**. The organisms in a community interact with each other. A plant may provide shelter for one organism and food for another. When an organism dies, decomposers return the nutrients from the organism to the soil, making them available to other organisms. A community and the abiotic parts of its environment make up an **ecosystem** (EK•oh•sis•tuhm). An ecosystem can be as small as a leaf or as large as a forest. Whatever its size, all of its biotic and abiotic parts interact with each other. Every ecosystem also interacts with other ecosystems.

✔ **Is every part of an ecosystem living? Explain your answer.**

▲ The monarch butterfly cannot survive in a cold environment. In summer it lives in Canada and the northern United States. It migrates up to 3000 km (about 1865 mi) to spend the winter months in California and Mexico.

▲ The monarch butterflies living together in this place make up a population.

▲ The monarch population and other populations, such as the fir trees the butterflies live in, make up a community.

The community of populations interacts with its abiotic surroundings to form an ecosystem. ▶

How Abiotic Factors Affect Ecosystems

Many land ecosystems such as grasslands, pine forests, and cornfields are named for the most common plants that grow there. Abiotic factors determine the kinds of plants and animals that can live in an ecosystem.

Plants, like other organisms, need certain things to support life. Water, air, and light are some of the things that different organisms need in different amounts. The climate of a region is one of the most important factors in determining a region's ecosystems. In the cold, dry climate of the arctic tundra, the ground is frozen most of the year and the growing season is short. Trees do not grow there. Mosses, grasses, and small shrubs make up the plant life. These plants can grow quickly. They have root systems that are close to the surface, where the ground sometimes thaws.

The large trees that make up rain forests need heavy rainfall. The trees grow tall, competing with one another to get sunlight. The only plants that can grow on the forest floor are those that don't need much light, such as ferns. Decomposition of the flowers, fruits, stems, and leaves that fall to the ground supplies the nutrients for all the forest's plant life.

Scientists have inferred that more species live in tropical rain forests than in all other environments combined. Tropical rain forests are unusual. Even though they have a vast number of species, each species has a small population. However, the more rainfall an ecosystem receives, the larger each of its populations will be. As plant populations increase in size, so do animal populations, because the many plants provide plenty of food. Warm, wet environments usually support the most life.

Every organism interacts with the biotic and abiotic parts of the ecosystem. An organism

THE INSIDE STORY

Habitats and Niches

How big is an ecosystem? It depends on how large an area you want to study. An ecosystem may be as small as a drop of water or as large as a forest. A forest ecosystem contains many smaller ecosystems. A rotting log that has fallen onto the forest floor can provide habitats for many populations that interact as a community.

Not all plants need soil. This moss grows on the decaying wood of the tree trunk. Mosses need moisture and shade.

These mushrooms are part of a fungus that grows in hairlike strands through the log. The fungus absorbs decaying wood as food.

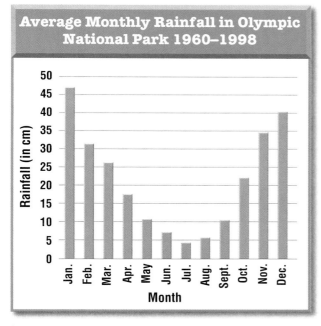

Average Monthly Rainfall in Olympic National Park 1960–1998

▲ Rain is one important abiotic factor in the environment. About how much rain does Olympic National Park receive a year?

lives in a certain place, acts in a certain way, requires certain food, needs a certain amount of heat and light, and may be food for other organisms. The role of an organism in an ecosystem is called its **niche** (NIHCH). It includes everything the organism needs and everything it does.

Even though several populations can live in the same habitat in an ecosystem, they usually do not have the same niche. When two populations in a habitat have the same needs, they have to compete for the same limited resources. As a result, one population may be pushed from the habitat. Populations that exist together usually find different niches, although the niches may overlap. For example, zebras, wildebeests, and gazelles share the same habitat on the African savanna. They all eat the savanna grass. However, zebras eat the top of the grass plant, wildebeests eat the middle, and gazelles eat the part of the grass closest to the ground.

✔ **What happens when two populations of organisms have the same niche in the same ecosystem?**

A wood roach burrows into the log, where it eats the wood and lays its eggs.

This millipede is a plant eater and a scavenger. It feeds on small plants or on decaying plant and animal materials.

Carpenter ants don't eat wood, but they bore their way into the log to make nests, where they lay their eggs.

How Biotic Factors Affect Ecosystems

An ecosystem is shaped by more than its abiotic factors. As you have read, the populations in a community interact, and their interactions help make their niches. The presence of one population in an ecosystem depends on what other populations are there. For example, the goshawk, a hunting bird, is found only in forests where fir trees grow. This is because the fir trees provide food for the larvae of a particular moth. The larvae are eaten by songbirds of the forest. The goshawk hunts these songbirds for food.

You can see how organisms interact by following the progress of an ecosystem after a natural disaster. Fire, flood, or volcanic eruption can kill or drive away most of the organisms in an area, but it doesn't take very long for life to begin to reappear. The first organisms to come back are small, weedy plants that grow fast and release seeds in one season. After a year or so, taller plants begin to appear. They also grow fast and tend to crowd out the smaller plants. As plants drop leaves or die, organisms decompose the plant matter. The soil now contains nutrients for other plants. Some seeds are carried to the area by the wind. Others arrive with animals that are beginning to return to the area. As new, taller plants grow, they attract other animals that use them for food or shelter. Soon, more kinds of plants and animals find niches in the growing ecosystem. After many years, the area's ecosystem may be very similar to the one that was destroyed.

✔ **What kind of plants are the first to grow after a natural disaster?**

In 1988, a fire that raged for months destroyed about half of the forest in Yellowstone National Park. The efforts of 25,000 firefighters were not enough to stop the fire, which died down only when the winter snows came. ▼

Among the first new plants to grow amid the ashes of the forest were fireweeds. These plants get their name from the fact that they are often the first plants to spring up in an area after a fire. ▼

The first trees to reappear were lodgepole pines. These unusual plants need the intense heat of a fire to release their seeds. ▼

Ecologists have observed that fires help some plants, such as certain species of pine trees, to increase in number. Forests like this one may experience fires from lightning once in a while.

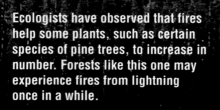

Summary

Organisms of the same species living in the same environment make up a population. Populations in the same environment make up a community. A community and the abiotic parts of its environment make up an ecosystem. Each species in an ecosystem lives in a habitat and has a niche that describes how it fits into the ecosystem.

Review

1. List four abiotic factors in an ecosystem.
2. How many different species can there be in a population?
3. Why can mosses and grasses survive in climates where tall trees cannot?
4. **Critical Thinking** Why are members of the same genus more likely to compete for a niche than organisms that are in different families?
5. **Test Prep** The role an organism plays in an ecosystem is its —

   A species
   B population
   C habitat
   D niche

LINKS

MATH LINK

Measurement How much water is in 1 in. of rain? Find out how much water falls in an inch of rain over an area of a square mile. First calculate the volume of rain in cubic inches. Convert the volume to gallons, and then find out how much this amount weighs. One gallon of water takes up 231 cubic inches and weighs about 8.35 pounds.

WRITING LINK

Expressive Writing—Friendly Letter Write a short letter to a friend in another state that describes how you interact with a part of your environment.

ART LINK

Architecture Find out what an architect means by the word *niche*. How is this meaning of the word similar to the ecological meaning? How is it different?

TECHNOLOGY LINK

Learn more about abiotic and biotic factors in ecosystems by visiting the Smithsonian Institution Internet Site.
www.si.edu/harcourt/science

Smithsonian Institution®

Why Are Natural Cycles Important to Ecosystems?

In this lesson, you can . . .

 INVESTIGATE the formation of groundwater.

 LEARN ABOUT three natural cycles and why they are important to ecosystems.

 LINK to math, writing, social studies, and technology.

 **INVESTIGATE**

Exploring Groundwater

Activity Purpose Water that lies under the ground, known as *groundwater,* makes up more than 90 percent of the liquid fresh water on Earth. It is the most important source of fresh water. Yet it accounts for less than 1 percent of the world's water. Most of the world's water is salt water. In this investigation, you'll find out where groundwater comes from.

Materials

- clear plastic box
- clay soil
- gravel
- sand
- topsoil or potting soil
- watering can
- water
- food coloring
- spoon
- book

Activity Procedure

1 Place a layer of clay soil in the plastic box and pack it down firmly. On top of the clay soil, place a layer of gravel. Cover the gravel with a layer of sand. Then add a layer of topsoil. (Picture A)

2 Add food coloring to water in the watering can. Make it "rain" over the soil by sprinkling water over the box. Sprinkle enough water to soak the topsoil. **Observe** the water moving through the soil layers by looking through the side of the box. (Picture B)

◄ Water is the most common liquid on Earth, and it is also the most precious—life depends on it. Earth's total supply of water does not change. It moves through the world's ecosystems in a natural cycle.

Picture A

Picture B

3 Make a pond at one end of the box. Spoon some soil from the topsoil layer to make a dip in the ground. Tilt the box by placing the book beneath the other end of the box. Sprinkle water gently over the raised end of the box. Watch the water movement through the side. Stop the rain when a pond forms in the dip.

Draw Conclusions

1. Describe how the "rain" soaked into the soil layers. Which layers did it move through? Which layer did the water not move through?

2. Most ponds and lakes form in places where dips in the ground fill with groundwater. How did the groundwater in your investigation reach the pond?

3. **Scientists at Work** Scientists **use models** in experiments to learn about natural processes. What did you learn about groundwater by using the model in the experiment?

Investigate Further Get permission from an adult to dig in an outdoor area near trees or bushes. Dig a narrow hole into the soil, and feel the bottom of the hole. Why is the soil moist at the bottom of the hole? Fill in the hole when you have finished, and leave the area as you found it.

Process Skill Tip

When you **use a model** and **experiment** with it, you can develop a new hypothesis about how the natural world works. The new hypothesis can be tested by more experiments.

Natural Cycles

Earth's Resources

Earth's ecosystems depend on energy from the sun, which will continue to supply sunlight for millions of years. However, ecosystems depend on other abiotic factors as well. Factors such as water, soil, and gases in the air are all limited resources. Living things are continually using them, so why aren't they all used up?

Abiotic materials can be used over and over again because living things return them to the environment. A substance moves through

FIND OUT

- what materials are cycled through Earth's ecosystems

- how living things get the materials they need

VOCABULARY

evaporation
water cycle
transpiration
condensation
precipitation
groundwater
carbon dioxide–oxygen
   cycle
nitrogen cycle

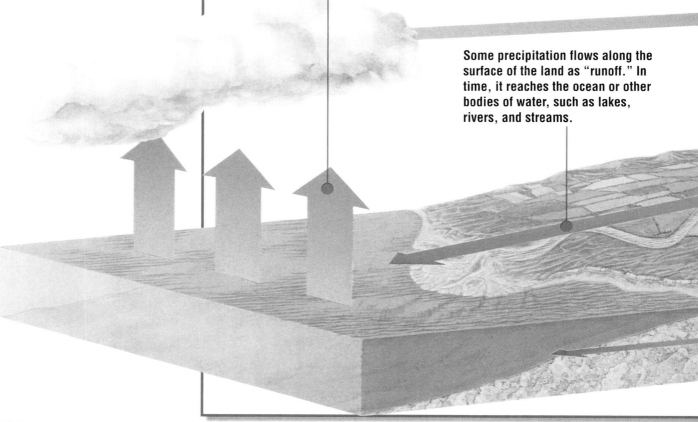

The Water Cycle

The water cycle is driven by energy from the sun and results in movement of water. Water moves from the oceans to the atmosphere, from the atmosphere to the land, and from the land back to the oceans.

The energy of the sun causes water in lakes, ponds, rivers, and oceans to change from liquid water to water vapor in a process called **evaporation**.

Some precipitation flows along the surface of the land as "runoff." In time, it reaches the ocean or other bodies of water, such as lakes, rivers, and streams.

the environment in a series of steps called a cycle. There are many important natural cycles, including the water cycle, the carbon dioxide–oxygen cycle, and the nitrogen cycle.

✔ **How are living things able to reuse abiotic materials?**

The Water Cycle

Most of Earth's water is in the oceans. Water is also found in freshwater lakes and ponds, and it flows in rivers and streams. All living things need water. The **water cycle** is the movement of water through Earth's ecosystems. In the course of the water cycle, water travels to all the parts of the environment, as you can see in the diagram.

Water that falls to Earth as precipitation is used by animals and plants. Animals consume water and return it as waste. Plants absorb water from the soil through their roots, and give it off through their leaves. All of the water that is used returns to the cycle to be used again.

✔ **What are two major processes that change the state of water in the water cycle? How do they work?**

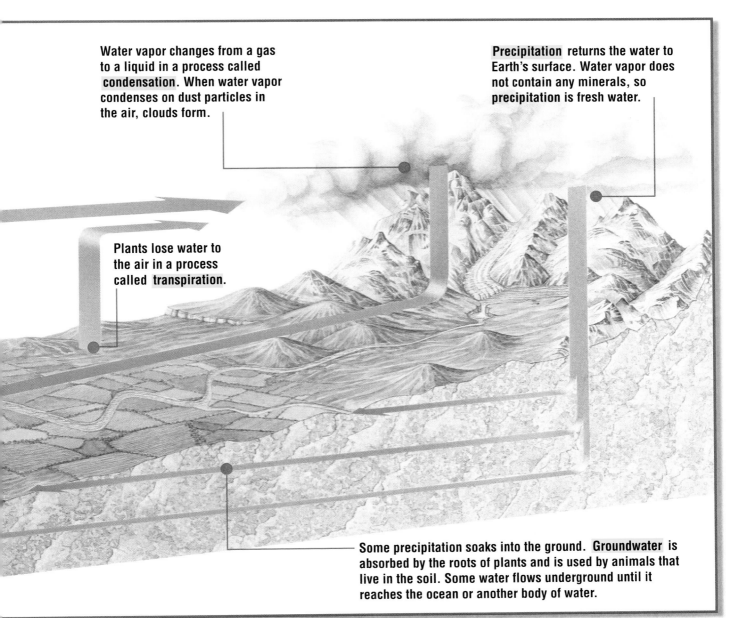

Water vapor changes from a gas to a liquid in a process called **condensation**. When water vapor condenses on dust particles in the air, clouds form.

Precipitation returns the water to Earth's surface. Water vapor does not contain any minerals, so precipitation is fresh water.

Plants lose water to the air in a process called **transpiration**.

Some precipitation soaks into the ground. **Groundwater** is absorbed by the roots of plants and is used by animals that live in the soil. Some water flows underground until it reaches the ocean or another body of water.

The Carbon Dioxide–Oxygen Cycle

Living things depend on the gases carbon dioxide and oxygen. Plants use carbon dioxide when they make food. Both animals and plants use oxygen to release the energy from food. The flow of these two gases through Earth's ecosystems is called the **carbon dioxide–oxygen cycle**.

You can study the diagram to see how the cycle works.

Carbon dioxide and oxygen are present in the atmosphere as gases. They also are dissolved in the world's fresh and salt water.

Photosynthesis, the process through which plants make food, takes place in chloroplasts in plant cells. In this process, plants make sugars

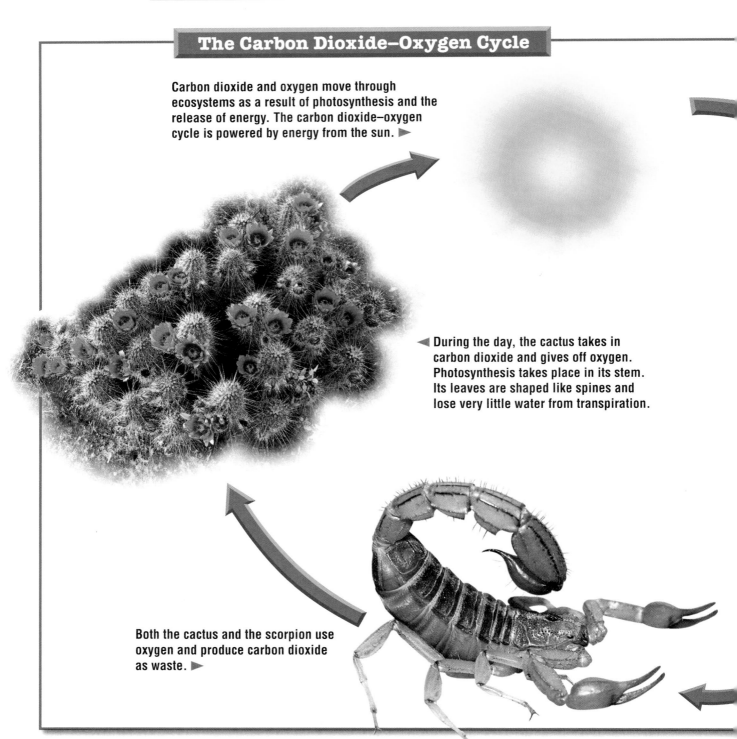

The Carbon Dioxide–Oxygen Cycle

Carbon dioxide and oxygen move through ecosystems as a result of photosynthesis and the release of energy. The carbon dioxide–oxygen cycle is powered by energy from the sun. ▶

◀ During the day, the cactus takes in carbon dioxide and gives off oxygen. Photosynthesis takes place in its stem. Its leaves are shaped like spines and lose very little water from transpiration.

Both the cactus and the scorpion use oxygen and produce carbon dioxide as waste. ▶

by combining carbon dioxide from the air with water that they absorb through their roots. Light from the sun provides the energy plants need for the process. Plants can use the sugars as food, or store them as starch for later use. In the process of making sugars, photosynthesis also produces oxygen, which plants release into the air as a gas.

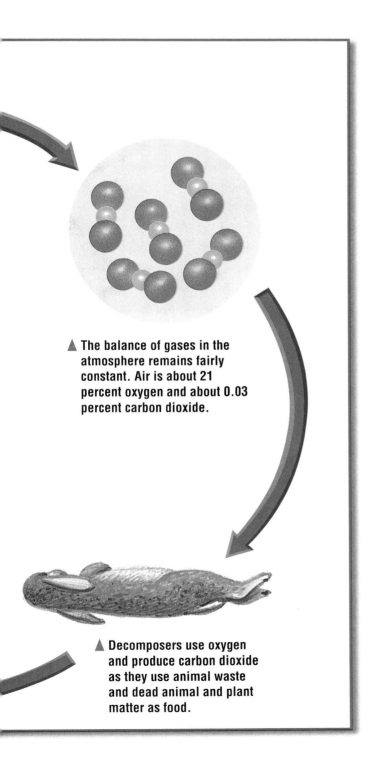

▲ The balance of gases in the atmosphere remains fairly constant. Air is about 21 percent oxygen and about 0.03 percent carbon dioxide.

▲ Decomposers use oxygen and produce carbon dioxide as they use animal waste and dead animal and plant matter as food.

Animals depend on the food produced by plants. They either eat plants themselves or eat other animals that eat plants. An animal's digestive system breaks down food. Starches are broken down into sugars. Along with other types of nutrients, sugars are carried to the animal's cells. All life processes require the energy that is stored in food.

Cells need oxygen to release the energy in food. Parts of an animal's body supply oxygen from the air to its cells. Within the mitochondria of the cells, oxygen combines with a kind of sugar to produce energy. In this process, carbon dioxide is also produced as a waste product. The carbon dioxide is released into the air as a gas.

All living things need energy. Even though plants make their own food, they still need the energy stored in it. They absorb oxygen from the air to release the energy, and return carbon dioxide into the air.

Decomposers such as fungi and bacteria use waste products and dead organisms as food. Most of them use oxygen to produce energy. They release carbon dioxide gas just as plants and animals do.

Most plants use up about the same amount of oxygen for life processes as they produce during photosynthesis. Animals and decomposers also use oxygen, but they don't produce it. Why doesn't the oxygen in the air get used up? Some very small living things called *phytoplankton* produce large amounts of oxygen. These plant-like protists live on the surface of the ocean. They make food by using photosynthesis and release energy by using oxygen. However, they produce much more oxygen than they use. Although these organisms are tiny, they have such large populations that they produce most of the oxygen in the atmosphere.

✔ **Why do plants need oxygen?**

The Nitrogen Cycle

Living things are made up of cells, and many of the cell parts are made of proteins. One of the important building blocks of a protein is nitrogen.

Nitrogen makes up about 78 percent of the air. Like water, carbon dioxide, and oxygen, nitrogen is used and returned by living things.

The movement of nitrogen through ecosystems is called the **nitrogen cycle**.

Most organisms cannot absorb nitrogen gas from the air as they do oxygen or carbon dioxide. In the nitrogen cycle, nitrogen is changed into nitrogen compounds that can be used by most living things. There are two ways in which nitrogen can be changed. In the first way, lightning passing through the air produces nitrogen

The Nitrogen Cycle

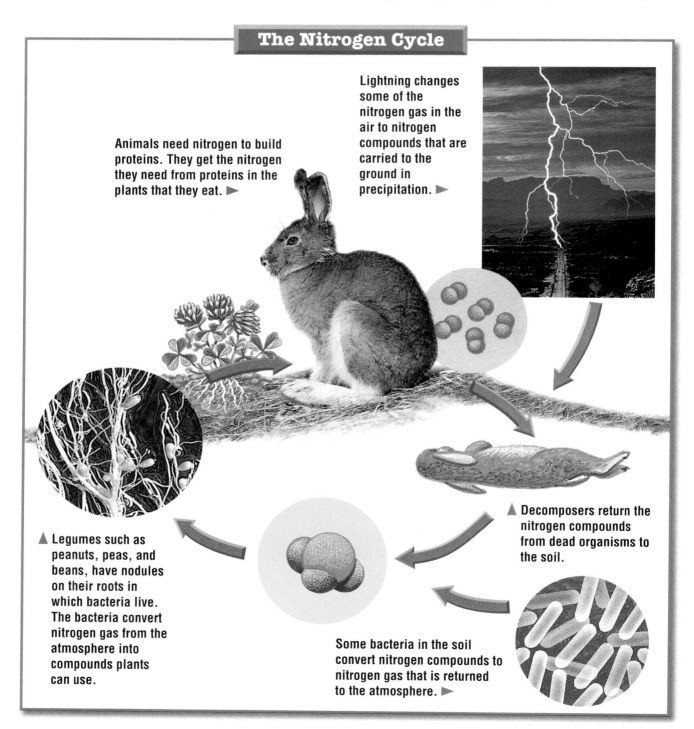

Animals need nitrogen to build proteins. They get the nitrogen they need from proteins in the plants that they eat. ▶

Lightning changes some of the nitrogen gas in the air to nitrogen compounds that are carried to the ground in precipitation. ▶

▲ Legumes such as peanuts, peas, and beans, have nodules on their roots in which bacteria live. The bacteria convert nitrogen gas from the atmosphere into compounds plants can use.

▲ Decomposers return the nitrogen compounds from dead organisms to the soil.

Some bacteria in the soil convert nitrogen compounds to nitrogen gas that is returned to the atmosphere. ▶

compounds that are carried to the ground by rain. In the second way, types of bacteria take in nitrogen directly from the air and change it into compounds. Either way, plants can then absorb and use the compounds to make proteins.

✔ **Why are the bacteria important that change nitrogen into compounds?**

Summary

Some of the materials that living things need move through Earth's ecosystems in natural cycles. The water cycle is powered by the energy of the sun. Water evaporates from the oceans into the atmosphere. The water vapor condenses when it cools, forming clouds, which return the water to the ground as precipitation. In the carbon dioxide–oxygen cycle, photosynthesis uses carbon dioxide and produces oxygen. Energy production in cells uses oxygen and produces carbon dioxide. The nitrogen cycle depends on bacteria that convert nitrogen to nitrogen compounds that can be used by organisms to build proteins.

Review

1. In what way is the water cycle powered by the sun?
2. What organisms produce most of the oxygen in the atmosphere?
3. How do plants use both carbon dioxide and oxygen?
4. **Critical Thinking** Native Americans placed a dead fish next to the seeds when they planted corn. Why did this result in a better crop?
5. **Test Prep** Plants can use nitrogen after it has been converted by —
   A photosynthesis
   B bacteria
   C evaporation
   D compounds

LINKS

MATH LINK

Circle Graph The atmosphere is about 78 percent nitrogen and 21 percent oxygen by volume. Carbon dioxide and other gases make up the remaining 1 percent. Make a circle graph to show the percentages of gases in the atmosphere by volume.

WRITING LINK

Informative Writing—Report Suppose that you are planning to build a base on the moon's surface. Write an essay for your teacher in which you list the organisms that you will need on the base so that astronauts can live there safely and comfortably.

SOCIAL STUDIES LINK

History of Science Joseph Priestley performed experiments to find out about oxygen in the air. Research Priestley's work, and illustrate the steps of one of his experiments.

TECHNOLOGY LINK

Visit the Harcourt Learning Site for related links, activities, and resources.
www.harcourtschool.com

WELCOME TO
THE
LEARNING
SITE

How Do People Use Natural Resources?

In this lesson, you can . . .

INVESTIGATE the recycling of paper.

LEARN ABOUT natural resources and how they are used.

LINK to math, writing, social studies, and technology.

INVESTIGATE

Making New Paper from Used Paper

Activity Purpose Some of the natural resources we use, such as air and water, are necessities. We can't live without them. Others are important to our way of life. For example, we use wood to build homes and furniture and to make paper for newspapers and books. Using resources wisely can help make sure they will be available for people in years to come. In this investigation, you will find out how trees can be conserved by making new paper from waste paper.

Materials

- scrap paper
- basin
- water
- laundry starch
- graduate or measuring cup and tablespoon
- safety goggles
- eggbeater

- wire window screen with taped edges
- newspaper, 2 sheets
- rolling pin or thick dowel

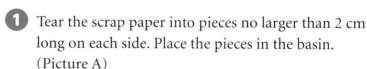

Activity Procedure

1 Tear the scrap paper into pieces no larger than 2 cm long on each side. Place the pieces in the basin. (Picture A)

2 Add water, keeping track of how many milliliters you add. For each 240 mL of water you use, add 16 mL of starch to the mixture.

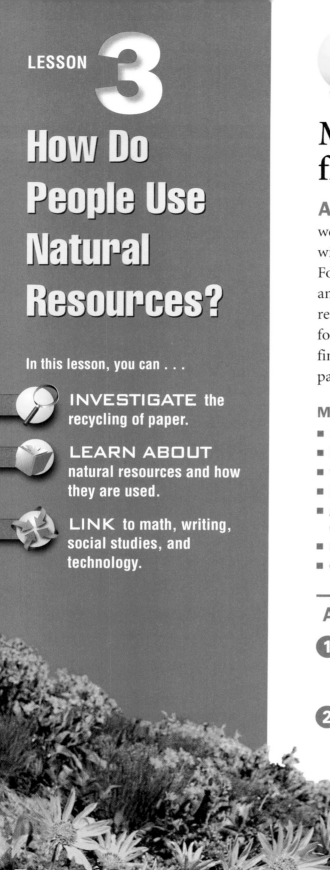

◀ Natural resources include things that contribute to our enjoyment as well as to our ecosystems. In many states, wildflowers like these are protected by laws against picking them.

Picture A

Picture B

3 **CAUTION** **Put on your safety goggles.** Beat the mixture with the eggbeater until it forms a watery pulp. (Picture B)

4 Dip the screen into the mixture, coating one side with a thin layer of pulp. Place the screen between sheets of newspaper. Roll the rolling pin over the newspaper to remove as much water as possible.

5 Allow the paper to dry.

Draw Conclusions

1. Compare the paper you made with paper you use in school. What might account for any differences?

2. Some of the paper and cardboard you use has been recycled from old paper. What factors might affect whether people make paper from waste materials or from trees?

3. **Scientists at Work** Scientists **use models** to help them develop ideas for how something might work on a larger scale. Using what you learned, suggest ways paper could be recycled in a large recycling plant.

Investigate Further Try making paper with other materials, such as cotton cloth or cardboard. Experiment with different methods of making paper. You can find plenty of ideas in craft books at the library.

Process Skill Tip

Scientists sometimes **use models** of a process. This allows them to compare how a number of processes would work without having to build expensive machinery for each.

How People Use Natural Resources

Renewable Resources

FIND OUT

- about Earth's renewable and nonrenewable resources
- how human activities affect Earth's resources

VOCABULARY

reusable resources
renewable resources
nonrenewable
    resources

Many of the resources we use are in limited supply. Some are **reusable resources**, or resources that can be used again and again. Resources such as water, carbon dioxide, oxygen, and nitrogen are reused in natural cycles. People's actions can make certain other materials reusable. For example, recycling cans makes aluminum reusable.

Other resources cannot be used again and again. Wood that is burned in a fireplace is gone forever. However, seeds from the tree that the wood came from can grow into new trees, replacing the wood that was used. Such resources are called **renewable resources**. A field of wheat can be replanted once the crop has been harvested. The offspring of a herd of beef cattle will grow up to replace the herd. Resources are considered renewable if they can be replaced within a human life span.

✔ **Give two examples of renewable resources not named on this page.**

Wetlands are natural resources that provide habitats for one third of the nation's endangered species, including vast numbers of birds, fish, and shellfish. Wetlands also act as natural filters and clean polluted water. ▼

Nonrenewable Resources

Some materials, once used, are gone forever. These resources that cannot be replaced within a human life span are called **nonrenewable resources**.

Many energy resources, materials that we use for fuel, are nonrenewable resources. Most of this country's electricity is generated in energy plants that burn coal. Coal forms over millions of years from plant matter that is buried. It takes so much time for new coal to form that, for human purposes, the coal that is used cannot be replaced. Oil is also formed over millions of years. Earth has a large supply of coal, but there is not as much oil available as there is coal. The graph on this page shows how Earth's reserves of oil are being produced and used up.

Some resources are not so easy to recognize as nonrenewable. Even though trees are renewable, an old-growth forest is not. It is a community of trees of all ages, including some that are hundreds of years old. Once it has been cut down, the forest takes hundreds of years to grow back to its old form. In some areas, groundwater is also a nonrenewable resource. Water is pumped from the ground faster than it can be replaced by precipitation.

Minerals are nonrenewable resources. For example, cinnabar is a mineral that is the chief source of mercury, a metal important in many industrial uses. ▶

Soil is another resource that takes a long time to form. Soil is formed of broken-up particles of rock, decomposed plant and animal matter, water, and air. Fertile soils are thick and rich in nutrients. Wind and water, which help form soil from rock, also erode it. In more than a third of the world's farmlands, soil is eroding faster than it forms. About 0.7 m (2 ft) of topsoil has been eroded from the Great Plains in the last century, leaving about 1.3 m (4 ft) of topsoil. In many areas of the United States, the topsoil is only a few inches deep.

✔ **What makes a resource nonrenewable?**

With no vegetation to anchor it, soil is unprotected against erosion by wind and water. This soil is barren and unproductive. ▼

This land is terraced so that rain does not easily wash the topsoil down the slope. Trees are often planted between fields to break the force of the wind. ▼

Production and Use of Oil

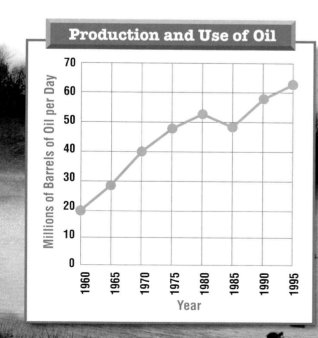

Millions of Barrels of Oil per Day (y-axis: 0, 10, 20, 30, 40, 50, 60, 70)

Year (x-axis: 1960, 1965, 1970, 1975, 1980, 1985, 1990, 1995)

Humans Can Alter Ecosystems

One of the factors affecting Earth's ecosystems is human activity. We get many of the resources we use through mining, agriculture, and forestry. These activities affect more than the appearance of the environment.

When we use more groundwater than is being replaced, there can be a water shortage. When we burn fossil fuels, the pollution can harm living things. Pollution can even be cycled through an ecosystem in much the same way as natural resources are. When we dump waste from the resources we use, we change the environment even more.

One way to reduce these effects on the environment is to use and throw away smaller amounts of resources. *Conservation*, or the saving of resources, helps prevent damage to the environment. It also helps make sure that the resources will not be used up.

There are several ways to conserve resources. One way is to use less of them. Turning off lights when they aren't in use saves electricity, which is usually made by burning fossil fuels. Many modern electric appliances are "energy efficient." This means that they use less energy than older appliances. Most modern cars use far less fuel than the older models. When people join a carpool or use public transportation, they save even more fuel. It takes energy to mine, transport, and process the natural resources we use for fuels. So saving energy saves *more* energy.

Another way to conserve resources is to recycle them. Recycling programs separate metals

Acid Precipitation

Chemicals from burning coal and other fuels enter the atmosphere and combine with water vapor to make acids. These acids can fall to Earth as rain or snow that is far more acidic than natural rain. This acid precipitation can damage stone and metal structures. When acid precipitation drains into a lake, it increases the acidity of the lake water. Acids may harm crops and forests. Acids can damage the leaves and stems of plants, and when it soaks into the soil, it also can harm their roots.

▲ The smoke contains chemicals that react with water vapor to form acid. The acid falls to the ground as acid rain.

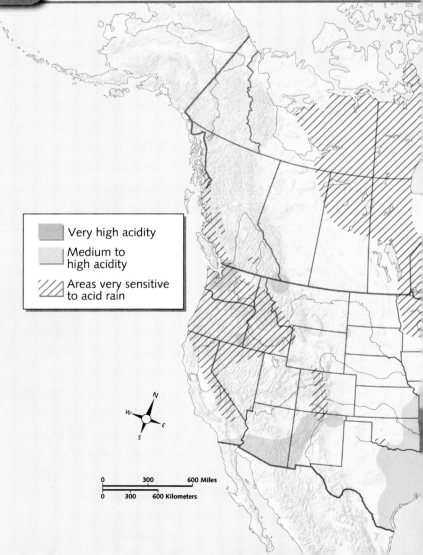

Very high acidity

Medium to high acidity

Areas very sensitive to acid rain

| 0 | 300 | 600 Miles |
| 0 | 300 | 600 Kilometers |

such as aluminum, iron, and steel from waste. They also separate glass, paper, and plastic. These materials can then be recycled and reused.

Using a substitute resource that is more plentiful is a good way to conserve limited resources. This may be an especially useful way to conserve energy resources. The energy of moving water at dams and waterfalls can be used to produce electricity without burning fossil fuels. Ocean water that moves with the tides can also be used to generate electricity. Wind energy and solar energy are being used on a small scale to supply electricity. Geothermal energy, or heat from deep within the Earth, is used in some areas. These substitute energy sources cause very little pollution.

Earth's natural resources are not limited to fuels and minerals. In fact, the diversity, or variety, of plant and animal life is one of Earth's

Planting wildflowers is one way to help preserve habitats. ▶

greatest resources. Large areas of land all around the world have been set aside for the *preservation* of the living resources there. The animals and plants in these areas are protected from hunting and other harmful activities of people. In some of these preservation areas, mineral resources are also protected.

✔ **Name two ways to conserve resources.**

The effect of acid rain on this forest can be seen in the damage to the trees, but there is also unseen damage to the soil. Sometimes the pollution in the air settles on the land in a dry state. The chemicals combine with dew or rain on the ground to form acids. ▶

◀ Few fish or other animals are found in this lake. Most of the plants that were here are gone, too. Acid rain eats away the shells of bird eggs and kills fish eggs, so fewer birds and fish hatch.

Treating the water with a chemical that will reduce its acidity may be an answer to the problems caused by acid rain in lakes. ▶

C25

Problems and Solutions

Sometimes even growing crops and raising livestock can harm the environment. In northern Africa, for example, cattle graze on the grasslands at the edges of the Sahara. There are now so many cattle that the land is overgrazed. As the grass is completely eaten, the plants die. The soil is no longer anchored in place, and it gets blown away. Sand from the desert takes its place, and the desert gets larger and larger. This results in even more overgrazing on the remaining grasslands. The pictures and the map below show some other problems and solutions that people have encountered all over the world.

✔ **How can introducing a new species to a place be harmful?**

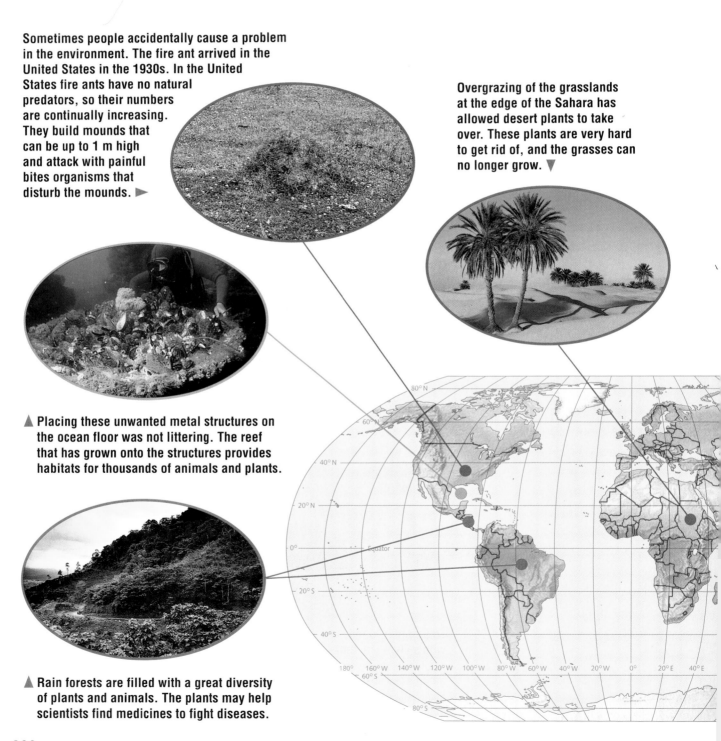

Sometimes people accidentally cause a problem in the environment. The fire ant arrived in the United States in the 1930s. In the United States fire ants have no natural predators, so their numbers are continually increasing. They build mounds that can be up to 1 m high and attack with painful bites organisms that disturb the mounds. ▶

Overgrazing of the grasslands at the edge of the Sahara has allowed desert plants to take over. These plants are very hard to get rid of, and the grasses can no longer grow. ▼

▲ Placing these unwanted metal structures on the ocean floor was not littering. The reef that has grown onto the structures provides habitats for thousands of animals and plants.

▲ Rain forests are filled with a great diversity of plants and animals. The plants may help scientists find medicines to fight diseases.

Summary

Natural cycles allow some resources to be reusable. Other resources are renewable; they can be replaced within a human life span. Non-renewable resources are depleted as they are used. The use of nonrenewable resources can be slowed down through conservation methods such as recycling.

Review

1. What is a renewable resource?
2. What is a nonrenewable resource?
3. How is acid rain able to affect lakes far from the source of the pollution?
4. **Critical Thinking** Why does conserving coal save more resources than just the amount of coal that would have been mined?
5. **Test Prep** Because they are cycled through ecosystems, nitrogen, carbon dioxide, and oxygen are —

   A conserved resources
   B renewable resources
   C nonrenewable resources
   D reusable resources

LINKS

MATH LINK

Percents and Fractions About 70 percent of the trash in the United States is dumped in landfills. This is $4\frac{2}{3}$ times as much trash as is recycled. What percent of trash is recycled?

WRITING LINK

Persuasive Writing—Opinion Suppose that you have started an electricity company that uses wind power as its energy source. Write an advertisement for your local newspaper to attract customers.

SOCIAL STUDIES LINK

The EPA Find out about the Environmental Protection Agency (EPA). Where was it founded? What is its mission? What kinds of jobs do people have who work for the EPA?

TECHNOLOGY LINK

To learn more about ways scientists are finding to extend the use of resources watch *Fuel Cell Cars* on the **Harcourt Science Newsroom Video**.

CNN
Turner
Le@rning

EXPLORING DEEP-OCEAN ECOSYSTEMS

Scientists have discovered some surprising new species on the ocean floor.

What is life like on the ocean floor?

When you think of new worlds or new forms of life, you probably think of outer space. Yet much of the ocean floor is also an unexplored world. Oceanographers have been able to look at only a few parts of the ocean floor from small submersible vehicles such as *Alvin*. Until 1977, in fact, they inferred that few species could live at great depth in the ocean. The complete lack of sunlight means that plants can't grow. The only food is what drifts down to the ocean bottom from above. The few fish species that live there have adaptations, such as huge mouths, to capture any food in the water.

What new kinds of living things did oceanographers find?

In 1977, oceanographers aboard *Alvin* were observing the ocean bottom near a mid-ocean ridge. There they found plumes, or columns, of hot water at a temperature of 370°C (about

Giant tube worms near deep-ocean vents

700°F) gushing from vents, or cracks, in the ocean floor. To their surprise, the scientists observed a variety of strange creatures living near the vents. They saw colonies of meter-long white tube worms with red feathery tips, snake-like fish with bulging eyes, and spindly crabs as big as manhole covers. At first, scientists were amazed to find so much life on the ocean floor. But even more surprising was the fact that this whole ecosystem was dependent on the chemicals coming out of the vents.

Scientists now know that vent ecosystems have living things found nowhere else on Earth. Until these ecosystems were found, plants were considered to be at the bottom of all food chains. But at the bottom of vent food chains are bacteria that use hydrogen sulfide from the vents instead of sunlight as their energy source.

Why is this discovery important?

Since 1977, vent ecosystems have been found in several hundred places on the sea floor. More than 300 new species from these areas have been identified. However, bacteria found living around vents by the *Alvin* expedition are completely different from other bacteria on Earth. Scientists call them archaea (ar•KEE•uh). All archaeans live

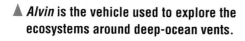

▲ *Alvin* is the vehicle used to explore the ecosystems around deep-ocean vents.

near the boiling waters of deep-ocean vents. They also live inside volcanoes and hot springs. The archaebacteria need neither oxygen nor sunlight. They can live on chemicals from Earth's crust. Because these life forms don't need oxygen, some scientists now hypothesize that similar forms of life could exist beneath the surface of Mars or in other places in the solar system.

THINK ABOUT IT

1. Why were scientists surprised to find a community of animals living near deep-sea vents?

2. Why is this discovery of life near ocean vents important?

WEB LINK:
For Science and Technology updates, visit The Learning Site.
www.harcourtschool.com

Careers   Oceanographer

What They Do
Oceanographers collect and study information about the ocean's water, life, and resources. Some oceanographers work in ships on the ocean, gathering data and doing experiments. Much of their work must also be done in laboratories.

Education and Training Oceanographers need to study basic sciences such as biology and chemistry, and they specialize in a particular area, such as biological oceanography. They also should have an interest in the environment. They should enjoy outdoor activities such as swimming and boating. An oceanographer must earn at least a bachelor's degree.

Carol Yoon
SCIENCE WRITER

"Being an academic biologist requires being able to focus on one particular thing for a very long time. . . . A career like journalism is just the opposite. You have to give up depth. . . . [But] you learn about a lot of things and talk to a lot of people. . . ."

Carol Yoon is one of the most successful and respected science writers in the country. As a writer for the *New York Times,* she has the chance to talk with the nation's leading scientists about their work. She then uses her knowledge of science and her abilities as a writer to turn that information into articles that the nonscientist can understand.

Although Dr. Yoon loves her work, she didn't always want to be a science writer. At one time, she wasn't thinking about a career in science at all. Then a college ecology course sparked her interest. She became so enthusiastic about science that she took more courses, did field work, and decided to make science her college major. But after getting a Ph.D. in molecular evolution, she stopped and asked herself, "Now what?"

With no definite plans, Dr. Yoon accepted a job as a science writer on the staff of an Oregon newspaper. She didn't expect to make a career of science writing. But after a couple of weeks, she knew she had found what she really wanted to do. "I realized, this is what I should have been doing all of my life," she says.

The job in Oregon led to Dr. Yoon's present job, in which she writes about ecology, conservation, biology, and evolution. The job is hard work. When Dr. Yoon starts a new story, she first reads to educate herself about the topic. She calls experts in the field to discuss questions that she has. Then she contacts the scientists whose work she will write about. She asks them about their research, why it interests them, and why it's important.

Even with all of the hard work and the need to "write and rewrite and rewrite and rewrite," Dr. Yoon finds her chosen career a perfect mix of her two loves—science and writing. It's also a great way for her to keep learning and to share the excitement of science with others.

THINK ABOUT IT

1. How did Dr. Yoon become interested in science?

2. How do you think being a science journalist differs from being a scientist?

◄ **Dr. Yoon often writes about ecological issues.**

Checking for Carbon Dioxide

Do plants produce carbon dioxide during photosynthesis?

Materials

- large bowl filled with small pieces of purple cabbage
- hot distilled water
- 3 large glass jars and 1 lid
- branch of a water plant, such as *Elodea*
- straw

Procedure

1. Pour the hot water over the cabbage and let it sit until it cools.

2. Discard the cabbage and pour the water into the three glass jars. Blue cabbage-water will change color if an acid is added. When carbon dioxide mixes with water, it forms a weak acid called carbonic acid.

3. Put the water plant into one jar, close the lid, and set it in the sun.

4. Using the straw, blow into the second jar until the water changes color.

5. Do nothing with the third jar.

Draw Conclusions

Did the water with the plant in it change color? Why? Why did the water that you blew into change color? Explain what happened in the third jar.

Raining Acid

How does acid rain affect plants?

Materials

- 2 spray bottles
- measuring cup
- distilled water
- vinegar
- adhesive labels
- 4 small, healthy, identical potted plants with saucers

Procedure

1. Fill a bottle with distilled water and label it *Water*.

2. Pour 240 mL (1 cup) distilled water and 240 mL vinegar into the other bottle. Label it *Acid Rain*.

3. Label two plants *Water* and two *Acid Rain*. Place them all in a warm, sunny window.

4. Every day for three weeks, spray the plant leaves and keep the soil moist. Use *Water* or *Acid Rain* as indicated by the plant labels.

Draw Conclusions

What differences do you observe between the two groups of plants? How might acid rain affect a field of corn? How might this acid rain affect crops planted in the same field the following year, even if no more acid rain fell?

Chapter 1 Review and Test Preparation

Vocabulary Review

Use the terms below to complete the sentences. The page numbers in ( ) tell you where to look in the chapter if you need help.

environment (C6)
abiotic (C6)
biotic (C6)
population (C7)
habitat (C7)
community (C7)
ecosystem (C7)
niche (C9)
evaporation (C14)
transpiration (C15)
water cycle (C15)

condensation (C15)
precipitation (C15)
groundwater (C15)
carbon dioxide–oxygen cycle (C16)
nitrogen cycle (C18)
reusable resources (C22)
renewable resources (C22)
nonrenewable resources (C23)

1. A ____ is a group of organisms of one species living in the same environment.

2. In the ____, liquid water is changed to water vapor by the process of ____. Water vapor forms into clouds by the process of ____.

3. Water that falls as ____ seeps through the soil to become ____.

4. An environment is made up of ____, or living, parts and ____, or nonliving, parts.

5. The role of an organism in an ecosystem is its ____, while the place where an organism lives is its ____.

6. All the populations living in the same environment at the same time make up a ____.

7. Carbon dioxide, oxygen, nitrogen, and water are called ____ because they are cycled through Earth's ecosystems.

8. Plants take water from the soil and lose water vapor to the air through ____.

9. The surroundings in which an organism lives are called its ____.

10. Communities and their abiotic surroundings make up an ____.

11. The ____ is made up of the paths taken by carbon dioxide and oxygen through Earth's ecosystems.

12. In the ____, nitrogen gas is changed into a form that plants can use.

13. Resources that can be replaced within a human lifespan are ____. Those that cannot are ____.

Connect Concepts

Use the terms from the Word Bank to complete the concept map.

abiotic   animals   biotic
water   plants   ecosystems
nitrogen   oxygen   carbon dioxide

Environments have

14. _____ parts and 15. _____ parts

such as bacteria,
16. _____,
and
17. _____,

such as oxygen,
carbon dioxide,
18. _____,
19. _____,

which use

cycled through Earth's
20. _____.

21. _____ for cellular respiration and use food made by plants, using

22. _____, water, and energy from the sun in photosynthesis.

Check Understanding

Write the letter of the best choice.

23. A millipede is a plant eater and a scavenger. Those terms describe its —

A population

B community

C ecosystem

D niche

24. After a forest fire, the first plants to re-appear are —

F small trees

G large trees

H weedy plants

J ferns

25. The process in the water cycle in which liquid water forms on dust particles in the air, resulting in clouds, is —

A evaporation

B condensation

C precipitation

D transpiration

26. Oxygen is needed by —

F plants for photosynthesis

G animals for cellular respiration

H plants and animals for photosynthesis

J plants and animals for cellular respiration

27. Nonrenewable resources take a long time to form. An example is —

A soil

B rain

C crop plants

D animals raised for food

28. Old-growth forests are examples of a —

F renewable resource

G nonrenewable resource

H reusable resource

J reusable and renewable resource

Critical Thinking

29. Some scientists hypothesize that cutting down tropical rain forests is adding to global warming, which may be caused by the increase of carbon dioxide in the atmosphere. Why might this be so?

30. Think about the everyday activities of you and your family. List the ways that you conserve resources. List some ways that you could increase your conservation efforts.

Process Skills Review

31. How does **graphing data** about rainfall and temperature help you understand an ecosystem?

32. Using your **observations** of a water cycle **model**, explain how groundwater is formed.

33. **Identify** the resource that is conserved when paper is recycled.

Performance Assessment

Experimenting with Plants

Work with a partner to plan an experiment to test this hypothesis: *Plants get the water they need from groundwater.* What materials would you need? What steps would you take? What would you expect to see if the hypothesis is correct?

Chapter 2

Interactions in Ecosystems

Ecosystems are full of interactions. Animals eat plants and other animals. Plants and animals defend themselves. New species are introduced. Old species die out. But any change, however small, shapes the ecosystem.

FAST FACT

Although most venomous snakes use their venom to paralyze or kill their prey, they can also be dangerous to people.

Human Deaths Due to Venomous Snakebites

Type of Snake	Number of Deaths per Year
Asian Cobras	15,000
Saw-scaled Vipers	10,000
Russell's Viper	5000
Krait	3000
Lance-headed Vipers	3000

Golden eyelash viper

Vocabulary Preview

producer
consumer
decomposer
predator
prey
scavenger
symbiosis
parasitism
mutualism
commensalism

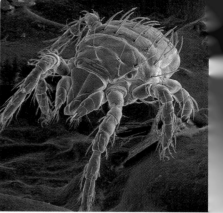

FAST FACT

There is one kind of mite whose only food source is the blood it sucks from the rear legs of a certain kind of South American army ant.

FAST FACT

Some animals have unusual ways of protecting themselves. The porcupine's hair is hard and flexible and has barbs on the end. The hairs stick in the skin of animals that attack the porcupine.

LESSON 1

How Do Organisms Get Energy?

In this lesson, you can . . .

 INVESTIGATE what owls eat.

 LEARN ABOUT feeding relationships in ecosystems.

 LINK to math, writing, social studies, and technology.

The Diet of Owls

Activity Purpose Studying animals to find out what they eat is often hard. You need to track the animals and watch them for a long time. However, some animals leave clues to what they eat. For example, owls produce pellets by regurgitating the materials from their food that they are unable to digest. In this investigation you'll **observe** an owl pellet to find out what the owl ate.

Materials

- safety goggles
- owl pellet
- paper towel or small aluminum tray
- toothpicks
- index card
- bone chart

Activity Procedure

1. **CAUTION** **Put on your safety goggles.** Your teacher will distribute owl pellets to the class. Place your pellet on the paper towel or aluminum tray.

2. Use toothpicks to take the pellet apart. (Picture A)

3. Separate the bones from the other material in the owl pellet. Place the bones in a pile. Your teacher will tell you where to dispose of the other material.

4. Place the bones on the index card. Using the bone chart, **classify** the bones into groups. All the bones in a group should be from the same kind of animal. (Picture B)

◀ Plants need nutrients to make their food and get energy. Some plants that grow in poor soil get the nutrients they need by "eating" animals. A sweet-smelling liquid attracts insects to a pitcher plant. Once an insect enters the tube-shaped leaf of the plant, hairs that point downward stop it from leaving. The insect falls into the pool of liquid inside the leaf. The liquid dissolves the insect, and the plant uses the nutrients.

Picture A

Picture B

Draw Conclusions

1. Do owls eat other animals, plants, or both? Explain your answer.

2. An owl usually produces one pellet a day. How many animals did the owl eat in one day? Explain your answer.

3. **Scientists at Work** Scientists **gather data** and use it to **infer** facts. How could you use the results of this investigation to determine whether owls hunt during the day or at night? What other information would you need?

Investigate Further Combine the class data. Make a bar graph to compare the numbers of different animals the owls ate. How might your results differ if you had used owl pellets from another area of the country?

How Organisms Get Energy

FIND OUT

- how energy flows in an ecosystem
- how the flow of energy is shown by food chains, food webs, and energy pyramids

VOCABULARY

producer
consumer
decomposer
predator
prey
scavenger

Energy in Ecosystems

Organisms need energy for all life processes. Owls get energy from the animals that they eat. But where do those animals get their energy? You know that water and nitrogen move through an ecosystem. Energy also moves through an ecosystem. As energy is passed along, some of it is not used. However, the ecosystem receives a new supply of energy from the sun every day.

The sun is the most important source of energy for life on Earth. Plants and algae capture the energy from the sun and use it to make their own food. The sun's energy is stored in the food these organisms make. An organism that makes its own food is called a **producer**. When an animal eats a producer, it takes in the producer's energy. If the animal is eaten by another animal, the energy is passed along. A **consumer** is an organism that eats other organisms.

A **decomposer** is a type of consumer that gets its food by breaking down animal wastes and the remains of dead plants and animals. Decomposers include some types of fungi and bacteria. They help ecosystems by recycling the important parts of dead material.

✔ **What is the difference between a producer and a consumer?**

Energy Flow in a Forest

The arrows show how energy flows from one organism to another in this forest ecosystem.

Deer eat plants to get energy. They are consumers. ▶

▲ Plants use energy from the sun to make food. They are producers.

◀ Puffballs are fungi. They have underground threads that absorb the waste and remains of animals and plants to get energy. They are decomposers.

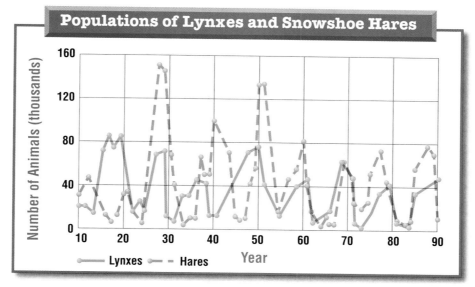

Populations of Lynxes and Snowshoe Hares

Number of Animals (thousands)

160

120

80

40

0

10 20 30 40 50 60 70 80 90

Year

— Lynxes --•-- Hares

The graph shows how the populations of lynxes and showshoe hares have changed over time in one area.

Predators and Prey

Energy passing through the forest ecosystem shown in the diagram on page C38 does not stop with the deer. Deer are food for animals such as wolves and coyotes. An animal that feeds on other living animals is called a **predator**. Predators are consumers that eat other consumers. The animals that predators eat are called **prey**.

The owl that produced the pellet you studied in the investigation is a predator. The bones you classified were the bones of the owl's prey. In a forest ecosystem, predators may include insects, birds, coyotes, and wolves. Some predators are also prey. Insects that eat smaller insects may be eaten by birds. Those birds may be eaten by larger birds or by mammals such as foxes.

Ecosystems also include animals called scavengers. **Scavengers** eat the remains of animals that have died. Vultures, jackals, and hyenas are common scavengers.

The interactions between predators and prey affect the populations of those animals. A large number of prey can feed a large number of predators. When the population of the prey decreases, however, it can no longer feed as many predators.

Snowshoe hares are the main food for lynxes. The graph shows the populations of lynxes and hares over time. The population of hares reaches a peak every 9 or 10 years. Then it decreases. The same changes can be seen with the lynx population.

There are several ways to explain the repeating pattern shown in the graph. One way scientists have explained it is that the large number of predators reduces the population of the prey. As the prey population decreases, it can't support as many predators. The population of predators then decreases. The smaller number of predators allows the population of prey to increase again. The increased number of prey once again supports an increased number of predators.

✓ **What is the difference between a predator and a scavenger?**

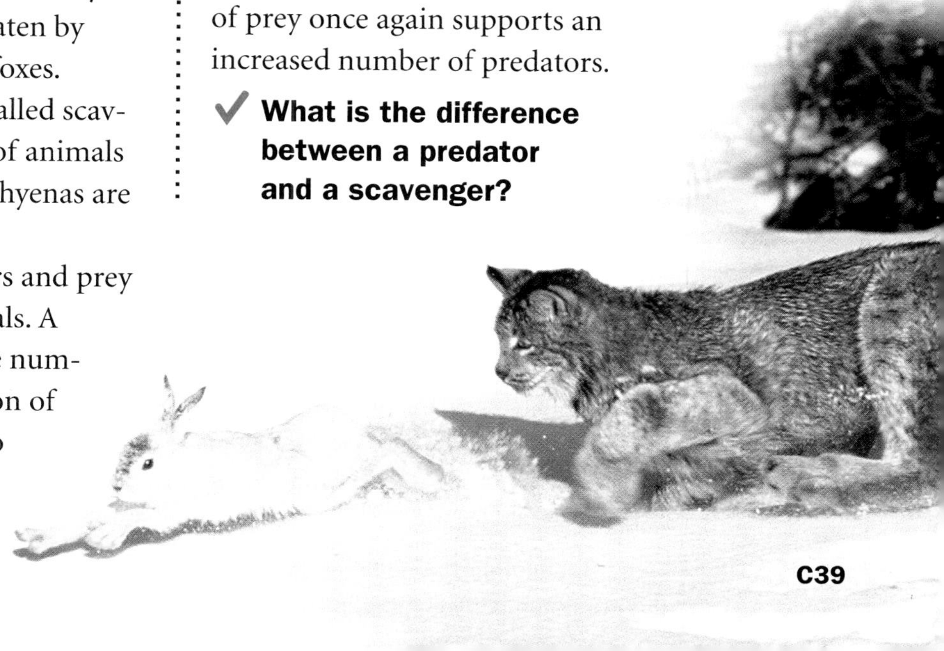

Food Chains and Food Webs

Simple paths of energy in an ecosystem can be shown by a food chain. A food chain shows how energy is passed through several organisms. **Plant → Deer → Coyote** is a food chain that shows energy passing from plants to deer to coyotes. The arrows in a food chain point *from* what is eaten *to* what eats it.

Feeding relationships in an ecosystem are usually not so simple. Producers are often eaten by more than one kind of consumer. Prey are often eaten by more than one kind of predator, and predators often have more than one kind of prey. For all these reasons, the food chains in an ecosystem overlap. For example, in the food chain **Plant → Deer → Coyote,** the same plant is food for insects as well as deer. The deer are prey for wolves as well as coyotes. The coyotes hunt rabbits and squirrels as well as deer.

The overlapping food chains in an ecosystem form a food web. Food webs are much more complicated than food chains. They show many more of the feeding relationships in an ecosystem. Also, an ecosystem's food web may change with the seasons.

The Arctic is a region of the Earth near the North Pole. During the summer small plants grow on the tundra. They provide food for insects, birds, rodents, and caribou. Arctic birds feed on the insects and plants. Weasels, snowy owls, and arctic foxes feed on the birds and small mammals. The arctic wolf eats almost every kind of animal in the ecosystem.

An Antarctic Food Web

The South Pole is a world away from the North Pole. The food web in the Antarctic is very different from the web in the Arctic. Most of the Antarctic's living things are found in the water around the huge southern icecap. The food web shows some of the feeding relationships between organisms in the Antarctic. In the food web below, find the food chain shown at the bottom of the page.

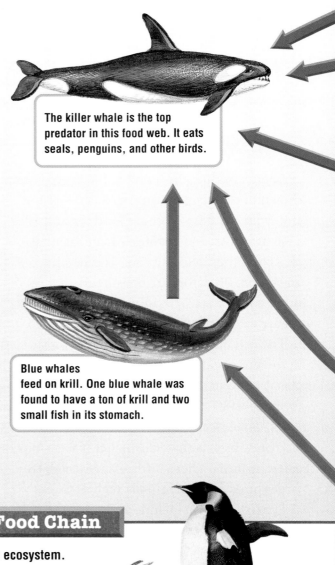

The killer whale is the top predator in this food web. It eats seals, penguins, and other birds.

Blue whales feed on krill. One blue whale was found to have a ton of krill and two small fish in its stomach.

Antarctic Food Chain

This food chain shows one energy path in an Antarctic ecosystem.

Diatoms are plantlike protists, the main producers in the ocean.

Krill, such as the one shown here, are small animals that feed on diatoms.

This squid feeds on krill and small fish.

The emperor penguin feeds on small squid. In this food chain the next organism could be a predator that eats penguins.

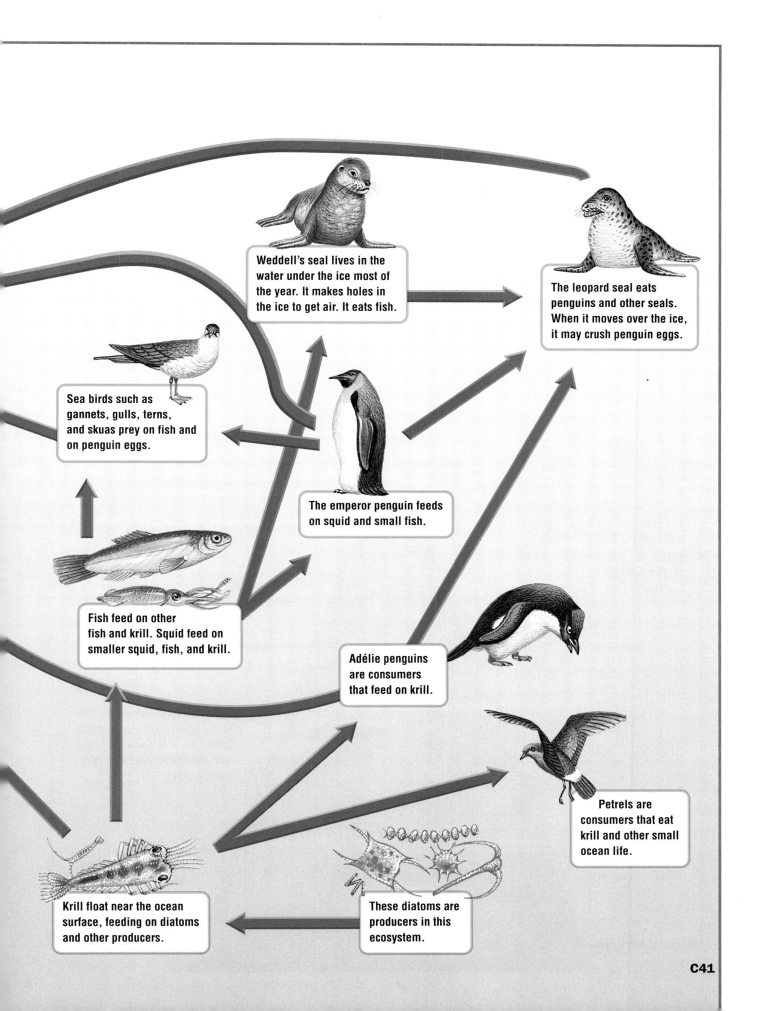

Weddell's seal lives in the water under the ice most of the year. It makes holes in the ice to get air. It eats fish.

The leopard seal eats penguins and other seals. When it moves over the ice, it may crush penguin eggs.

Sea birds such as gannets, gulls, terns, and skuas prey on fish and on penguin eggs.

The emperor penguin feeds on squid and small fish.

Fish feed on other fish and krill. Squid feed on smaller squid, fish, and krill.

Adélie penguins are consumers that feed on krill.

Petrels are consumers that eat krill and other small ocean life.

Krill float near the ocean surface, feeding on diatoms and other producers.

These diatoms are producers in this ecosystem.

In the winter, conditions in the ecosystem are different. Plants no longer have leaves. The insects have died, leaving their eggs to hatch the following spring. The small mammals search for seeds to eat. While the mammals are looking for food, they are prey to snowy owls. Most of the other birds have flown south in search of food. The caribou and the wolves have also migrated south. The food web of the tundra has fewer overlapping food chains in the winter than in the summer.

✔ **What is the difference between a food web and a food chain?**

Energy Pyramids

Producers are able to capture energy from the sun and use it to make food. They use some of the energy from that food to stay alive, grow,

and reproduce. They lose some of the energy as heat. They store the rest of the energy as extra food.

When a consumer eats a producer, it takes in the energy stored in the producer. The consumer also uses some of the energy for its life processes and loses some as heat. It, too, stores some of the energy in its body. However, scientists have found that a *herbivore*, or a consumer that eats plants, can use only about 10 percent of the energy that was stored in the producer.

This decrease in energy continues through a food chain. A *carnivore*, or consumer that eats other animals, can use only about 10 percent of the energy from a herbivore's body. Energy is lost at each level in the food chain. Because of this loss of energy, most food chains have no more than five levels. The number of organisms generally decreases from one level to the next.

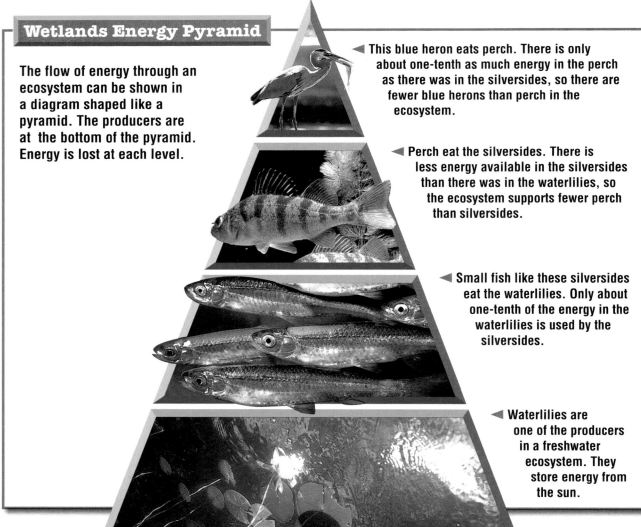

Wetlands Energy Pyramid

The flow of energy through an ecosystem can be shown in a diagram shaped like a pyramid. The producers are at the bottom of the pyramid. Energy is lost at each level.

◀ This blue heron eats perch. There is only about one-tenth as much energy in the perch as there was in the silversides, so there are fewer blue herons than perch in the ecosystem.

◀ Perch eat the silversides. There is less energy available in the silversides than there was in the waterlilies, so the ecosystem supports fewer perch than silversides.

◀ Small fish like these silversides eat the waterlilies. Only about one-tenth of the energy in the waterlilies is used by the silversides.

◀ Waterlilies are one of the producers in a freshwater ecosystem. They store energy from the sun.

For example, there are far fewer fish than there are krill and far fewer penguins than there are fish.

An energy pyramid is one way to show how energy is used in an ecosystem. Each level of the pyramid has only about one-tenth as much energy as the level below.

✓ **What happens to energy as it passes through a food chain?**

Summary

All organisms need energy. Producers get energy from the sun. Consumers get energy from producers or from other consumers. Decomposers get energy from the wastes or remains of other organisms. Some consumers are predators. They hunt prey, or other live animals.

The movement of energy from organism to organism can be shown in a food chain. A food web shows the overlapping food chains in an ecosystem. It shows more clearly how energy moves. Some energy is lost each time energy passes from one organism to another. The energy pyramid shows how energy is lost at each level of the food chain.

Review

1. What is the difference between a producer and a consumer?
2. What kind of organism always comes first in a food chain?
3. What is a scavenger?
4. **Critical Thinking** Can a predator be prey? Explain.
5. **Test Prep** A barn owl is —
   A both producer and predator
   B both producer and prey
   C both consumer and predator
   D both consumer and prey

LINKS

MATH LINK

Vanishing Energy Only 10 percent of the energy at one level is passed on to the next level of an energy pyramid. In a pyramid with four levels, what percent of the energy on the bottom level reaches the top level? Convert the percent to a decimal and a fraction.

WRITING LINK

Persuasive Writing—Opinion Write a magazine editorial to persuade readers to eat mostly from the two lowest levels of an energy pyramid. That is, persuade them to eat mostly producers or herbivores.

SOCIAL STUDIES LINK

American Bison Find out what happened to the American bison in the 1700s and 1800s. What predator caused the bison population to drop? How has the population been protected? Make a graph to show the changes in the American bison population over the past 200 years.

TECHNOLOGY LINK

Learn more about relationships of organisms in ecosystems by visiting this Internet Site.
www.scilinks.org/harcourt

LESSON 2

What Is Symbiosis?

In this lesson, you can . . .

INVESTIGATE hydras.

LEARN ABOUT three kinds of relationships between living things of different species.

LINK to math, writing, health, and technology.

INVESTIGATE

Hydras

Activity Purpose   You've seen that some organisms in an ecosystem use other organisms for food. There are other kinds of relationships between some organisms. In this activity you'll investigate an animal that has food-making algae in its body.

Materials

- Microslide Viewer
- Microslides of hydras

Activity Procedure

1. Set up your Microslide Viewer, and place the Microslide of the hydra on the viewer platform.

2. Carefully **observe** the hydra. Draw a picture of what you see. Include all the important details, such as colors or body parts you might see.

3. Now **observe** the Microslide showing the hydra and *Daphnia*. Draw a picture of this interaction. (Picture A)

4. **Observe** the Microslide of the hydra and the worm. Draw a picture of what you see.

◀ A rhinoceros and oxpeckers form an unlikely partnership. The birds feed on ticks on the rhino's skin. As the oxpeckers get food, the rhino gets rid of pests.

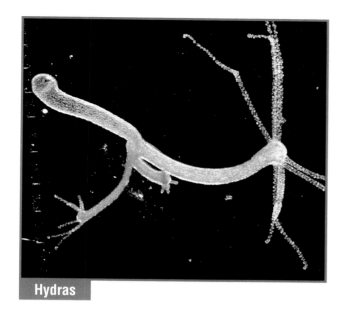

Hydras

Picture A

Draw Conclusions

1. What did you **infer** the interaction was between the hydra and *Daphnia*? Explain your answer. Is the hydra a producer or a consumer?

2. The green objects you saw in the hydra are green algae that carry out photosynthesis. What did you **observe** about the algae? What is their habitat?

3. **Scientists at Work** Scientists make drawings and collect other information to **record data** about living things and processes. From their data, they can **make inferences**. Think of what you know about photosynthesis and what you **observed** and recorded in your drawings. What can you infer about what a hydra might get from the algae? What might the algae get from a hydra? What can you infer about the habitat of a hydra?

Investigate Further Use a microscope to look for hydras and *Daphnia* in a drop of pond water. See page R5 for help in using a microscope.

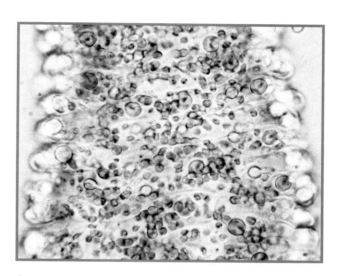

▲ Closeup of hydra showing algae.

Process Skill Tip

You **record data** when you collect numbers, write a description, or draw a picture. Anything you do to help **communicate** your **observations** to another person is a way of recording data.

Symbiosis

Three Types of Close Relationships

FIND OUT

- what symbiosis is
- what the three kinds of symbiosis are
- how organisms are helped or harmed in symbiotic relationships

VOCABULARY

symbiosis
parasitism
mutualism
commensalism

Millions of species live together in the Earth's ecosystems. Some organisms are producers, and some are consumers. Some are predators, and some are prey. The feeding relationships you have read about are not the only relationships between organisms of different species. Many organisms, such as the hydras and the algae you investigated, live in a close association called **symbiosis** (sim•by•OH•sis). Symbiosis means "living together." It is a relationship between two organisms of different species that benefits one or both of the organisms.

If you have a pet dog, you're part of a symbiotic relationship. You provide your pet with food and shelter, and your pet provides you with companionship. Two organisms of different species benefit from the relationship.

There are three kinds of symbiosis. In one kind of symbiosis, one organism benefits while the other is harmed. In a second kind, both organisms benefit. In a third kind, one organism benefits while the other is neither helped nor harmed.

✔ **Which kind of symbiosis is the relationship between a human and a pet dog?**

Symbiosis

Parasitism	Mutualism	Commensalism

▲ Head lice are insects whose habitat is human hair. They feed on blood from the scalp. The head lice benefit, but they harm the human.

▲ This hermit crab carries a sea anemone on its shell. The anemone's stinging cells protect the crab from predators. The anemone gets carried to new feeding areas. Both organisms benefit.

▲ Birds build their nests in trees for protection against predators. The birds benefit, and the tree is neither helped nor harmed.

◄ Mistletoe is a parasitic plant that grows on trees. Its roots take sap from the trees.

These are larvae of the *Trichinella* roundworm. These parasites burrow into the muscles of animals, including humans, causing great pain. ►

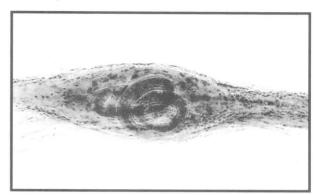

Parasitism

When one organism in a symbiotic relationship benefits and the other organism is harmed, the relationship is called **parasitism**. In a parasitic relationship, only the parasite benefits. The other organism, the host, is harmed by the relationship. In many ways, parasitism is like a predator-prey relationship. However, parasites generally live in or on an organism that is much larger than they are, and they usually don't kill their host.

Some parasites live on the outer surface of their hosts. Ticks and fleas are parasites that live in a host animal's fur. They bite the animal's skin and drink its blood. They move from one host to another by jumping or crawling. Sometimes ticks carry a disease, such as Rocky Mountain spotted fever or Lyme disease.

Some parasites, such as tapeworms, live inside their hosts' bodies. Tapeworms are flatworms that have adapted to being parasites. They absorb food directly through their body walls. They live in the intestines of many vertebrates, where they attach themselves with hooks and suckers on their heads.

Tapeworms can harm a host. They use the host's food and water, they produce waste, and they may block the host's digestive system. In some parts of the world, it is common for people to have tapeworms. In the United States, however, meat-processing laws have made tapeworms and other parasitic worms rare in humans.

Some parasites have plant hosts. Red spider mites are ticklike animals that infest house plants. They suck out of the plants the sugars that the plants produce. Red spider mites and organisms like them are common plant parasites. They infest many crop plants and sometimes kill them. But by the time the parasites kill a host plant, they have reproduced and infested other plants.

✔ **What are parasites?**

Tapeworms can reach lengths of 6 m (about 20 ft). But those that are most dangerous to people are only about 1 cm (less than half an inch) long. ▼

Mutualism

Not all symbiotic relationships result in harm. **Mutualism** is a symbiotic relationship that benefits both organisms involved. One well-known example of mutualism is the relationship between flowers and bees. Flowers provide bees with nectar for food, and bees pollinate flowers.

In many examples of mutualism, microscopic organisms live within larger organisms. Many herbivores, such as cows, sheep, deer, horses, and rabbits, depend on bacteria and protists that live in their stomachs or intestines. These microorganisms break down cellulose, the material in the cell walls of plants. The herbivores can then digest the plant material efficiently. In turn, the bacteria and the protists get a habitat and food from the herbivores.

Plants called legumes, such as peas and peanuts, and nitrogen-fixing bacteria also live together in a mutualistic relationship. The bacteria live in cells in the roots of legumes. They convert nitrogen into a form that plants can use.

Lichens, which grow on trees, rocks, and bare soil, look like small plants. But they are made up of two organisms: a fungus and an alga or bacterium. The two organisms help each other grow in places where neither could grow alone. The alga gets water and nutrients from the fungus. The fungus gets food from the alga.

Mutualistic relationships between animals are easier to see. The snapping shrimp is almost

▲ Corals are animals that have algae in their tissues. The corals provide protection for the algae. The algae provide food for the corals. This mutualistic pair needs the sunlight and warm water found near the surface of tropical seas.

blind. It lives with a goby fish, which alerts it to danger. The goby, in turn, shares the burrow the shrimp builds on the sea floor. Other kinds of small fish and shrimp eat algae and parasites from the scales and gills of larger fish. The "cleaners" could be prey for the larger fish, but they are not harmed.

Cleaning relationships exist on land as well, where the cleaners are usually birds. The Egyptian plover picks insect pests from the skin of animals such as giraffes and buffaloes. The plover will even enter a crocodile's mouth to eat parasites that are there.

✓ **How does mutualism differ from parasitism?**

The ratel (RAY•tuhl), or honey badger, likes honey but is not very good at finding beehives. The honeyguide bird leads the honey badger to a beehive. The badger tears open the hive with its paws. Both the badger and the honeyguide get food. ▶

◀ The honeyguide's diet includes beeswax and bee larvae. The bird finds beehives easily, but is too small to break them open.

Mutualism—The Acacia and the Ants

Plant-eating insects can harm plants and even kill them. However, not all relationships between plants and insects are harmful to the plants. The ants that live on bull's-horn acacia trees in Central America have a mutualistic relationship with the trees. The trees provide the ants with food and shelter, and the ants protect the trees from many other organisms.

Ants live inside the large, hollow thorns of the acacia. In this picture you can see the small hole through which the ants enter the thorn.

Acacia leaves contain small structures filled with proteins and oils. The ants eat the proteins and oils and feed them to their larvae. The ants also eat the nectar that these round, green organs produce at the bases of the leaves.

The ants chew the stems of vines and other plants that might grow over the acacia or compete with it for soil resources. The ants clear the area around the acacia. As a result, the acacia tree grows faster and taller than the plants around it. The ants also attack and kill any leaf-eating insects that they find on the tree. If a large animal rubs against the tree, the ants swarm onto the animal. They drive it away by biting it.

▲ Orchids grow high in tall trees in tropical forests. Through their roots they take in water and nutrients from decaying tree limbs and rainwater. They do not harm the trees, but the trees help them get water, sunlight, and nutrients.

Commensalism

Some organisms depend on other living things that they neither help nor harm. **Commensalism** is a symbiotic relationship that benefits one organism and doesn't harm or help the other organism. One example is the relationship of the egret, an insect-eating bird, and large herbivores such as cattle and horses. Egrets hunt for insects near a grazing animal's mouth. They eat the insects that escape from the plants the herbivore is eating. By feeding near the large grazers, the egrets have a better food supply than they might find elsewhere. The egrets neither help nor harm the grazing animals.

In many commensal relationships, one organism uses the other as a means of transportation. Barnacles are shelled organisms. They are filter feeders. That is, they feed on tiny organisms they take from the water. Barnacles produce a cement that helps them stick to objects such as piers and rocks. But they also attach themselves to whales. The whales take the barnacles to new food supplies and enable them to release their eggs over a large area. The barnacles do not seem to affect the whales at all.

Some kinds of fish live among the tentacles of sea anemones. Anemones and some kinds of fish also have a commensal relationship. Anemones use their tentacles to sting their prey. Fish like the clown fish, however, aren't harmed by the anemone's sting. They live among the tentacles, which protect them from predators. The fish don't seem to harm or help the anemone.

You can even find commensalism on yourself. Millions of bacteria live on your skin, where dead cells give them shelter and food. Because this doesn't help you or harm you, you and the bacteria are partners in commensalism.

✔ **What is a commensal relationship?**

Summary

Organisms of different species sometimes live in symbiosis, a close relationship with each other. Parasitism is a symbiosis in which one organism benefits and the other is harmed. Mutualism benefits both organisms. Commensalism benefits one of the organisms in the relationship, while the other is neither helped nor harmed.

Review

1. Give an example of parasitism.
2. What is mutualism?
3. How does commensalism differ from parasitism?
4. **Critical Thinking** Why is it important to a parasite not to kill the host?
5. **Test Prep** In the symbiosis between a virus and a human, the human is —

   A the host   **C** prey
   B the parasite   **D** commensal

Remoras are jawless fish that attach themselves to larger organisms, such as sharks, turtles, and even whales. Remoras benefit by being carried to new locations and sharing leftover food. They do not harm their carriers. ▼

LINKS

MATH LINK

Millions of Relationships One scientist has estimated that there are about 4 million bacteria on each square centimeter of a person's skin. How many bacteria might there be on your hand? Figure out a way to estimate the area of the skin on your hand. Then calculate the approximate number of bacteria there. (**Hint:** You might try tracing your hand on a piece of graph paper.)

WRITING LINK

Expressive Writing—Poem Mutualism exists in all sorts of situations: between gardeners and their gardens, between shepherds and their sheep, even between cats and their human owners. Write a poem for your classmates about a situation that involves mutualism.

HEALTH LINK

Bacteria and You You have a mutualistic relationship with a bacterium, *Escherichia coli*, which lives in your digestive system. Find out and report on how you benefit from this relationship.

TECHNOLOGY LINK

To find out more about symbiotic relationships, watch *Blueberry Bees* on the **Harcourt Science Newsroom Video.**

BIOLOGICAL Control of Pests

Scientists are finding ways to get rid of insect pests without using toxic chemicals.

Why do we need to control insect pests?

Moths, aphids, mealybugs, and leafhoppers are just a few of the thousands of pests that attack food crops. Each year they damage crops all over the world, resulting in a loss of huge amounts of food. Farmers use pesticides to try to control these insects and save their crops.

What kinds of problems can result from improper use of pesticides?

The substances in many pesticides are harmful to the environment. Pesticides can pollute soil as well as ground and surface waters. The

Cabbage worms

Cabbage worm wasp

chemicals they contain can sicken or kill animals, plants, and people. For example, the pesticide DDT was considered perfectly safe at first. But as scientists continued to study its effects on the environment, they found evidence that it harmed the environment and perhaps even contributed to causing some cancers in humans. It is now illegal to use DDT in the United States.

How is biological pest control different?

Biological pest control kills pests without the use of toxic chemicals. Methods of biological pest control include introducing a carefully chosen parasite, predator, or disease—one that kills a pest without harming other organisms—into the pest population. One method involves using a type of roundworm to kill corn earworms. The roundworms carry a type of bacteria that infects the earworms in their early stages of development. The corn earworm larvae die within 48 hours, so they are unable to reproduce.

Plants can help in biological pest control, too. Cabbage worms are common pests in cabbage fields. Planting buckwheat next to cabbage fields can help get rid of the worms. The buckwheat flowers produce nectar that is food for tiny wasps. The wasps lay eggs in the cabbage worms. As the wasp eggs mature, they destroy the worms. This cuts down on the number of worms that can damage the cabbage.

Why is biological pest control good for the environment?

Biological pest control was developed to kill insect pests without using toxic chemicals. It prevents the pollution of the soil, the water supply, and the air in and around gardens and farm fields. It also saves plants and animals that are not pests from being harmed by pesticides.

THINK ABOUT IT

1. What is biological pest control?
2. Why is biological pest control an improvement over the use of chemical pesticides?

WEB LINK:
For Science and Technology updates, visit The Learning Site.
www.harcourtschool.com

Careers | Companion Dog Trainer

What They Do
Companion dog trainers teach dogs to obey commands and perform tasks for people who need assistance. Trainers are often responsible for care and feeding of animals as well.

Education and Training Companion dog trainers should have some background in biology. They should enjoy being around and working with animals. Dog trainers should have a high school education. Many gain experience by working with other more experienced trainers.

Verma Miera

WILDLIFE BIOLOGIST

"I get an early start . . . surveying frogs, measuring water quality and other habitat variables, and generally mucking around in some nasty places. . . . Other times, I get to hike in some of the most beautiful places I've ever seen."

Frogs are often pictured sitting on lily pads in watery environments. But Verma Miera studies frogs by "mucking around" in the Arizona desert. Her job is to help solve a mystery: Why are the populations of Arizona's native frog species decreasing? Ms. Miera says that finding out what's killing the frogs could help save them. The work is important because no one knows how the elimination of Arizona's native frog species could affect other parts of the desert ecosystem. And whatever is wiping out frogs in some areas could be dangerous for other species as well.

Verma Miera has been interested in environmental issues all of her life. She graduated from the University of Arizona with a degree in ecology. Then she immediately began working in the desert, trapping frogs, snakes, and lizards for a researcher. This field experience prepared her for her present job as a

wildlife biologist with the Arizona Department of Game and Fish.

Ms. Miera puts in long days in the field. She catches frogs in one place and releases them in others to form new populations or increase shrinking ones. "We have been generally encouraged by our results and have learned quite a lot," she says. She and her colleagues have learned that the introduction of nonnative species such as bullfrogs, crayfish, and certain fish has made it harder for native frogs to thrive. Ms. Miera hopes to reduce or eliminate the introduction of these nonnative species.

THINK ABOUT IT

1. How does Verma Miera hope to improve the environment for native frogs?
2. Why is it important to find out why the number of Arizona's native frogs is decreasing?

Native Arizona leopard frog

Producing Food

Where is energy stored in plants?

Materials

- green leaf
- small jar of rubbing alcohol with a lid
- paper towel
- saucer
- bottle of iodine

Procedure

1. Put the leaf in the jar of rubbing alcohol, close the lid, and let it sit for one day. The alcohol will remove some of the leaf's chlorophyll, making it easier to see food (starch) in the leaf. **CAUTION** Be very careful handling the alcohol. It is poisonous and catches fire easily.

2. Take the leaf out of the jar, and blot it dry with the paper towel.

3. Put the leaf in the saucer, and carefully cover the leaf with iodine. The iodine will turn starchy areas purple or black. **CAUTION** Wash your hands carefully after using the iodine. Too much iodine is poisonous.

Draw Conclusions

How much of the leaf contained food in the form of starch? What other parts of plants do you think would have more food? How could you find out?

Examining Symbiosis

How can organisms from two different kingdoms work together?

Materials

- lichen (Look for pale green patches of lichen on the north side of trees.)
- water
- hand lens
- bright light, such as a desk lamp
- sewing needles

Procedure

1. Moisten the lichen with water. Notice which parts of the organism soak up the water. Lichen is a combination of cyanobacteria from the kingdom Monera and a fungus from the kingdom Fungi.

2. Use the hand lens to examine a piece of lichen under the light.

3. Use the needles to try to separate the cyanobacteria from the colorless fungus.

4. Look for the tiny, pale rootlike structures that attach the fungus to the tree bark.

Draw Conclusions

Cyanobacteria contain chlorophyll, so they can produce food. How could this help the fungus? Cyanobacteria must have water to survive. How does the fungus help? What kind of symbiosis is this?

Chapter 2 Review and Test Preparation

Vocabulary Review

Use the terms below to complete the sentences. The page numbers in ( ) tell you where to look in the chapter if you need help.

producers (C38)   **scavengers** (C39)
consumers (C38)   **symbiosis** (C46)
decomposers (C38)   **parasitism** (C47)
predator (C39)   **mutualism** (C48)
prey (C39)   **commensalism** (C50)

1. Plants and algae that make food are called ____.

2. The organism eaten by a predator is called ____.

3. ____ is a symbiotic relationship in which both organisms benefit.

4. A symbiotic relationship in which one organism is harmed and the other benefits is called ____.

5. Organisms that eat other organisms are called ____.

6. A consumer that eats other living animals is called a ____.

7. In the symbiotic relationship called ____, one organism benefits and the other neither benefits nor is harmed.

8. ____ is a close association between members of two different species living together.

9. Organisms that get their food by breaking down the wastes and remains of other organisms are called ____.

10. Animals that eat the remains of another animal are called ____.

Connect Concepts

Choose items from the word bank to provide examples for each category. Most of the items are pairs of organisms. Use each item only once.

rhinoceros—oxpecker   **tree—orchids**   **lichens**
honeyguide—badger   **shark—remora**   **dog—tick**
clownfish—sea anemone   **human—tapeworm**

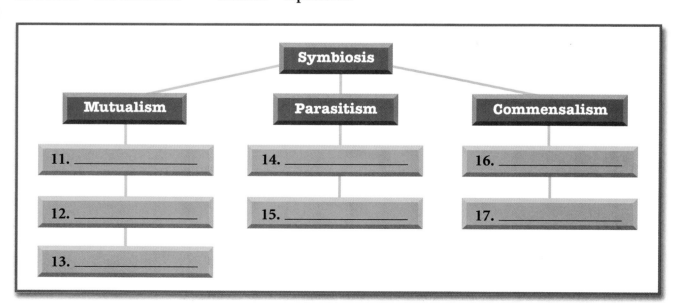

Symbiosis

Mutualism
11. _____
12. _____
13. _____

Parasitism
14. _____
15. _____

Commensalism
16. _____
17. _____

Check Understanding

Write the letter of the best choice.

18. Most energy in an ecosystem is found in —

A consumers C prey

B predators D producers

19. Bull's-horn acacia trees and the ants that protect them are an example of —

F parasitism

G commensalism

H predators and prey

J mutualism

20. In the Antarctic Ocean ecosystem there are fewer krill than —

A algae C fish

B seals D whales

21. ____ means "together living."

F Commensalism

G Mutualism

H Parasitism

J Symbiosis

22. Going from producers to consumers in an energy pyramid, —

A the number of individuals at each level decreases

B the number of individuals at each level increases

C the energy in each level increases

D the number of individuals in each level increases as the energy decreases.

23. When the number of prey in an ecosystem increases, their predators —

F capture fewer prey

G increase in number

H decrease in number

J remain the same

Critical Thinking

24. Some fish live in the tentacles of sea anemones. They show a commensal relationship, with anemones providing protection for the fish. If it were discovered that the fish protect the anemones, what kind of symbiosis would these organisms show?

25. How are parasites different from predators? Use the tapeworm and the barn owl as examples in your answer.

Process Skills Review

26. Based on your **observations** of what is in barn owl pellets, what can you **infer** about what barn owls eat?

27. You **observed** algae in some cells of *Hydra*. What **hypothesis** can you test about the role of the algae?

28. Think of two organisms that have a symbiotic relationship. Write an article for *Science* magazine to **communicate** how this relationship works.

Performance Assessment

Energy Users

Make an energy pyramid that includes examples of producers and consumers. Label the levels of your pyramid. You may wish to draw or cut out pictures to include in your pyramid.

Chapter 3

Earth's Oceans

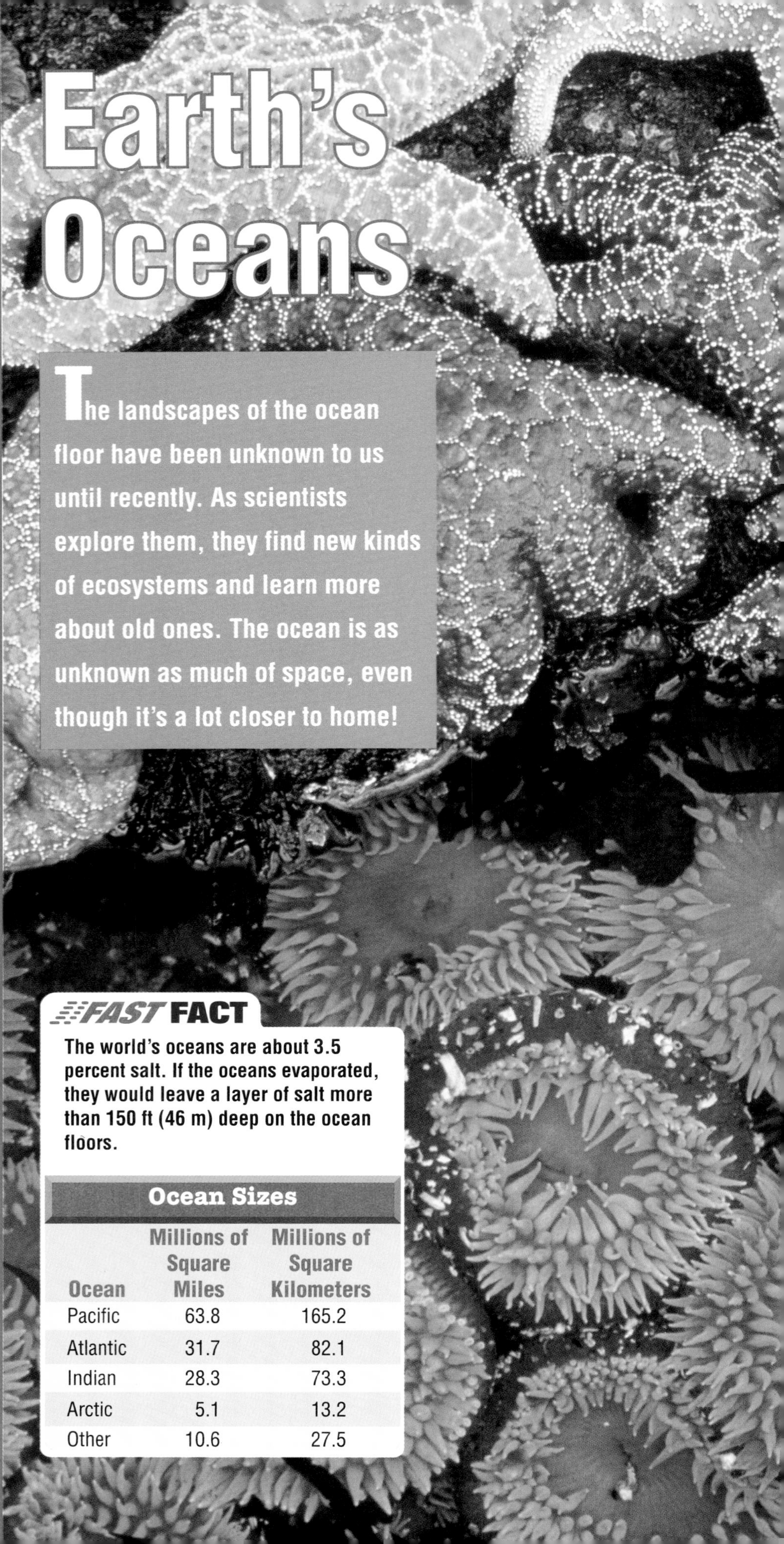

The landscapes of the ocean floor have been unknown to us until recently. As scientists explore them, they find new kinds of ecosystems and learn more about old ones. The ocean is as unknown as much of space, even though it's a lot closer to home!

Vocabulary Preview

continental shelf
continental slope
abyssal plain
mid-ocean ridge
trench
seamount
atoll
intertidal zone
coral reef
estuary

FAST FACT

The world's oceans are about 3.5 percent salt. If the oceans evaporated, they would leave a layer of salt more than 150 ft (46 m) deep on the ocean floors.

Ocean Sizes

Ocean	Millions of Square Miles	Millions of Square Kilometers
Pacific	63.8	165.2
Atlantic	31.7	82.1
Indian	28.3	73.3
Arctic	5.1	13.2
Other	10.6	27.5

LESSON 1

What Are the Characteristics of the Ocean Floor?

In this lesson, you can . . .

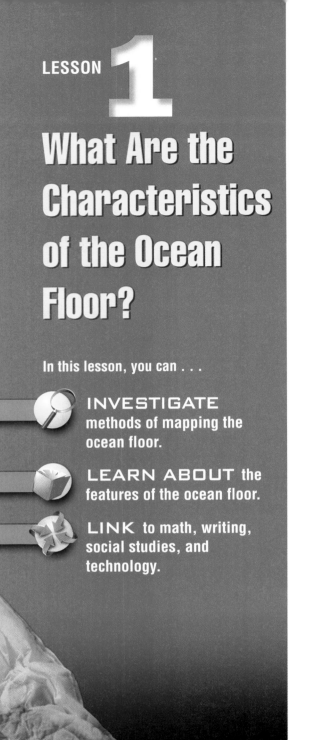

INVESTIGATE methods of mapping the ocean floor.

LEARN ABOUT the features of the ocean floor.

LINK to math, writing, social studies, and technology.

Mapping the Ocean Floor

Activity Purpose When you run your fingers over some world globes, the oceans feel smooth compared with the jagged mountains. That's because you're feeling only the surface. Below the surface of the oceans are Earth's most dramatic features. There are gigantic volcanoes and amazingly deep canyons. Scientists have revealed these features by mapping the depth of the ocean floor. In this activity you'll explore a method of **measuring** ocean depth.

Materials

- scissors
- poster board
- shoe box with lid
- tape
- chopstick or straw
- centimeter ruler
- centimeter graph paper

Activity Procedure

1. Cut a strip of poster board about $1\frac{1}{2}$ times as long as the shoe box but just wide enough to fit into it. Fold the strip to **make a model** of an ocean floor. It can show mountains, plains, slopes, and canyons. Trim your model so that it fits exactly into the shoe box. Tape the ends in place. (Picture A)

2. Cut a slit about 0.5 cm wide along the length of the lid. Then tape the lid to the box.

◄ Many strange-looking animals, including this gulper eel, live in the deepest parts of the ocean.

Picture A

Picture B

3 Trade models with another group. Do not open the lid on the model you get.

4 Plan a way to use the chopstick and the ruler to **measure** the depth of the ocean floor at different places in the model. **Collect the data** you need to make a cross section. On the graph paper, draw a cross section that shows the shape of the ocean floor as it would look from the side. (Picture B)

5 Now open the lid of the box, and compare your drawing to the actual model.

Draw Conclusions

1. How did you use the materials to **measure** the depth of the ocean floor in the model?

2. How did you use the data you collected to draw the side view of the ocean floor in the model? What scale did you use?

3. **Scientists at Work** Scientists sometimes **use models** to get data about things that are hard to **observe** directly. They also use models to develop methods for **gathering data** in real situations. For which purpose did you use a model in this activity?

Investigate Further Suppose you wanted to map the bottom of a lake. Describe a way for doing this that uses simple equipment and a small boat. What steps would you take?

Process Skill Tip

You can **use a model** to help you develop methods for collecting data. First, find out what works well on the model. Then, adapt your method to work in the real situation.

Features of the Ocean Floor

The Bottom of the Ocean

FIND OUT

- the features of the ocean floor
- how some features of the ocean floor become visible above the ocean's surface

VOCABULARY

continental shelf
continental slope
abyssal plain
mid-ocean ridge
trench
seamount
atoll

As you walk from the beach into the ocean, the water gradually gets deeper and deeper. Does the ocean floor slope slowly down to the middle of the ocean? Does it stay sandy and smooth, or does the ocean floor have features similar to those found on land?

To answer some of these questions, scientists set sail on the British ship H.M.S. *Challenger* in 1872. The ship went around the world on a voyage that lasted three and a half years and covered 110,000 km (about 68,000 mi). The scientists made the first major study of the world's oceans. Among other activities, they mapped the depth of areas of ocean floor. As you did in the investigation, these explorers used a measuring tool that touched the ocean floor. They lowered a

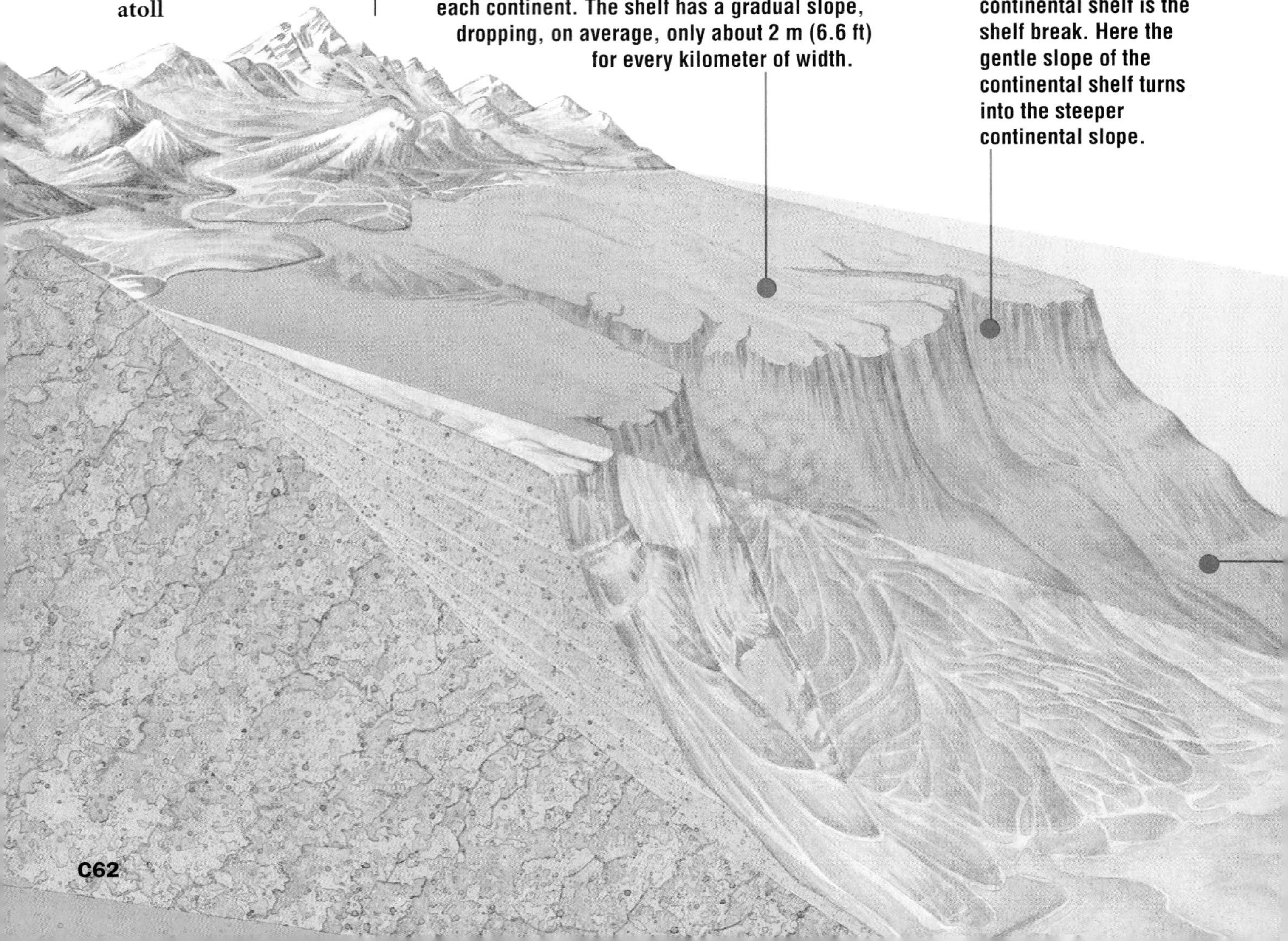

Like the brim of a hat, a continental shelf rings each continent. The shelf has a gradual slope, dropping, on average, only about 2 m (6.6 ft) for every kilometer of width.

At the edge of the continental shelf is the shelf break. Here the gentle slope of the continental shelf turns into the steeper continental slope.

weighted rope from the ship. When the rope hung loosely, the scientists knew the weight had reached the bottom.

Starting in the 1920s, a new invention allowed more accurate measurements of the depth of the ocean. Scientists began mapping the ocean floor by using an echo sounder. Today the machine that does echo sounding is called *sonar*. It works by sending sound waves toward the ocean bottom and finding how long they take to bounce back up to the surface. Scientists know how fast sound travels through seawater. They use this information to calculate how far the sound waves travel, from the ship to the ocean floor and back again. Half of that distance is the depth of the ocean floor.

Using sonar, scientists have found that around each continent is a gently sloping **continental shelf**. When you walk into the water at an ocean beach, you walk onto the continental shelf. Where the coastline is mountainous, the shelf is narrow. It may extend into the ocean as little as 30 km (about 19 mi). Where the land slopes gently to the water, the shelf is usually wider. It may extend as much as 1100 km (about 680 mi) into the ocean.

Continental shelves are the shallowest parts of the ocean. Their greatest depth is 140 m (about 460 ft). Because they are shallow, they have the greatest variety of ocean, or marine, life. Most undersea life needs sunlight, which can't reach the ocean bottom in deeper waters.

The continental shelf ends at the shelf break. This is the point at which the continental shelf becomes the **continental slope**. The slope of the ocean floor suddenly becomes much steeper. The continental slope goes down from the shelf break all the way to the deep-ocean floor. This is a drop of as much as 4 to 5 km (about 2.5 to 3 mi). In some places, steep-sided canyons cut into the continental slope. They stretch for lengths of up to 100 km (about 62 mi) and have walls as high as 2300 m (about 7500 ft). These underwater canyons are as spectacular as canyons on land.

At the end of the continental slope, the ocean floor gradually flattens out into the **abyssal plain** (uh•BIS•uhl PLAYN), the vast floor of the deep oceans. The abyssal plain covers almost one-half of Earth's surface. It lies under a layer of sediment 500 to 1000 m (about 1600 to 3300 ft) thick. The sediment has made the abyssal plain the flattest place on Earth. But on this flat plain are some deep trenches and underwater mountains.

✔ **Name three regions of the ocean floor.**

The continental slope is the edge of a continent. The ocean floor here drops, on average, about 70 m (230 ft) for every kilometer of width. In some places, however, the slope is very steep. Underwater landslides often carry sediments down the slope to the abyssal plain below.

Thousands of meters below sea level lies the abyssal plain. It is covered with a thick layer of sediments carried by currents. The remains of marine plants and animals drift down from the waters above and settle on the abyssal plain.

The Shape of the Ocean Floor

If you could drain the world's oceans, you would uncover Earth's highest mountains and deepest canyons. The map at the right shows the topography, or rise and fall, of most of the ocean floor.

Along the middle of the ocean floor are **mid-ocean ridges**. Here the plates of the Earth's crust are being split apart. Molten rock pushed up from below forms new ocean floor and a vast mountain range. The mountains stretch through the Atlantic, Pacific, and Indian Oceans. They rise about 2500 to 3000 m (8000 to 10,000 ft) above the ocean floor. As you can see on the map, the mid-ocean ridges extend for great distances on both sides of each split in the crust.

As the rocky plates of Earth's crust move apart at the mid-ocean ridges, they push into other plates. Where two plates hit each other, deep-ocean **trenches** form. These trenches are the deepest parts of the ocean. Some of them plunge more than 10,000 m (about 33,000 ft) below the surface.

At other parts of the ocean floor, steep-sided volcanic mountains called **seamounts** rise hundreds or even thousands of meters above the abyssal plain. Researchers have drilled through the sediments on these underwater peaks. Underneath they have found volcanic rock. This helps to show that seamounts formed from molten rock bubbling up through the ocean floor.

Most seamounts remain under water, but as molten rock continues to build them up, some rise above the water's surface. The peaks become islands. Seamounts that have become islands are found mainly in the Pacific Ocean.

✔ **At what part of the ocean is new ocean floor being formed?**

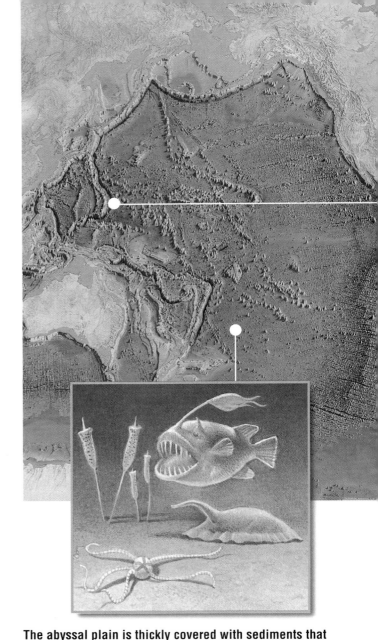

The abyssal plain is thickly covered with sediments that have built up over millions of years. These sediments are mostly clay but include silt, sand, and rock that have been washed into the ocean. They also contain the remains of billions of sea creatures, large and small, that have lived and died during that time.

Seamounts rise above the abyssal plain. These volcanoes are common along *fracture zones*, areas of deep cracks in the rocks of the ocean floor. ▶

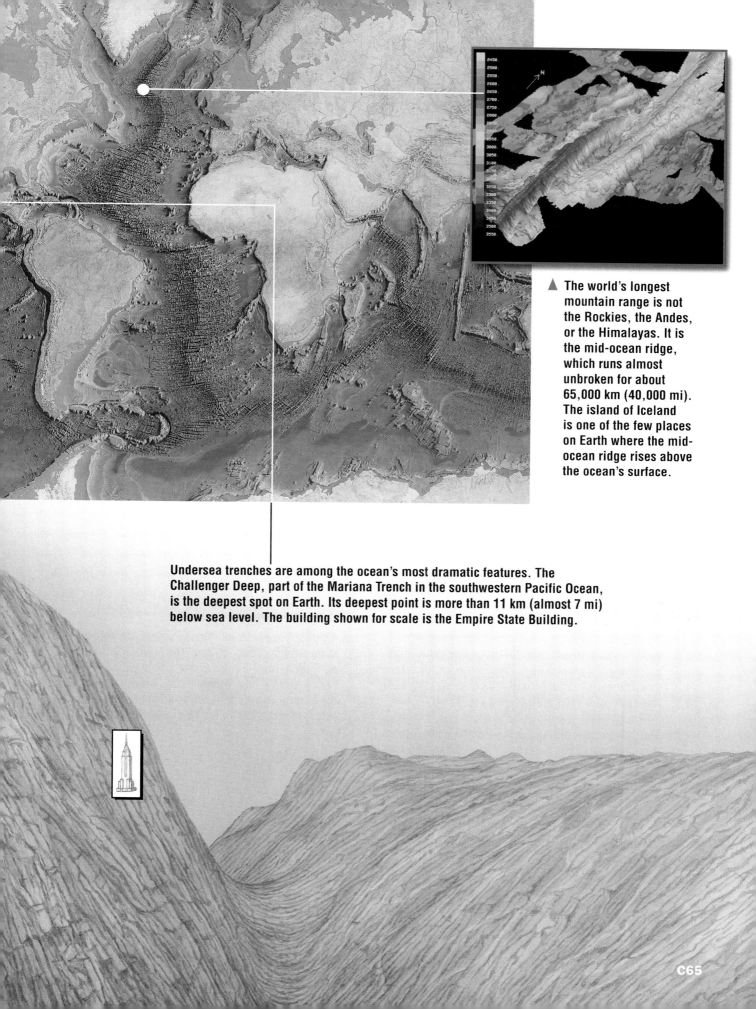

▲ The world's longest mountain range is not the Rockies, the Andes, or the Himalayas. It is the mid-ocean ridge, which runs almost unbroken for about 65,000 km (40,000 mi). The island of Iceland is one of the few places on Earth where the mid-ocean ridge rises above the ocean's surface.

Undersea trenches are among the ocean's most dramatic features. The Challenger Deep, part of the Mariana Trench in the southwestern Pacific Ocean, is the deepest spot on Earth. Its deepest point is more than 11 km (almost 7 mi) below sea level. The building shown for scale is the Empire State Building.

Islands and Atolls

It may seem as though Earth hasn't changed much for thousands or even millions of years. The names of countries on a map may change, but the land itself doesn't. Or does it? In 1963 a brand-new island named Surtsey appeared in the northern Atlantic Ocean near Iceland. Molten rock breaking through the ocean floor at the mid-ocean ridge formed a volcano. It finally grew large enough to rise above the surface of the ocean. Within months of Surtsey's birth, plants and sea birds started living on the rocky island.

Volcanoes also form near deep-ocean trenches, where one plate slides under another. When the descending plate reaches a depth of about 100 km (62 mi), some of the material begins to melt. The molten rock rises and may break through the ocean floor, forming a volcano. If this continues for long enough, the volcano becomes an island.

Undersea volcanoes formed the Hawaiian Islands. These volcanoes formed in the middle of one of Earth's plates, not near a place where two plates meet. The most recent Hawaiian volcanoes are still active. They make up the larger islands to the southeast. The older Hawaiian islands, to the northwest, are smaller. Their volcanoes are no longer active, and they are slowly eroding back into the Pacific.

The Formation of an Atoll

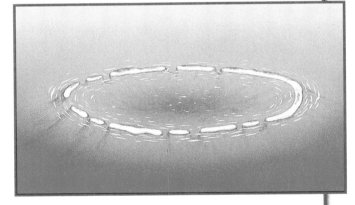

▲ An undersea volcano rises above the ocean's surface. As it develops, millions of tiny coral animals grow around its slopes in the sunlit waters near the surface. Over thousands of years, the hard skeletons of these corals form a stony reef.

▲ After thousands or millions of years, the volcano is no longer active. Without the magma pushing up from below, the volcano wears down and slowly sinks. If the volcano sinks slowly enough, the coral reef around it can continue to grow. The reef forms islands on which plants can grow.

▼ Atolls are most common in the South Pacific ocean. In this photograph you can see an atoll where the coral has grown into a chain of islands around a calm lagoon.

Another type of island grouping is an atoll (A•tawl). An **atoll** is a ring of islands around a shallow central lagoon. In the middle of the nineteenth century, Charles Darwin suggested that atolls began as coral reefs around volcanic islands. The crust beneath the volcano sank over thousands or millions of years, but the coral reef kept growing. It became a ring of barrier islands around the original island, which gradually sank into the ocean. Most scientists today accept Darwin's theory of how atolls form.

✔ **How are the formation of Surtsey and the formation of an atoll similar? How are they different?**

Summary

The ocean floor begins at the edge of a continent, with a shallow continental shelf that leads to a much steeper continental slope. This slope can carry sediments down to the flat abyssal plain—the deep-ocean floor. Ocean features include mid-ocean ridges and volcanic seamounts, which are like mountains, and deep trenches, which are like enormous valleys. Underwater volcanoes can form islands in different ways.

Review

1. Why are continental shelves the areas of the ocean richest in marine life?

2. Why is the abyssal plain so flat?

3. Where do deep-ocean trenches occur?

4. **Critical Thinking** Why don't scientists bounce light, rather than sound, off the ocean floor to measure depth?

5. **Test Prep** An atoll is a ring of islands that forms because of the growth of a —

   A coral reef

   B trench

   C mid-ocean ridge

   D seamount

LINKS

MATH LINK

Speedy Sound Sound travels through seawater at about 1500 m per second. A research ship sends out a pulse that takes 4 seconds to travel to the ocean floor and back. How deep is the ocean at that point? How deep would it be if the pulse took only 1 second?

WRITING LINK

Informative Writing—Description What might it have been like to work on a research ship like the H.M.S. *Challenger* in 1872? Write diary entries for one week. Suppose that you have been measuring water depth along the abyssal plain and have come upon a mid-ocean ridge. Tell how your discovery will change people's ideas about the ocean floor.

SOCIAL STUDIES LINK

Which Is Taller? Mount Everest rises about 9.8 km above sea level. Hawai'i's Mauna Loa rises about 4 km above sea level, but it also extends almost 6 km below the ocean's surface. In your judgment, which mountain is taller? Give reasons to support your view.

TECHNOLOGY LINK

To find out more about how scientists study and map the ocean floor, watch *Ocean Floor* on the **Harcourt Science Newsroom Video**.

 Turner Le@rning

What Are Some Ocean Ecosystems?

In this lesson, you can . . .

INVESTIGATE two ocean ecosystems.

LEARN ABOUT the variety of life in the ocean's biological communities.

LINK to math, writing, social studies, and technology.

Comparing Ocean Ecosystems

Activity Purpose From the shallow, sunlit waters of the continental shelf to the dark and frigid depths of the abyssal plain, the ocean has many kinds of environments. Warm waters are filled with an amazing display of life. But organisms have also adapted to the harshest ocean environments. In this activity you'll **compare** two ocean ecosystems. You'll discover some of the ways in which living things interact beneath the waves.

Materials

■ ecosystem pictures (on page C69)

Activity Procedure

1 The pictures on page C69 show two ocean ecosystems and some of the organisms that are part of them. Study each picture. Pay special attention to the conditions in which the organisms live.

2 Make a chart like the one shown on page C69. In the first row, describe the environmental conditions in each ecosystem.

3 Now study the organisms in each picture to see how they are adapted to the conditions you noted in Step 2. For each organism, list the adaptations you **observe** that allow it to survive in its environment.

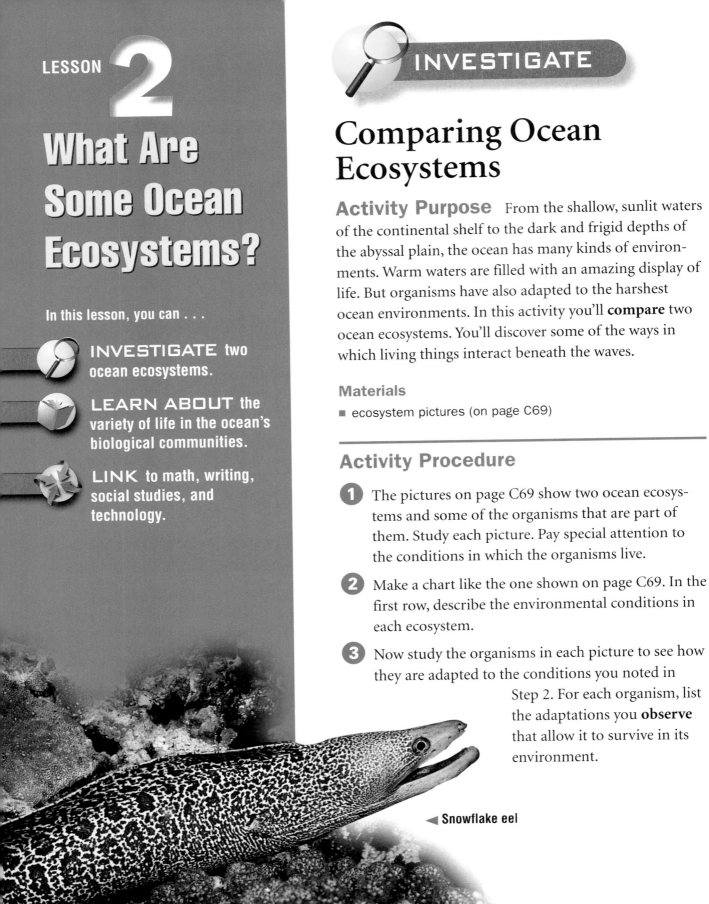

◀ **Snowflake eel**

Coral Reef Ecosystem

Comparing Ocean Environments		
	Coral Reef	Intertidal Zone
Environmental Conditions		
Organisms & Adaptations		

Intertidal Ecosystem

Draw Conclusions

1. How are the two ecosystems alike? How are they different?

2. How have the organisms adapted to their environments?

3. **Scientists at Work** Scientists **compare** organisms in an ecosystem to see how the organisms have adapted to the same environment. What similarities and differences did you notice in the way different organisms had adapted to the same environment?

Investigate Further Some of the organisms living on the abyssal plain make their own light. Find out how this light helps the animals survive.

Process Skill Tip

To **compare** organisms, **observe** and record how the organisms are alike and how they are different.

Life in the Oceans

Ocean Environments

FIND OUT

- the kinds of ecosystems in the ocean

- what environmental conditions help define each ocean ecosystem

VOCABULARY

intertidal zone

coral reef

estuary

Most of the organisms in the ocean live in shallow water near land. Ecosystems such as coral reefs and oyster banks can be found in these shallow waters. In the open ocean farther from land, large and very fast fish, such as sailfish, tuna, marlin, and swordfish, swim near the surface. Life in the deep waters includes fish that make their own light and communities of organisms around volcanic vents, or openings, on the ocean floor.

Like those on land, all ocean ecosystems rely on producers. The primary producers in the ocean are *phytoplankton* (FY•toh•plank•tuhn). Plankton are organisms, including plants, animals, and protists, that float freely on the ocean currents. Phytoplankton are microscopic plankton that make their own food by photosynthesis. They are protists, such as diatoms and other algae. By producing food, they support all ocean life, and the oxygen they give off during photosynthesis helps support life on land, too. Phytoplankton exist in huge numbers. A single gallon of seawater may contain more than a million diatoms.

Ocean environments are often classified by depth. As depth increases, there is less light. The water temperature drops, and water pressure increases. As the conditions change, so do the organisms that can survive in them.

✓ **How does the ocean environment change with depth?**

There are nearly 10,000 species of diatoms, single-celled protists with glassy, jewel-like shells. Diatoms are the most common floating algae in the oceans. They make their own food. ▶

◀ Algae are producers in the food webs of many ocean ecosystems.

The barracuda's niche is near the top of a food chain. The chain starts with microscopic phytoplankton such as diatoms.

The Photic Zone

The top layer of the oceans is called the *photic* (FOH•tik) *zone*. It is lit by sunlight, and it extends to about 200 m (650 ft) below the surface. This is as deep as light can reach in clear water. Ocean producers that use energy from sunlight live in the photic zone. So do most of the consumers that eat these producers. Because of this, most ocean life is found in the photic zone.

The Aphotic Zone

The water below 200 m is totally dark. It is called the *aphotic* (ay•FOH•tik) *zone*. Almost all life in this region depends on energy from the photic region above. Organisms that move between light and dark zones may get eaten in the aphotic zone, providing energy for animals that live there. Organisms in the aphotic zone also feed on dead plants and animals that drift down from above.

The Bathyal Zone

The aphotic zone can be divided into two parts—the *bathyal* (BATH•ee•uhl) *zone* and the *abyssal zone*. The bathyal zone extends from 200 to 2000 m (about 650 to 6500 ft), about the same depth as the continental slope.

The Abyssal Zone

Below 2000 m is the abyssal zone. Creatures in the abyssal zone must be able to live in complete darkness at a temperature of between 2°C and 4°C (about 36°F to 39°F). They also must be able to survive the crushing pressure of the tons of water above them. At 2000 m the pressure is 200 times the pressure at the surface.

Intertidal Ecosystems

In many places on Earth, the location of the shoreline at the edge of the ocean changes two to four times a day. The area between the high-tide mark and the low-tide mark is the **intertidal zone**. The intertidal zone is an environment that is always changing. At low tide, organisms in this zone may have to find shelter from the hot sun. Hours later, they must survive the rough water of incoming waves as the tide rises. They may then spend hours in an undersea world until the tide is low again.

Intertidal organisms handle the changes in their surroundings in different ways. Many of them, such as the sand dollar, bury themselves in the mud during low tide to stay moist and protected. Crabs hide under rocks and in other sheltered, moist spots when the tide goes out.

Mussels and barnacles close their shells tightly during low tide, trapping water inside. During high tide they open up to feed on plankton and other organic matter. Periwinkles, or small snails, which live at the upper edge of the intertidal zone, can seal their shells to rocks when conditions get too dry. They feed by scraping algae off the rocks.

Not all the water leaves the intertidal zone when the tide goes out. Tidal pools hold water even at low tide. The pools are habitats for sea anemones, sea urchins, and other organisms that would die if they dried out.

The intertidal zone is an important feeding ground for many birds, such as piping plovers and gulls. Humans also collect many kinds of seafood there at low tide.

✔ **How does the environment of the intertidal zone change?**

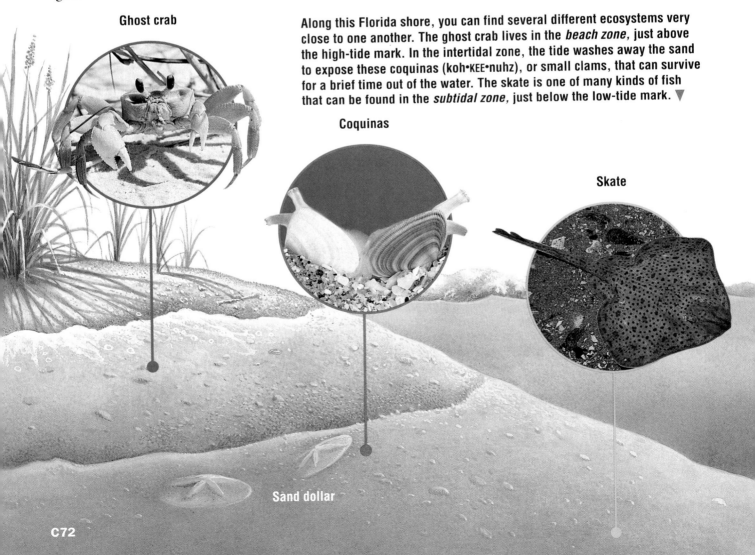

Ghost crab

Along this Florida shore, you can find several different ecosystems very close to one another. The ghost crab lives in the *beach zone,* just above the high-tide mark. In the intertidal zone, the tide washes away the sand to expose these coquinas (koh•KEE•nuhz), or small clams, that can survive for a brief time out of the water. The skate is one of many kinds of fish that can be found in the *subtidal zone,* just below the low-tide mark. ▼

Coquinas

Skate

Sand dollar

Coral Reef Ecosystems

Coral reefs are some of the largest structures on Earth that are built by living creatures. They are formed by small animals called corals, which live in warm, sunlit water. Corals use minerals dissolved in ocean water to form hard outer skeletons. Living corals don't move from place to place. They attach themselves to the skeletons of dead corals, and very slowly a reef is formed. Many kinds of algae and some kinds of plants live on reefs. The reefs provide underwater surfaces that sunlight can reach easily. They also provide shelter for many kinds of animals.

Producers in coral-reef food webs include cyanobacteria, seaweed, and algae that live within the corals. These reef producers provide food for consumers from almost every animal phylum. Important consumers include sea urchins and surgeonfish. Some species of fish eat the coral itself. Parrotfish actually bite chunks off the reef, grinding up the coral skeletons with teeth in their throats. Butterfly fish eat only living corals. Larger predators prey on these consumers.

✔ **What material are coral reefs made of?**

Coral reefs need warm water year-round. They also must be close to the ocean's surface, where plenty of sunlight can reach them. This coral reef is in the Red Sea, between Africa and the Arabian Peninsula. ▼

▲ Vent ecosystems in the deep ocean do very well without depending on energy from sunlight. Sea anemones (uh•NEM•uh•neez), sea cucumbers, white crabs, red-tipped tube worms, and giant clams are found here and nowhere else on Earth.

Deep-Ocean Vent Ecosystems

Until recently, scientists hypothesized that all of Earth's ecosystems use sunlight as their energy source. But researchers discovered new kinds of ecosystems in the deep oceans. These ecosystems seem to get all their energy from chemical reactions.

On some parts of the ocean floor in the abyssal zone, volcanic vents release heated water containing dissolved chemicals. Certain bacteria use these chemicals rather than sunlight to produce and store energy. These bacteria are the primary producers in vent ecosystems. All other members of the ecosystem depend on the energy the bacteria store. In fact, some species in these ecosystems have no stomachs or mouths. Instead, they live with these bacteria in their bodies. They take nutrients from the bacteria directly into their blood. Deep-ocean vents are the habitats of many species that weren't known before these ecosystems were discovered.

✔ **What are the primary producers in deep-ocean vent ecosystems?**

Estuary Ecosystems

The place where a freshwater environment and a saltwater environment meet is called an **estuary** (ES•tyoo•air•ee). Bays, inlets, river deltas, sounds, marshes, and swamps can all be estuaries.

Many estuaries are very fertile. They are shallow, and sunlight reaches all levels of the water, so algae and water plants grow well. These in turn provide food for many other organisms. The shelter from ocean predators that estuaries offer makes them ideal places for young marine life to grow and develop before moving to the open ocean. Estuaries are known as the nurseries of the sea.

Producers in estuaries include phytoplankton as well as land plants and water plants. Decaying plant matter provides food for the estuary's decomposers. Estuaries attract many consumers, including birds, mammals, and reptiles, as well as fish and other marine organisms. Many of these animals live their entire lives in estuaries.

Estuaries are the oceans' most important ecosystems for people. They are breeding grounds for much of the seafood people eat. Researchers have found that, per unit of area, shallow natural estuaries produce as much living matter as the most productive farmland. The open ocean, on the other hand, is only about as productive as desert land.

Spartina grass

Oysters

Blue crab

The Chesapeake Bay estuary, along the coast of Maryland, produces much of the seafood eaten by people in the mid-Atlantic states. Spartina (spar•TY•nuh), a type of sea grass, provides a habitat and food for many marine creatures. Oyster beds are not only food sources, but, like coral reefs, they are also habitats for other sea life, such as the blue crab.

Estuaries are also important for the roles they play for other ecosystems. They absorb heavy rains and floodwaters like sponges and then slowly release them. Microorganisms in swamps and marshes can clean polluted water, serving as natural water filters.

✓ **Why are estuaries important to life in the open ocean?**

Summary

Oceans contain a wide variety of ecosystems. Most of these ecosystems depend on phytoplankton that live near the surface of the ocean. Most ocean life exists in the upper layer of the oceans. However, even the cold, dark abyssal zone has ecosystems.

Coral reefs form in warm, shallow, well-lit water. They are some of the most diverse ecosystems in the world. Estuaries, where fresh water and salt water meet, are important producers of food for humans. Estuaries are nurseries for many ocean organisms.

Review

1. What organisms are the primary producers in the oceans?

2. In which ecosystem must organisms survive an environment that constantly changes between being wet and dry?

3. What conditions help make coral reefs such diverse ecosystems?

4. **Critical Thinking** How does life in the aphotic zone depend on sunlight?

5. **Test Prep** Deep-ocean vent ecosystems depend on energy stored by —

   A photosynthesis

   B algae

   C bacteria

   D tube worms

LINKS

MATH LINK

Feeling the Pressure Air pressure at sea level is about 14.7 pounds per square inch (psi). Near the bottom of the Mariana Trench, the water pressure is an amazing 16,883 psi. About how many times as great as the pressure at sea level is this?

WRITING LINK

Informative Writing—Description Take a walk along the shore of the ocean or a nearby lake or stream. Write detailed descriptions for your teacher of at least three organisms you see on your walk. Observe the organisms long enough so that you can record not only what they look like but also how they behave.

SOCIAL STUDIES LINK

Caribbean Cultures Learn more about the cultures of the islands of the Caribbean. How are the lives of the people who live on these islands in harmony with the oceans around them?

TECHNOLOGY LINK

Learn more about the ecosystems and landforms of the oceans by investigating *Landscapes of the Ocean Floor* on **Harcourt Science Explorations CD-ROM.**

Exploring the Oceans

Early Oceanography

Since ancient times the ocean has fascinated and terrified people, and for hundreds of years only the bravest explorers dared to sail far from land. One of the earliest explorers was Pytheas, a Greek who lived around 300 B.C. His travels took him far north of his native Mediterranean Sea, close to the Arctic Circle.

During the period known as the Age of Exploration (about A.D. 1400–1600), the number of ocean voyages greatly increased, and so did the demand for better navigational instruments. In the mid-1700s, the invention of accurate instruments allowed sailors to determine their exact position on the ocean.

In 1872 the *Challenger* set sail from England for a two-and-a-half year expedition. Scientists aboard the *Challenger* sank nets 5500 m (18,000 ft) below the surface, bringing up creatures that had never been seen before. The voyage, which produced 50 volumes of scientific reports, marks the true beginning of oceanography.

Diving into a New Frontier

As people's knowledge of the ocean grew, so did their determination to investigate it first-hand. As early as the 1830s, divers began to use diving suits that had helmets with air hoses connecting them to the surface. However, these early suits were heavy and dangerous. In 1943 Jacques-Yves Cousteau and Emile Gagnan invented scuba equipment. Scuba stands for self-contained underwater breathing apparatus. A scuba diver has complete freedom of movement, carrying only a tank of compressed air on his or her back.

Ocean Explorations

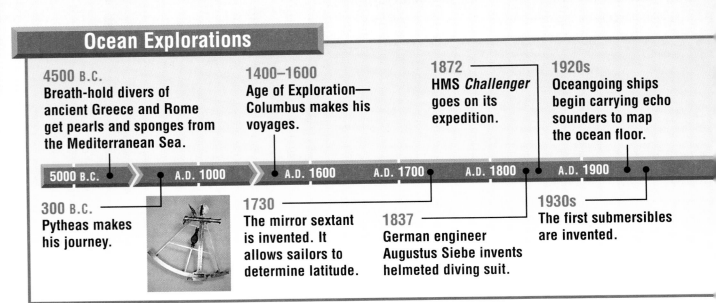

4500 B.C.
Breath-hold divers of ancient Greece and Rome get pearls and sponges from the Mediterranean Sea.

1400–1600
Age of Exploration—Columbus makes his voyages.

1872
HMS *Challenger* goes on its expedition.

1920s
Oceangoing ships begin carrying echo sounders to map the ocean floor.

5000 B.C.   A.D. 1000   A.D. 1600   A.D. 1700   A.D. 1800   A.D. 1900

300 B.C.
Pytheas makes his journey.

1730
The mirror sextant is invented. It allows sailors to determine latitude.

1837
German engineer Augustus Siebe invents helmeted diving suit.

1930s
The first submersibles are invented.

Exploring the Deep

Today even experienced scuba divers are cautioned to descend only to about 40 m (about 130 ft). The water pressure below that depth is too great. In 1948 Auguste Piccard built the first bathyscaph, a submersible able to descend to great depths. While a bathyscaph can withstand great pressure, it can't move around well. In 1964 scientists in the United States designed *Alvin*, a motor-driven submersible that can move around on the ocean floor. The capsule, which is 2 m (7 ft) wide, can dive below 3300 m (about 11,000 ft). Three people can stay in it for about 8 hours.

Ocean Discoveries

Until the development of sonar, many people thought the ocean floor was a flat plain. Today oceanographers know that it is as varied as dry land, with canyons, plains, mountains, and deep trenches. High-tech submersibles have taken scientists into these trenches, where they have made startling discoveries. In 1977 scientists found communities of organisms living around hot ocean vents.

In some ways the ocean is still as mysterious as the moon and planets in our solar system. But new inventions will continue to allow people to explore and make new discoveries about the ocean and planet Earth itself.

THINK ABOUT IT

1. Why do people want to explore the ocean?
2. How did improved technology help people better understand the ocean?

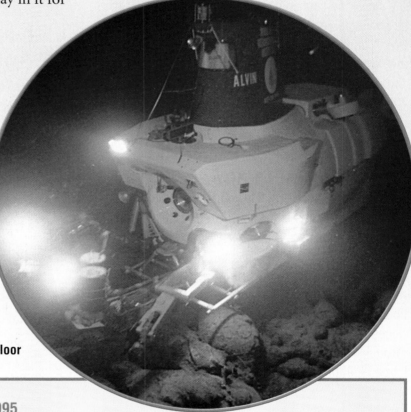

Alvin **exploring the ocean floor**

1940s
Cameras and other equipment that are not damaged by salt and can operate in the deep ocean are invented.

1995
The Japanese submersible *Kaiko* descends into the Mariana Trench.

2000

1960
The bathyscaph *Trieste* descends 10.9 km (about 6.8 mi) below the surface.

Today
Scientists continue to make discoveries about living organisms in the deepest parts of the ocean.

Hardened lava from the deep ocean ▼

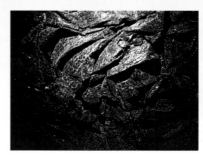

Harry Hammond Hess

GEOLOGIST

Harry Hammond Hess was one of our nation's most important geologists. His ideas about sea-floor spreading became an important part of the plate tectonics theory—a theory that few scientists accepted at first.

Dr. Hess began his research while he was in the U.S. Navy. As captain of a ship during World War II, he conducted echo-sounding surveys of the Pacific Ocean floor as the ship travelled from one battle to the next. The surveys assembled a great deal of data about features of the sea floor.

Years later, while teaching geology at Princeton University, Dr. Hess published some of his findings. In his 1962 paper called "History of the Ocean Basins," he described what he called the process of sea-floor spreading at ocean ridges. Dr. Hess discovered that ocean-floor rock is younger near the mid-ocean ridges than it is farther from them. To explain this, he hypothesized that the sea floor was spreading.

Other scientists did not agree at first, but later research has supported Dr. Hess's theory. The sea-floor plates do spread apart along the mid-ocean ridges. As the plates move apart, magma bubbles up through the crack between them. As the magma hardens, it forms new sea floor. The oldest sea-floor

rock is found far from the ridges, along deep ocean trenches, where the sea floor moves down into the crust to melt into magma.

Because of Dr. Hess's important contribution to science, President John Kennedy made him chairman of the Space Science Board in 1962. So in addition to advancing the theory of plate tectonics, Dr. Hess helped design the space program.

THINK ABOUT IT

1. What did Dr. Hess contribute to the science of geology?
2. When did Dr. Hess do some of his field research on the ocean basins?

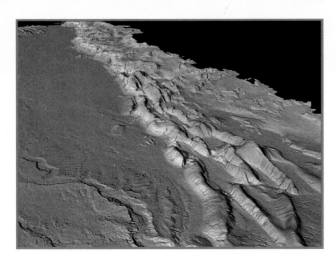

◀ **This is an example of a sonar image. It is a computer-colored image of the continental shelf off the coast of Oregon.**

Bouncing Sound

Can you locate a wall by listening to echoes?

Materials
- concrete wall (or wall with hard surface)
- toy clicker (or two small wood blocks)

Procedure

1. Stand about 3 m (10 ft) from the wall. Close your eyes as your partner turns you in circles.

2. Once you've stopped turning, keep your eyes closed and snap the clicker as you point it in several directions. Listen for an echo and guess the direction of the wall. Open your eyes to see if your guess is correct.

3. Close your eyes again. Have your partner turn you in circles and then lead you closer to or farther from the wall.

4. Snap the clicker to locate the wall. Tell your partner whether you think you're closer to or farther from the wall. Open your eyes and check.

5. Give your partner a turn at locating the wall and guessing the distance.

Draw Conclusions

How do you think a process similar to the one in Step 4 can be used to map the ocean floor? If you decide to use clicker echoes to figure out the exact distance to a large object, what two things would you have to know?

Pressure and Depth

How does water pressure change as water depth increases?

Materials
- large balloon with a 60-cm (2-ft) plastic tube attached to it
- deep container of water, such as an aquarium or a bucket

Procedure

1. Blow through the tube to inflate the balloon. Then let the air out.

2. Hold the balloon just under the surface of the water, and inflate it again. Let the air out.

3. Push the balloon to the bottom of the container of water and inflate it again.

Draw Conclusions

When was it easiest to inflate the balloon? Hardest? Why was Step 3 harder than Step 2? Why do you think it is impossible for a scuba diver to breathe in the deepest parts of the ocean?

Chapter 3 Review and Test Preparation

Vocabulary Review

Use the terms below to complete the sentences. The page numbers in ( ) tell you where to look in the chapter if you need help.

continental shelf (C62)   **seamount** (C64)

continental slope (C63)   **atoll** (C67)

abyssal plain (C63)   **intertidal zone** (C72)

mid-ocean ridge (C64)   **coral reef** (C73)

trench (C64)   **estuary** (C74)

1. Molten rock rises along the ___ to form new ocean floor.

2. The ecosystem found at the shore between the low- and high-tide lines is the ___.

3. An ecosystem in which fresh water and salt water mix is an ___.

4. The gently sloping ocean floor known as the ___ is found at the edge of continents.

5. Under the oceans a deep ___ forms where crustal plates collide.

6. The steep incline from the continental shelf to the abyssal plain is the ___.

7. An underwater ridge, usually made up of coral skeletons, is a ___.

8. A ring of islands that forms around a volcano is an ___.

9. A ___ is an undersea volcano that rises above the surrounding ocean floor.

10. The floor of the deep ocean, known as the ___, includes some of the flattest places on Earth.

Connect Concepts

Complete the concept map by filling in terms from the Word Bank.

deep-ocean vent   **continental shelf**   **estuary**

abyssal plain   **continental slope**   **coral reef**

intertidal zone

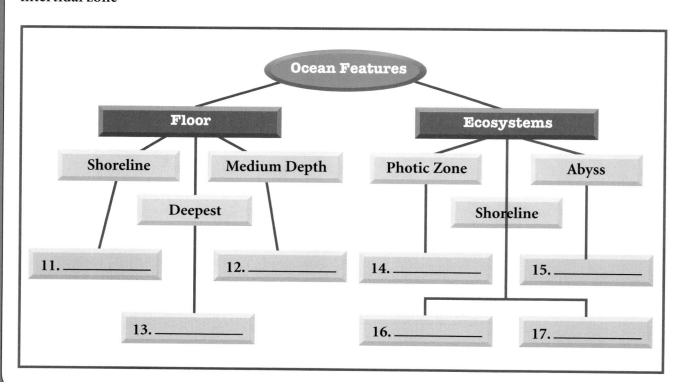

Ocean Features

Floor — Shoreline, Medium Depth, Deepest

Ecosystems — Photic Zone, Abyss, Shoreline

11. _____   12. _____   14. _____   15. _____

13. _____   16. _____   17. _____

Check Understanding

Write the letter of the best choice.

18. From an economic standpoint, ____ ecosystems are the most important to humans.
    - A intertidal zone
    - B estuary
    - C deep-sea vent
    - D coral reef

19. The primary producers in most ocean ecosystems are ____ , which produce energy through photosynthesis.
    - F zooplankton
    - G mollusks
    - H phytoplankton
    - J coral polyps

20. An ecosystem that does not depend on sunlight as its primary source of energy is —
    - A a deep-sea vent
    - B an intertidal zone
    - C a coral reef
    - D an estuary

21. The abyssal plain is flat because of —
    - F water pressure
    - G trenches
    - H gravity
    - J sediment

22. The presence of ____ helps make the continental shelf rich in marine life.
    - A sunlight
    - B coral
    - C warm water
    - D sediment

Critical Thinking

23. Why could a rapid increase in global ocean levels be a disaster for coral reef ecosystems?

24. Why couldn't organisms from the intertidal zone thrive in a deep-sea vent ecosystem?

25. The ocean floor stretching from the mid-ocean ridge to undersea trenches is sometimes described as a "crustal conveyor belt." Explain.

26. Why is so much of the ocean floor an unknown region of Earth?

Process Skills Review

27. How can you **model** the stages in the formation of an atoll?

28. You want to **compare and contrast** two ocean ecosystems. What features should you look at?

Performance Assessment

Living Under the Sea

Choose one ocean environment. Draw a picture or make a diorama showing the conditions in which organisms in that environment must live. List the particular challenges organisms face in meeting their needs. Include in your drawing or diorama some of the producers and consumers in the ecosystem of your ocean environment.

Weather Changes

Everyone talks about the weather, but no one can control it. Plenty of people have tried, but none have found a way. So far, the best we have been able to do is to improve our ability to predict weather and to warn people when it threatens to become dangerous.

Vocabulary Preview

troposphere
thermosphere
mesosphere
stratosphere
air mass
air pressure
relative humidity
front
forecast
station model
surface map
weather balloon
weather map
thunderstorm
hurricane
tropical storm
tornado

⚡FAST FACT

There are places on Earth where lightning can strike 1000–2000 times an hour during a thunderstorm.

Lightning Strike Facts

Frequency	100 times/sec (world) 20 million/year (U.S.A.)
Temperature	50,000°F (about 28,000°C)
Length (from cloud to ground)	5 mi (about 8 km)
Electric Energy	100 million volts

Tropical storms that form north of the equator spin in a counterclockwise direction. Tropical storms that form south of the equator spin clockwise.

Most tornadoes last only from 5 to 10 minutes and travel only a few miles. However, their winds may reach 360 mi/hr (600 km/hr) and do enormous damage.

LESSON

1

What Makes Up the Atmosphere?

In this lesson, you can . . .

INVESTIGATE the layers of the atmosphere.

LEARN ABOUT what the atmosphere is made of and how it is layered.

LINK to math, writing, social studies, and technology.

Layers of the Atmosphere

Activity Purpose The atmosphere is a thick ocean of air that surrounds all of Earth. Just like the ocean, the atmosphere has layers. In this investigation you will make a diagram and **infer** what the layers are and where their boundaries are.

Materials

- graph paper
- ruler

▼ Electrically charged particles from the sun collide with particles in the upper atmosphere. The collisions produce curtains of brilliant light called auroras.

Average Temperatures in Earth's Atmosphere	
Height Above Sea Level (km)	**Average Temperature (°C)**
0	12
5	-30
10	-60
15	-60
20	-60
25	-55
30	-50
35	-30
40	0
45	0
50	0
60	-30
70	-60
80	-90
85	-90
90	-85
100	-60
500	-30
600	0

Activity Procedure

1 The data in the table is temperature information collected by different atmospheric probes. The data was not collected at equal intervals—so be careful when graphing! **Use the numbers** in the table to plot each point for temperature in the atmosphere. Let the *y*-axis be the height above sea level. Let the *x*-axis be the average temperature. Use the grid on the right to set up your graph.

2 Connect all of the points in your graph with a smooth line. (Picture A)

3 Scientists **infer** that the atmosphere can be divided into layers based on temperatures and temperature changes. Now, **analyze the data** you just plotted. Look for places where the temperature changes and places where the temperature stays the same. Look for three different boundaries, where the temperature levels off. Draw a straight line to mark the boundaries.

4 Label each of the layers, from the bottom up. The first layer is the *troposphere*. The second is the *stratosphere*. The third is the *mesosphere*. The fourth is the *thermosphere*.

Draw Conclusions

1. Did the temperature in the atmosphere change in the way you expected it to? Explain.

2. What happens to the temperature of the atmosphere as you go up through the stratosphere?

3. What would you expect the temperature to be at the top of Mount Everest? (The top of Mount Everest is about 9000 m above sea level.)

4. **Scientists at Work** Scientists sometimes **use numbers** in many different ways to help them **interpret data**. Would a bar graph have been more helpful in interpreting this data? Explain.

Investigate Further Find out where most of Earth's weather takes place and where most airplanes fly. Explain why the weather and the planes are in different places.

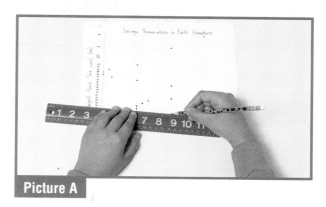

Picture A

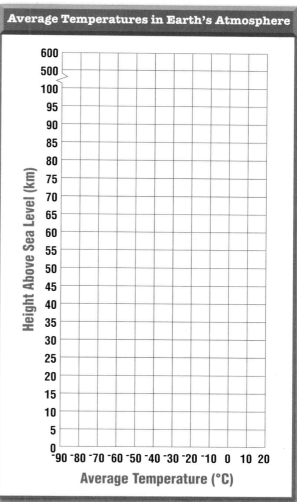

Average Temperatures in Earth's Atmosphere

Height Above Sea Level (km)

600 500 100 95 90 85 80 75 70 65 60 55 50 45 40 35 30 25 20 15 10 5 0

⁻90 ⁻80 ⁻70 ⁻60 ⁻50 ⁻40 ⁻30 ⁻20 ⁻10 0 10 20

Average Temperature (°C)

Process Skill Tip

Sometimes you need to **use numbers** when you try to **interpret data**. You can use formulas, tables, and graphs. You need to pick the right tool to help make sense of the numbers.

Earth's Atmosphere

Atmospheric Gases

Earth's atmosphere is an ocean of air hundreds of kilometers thick. The air is densest at the Earth's surface. In fact, about 90 percent of the atmosphere by weight is within 16 km (10 mi) of Earth's surface. The greater the height above sea level, the thinner the air is. The atmosphere eventually fades into the emptiness of outer space.

Air contains many gases, but most of its volume is made up of only two of them. Nitrogen and oxygen make up 99 percent of dry air. These two gases are necessary for life processes. Another gas necessary for life is carbon dioxide, which is used by plants in photosynthesis. Carbon dioxide makes up only about 0.035 percent of dry air.

The atmosphere also contains small amounts of several other gases. Water vapor ranges from almost none to about 4 percent of the air. Water vapor in the atmosphere is an important part of the water cycle.

Another gas that exists in tiny quantities is ozone. A molecule of ozone is made up of three oxygen atoms. A molecule of oxygen gas is made up of two. Most of the ozone is in the layer of the atmosphere that is between 10 and 50 km (between about 6 and 30 mi) high. There it absorbs ultraviolet light from the sun, shielding Earth from rays that can be harmful to life.

Throughout the atmosphere, there are also varying amounts of dust particles. These particles are not just dirt or soot. Some, such as pollen grains, are from living things. Others are the remains of meteors that entered Earth's atmosphere. Dust particles affect the weather by providing a surface for water vapor to condense on so that it can become precipitation.

✔ **Where is about 90 percent of Earth's atmosphere found?**

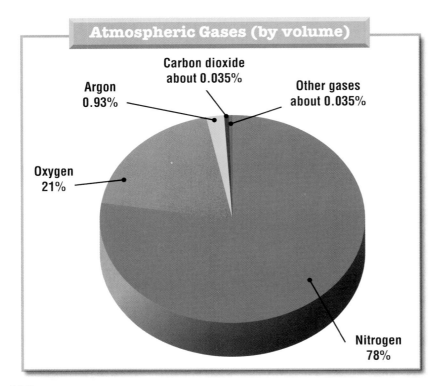

Atmospheric Gases (by volume)

Carbon dioxide
about 0.035%

Argon
0.93%

Other gases
about 0.035%

Oxygen
21%

Nitrogen
78%

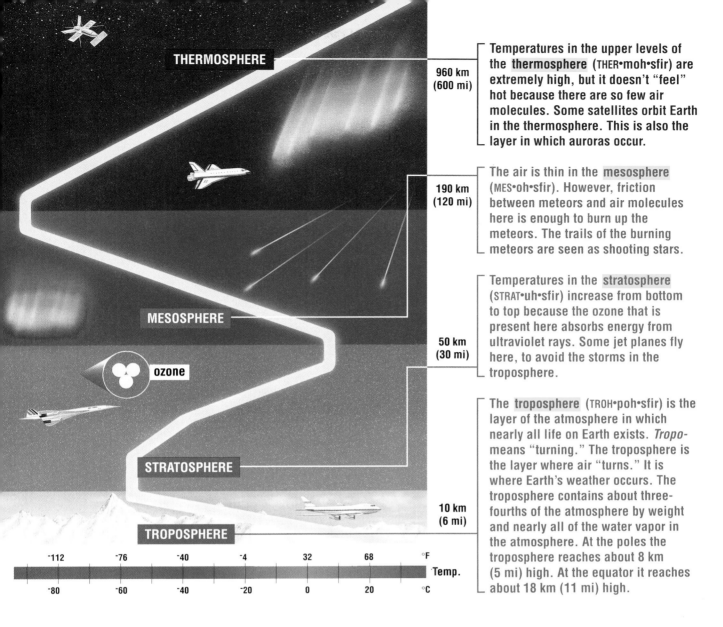

THERMOSPHERE

960 km
(600 mi)

Temperatures in the upper levels of the **thermosphere** (THER•moh•sfir) are extremely high, but it doesn't "feel" hot because there are so few air molecules. Some satellites orbit Earth in the thermosphere. This is also the layer in which auroras occur.

190 km
(120 mi)

The air is thin in the **mesosphere** (MES•oh•sfir). However, friction between meteors and air molecules here is enough to burn up the meteors. The trails of the burning meteors are seen as shooting stars.

MESOSPHERE

Temperatures in the **stratosphere** (STRAT•uh•sfir) increase from bottom to top because the ozone that is present here absorbs energy from ultraviolet rays. Some jet planes fly here, to avoid the storms in the troposphere.

50 km
(30 mi)

ozone

STRATOSPHERE

The **troposphere** (TROH•poh•sfir) is the layer of the atmosphere in which nearly all life on Earth exists. *Tropo-* means "turning." The troposphere is the layer where air "turns." It is where Earth's weather occurs. The troposphere contains about three-fourths of the atmosphere by weight and nearly all of the water vapor in the atmosphere. At the poles the troposphere reaches about 8 km (5 mi) high. At the equator it reaches about 18 km (11 mi) high.

10 km
(6 mi)

TROPOSPHERE

⁻112	⁻76	⁻40	⁻4	32	68	°F

Temp.

⁻80	⁻60	⁻40	⁻20	0	20	°C

Structure of the Atmosphere

The atmosphere changes as the height above sea level increases. That's why climbers who challenge Mount Everest face more than sheer rock walls. As they climb higher, the air grows colder and thinner. So they carry supplies of oxygen. Often mountain climbers must use the supplies of oxygen because the air is too thin for them to breathe easily. The top of Mount Everest is near the upper limit of the troposphere, the bottom layer of Earth's atmosphere. The troposphere stretches from sea level to about 10 km (6 mi) above sea level.

Scientists have used information from weather balloons, research planes, and spacecraft to divide the atmosphere into four layers. The divisions are based on temperature. The diagram above shows the changes in temperature throughout the atmosphere.

The place where the atmosphere begins is clear. It begins at the surface of the land or sea. However, there is no exact border between the atmosphere and outer space. There are just fewer molecules of the atmosphere at greater heights. Hundreds of kilometers above Earth, the atmosphere thins out into space.

✔ **According to the diagram above, does the temperature rise or fall as you travel upward through the stratosphere?**

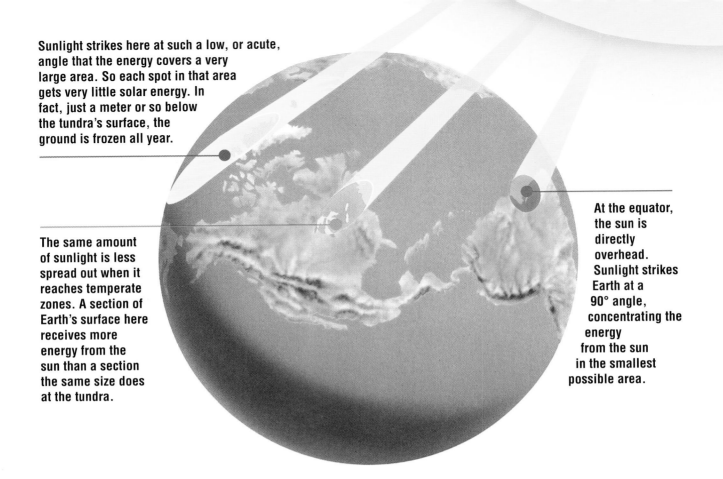

Sunlight strikes here at such a low, or acute, angle that the energy covers a very large area. So each spot in that area gets very little solar energy. In fact, just a meter or so below the tundra's surface, the ground is frozen all year.

The same amount of sunlight is less spread out when it reaches temperate zones. A section of Earth's surface here receives more energy from the sun than a section the same size does at the tundra.

At the equator, the sun is directly overhead. Sunlight strikes Earth at a 90° angle, concentrating the energy from the sun in the smallest possible area.

Uneven Heating by the Sun

Earth is heated by energy from the sun. However, the sun doesn't heat all of Earth's regions evenly.

The diagram shows how the same amount of light lands on three parts of the planet. When sunlight hits Earth at an angle of 90°, the sunlight spreads out over the smallest possible area. But when it hits Earth at an acute angle, an angle that measures less than 90°, the same amount of light spreads out over a larger area. Because the same amount of energy covers a larger area, each part of the area gets less energy. The more acute the angle of the light hitting Earth's surface, the less thermal energy a particular place gets. The Earth gets less energy from the sun at the poles than it does at the equator.

There is another reason that Earth is heated unevenly. Light loses some of its energy as it travels through air. When the sun is directly overhead, light travels the shortest distance through the atmosphere before reaching Earth's surface. The smaller the angle the light makes, the farther it has to travel through the atmosphere. More of its energy is absorbed or reflected before it reaches Earth's surface.

The uneven heating of Earth's surface has a great effect on the air in the troposphere. For example, the air in the troposphere above a Canadian forest is colder and drier than the air above the ocean near the equator. A large body of air that has the same characteristics throughout is called an **air mass**. Air masses form in the troposphere and help determine the weather. The heat and humidity of an air mass are determined by the conditions where it forms.

However, air masses can travel thousands of kilometers. In this way they bring their temperature and humidity to other regions.

✓ **Name two factors that affect the amount of energy Earth's surface receives from the sun.**

Summary

The atmosphere is an ocean of air that extends hundreds of kilometers above Earth's surface. It is divided according to temperature into four layers—the troposphere, the stratosphere, the mesosphere, and the thermosphere. The lowest layer, the troposphere, is where air masses form. Air masses have different characteristics because the areas over which they form receive different amounts of energy from the sun.

Review

1. Why are dust particles an important component of the atmosphere?
2. Why is the temperature greater in the upper part of the stratosphere?
3. What is an air mass?
4. **Critical Thinking** Why don't meteors burn up when they first enter Earth's atmosphere?
5. **Test Prep** An area receives the most energy from sunlight if the light hits the Earth at —

   A the mesosphere

   B the poles

   C a 90° angle

   D a low height above sea level

LINKS

MATH LINK

High Pressure About 99 percent of the atmosphere's air by weight lies below an altitude of 22 mi. Air pressure at the bottom of the atmosphere (sea level) is 14.7 pounds per square inch (psi). What would you expect air pressure to be at 22 mi?

WRITING LINK

Persuasive Writing—Request The ozone layer that protects Earth from harmful ultraviolet light has been damaged by the use of chemicals called CFCs. Find out about CFCs. Write a pamphlet that encourages people in your community to discuss this problem and come up with solutions.

SOCIAL STUDIES LINK

History of Science The first explorations of the atmosphere took place in hot-air balloons. Find out about these first voyages into the atmosphere and share your findings with the class.

TECHNOLOGY LINK

Learn more about Earth's atmosphere by visiting the National Air and Space Museum Internet Site.
www.si.edu/harcourt/science

Smithsonian Institution®

LESSON **2**

What Are Weather Fronts?

In this lesson, you can . . .

INVESTIGATE the effects of air pressure.

LEARN ABOUT how air masses with different properties cause our weather.

LINK to math, writing, social studies, and technology.

INVESTIGATE

Air Pressure

Activity Purpose We live at the bottom of an ocean of air called the atmosphere. Air pressure, or the weight of the atmosphere on an area, is like water pressure. Both increase as depth increases. So air pressure is greatest at the bottom of the atmosphere, the Earth's surface. In this investigation you will see what air pressure can do.

Materials
- bucket or other deep container
- hot tap water
- 0.5-L plastic bottle with cap
- cold tap water

Activity Procedure

1 Carefully pour hot water into the bucket until it is about three-fourths full. Remove the cap from the bottle. Hold the bottle in the container of hot water so that the water reaches up to its neck. (Picture A) Keep it there for two minutes.

2 While the bottle is still in the hot water, screw the cap on tightly.

3 Remove the bottle from the water. Pour the hot water out of the bucket and replace it with very cold water. Without removing the cap, hold the bottle in the water. (Picture B) **Observe** what happens.

4 Remove the bottle from the water. Listen as you slowly twist open the bottle cap.

◄ On a spring day, ice has coated this young seedling.

C90

Picture A

Picture B

Draw Conclusions

1. When air is warmed, it expands. Use this information to **infer** whether the air inside the bottle was more or less dense than the air in the room when you put the cap on.

2. Did cooling the air in the bottle increase or reduce the pressure inside the bottle?

3. How can you explain what you **observed** when you cooled the bottle?

4. **Scientists at Work** Scientists often **make inferences** about things they cannot see directly. What can you infer about the cause of the sound you heard when you opened the cap on the bottle?

Investigate Further Use a weather map to find areas of high and low pressure. Find out what kinds of winds and temperatures tend to be associated with each type of pressure.

Process Skill Tip

Many events occur because of changes in physical conditions. When you **compare** the physical conditions at different stages in an experiment, you can often **infer** why an event occurs.

Weather Fronts

FIND OUT

- how air masses and the collision of air masses cause weather conditions

- which air masses, global wind belts, and types of fronts usually control weather in the United States

VOCABULARY

air pressure
relative humidity
front

Air Masses

Gravity keeps Earth's atmosphere in place. It also causes the mass of hundreds of kilometers of air to push down, causing air pressure. **Air pressure** is the weight of air pressing down on an area. At sea level, normal air pressure is about 14.7 pounds per square inch. In the investigation, you saw one effect of this pressure.

The air pressure at Earth's surface is not always the same. A change in air pressure is a sign of a change in the weather. As an air mass moves into a region, it replaces the air mass that was there before. An air mass has about the same temperature, amount of moisture, and air pressure all through it. Because of this, a change in air pressure in a region shows that a new air mass has arrived, bringing new weather with it.

Air masses can be thousands of kilometers wide and several kilometers high. Seven major air masses usually affect the weather in the United States. They are shown on the map below.

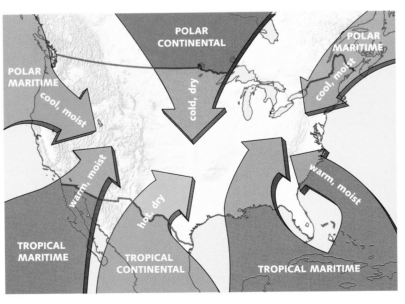

CONTINENTAL POLAR AIR a cold, dry air mass that forms over Alaska and northern Canada

ARCTIC AIR very cold, very dry air from the Arctic Circle that sometimes reaches the northern United States

PACIFIC MARITIME POLAR AIR cool, moist air that brings moisture from the northern Pacific Ocean

PACIFIC MARITIME TROPICAL AIR warm, moist air from the Pacific Ocean west of Mexico that sometimes brings summer showers to the dry southwestern United States

ATLANTIC MARITIME POLAR AIR cool, moist air from the North Atlantic that can bring clouds or cooler weather

ATLANTIC MARITIME TROPICAL AIR warm, moist air from the Gulf of Mexico and the Caribbean Sea that brings summer heat and humidity

CONTINENTAL TROPICAL AIR a very hot, dry air mass that forms over the deserts of Mexico and the southwestern United States and can bring drought conditions to the Great Plains

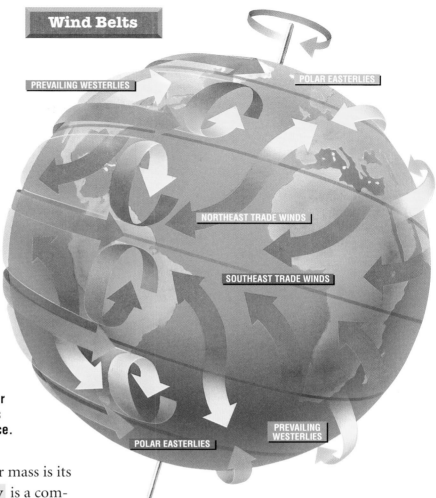

POLAR EASTERLIES

These winds blow from the east, bringing polar air masses south.

PREVAILING WESTERLIES

Blowing from west to east, these winds cause most of the weather in the United States.

NORTHEAST TRADE WINDS

These are the winds that took sailors in earlier centuries from Europe to the New World.

SOUTHEAST TRADE WINDS

These winds, blowing from southeast to northwest, also helped ships sail across the Atlantic Ocean.

PREVAILING WESTERLIES

These winds cause the weather patterns in southern Africa and South America.

POLAR EASTERLIES By moving cold polar air toward the equator, the polar easterlies help keep the global temperature in balance.

One of the characteristics of an air mass is its relative humidity. **Relative humidity** is a comparison of the actual amount of moisture in the air to the greatest possible amount that could be in the air at the same temperature and pressure. Air that has as much water vapor as possible has a relative humidity of 100 percent. At 100 percent relative humidity, the water vapor condenses as fog or precipitation, such as rain or snow. An air mass that has only half of the maximum possible water vapor has a relative humidity of 50 percent.

The relative humidity and temperature of an air mass depend on the area of land or ocean where the air mass formed. This area is usually fairly large and uniform. Air that has been in the same place for days or even weeks gets its characteristics from that area. Maritime air masses, or air masses that form over oceans, are humid. Continental air masses, which form over land, are usually dry. Polar air masses are cooler than tropical air masses.

Wind is the movement of air from an area of high pressure to an area of low pressure. Wind carries an air mass from one region to another.

Some winds form because of local differences in air pressure, such as those around a mountain range. Other winds occur on a larger scale and are more constant and easier to predict. They are caused by the uneven heating of the Earth, and they move the air masses that cause the weather.

The diagram above shows the six major "belts" of winds that circle the globe. Each of these winds always blows in the same direction. Two of them are called trade winds. Before steam power came into use, sailing ships carried trade goods between many of the countries of the world. Some of these ships relied on the dependable trade winds to push them across the Atlantic Ocean.

✔ **What is an air mass?**

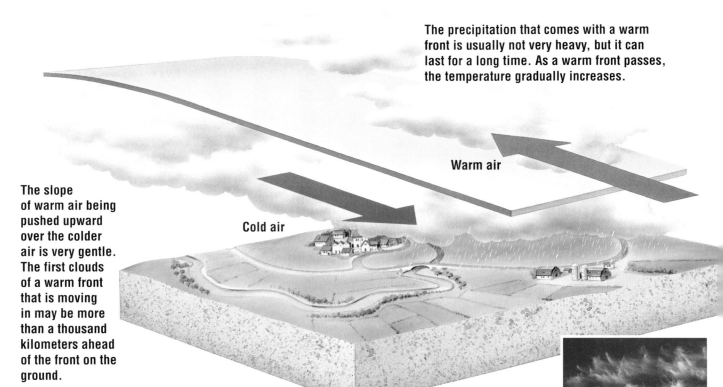

The precipitation that comes with a warm front is usually not very heavy, but it can last for a long time. As a warm front passes, the temperature gradually increases.

Warm air

Cold air

The slope of warm air being pushed upward over the colder air is very gentle. The first clouds of a warm front that is moving in may be more than a thousand kilometers ahead of the front on the ground.

High, thin cirrus clouds are a sign that a warm front is on the way. ▶

Fronts

As air masses move across the surface of the Earth, some of them collide. Collisions of air masses usually happen in the regions halfway between one of the poles and the equator. Most of the United States is in one of these regions.

The border between two air masses that collide is called a **front**. The two air masses don't mix very much at a front. They each keep their own characteristics. However, the air masses are probably moving at different speeds, so the faster one will push against the other. No matter which air mass is doing the pushing, the warmer air will always be pushed up over the denser, cooler air. This results in changes in the weather that are not just the replacement of the weather of one air mass by the weather of another. Fronts cause entirely new kinds of weather.

Meteorologists (meet•ee•er•AHL•uh•juhsts), or scientists who study the weather, classify fronts into four types. They are warm fronts, cold fronts, stationary fronts, and occluded fronts.

✔ **What is a front?**

Warm Fronts

When a warm air mass moves into an area of cooler air, the boundary that forms between the air masses is called a warm front. The leading edge of the warm air is pushed up over the cooler air in a wide, gentle slope. This warm air is usually more humid than the cool air. As this humid air runs over the cooler air along the front and moves upward, it cools. Its relative humidity increases until its moisture condenses into clouds. Because of the gentle slope of warm air, the highest clouds—cirrus clouds—are a long way ahead of the front.

Cirrus clouds are a sign that a warm front is coming. They are followed by lower clouds that cause precipitation. These clouds stretch over a long distance, and steady rain, sleet, or snow with gray, cloudy skies usually follows. The precipitation may last for several days before the actual warm front arrives.

✔ **What is one of the first signs that a warm front is on the way?**

Cold Fronts

The leading edge of a cold air mass causes a cold front as it collides with a warm air mass. The weather changes that occur with cold fronts are more extreme than those that occur with warm fronts. These changes also take place much closer to the front itself.

Cold air masses usually move more quickly than warm ones. When cold air moves into warmer air, the cold air, being denser, is able to edge its way under the warm air mass. The cool air forces the warmer air rapidly upward, where it cools and its moisture begins to condense. This results in towering cumulonimbus (kyoo•myoo•loh•NIM•buhs) clouds. These can rise up to 18,000 m (about 60,000 ft) in the atmosphere—up to the bottom of the stratosphere. These clouds often bring heavy precipitation. As a cold front comes closer, the towering clouds can usually be seen in the distance.

Because cold fronts move so much warm air high into the troposphere so quickly, they can cause thunderstorms and even tornadoes, especially during the summer. However, the clouds do not spread over long distances, and the storms don't last long. The skies clear fairly soon after the front has passed. The cooler air mass has replaced the warmer air mass.

✔ **Why can a cold front bring strong storms?**

At a cold front, warm air is forced upward in a steep, narrow band. When the warm air's water vapor condenses, it releases heat, pushing the air up even faster.

Stormy weather often comes with a cold front. The temperature usually drops quickly, and the wind direction changes.

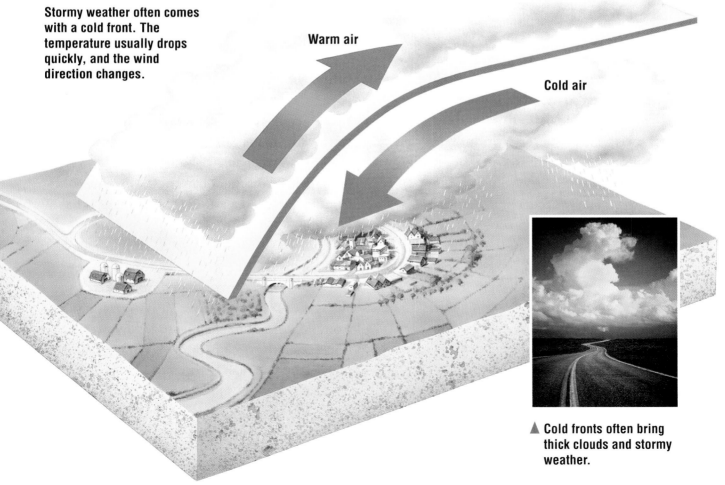

Warm air

Cold air

▲ Cold fronts often bring thick clouds and stormy weather.

A stationary front occurs where cold and warm fronts meet.

▲ As with other fronts, the weather differs on each side of a stationary front. This kind of front can bring many days of rainy weather to an area. By blocking the usual flow of air masses over a region, however, it can also result in drought or heat waves. Stationary fronts may not move for long periods of time.

Stationary Fronts

Sometimes the boundary between two air masses doesn't move. Neither air mass pushes against the other, so the front is not described as either warm or cold. When this occurs, the boundary is called a stationary front.

Even though the air masses are not moving, the weather at a stationary front is not the weather that usually occurs under an air mass. Often, warm air mixes with cooler air, and clouds form on both sides of the front. The clouds are pushed upward and cool, and precipitation occurs. This is usually light. But because the front is not moving, the precipitation lasts for a long time.

When a warm front or a cold front stalls, or stops moving, it becomes a stationary front. When the front starts moving again, it is once again a warm front or a cold front, and it produces the weather that is typical of it.

✔ **What is a stationary front?**

Occluded Fronts

Another type of front is the occluded (uh•KLOOD•uhd) front. This takes place when a cold front overtakes a warm front. At the cold front, a cool air mass wedges itself under a warmer air mass. The cold front moves faster than the warmer air mass and catches up with the other side of the warm front. Now the cold front has reached another cool air mass. It has lifted the warm air mass completely off the ground. The warm air mass sits trapped above the cooler air of the two cool air masses.

The weather at an occluded front often changes as the front forms. Heavy precipitation from the cold front changes to lighter precipitation. When the occluded front is fully formed, the weather is much like that of a warm front. Light rain or snow falls steadily.

✔ **What happens to the warmer air mass at an occluded front?**

Summary

The air masses that pass over an area control its weather. Where the air masses collide, fronts occur. Warm fronts often bring steady rain and cloudy skies that stay in an area for several days. Cold fronts move through more quickly, causing brief, sometimes strong, showers or thunderstorms. Fronts that stall in place are called stationary fronts. When a cold front overtakes a warm front and pushes the entire warm air mass upward, an occluded front forms.

Review

1. What are the characteristics of the air in a maritime polar air mass?
2. What is relative humidity?
3. What causes the global wind belts?
4. **Critical Thinking** Death Valley runs along the east side of the Sierra Nevada, only a few hundred kilometers from the Pacific Ocean. Why doesn't it get precipitation from the maritime air masses that reach the western United States?
5. **Test Prep** Thunderstorms often occur with —

   A cold fronts

   B warm fronts

   C the stratosphere

   D trade winds

LINKS

MATH LINK

Decimals Warm air pushed up along a cold front cools about 5.4°F for every 1000 ft of increase in altitude. If air that has a temperature of 80°F is forced 5000 ft higher by a cold front, what would the new temperature be?

WRITING LINK

Expressive Writing—Poem A haiku is a kind of poem that has three lines. The first and third lines each have five syllables, and the second has seven syllables. Poets who write haiku often choose subjects from nature, as in this example:

A stray summer storm—
we get soaked to the bone; then
the wind dries us off

Write a haiku for your classmates that describes your favorite kind of weather.

SOCIAL STUDIES LINK

Ocean History Find out more about the area of the ocean called "the doldrums." How did this area get its name? What causes the weather conditions in the doldrums?

TECHNOLOGY LINK

Visit the Harcourt Learning Site for related links, activities, and resources.
www.harcourtschool.com

How Can Weather Be Predicted?

In this lesson, you can . . .

 INVESTIGATE how to make a station model.

 LEARN ABOUT methods and tools for predicting weather.

 LINK to math, writing, social studies, and technology.

One way to learn about conditions in a violent storm is to collect data from inside it. Planes like this one can carry meteorologists into the heart of a hurricane.

INVESTIGATE

Making a Station Model

Activity Purpose Throughout the United States hundreds of weather stations **collect data** on local weather conditions. The pieces of data from all of the stations are put together on maps. In this investigation you will learn how to make a station model that records weather conditions in your area.

Materials

■ weather station

Symbols Used on a Station Model

Precipitation	Wind Speed and Direction (mi/hr)	Cloud Cover
☰ Fog	○ No wind	○ No cover
• Snow	1–3	$\frac{1}{10}$ or less
● Rain	4–7	$\frac{2}{10}$ to $\frac{3}{10}$
⊼ Thunder-storm	8–14	$\frac{4}{10}$
' Drizzle	15–20	$\frac{1}{2}$
▽ Showers	21–26	$\frac{6}{10}$
	27–31	$\frac{7}{10}$
		Overcast with openings
		● Completely overcast

Activity Procedure

1 On a sheet of paper, **record** the current weather conditions. Include temperature, air pressure, wind speed and direction, amount of precipitation, and cloud cover.

2 Use the symbols to **record** your station model for the day in a chart like the one below.

Day 1	Day 2	Day 3	Day 4	Day 5
♀				

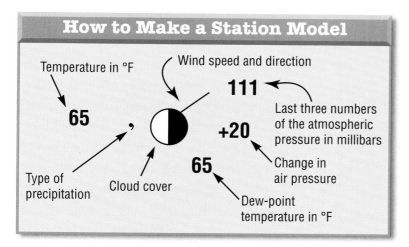

How to Make a Station Model

Temperature in °F

Wind speed and direction

111 ← Last three numbers of the atmospheric pressure in millibars

65

+20 Change in air pressure

65

Type of precipitation

Cloud cover

Dew-point temperature in °F

3 Repeat Steps 1 and 2 for three more days. Make sure your measurements are taken at the same time of day. You should have a total of four observations.

4 Use your observations to **predict** what the weather for Day 5 will be like. **Record** your prediction in the box for Day 5.

5 **Record** the actual weather for Day 5.

Draw Conclusions

1. How did the station-model symbols help you summarize and **record data**?

2. How were your **prediction** and the actual weather on Day 5 different?

3. How did making station models for four days give you information to **predict** the weather? What other information might be useful in predicting the weather?

4. **Scientists at Work** Meteorologists must carefully **measure** conditions to **gather** and **record data** for maps that will help them **predict** the weather. How would the measurements from an electronic weather station differ from those that you took? How would the electronic station be helpful to meteorologists?

Weather Prediction

Forecasting the Weather

FIND OUT

• how meteorologists make station models and surface maps

• the tools and technology that meteorologists use to forecast weather

VOCABULARY

forecast
station model
surface map
weather balloon
weather map

Meteorologists have identified the causes of change in the atmosphere. They have also discovered how these causes lead to different kinds of weather. One of the greatest benefits of meteorology is the weather **forecast**, a prediction of what the weather will be like in the future.

To make their forecasts, meteorologists make a station model for each location from which they have data. A **station model** is an arrangement of symbols and numbers that show the weather conditions recorded at a weather station. Each piece of data is printed in a certain position on the model. Station models are shown on daily maps from the National Weather Service. From the station models meteorologists construct a surface map. A **surface map** includes station models and information about fronts and about centers of high pressure and low pressure.

Because of advances in technology, meteorologists can make accurate forecasts of the next day's weather. They can also make fairly

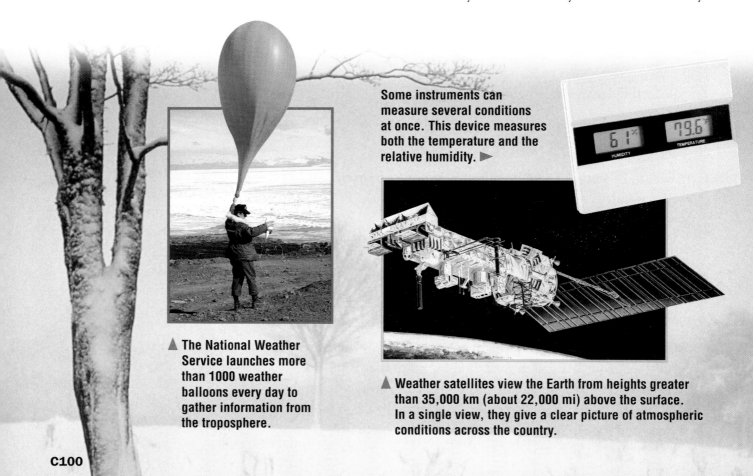

Some instruments can measure several conditions at once. This device measures both the temperature and the relative humidity. ▶

▲ The National Weather Service launches more than 1000 weather balloons every day to gather information from the troposphere.

▲ Weather satellites view the Earth from heights greater than 35,000 km (about 22,000 mi) above the surface. In a single view, they give a clear picture of atmospheric conditions across the country.

accurate weather forecasts for up to five days into the future. Beyond five days, meteorologists can make fairly accurate long-term forecasts about an area's general climate. But they can't make accurate long-term forecasts of the area's daily weather.

Although large weather systems are complex, most of the tools for collecting data at each station are simple. Many of these tools are attached to an instrument shelter. The shelter protects the instruments inside from sun, rain, and wind, but it allows air from outside to reach them. It is usually placed in a grassy area that does not collect or reflect heat as concrete does.

Instruments inside the shelter include a thermometer to measure temperature and a barometer to measure air pressure. They may also include thermometers that record the highest and lowest temperatures of the day, and instruments that keep a continual record of changes in temperature and air pressure. Outside the shelter is a *rain gauge*, which measures the amount of precipitation that has fallen. Also

outside is an *anemometer* (an•uh•MAHM•uht•er), which measures wind speed.

Meteorologists read the shelter's instruments at regular intervals. They also take measurements to find the *dew point*, the temperature at which water vapor in the air will condense. The closer the temperature of the air is to the dew point, the higher is the air's relative humidity.

Weather forecasters also use information about conditions high above the ground. They record data on how cloudy it is, the types of clouds, their movement, and their height. Forecasters may also release weather balloons into the atmosphere. A **weather balloon** carries a package of instruments that records data about temperature, air pressure, and humidity. This data is transmitted back to the ground by radio. The instruments work at heights up to about 30,000 m (100,000 ft).

✓ **Name three instruments used in weather forecasting.**

A barometer measures air pressure. Weather forecasters are often more interested in how the pressure has changed than in its current measurement. Some barometers are connected to instruments that keep a record of every change. ▶

▲ As the cups of an anemometer catch the wind, they spin. A dial shows the wind speed. The wind vane swings with the wind and shows wind direction.

◀ Doppler radar is one of meteorology's newest tools. Not only can it identify storms, but it can also detect the motion of the winds inside a storm. This is especially useful in forecasting severe weather conditions such as hurricanes and tornadoes.

Weather Maps

The weather in any one place is part of a larger pattern. Local weather is produced by a combination of atmospheric conditions that are both nearby and far away. Because of this, the best way to communicate information about the weather is with a map. A **weather map** shows data about recent weather conditions across a large area. It shows precise data for separate locations, and it shows how this data relates to each other. Weather maps are useful tools for making forecasts.

The National Weather Service (NWS) is the main source of weather maps in the United States. Several times each day, forecasters at about 350 major weather stations (and many smaller ones) around the country send data to the NWS. The NWS plots this information on surface maps. New surface maps are prepared every three or six hours.

A surface map may show station models for hundreds of weather stations. Each station model may include up to about 20 different pieces of data. For example, there can be data on the kinds of clouds at different altitudes, the amount of precipitation over the previous six hours, and the change in air pressure over the previous three hours.

By comparing the information from the station models on a surface map, NWS meteorologists can identify larger patterns in the weather. They mark maps to show storms, regions of high or low pressure, and fronts. They add information sent by radio from weather satellites, weather balloons, and ocean buoys. The final maps show recent weather conditions across the nation.

A weather map helps to show what is happening nearby. Fronts, pressure systems, precipitation, and temperature are all often shown on weather maps. When you want more precise information, a general weather map can be combined with station models. The symbols used on weather maps are the same all over the world. Using standard symbols allows everyone to share data about the weather, wherever the data has been collected. What would you expect the temperature in Louisville to be if the cold front moves south?

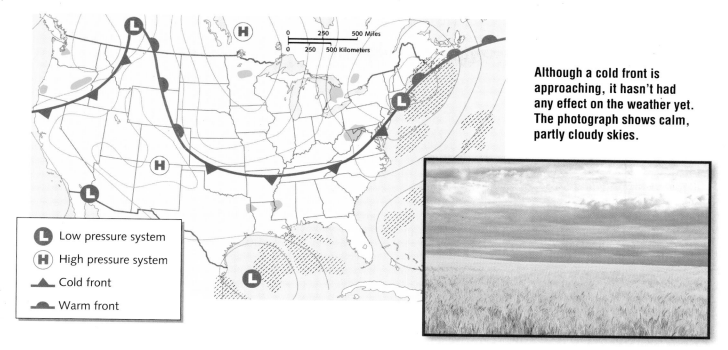

Although a cold front is approaching, it hasn't had any effect on the weather yet. The photograph shows calm, partly cloudy skies.

The two maps on this page show a cold front passing through the United States. On the top map, the areas ahead of the cold front have fair weather, because of the air mass that hangs over the land. Station models in this area would show warm temperatures, gentle winds, and little cloud coverage.

The map at the bottom of the page shows the United States 48 hours later. A cold front has moved into the area, bringing the changes that you might expect. The warm, humid air has been pushed upward, forming towering clouds and causing brief, strong showers or thunderstorms. These conditions are common when there is a great difference between the temperature and humidity of the air masses that are colliding.

Meteorologists can use weather maps like these to predict how the weather will change. By reading the station models on both sides of the front, meteorologists can know what the air masses will do next. Unless conditions change, the front shown on these two maps will probably continue to move across the area at a constant speed.

✔ **What will the weather just ahead of the cold front be like in another 24 hours?**

Two days later, the weather has changed. The cold front has collided with the warm, wet air, causing winds and rain.

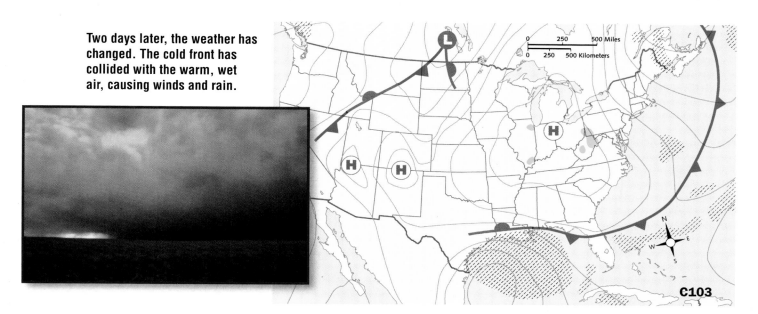

C103

A satellite image shows the intensity of these thunderstorms, but it cannot pinpoint locations where tornadoes are likely to form.

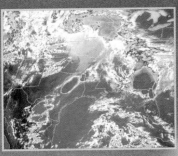

Winds blowing toward the Doppler radar tower show up as blue-green. Winds blowing away show up as yellow-red. When these colors appear next to each other, a tornado is likely to form.

Satellite and Doppler Technology

Advances in technology have helped make weather forecasts more and more accurate. Two new developments, weather satellites and Doppler radar, have actually helped save many lives. Because of these devices, forecasters have been able to warn people of dangerous weather.

Weather satellites have been orbiting Earth since the 1960s. They are especially useful for tracking the paths of hurricanes and other severe storms. The earliest satellites gave meteorologists their first overall view of the clouds over the Earth and allowed them to track storms far out at sea. Today satellites can measure humidity and temperature and even detect fog forming at night. Most of the United States can be viewed by two satellites that stay in position over the equator. They orbit Earth at the same speed as it rotates, so they always view the same areas. There are also two weather satellites that view different areas as they circle the Earth.

Additional weather data is collected by a network of Doppler radar stations across the country. Doppler radar uses the reflection of radio waves to accurately measure wind speeds and precipitation. It can also determine the direction of winds. Information

◀ Tornadoes form from funnel-shaped thunderclouds. Although these storms last a short time and cover a small area, they cause extreme damage. The winds in a tornado can approach speeds of 480 km/hr (about 300 mi/hr).

about wind direction is extremely important in forecasting tornadoes. Tornadoes are formed by strong winds that rotate within a thunderstorm. Doppler radar detects the opposing directions of rotating winds. When meteorologists see these conditions, they can issue tornado watches and warnings to communities that are likely to be affected.

✓ **How do weather satellites and Doppler radar help meteorologists forecast violent weather conditions?**

Summary

Meteorologists use data collected at weather stations to make surface maps. These maps include station models and symbols for systems such as fronts and for centers of high and low pressure. The information in station models is gathered using a variety of tools. Weather maps also use data collected by weather satellites, Doppler radar, and weather balloons.

Review

1. What is a station model?
2. What does an anemometer measure?
3. Why aren't instrument shelters built on concrete surfaces?
4. **Critical Thinking** If the National Weather Service doubled the number of its employees and the amount of its equipment, would its forecasts become twice as accurate as they are now? Explain your answer.
5. **Test Prep** Which weather prediction tool is most useful for identifying conditions under which a tornado might form?
   A weather maps
   B surface maps
   C Doppler radar
   D weather satellites

LINKS

MATH LINK

Forecasting The trends method of weather forecasting uses general changes in the past to predict future weather. A cold front has traveled 800 km from the Great Plains to the Great Lakes area over the past 24 hours. Buffalo, New York, is 400 km from the cold front now. Assuming that the front continues to travel at the same speed, in about how many hours will the front pass over that city?

WRITING LINK

Narrative Writing—Story The writer Mark Twain once said, "Everyone talks about the weather, but no one does anything about it." Write a story that includes a weather saying that you have made up and an explanation of how it came to be.

SOCIAL STUDIES LINK

How Weather Shaped the Modern World In 1588 the English navy won an important sea battle against the Spanish Armada. This event helped shape the history of the modern world. Find out how weather played an important role in this historic event.

TECHNOLOGY LINK

Learn more about weather and weather forecasting by visiting this Internet Site. **www.scilinks.org/harcourt**

SCI LINKS
THE WORLD'S A CLICK AWAY

LESSON 4

What Causes Severe Storms?

In this lesson, you can . . .

INVESTIGATE how meteorologists track the paths of hurricanes.

LEARN ABOUT how storms develop and what you can do to protect yourself from them.

LINK to math, writing, social studies, and technology.

Tracking Hurricanes

Activity Purpose Meteorologists at the National Weather Service track dangerous storms so that, if necessary, they can tell people to prepare or to move. In this investigation you will get an inside view of one of a meteorologist's most important jobs—tracking the movement of a hurricane. You will track the progress of a fictional storm—Hurricane Zelda.

Materials

- hurricane tracking chart
- 3 different-colored pencils or markers
- history table for Hurricane Zelda
- current advisory for Hurricane Zelda

Activity Procedure

1 On the hurricane tracking chart, plot the path taken by Hurricane Zelda. Use the data from the history table and the current advisory. On the tracking chart, draw a small circle for each location listed on the history table. Use an ordinary pencil for this step.

▼ Satellite images like this one help meteorologists track hurricanes, Earth's largest storms.

2. Your first circles show Zelda as a tropical depression. When winds exceed 39 mi/hr, a tropical depression is classified as a tropical storm and is given a name. Fill in the tropical depression circles with one color. Write *Tropical Storm Zelda* under the location where the tropical depression first becomes a tropical storm. Choose a different color for the tropical storm circles.

3. When winds exceed 74 mi/hr, a tropical storm becomes a hurricane. Write *Hurricane Zelda* under the location where Zelda first reaches hurricane strength. Use the color for the tropical storm to fill in all the circles from the one labeled in Step 2 to the one labeled here. Choose a different color for the hurricane circles, and fill in all of those.

History of Hurricane Zelda

Date and Time	Latitude	Longitude	Maximum Wind Speed
07/27 3:00 UT*	23.0°N	66.0°W	35 mi/hr
07/27 9:00 UT	23.5°N	67.0°W	35 mi/hr
07/27 15:00 UT	24.0°N	67.5°W	40 mi/hr
07/27 21:00 UT	24.5°N	67.5°W	45 mi/hr
07/28 3:00 UT	25.5°N	69.0°W	55 mi/hr
07/28 9:00 UT	27.0°N	72.0°W	60 mi/hr
07/28 15:00 UT	29.0°N	72.5°W	70 mi/hr
07/28 21:00 UT	31.0°N	73.0°W	75 mi/hr
07/29 3:00 UT	31.0°N	76.0°W	85 mi/hr

*UT means Universal Time and is the same as Greenwich Mean Time. In this 24-hour system, the time one hour after 12:00 noon is 13:00.

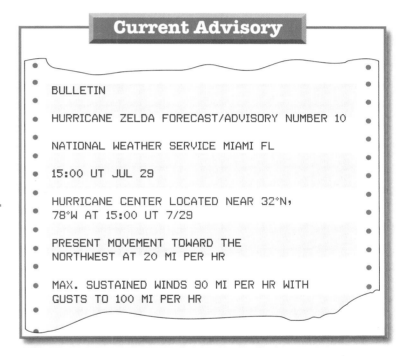

Current Advisory

BULLETIN

HURRICANE ZELDA FORECAST/ADVISORY NUMBER 10

NATIONAL WEATHER SERVICE MIAMI FL

15:00 UT JUL 29

HURRICANE CENTER LOCATED NEAR 32°N, 78°W AT 15:00 UT 7/29

PRESENT MOVEMENT TOWARD THE NORTHWEST AT 20 MI PER HR

MAX. SUSTAINED WINDS 90 MI PER HR WITH GUSTS TO 100 MI PER HR

Draw Conclusions

1. Look at the track of the storm on the map. What general patterns can you see in the storm's direction and wind speed?

2. Use the tracking chart and the latest data on Zelda's speed and direction to **predict** where and when the storm will strike the coast.

3. **Scientists at Work** Scientists who track hurricanes often **predict** using probabilities. They list the probability of a storm's striking a spot on the coast as low, medium, or high. To which parts of the coastline would you give low, medium, and high probabilities of being hit by Hurricane Zelda?

Investigate Further Hurricane Zelda's path does not cross any land. Find out what happens to hurricanes that travel across islands in the Caribbean. Do they continue to travel as hurricanes?

Process Skill Tip

When you use data to **predict**, you need to decide whether you should use only the most recent patterns shown by the data or the pattern shown overall, by the whole set of data.

Severe Storms

Thunderstorms

About 2000 thunderstorms are taking place on Earth at any given moment. A **thunderstorm** can be a very strong storm with a lot of rain, thunder, and lightning.

A thunderstorm begins to form when warm, humid air is pushed high into the atmosphere. Wind, the sun's heating of the Earth's surface, or the arrival of a cold front may do this. As the warm air is pushed upward, it begins to cool. When it reaches the dew point, the water vapor in the air begins to condense, and a cloud forms.

Soon, the weight of the condensed water vapor becomes too much for the air to support. The water falls to the ground, pulling cool air with it. At this time winds blow both upward and downward in the cloud.

Electric charges build up in the cloud. This is similar to static electricity collecting when clothes rub against each other. The charges increase until they are so strong that electricity travels through the air as lightning. It may travel between parts of the cloud or between the cloud and the Earth's surface.

The air along the path of a lightning bolt is heated to temperatures that can be greater than 28,000°C (about 50,000°F), which is about four times the temperature at the surface of the sun. This intense heat makes the air expand so fast that the shock waves make the sound of thunder.

FIND OUT

- how thunderstorms, hurricanes, and tornadoes form

- what to do to stay safe in severe storms

VOCABULARY

thunderstorm
hurricane
tropical storm
tornado

About 45,000 thunderstorms occur on Earth every day. They result in lightning, thunder, heavy precipitation, and sometimes hailstones as big as tennis balls. ▼

The large volumes of warm air being pushed upward add height to the cloud that forms. These upward movements of air, called updrafts, can reach speeds of 100 km/hr (62 mi/hr).

Most thunderstorms are over within an hour. The precipitation and cool air moving downward through a thundercloud stop more warm air from moving up into the cloud. Sometimes, however, the cool air rushing down to the Earth's surface pushes more warm air upward to form a neighboring thundercloud.

✔ **Why do most thunderstorms stop?**

Thunderstorm Safety

Lightning that travels between a cloud and the Earth's surface can be deadly. It is usually attracted to the highest point in the area and to materials that easily conduct electricity, such as water, wiring, and metals. Here are some rules that can protect you in a thunderstorm:

1. If you are outside, try to get indoors. Avoid small buildings that are far from other buildings.
2. Don't touch faucets, plumbing pipes, electric outlets, or telephones with cords, except in an emergency.
3. If you can't get indoors, you will be safe in a car, as long as you are not touching any of the car's metal parts.
4. If you are out in the open, lie down flat.
5. Don't take shelter under a tree.
6. Stay out of water. If you are in a boat, get to shore as soon as a storm threatens, even if it seems far away.

Precipitation forms a cool downdraft, a downward movement of air, near the original warm updraft. This cool air eventually shuts off the thunderstorm's fuel supply, the warm air below. When it does, the storm weakens and breaks up.

Thunderstorm updrafts can carry moisture all the way to the edge of the stratosphere, where it forms a flat-topped, anvil-shaped cloud.

Falling ice crystals can gather water droplets that freeze to form a coating around them. The balls or lumps—called hailstones—may be carried upward by updrafts and fall again. Each time this happens, the hailstones gain another layer of ice.

Hurricanes

Much fiercer weather than thunderstorms can form in the tropics. **Hurricanes** are large, spiraling storm systems that can be as much as 600 km (about 372 mi) across. They can travel for thousands of kilometers and last for more than a week. Their winds can reach 300 km/hr (186 mi/hr).

A hurricane starts as a low-pressure area over an ocean. This area is called a tropical depression, because the air pressure is low, or "depressed." Winds blow into the low-pressure area, and the rotation of the Earth causes them to spiral around that area. If the winds reach a constant speed of 63 km/hr (about 39 mi/hr), the tropical depression is classified as a **tropical storm**. About half of the tropical storms that form each year develop winds that exceed 119 km/hr (about 74 mi/hr). When the wind reaches this speed, the storms are classified as hurricanes.

When a hurricane reaches land, extremely strong rains can cause flooding, and violent

THE INSIDE STORY

Anatomy of a Hurricane

The center of a hurricane, called the eye, is about 20 km (12 mi) wide. Within the eye the winds drop and there is no rain. The eye is caused by dry, cool air that is pulled down from above.

Around the eye is the eye wall. This area is the most intense part of the storm. The warm, wet air that rushes to the center of a hurricane is pulled upward in the eye wall. As the air travels upward, it causes low pressure at the surface, pulling in more air. When the water vapor in the air that is being pushed upward condenses into rain, it releases heat, strengthening the storm.

Heat and moisture from below feed both the upward-moving and the downward-moving air. As long as the storm stays over warm water, it can continue to strengthen.

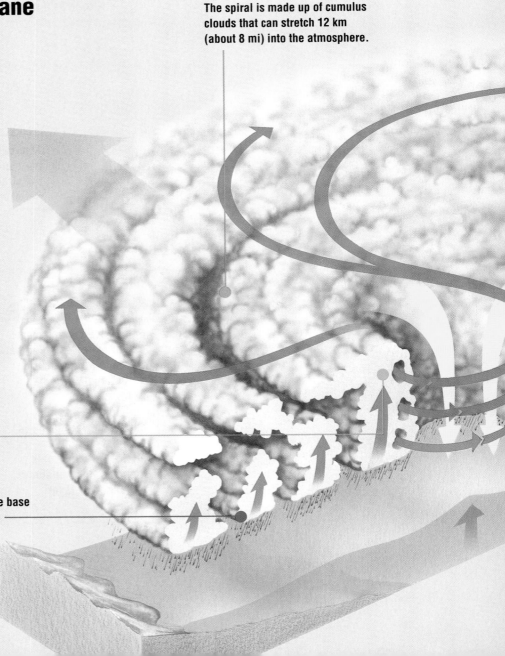

The spiral is made up of cumulus clouds that can stretch 12 km (about 8 mi) into the atmosphere.

The hurricane's fastest winds spiral around the eye in the eye wall.

Warm, wet air is pulled into the base and the sides of the hurricane.

winds can destroy buildings. Waves of up to 12 m (about 40 ft) high hit the shoreline, and a storm surge of water up to 3 m (about 10 ft) high is also pushed ahead of the storm. These can cause serious damage to beaches and barrier islands.

Large amounts of warm, humid air keep hurricanes in motion. When they reach cooler seas or move across land, where the air is less humid, hurricanes may die out.

✓ **What causes the winds to rush toward hurricane areas?**

Cool, dry air is pulled down into the eye of the hurricane. As a result the eye is a place of calm and quiet. However, it is quiet only for a short time. As the storm moves, the eye wall with its extreme weather once again moves over an area.

The hurricane is pushed by the prevailing winds at 15–40 km/hr (about 9–25 mi/hr).

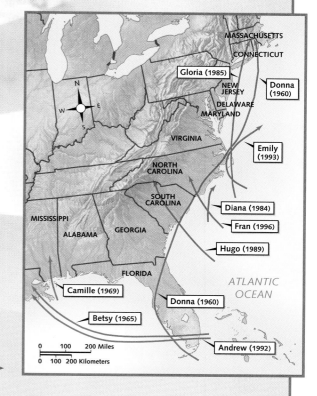

This map shows the tracks of some of the strongest hurricanes to reach the United States since 1960. Which states seem most at risk from these storms? ▶

C111

Tornadoes

Far from the ocean, a stretch of the Great Plains from northern Texas through North and South Dakota has hundreds of Earth's most violent storms each year. This stretch is known as Tornado Alley.

A **tornado** is an intense windstorm that often forms within a severe thunderstorm. The winds of a tornado spin in a column of air that extends from the bottom of a thundercloud. Warm, humid air is pulled into the funnel-shaped column. The swirling updrafts can reach speeds of 480 km/hr (about 300 mi/hr). A tornado may also form because of winds associated with a hurricane. When a tornado touches the ground, its winds can pick up or destroy almost everything in their path, including buildings, railroad cars, and buses.

✔ **What kinds of storms can cause tornadoes?**

Tornado Safety

When you hear a tornado warning or see a tornado, act quickly.

1. Stay inside, if possible. However, some homes, such as mobile homes, are not sturdy enough to withstand the force of a tornado.
2. If you look for shelter inside, go to an inside room on the lowest floor of the building. A basement is best, but an inside hallway or bathroom is a good second choice. Stay away from windows and doors.
3. Stay underneath a staircase, a bed, or a strong table or desk.
4. If you can't get inside a building, lie in a ditch with your hands over your head. Don't stay in a car or other vehicle.

◄ A small funnel begins to form at the bottom of a wall cloud, a circular bulge on the bottom of a thundercloud. Strong updrafts are already present in this bulge. With modern Doppler radar, meteorologists can detect tornadoes as they form in clouds.

◄ The swirling funnel starts to descend. By the time the funnel is visible, the winds may already be swirling debris around on the ground below. Flying debris is one of the greatest dangers from a tornado.

Summary

Thunderstorms often form at cold fronts and move into an area of warm, humid air. Lightning, thunder, high winds, hail, and tornadoes can accompany thunderstorms. Hurricanes are large, spiraling storms with high winds and heavy rain. Tornadoes are violently rotating columns of air that can form in thunderstorms and hurricanes. The winds of a tornado can be exceptionally destructive.

Review

1. Does thunder cause lightning, or does lightning cause thunder? Explain.
2. Why do hurricanes form over oceans?
3. Why is a mobile home an unsafe place to be during a tornado?
4. **Critical Thinking** Why do most thunderstorms form in the afternoon?
5. **Test Prep** The most violent weather in a hurricane is in the —

   A eye
   B eye wall
   C downdraft
   D spiral

◄ The funnel touches ground. If this tornado is like many others, it will travel for about 15 minutes in a northeasterly direction at about 55 km/hr (34 mi/hr). It may cause a path of destruction about 140 m (459 ft) wide and about 15 km (9 mi) long. But tornadoes are not predictable. They vary greatly in their size, speed, duration, and strength.

LINKS

MATH LINK

Rates During a thunderstorm, you hear thunder after you see the lightning that causes it. You can figure out how far away a thunderstorm is, based on the difference between the speed of light and the speed of sound. If there is a lapse of 5 seconds between seeing the lightning and hearing the thunder, the storm is about 1.6 km away. How far away is the storm if the lapse is 12 seconds?

WRITING LINK

Informative Writing—Explanation Find out about waterspouts. Write and illustrate a short magazine article for your classmates that explains what waterspouts are, how and where they form, and what effects they have.

SOCIAL STUDIES LINK

Geography Rotating tropical storms can form over the Indian and western Pacific Oceans. Learn more about these storms and the damage they can do. What are these storms called?

TECHNOLOGY LINK

To learn more about tornadoes and the people who study them, watch *Hurricane Warning* on the **Harcourt Science Newsroom Video.**

TRACKING EL NIÑO

Scientists use satellites and other technology to scan the ocean for changes that can cause severe weather.

Why look at the ocean for weather changes?

The temperature of the ocean affects the air above it. The effects on air masses help determine the weather. Warm water evaporates faster than cold water and can cause more storms to form. Depending on wind patterns, the storms can affect nearby land. The cooling of ocean waters can cause different weather patterns.

What is El Niño?

Winds normally push a current of warm water westward across the Pacific, toward Australia. El Niño begins when those winds change direction and push warm water eastward, toward South America. As a result, a band of unusually warm water—an El Niño current—forms across the Pacific. It blocks the colder water that usually flows along the western coast of South America. The warmer ocean increases the formation of clouds and storms in the Pacific. This changes weather patterns in Australia, East Africa, and Southeast Asia, as well as North and South America.

How do satellites and other hardware help forecast El Niño?

Meteorologists use satellites, weather balloons, ground weather stations, and radar to gather data on the atmosphere and the ocean each day. They also collect data from buoys, ships, and airplanes. They feed the data into computers that make models of the atmosphere. Forecasters use the models to predict the weather.

To forecast El Niño, meteorologists add a couple of extra tools. The TOPEX/Poseidon satellite measures the surface level of the Pacific every 10 days. Although the satellite orbits 1336 km above Earth's surface, its measurements are accurate to 13 cm. Because the winds that form an El Niño current raise ocean water levels in the eastern Pacific, a rise in ocean levels is a clue that El Niño is beginning.

Meteorologists also get data from a group of buoys, the Tropical Atmosphere Ocean Array. The array stretches from New Guinea across the Pacific to Peru. The buoys send data on air temperature, water temperature, wind, and humidity to data centers in the United States. The information allows forecasters to quickly spot weather changes caused by El Niño.

A new supercomputer at NASA's Goddard Space Flight Center in Maryland will be able to use even more detailed data from satellites and buoys to make models that will better predict El Niño events. In the year 2000, NASA and the French space agency plan to launch *Jason-1,* a satellite that will have twice the ocean-measuring ability of the present network.

Why is it important to know when an El Niño pattern will occur?

An El Niño pattern in the Pacific causes severe weather that can harm millions of people. An El Niño pattern occurred between late 1997 and mid-1998. As a result, storms from the Pacific pounded the west coast of North and South America. Drought struck Australia. Floods destroyed crops in Africa. Predicting El Niño events can help people prepare for these storms' damaging effects.

THINK ABOUT IT

1. Why is it important to track El Niño systems?
2. How do meteorologists use satellites to track El Niño?

WEB LINK:
For Science and Technology updates, visit The Learning Site.
www.harcourtschool.com

Careers   Tornado Chaser

What They Do
Tornado chasers work in areas where tornadoes are common. They place instruments in the paths of tornadoes to collect information. They also use computer models to forecast the formation and movement of tornadoes.

Education and Training A tornado chaser must have a background in geography, physics, chemistry, mathematics, and computer science. Those who work in the field need at least a bachelor's degree in meteorology.

Edward Lorenz

METEOROLOGIST

Edward Lorenz teaches meteorology at the Massachusetts Institute of Technology (MIT). He is best known for his contributions to chaos theory, an important new understanding of natural occurrences. Dr. Lorenz used the ideas of chaos theory to show why accurate long-range weather prediction is not possible. In his studies he observed that even the smallest change in one variable that contributes to a weather system can have a big effect on how the system develops. That means that all atmospheric conditions measured to the smallest fraction of a degree would have to be known completely to make long-range predictions, predictions more than four or five days into the future. Because that's impossible, so are long-range weather predictions.

Dr. Lorenz came up with his contribution by accident. After serving as a weather forecaster in the U. S. Army, he began to wonder if weather forecasting could be improved. He decided to write a computer program that would make long-range predictions. While a meteorologist at MIT in the early 1960s, Dr. Lorenz set up his computer program. He

programmed a set of equations that defined weather conditions and set the computer model in motion. The computer showed how weather conditions would change over time.

At a certain point, Dr. Lorenz wanted to repeat a weather pattern. He found the numbers from an earlier run that had produced that pattern. He put the numbers back into the computer, expecting the computer to produce the same pattern. But instead of using the exact numbers carried out to six decimal places (for example, 0.506127), he rounded to three (0.506). The change was so small that he thought it wouldn't matter. But it did. The resulting weather pattern varied from the original—first a little and then more and more. After a few months of simulated time, the second weather pattern was completely different from the first. He called this "the butterfly effect," because a tiny difference in conditions, such as the breeze caused by the flapping of the wings of a butterfly in China could alter the weather over the United States weeks later.

THINK ABOUT IT

1. What is chaos theory, and what does it have to do with weather?

2. Why did Dr. Lorenz hypothesize that accurate long-range weather forecasting would be impossible?

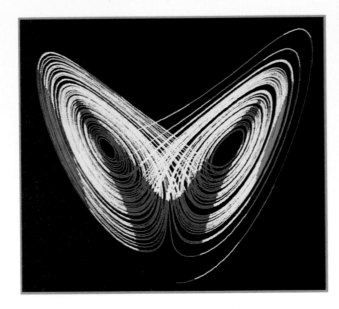

The shape produced by a computer graphing Dr. Lorenz's equations.

Figuring Out Fronts

How do air masses behave when they meet?

Materials
- 22.5-cm (9-in.) glass pie plate
- 240 ml (1 cup) water, colored blue
- 240 ml (1 cup) cooking oil
- clay

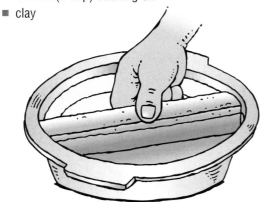

Procedure

1 Use the clay to build a barrier across the middle of the pie plate.

2 Gently pour the colored water into one side of the plate and the oil into the other side.

3 Remove the barrier, disturbing the liquids as little as possible.

4 Quickly bend down and observe how the liquids move in the plate.

Draw Conclusions

Which liquid is heavier or more dense? How can you tell? What kind of air mass do you think the water represents? What does the oil represent? Where is the front?

Low Pressure

How does low pressure affect weather?

Materials
- 2 medium-sized balloons
- 2 lengths of string, each 30 cm (1 ft)

Procedure

1 Inflate the balloons to equal sizes and knot them shut.

2 Tie one end of one string to a balloon. Tie one end of the other string to the second balloon.

3 Hold the other ends of the strings and position the balloons about 7.5 cm (3 in.) apart in front of your face.

4 Blow a steady stream of air between the balloons and observe how they respond.

Draw Conclusions

The "wind" blowing between the balloons lowered the air pressure between them. How did the balloons respond? How do you think that blowing between the balloons is similar to what happens when a tornado forms?

Vocabulary Review

Use the terms below to complete the sentences. The page numbers in ( ) tell you where to look in the chapter if you need help.

thermosphere (C87)   **surface map** (C100)
mesosphere (C87)   **station model** (C100)
stratosphere (C87)   **weather balloon** (C101)
troposphere (C87)   **weather map** (C102)
air mass (C88)   **thunderstorm** (C108)
air pressure (C92)   **hurricane** (C110)
relative humidity (C93) **tropical storm** (C110)
front (C94)   **tornado** (C112)
forecast (C100)

1. The line at which two air masses collide is a ____.

2. The force of all the air pressing down on Earth is called ____.

3. A violent storm that rotates around a central eye is a ____, which begins as a ____.

4. A weather condition called a ____ often produces the rapidly swirling winds of a ____.

5. The conditions near the ground can be shown on a ____, a type of ____.

6. The current weather at a particular weather station can be shown by the numbers and symbols of a ____.

7. The levels of the atmosphere in order from Earth's surface, are the ____, the ____, the ____, and the ____.

8. The amount of moisture in the air compared with the amount that could be in the air is known as the ____.

9. A large body of air that has the same overall characteristics throughout is an ____.

10. A prediction of upcoming weather called a ____ can be made with the help of data from a ____, which is released into the atmosphere.

Connect Concepts

Complete the chart with terms from the word bank.

thunderstorm   tornado   barometer
anemometer   uneven heating   hurricane
weather map   fronts

```
                        Weather
                           |
   ┌───────────────────────┼───────────────────────┐
Storms include          Caused by            Forecasting tools

11. _____        14. _____        16. _____

12. _____     air masses colide at     17. _____

13. _____        15. _____        18. _____
```

Check Understanding

Write the letter of the best choice.

19. The winds that move air masses around the globe are caused by —
    A the thinning of the atmosphere at higher elevations
    B uneven heating of Earth by the Sun
    C Earth's ozone layer absorbing ultraviolet energy
    D the aurora borealis

20. A passing front usually brings —
    F a change of weather
    G a hurricane or tornado
    H warmer weather
    J cooler weather

21. Comparing the temperature and the dew point can tell you the air's —
    A anemometer
    B relative humidity
    C speed
    D direction

22. For which type of severe storm can forecasters give us the earliest warning?
    F air mass
    G thunderstorm
    H tornado
    J hurricane

23. A continental polar air mass is about to move into your area. What can you expect the weather to become?
    A warmer and drier
    B warmer and wetter
    C cooler and wetter
    D cooler and drier

Critical Thinking

24. Hot-air balloons, or balloons that people use for flight, generally travel at fairly low altitudes. What are some reasons for this?

25. An occluded front forms when a warm air mass is trapped above two cooler air masses. Can a cool air mass be trapped above two warmer air masses? Explain.

26. It is summer, and a cold front is moving into the Great Plains. Predict what will happen when the front meets a warmer air mass.

Process Skills Review

27. You hear a clap of thunder. What can you **infer** about its cause?

28. Why are station models useful for **comparing** local weather conditions?

29. Which would be more helpful to you to **interpret data** about weather patterns—a written paragraph or a list of monthly average temperatures. Explain your answer.

Performance Assessment

Recording Weather Conditions

You receive the following report of weather conditions:

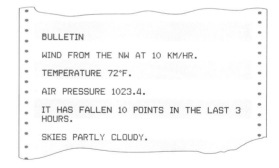

BULLETIN
WIND FROM THE NW AT 10 KM/HR.
TEMPERATURE 72°F.
AIR PRESSURE 1023.4.
IT HAS FALLEN 10 POINTS IN THE LAST 3 HOURS.
SKIES PARTLY CLOUDY.

Make a station model from the weather report. List the other information you would need to complete the station model.

Unit Project Wrap Up

Here are some ideas for wrapping up your unit project or doing other projects.

Demonstrate at a Science Fair

Demonstrate your weather reports and instruments in a school science fair. Describe how you observe, measure, and predict the weather. Videotape sample weather reports, and play them at the Science Fair.

Make a Bulletin Board Display

Use yarn, paper, and other art materials to make a bulletin board display of an ecosystem. Show how the things in the ecosystem interact with each other.

Make an Ocean Model

Use clay to make a model of the ocean bottom. Write a report about ocean ecosystems.

Investigate Further

How can you make your project better? What other questions do you have? Plan ways to find answers to your questions. Use the Science Handbook on pages R2–R9 for help.

Today's Weather

Cycles in Earth and Space

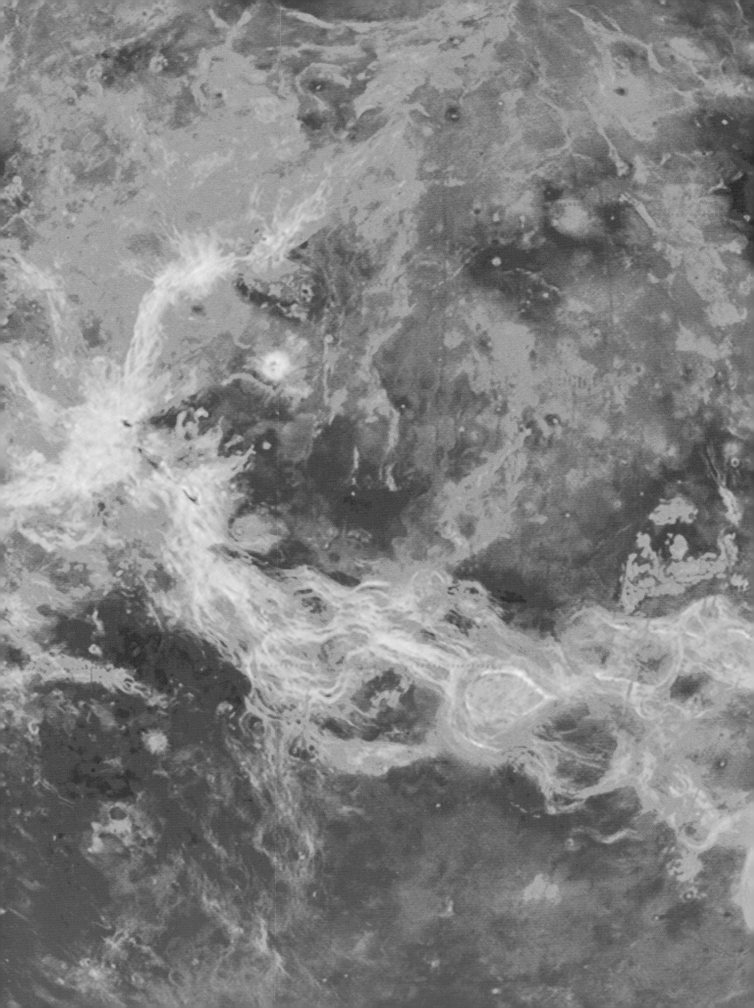

UNIT D

EARTH SCIENCE

Cycles in Earth and Space

Unit Project

Game Show

Write game show questions about cycles in Earth and space. Use the chapter titles in this unit for question categories. Write ten questions and answers for each category. Make plans to produce the game show during the unit.

Movement of Earth's Crust

Maps made decades or even centuries ago are often still accurate and useful because Earth changes very slowly. But over longer periods of time, it changes greatly.

Vocabulary Preview

crust
mantle
core
lithosphere
asthenosphere
plate tectonics
divergent boundary
convergent boundary
transform fault boundary
mid-ocean ridge
rift
sea-floor spreading
earthquake
focus
epicenter
P wave
S wave
surface wave
Richter scale
volcano

FAST FACT

Most active volcanoes have erupted within the last 2000 years. The United States has at least 58 active volcanoes.

Some U.S. Volcanoes	
State	**Number**
Alaska	43
Hawai'i	5
Washington	4
Oregon	3
California	3

FAST FACT

Earthquake waves travel more slowly through warm rocks than they do through cool rocks. Scientists have used earthquake waves to locate the "hot spot" that lies under Yellowstone National Park.

FAST FACT

The Himalayas are still being formed by the collision of two parts of Earth's surface. The mountains are rising at the rate of about 5 mm per year.

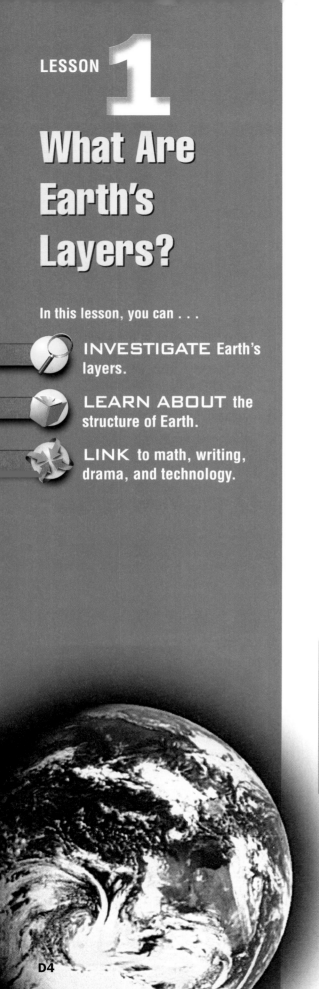

What Are Earth's Layers?

In this lesson, you can . . .

INVESTIGATE Earth's layers.

LEARN ABOUT the structure of Earth.

LINK to math, writing, drama, and technology.

INVESTIGATE

Earth's Layers

Activity Purpose   Have you ever thought about digging a hole to the other side of the Earth? If so, you've probably realized that the distance is much too great. In fact, you could dig for years and never get past Earth's thin outer layer, or crust. Even if you did get past the crust, what other layers would you have to go through? And how thick are they compared to the crust? In this investigation you will **use a model** of Earth's layers to find out more about our planet's structure.

Materials

- newspaper
- modeling clay—yellow, brown, red, green
- metric ruler
- clear plastic straw

Activity Procedure

1. You will **make a model** of Earth's layers. The model should be made to scale. Let 1 cm = 1000 km.

2. Use the measurements in the table to help you. Copy and complete the table for your model.

Earth's Layers		
Layer	Approximate Thickness	Model
Crust	8 km	0.008 cm
Mantle	3000 km	
Outer core	2500 km	
Inner core	1000 km	

Picture A

Picture B

3 Before you make your model, cover your work area with newspaper. From the inside out, Earth's layers are in this order: inner core, outer core, mantle, and crust. Use the yellow clay for the inner core, brown clay for the outer core, red clay for the mantle, and green clay for the crust. (Picture A)

4 Use the plastic straw to take a sample of your model. Push the straw through the layers. Then pull it out. Draw a picture of the layers in the straw. (Picture B)

Draw Conclusions

1. From your model, what can you tell about the thickness of the crust compared to the other layers?

2. The core and mantle are too far below the surface for scientists to sample. But they can take samples of the layers in the crust in the same way that you used the straw to take a sample of your model. What does your sample show?

3. **Scientists at Work** Scientists **use models** to study the parts of Earth that they can't **observe** directly. From your model, what did you find out about Earth's layers?

Investigate Further Think about a way to use your model to find the volume of each of Earth's layers. Which of Earth's layers has the greatest volume? Which has the least volume?

Process Skill Tip

Earth's mantle and core are too deep for us to observe directly. You can **use a model** to compare the positions of the layers and the thicknesses of the layers.

Earth's Structure

Earth's Layers

FIND OUT

- about Earth's structure
- about Earth's plates and where they are located
- some of the ways that Earth's surface changes

VOCABULARY

crust
mantle
core
lithosphere
asthenosphere
plate tectonics

We live on Earth's crust, which is about 32 km (20 mi) thick under the surface of the continents and about 8 km (5 mi) thick under the ocean floor. Earth's outermost layer is the **crust**. The layer directly beneath the crust is the **mantle**. The innermost layer is the **core**.

INNER CORE

Evidence shows that the inner core, which is mainly iron, is solid. The inner core is also extremely hot. It is estimated to be more than 5500°C (about 10,000°F). At this temperature metals should melt. However, the inner core is pressed into a solid by the weight of all the layers around it.

If you could tunnel from Earth's surface to the center of the core, you would travel about 6400 km (4000 mi). It would be an amazing trip, but it's not possible. Temperatures at the core are more than 5500°C (about 10,000°F), and the pressures deep inside Earth are crushing.

How, then, do we have information about Earth's structure? For the first 10 or 12 km (about 6 or 7 mi), scientists use drills to take samples of the crust. Below that they must hypothesize what the layers are made of. They base their hypotheses on the patterns of waves that travel through Earth after an earthquake and on the materials that come to the surface in an active volcano. From this information scientists have put together a picture of Earth's structure.

✓ **What are the three main layers of Earth?**

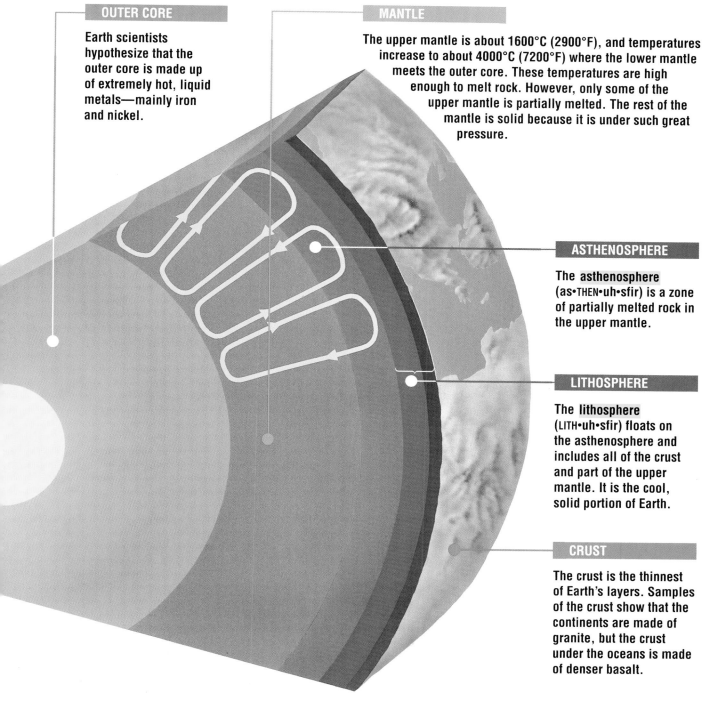

OUTER CORE

Earth scientists hypothesize that the outer core is made up of extremely hot, liquid metals—mainly iron and nickel.

MANTLE

The upper mantle is about 1600°C (2900°F), and temperatures increase to about 4000°C (7200°F) where the lower mantle meets the outer core. These temperatures are high enough to melt rock. However, only some of the upper mantle is partially melted. The rest of the mantle is solid because it is under such great pressure.

ASTHENOSPHERE

The asthenosphere (as•THEN•uh•sfir) is a zone of partially melted rock in the upper mantle.

LITHOSPHERE

The lithosphere (LITH•uh•sfir) floats on the asthenosphere and includes all of the crust and part of the upper mantle. It is the cool, solid portion of Earth.

CRUST

The crust is the thinnest of Earth's layers. Samples of the crust show that the continents are made of granite, but the crust under the oceans is made of denser basalt.

Earth's Plates

The lithosphere is divided into seven major plates, as shown on the map. All of Earth's land and oceans are on these plates. The plates float on a layer of partially melted rock of the asthenosphere. The huge, stiff plates float because the asthenosphere has a property called *plasticity,* which means that it can flow. Think of the plastic putty that children play with. Even though it is a solid, it can be pulled and pushed into different shapes. And when left in a ball, the putty slowly flows into a puddle.

Heat from the center of Earth causes currents in the asthenosphere. Hot mantle rock is pushed up by cooler rock flowing in underneath it. The rock spreads out, cools, and then sinks again. As the asthenosphere flows, the plates of the lithosphere move with it. In fact, the plates are in constant motion. However, their motion is so small—just a few centimeters a year—that it must be carefully measured to be detected.

The plates of the lithosphere constantly change in shape and size. A plate may split along new lines or combine with another plate. A plate may even slide under another plate to become mantle rock again. The boundaries where plates meet are usually the sites of earthquakes and volcanoes. **Plate tectonics** is the

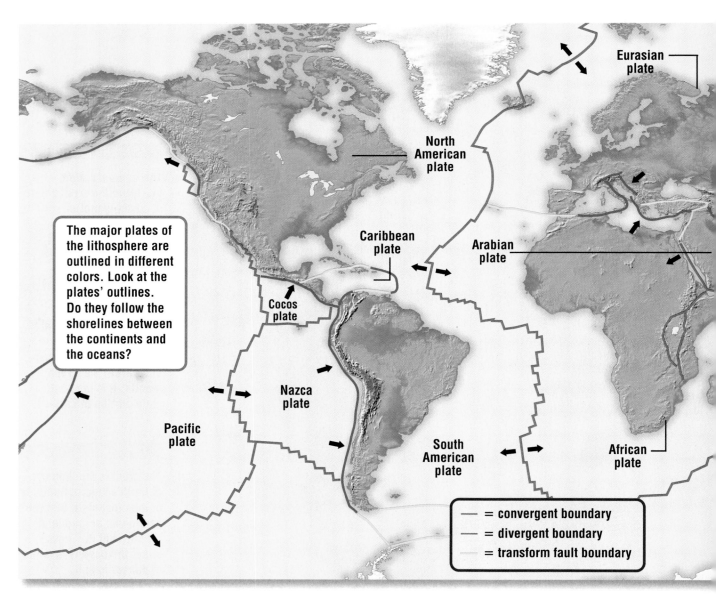

The major plates of the lithosphere are outlined in different colors. Look at the plates' outlines. Do they follow the shorelines between the continents and the oceans?

Eurasian plate

North American plate

Caribbean plate

Arabian plate

Cocos plate

Nazca plate

Pacific plate

South American plate

African plate

— = convergent boundary
— = divergent boundary
— = transform fault boundary

theory scientists use to explain plate movements. The word *tectonics* comes from the Greek word meaning "builder," because plate movements build Earth's largest landforms.

The major plates are named for the continents or oceans they carry. You can see from the map that the major plates are huge. For example, the American plates carry most of the United States, Canada, and Mexico, as well as South America.

Look at the boundaries of the North and South American plates. Notice that the plates include about half of the Atlantic Ocean as well as the continents of North and South America.

The crust under the ocean is the newer, thinner oceanic crust. The crust at the continents is the older, thicker continental crust. Most plates contain both oceanic and continental crust.

Find the Pacific plate. This is the largest one, covering about one-fifth of Earth's surface. It stretches from the western coast of North America to the Philippine Islands. Unlike the North American plate, the Pacific plate is composed almost entirely of oceanic crust. It carries only the Pacific Ocean floor, its islands (including Hawai'i), and a narrow strip of the California coast.

✔ **What is plate tectonics?**

This cross section shows the Earth's crust and the upper layers of its mantle. The lithosphere is like a jigsaw puzzle of huge, rigid plates that float on the asthenosphere of hot, plastic rock. ▼

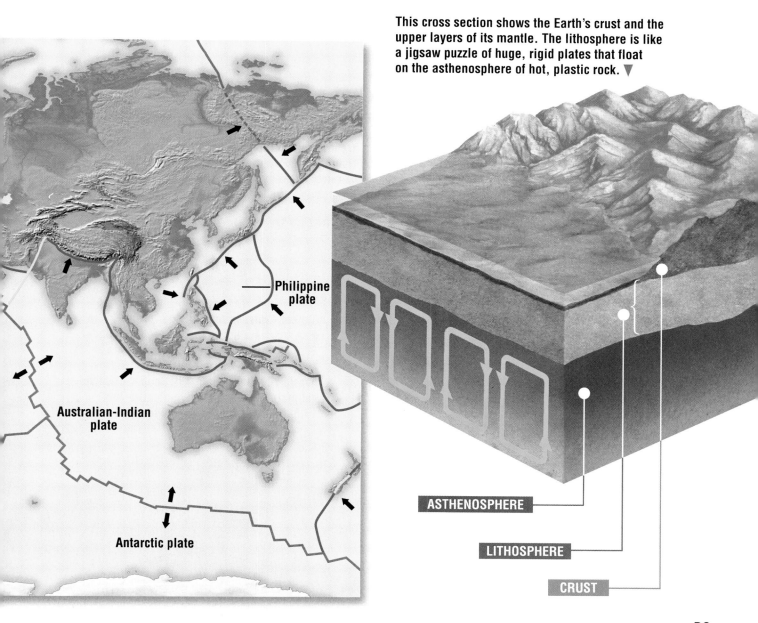

Philippine plate

Australian-Indian plate

Antarctic plate

ASTHENOSPHERE

LITHOSPHERE

CRUST

Changes to Earth's Surface

You will find out that the movement of plates causes Earth's surface to change constantly and dramatically. The plates move continents around the globe, forming mountains and causing earthquakes and volcanic eruptions. But there are other processes that cause Earth's surface to change all the time. Some of these are constant. Others occur only once in a while. But they all change Earth in observable ways.

Earth's surface is changed by the constant processes of erosion and deposition. Water and wind erosion carve out valleys, cliffs, and caves. A river may carry along sand and rocks and deposit them on its banks and at its mouth. Wind may pick up sand and deposit it on dunes.

Glaciers also change Earth's surface. When Earth was cooler, a dense blanket of ice spread over much of North America. Remains of that glacier still cover most of Greenland. Today most glaciers form slow-moving rivers of ice in cold mountain valleys.

A glacier can erode the land and deposit rock, sand, and mud. As the ice is pulled downhill by gravity, it drags rocks and pebbles along with it, acting as a sort of sandpaper that grinds away the land beneath. When the ice melts, the

◄ The dark stripes on this valley glacier in Alaska are made up of rock that has been torn up from the land's surface underneath. The glacier acts like a huge river of ice, tearing up rock and moving it.

Meteor Crater in Arizona was formed by an enormous meteorite that hit the Earth about 20,000 years ago. The meteorite made a hole about 1.2 km (0.7 mi) across and nearly 180 m (about 591 ft) deep. Scientists estimate the mass of the meteorite was 13,600,000 kg (about 15,000 tons)! ▼

material carried by the glacier is deposited to form ridges, hills, and gravel-covered plains.

Still another way that Earth's surface changes is when it is hit by objects from space, such as meteorites and comets. Meteoroids are pieces of rock that move through the solar system. When a meteoroid enters Earth's atmosphere, friction causes it to heat up and burn. At night this event is seen as a "shooting star," or meteor. Meteoroids that reach the surface of Earth are called meteorites. Each year, about 19,000 meteorites fall to Earth. Most of them are so small that no one notices them.

✓ **What changes Earth's surface?**

Summary

Earth is composed of the inner core, outer core, mantle, and crust. The crust plus part of the upper mantle make up the lithosphere—the place where Earth's land and oceans are found. The theory of plate tectonics explains how the plates of the lithosphere move around, causing changes to Earth's surface. Other changes to Earth's surface are caused by wind and water, glaciers, and objects from space that hit Earth.

Review

1. Draw and label a diagram of Earth's layers.
2. Compare the lithosphere and the asthenosphere.
3. Why do the plates of the lithosphere move?
4. **Critical Thinking** The rock below the asthenosphere is more stiff and rigid than the rock near the outer core. Use what you know about the temperatures of Earth's layers to explain why.
5. **Test Prep** The lithosphere includes —
   A all of the crust
   B the crust and part of the lower mantle
   C the core and part of the upper mantle
   D the crust and part of the upper mantle

LINKS

MATH LINK

Comparing Depths The distance from Earth's surface to its center is about 6400 km. The deepest anyone has ever been inside Earth is 5 km down a South African mine. How many times as great as the depth of the mine is the distance to the center of Earth?

WRITING LINK

Narrative Writing—Story Choose a nearby place such as a field, a mountain, a riverbank, or even the land under a sidewalk. Write a story for your classmates describing how the surface of Earth in that area might have changed over time.

DRAMA LINK

Skit Write and perform a skit describing a journey to the center of the Earth. Include information about how the temperature and pressure might change during the journey.

TECHNOLOGY LINK

Learn more about Earth's plates by visiting the National Air and Space Museum Internet site.
www.si.edu/harcourt/science

 Smithsonian Institution®

How Do Earth's Plates Move?

In this lesson, you can . . .

INVESTIGATE how the movement of Earth's plates affects the continents.

LEARN ABOUT how Earth's plates move.

LINK to math, writing, literature, and technology.

Mountain building is one effect of the movement of Earth's plates. ▽

How Earth's Plates Move

Activity Purpose Earth's plates are creeping along at the rate of a few centimeters a year. Some plates are moving toward each other, some are moving away from each other, and some are sliding past each other. How does this movement affect the continents on the surface of the plates? In this investigation you will **make and use a model** of a split in the floor of the Atlantic Ocean. Then you will **make inferences** based on what you **observe**.

Materials
- shoe box
- metric ruler
- scissors
- paper
- modeling clay

Activity Procedure

1 Turn the shoe box upside down, and cut a 1-cm by 10-cm slit across the bottom. Then cut out a hole large enough for your hand in the center of one of the box's long sides.

2 Cut two 8-cm by 25-cm strips of paper. Run the strips through the slit in the box. Leave about 10 cm sticking out of the box. Fold the strips of paper back on opposite sides of the slit. (Picture A)

3 Use modeling clay to make a model of the continents of North America and South America. Press down your model on the left strip of paper. Make a model of Europe and Africa, and press it down on the right strip. (See pages D8–D9 for a map of the world.)

4 From beneath the box, slowly push the strips up through the slit. **Observe** what happens to the clay. (Picture B)

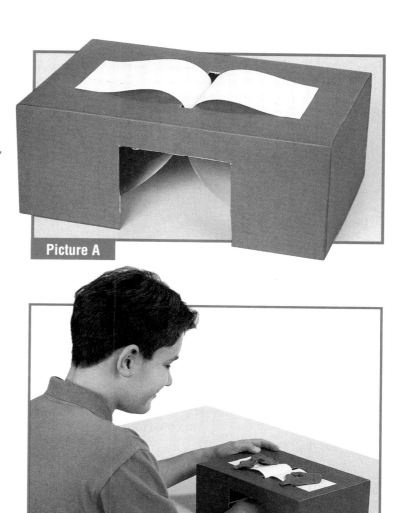

Picture A

Draw Conclusions

1. The clay in your model represents the continents bordering the Atlantic Ocean. The rising paper acts like the molten rock that is moving out of a crack between plates, pushing the plates apart. **Use your model** to **infer** what happens to the continents as the plates they are on move apart.

2. Plates can also move toward each other or slide past each other. **Use your model** to demonstrate these two other kinds of plate movement. Describe what happens to the continents.

3. **Scientists at Work** From **observations** of the natural world and from **using models**, scientists **infer** how the continents move. Based on your model, what can you infer about the positions of the continents millions of years ago?

Investigate Further **Use a model** to show what happens to Earth's surface when plates collide. Wet a paper towel, and then spread it out on a flat surface. Place your hands on either side of the towel, and slowly move your hands toward each other. What happens to the paper towel? What might this be a model of?

Process Skill Tip

When you **infer**, you explain an event. An inference is your best guess, or judgment, based on observations and any other evidence you have. Not all inferences are correct, even if they seem to make sense. As you gather more evidence, your inferences may change.

How Earth's Plates Move

The Movement of Earth's Plates

FIND OUT

- about divergent, convergent, and transform fault boundaries

- how continents move and change

VOCABULARY

divergent boundary
convergent boundary
transform fault
  boundary
mid-ocean ridge
rift
sea-floor spreading

The lithosphere is broken into huge, stiff plates that fit together like the pieces of a puzzle. These plates float on the asthenosphere. As Earth's plates move, they interact in one of several ways. Plates move away from each other along a **divergent boundary**. They collide along a **convergent boundary**. They grind past each other along a **transform fault boundary**.

Plate movements have produced most of the world's volcanoes, earthquakes, high mountain ranges, and deep-ocean trenches. All of these can occur along plate boundaries or former plate boundaries. The three different kinds of boundaries are shown in the diagram below. A map showing the location of these boundaries is on pages D8–D9.

✔ **How does the movement of plates affect Earth's surface?**

— = convergent boundary
— = divergent boundary
— = transform fault boundary

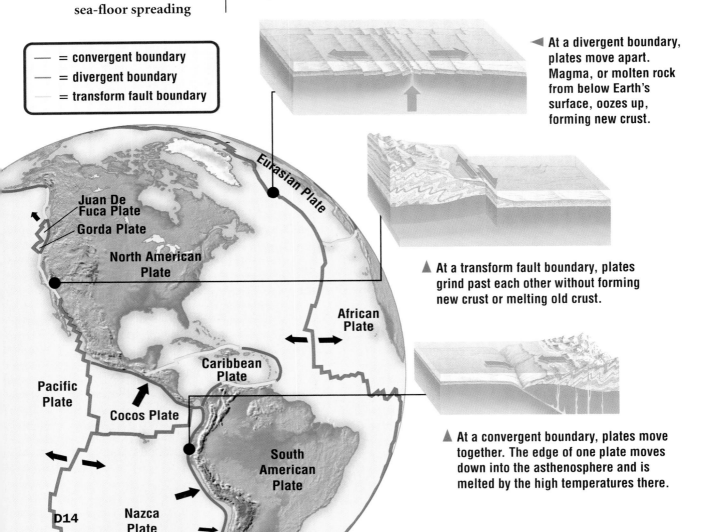

◄ At a divergent boundary, plates move apart. Magma, or molten rock from below Earth's surface, oozes up, forming new crust.

▲ At a transform fault boundary, plates grind past each other without forming new crust or melting old crust.

▲ At a convergent boundary, plates move together. The edge of one plate moves down into the asthenosphere and is melted by the high temperatures there.

Juan De Fuca Plate
Gorda Plate
North American Plate
Eurasian Plate
African Plate
Caribbean Plate
Pacific Plate
Cocos Plate
South American Plate
Nazca Plate

D14

Divergent Boundaries

Scientists have hypothesized that divergent boundaries are caused by magma being pushed upward under a plate. The magma presses against the plate, melting and stretching the lithosphere until it cracks. Then the magma oozes into the gap and cools to form new crust. Where the pressure is great enough, the magma erupts as a volcano.

Most divergent boundaries are found along the **mid-ocean ridge**, a chain of mountains that runs 83,000 km (about 52,000 mi) through all the world's oceans. Along the highest part of the mid-ocean ridge runs a deep valley, or **rift**. A rift forms where two plates move apart.

Magma is slowly pushed up through cracks in the rift and then cools to form new sea floor. The process is called **sea-floor spreading**. The rocks on each side of the rift are slowly pushed away from it. This is how the floor of the Atlantic Ocean has formed over the last 165 million years.

Some divergent boundaries occur within continents. One is in East Africa, at the Great Rift Valley. Here, two small plates are moving away from the African plate. Some day East Africa will split apart from the rest of the continent.

At divergent boundaries, continents or ocean floors are spreading apart. As new crust forms, it pushes the plates on either side of the boundary farther and farther away from each other. ▼

The Great Rift Valley started millions of years ago. The crust in East Africa was stretched thin by the spreading plates. Two great cracks in Earth's surface opened up, and what would become the floor of the Great Rift Valley slowly dropped hundreds of feet. Today there are cliffs and volcanoes on both sides of the valley.

✔ **What happens along a divergent boundary?**

▲ In a few places, the mid-ocean ridge is above the ocean's surface, forming islands. On Iceland, one of these islands, you can see the rift at the top of the ridge.

D15

Convergent Boundaries

When new crust forms at a divergent boundary, somewhere on Earth crust must be melting. If it did not, Earth would keep growing larger. But scientists know that Earth's size has not changed over a long period of time. So old crust must be melting to balance new crust that is forming. The melting often occurs at convergent boundaries, where plates collide.

Three kinds of collisions are possible. First, an oceanic plate can collide with another oceanic plate. When this happens, one of the two plates is pushed down under the other. The plate that is forced down melts in the asthenosphere. The collision can cause a deep-ocean trench to form. The deepest trench on Earth, the Mariana Trench, is at the boundary where the Pacific plate is moving beneath the Philippine plate. The Mariana Trench is 11 km (about 6.8 mi) deep, more than six times the depth of the Grand Canyon.

In the second kind of collision, two continental plates collide and one is forced down beneath the other. The plates crumple and fold, forming mountain ranges. This process has formed some of the world's highest mountains. The Himalayas, for example, are forming where the plate carrying India is crashing into the Asian plate. The Himalayan peaks are still rising about 5 mm (0.2 in.) a year.

At this convergent boundary, an oceanic plate and a continental plate collide. As the denser rock of the ocean floor moves down into the asthenosphere, it begins to melt. The melted rock may return to the surface in a volcanic eruption. ▼

In the third kind of collision, an oceanic plate collides with a continental plate and the oceanic plate is forced downward. This happens because oceanic crust is denser than continental crust. Mountains and volcanoes form along the boundary between the plates. The Andes Mountains in South America are one result of this kind of collision.

The destruction of a plate causes a lot of activity along convergent boundaries. Eighty percent of the world's volcanoes and 90 percent of all earthquakes occur along convergent boundaries. For example, the Mount St. Helens volcano in Washington State is the result of a collision between the American plate and another, smaller plate. Sometimes violent activity continues at very old convergent boundaries.

✔ **What happens along a convergent boundary?**

This photograph shows the movement that occurs along a transform fault. ▶

Many volcanoes form along a convergent boundary. Melted oceanic crust is slowly pushed upward and then erupts to the surface.

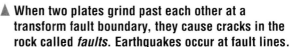

▲ When two plates grind past each other at a transform fault boundary, they cause cracks in the rock called *faults*. Earthquakes occur at fault lines.

Transform Fault Boundaries

At a transform fault boundary, two plates move past each other in opposite directions. Most transform faults are in oceanic crust. However, a few are within continents.

One famous transform fault is located where the Pacific plate moves past the American plate. This is called the San Andreas fault. It zigzags for about 1280 km (800 mi) through parts of coastal California. Land west of the fault is on the Pacific plate. It moves northwest about 5 cm (2 in.) per year. Land east of the fault is on the American plate. If the movement continues for millions of years, the part of California that is west of the fault will become an island off the west coast of the United States. Some day it could reach Alaska!

Earthquakes are common along a transform fault boundary. As you may know, the area near the San Andreas fault has many earthquakes. However, volcanoes and other mountains usually do not form along a transform fault boundary.

✓ **What happens along a transform fault boundary?**

Earth's Surface Changes Over Time

Remember that the continents and oceans are on Earth's plates. Because the plates move, the continents we live on today were in different places in the past. They will continue to move and will be in other positions in the future. If you could see Earth 200 million years from now, it would look nothing like the way it looks today. Old oceans will have closed up, and new oceans will have formed.

Using clues from rocks, volcanoes, and earthquake patterns, Earth scientists have formed a hypothesis about how Earth's surface has changed over the past 500 million years. The maps below show this hypothesis. Ancient continents moved away from each other and then collided again at different locations.

The collisions produced many of Earth's great mountain ranges. For example, the plates carrying Africa and North America collided about 225 million years ago as the supercontinent of Pangea (pan•JEE•uh) formed. This collision produced the southern Appalachian Mountains. Long ago those mountains may have towered higher than Mount Everest does today.

The movement of the continents causes oceans to disappear and new oceans to form. About 135 million years ago, the plates carrying South America and Africa began splitting apart to form the South Atlantic Ocean. Notice the shapes of these two continents, and think of South America next to Africa. You can see that they fit together like two pieces of the same puzzle.

✔ **How do Earth's plates affect the positions of the continents?**

500 million years ago
Earth's continents formed three distinct land masses.

Between 500 and 225 million years ago, these land masses began to come together.

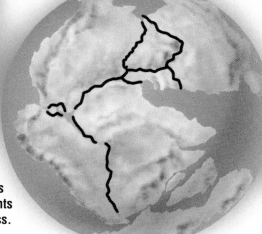

225 million years ago
The supercontinent Pangea was formed when all of the continents came together as one land mass.

Summary

As Earth's plates move, they interact in several different ways. Plates move away from each other along divergent boundaries. They collide along convergent boundaries. They grind past each other along transform fault boundaries. The movement of the plates causes Earth's continents to move apart, move together, or slide past one another as well.

Review

1. Compare the three types of plate boundaries.

2. How does new crust form along divergent boundaries?

3. How are most mountain ranges produced?

4. **Critical Thinking** Scientists can tell how old the rocks are along a rift. Which ones do you think will be older: the rocks found within a few meters of the rift or rocks found farther away? Explain.

5. **Test Prep** Which of the following is most likely to occur along a transform fault boundary?

   A an earthquake   **C** a mountain range

   B a volcano   **D** a mid-ocean ridge

Today
Pangea broke up into the pieces that make up the continents we know today.

LINKS

MATH LINK

Metric Distances New York City is about 5800 km from Paris. The two cities are on different plates that are moving away from each other at an average speed of about 2.5 cm per year. At this speed, how long would it take New York and Paris to be twice as far apart as they are today? Hint: There are 100,000 cm in a kilometer. So the cities are moving apart at a speed of 0.000025 km per year.

WRITING LINK

Informative Writing—Report Find out more about Alfred Wegener, the first person to hypothesize that Earth's continents move around the globe. Write a short report for your teacher describing Wegener's life and work.

LITERATURE LINK

Our Patchwork Planet Read this book by Helen Roney Sattler to find out more about Earth's plates and how they move. You will also find out how scientists are learning to predict the earthquakes and volcanic eruptions caused by plate movements.

TECHNOLOGY LINK

Learn more about how scientists and engineers are working to make buildings and structures more earthquake resistant by watching *Earthquake Building Codes* on the **Harcourt Science Newsroom Video.**

LESSON 3

What Causes Earthquakes and Volcanoes?

In this lesson, you can . . .

INVESTIGATE how to find the location of an earthquake.

LEARN ABOUT the causes of earthquakes and volcanoes.

LINK to math, writing, art, and technology.

Volcanologists (vahl•kuh•NAHL•uh•jists), or scientists who study volcanoes, collect lava and gas samples. ▼

How You Can Locate an Earthquake

Activity Purpose Suppose there's an earthquake. The ground trembles, and buildings, bridges, and roads shake. Then, just seconds later, it's over. What can scientists learn about an event that is less than a minute long? How do they know precisely where the earthquake occurred? The waves an earthquake produces can offer a lot of information. In this investigation you'll find out how you can **interpret data** on wave-travel times to determine an earthquake's location.

Materials

■ map of the western United States   ■ drawing compass

Activity Procedure

1 An earthquake produces different kinds of waves that travel inside Earth. They travel at different speeds. The table shows the difference in arrival times between two types of waves. Scientists have discovered that they can tell how far away an earthquake is by using the difference in travel time for the waves. For each 100 km traveled, there is an 8-sec time difference.

2 Copy and complete the data table. **Calculate** the distance from each city to the source of the earthquake. First, divide each time by 8 sec. Then, multiply the result by 100 km.

Earthquake Wave Data		
City Where Waves Were Recorded	Time Difference	Distance from Earthquake
Carson City, Nevada	20.8 sec	
Los Angeles, California	44.4 sec	
Phoenix, Arizona	83.2 sec	

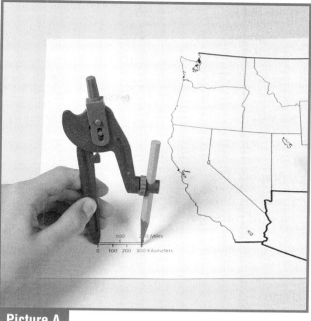

Picture A

③ Use the map scale to set the radius of your compass to match the distance from the earthquake to one of the cities. (Picture A)

④ Center your compass on the city you selected. Draw a circle to show all the points that are the calculated distance from that city.

⑤ Repeat Steps 3 and 4 for the other cities in the table. You should draw three circles that all intersect at or near one city. This is where the earthquake occurred.

Draw Conclusions

1. According to your **data** and **calculations**, where did the earthquake occur?

2. Why do you think you needed **data** from three different cities to find the earthquake's location?

3. **Scientists at Work** Scientists **interpret data** and **use numbers** to study earthquakes and other natural disasters. Based on the activity, what are some of the ways scientists use the data they get from earthquake waves?

Investigate Further What else can earthquake waves tell scientists? Go to the library to research these waves, which are also called seismic (SYZ•mik) waves. Report on your findings.

Process Skill Tip

When you measure, you are making observations that can often be summarized by **using numbers**. Later, you need to **interpret your data**, the numbers, to draw conclusions about what you are studying.

Earthquakes and Volcanoes

Plate Movements Cause Earthquakes

VOCABULARY

earthquake
focus
epicenter
P wave
S wave
surface wave
Richter scale
volcano

You've already found out that the crust of Earth is constantly moving. Strong forces shape its rocks—crumpling them, folding them, and stretching them until they crack and break apart. Most of these changes take place along plate boundaries. The changes are usually slow, so you don't notice them—until a major earthquake takes place.

About 95 percent of all earthquakes occur at or near the edges of moving plates, along great cracks in Earth's crust called *faults*. As the plates move, the rocks on either side of the fault do not slide freely past each other. Instead, they become tightly locked together. As the plates continue to move, the rocks are put under great strain. They bend and stretch until they reach their breaking point. Suddenly, the rocks snap and then shift into a new position. This sudden jolt releases energy as vibrations that are felt as an **earthquake**.

Each year, about 200 earthquakes around the world are large enough to cause major damage. But scientific instruments can detect

The sudden movement of rocks along a fault releases energy. The energy travels in all directions from the earthquake's **focus**, the point in Earth's crust where the first major movement along the fault occurred. The point on Earth's surface directly above the focus is called the **epicenter**.▼

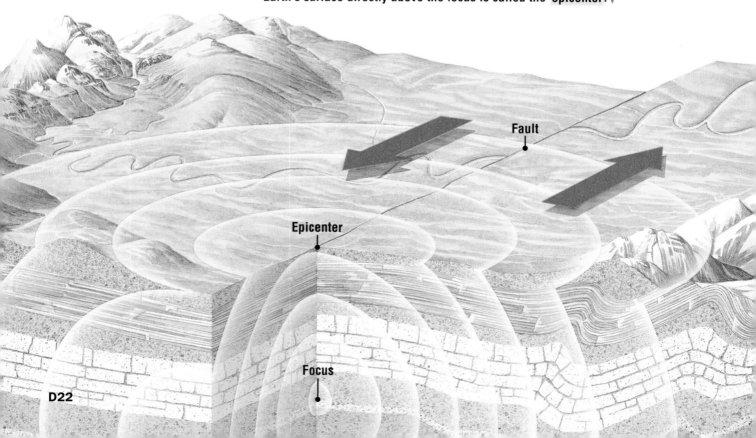

Fault

Epicenter

Focus

many earthquakes that people can't. Scientists have discovered there are actually about 1 million earthquakes each year.

✔ **How does the movement of plates cause earthquakes?**

Earthquake Waves

The energy from an earthquake travels away from the focus in waves. In the investigation, you read that when an earthquake occurs, it produces different kinds of waves that travel at different speeds. Scientists put these waves into two categories: those that travel inside the Earth and those that travel only at the surface.

Two main kinds of waves travel inside the Earth. The faster kind is called a primary wave,

or **P wave**. P waves are "push-pull" waves that cause back-and-forth vibrations in the same direction as the waves move. These are like the waves made by suddenly pushing or pulling on the end of a stretched-out spring toy.

The slower kind of wave is called a secondary wave, or **S wave**. S waves cause vibrations at right angles to the waves' direction of travel. S waves travel like the waves on a rope that is shaken up and down.

Surface waves travel only at the surface and move less quickly than the other two kinds. These powerful waves make the ground roll and sway. They often cause a great deal of damage to buildings, roads, and other surface features. The surface waves are the chief cause of damage during an earthquake.

During a major earthquake, people feel an initial jolt, caused by the arrival of the P waves. Then, there is a second, larger jolt, when the S waves arrive. Finally, people feel a rolling and swaying motion caused by surface waves.

✔ **How is the motion of a P wave different from the motion of an S wave?**

◀ Most earthquakes occur along fault lines like this one in California. This is the San Andreas fault.

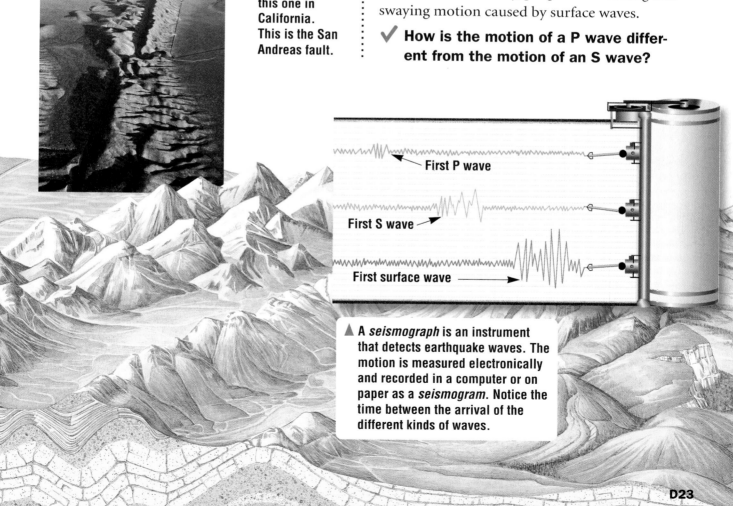

First P wave

First S wave

First surface wave

▲ A *seismograph* is an instrument that detects earthquake waves. The motion is measured electronically and recorded in a computer or on paper as a *seismogram*. Notice the time between the arrival of the different kinds of waves.

Earthquake Safety

Scientists measure earthquakes in different ways. Two of these are the Richter scale and the Mercalli intensity scale. The **Richter scale** measures the amount of energy released during an earthquake. The largest earthquakes ever recorded were about 8.5 on the Richter scale. They released energy equal to that from an explosion of one billion tons of TNT.

The Mercalli intensity scale measures the amount of damage that an earthquake causes. The amount of damage depends on how close communities are to the epicenter, how well structures are built, and the kind of ground on which the buildings stand. The numbers on the scale range from I to XII. An earthquake with an intensity of I is felt by very few people. An earthquake with an intensity of XII causes total destruction.

Scientists try to predict earthquakes. However, it is difficult to tell exactly where and when an earthquake will strike. People who live in earthquake zones need to be prepared. Often buildings in these areas are made to withstand the shocks.

Most communities and families in earthquake zones have disaster plans. If you live in an earthquake zone, you should take part in earthquake drills. That way you know what to do, where to go, and how to communicate if telephone and transportation systems are destroyed. Look at the chart above for earthquake safety tips.

✔ **What is the difference between the Richter scale and the Mercalli intensity scale?**

Average Yearly Earthquakes		
Richter Scale Magnitude	Approximate Number Each Year	Damage Done
Less than 2.5	900,000	Most people don't feel them.
2.5–5.4	30,000	Little damage, mostly caused by falling objects.
5.5–6.0	500	Some buildings may be damaged.
6.1–6.9	100	Many buildings will suffer some damage.
7.0–7.9	20	Major earthquakes with extensive damage to almost all buildings and structures.
8.0 or greater	1 every 5–10 years	Buildings totally destroyed.

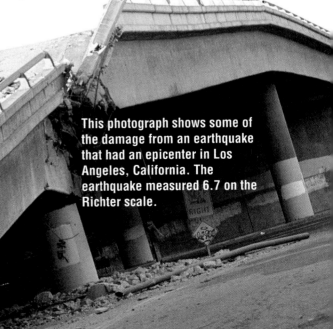

This photograph shows some of the damage from an earthquake that had an epicenter in Los Angeles, California. The earthquake measured 6.7 on the Richter scale.

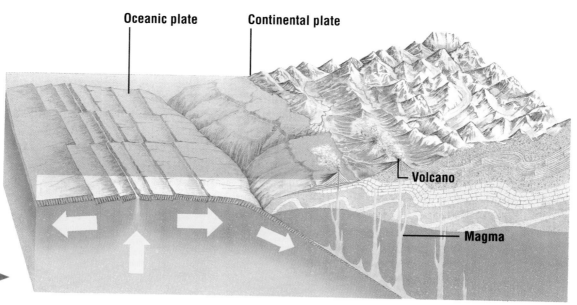

Oceanic plate   Continental plate

An oceanic plate moves down and under a continental plate along a convergent boundary. As the oceanic plate enters the mantle, it melts to form magma. The magma is pushed up through cracks in the crust to form a range of volcanoes. ▶

Volcano

Magma

How Volcanoes Form

Sometimes magma, or molten rock beneath Earth's surface, is forced up through an opening in Earth's surface. The molten rock erupts as lava, or molten rock at Earth's surface. Sometimes it can erupt as ashes and cinders. A **volcano** is a mountain that may form around the opening as the lava or cinders build up.

An erupting volcano is one of the Earth's most spectacular fireworks shows. A volcano may erupt with a violent explosion of lava, ash, and gas. It may produce a glowing cloud that reaches into the stratosphere. Other volcanoes may slowly ooze red-hot lava in long ropes or sheets. There are about 600 volcanoes on land and many more on the ocean floors. Some are active. Others are not active right now, but they may erupt in the future.

Although volcanic flows and eruptions can be destructive, they are also useful. In a few places, such as Iceland, the heat they produce is a source of low-cost energy. More importantly, volcanoes are Earth's chief land builders. Scientists estimate that about 80 percent of the area of the continents and ocean floors was formed by volcanic flows and eruptions.

Like earthquakes, most volcanoes occur at plate boundaries. Along a mid-ocean rift, where two plates move apart, a ridge of underwater volcanoes is formed. Iceland's volcanoes are part of this kind of ridge. Other rift volcanoes are found on continents, such as those that make up the East African rift system.

At convergent boundaries where an oceanic plate collides with a continental plate, the denser oceanic plate moves down and under the continental plate. The sinking plate begins to melt. The hot molten rock is pushed upward to form volcanic mountains, such as the Andes in South America. This volcanic range is located along the edge of the continental plate bordering the Pacific Ocean.

The Andes are part of an amazingly long chain of volcanoes known as the Ring of Fire. This chain is nearly 50,000 km (about 30,000 mi) long. It almost completely surrounds the Pacific Ocean.

When the Andes formed, crust was destroyed by a collision at the edge of a plate. At a rift new plate material is formed. These two processes always balance. As one edge of a plate is destroyed, another edge is built up. Volcanoes form at both edges.

✔ **How does a volcano form?**

Types of Volcanoes

You probably picture a volcano as a cone-shaped mountain. But in fact, volcanoes have many sizes and shapes. Some are cone-shaped, but others are wide and flat. Scientists classify volcanoes into three general forms: shield volcanoes, cinder cones, and composite cones.

The size and shape of a volcano depend on the type of lava that erupts. For example, lava that flows easily can spread over great distances and form a shield volcano. The lava builds up in layers to form a low, wide mountain.

Thicker lava may erupt more violently, throwing volcanic fragments high into the air. When the fragments land near the vent, they form steep-sided cinder cones.

Some volcanoes erupt quietly at first, like a shield volcano, and then violently, like a cinder cone volcano. The result is a steep, cone-shaped volcano called a composite volcano.

A *composite volcano* switches between quiet eruptions of flowing lava and violent eruptions of thick, gas-rich lava. This type of volcano has the most powerful eruptions of all. ▼

Steeply sloping cone formed of layers of ash and lava

◄ Even the shattered remains of Mount St. Helens have the usual steep cone shape of a composite volcano. Like shield volcanoes, a composite volcano may erupt on and off for a period as long as a million years.

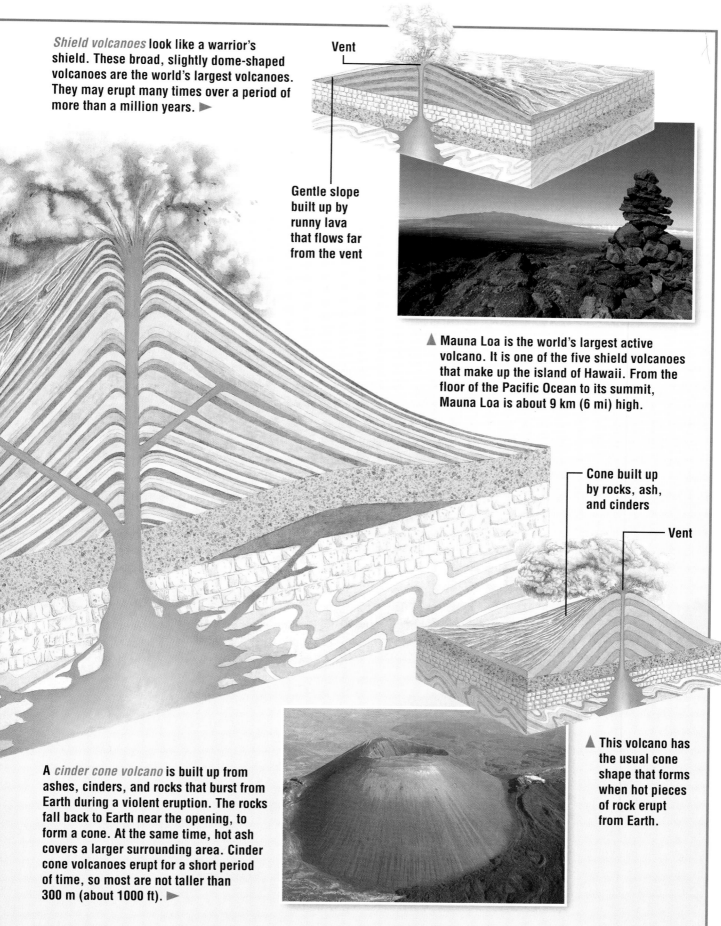

Shield volcanoes look like a warrior's shield. These broad, slightly dome-shaped volcanoes are the world's largest volcanoes. They may erupt many times over a period of more than a million years. ▶

Vent

Gentle slope built up by runny lava that flows far from the vent

▲ Mauna Loa is the world's largest active volcano. It is one of the five shield volcanoes that make up the island of Hawaii. From the floor of the Pacific Ocean to its summit, Mauna Loa is about 9 km (6 mi) high.

Cone built up by rocks, ash, and cinders

Vent

A *cinder cone volcano* is built up from ashes, cinders, and rocks that burst from Earth during a violent eruption. The rocks fall back to Earth near the opening, to form a cone. At the same time, hot ash covers a larger surrounding area. Cinder cone volcanoes erupt for a short period of time, so most are not taller than 300 m (about 1000 ft). ▶

▲ This volcano has the usual cone shape that forms when hot pieces of rock erupt from Earth.

Hot-Spot Volcanoes

Not all of Earth's volcanoes form at the edges of plates. Sometimes a volcano forms when a narrow column of hot molten rock breaks through the lithosphere in the middle of a plate. This single column of magma is called a *hot spot*. A hot spot does not move. However, the plate above it moves, forming a chain of volcanoes.

If the hot spot is under the ocean, it may deposit layers of lava on the ocean floor. Sometimes these layers build up high enough to break through the ocean's surface, forming an island. As the plate drifts over the hot spot, a chain of volcanic islands is produced. Most of these volcanoes are shield volcanoes.

The Hawaiian Islands were formed by a hot spot near the middle of the Pacific plate. They are part of a long chain of islands and

Step 1
Within a plate, a hot-spot volcano forms above a column of hot magma from deep in the mantle. ▶

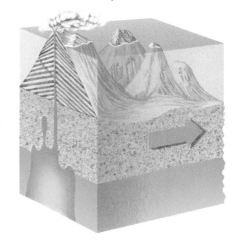

Step 2
As the plate moves, the hot spot below stays where it is. The first volcano moves away from the hot spot and so away from the source of magma. A new location on the plate is over the hot spot, and a second volcano starts to form. ▶

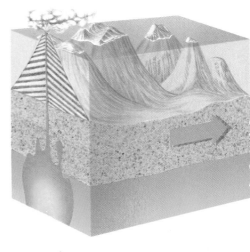

Step 3
As the plate continues to slide across the hot spot, still another volcano starts to form. In this way a chain of islands can form. ▶

The Hawaiian Islands were formed by a hot spot under the Pacific plate. Today only the island of Hawai'i, located directly over the hot spot, has active volcanoes. ▼

seamounts that stretches from the island of Hawai'i to a seamount 5920 km (about 3680 mi) away.

You can tell that the Pacific plate is moving northwest by following the trail of volcanic islands and seamounts. The youngest is the island of Hawai'i—less than 1 million years old. The oldest, now a seamount, formed 70 million years ago.

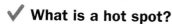 **What is a hot spot?**

Summary

Most earthquakes and volcanoes are caused by the movements of Earth's plates. Earthquakes result when the rocks along plate boundaries are bent and stretched to their breaking point. Then the rocks snap, releasing energy that travels through the Earth. Volcanoes form when hot, molten rock erupts as lava at the Earth's surface.

Review

1. Compare the three types of waves produced by earthquakes.

2. How does the Richter scale differ from the Mercalli intensity scale?

3. How does a volcano form?

4. **Critical Thinking** Which of the Hawaiian Islands is the oldest—the island directly over the hot spot or the island that is farthest from the hot spot? Explain.

5. **Test Prep** Which of the following types of volcanoes are most likely to erupt violently?

   A shield and cinder cone volcanoes

   B shield and composite volcanoes

   C cinder cone and composite volcanoes

   D cinder cone and hot-spot volcanoes

LINKS

MATH LINK

Richter Scale Multiplication On the Richter scale, an increase of 1 means 32 times as much energy. Thus, an earthquake that measures 6.5 on the scale releases 32 times the energy of an earthquake that measures 5.5. How many times as much energy is released by a 7.2 earthquake as compared with a 4.2 earthquake?

WRITING LINK

Informative Writing—Description Choose one of the three types of volcanoes. Suppose you are viewing that type of volcano from a safe distance as it erupts. Write an article for a school newspaper to describe what you see.

ART LINK

Views of Mount Fuji Katsushika Hokusai (1760–1849) was an artist who painted many views of Mount Fuji, a composite volcano in Japan. Go to the library and find an example of his paintings in an art book or a book about volcanoes. If you like, try painting your own view of Mount Fuji.

TECHNOLOGY LINK

Learn more about volcanoes and plate tectonics by investigating *Volcanoes— Construction and Destruction* on **Harcourt Science Explorations CD-ROM.**

HISTORY OF Plate Tectonics

The Old View of Earth

In ancient times most people believed that Earth's continents had always been and would always be in the same place. During the Age of Exploration (1400s–1600s), explorers gave people the first accurate view of the world's oceans and continents. A few people noticed that, with a little adjusting, the continents fit together like a jigsaw puzzle. For most scientists, this was no more than a curious observation.

Fossil Evidence for Continental Drift

In 1912 Alfred Wegener, a German scientist, described a theory of continental drift and gave evidence for it. One part of his evidence came from fossils he had found while working with other scientists. Wegener had found fossils of the same species in areas of Africa and South America. The species included a lizard and a plant. Neither species could have crossed from Africa to South America by swimming. The fossils, he said, along with other evidence, showed that at one time all the continents had formed one giant supercontinent.

Even with the evidence, many scientists found Wegener's ideas hard to believe. How could huge land masses move such great distances? Scientists continued to look for more evidence.

The Sea Floor

In the 1960s more evidence was found to support Wegener's theory. By careful exploration, scientists found evidence that the ocean floor was spreading. When sea-floor spreading occurs, hot magma from inside Earth flows onto the surface, forming new crust. Scientists reasoned that since new crust was being formed and Earth was not getting larger, something must be happening to remove some of the old crust.

Changing Views of Earth

1492
Mapmakers and navigators begin to make accurate world maps and globes.

1950s
Scientists start using magnetism to study rocks.

1963
Scientists use magnetic stripes to confirm sea-floor spreading. With this confirmation, the theory of plate tectonics continues to develop.

1400   1900

1912
Alfred Wegener proposes his theory of continental drift.

1960s
Scientists studying the sea floor find evidence for sea-floor spreading.

The discovery of sea-floor spreading was the first step toward the theory of plate tectonics. Further investigation showed that Earth's crust is made up of about 20 rigid slabs, called tectonic plates. These plates float on top of Earth's hot liquid mantle. Where plates collide, under the sea or on land, mountains form.

Shifting Magnetism

By the 1950s scientists were using new technology as well as their understanding of plate tectonics to study the ocean floor. Ocean researchers discovered that the magma contains a magnetic material called magnetite. As the magma cools, the magnetite hardens, pointing to the magnetic North Pole. The stripes in which magnetite is found are called magnetic stripes.

By the early 1960s this discovery tool was being used to check the idea of sea-floor spreading. Researchers found that not all the magnetite in rocks points to today's magnetic north. This led them to conclude that the location of the magnetic North Pole has changed throughout Earth's history. When they studied the width and the pattern of magnetic stripes on

the sea floor, they found the same pattern and width on each side of a mid-ocean ridge. The stripes were symmetrical. The only way this could occur would be if the rock on both sides of the ridge cooled at the same time. So scientists had further evidence for sea-floor spreading and were able to continue to develop the theory of plate tectonics.

Studying the width of the stripes has helped scientists estimate how fast the sea floor is spreading.

THINK ABOUT IT

1. Another piece of evidence that Wegener found was a similarity of layering of rocks in Africa and South America. How would this show the two continents were once joined?
2. Why were scientists reluctant to accept the idea of continental drift?

Lasers and other advanced equipment on satellites can detect movement as small as one centimeter. Scientists' calculations of tectonic plate movements show that Hawaii is moving northwest toward Japan at a rate of 8.3 cm (3 in.) per year.

1990s
Movements of tectonic plates are measured by instruments on satellites orbiting Earth.

2000

1980s
Ocean researchers continue to study magnetic striping. They discover that the average rate of sea-floor spreading is 1–2 cm (less than 1 in.) per year.

Waverly Person

GEOPHYSICIST

When an earthquake occurs somewhere in the world, Waverly Person is one of the first people to find out about it. Dr. Person is chief of the National Earthquake Information Service (NEIS), a government agency that keeps track of earthquakes all over the world. NEIS uses sensitive instruments, both on the ground and on satellites, to record even the slightest movement of Earth's crust. When NEIS detects a quake, it helps notify government officials, relief agencies, and the media in the affected area. As a result, aid can reach earthquake victims as soon as possible. For earthquakes in some remote parts of the world, information from NEIS is the first clue that a natural disaster has occurred and that people may need help.

Dr. Person's curiosity about the world began at an early age. "I was always asking questions," he says. His curiosity about Earth's physical properties led him to pursue a college degree and then a career as a geophysicist.

Today Dr. Person supervises a staff of 15 geophysicists at NEIS. A geophysicist studies the physical properties of Earth and uses data from satellites, Earth-based instruments, and computers to track geological events. Geophysicists that study earthquakes are called seismologists.

Waverly Person has been a geophysicist and a seismologist for more than 30 years. After all that time, he still loves what he does. What are the best parts? It's exciting, and he has the opportunity to help people. Plus, he says, there's always a chance to learn something new.

THINK ABOUT IT

1. Why is the work of NEIS important?
2. What makes Waverly Person enjoy working in this field?

A parking garage tower toppled by an earthquake near Los Angeles

Producing a Tsunami

How do Earth's plate movements cause a huge ocean wave?

Materials
- large, deep baking pan or sink
- 2 wooden blocks, each about 15 × 10 × 5 cm (6 × 4 × 2 in.)
- water

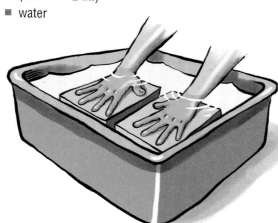

Procedure

1. Put the blocks in the pan or sink. Add water until they are about 5 cm (2 in.) under the surface. (If they start to float, hold them down.)

2. Hold the blocks about 5 cm (2 in.) apart. Move them together quickly.

3. Repeat this action several times and observe how the water moves.

Draw Conclusions

What do the blocks represent? What happens to the water when they move quickly?

Studying Earth's Core

How do scientists use S waves to study Earth's core?

Materials
- large bowl or cake pan
- clean, empty glass jar
- water

Procedure

1. Fill the jar and the bowl half-full of water.

2. Place the jar in the center of the bowl.

3. Use your finger to tap the water surface several times near the side of the bowl, creating ripples.

4. Observe how the ripples react when they reach the jar.

Draw Conclusions

What do the ripples represent? What does the jar represent? How do the ripples react when they reach the jar? S waves can move through solids, but not liquids, such as the liquids in Earth's core. The ripples in this experiment also cannot move through "Earth's core." What could scientists learn by studying the reflection of S waves?

Vocabulary Review

Use the terms below to complete the sentences. The page numbers in parentheses ( ) tell you where to look in the chapter if you need help.

crust (D6)

mantle (D6)

core (D6)

lithosphere (D7)

asthenosphere (D7)

plate tectonics (D8)

divergent
   boundary (D14)

convergent
   boundary (D14)

transform fault
   boundary (D14)

mid-ocean ridge (D15)

rift (D15)

sea-floor
   spreading (D15)

earthquake (D22)

focus (D22)

epicenter (D22)

P wave (D23)

S wave (D23)

surface wave (D23)

Richter scale (D24)

volcano (D25)

1. The cool solid blocks of the ___ float on the asthenosphere.

2. At a ___ Earth's plates collide.

3. Iceland is part of a long underwater range of mountains known as a ___.

4. From the innermost to the outermost, Earth's main layers are ___, ___, and ___.

5. At a ___, plates grind by each other.

6. After an earthquake, the first wave to reach a recording station is a ___, followed by an ___.

7. In an earthquake, the ___ is the point in Earth's crust where rocks first break and move.

8. When rocks on a fault pass their stretching point and snap, the energy they release is known as an ___.

9. A theory called ___ explains the movement of Earth's plates.

10. A theory called ___ explains how new crust is formed along a great crack, or ___ in Earth's ocean floors.

11. A ___ is the slowest but most destructive wave generated by an earthquake.

12. Located in the upper mantle, the ___ is a zone of solid rock that flows.

13. The mountain formed when molten rock reaches Earth's surface through a vent is known as a ___.

14. The ___ measures the energy released by an earthquake.

15. The ___ of an earthquake is located directly above the focus.

16. Earth's plates move apart along a ___.

Connect Concepts

Write the terms that belong in the concept map showing how plate tectonics shapes Earth's crust. You will use some terms more than once.

convergent boundary

divergent boundary

earthquake

transform fault
   boundary

sea-floor spreading

mountain building

volcano

Type of Boundary	Activity Found Along Boundary
17. _____	20. _____
18. _____	21. _____
19. _____	22. _____

Check Understanding

Write the letter of the best choice.

23. The arrow in the illustration below is pointing to Earth's —

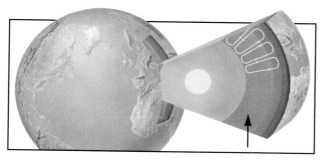

   A crust   **C** outer core

   B mantle   **D** inner core

24. The plates of the lithosphere float on the —

   F asthenosphere   **H** crust

   G inner core   **J** oceans

25. The Great Rift in East Africa is found along a ____ boundary.

   A transform fault

   B sea-floor

   C convergent

   D divergent

26. Earthquakes are associated with —

   F transform fault boundaries

   G convergent boundaries

   H transform fault and convergent boundaries

   J divergent boundaries

27. A hot spot under the ocean floor is most likely to —

   A cause an earthquake

   B build a chain of islands

   C push apart two plates

   D cause sea-floor spreading

Critical Thinking

28. The crust along a divergent boundary is some of the newest crust on Earth. Explain why.

29. A certain earthquake that measures 7.0 on the Richter scale hits two different cities. In one city, the damage on the Mercalli intensity scale is IX (9). In the other city, the damage on the Mercalli intensity scale is V (5). What might explain the difference in damage done to the two cities?

Process Skills Review

30. What can a **model** tell you about the structure of Earth?

31. The Appalachians are a mountain range that run through the eastern United States and Canada. Mountains of about the same age and structure are found across the Atlantic Ocean in the British Isles and Scandinavia. From this evidence, what can you **infer** about the position of the continents of North America and Europe? Explain.

32. How do scientists **interpret data** from earthquake waves to determine the location of an earthquake?

Performance Assessment

Journey to the Surface of Earth

Magma is hot molten rock. Draw a diagram illustrating magma's journey through different layers of Earth from the asthenosphere to Earth's surface. Use a caption to describe what happens as the magma moves to the surface.

Rocks and the Rock Cycle

Rocks first formed from melted material that cooled. Later, other rocks resulted from the grinding forces of water, wind, and ice, and from years and years of materials being glued together by natural processes. Still other rocks formed when rocks were crushed and heated by processes such as the collision of Earth's plates. However they formed, there is a surprising number of different kinds of rocks at Earth's surface today.

Vocabulary Preview

mineral
magma
igneous rock
lava
weathering
erosion
deposition
sedimentation
cementation
clastic rock
chemical rock
metamorphism
rock cycle

⊫FAST FACT

There are mountains on every continent—some even rise from ocean floors. Many land mountains are near the edges of continents, where undersea plates push up against the land.

Highest Mountain on Each Continent			
Name	Height in feet	in meters	Continent
Mount Everest	29,028	8848	Asia
Aconcagua	22,834	6960	South America
Mount McKinley	20,320	6194	North America
Kilimanjaro	19,340	5895	Africa
Mount Elbrus	18,481	5633	Europe
Vinson Massif	16,864	5140	Antarctica
Mount Kosciusko	7,310	2228	Australia

Petrified wood forms when the cells of a tree are slowly replaced by minerals. The logs in Arizona's Petrified Forest National Park were the trunks of living trees 150 million years ago.

Giant's Causeway, in Ireland, is a natural rock formation. It is made of basalt, a volcanic rock that takes the shape of columns as it cools.

LESSON 1

What Are Igneous Rocks?

In this lesson, you can . . .

INVESTIGATE types of igneous rock.

LEARN ABOUT igneous rocks.

LINK to math, writing, social studies, and technology.

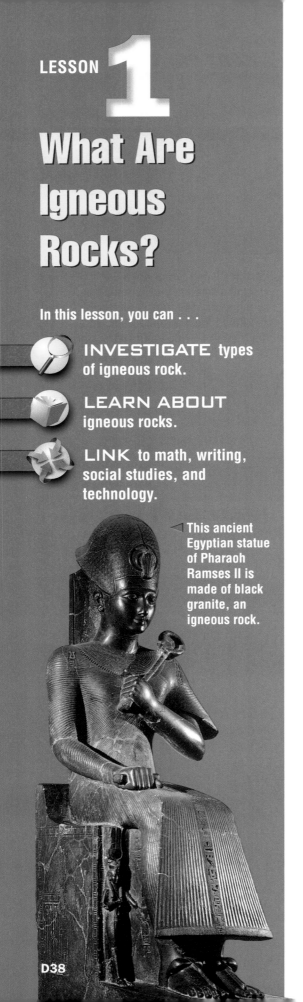

◁ This ancient Egyptian statue of Pharaoh Ramses II is made of black granite, an igneous rock.

INVESTIGATE

Types of Igneous Rock

Activity Purpose The word *igneous* comes from a word meaning "fire." So why do we call a type of rock igneous? It is because igneous rock forms from red-hot material. Igneous rock forms in two ways. The red-hot material can be pushed up into Earth's crust, where it hardens into rock underground. Or the material can be squeezed to the surface, where it hardens in the cool air. The two main groups of igneous rocks form in these two different ways. You can often tell which group an igneous rock belongs to by observing the texture of the rock. In this investigation you will **observe** igneous rocks and **classify** them into one of the two groups.

Materials

- 6 igneous rock samples
- hand lens

Activity Procedure

1 Copy the following chart.

Comparing Rocks

Sample	Texture	Other Observations
A		
B		
C		
D		
E		
F		

2 Use the hand lens to **observe** the texture of each rock sample. (Picture A) Texture is the size and shape of the grains, or particles, in the rock. Texture also includes the way the grains fit together. For example, grains can look completely separate or can appear locked together like the pieces of a jigsaw puzzle.

3 **Record** the textures you **observe.** Also record any other information that helps you tell the rocks apart, such as differences in color.

4 **Compare** the properties you **observed.**

5 **Classify** the rock samples into two groups, according to the textures you **observed.**

Picture A

Draw Conclusions

1. What rock textures did you **observe**?

2. How did you **classify** the rocks into two groups? Describe the rocks that you put into each group. In what other ways could you classify the rocks?

3. **Scientists at Work** Scientists often learn from other scientists. **Observe** how other students **classified** the rocks. What did you learn from other students? You might use what you learned from others to reclassify the igneous rocks into two groups.

Investigate Further Look for other rocks in your area that you can **observe** and **classify** into your two groups.

Process Skill Tip

When you **observe** objects, you use your senses to examine them. When you **classify** objects, you use your observations to put the objects into groups.

Igneous Rocks

Minerals

FIND OUT

- **how igneous rocks form**
- **how we use igneous rocks**

VOCABULARY

mineral
magma
igneous rock
lava

▲ Different kinds of feldspar, along with quartz, are the main minerals in granite. Granite is the most common rock on Earth.

Wherever you go on Earth, you can find rock. Mountains and canyons are rock. Soil contains small particles of rock. Sandy deserts are made of finely ground rock. If you could dive to the ocean floor or dig through the polar ice, you would find rock. Rocks are divided into three main types according to how they formed: igneous, sedimentary, and metamorphic.

Just as rocks are the building blocks of landforms, minerals are the building blocks of rocks. A **mineral** is a natural, solid substance that has a definite chemical composition and physical structure. Minerals always form as crystals, or solids that have a regular geometric shape that reflects the way the atoms are arranged within it. There are more than 4000 different minerals. They include substances as different as gold and the gray piece of graphite in your pencil. In recent years scientists have discovered hundreds of new minerals. But only a dozen minerals are common. They make up most of the rock in Earth's crust.

To identify a mineral, scientists observe the properties. Hardness is one property they observe. Some minerals are very hard. Diamond is the hardest mineral and can scratch any other substance. On the other hand, chalk is such a soft mineral that you can write with it. Other properties include color, crystal shape, the color of the streak the mineral leaves when rubbed on tile, and density.

The properties of the minerals that form a rock give the rock some of its properties. A rock that contains the hard mineral quartz is usually much harder than a rock made of the softer, chalky mineral calcite.

✔ **What is a mineral?**

◄ Quartz is one of the most common rock-forming minerals. It often develops in groups of six-sided prisms tipped with a pyramid.

Pyroxene crystals are short, stubby, and dark. ▼

Formation of Igneous Rocks

If you dig into a sandy beach or into garden dirt, the sand or dirt seems cool. But if you could dig past the cool layer of Earth's crust, you would reach part of the mantle—a thick layer where temperatures climb to thousands of degrees. The pressure at this depth is crushing. The heat and the pressure are great enough to melt rock. Melted rock within the Earth is called **magma**.

Igneous rock forms when magma is pushed up from the mantle into the cool crust and hardens into rock. The process of hardening is sometimes called crystallization. Some magma crystallizes into rock underground. Other magma crystallizes into rock when it reaches Earth's surface.

Magma that hardens within Earth's crust is called *intrusive* rock because the magma intrudes, or pushes into, the crust. Intrusive rock is also called *plutonic* rock, from the name Pluto, the Greek god of the world below the surface.

Magma that hardens on Earth's surface is called *extrusive*, or volcanic, rock. Sometimes magma is pushed up through the crust and flows or even explodes from cracks in Earth's surface. Magma that reaches the surface is called **lava**. Lava oozes or explodes over the surface from volcanoes. Once lava reaches the air or ocean water, it cools and hardens into extrusive igneous rock.

✔ **What are igneous rocks?**

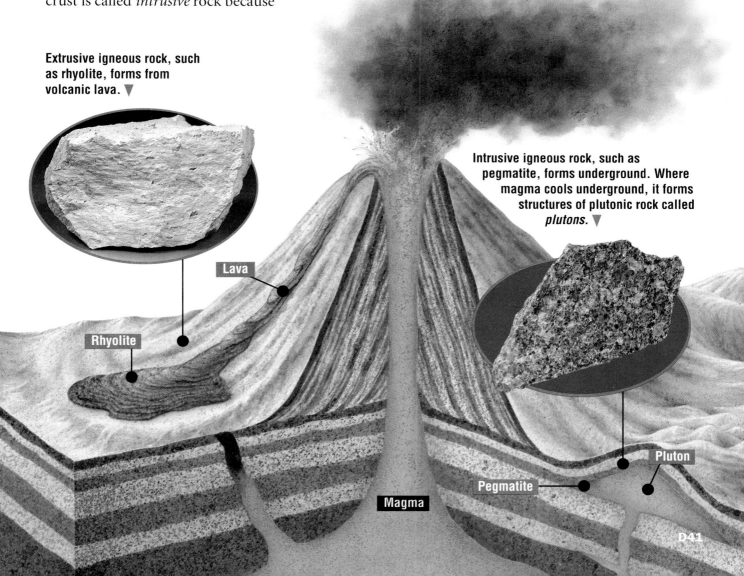

Extrusive igneous rock, such as rhyolite, forms from volcanic lava. ▼

Intrusive igneous rock, such as pegmatite, forms underground. Where magma cools underground, it forms structures of plutonic rock called *plutons*. ▼

Lava

Rhyolite

Pluton

Pegmatite

Magma

Gabbro				
Type	**Texture**	**Density**	**Color**	**Main Minerals**
intrusive, formed from magma	coarse-grained	dense	dark	feldspar, pyroxene

Intrusive Igneous Rocks

Intrusive igneous rocks share some characteristics. Because they form underground, they cool very slowly—sometimes over millions of years. The minerals in these rocks have a long time to form, so the crystals they form can become large. This gives intrusive rocks a coarse texture. In the investigation the coarse-grained rocks diorite, granite, and gabbro were intrusive.

Intrusive igneous rocks form a number of structures. Because melted rock is less dense than solid rock, magma is pushed toward the surface. It forces its way into cracks and holes in the crust and may push up the land above it. As it cools, this magma forms plutons, which are underground structures of igneous rock.

Large plutons that are exposed at Earth's surface by erosion are called batholiths. Some mountain ranges, such as the Sierra Nevada in California, are batholiths.

Batholith rock formations can be dramatic landforms. Shiprock is the name of a huge tower of rock that rises straight up 425 m (about 1400 ft) from a flat plain in New Mexico.

◄ Shiprock, in New Mexico, is one example of the unusual landforms that can result from intrusive igneous rock.

Pumice				
Type	**Texture**	**Density**	**Color**	**Main Minerals**
extrusive, formed from lava	fine-grained	light, full of bubbles; only rock that can float	light	feldspar, quartz

This towering rock was produced when magma cooled and formed intrusive rock in the vent of a volcano. Over millions of years, weathering and erosion wore away the softer rock and soil of the volcano. Only the hard igneous rock core remains.

✔ **Why are the crystals in intrusive igneous rock large?**

Extrusive Igneous Rocks

Magma can explode from some volcanoes. It can ooze out of others and pour along the ground like thick mud. When magma comes out of the Earth, it is a red-hot liquid. In the air or water, the lava cools and crystallizes into extrusive rock.

The rate of cooling determines the texture of the rock. Magma, which cools slowly, forms large crystals. So, intrusive rock has larger crystals and a coarse-grained texture. Lava, which cools in air or water, hardens quickly. Crystals do not have much time to grow and develop. As a result, the crystals in extrusive rock are smaller. Extrusive rock has a fine-grained texture. Some extrusive rocks have particles so small that a microscope is needed to see them. In the investigation the fine-grained rocks rhyolite, andesite, and basalt (buh•SAWLT) were extrusive rocks.

Extrusive igneous rocks take many forms. Obsidian is a dark, glassy rock. Lava that becomes obsidian cools and hardens so quickly that crystals do not have time to form. Pumice (PUM•is) is a lightweight rock full of small holes. It forms when lava becomes foamy and then quickly hardens. Pumice is so light that it can float in water—the only rock that can.

✔ **What can texture tell you about the formation of an igneous rock?**

◄ You can see grains of three minerals in this piece of granite. The gray and some white grains are quartz, the pink and other white grains are feldspar, and the black grains are mica.

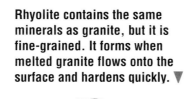

Rhyolite contains the same minerals as granite, but it is fine-grained. It forms when melted granite flows onto the surface and hardens quickly. ▼

▲ Diorite is a kind of slow-cooling igneous rock. The large black and white crystals are clearly visible, a sure sign of slow cooling.

Uses of Igneous Rocks

Igneous rocks are some of the most common rocks on Earth. They are used in many things, from building materials to jewelry.

The igneous rock granite is durable and looks good. It also resists weathering better than many other types of rock. As a result, granite is often used as a building material. Famous structures such as the Empire State Building in New York and the Great Wall of China are made partly of granite.

The extrusive igneous rock obsidian has been used for tools and for jewelry. Obsidian breaks with sharp edges, so it was used to make cutting tools in ancient times. Because of its glassy surface, people also used obsidian as a mirror. The beauty of this shiny, black rock made it useful for jewelry as well.

Pumice is an extrusive rock that can be pounded into powder. It is used as a scouring substance in soaps and cleaners. Pumice was used as a tooth cleaner in the past. However, it is so gritty that it not only cleaned teeth but also filed them down.

Igneous rocks are sources of many important ores. Ores are useful minerals or mixtures of minerals that are mined. The ores contain large amounts of chromium, platinum, and diamond. Rich deposits of nickel and copper are also found in some igneous rocks.

✓ **List three ways that igneous rocks are used.**

Granite is a common building material because it is beautiful, hard, and strong. The state capitol building in Austin, Texas, is made of pink granite. ▶

Obsidian breaks with sharp edges. It was used by some Native American tribes for arrowheads and cutting tools.

Summary

Igneous rocks form when magma or lava cools and crystallizes. Igneous rocks can form in Earth's crust or from lava that erupts from volcanoes on Earth's surface. Igneous rocks are often used as building materials.

Review

1. What is igneous rock?

2. How does intrusive igneous rock form?

3. Where would you expect to find extrusive igneous rock?

4. **Critical Thinking** Why would it be easier for geologists to study extrusive igneous rocks than intrusive igneous rocks?

5. **Test Prep** What igneous rock is often used as a building material?

   A cement

   B obsidian

   C pumice

   D granite

LINKS

MATH LINK

Circle Graph To identify and compare rocks, scientists analyze the percentage of minerals or compounds. One sample of granite that was analyzed contained the following minerals: 50% orthoclase feldspar, 22% quartz, 14% plagioclase feldspar, 6% amphibole, 5% muscovite, 3% biotite. Show this in a circle graph.

WRITING LINK

Informative Writing—Description Write a one-page essay for a younger student that describes a mineral or rock and its use.

SOCIAL STUDIES LINK

Mineral Map Join your classmates in making a world or U.S. map that shows the locations of several major mineral and ore deposits. Are there any major deposits near where you live?

TECHNOLOGY LINK

Learn more about igneous rocks and the processes that form them by visiting this Internet site.
www.scilinks.org/harcourt

SCi LINKS
THE WORLD'S A CLICK AWAY

LESSON 2

What Are Sedimentary Rocks?

In this lesson, you can . . .

 INVESTIGATE how flowing water erodes sediment.

 LEARN ABOUT sedimentary rocks.

 LINK to math, writing, social studies, and technology.

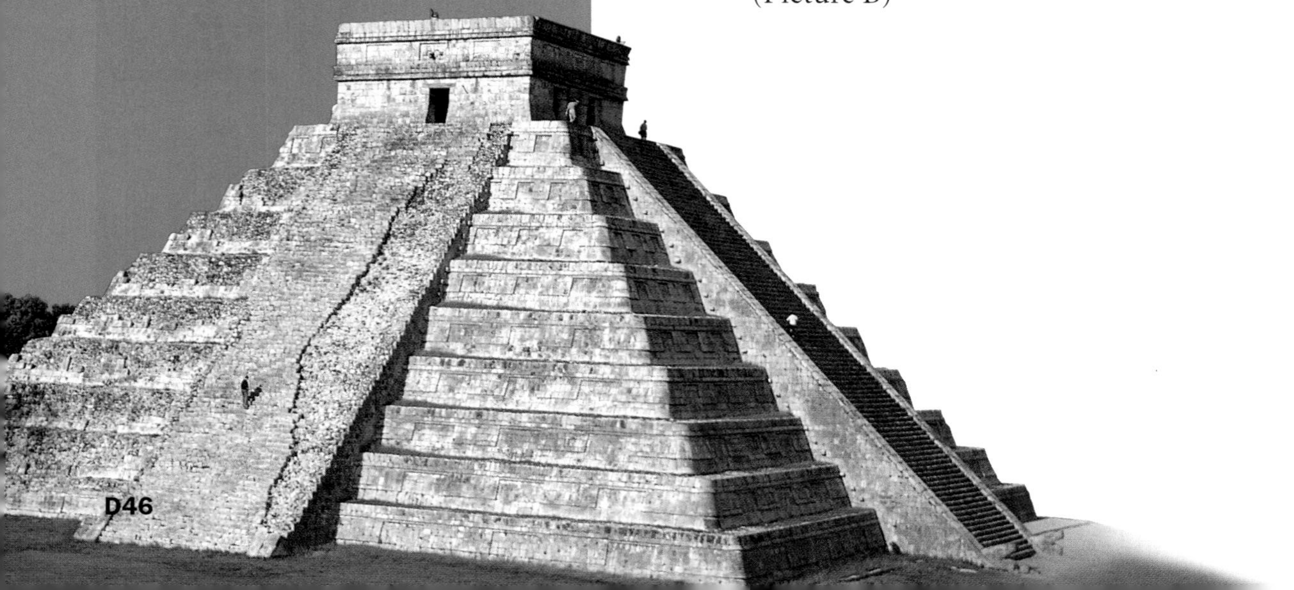

The Mayas of Central America built many limestone pyramids during the height of their civilization. This is only one way in which people have used sedimentary rocks. ▽

 **INVESTIGATE**

Stream Erosion

Activity Purpose As water flows over land, it may become dark and muddy. For example, the Rio Grande in Texas is often the color of the surrounding land. This is because flowing water can pick up particles of rock and soil from the land and carry the particles away. In this investigation you will **control variables** in an **experiment** to see the effects of flowing water.

Materials

- stream table
- sand
- 2 buckets
- 2 30-cm pieces of rubber tubing
- 7 books
- screw clamp
- water
- clock or watch with second hand

Activity Procedure

1 Set up the stream table with the sand smoothed out. Place two books under the upper end of the stream table. (Picture A)

2 Open the clamp to allow a narrow stream of water to run over the sand in the stream table. Use the clamp to stop the flow of water after 20 seconds. **Record** your **observations** of the stream channel and the amount of erosion. After you have recorded your observations, smooth out the sand again. (Picture B)

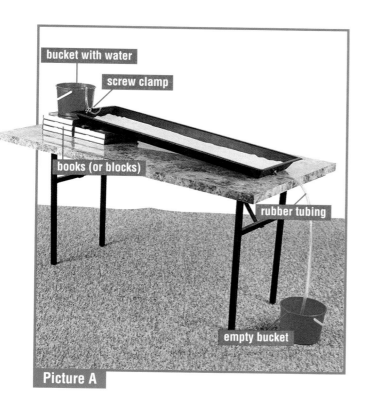

Picture A

bucket with water
screw clamp
books (or blocks)
rubber tubing
empty bucket

Picture B

3 Place a third book under the upper end of the stream table. (You will need to add a book to the stack under the bucket.) Open the clamp to produce a stream of the same width as in Step 2. Stop the stream after 20 seconds. **Record** your **observations.** Smooth out the sand again.

4 Open the clamp to allow a larger, wider stream of water to flow over the sand. Stop the flow after 20 seconds. **Record** your **observations.**

Draw Conclusions

1. How did you change the speed of the water flow? How did you change the amount of the water flow?

2. What did you **observe** when you changed the speed of the water flow? What did you **observe** when you changed the amount of water flow?

3. **Scientists at Work** Scientists **control variables** in an **experiment** to **gather data** about a process. What can you **infer** about the effect of flowing water on soil in the mountains?

Investigate Further **Experiment** by **controlling variables** you have not tested. Repeat Steps 2 and 3 of the investigation, but use a different type of soil or add leaves and twigs to the sand. **Record** your **observations**.

Process Skill Tip

When you **experiment**, you carry out a procedure to gather data. During the experiment, you control one or more variables. When you **control variables**, you control factors that affect the outcome of the experiment.

Sedimentary Rocks

Formation of Sedimentary Rocks

FIND OUT

- about the types of sedimentary rocks
- how sedimentary rocks form
- how we use sedimentary rocks

VOCABULARY

weathering
erosion
deposition
sedimentation
cementation
clastic rock
chemical rock

Have you ever seen a rock with stripes or layers of different colors? That is probably a sedimentary rock. Of all the rock on Earth's surface, 75 percent is sedimentary rock. But sedimentary rock is only about 5 percent of the whole crust. Why can you find so much sedimentary rock at Earth's surface? Unlike igneous rock, which forms from materials deep underground, sedimentary rock forms from materials at Earth's surface.

Weathering is the process of breaking rock into smaller pieces. It occurs because of natural forces such as flowing water or moving ice and freezing and thawing, which cause contraction and expansion.

Conglomerate is a sedimentary rock formed from pebbles and sand that are cemented together. ▶

① Cementation begins when particles of sediment are deposited in layers.

② Water with minerals in it flows through the spaces between the particles.

③ Cementation is completed when minerals in the water are deposited in the spaces between the particles. First, the minerals line the spaces and cement the particles together. After some time, the minerals can seal all the open spaces.

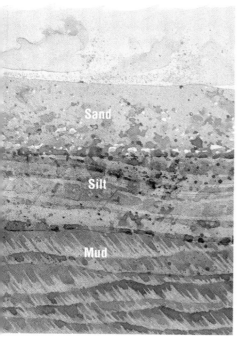

① The compaction of sediment begins when a layer of sediment is deposited. The particles do not fit together tightly, and water fills the spaces between them.

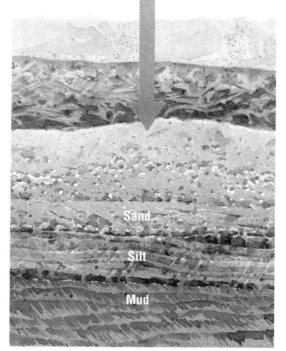

② More layers of sediment are deposited. The weight of new layers presses down on layers underneath. The water is squeezed out, the spaces get smaller, and the particles are forced together.

③ Eventually, the layers are compacted into solid rock.

The growth of plants in rock also causes weathering.

After weathering breaks rock into bits, water, wind, or ice may move it away. The movement of sediment to new locations is called **erosion** or transportation.

The next step is deposition. **Deposition** is the dropping of sediment from wind or water that slows down, or from ice that melts. For example, as moving water slows down, it has less energy and can carry less sediment. A river will slow as it empties into a larger body of water, such as a lake or ocean. Rivers often slow down at their mouths and drop layer upon layer of sediment there.

Layers of sediment build up over millions of years in a process called **sedimentation**. The weight of the upper layers presses down on the

Shale forms from layers of compacted clay. You can see the layers in this piece of shale. ▶

lower layers. This *compacts*, or packs down, the sediment. **Cementation** then glues the compacted particles together.

Sedimentary rocks are classified into two main groups. **Clastic rocks** are made of sediments that were weathered, transported, and deposited in layers. **Chemical rocks** are formed from minerals that were dissolved in water, came out of solution, and were then deposited.

✔ **How do sedimentary rocks form?**

Breccia

Clastic Rocks

Clastic rocks are classified by the size of the sediment particles that form them. The particles can be fine, medium, or coarse. The smallest particles of sediment are too fine to see without a microscope. The largest particles can be as big as boulders.

Fine particles form rocks such as shale. Shale is the most common sedimentary rock. Fossil imprints often occur in the layers of shale.

Medium-sized particles form rocks called sandstone. Sandstone can be made from several different minerals. However, most sandstone has a lot of quartz in it.

Coarse, pebble-sized particles with smooth, rounded edges are in conglomerates. The spaces between the larger particles are filled with sand

Clastic Rocks		
Rock	**Composition, Particle Size**	**Environments and Processes of Formation**
Conglomerate	contains rounded pebbles, greater than 4 mm	swift rivers, glaciers, beaches
Breccia	sharp pebbles, greater than 4 mm	glaciers, cave-ins, landslides
Sandstone	sand, $\frac{1}{16}$ to 2 mm	deserts, deltas, beaches
Siltstone	silt, $\frac{1}{256}$ to $\frac{1}{16}$ mm	deltas, shallow seas, lagoons
Shale	clay, less than $\frac{1}{256}$ mm	shallow seas, lagoons, lakes

or mud. Pebble-sized particles with sharp edges form a rock called *breccia* (BRECH•ee•uh).

The shape of particles in a clastic rock helps you infer how far from the source the particles were deposited. Particles with rounded edges were probably moved a long distance by water. Bumping against other particles in flowing water gradually smoothed their edges. Particles with sharp edges were not transported for as long a time or as far.

✔ **What is conglomerate?**

Sandstone often forms in very dry places, such as deserts. It also forms in sea water or river water. About 11 percent of sedimentary rock is sandstone. ▼

Shale forms from the smallest particles of sediment that drop out of very still water. About 75 percent of sedimentary rock is shale or siltstone. ▶

Chemical Rocks		
Rock	Composition	Environments and Processes of Formation
Chalk	tiny sea protists	shallow seas
Coquina	shells	shallow seas, beaches
Limestone	calcite from shells	sea water
Chert	quartz, tiny sea protists	groundwater
Gypsum	gypsum	places where sea water evaporated
Halite	rock salt	places where sea water evaporated

▲ In Yellowstone National Park, a hot spring rich in dissolved minerals leaves growing deposits of limestone.

Chemical Rocks

Have you ever mixed sugar into a cup of hot tea? The sugar dissolves. But if you mix in enough sugar and then let the tea cool, some sugar will come out of the solution. It will settle to the bottom of the cup. This is the way some sediments build up to form chemical sedimentary rocks.

Like clastic rocks, chemical sedimentary rocks begin with weathering. Chemical weathering causes rocks to break down into chemicals that can dissolve in water. There are no large pieces of rock or sand in the solution. Rain, for example, can remove minerals from the surface of rock. Some of the chemical substances from the rock dissolve. However, just like the sugar in a glass of tea, the dissolved chemicals can settle out of water when conditions change. The chemical sediment collects at the bottom of calm water in layers.

Once the chemicals are in water, chemical sedimentary rocks form in two ways. Evaporation can leave chemical sedimentary rocks behind. For example, evaporation may leave a layer of salt at the bottom of a dried-up lake.

Chemical sedimentary rocks can also form from animal shells or skeletons. Animals such as corals take chemicals from sea water to make their shells. Their skeletons build up to form large limestone reefs on the ocean floor. Animal shells can also pile up on the bottom of a lake or ocean. Over long periods of time, compaction and cementation can form rock from these shells. Large deposits of limestone that are now far from the coast are clues to where there were seas millions of years ago.

✔ **What is a chemical sedimentary rock?**

Limestone is the most common chemical sedimentary rock. It is made mostly of a mineral called calcite. Limestone can form from the shells and skeletons of invertebrates that lived in the ocean. Limestone often contains many fossils. ▼

Gypsum is a chemical sedimentary rock that can form when ocean water evaporates and cannot be replaced with more ocean water or fresh water. ▶

Uses of Sedimentary Rocks

People use sedimentary rocks for many purposes, from building to learning about Earth's history.

Many building materials are made from sedimentary rocks. Shale and mudstone, a kind of shale with a lot of silt in it, are used to make bricks, tiles, pottery, and china. Many buildings are made of sandstone. Rock gypsum, a chemical rock formed by evaporation, is used to make plaster.

Rock salt, or halite, is used to season and preserve food. It is also used to melt snow and ice on roads and sidewalks in cold weather.

Sedimentary rocks often contain important energy resources. Petroleum and natural gas are found in sedimentary rocks.

Farmers depend on sedimentary rocks, too. Limestone is used to make agricultural lime for treating acidic soils. Potassium salts and phosphate rocks are made into fertilizer.

Sedimentary rocks are the kinds most likely to contain fossils. Scientists observe fossils in order to piece together information about what life was like in the past. We would not know about animals of the past, such as dinosaurs, without their fossils. Most of these were found in sedimentary rocks.

✔ **Name three uses of sedimentary rocks.**

The front of one of the main buildings in the ancient city of Petra, Jordan, was carved from a wall of sedimentary rock. ▼

Native American tribes of Central America used shallow platforms called metates (muh•TAH•tehz) for grinding corn. Some of these platforms were made of sedimentary rock.

Summary

Sedimentary rocks form from the deposition of sediment. Sediment that was compacted and cemented forms clastic rock. Chemicals that were in solution and came back out form chemical rock. Sedimentary rocks are used as building materials, are sources of important energy resources, and have many other uses.

Review

1. What part does weather play in the formation of sedimentary rocks?

2. What is erosion?

3. What is cementation?

4. **Critical Thinking** Are you more likely to see sedimentary rocks on the surface or deep in Earth's crust? Explain.

5. **Test Prep** Chemical and ___ are the two groups of sedimentary rock.
   A clastic   C extrusive
   B igneous   D sandstone

LINKS

MATH LINK

Rock Analysis A conglomerate rock is analyzed. Scientists use sieves that have metric measures based on powers of two. You find that the average diameter of pebbles in the rock is 32 mm. The average diameter of clay particles that fill the spaces in the rock is $\frac{1}{256}$ mm. What is the difference in diameter between the pebbles and the clay particles? Express your answer as a decimal rounded to the nearest thousandth.

WRITING LINK

Expressive Writing—Poem Write a short poem for your teacher about rocks. It can be about what they look like, what they feel like, how you use them, or how they make you feel.

SOCIAL STUDIES LINK

Pyramids of Rock The pyramids of ancient Egypt were made of sedimentary rock. Find out what kind was used and where it came from. Learn how the builders made the huge pyramids without modern tools. Share the information in class.

TECHNOLOGY LINK

To learn more about the structures that can form from sedimentary rocks, watch *Caves on Barbados* on the **Harcourt Science Newsroom Video.**

What Are Metamorphic Rocks?

In this lesson, you can . . .

INVESTIGATE the formation of metamorphic rocks.

LEARN ABOUT metamorphic rocks.

LINK to math, writing, art, and technology.

◀ **Many statues and sculptures, such as this sculpture of Julius Caesar, are made of marble.**

INVESTIGATE

Changes in Rock

Activity Purpose The word *metamorphose* means "to change form." Metamorphic rock has changed from one kind of rock into another. In this investigation you will **make a model** of a rock and then change it into a model of a metamorphic rock.

Materials

- clay of 3 different colors
- 2 sheets of wax paper
- plastic foam pellets
- rolling pin
- 2 heavy blocks of wood

Activity Procedure

1 Use clay of one color to **make a model** of a layer of sediment about 12 cm square and 2 cm thick. Place your model on a sheet of wax paper.

2 Use clay of a different color to make 5–10 clay pellets, each about 2 cm in diameter. Add a layer of plastic foam pellets and your clay pellets on top of the sediment model. (Picture A)

3 Use clay of the third color to make a second layer of sediment about 12 cm square and 2 cm thick. Place this layer on top of the layer of pellets.

4 Place a sheet of wax paper on top of the model. Very gently press down on the top layer to form your model rock. Make a drawing of what you **observe.**

Picture A

Picture B

5 Using the rolling pin, apply more pressure to your "rock." Then place a block of wood on either side of your rock. Slowly, but firmly, slide the two blocks toward each other until your rock is squeezed into a new shape. (Picture B) Make a drawing of what you **observe.**

Draw Conclusions

1. Look at your first drawing (Step 4). What type of rock did you **model**?

2. **Compare** the first drawing of the model with the drawing of the model after you changed it (Step 5). How did the model stay the same? How did it change?

3. **Scientists at Work** Scientists **use models** to study how a natural process works. What can you **infer** from your model about the processes that form metamorphic rock? In what part of Earth might these forces occur?

Investigate Further Design an edible model of a metamorphic rock. The materials should be your favorite sandwich makings. What forces would you apply to **make your model?**

Process Skill Tip

You can **use a model** to study a process that is too slow or too fast to observe in nature.

Metamorphic Rocks

Formation of Metamorphic Rocks

FIND OUT

- how metamorphic rocks form
- about types of metamorphic rock
- how we use metamorphic rocks

VOCABULARY

metamorphism

Unlike sedimentary rocks, metamorphic rocks are not common on Earth's surface. Metamorphic rocks form in Earth's crust. We see them only when forces in the Earth lift them up and weathering wears away the rocks and soil on top of them.

Metamorphism is the process by which any kind of rock is changed into metamorphic rock. Metamorphism occurs deep in Earth's crust, where intense heat and pressure can change the properties of rock. As you saw in the investigation, metamorphism can also change the appearance of rock.

The type of metamorphic rock that forms depends on the parent rock, the rock that existed before metamorphism. The type of rock that forms also depends on the degree of metamorphism.

Metamorphism can be low-grade or high-grade. In low-grade metamorphism, pressure and heat are less intense. Rocks change only slightly. Low-grade metamorphism can turn shale, a sedimentary rock, into slate. The pressure of metamorphism makes slate more compact than shale. But the two rocks are not very different. High-grade metamorphism is intense enough to change rock completely.

Deep in Earth's crust, extreme pressure and high temperatures produce the metamorphic rock eclogite. ▼

Marble forms from limestone that has gone through metamorphism. Pure marble is white. The pink color of the marble in this photo is due to small amounts of other substances. ▶

Slate forms from shale that has been compressed by metamorphism. ▶

Compaction can turn granite, an igneous rock, into gneiss (NYS), a metamorphic rock. Compression during metamorphism forms the bands you see in gneiss. ▼

Metamorphism usually occurs under two conditions. *Regional metamorphism* occurs in large areas around plate boundaries. Most metamorphic rock forms this way. Where plates carrying land masses collide, tremendous pressure and stress affect large areas of crustal rock. The rock crumples and folds, and metamorphism occurs. The pushing together of plates can cause a huge pileup, building mountain ranges that have cores of metamorphic rock. For example, in the Himalayas the crust has piled up to a thickness of 64 km (about 40 mi). This is the thickest crust on Earth.

Contact metamorphism occurs when magma rises through Earth's crust and touches existing rock. The hot magma "bakes" the rock, changing its structure and making it metamorphic. Contact metamorphism occurs deep in Earth's crust and under volcanoes.

Geologists classify metamorphic rocks into two groups. These are *foliated* and *nonfoliated* rocks. Foliated rocks have layers or bands you can see. As you observed in the investigation, pressure folds rock, giving foliated rock its layered look. Nonfoliated rocks, such as marble, do not appear layered.

✔ **What is a metamorphic rock?**

Metamorphic Rock Types		
Metamorphic Rock	**Parent Rock**	**Texture**
Slate	shale	fine, foliated
Phyllite	shale or slate	medium, foliated
Schist	shale, slate, or phyllite	coarse, foliated
Gneiss	shale, granite, slate, phyllite, or schist	coarse, foliated
Marble	limestone	medium/coarse, nonfoliated
Quartzite	sandstone	medium, nonfoliated
Hornfels	any fine-grained material	fine, nonfoliated

Processes That Cause Metamorphism

The main causes of metamorphism are heat and pressure. In some cases hot water can cause metamorphism. Most metamorphism occurs in the middle to lower parts of the crust—from about 10 to 30 km (6 to 19 mi) below the surface.

Heat is the most important cause of metamorphism. On the surface you're not aware of Earth's heat, but the deeper you go in the crust, the hotter it gets. Temperatures increase by 20°–60°C (about 36°–108°F) per kilometer of depth. Under extreme heat metamorphic rock gets very close to its melting point. However, once the rock melts, it becomes a source of igneous rock.

Heat breaks the chemical bonds in the minerals of rock. When the rock cools, it can crystallize into new minerals. This happens in regional metamorphism, when surface rock is pushed deep into Earth. It also happens in contact metamorphism, when rock comes into contact with hot magma.

Pressure is another cause of metamorphism. Just as heat does, pressure increases with depth. Pressure acts in two ways. First, the weight

THE INSIDE STORY

Magma intrusion
Columns of magma from Earth's mantle flow up through cracks in the crust. They form areas of hot, melted rock that intrude into the solid rock of the crust.

Contact metamorphism
Magma heats the solid rock around it, changing the structure of the rock. The process turns igneous and sedimentary rock into metamorphic rock. And it turns some metamorphic rock into other types of metamorphic rock.

of rock and soil on top presses down on rock that is underneath, making it denser. Second, crustal movement can squeeze rock and bend it. Where Earth's plates collide or where they grind past each other, crustal rock is squeezed. Because heat has already softened the rock, the pressure can fold the rock more easily. You can often see folds in rock that has gone through metamorphism. You made a model of this process in the investigation.

Rock can also be metamorphosed by mineral-rich water that is extremely hot—about 300°–500°C (570°–930°F). Usually, water this hot is near magma. The superheated water heats the surrounding rock and changes its minerals. Minerals may be added to the surrounding rock, or the hot water may take minerals away. Gold, silver, and copper are often deposited in rock that was metamorphosed by superheated water.

The texture and minerals of a metamorphic rock can tell scientists about the heat, pressure, or hot water that caused the metamorphism.

✔ **What are the three main causes of metamorphism?**

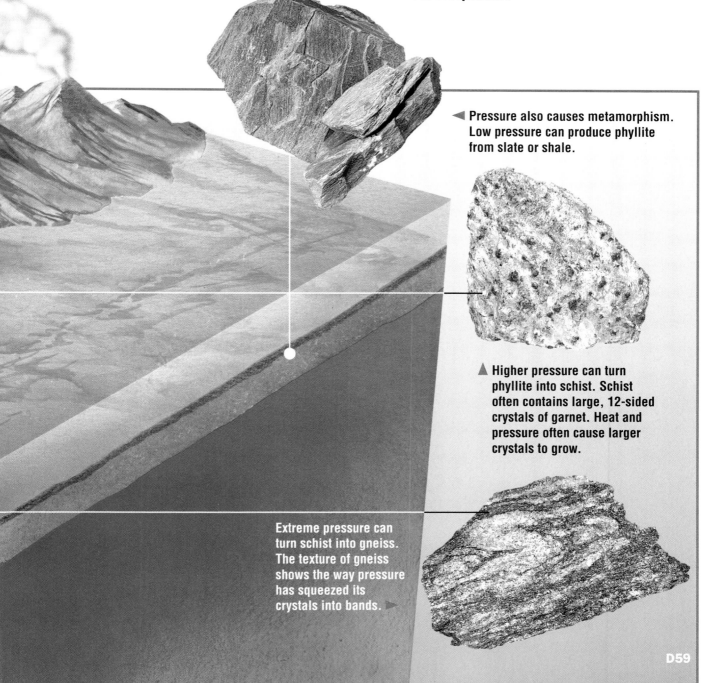

◀ **Pressure also causes metamorphism. Low pressure can produce phyllite from slate or shale.**

▲ **Higher pressure can turn phyllite into schist. Schist often contains large, 12-sided crystals of garnet. Heat and pressure often cause larger crystals to grow.**

Extreme pressure can turn schist into gneiss. The texture of gneiss shows the way pressure has squeezed its crystals into bands. ▶

Uses of Metamorphic Rocks

Metamorphic rocks have many uses. They are used as building materials and in writing materials and cosmetics.

You've probably seen metamorphic rocks as parts of buildings. Marble is a beautiful and durable metamorphic rock. Pure white marble is used for statues and public buildings. India's Taj Mahal is made of this gleaming rock. Other substances in marble can give it many colors such as red, green, or black.

Slate is another metamorphic rock used for buildings. Slate is a foliated rock that splits easily into thin sheets. Years ago builders often used slate for roofs. It was also used for

◀ Chefs use marble tools. This mortar and pestle is used to grind spices.

chalkboards. Today, slate is still used for pavement stones and floors.

Talc is a common powder used for lubrication. It is also used in cosmetics and as a dusting powder. Talc is a mineral that comes from schist, a metamorphic rock.

Graphite is another mineral found in some metamorphic schists. You probably know that the "lead" in your pencil is graphite. Because of its slippery texture, graphite is also used as a lubricant.

✔ **Name three uses of metamorphic rocks.**

The Taj Mahal is an elaborate tomb made of marble. It is considered one of the most beautiful buildings in the world. The Taj Mahal was built between 1632 and 1654 outside of Agra, India.

Summary

Metamorphic rocks are rocks that have been changed because of heat, pressure, or hot water deep in Earth's crust. Metamorphic rocks are used as building materials and as ingredients in cosmetics.

Review

1. What is low-grade metamorphism?
2. What is high-grade metamorphism?
3. Where do metamorphic rocks form?
4. **Critical Thinking** What kind of metamorphism do you think might take place at divergent plate boundaries? Explain.
5. **Test Prep** Metamorphic rocks are formed by heat, hot water, and —
   A sedimentation
   B cementation
   C pressure
   D weathering

LINKS

MATH LINK

Comparisons Work with classmates to make a diagram comparing the heights of famous marble buildings. Make a scale, and use it to draw outlines of the buildings next to each other.

WRITING LINK

Persuasive Writing—Opinion Write a composition that will make a student in a lower grade agree that rocks are important resources. Give examples to back up this opinion.

ART LINK

Landscapes of Rock Find a photograph of a landscape that includes metamorphic rocks. Bring the photo or a copy of it to class. Add it to a classroom gallery called "Metamorphic Rock Landscapes." Discuss the features of the rocks shown in the gallery.

TECHNOLOGY LINK

Visit the Harcourt Learning Site for related links, activities, and resources.
www.harcourtschool.com

WELCOME TO **THE LEARNING SITE**

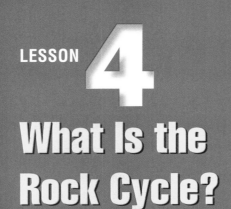
What Is the Rock Cycle?

In this lesson, you can . . .

INVESTIGATE the relationships of the three types of rock.

LEARN ABOUT how rocks change.

LINK to math, writing, language arts, and technology.

Weathering and erosion caused by blowing wind have carved this sandstone into elaborate shapes and arches. ▽

INVESTIGATE

The Classification of Rocks

Activity Purpose Do igneous, sedimentary, and metamorphic rocks look different from one another? In many cases they do—even when they contain some of the same minerals. In this investigation you will **observe** a rock from each of the three main groups, and each rock will contain a lot of quartz. You will **compare** the appearances of the rocks to **classify** them as igneous, metamorphic, or sedimentary.

Materials
- 3 rock samples
- hand lens

Activity Procedure

 Copy the chart below.

The Classification of Rocks

Rock Sample	Observed Properties
A	
B	
C	

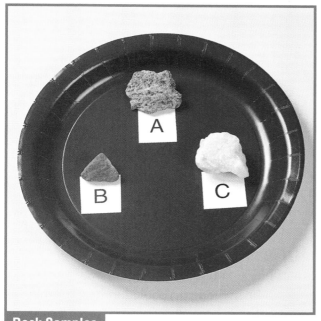

Rock Samples

Picture A

2 Examine Sample A with the hand lens. **Observe** the color, texture, and patterns of the rock. **Record** your observations on the chart. (Picture A)

3 Repeat Step 2 but with Samples B and C. **Record** your **observations** on the chart.

Draw Conclusions

1. Describe what you **observed** about each sample. **Compare** your observations for the three samples. What differences did you observe?

2. Based on your **observations** and your knowledge of the three groups of rocks, how would you **classify** the samples? Which is igneous? Sedimentary? Metamorphic?

3. **Scientists at Work** Scientists often learn from their peers by **comparing** their **observations** with those of other scientists. Find out how other student groups **classified** the rocks. What can you learn from the other groups? You might use what you learn from others to reclassify your rocks.

Investigate Further Look in your community for examples of the three groups of rocks. You can look for rocks in nature or rocks used as building materials. Make a chart of the rocks you see. Describe each rock and where you **observed** it. Name what type of rock you think it is.

The Way Rocks Can Change

The Rock Cycle

FIND OUT

- about the rock cycle
- where the rock cycle occurs

VOCABULARY

rock cycle

Some minerals are found only in certain types of rock. For example, calcite is found in sedimentary rock but not usually in igneous rock. But that is not the case with quartz. Quartz is a common mineral found in all three types of rock. Because of this, it is in all parts of the rock cycle.

The **rock cycle** shows the processes by which rocks are formed from one another. For example, a conglomerate can be weathered and become a sandstone, or it can be melted and cooled to become an igneous rock. You can think of the rock cycle as Earth's way of recycling its rocks.

When Earth's surface first cooled, all rock was igneous. Then wind, water, and ice began to weather and erode the igneous rock. Particles of sediment were carried away and deposited. Eventually, sedimentary rock formed. After millions of years, heat and pressure deep in Earth changed sedimentary rock and igneous rock into metamorphic rock. Since that time, each type of rock has been changing continuously into other types of rock through the rock cycle.

The rock cycle shows how different types of rocks are related and how rock material is recycled. There are five main groups of processes in the rock cycle.

Microscopic view of granite ▼

When weathering breaks down igneous rock, particles of quartz are carried away. The particles are deposited in layers that become quartz sandstone, a sedimentary rock. ▼

▲ Crystals of quartz are common in granite, an igneous rock.

◄ Microscopic view of quartzite

▲ Microscopic view of sandstone

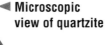◄ When sandstone is compressed and changed under Earth's surface, it becomes quartzite, a metamorphic rock.

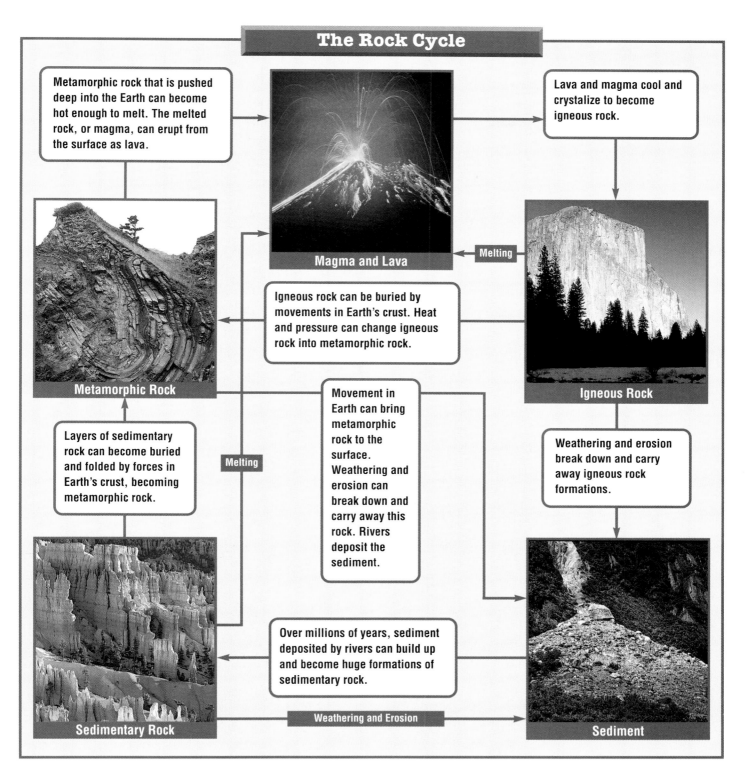

The Rock Cycle

Metamorphic rock that is pushed deep into the Earth can become hot enough to melt. The melted rock, or magma, can erupt from the surface as lava.

Lava and magma cool and crystalize to become igneous rock.

Magma and Lava

Melting

Igneous rock can be buried by movements in Earth's crust. Heat and pressure can change igneous rock into metamorphic rock.

Metamorphic Rock

Igneous Rock

Layers of sedimentary rock can become buried and folded by forces in Earth's crust, becoming metamorphic rock.

Melting

Movement in Earth can bring metamorphic rock to the surface. Weathering and erosion can break down and carry away this rock. Rivers deposit the sediment.

Weathering and erosion break down and carry away igneous rock formations.

Over millions of years, sediment deposited by rivers can build up and become huge formations of sedimentary rock.

Sedimentary Rock

Weathering and Erosion

Sediment

Melting—The melting of sedimentary, igneous, and metamorphic rock forms magma.

Cooling and solidification—As magma cools, it solidifies into igneous rock.

Weathering, erosion, and deposition—The weathering of all three rock types forms sediment that is carried away and deposited.

Compaction and cementation—Sediment that is compacted and cemented forms sedimentary rock.

Heat and pressure—All three rock types exposed to heat and pressure are changed into metamorphic rock.

✔ **What is the rock cycle?**

The Rock Cycle and Plate Boundaries

A good place to see the rock cycle at work is at a boundary between plates of Earth's crust. At a boundary where an ocean plate and a land plate collide, all three rock types are being formed and changed. You can see this in the diagram.

Sediment is deposited where rivers end. Over a long time, large amounts of sedimentary rock form at those places, where land plates and ocean plates meet.

Ocean plates are made of dense igneous rock. When an ocean plate collides with a less-dense land plate, the ocean plate is pushed downward. As it sinks, it drags some sedimentary rock with it. Both the sedimentary rock and the igneous rock are changed into metamorphic rock. Then the metamorphic rock that continues to sink is destroyed by melting and becomes magma.

Magma is pushed up through cracks in the crust. As it is pushed up, it bakes the surrounding rock, forming metamorphic rock. Magma that cools in the crust or on the surface will form igneous rock.

✔ **Describe the changing of sedimentary rock into igneous rock at the plate boundary shown on this page.**

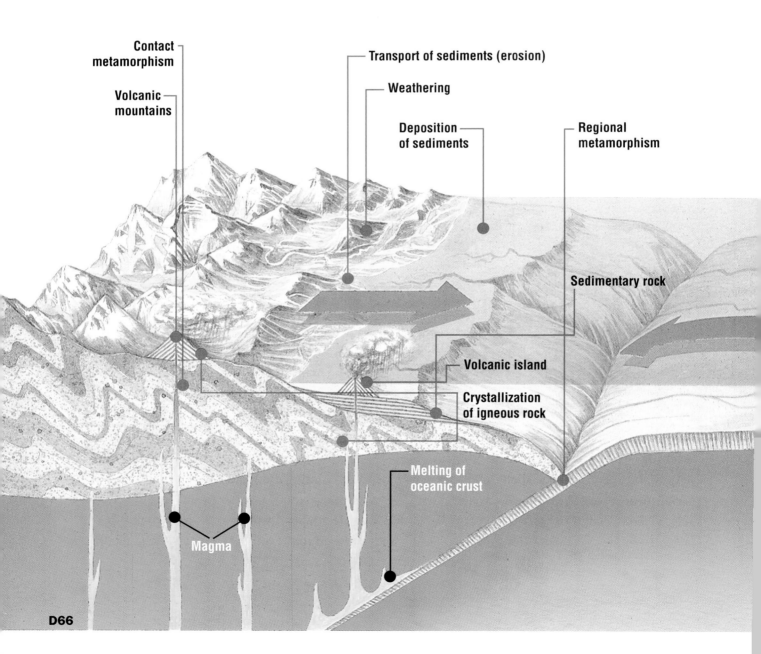

Contact metamorphism

Volcanic mountains

Transport of sediments (erosion)

Weathering

Deposition of sediments

Regional metamorphism

Sedimentary rock

Volcanic island

Crystallization of igneous rock

Melting of oceanic crust

Magma

Summary

The rock cycle shows the processes by which rocks are formed from one another. The stages of the rock cycle are happening on Earth all the time.

Review

1. For each of the three types of rock, name a rock that contains quartz.
2. Describe how igneous rock can become sedimentary rock.
3. Describe how metamorphic rock can become igneous rock.
4. **Critical Thinking** Can all three types of rock be formed on Earth's surface? Explain.
5. **Test Prep** All three types of rock can form at a boundary where plates are —
   A colliding
   B pulling apart
   C sliding by each other
   D standing still

LINKS

MATH LINK

Metamorphism Make a graph that shows the following information: Shale can form at surface temperatures, about 0°–100°C. Slate begins to form at temperatures of about 150°C. Schist begins to form at 250°C. Gneiss begins to form at 600°C, and granite can begin to form at 700°C.

WRITING LINK

Informative Writing—Compare and Contrast Write a composition for a classmate, explaining two ways in which a rock becomes a different type of rock.

LANGUAGE ARTS LINK

Analogies Analogies are comparisons between objects or events. They are often used to explain something unfamiliar by using something that is familiar. For example, an analogy between Earth's crust and an eggshell might be used to explain the thickness of the crust. Make up an analogy between the rock cycle and neighborhood recycling. Write it down in a paragraph, and share it with another student. Use your classmate's questions and comments to help you revise the analogy.

TECHNOLOGY LINK

Visit the Harcourt Learning Site for related links, activities, and resources.
www.harcourtschool.com

WELCOME TO
THE
LEARNING
SITE

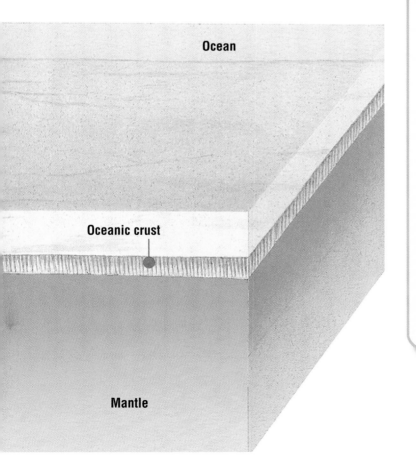

Ocean

Oceanic crust

Mantle

FINDING BURIED TREASURE

Oil companies rely on sound waves and specialized computer programs to decide where to drill for oil.

Look!

Finding oil used to be easy. It seeped out of the ground, so you just looked for it. For thousands of years, people got the oil they used for lamps or medicines by simply scooping it up. Underground oil used to be easy to find too. About 150 years ago, Colonel Edwin Drake drilled the world's first oil well when he drove a pipe 69 feet into the ground near an oil seep in Titusville, Pennsylvania.

But the "easy" oil has all been found. Now oil companies have to look harder to find the right places to drill. The search starts with geologists, who look for rock formations that are known to be associated with underground oil. They gather some clues on the ground, but they also rely on photographs taken from satellites. These overhead images let the geologists look at hundreds of square miles of land. When they spot places that look promising, they investigate more closely—by listening for oil.

The first oil well in the world

Seismic vibrator truck

Listen?

Oil companies use sound to "see" beneath the surface of the Earth in much the way bats use sound to "see" in the air. The echoes that bounce back to a bat's ears tell the animal what's moving around in the darkness. Echoes that bounce back to a geologist's electronic "ears" provide information about what's buried deep underground. The technique geologists use is called seismic stratigraphy (struh•TIG•ruh•fee).

Seismic stratigraphy starts off with a bang. On land, geologists use small explosions or a "vibrator truck" that pounds a heavy metal plate against the ground to produce sound waves. In the ocean, scientists make sound waves with blasts of compressed air. The sound waves travel as far as 20,000 feet underground. Each layer of the Earth reflects some of the sound back to the surface. Microphones (called geophones if they are listening for echoes for land and hydro-phones for the ocean) detect the echoes. Scientists know how far each microphone is from the sound source. By measuring the time it takes for echoes to reach the microphones, scientists can calculate the speed of the sound waves that bounce off each underground layer. The geologists also know how fast sound travels through different types of underground material. They use computer programs to turn all this information into a picture of the hidden world beneath them. If they have interpreted all the clues correctly, that picture shows the geologists where to drill for oil.

Luck?

Before oil companies had seismic stratigraphy to help them, they had to drill dozens of wells that may not have yielded any oil at all. During the 1980s, when they started using Earth's echoes to help them, their luck got better—one well out of ten produced oil. Now the seismic technique is even more accurate, and oil companies hit oil in one well out of four. Seismic stratigraphy works so well that oil companies spend $4 billion each year to "look" into the Earth with sound.

THINK ABOUT IT

1. What is the name of the process in which echoes that bounce back to a geologist's electronic "ears" provide information on where oil can be found?

2. What other underground features could seismic stratigraphy "look" for?

WEB LINK:
For Science and Technology updates, visit The Learning Site.
www.harcourtschool.com

Careers — Petroleum Exploration Engineer

What They Do
Exploration engineers study information gathered from photographs and ground surveys to determine where to put the sound source and microphones for seismic stratigraphy

projects. They use information from seismic "shots" to reposition their equipment until the area has been surveyed completely.

Education and Training Exploration engineers study geology and electronic engineering in college and graduate school. They also need on-the-job training.

August F. Foerste
PALEONTOLOGIST

Now known for his work as a paleontologist, August Foerste always studied and enjoyed nature. As a young teen, he liked to hike in the hills near his hometown of Dayton, Ohio. At that time he was primarily interested in looking for plants. Before he graduated from high school, his collection included more than 1000 species of local flowering plants.

When a high-school teacher gave him the book *Paleontology of Ohio,* August Foerste began seriously collecting and studying local fossils. By the time he entered college, his collection of fossils from the limestone layers that he later named the Brassfield Formation was the most complete in the world. He used his fossils to describe, illustrate, and classify hundreds of species of ancient invertebrates. Many of the species had been incorrectly classified by other scientists before him.

After high school, August Foerste went on to earn a Ph.D. in physical geography and petrography—the classification of rocks. He spent several years doing

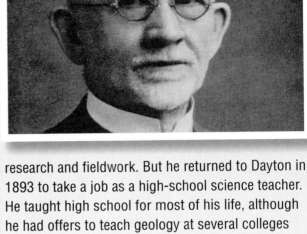

research and fieldwork. But he returned to Dayton in 1893 to take a job as a high-school science teacher. He taught high school for most of his life, although he had offers to teach geology at several colleges and universities. Foerste considered teaching high school a service to his community, but teaching also allowed him free time during holidays and summers to collect fossils in the field and write papers on his discoveries.

Foerste's work includes thousands of pages of text and hundreds of sketches of rocks and fossils. For a part-time collector and researcher, he accomplished a great deal. His work is also an important resource for paleontologists trying to piece together what life was like on Earth millions of years ago.

THINK ABOUT IT

1. How did Dr. Foerste show his interest in science at any early age?
2. Why did Dr. Foerste want to teach high school?

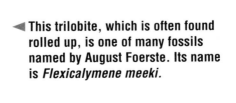

◀ This trilobite, which is often found rolled up, is one of many fossils named by August Foerste. Its name is *Flexicalymene meeki.*

Forming Crystals

How do crystals form in igneous rock?

Materials
- lid from a large jar
- circle of black paper cut to fit inside the lid
- 2 tablespoons of Epsom salts
- 1/2 cup of water

Procedure

1. Turn the lid upside down and put the paper inside it.

2. Stir the Epsom salts into the water.

3. Pour a thin layer of the mixture into the lid.

4. Allow the lid to sit undisturbed for a day or two. Observe and record what happens as the water evaporates.

Draw Conclusions

What shape were the salts after the water evaporated? These new shapes are crystals that formed as the water slowly evaporated and the molecules of salt moved closer together. If the water containing the salts evaporated very quickly, how might the crystals change? How could you test this?

Identifying Rocks

How do clastic and chemical sedimentary rocks differ?

Materials
- samples of sedimentary rock
- white vinegar
- dropper

Procedure

1. Separate the rock samples into clastic and chemical groups, using what you have learned about sedimentary rocks.

2. Use the dropper to place a few drops of vinegar on each sample that you believe is a clastic rock. Record what happens.

3. Test the chemical rocks in the same way, recording the results.

4. Rearrange your groups, if necessary, so all the rocks that reacted to the vinegar are in the same group.

Draw Conclusions

Calcium carbonate, or calcite, the mineral that makes up limestone, reacts to the acid in vinegar by producing bubbles of carbon dioxide. Are the samples that bubbled mostly clastic or mostly chemical rocks? How do you know? Why would a rock that is mostly clastic react to vinegar by forming bubbles?

Chapter ② Review and Test Preparation

Vocabulary Review

Use the terms below to answer Questions 1 through 12. The page numbers in ( ) tell you where to look in the chapter if you need help.

mineral (D40)   **sedimentation** (D49)

magma (D41)   **cementation** (D49)

igneous rock (D41)   **clastic rocks** (D49)

lava (D41)   **chemical rocks** (D49)

weathering (D48)   **metamorphism** (D56)

erosion (D49)   **rock cycle** (D64)

deposition (D49)

1. The movement of weathered rock material is called ____.

2. The process that builds up sediment over millions of years is ____.

3. A natural solid with a definite chemical and physical structure is a ____.

4. The ____ shows the processes by which rocks are formed from one another.

5. Rock that forms when magma cools in or on Earth's crust is ____.

6. ____ are made of sediments that have been weathered and eroded from other rocks, but ____ are formed from minerals dissolved in sea water.

7. The changing of any kind of rock into metamorphic rock is ____.

8. Magma that reaches the surface is ____.

9. ____ is the breakdown of rock into smaller pieces.

10. The gluing together of particles of sediment is ____.

11. ____ is the dropping of sediment by wind, water, or ice.

12. Melted rock in the upper mantle is ____.

Connect Concepts

Write a correct term for each place in the concept map. Use all the terms in the box.

extrusive   **clastic**   **intrusive**

foliated   **nonfoliated**   **sedimentary**

metamorphic   **chemical**   **igneous**

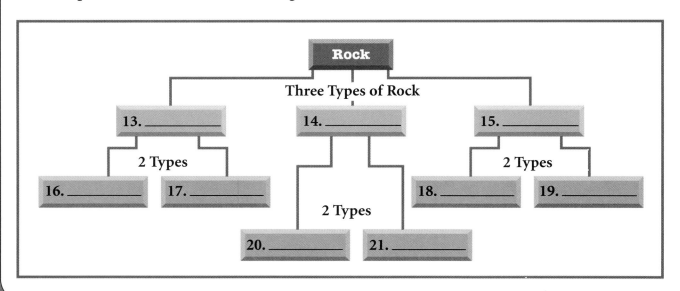

Check Understanding

Write the letter of the best choice.

22. The building blocks of rocks are —
    A minerals
    B ores
    C gemstones
    D sediment

23. Extrusive igneous rock forms from —
    F iron
    G lava
    H mountains
    J earthquakes

24. A clastic sedimentary rock with very large particles is —
    A chemical
    B conglomerate
    C igneous
    D metamorphic

25. Chemical sediment can form as a result of —
    F eruptions
    G cementation
    H evaporation
    J metamorphism

26. One cause of metamorphism is —
    A cold
    B pressure
    C sedimentation
    D weathering

27. The cycle that includes the transformation of sandstone into quartzite is the —
    F metamorphic cycle
    G igneous cycle
    H rock cycle
    J quartz cycle

Critical Thinking

28. Would new igneous rock be formed if Earth's temperature did not increase with depth? Explain.

29. Why are most sedimentary rocks clastic rocks?

30. Why are metamorphic rocks not common on Earth's surface?

31. Explain why geologists say that all rock was originally igneous rock.

Process Skills Review

32. Give examples of the properties you would **observe** to **classify** rocks.

33. Suppose you need to find out how much time it takes for flowing water to smooth the rough surfaces of a certain type of rock. What **variables** would you need to **control** in an experiment on this topic?

34. Describe how you would **model** the formation of sedimentary rock.

35. **Compare** the formation of intrusive and extrusive igneous rocks.

Performance Assessment

The Rock Cycle

Make a simple drawing of the rock cycle. Label it so that all of the stages are clear. Give one example of each kind of rock that is present in the cycle.

Chapter 3

Vocabulary Preview

planetary system
asteroid
meteoroid
comet
astronomical unit
rotation
axis
revolution
orbit
ellipse
season
axial tilt
phases
first quarter
third quarter

Cycles in the Solar System

Every day, you experience the effects of outer space on Earth. The cycles of day and night, the phases of the moon, and the seasons are all determined in part by the motions of objects through space.

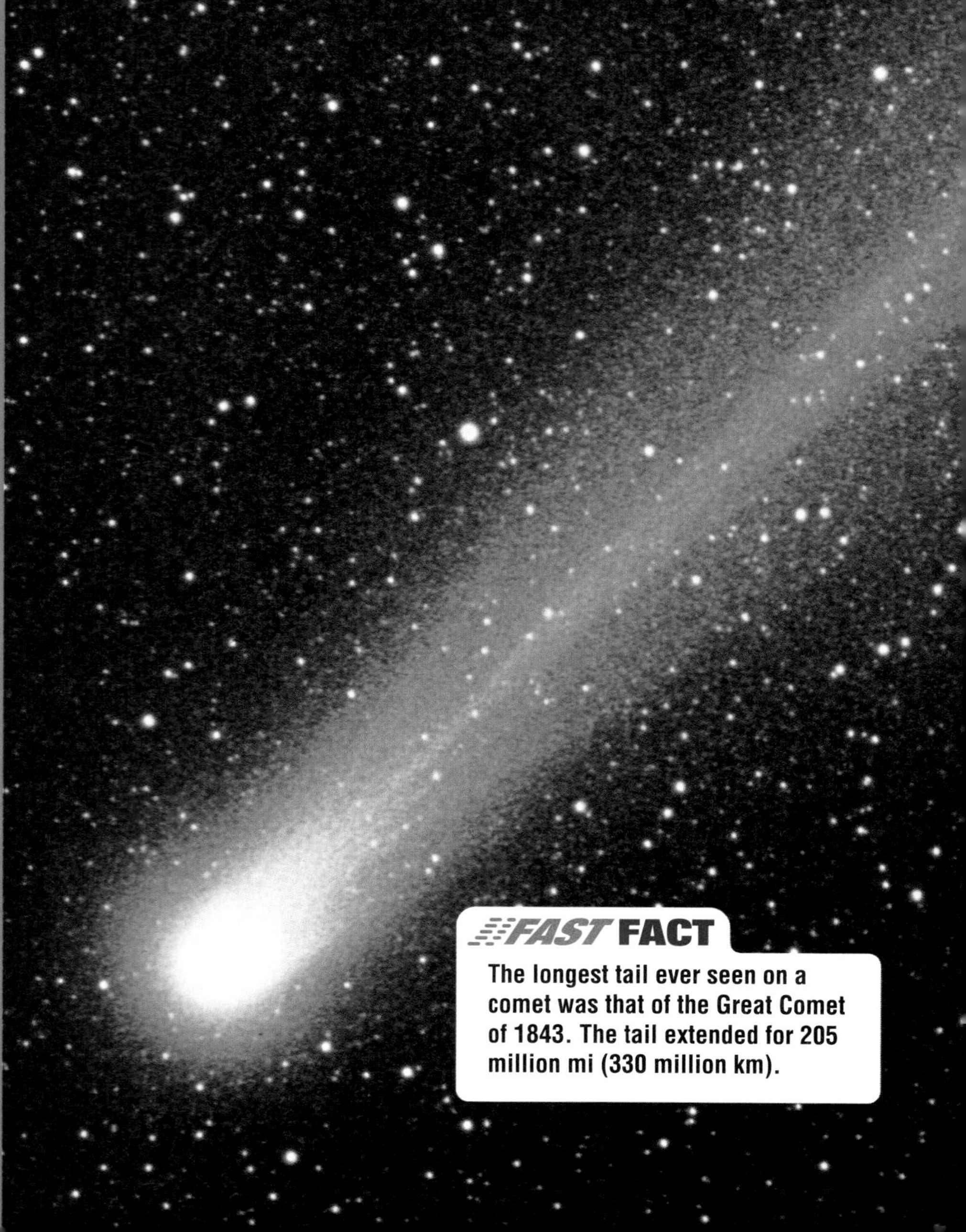

FAST FACT

The longest tail ever seen on a comet was that of the Great Comet of 1843. The tail extended for 205 million mi (330 million km).

What Are the Parts of the Solar System?

In this lesson, you can . . .

INVESTIGATE the sizes of the planets.

LEARN ABOUT the parts of the solar system.

LINK to math, writing, art, and technology.

This old model shows how the known planets were thought to revolve around the sun. ▼

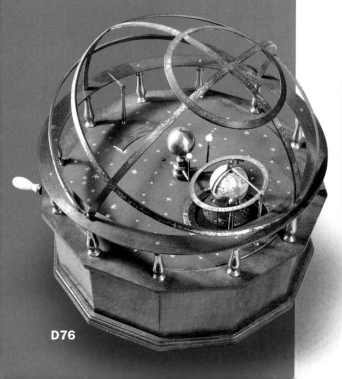

INVESTIGATE

The Sizes of the Planets

Activity Purpose Each of the planets in our solar system is a different size. But how do they compare? In this investigation you will **make a model** of the planets to **compare** their sizes. Then you will decide whether you can use the same scale to compare the distances of the planets from the sun.

Materials
- large sheet of white paper
- drawing compass
- string
- ruler
- colored pencils

Activity Procedure

1 Copy the table below onto a separate sheet of paper. Round each diameter to the nearest hundred kilometers.

2 Decide on a scale for your model. Think about the sizes of the smallest planet and the largest planet. Make 1 cm in your model represent a number of kilometers. The scale must be large enough for you to see the smallest planet easily. The scale must be small enough for the largest planet to be shown completely.

Planetary Information		
Planet	Diameter (km)	Distance from Sun (km)
Mercury	4,878	58 million
Venus	12,100	108 million
Earth	12,756	150 million
Mars	6,786	228 million
Jupiter	142,984	778 million
Saturn	120,536	1,424 million
Uranus	51,108	2,867 million
Neptune	49,538	4,488 million
Pluto	2,350	5,909 million

3 **Calculate** the diameter in centimeters for each planet in the model. Then calculate the radius. To do this, divide the diameter by 2. Plan the position of each planet in order from Mercury to Pluto. Do not include the sun.

4 On the paper, use the compass to draw an outline of each planet. Set the opening of the compass to the planet's radius for the model. (Remember to divide the diameter by 2 to find the radius.) If the compass is not big enough, **measure** a length of string about 5 cm greater than the radius. Tie a pencil to one end of the string with a loop. Measure your radius again and mark the string. Position the mark at a central point on the paper. Use your index finger to hold the string in place at that point. Then pull the string tight, and trace a circle around that point. (Picture A)

5 After you draw the planets, color their surfaces. (Picture B) Use photos from books as a guide. Write your scale on the drawing. Label the planets.

Picture A

Picture B

Draw Conclusions

1. What scale did you work out for your planets?

2. Is it possible to **make a model** in class using the same scale to show the distances between the planets and the sun? Explain your answer.

3. **Scientists at Work** Scientists often **make models** of things to see how they work or to **compare** them. In the investigation, how did making a model of the planets help you compare them?

Investigate Further Make a plan for a model that would show the distances between the planets but not their sizes. Describe your plan. What scale would you use?

Process Skill Tip

When something is too big or too small to see with your eyes, **making a model** of it can help you learn how it looks. You can't look at the planets of the solar system close up. So making a model helps you compare their sizes.

The Solar System

Organization of the Solar System

FIND OUT

- about the parts of the solar system
- how far stars are from Earth

VOCABULARY

planetary system
asteroid
meteoroid
comet
astronomical unit

When people looked at the sky in ancient times, they saw the sun rise in the east, move across the sky, and set in the west. The moon and the stars moved across the sky at night. Naturally, people thought that the Earth was the center of the universe and that all the other bodies moved around it.

In about A.D. 140, the respected astronomer Claudius Ptolemy (TAHL•uh•mee) of Alexandria, Egypt, wrote an explanation that filled 13 volumes, about how objects move in space. In his model, Earth was the center of the universe and didn't move at all. The moon, sun, and planets revolved in circular orbits around Earth. Outside the orbit of the planets was a rotating sphere studded with stars. As the sphere turned, the stars moved across the sky.

Ptolemy's model was wrong. However, it was so carefully worked out that astronomers and navigators used it successfully for more than a thousand years to predict the positions of objects in space. Governments and religions accepted the model as law. Ptolemy's books became known as *Almagest,* which means "the greatest."

After five or six centuries, people began to find problems with the model. The model was not successfully challenged, however, until the early 1500s, when the Polish astronomer Nicholas Copernicus (koh•PER•nih•kuhs) thought of a different model. Copernicus placed

Ptolemy's model of the universe is called geocentric, from the Latin words *geo,* meaning "Earth," and *centric,* meaning "in the center." The Copernican model is called heliocentric, from the Latin words *helio,* meaning "sun," and *centric.* ▼

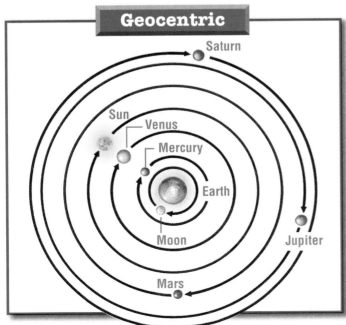

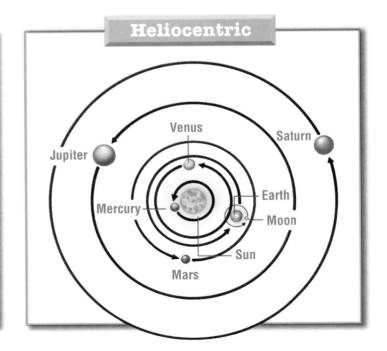

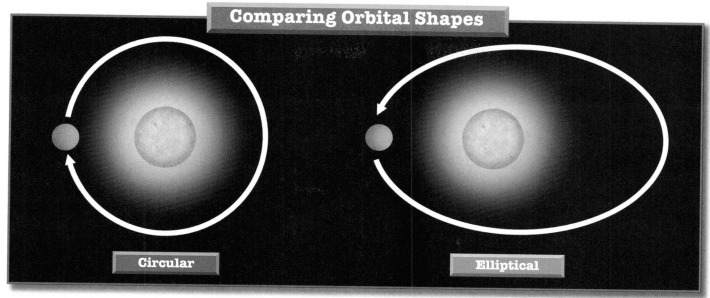

Comparing Orbital Shapes

Circular

Elliptical

▲ Astronomers once thought that planetary orbits were circular and that the sun was in the center. Kepler showed that the orbits are elliptical. The sun is not at the center but slightly to one side.

the sun at the center of the solar system—an idea that most people of the time did not accept.

Copernicus was right about the organization of the solar system, but he was wrong about the shape of planetary orbits. Like Ptolemy, he thought they were circular.

A German astronomer, Johannes Kepler, found the error. He discovered that Mars does not have a circular orbit. Its orbit is elliptical. An ellipse is shaped like a flattened circle. (You will learn more about ellipses in the next lesson.) Kepler inferred that if Mars's orbit is elliptical, then the other planets must have elliptical orbits, too.

In 1609 Kepler published his laws of planetary motion. His first law stated that the orbits of the planets are elliptical.

While Kepler was figuring out the shape of the orbits, the Italian astronomer Galileo was studying the planets with the newly invented telescope. Galileo's observations convinced him that Copernicus was right. The sun is the center of the solar system, and Earth is one of several planets revolving around it.

The idea that Earth moved was not accepted in the early 1600s. But people gradually became

convinced that it was the correct model and that Copernicus and Galileo were right. Earth is part of a **planetary system**, a system of planets revolving around a star.

Today we know that the solar system has even more major parts than Copernicus and Galileo knew about. It has nine planets orbiting the sun and more than 60 moons orbiting the planets. All of these movements together make the solar system seem like a complex dance of planets and moons.

✔ **Compare the geocentric and heliocentric models of the solar system.**

Solar System's Planets and Known Moons

Planet	Moons
Mercury	0
Venus	0
Earth	1
Mars	2
Jupiter	16
Saturn	19
Uranus	17
Neptune	8
Pluto	1

MERCURY

Surface: **rocky, with craters**

Atmosphere: **thin, containing oxygen and helium**

Diameter: **4878 km (about 3031 mi)**

Interesting Fact: **In sunlit areas the surface is hot enough to melt lead.**

VENUS

Surface: **rocky**

Atmosphere: **thick, mostly carbon dioxide and nitrogen, heavy enough to crush humans**

Diameter: **12,100 km (about 7519 mi)**

Interesting Fact: **Venus rotates backward compared with other planets.**

The Structure of the Solar System

In addition to its planets and moons, the solar system has many smaller bodies called asteroids, meteoroids, and comets.

An **asteroid** is a chunk of rock and metal that orbits the sun. Too small to be called planets, most asteroids are less than 1 km (about 0.6 mi) across. The largest known asteroid, Ceres, is about 1000 km (620 mi) in diameter. Most of the asteroids are located between the orbits of Mars and Jupiter.

EARTH

Surface: **mostly water, with areas of soil-covered rock**

Atmosphere: **mostly nitrogen and oxygen**

Diameter: **12,756 km (about 7926 mi)**

Interesting Fact: **Earth has the only known life in the solar system.**

MARS

Surface: **rocky, covered with dust**

Atmosphere: **thin, mostly carbon dioxide**

Diameter: **6786 km (about 4217 mi)**

Interesting Fact: **Mars has the solar system's largest volcano, Olympus Mons, whose base is larger than the state of New Mexico.**

JUPITER

Surface: **gaseous planet, possibly with liquid hydrogen surface**

Atmosphere: **mostly hydrogen and helium**

Diameter: **142,984 km (about 88,849 mi)**

Interesting Fact: **The Great Red Spot on Jupiter is a huge storm that has lasted at least since the time of Galileo.**

ASTEROID BELT

Number of Asteroids: **about 50,000 known**

Largest Asteroid: **about 1000 km (620 mi) in diameter**

Composition of Asteroids: **rock and metal**

Orbits: **most located in a belt between Mars and Jupiter; about 1000 with orbits near Earth**

The space between the planets is full of rocks and bits of dust that orbit the sun. A chunk smaller than an asteroid is a **meteoroid**. Earth collides with thousands of meteoroids each day. Friction with the atmosphere heats the meteoroid and the air around it, producing a glowing trail of light called a meteor. Most meteors burn up before reaching Earth's surface. A meteor that survives the atmosphere and the fall to Earth's surface is a meteorite.

A **comet** is a ball of ice, rock, and frozen gases that orbits the sun. At one end of the orbit, the comet may pass near the sun. At the opposite end, it may swing far out past Pluto to the edge of the solar system.

As a comet approaches the sun, heat may turn some of its frozen matter into gas. Energy from sunlight causes the gas to glow, and pressure from particles that are given off by the sun pushes the glowing gas. As a result, the comet appears to have a tail—a streak of light that extends beyond the comet for millions of kilometers. A comet's tail always points away from the sun.

✓ **What do all the planets in the solar system have in common?**

KUIPER BELT An area beyond the orbit of Neptune that is the source of short-period comets. Short-period comets have orbits that bring them near the sun fairly regularly. Encke's comet has a 3.3-year period. Halley's comet swings by the sun every 76 years.

SATURN
Surface: **gaseous planet with no known solid surface**
Atmosphere: **mostly hydrogen and helium**
Diameter: **120,536 km (about 74,900 mi)**
Interesting Fact: **Saturn has a wide, thin system of rings made of small pieces of ice and rock.**

URANUS
Surface: **gaseous planet with no known solid surface**
Atmosphere: **mostly hydrogen and helium**
Diameter: **51,108 km (about 31,758 mi)**
Interesting Fact: **A possible collision with an Earth-sized object may have knocked Uranus on its side. As a result, it rolls around in orbit.**

NEPTUNE
Surface: **gaseous planet with no known solid surface**
Atmosphere: **mostly hydrogen, helium, methane**
Diameter: **49,538 km (about 30,782 mi)**
Interesting Fact: **Neptune is one of the windiest places in the solar system. Winds top 1000 km per hour (about 620 mi per hour).**

PLUTO
Surface: **water and methane ice**
Atmosphere: **mostly methane**
Diameter: **about 2350 km (1460 mi)**
Interesting Fact: **Pluto is usually the ninth planet, but part of its orbit is inside the orbit of Neptune, making Pluto sometimes the eighth planet.**

OORT CLOUD A large area, much farther from the sun than the Kuiper Belt, that contains a trillion comets. It is the source of long-period comets. Long-period comets may come close to the sun only once in thousands or millions of years.

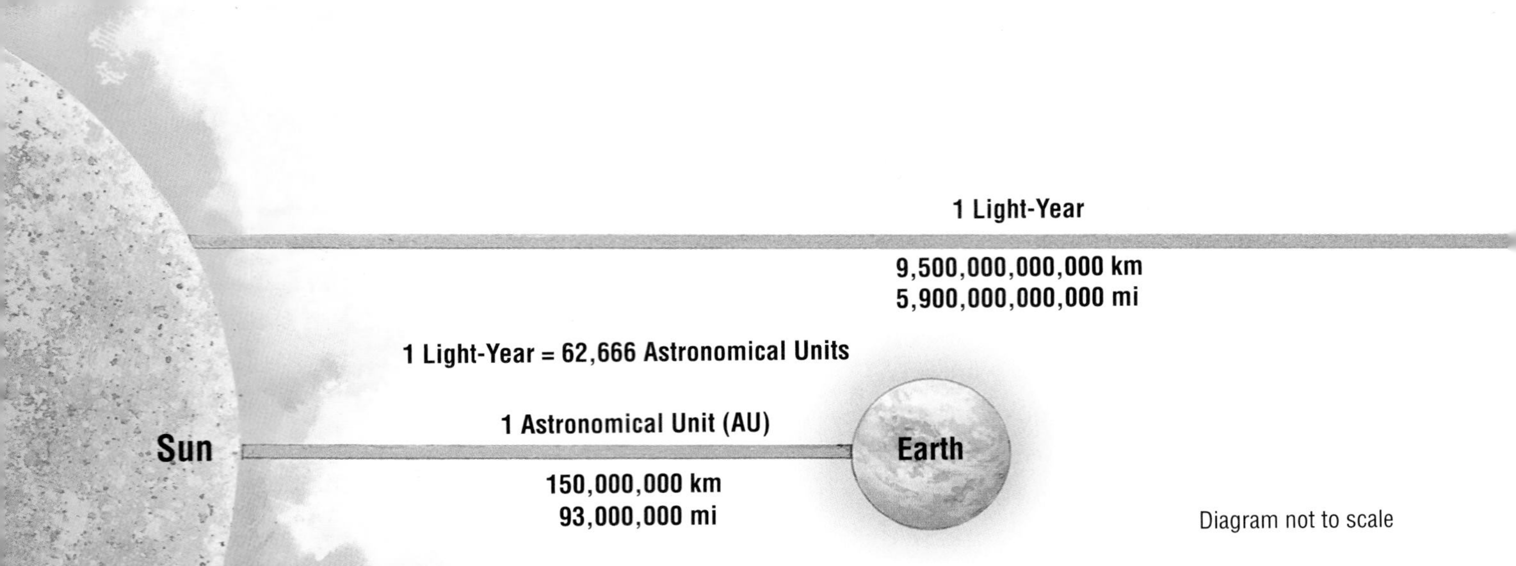

1 Light-Year

9,500,000,000,000 km
5,900,000,000,000 mi

1 Light-Year = 62,666 Astronomical Units

1 Astronomical Unit (AU)

Sun

Earth

150,000,000 km
93,000,000 mi

Diagram not to scale

Distances of Planets from Sun

Planet	AU from Sun
Mercury	0.39
Venus	0.72
Earth	1.00
Mars	1.52
Jupiter	5.19
Saturn	9.49
Uranus	19.11
Neptune	29.92
Pluto	39.39

Distances of Stars from Earth

Star	Light-Years from Earth
Proxima Centauri	4.2—second-closest star to Earth
Alpha Centauri	4.3—third-closest star to Earth
Sirius	8.8—brightest star visible from Earth
Betelgeuse	300.0—giant star, far from Earth
Deneb	1600.0—big and bright, far from Earth

Astronomical Units and Light-Years

Distances in space are gigantic. There are tens of millions of kilometers between Earth and the sun. Alpha Centauri, a star near Earth, is 270,000 times as far away as the sun. Measuring such distances requires large units.

Astronomers often measure distances in our solar system with astronomical units. An **astronomical unit**, or AU, is equal to the distance between Earth and the sun. That distance is about 150 million km (93 million mi). The chart at the left shows the distances of the planets from the sun in astronomical units. It is easier to write that Mars is 1.52 AU from the sun than to write that it is 228,000,000 km (about 142,000,000 mi) from the sun.

But even the astronomical unit is too small to conveniently measure distances to stars. Alpha Centauri is 270,000 AU from Earth. Consider the large figures you would need to show the distance to stars a million times as far away.

For distances to the stars, scientists use a larger unit called the light-year. A *light-year* is equal to the distance light can travel in a vacuum in one year—9.5 million million km (about 5.9 million million mi). Instead of writing a long number to show Alpha Centauri's distance from Earth in kilometers or astronomical units, you can write the distance as 4.3 light-years.

Star

The fact that Alpha Centauri is 4.3 light-years away means that its light has taken 4.3 years to reach Earth. You see the star as it looked 4.3 years ago, not the way it looks now. For stars that are thousands of light-years away, you see light that left the star thousands of years ago. The star itself might no longer exist.

 What is an astronomical unit?

Summary

The solar system consists of the sun, nine planets, and more than 60 moons. Asteroids, comets, and meteoroids are also part of the solar system. Stars, except for the sun, are very distant. The closest stars are light-years from the solar system.

Review

1. What is the difference between the solar system models of Ptolemy and Copernicus?
2. What did Kepler discover about the orbits of the solar system's planets?
3. What is an asteroid?
4. **Critical Thinking** Why are comets visible only when they are near the sun?
5. **Test Prep** A large unit for measuring distances beyond the solar system is a —
   A kilometer
   B solar unit
   C light-year
   D nautical mile

LINKS

MATH LINK

Planet Chart Make a chart of the nine planets, showing date of discovery, comparison with Earth's gravity (greater or less than), mass of the planet, and one other category of information of your choosing. Compare your chart with those of your classmates. What seems to be the relationship between the mass of the planet and its gravity?

WRITING LINK

Informative Writing—Description Write a composition for a child in first grade. Explain the organization of the solar system. Describe all of its parts in a way that a young child can understand.

ART LINK

Planet Surfaces Draw a picture of the landscape you might see if you were standing on another planet or on a moon. Choose any planet or moon in the solar system except Earth. Use the information in this book and in books on the solar system.

TECHNOLOGY LINK

To learn more about parts of the Solar System, watch *Photos of Europa* on the **Harcourt Science Newsroom Video**.

What Are Planetary Cycles?

In this lesson, you can . . .

INVESTIGATE the orbits of the planets in the solar system.

LEARN ABOUT the way the planets move.

LINK to math, writing, social studies, and technology.

INVESTIGATE

Planetary Orbits

Activity Purpose Almost everything in the solar system, from planets to bits of dust, orbits the sun. Some orbits, like those of comets, are long ellipses. Other orbits are shorter and more circular. Did you ever wonder what a planet's orbit looks like? In this investigation you will **make a model** of the orbit of a planet to find out.

Materials

- sheet of construction paper
- ruler
- section of a newspaper
- 2 pushpins
- piece of string, 35–40 cm long
- penny or nickel

Activity Procedure

1 Start by drawing two dots 10 cm apart in the center of the construction paper.

2 Fold the newspaper two or three times so it makes a thick, flat surface. Place it on a table. Put the construction paper on top of the newspaper. At each dot, stick a pushpin through the construction paper and into the newspaper.

3 Tie the ends of the string to make a loop. Place the loop around the pushpins. The loop should be loose. (Picture A)

◀ As any planet rotates, part of its surface is lit by the sun and the rest is in darkness. On a planet or moon, the line that separates darkness from light is the *terminator*.

Picture A

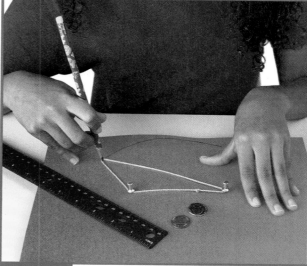

Picture B

4 Put the point of a pencil inside the loop. A partner may need to press down on the pushpins as you pull the pencil point outward until the string makes a tight triangle shape. (Picture B) Move the pencil point all the way around the pushpins, keeping the string tight and drawing a line as you go. The shape you will draw is an ellipse. Each pushpin is at a *focus* of the ellipse. An ellipse has two foci.

5 Trace the penny or nickel to draw a planet on the ellipse. Draw the sun at one focus of the ellipse.

Draw Conclusions

1. What are the features of an elliptical orbit? How does an elliptical orbit differ from a circular orbit?

2. Where is the sun in relation to a planet's orbit?

3. **Scientists at Work** Scientists **make models** to find out how things work or what they're like, especially when the things themselves are too large to see. In the investigation, what did your model help you learn?

Investigate Further Figure out a way to **make your model** of an elliptical orbit fatter and then thinner.

> **Process Skill Tip**
>
> You can **make a model** by drawing, by building, or by using a computer to simulate an object or event.

D85

The Cycles of Planets

Planets Rotate on Their Axes

FIND OUT

- how the planets move on their axes
- how the planets move around the sun

VOCABULARY

rotation
axis
revolution
orbit
ellipse

Earth rotates from west to east. At dawn your location moves toward the sun's light. The sun appears to rise above the eastern horizon. ▼

Suppose there were a world in which the sun shone for 6 months followed by 6 months of darkness. If you woke up to a gray dawn, it could be weeks before the sky was bright. That is what a day on Earth would be like if the planet did not spin, or rotate.

Earth has a day that lasts about 24 hours because of the planet's rotation. **Rotation** is the turning of an object on an axis. Earth's **axis** is an imaginary line through the planet's center, from the North Pole to the South Pole. Because Earth rotates, locations on its surface move from daylight to darkness and back to daylight again. The half of Earth facing the sun is in sunlight and has day. The half of Earth facing away from the sun is in darkness and has night.

All planets rotate on their axes, as Earth does. But each planet rotates at a different speed. The amount of time it takes for a planet to complete one rotation is its *period of rotation*.

✔ **What is rotation?**

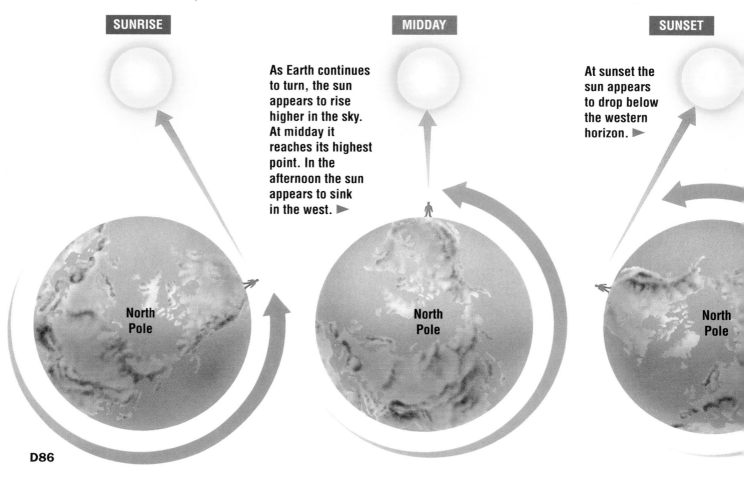

SUNRISE

MIDDAY

As Earth continues to turn, the sun appears to rise higher in the sky. At midday it reaches its highest point. In the afternoon the sun appears to sink in the west. ►

SUNSET

At sunset the sun appears to drop below the western horizon. ►

North Pole

North Pole

North Pole

Days and Years

You think of a day as 24 hours, the length of a day on Earth. But because the planets in the solar system have different periods of rotation, each planet has a day of a different length. Jupiter has the shortest day of all the planets. It rotates in 9.8 hours, so its day is just that long. You could spend two full days on Jupiter in less than one Earth day! On the other hand, Venus has a day that lasts 243 Earth days. In one day on Venus, about two-thirds of an Earth year would pass. As you can see on the chart, the lengths of the planets' days do not form a pattern.

As a planet rotates on its axis, it also revolves around the sun. **Revolution** is the movement of one object in an orbit around another object. An **orbit** is the path an object follows as it revolves around another object. In the investigation you saw that orbits are elliptical. An **ellipse** is an oval path.

The length of time that a planet takes to complete one revolution around the sun is a year. Because the planets' periods of revolution differ, their years differ. The length of Earth's year is $365\frac{1}{4}$ days. You can see in the chart that the lengths of the planets' years vary widely.

A planet's year depends on its distance from the sun. Johannes Kepler, who discovered that the planets have elliptical orbits, also discovered that the speed of a planet in orbit decreases as the distance from the sun increases. So the planets farthest from the sun cover the greatest distance in orbit but move the slowest.

Mercury, the closest planet to the sun, has the shortest year because it moves around the sun the fastest and has the shortest distance to travel. Pluto, the planet usually farthest from the sun, takes about 248 Earth years to make one revolution.

✔ **What is planetary revolution?**

Planets: Length of Day and Year in Earth Equivalents

MERCURY
Day = 59 Earth days
Year = 88 Earth days

VENUS
Day = 243 Earth days
Year = 225 Earth days

EARTH
Day = 24 hours
Year = 365 days

MARS
Day = 25 Earth hours
Year = 687 Earth days

JUPITER
Day = 10 Earth hours
Year = 12 Earth years

SATURN
Day = 10 Earth hours
Year = 29.5 Earth years

URANUS
Day = 18 Earth hours
Year = 84 Earth years

NEPTUNE
Day = 19 Earth hours
Year = 165 Earth years

PLUTO
Day = 6 Earth days
Year = 248 Earth years

All times have been rounded to the nearest hour, day, or half year.

Orbits and Seasons

If you could look at a planet's orbit from above, you would see that the sun is not at the center of the ellipse. The sun is at one focus of the ellipse, slightly away from the center.

Because planetary orbits are elliptical, each planet is closer to the sun at some times than at others. The point in orbit where a planet is closest to the sun is called *perihelion* (pair•ih•HEE•lee•uhn). The point where the planet is farthest from the sun is called *aphelion* (ap•HEE•lee•uhn).

Earth has different seasons as it revolves around the sun. But Earth's changing distance from the sun does not cause seasonal temperature changes. In fact, Earth is closest to the sun in mid-winter in North America. It is then 5 million km (about 3 million mi) closer to the sun than in summer.

✔ **Where is the sun with respect to the shape of the planets' orbits?**

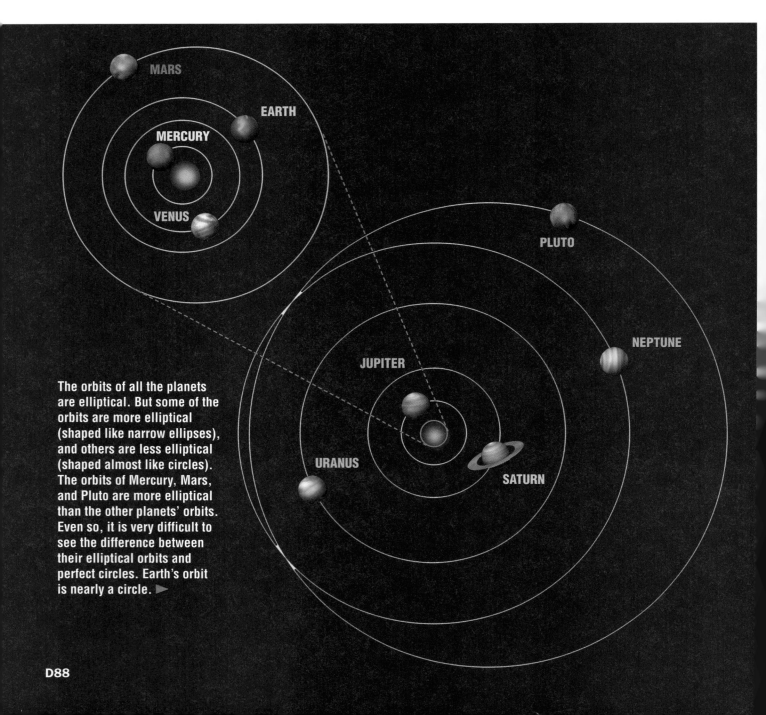

MARS

EARTH

MERCURY

VENUS

PLUTO

NEPTUNE

JUPITER

URANUS

SATURN

The orbits of all the planets are elliptical. But some of the orbits are more elliptical (shaped like narrow ellipses), and others are less elliptical (shaped almost like circles). The orbits of Mercury, Mars, and Pluto are more elliptical than the other planets' orbits. Even so, it is very difficult to see the difference between their elliptical orbits and perfect circles. Earth's orbit is nearly a circle. ▶

SEPTEMBER 22 OR 23
Earth's axis tilts neither toward nor away from the sun. Daytime and nighttime are of equal length in both hemispheres. This day, which is called an equinox (EE•kwih•nahks),marks the beginning of fall in the Northern Hemisphere and the beginning of spring in the Southern Hemisphere.

ON OR AROUND JULY 4,
Earth is at aphelion (the point where it's farthest from the sun) at a distance of 152 million km (about 94 million mi).

JUNE 21 OR 22
Tilted toward the sun, the Northern Hemisphere has its longest day and short-est night. This marks the beginning of summer. The Southern Hemisphere has its shortest day, marking the beginning of winter.

DECEMBER 21 OR 22
Tilted away from the sun, the Northern Hemisphere has its shortest day and longest night. This marks the beginning of winter. The Southern Hemisphere has its longest day, marking the beginning of summer.

ON OR AROUND JANUARY 3,
Earth is at perihelion (the point where it's closest to the sun) at a distance of 147 million km (about 91 million mi).

MARCH 20 OR 21
Earth's axis tilts neither toward nor away from the sun. This equinox marks the beginning of spring in the Northern Hemisphere and the beginning of fall in the Southern Hemisphere.

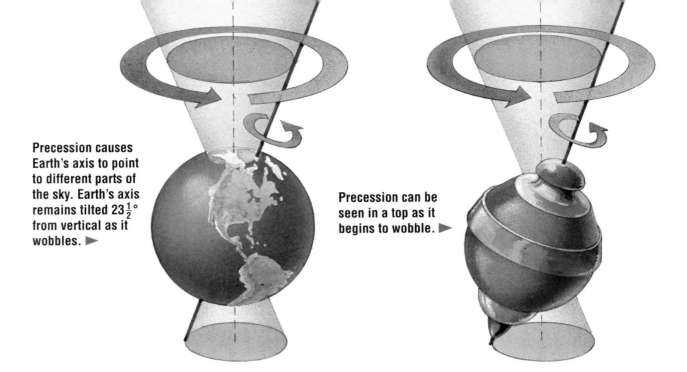

Precession causes Earth's axis to point to different parts of the sky. Earth's axis remains tilted $23\frac{1}{2}°$ from vertical as it wobbles. ▶

Precession can be seen in a top as it begins to wobble. ▶

Planets Wobble on Their Axes

Earth rotates and revolves fairly fast. But a third movement of Earth is very slow. If you have ever spun a top, you know that it stands straight up and down when it is spinning fast. As the top slows, it starts to wobble.

The Earth wobbles like a top—just not as quickly. In 26,000 years, the Earth makes one huge wobble. The poles slowly trace huge circles. This wobble is called *precession.*

Because the wobble is so slow, people don't see its effects in one lifetime. But the effects are clear over thousands of years. One important long-term effect of precession is that Earth's axis at the North Pole points at different stars in the night sky.

In the Northern Hemisphere, Earth's axis now points to a star called Polaris. For this reason, Polaris is also called the North Star. Because of its location, Polaris doesn't seem to move as Earth rotates. It appears to stay in one spot, while all the other stars appear to move in circles around it. Because Polaris appears fixed, navigators have used it for hundreds of years to find their position. The angle made by Polaris and the horizon shows latitude.

During Earth's slow wobble, the North Star changes. At the time of the ancient Egyptians, in 2700 B.C., the North Star was Thuban. Thuban is in the constellation Draco, the dragon. Twelve thousand years from now, the North Pole of the axis will be on the other side of its precession circle. At that time, the axis will point to a place very near a bright star named Vega.

✔ **What is precession?**

The North Star and Precession of Earth					
	2700 B.C.	A.D. 2000	A.D. 14,000	A.D. 23,000	A.D. 28,000
Vega			North Star		
Polaris		North Star			North Star
Thuban	North Star			North Star	

Summary

All planets rotate on their axes. One rotation defines a day. Planets revolve around the sun in elliptical orbits. One revolution defines a year. The length of days and years differs for the different planets of the solar system.

Review

1. What is a planet's revolution?
2. What is aphelion?
3. What is perihelion?
4. **Critical Thinking** How would Earth's year be different if it were farther from the sun? Explain your answer.
5. **Test Prep** Precession causes Earth to wobble slowly on its —

    A poles

    B equator

    C orbit

    D axis

LINKS

MATH LINK

Earth's Orbit Earth's elliptical orbit is almost a circle. How can you change the method you used in the investigation to make the ellipse more circular? Experiment to find out. Use the method to draw Earth's orbit.

WRITING LINK

Narrative Writing—Story What would a day on another planet be like? Choose a planet and find information about it in this book or other sources. Then write for your classmates a description of a day's experience on the planet.

SOCIAL STUDIES LINK

Seasonal Celebrations Throughout history, people have used events in the sky to mark the changing seasons. Find out how another culture determined when the seasons began. Share your findings with your classmates.

TECHNOLOGY LINK

Learn more about planets and their moons by visiting the National Air and Space Museum Internet site.
www.si.edu/harcourt/science

Smithsonian Institution®

◄ In addition to moons, millions of chunks of ice and rock revolve around Saturn. The chunks form Saturn's rings.

LESSON 3

Why Do Planets Have Seasons?

In this lesson, you can . . .

INVESTIGATE why temperatures change during the year.

LEARN ABOUT the seasons.

LINK to math, writing, music, and technology.

In some parts of the country, crocuses are one of the first signs of spring. ▼

How Sunlight Affects Temperature

Activity Purpose The sun shines all year round. But in most places, the sun feels a lot warmer in summer than it does in winter. Have you ever wondered why? In this investigation you will **gather and interpret data** to **form a hypothesis** about how the angle of light affects temperature.

Materials

- 2 sheets of graph paper
- ruler
- small flashlight
- 2 pencils, red and blue
- 2 sheets of black paper
- 2 thermometers
- lamp with 60-watt bulb
- clock or watch

Activity Procedure

1 Shine the flashlight on one sheet of graph paper from 15 cm directly above a point in the middle. Use the red pencil to trace around the area of bright light that falls on the paper. **Record** your **observations**. (Picture A)

2 Shine the flashlight at the same point on the graph paper but at a 45° angle. Keep the lamp 15 cm from the point in the middle. Use the blue pencil to trace around the area of bright light. **Record** your **observations**. (Picture B)

3 **Predict** which area would get warmer, the one that gets direct light or the one that gets indirect light. **Record** your prediction.

4 Place a thermometer on a sheet of black paper. **Measure** and **record** the temperature. For five minutes, shine the lamp from a distance of 15 cm directly over the bulb of the thermometer. Measure and record the temperature every 30 seconds. (Picture C)

Picture A

Picture B

5 Place the second thermometer on the other sheet of black paper. **Measure** and **record** the temperature. For five minutes, shine the light at a 45° angle, 15 cm from the bulb of the thermometer. Measure and record the temperature on the thermometer every 30 seconds.

6 Use your temperature data to draw one graph with two lines on the second sheet of graph paper. Draw a red line for the temperature data from Step 4. Draw a blue line for the temperature data from Step 5. **Compare** the two lines.

Picture C

Draw Conclusions

1. Which area did you **predict** would get warmer? Why? Was your prediction correct?

2. Did the temperature rise faster with direct light or indirect light?

3. **Scientists at Work** Scientists **gather and interpret data** to **form a hypothesis**. Using the data, form a hypothesis about the relationship between temperature and the angle at which light rays hit a surface. Think of the lamp as the sun and the sheets of paper as Earth. **Infer** the time of year that the sun's rays shine on your area most directly.

Investigate Further Hold the lamp at a different angle while shining it on a thermometer. **Predict** how the result will **compare** with your findings in the investigation. Test your prediction.

Why Planets Have Seasons

Seasons on Earth

FIND OUT

- why there are seasons on Earth
- what seasons are like on other planets

VOCABULARY

season
axial tilt

In most places on Earth, the weather changes with the season. A **season** is a period of the year with a certain level of temperature and type of weather. Winter can bring lower temperatures and sometimes ice and snow. Summer can bring hot, sunny days and thunderstorms. Why does the temperature change from one season to another?

In the investigation you saw the reason for seasonal temperature differences. When the sun's rays hit Earth's surface directly, the surface absorbs more energy and the temperatures are high. When rays hit at

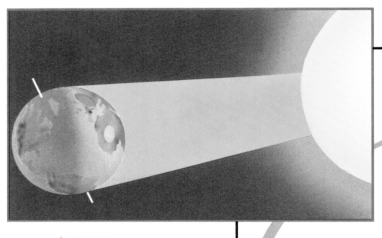

September 23—Autumnal Equinox
This is one date of almost equal daylight and darkness in both hemispheres. Neither hemisphere receives more direct sunlight. Fall begins in the Northern Hemisphere, and spring begins in the Southern Hemisphere.

▲ **WINTER**
Rays from the sun hit the Northern Hemisphere indirectly in winter. The slanting rays spread the solar energy over a larger area than in summer, causing lower temperatures.

December 22—Winter Solstice
The date with the least daylight in the Northern Hemisphere marks the beginning of winter. The Southern Hemisphere receives more direct sunlight. In the Southern Hemisphere, summer begins on this date.

an angle of less than 90°, the surface absorbs less energy and the temperatures are lower.

If Earth rotated on a vertical axis, the angle of the sun's rays at each location on Earth would be the same all year. There would be no seasons. But Earth's axial tilt causes the angle of the sun's rays to change during the year. **Axial tilt** is the angle that a planet's axis is tilted from vertical. Earth's axis is tilted 23.5°, enough to cause seasons.

Earth's axis remains tilted in the same direction all year. As Earth revolves around the sun, the axial tilt causes the Northern Hemisphere to be pointed toward the sun for part of the year and away from the sun for another part.

When the Northern Hemisphere is pointed toward the sun, the sun's rays hit it more directly and there are more hours of daylight. More solar energy is absorbed. The hemisphere's climate grows warmer, and summer occurs.

As Earth continues to revolve, it reaches a point in its orbit where the axial tilt is neither toward nor away from the sun. The angle of sunlight is less direct than in summer. Hours of daylight and darkness are almost equal. The hemisphere's temperatures are cooler, and fall begins.

When the Northern Hemisphere is pointed away from the sun, the sun's rays are the most slanted and indirect. There are fewer hours of daylight. The hemisphere's climate grows cooler, and winter occurs.

When Earth reaches the second point in its orbit where the axial tilt is neither toward nor away from the sun, spring begins.

✔ **Why is it warmest in the summer?**

June 21— Summer Solstice
The date with the most daylight in the Northern Hemisphere marks the beginning of summer. The sun's rays more directly strike the Northern Hemisphere. This date in the Southern Hemisphere marks the beginning of winter.

March 21—Vernal Equinox
This is one date of almost equal daylight and darkness in both hemispheres. Spring begins in the Northern Hemisphere, and fall begins in the Southern Hemisphere.

SUMMER
Solar energy hits the Northern Hemisphere more directly in summer than in winter. Direct rays concentrate the solar energy on a smaller area, causing higher temperatures. ▼

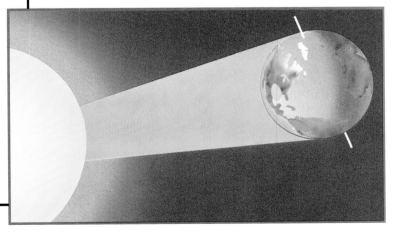

The Seasons on Mars

No one has ever experienced summer on Mars or winter on Pluto. But astronomers know that these planets and several others have axial tilts that can cause seasons.

The axial tilts of the planets differ. For example, Mercury, Venus, and Jupiter have almost no axial tilt. The three planets have axes almost vertical to their orbits, so they have no seasons. Uranus and Pluto have extreme axial tilts. Uranus is tilted 97.9° from vertical. Pluto has an even greater axial tilt of 122.5°.

The amount of axial tilt affects seasons. In some cases so does a planet's orbit. Earth's orbit is nearly circular, so it does not have much effect on the seasons. However, Mars has a much more elliptical orbit that affects the amount of solar energy it receives at different times of the year.

For years people observed seasonal changes on Mars. Polar icecaps grew each winter, and large greenish regions appeared to grow every summer. Some people also thought they saw canals. They imagined vast areas of Martian plants being watered every summer by Martians.

Today we know that Mars has no canals, no plants, and no Martians. But it does have seasons. Mars is farther from the sun than Earth

THE INSIDE STORY

Seasons on Mars

SUMMER SOLSTICE

March 1997

Northern Polar Summer
The permanent icecap is mostly water ice. In summer a frost of mostly carbon dioxide evaporates away. The polar icecap shrinks.

NORTHERN SUMMER
Mars reaches its farthest point from the sun, causing a long, cool summer in the northern hemisphere and a long, very cold winter in the southern hemisphere. Winds may uncover dark stone, causing seasonal patches of "green."

177 Martian days

Fall Equinox
As Mars approaches perihelion, the shortest season occurs. It is fall in the north and spring in the south.

142 Martian days

and takes a longer time to orbit the sun. So Martian seasons are colder and twice as long as Earth's. The hottest Martian summer day reaches only 20°C (68°F). A winter day might reach ⁻140°C (⁻220°F).

Because of the 25.2° tilt and elliptical orbit, Martian seasons are more extreme than Earth's. The difference between Earth's greatest distance from the sun and its least distance is relatively small—just 5 million kilometers (about 3 million mi). That is because Earth's orbit is almost circular. For Mars the difference between the greatest distance from the sun and the least distance is 43 million km (about 27 million mi).

So, unlike Earth's seasons, the seasons on Mars are affected by both the axial tilt and the shape of the orbit. You can see this in the diagram.

Mars has higher summer temperatures in the southern hemisphere than in the northern hemisphere because the southern summer comes at perihelion. The southern hemisphere winter occurs when Mars is at its greatest distance from the sun. This causes southern hemisphere winters to be much colder than those in the northern hemisphere.

✓ **Why do astronomers think that, besides Earth, other planets in the solar system also have seasons?**

194 Martian days

Spring Equinox
As Mars approaches aphelion, the longest season occurs. It is spring in the north and fall in the south.

165 Martian days

WINTER SOLSTICE

October 1996

Winter Solstice
Mars orbits close to the sun, causing a short, mild winter in the north. In the southern hemisphere, summer is short and hot.

NORTHERN WINTER
In winter, temperatures drop below ⁻125°C (⁻193°F). Carbon dioxide in the atmosphere freezes, covering the ground with a thin layer of dry-ice snow. The polar icecap grows large.

Seasons and Other Planets

The amount of axial tilt affects seasons. How far a planet is from the sun can determine temperature patterns. The planets with the least axial tilt, Mercury and Venus, are near to the sun. They have no seasons. All of Venus and the sunlit side of Mercury are always hot.

The planets with the greatest axial tilt are Uranus and Pluto. Astronomers hypothesize that a collision with an Earth-sized object changed Uranus's axial tilt. As a result, Uranus now lies on its side. This position gives Uranus a pattern of sunlight and darkness rather than seasonal change.

Because of its tilt, Uranus seems to roll on its orbit, with one pole facing the sun for about one-fourth of its year—about 21 Earth years. At the same time, the other pole has 21 Earth

MERCURY AND VENUS ▶ Mercury and Venus have the smallest axial tilts in the solar system. Mercury is tilted about 2°. Venus has a 2.7° tilt. These slight tilts mean that Mercury and Venus do not have seasons.

2°

2.7°

MERCURY 2°

VENUS 2.7°

URANUS AND PLUTO ▶ Uranus and Pluto have the greatest axial tilts in the solar system. Uranus is tilted 97.9°. Pluto is tilted 122.5°.

97.9°

122.5°

URANUS 97.9°

PLUTO 122.5°

years of continuous night. As the planet revolves, the pole that was in daylight moves into darkness, while the pole that was in darkness moves into light.

Pluto does have seasonal temperature changes. But Pluto is so far from the sun—5.9 billion km (about 3.7 billion mi)—that temperatures range from cold for the part facing the sun to even colder for the part facing away. The average temperature on Pluto is about ⁻210°C (⁻346°F). From Pluto the sun looks like a very bright star, and it casts a dim light. Pluto's sky is always dark. Its surface is always icy, and its temperatures are always bitterly cold—regardless of which pole is tilted toward the sun.

✔ **Why don't Mercury and Venus have seasons?**

Summary

Earth's axial tilt causes seasons. Its distance from the sun has little effect on the seasons. Some other planets are also tilted on their axes, so some of these planets also have seasons. For other planets, both the axial tilt and the distance from the sun affect their seasons.

Review

1. What is axial tilt?
2. How do seasons of the Northern Hemisphere relate to seasons of the Southern Hemisphere on Earth?
3. Name two factors that affect Mars's seasons.
4. **Critical Thinking** How would Earth's seasons be different if it had no tilt?
5. **Test Prep** One visual sign of seasons on Mars is the change in the planet's —
   A icecaps
   B axes
   C moons
   D plant life

LINKS

MATH LINK

Axial Tilt Use a ruler, a protractor, and a drawing compass to draw one of the planets with the correct axial tilt.

WRITING LINK

Persuasive Writing—Opinion Which season is your favorite? Write a composition for your classmates to persuade them that the season you chose is the best.

MUSIC LINK

Seasonal Songs Find music connected to winter, spring, summer, or fall. What adjectives would you use to describe the music and the lyrics? Explain why you think the music fits the season or why it does not. Share your music selections with the class.

TECHNOLOGY LINK

Learn more about Mars by visiting The National Air and Space Museum Internet site.
www.si.edu.harcourt.science

 Smithsonian Institution®

Why Do Moons Have Phases?

In this lesson, you can . . .

INVESTIGATE the phases of the moon.

LEARN ABOUT the phases of moons and planets.

LINK to math, writing, art, and technology.

◀ The full moon is one of the phases of the moon.

INVESTIGATE

Views of the Moon

Activity Purpose If you look at the moon each night, it seems to change shape. You know its shape doesn't really change. So what is happening? In this investigation you will **observe** a model of the moon's movements. Then you will **infer** what causes the moon to "change its shape."

Materials
- yellow construction paper
- scissors
- tape
- 8 sheets of white paper ($8\frac{1}{2} \times 11$ in.)
- black marker
- 3-in. white plastic foam ball
- toothpick

Activity Procedure

1 From the yellow construction paper, cut out a sun and tape it to the front wall of the classroom. Write the letters *A* through *H* on the eight sheets of paper so that one letter fills each sheet. Tape the sheets of paper to the walls of the classroom as shown. (Picture A)

2 Use the marker to blacken one-half of the foam ball. Give it two or three minutes to dry. This ball will be the moon. Stick the toothpick into the foam moon at any spot where the black and white parts meet. Use the toothpick as a handle.

3 You will be Earth in this model. Stand in the middle of the room. (Take turns so that everyone has a chance to be Earth.)

4 Another person should hold the moon and move slowly around you from Point A to Point H, stopping briefly in front of each letter on the wall. This person must hold the moon so that its white half is always facing the sun at the front of the classroom. The white half represents the moon's sunlit side. (Picture B)

5 **Observe** the moon carefully as it moves. Turn as needed to keep the moon in sight. Identify the white shapes you see as the moon completes one revolution around you. When the moon stops in front of each letter, record your observations by drawing what you see.

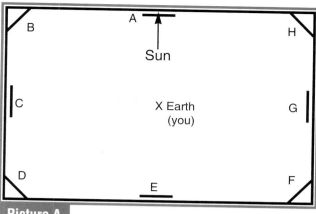

Picture A

Draw Conclusions

1. At what point did you **observe** the most of the white half of the foam moon? What shape did you observe?

2. At what point did you **observe** the least of the white half of the foam moon? What did you observe?

Picture B

3. **Scientists at Work** Scientists **observe** things and then **infer** how they work. Use your observations to infer why the moon seems to change shape.

Investigate Further How could you change your model to see if Earth appears to change its shape when viewed from the moon?

Process Skill Tip

One way to **observe** is to use your eyes to examine things. Then you record what you see. When you **infer**, you use what you observe to form an opinion.

The Phases of Moons

Phases of Earth's Moon

FIND OUT

- why we see phases of the moon
- what planetary phases are

VOCABULARY

phase
first quarter
third quarter

If you observe the moon, you will find that on some nights it rises in the evening sky as a big, round disk. On other nights, after hours of darkness, just a thin crescent appears. You are seeing the moon's phases. **Phases** are the different shapes the moon seems to have when it is viewed from Earth. In the investigation, you saw how the phases change as the moon revolves around Earth. The diagram on the next page shows the eight main phases of the moon.

If the moon produced light, it would always appear as a bright round disk. But the moon does not produce light. It reflects light from the sun. As the moon revolves around Earth, one-half of the moon is always lit by the sun. Depending on where the moon is in its orbit, you see different amounts of its lit side. The shape you see depends on how much of the moon's lit side is visible from Earth.

The moon takes $29\frac{1}{2}$ days to go through its cycle of phases—from new moon to full moon and back to new moon again. Between the new moon and the full moon, the visible part of the lit side gets larger. The shapes you see are called the *waxing phases*. From full moon to new moon, the visible part of the moon's sunlit side gets smaller. The shapes you see are called the *waning phases*.

During a full moon, you see all of the moon's sunlit side. ▼

The new moon can barely be seen because the unlit half of the moon is facing Earth. The moon's lit half faces away from Earth. There is, however, enough sunlight reflected from Earth to light the dark side of the moon very dimly.

In later phases, the moon's sunlit side comes into view. First, you see just an edge. This is the waxing (growing) crescent. The next phase is the first quarter. In the **first quarter**, half the moon's lit side is visible. It is called the first quarter because it occurs when the moon is one-quarter of the way through its orbit. The waxing gibbous moon appears next. In this phase about three-fourths of the moon's lit side is visible. When the moon is halfway around its orbit, its whole lit side is visible. This phase is the full moon.

After the full moon, less and less of the moon's sunlit side is visible and the moon wanes (grows smaller) through its phases. The waning gibbous moon is followed by the third quarter moon. In the **third quarter**, half of the moon's lit side is visible—the half that was dark in the first quarter. This phase is called the third quarter because it happens when the moon is three-quarters of the way through its orbit. The last phase is the waning crescent. Then a new moon starts the cycle again.

✔ **What is meant by *phases* of the moon?**

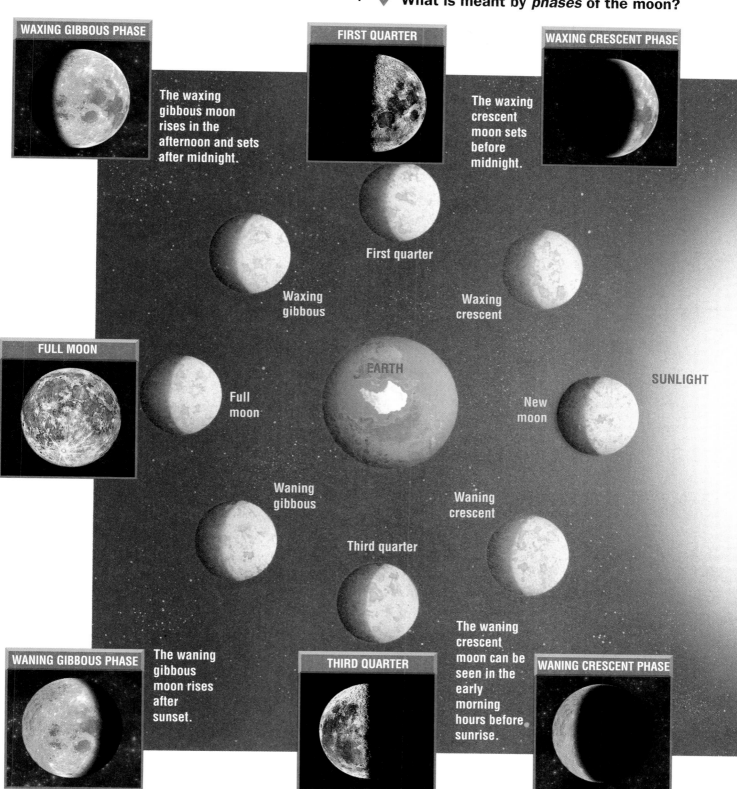

WAXING GIBBOUS PHASE

The waxing gibbous moon rises in the afternoon and sets after midnight.

FIRST QUARTER

WAXING CRESCENT PHASE

The waxing crescent moon sets before midnight.

First quarter

Waxing gibbous

Waxing crescent

FULL MOON

EARTH

SUNLIGHT

Full moon

New moon

Waning gibbous

Waning crescent

Third quarter

WANING GIBBOUS PHASE

The waning gibbous moon rises after sunset.

THIRD QUARTER

The waning crescent moon can be seen in the early morning hours before sunrise.

WANING CRESCENT PHASE

From Earth the new phase and the full phase of Venus cannot be seen. However, the crescent phases and "quarter" phases can be seen clearly.

Although you can see more of its lit side, Venus looks smallest near its full phase because then it is farthest from Earth. The planet disappears from our skies because it moves behind the sun in full phase. ▶

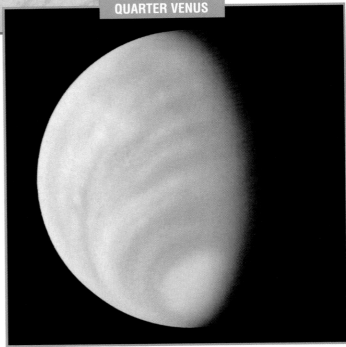

NEAR FULL VENUS

QUARTER VENUS

▲ This view of Venus occurs one-quarter through its cycle of phases. The phases of Venus as seen from Earth follow a 584-day cycle.

Phases of Other Moons and Planets

You see the moon's phases because, as the moon revolves, different amounts of its lit side are visible from Earth. What about other bodies in the solar system? Do they have phases?

There are more than 60 known moons in our solar system. If you could stand on the surface of one of the other planets with moons, you would see phases like those of Earth's moon.

In 1609 Galileo showed that planets also have phases. He was the first astronomer to see the phases of Venus. Galileo's observations helped him show that Venus and the other planets orbit the sun.

During much of the year, Venus appears as a bright star in either the morning or evening sky. Depending on its position in orbit, you can see different phases of Venus from Earth with a small telescope or binoculars.

Viewed from Earth, Mercury also has phases. However, Mercury's phases are difficult to see because the planet is close to the sun. Mercury's phases are best seen when Mercury and the sun are farthest apart as viewed from Earth.

If we send a probe out beyond other planets such as Mars and Jupiter, we see that they also have phases. But because the planets beyond Earth are so far from the sun, their phases are much harder to see.

✔ **Why does Venus have phases?**

Summary

Phases are the different amounts that you see of the moon's sunlit side as the moon orbits Earth. Some other moons and planets of the solar system also have phases.

Review

1. What is a new moon?
2. What are waxing phases?
3. What are waning phases?
4. **Critical Thinking** Would it be possible to see phases of Earth from Mars? Explain your answer.
5. **Test Prep** It is easiest to see the phases of the moon and —

   A Pluto

   B Neptune

   C Venus

   D the sun

Although you cannot see much of it, Venus looks largest in the crescent phase because then it is closest to Earth. When Venus moves in front of the sun (during the "new Venus" phase), it disappears in the glare of sunlight for a second time. ▼

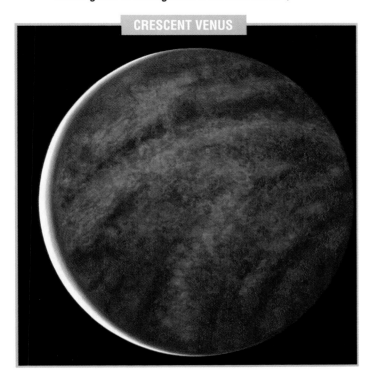

CRESCENT VENUS

LINKS

MATH LINK

Lunar Cycle Starting with the next new moon, predict the times of the moon's phases for a month. Keep in mind that the whole cycle takes $29\frac{1}{2}$ days and that there are eight major phases. Draw a calendar, and mark the phases on the proper days. Check your accuracy during the month.

WRITING LINK

Persuasive Writing—Business Letter Write a letter to NASA, asking for a photo of astronauts on the moon's surface or of "Earthrise" as seen from the moon. Find out where to send the letter. Make your request clear, short, and polite.

ART LINK

Lunar Phases Make a piece of art showing one phase of the moon. Choose any material, such as paper, paint, foil, charcoal, or clay, or take a photograph. Show the moon alone or the moon as part of a landscape. Display your art in class.

TECHNOLOGY LINK

Visit the Harcourt Learning Site for related links, activities, and resources.
www.harcourtschool.com

WELCOME TO THE LEARNING SITE

EXPLORING MARS

Scientists used a tiny remote-controlled vehicle called a rover to make new discoveries on Mars.

Why do scientists want to explore Mars?

Exploring Mars could provide scientists with clues about the formation of the planets in the solar system, including Earth. Scientists also want to find out whether life exists on Mars.

How was *Pathfinder* different from other probes that have explored Mars?

The *Pathfinder* probe was one of many probes sent to explore Mars. It was smaller and cheaper than most of the others. It cost about one-fifth of what the Mars Viking probes cost in 1976. *Pathfinder* was a small, 600-pound lander that carried a tiny, six-wheeled rover (named *Sojourner*) not much bigger than a large toy truck. The mission tested how well scientists on Earth could guide the rover over the surface of Mars by remote control.

How has *Pathfinder* helped scientists find out more about Mars?

Pathfinder sent back thousands of images of the surface of Mars at a faster rate than any other planetary probe had been able to. Scientists used the pictures to study the geology of

Pathfinder and *Sojourner* on Mars

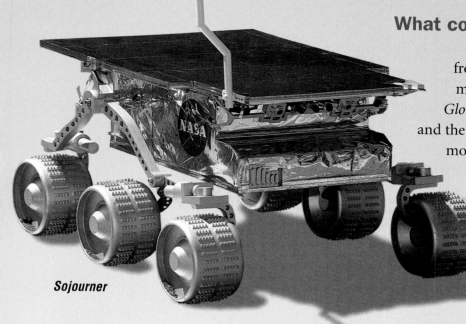
Sojourner

What comes after *Pathfinder*?

It will take years to analyze the data from *Pathfinder's* mission. In the meantime, NASA has sent the *Mars Global Surveyor,* the *Mars Polar Lander,* and the *Mars Climate Orbiter* to collect more information about Mars. NASA has plans for several more crewless missions to Mars over the next few years. Some of the missions will collect information necessary to prepare for future human missions to Mars.

THINK ABOUT IT

1. What did *Pathfinder* find out about Mars?
2. What information from the *Pathfinder* mission might be useful for future missions?

WEB LINK:
For Science and Technology updates, visit The Learning Site.
www.harcourtschool.com

the planet and to locate the most interesting places to send *Sojourner.*

Sojourner explored Martian rocks with an instrument called an alpha proton X-ray spectrometer. The instrument bombards rocks with high-energy particles. The particles given off by the target rock tell scientists which elements are in the rock and in what amounts. Surprisingly, the spectrometer showed that one rock on Mars contains a lot of quartz. Scientists hypothesize the rock, which they called "Barnacle Bill," might also contain equal amounts of the minerals feldspar and pyroxene. This would make it similar to andesite, a type of rock found on Earth. Andesite on Earth forms only along plate boundaries. This suggests that Mars may at one time have had moving tectonic plates.

Meteorologists looked at the weather data from Mars. They found that the Martian atmosphere is colder and dustier than they had thought. High temperatures on Mars were about ⁻18°C (0°F) each day, with lows of about ⁻73°C (⁻100°F) at night. Mars would be warmer if it weren't for the large amount of atmospheric dust, which absorbs and scatters sunlight.

Careers   Robotics Engineer

What They Do Any engineer who works with robots can be called a robotics engineer. Robotics engineers design, build, and program robotic devices and other automated equipment. They also develop computer software to control these devices.

Education and Training Robotics engineers must study computer science and mathematics. They should enjoy building things and finding out how things work. Robotics engineers need at least a bachelor's degree but often have advanced degrees.

Carolyn Shoemaker

ASTRONOMER

Carolyn Shoemaker likes to watch the night sky. She has been doing it for almost 20 years. So far, she has discovered 27 comets—more than any other person now living. She has also discovered more than 300 asteroids.

Dr. Shoemaker is a visiting scientist in the Astrogeology Branch of the U.S. Geological Survey. She uses one of the Mount Palomar telescopes in California to do her sky watching. She works with the telescope seven nights each month. She takes photos, which she later examines carefully for comets and asteroids. She has developed very efficient ways to examine the photos. She uses a stereo microscope, which cuts in half the time needed to survey the whole sky.

Dr. Shoemaker worked with her husband, a planetary geologist, until his death. The two scientists spent their summers investigating meteorite impact sites and collecting meteorites for study.

Eugene and Carolyn Shoemaker

That Dr. Shoemaker is now making her mark in astronomy is remarkable because she didn't originally intend to pursue science. In college she majored in history and political science. Her career change began when her husband encouraged her to help him with some projects on asteroids. She became fascinated by astronomy and soon knew she had found her field.

Today she says that she "could spend 48 hours a day" pointing the big telescope at the sky and looking for comets and asteroids. It's work that she finds fascinating—and fun!

THINK ABOUT IT

1. What discoveries has Carolyn Shoemaker made?
2. How did she make these discoveries?

◄ This is a sequence of images taken by the Hubble Space Telescope that shows Comet Shoemaker-Levy (named for its finders) crashing into Jupiter. This is only one of many comets found by Dr. Shoemaker.

Spinning Planets

How does rotation help planets maintain their position in orbit?

Materials

- 25-cm (10-in.) cardboard circle with a small hole in the exact center
- 0.9 m (1 yd) of heavy string
- 4 large, metal paper clips

Procedure

1. Push one end of the string through the hole in the cardboard disk. Knot the other end so that it will not pull through. The disk represents an orbiting planet.

2. Attach the paper clips evenly around the outside of the planet.

3. Holding the end of the string, swing the planet back and forth. Observe how it moves.

4. With your hand, quickly spin the planet toward you. Then swing it again as it spins and observe how it moves.

Draw Conclusions

What happened when you swung the planet in Step 3? What happened when you swung the planet in Step 4? What does the spinning represent?

Plants on Other Planets

Why do the conditions on Earth support life?

Materials

- 6–9 seeds, such as dried beans or sunflower seeds
- 3 small, plastic cups nearly filled with soil
- 1 shoe box lined with aluminum foil
- refrigerator freezer
- water

Procedure

1. Plant two or three seeds in each cup, water lightly, and put them in a sunny spot until they sprout. Water whenever the soil is dry.

2. Label the pots "Earth," "Jupiter," and "Mercury."

3. Leave "Earth" where it is, and water its soil when it feels dry.

4. Put "Jupiter" in the freezer. Do not water it.

5. Put "Mercury" in the box, put the box in the sun, and do not water.

6. Observe the seedling growth in all three cups for a week.

Draw Conclusions

Why did you withhold water from Jupiter and Mercury? Should the Jupiter cup be in the sunlight? How does this experiment model growth on other planets?

Chapter ③ Review and Test Preparation

Vocabulary Review

Use the terms below to complete the sentences. The page numbers in ( ) tell you where to look in the chapter if you need help.

planetary system (D79)　**orbit** (D87)

asteroid (D80)　**ellipse** (D87)

comet (D81)　**season** (D94)

meteoroid (D81)　**axial tilt** (D95)

astronomical unit (D82)　**phase** (D102)

rotation (D86)　**first quarter** (D102)

axis (D86)　**third quarter** (D103)

revolution (D87)

1. A shape like a flattened circle is an ____.

2. The phase that shows half the moon's lighted face while it is waning is the ____.

3. The turning of a planet on its axis is ____.

4. A planet and the moons that revolve about it form a ____.

5. The crescent moon is an example of one ____ of the moon.

6. A division of the year that has a certain type of weather is a ____.

7. A unit of measurement that equals the average distance between Earth and the sun is an ____.

8. The phase that shows half the moon's lighted face while it is waxing is the ____.

9. A ball of ice, rock, and frozen gases that orbits the sun is a ____.

10. An imaginary line that runs through the middle of a planet from pole to pole is an ____.

11. The path an object in space follows as it revolves around another object is an ____.

12. A chunk of rock and metal that is smaller than a planet and that orbits the sun is an ____.

13. The movement of one object in orbit around another object is ____.

14. A particle of rock that is smaller than an asteroid and that orbits the sun is a ____.

15. The angle that a planet's axis is tilted from vertical is its ____.

Connect Concepts

Write the names of the objects in the diagram.

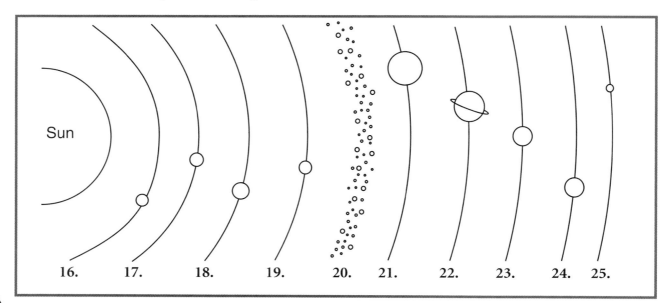

Sun

16.　17.　18.　19.　20.　21.　22.　23.　24.　25.

Check Understanding

Write the letter of the best choice.

26. The solar system's asteroid belt is between —
    A Earth and Mars
    B Mars and Jupiter
    C Jupiter and Saturn
    D Earth and Venus

27. The sun is located ____ of the orbits of the planets.
    F exactly in the center
    G at the edge
    H above and to the right
    J slightly away from the center

28. Rotation causes a planet to have —
    A years
    B phases
    C day and night
    D winter and summer

29. A planet completes one revolution in that planet's —
    F year
    G day
    H month
    J week

30. Precession of Earth's axis causes —
    A axial tilt
    B a change in the North Pole star
    C seasons
    D day and night

31. The axial tilt of Earth causes its —
    F revolution
    G phases
    H seasons
    J rotation

Critical Thinking

32. If you could view the phases of Earth's moon from the sun, what would you see?

33. Would astronomical units be practical for measuring distances on Earth? Explain your answer.

34. How might seasons on Earth be affected if Earth's orbit were more elliptical? Explain your answer.

Process Skills Review

35. If you had paper, a pencil, scissors, string, and a ruler, how could you **make a model** of Earth's planetary system? Describe each step.

36. How would you **gather and interpret data** to compare the characteristics of each season?

37. List characteristics of the moon that you can **observe**.

38. What can you **infer** about the relative sizes of Pluto and Earth if Pluto is smaller than the moon? Explain your answer.

Performance Assessment

Phases of the Moon

Draw a diagram showing the moon's phases. Show Earth and the position of the moon in relation to Earth during each phase. Include the name and shape of each phase.

Exploring the Universe

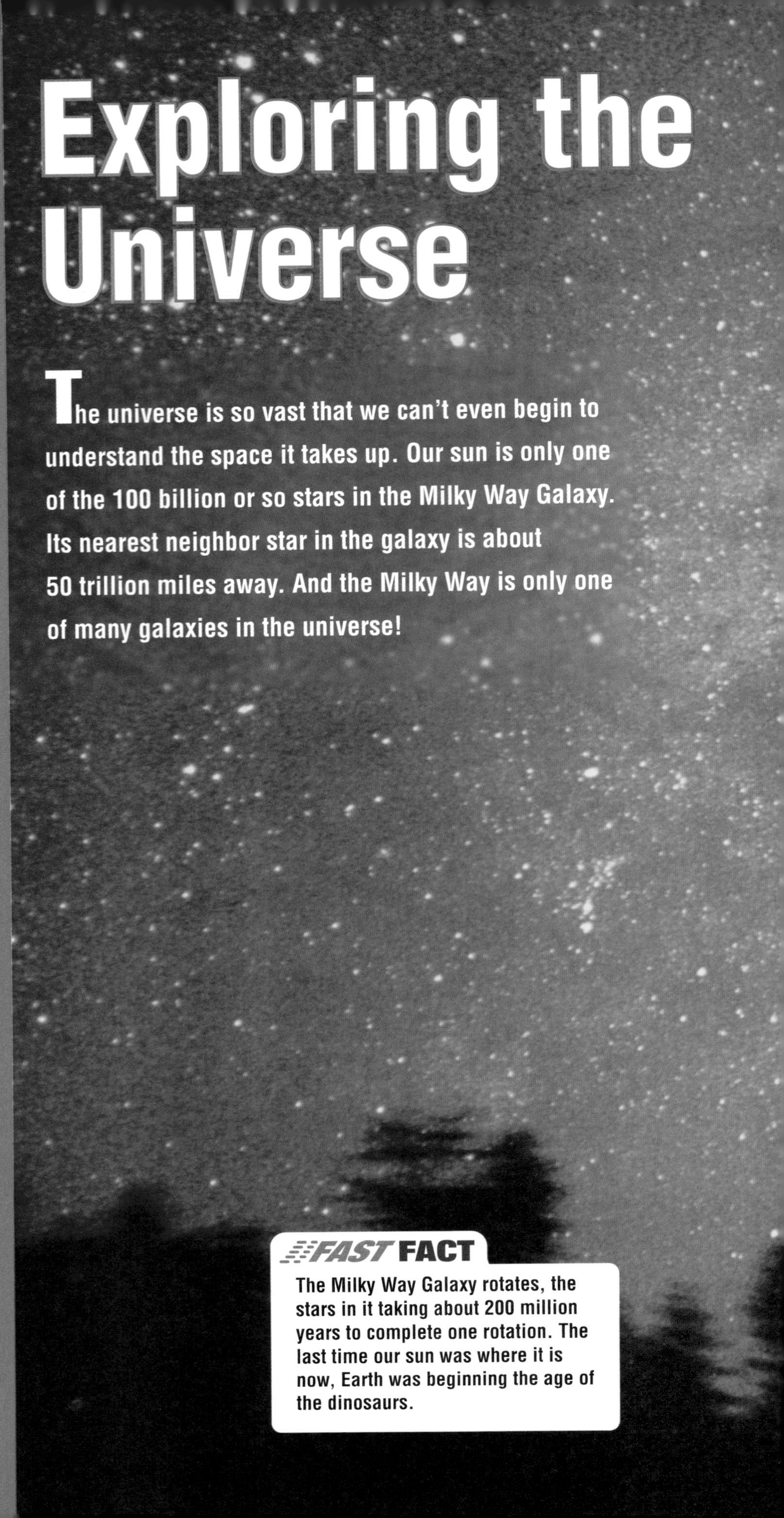

The universe is so vast that we can't even begin to understand the space it takes up. Our sun is only one of the 100 billion or so stars in the Milky Way Galaxy. Its nearest neighbor star in the galaxy is about 50 trillion miles away. And the Milky Way is only one of many galaxies in the universe!

Vocabulary Preview

fusion
main sequence
nebula
nova
supernova
galaxy
galactic cluster
refracting telescope
reflecting telescope

FAST FACT

The Milky Way Galaxy rotates, the stars in it taking about 200 million years to complete one rotation. The last time our sun was where it is now, Earth was beginning the age of the dinosaurs.

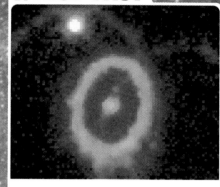

The exploding star Supernova 1987a, which was named for the year in which it was first seen on Earth, actually exploded more than 170,000 years ago.

Laika, first dog in space

Although rockets have existed for almost 1000 years, it was only toward the end of the twentieth century that they were powerful enough to orbit Earth.

Rockets	
Event	**Year**
Invention of gunpowder	300 B.C.
Rockets used as weapons	A.D. 1045
Liquid-fuel rocket	1926
Long-range guided rocket	1942
First animal in space—Laika, the dog	1957
Astronaut launched with rocket	1958
Saturn rocket moon launch	1969

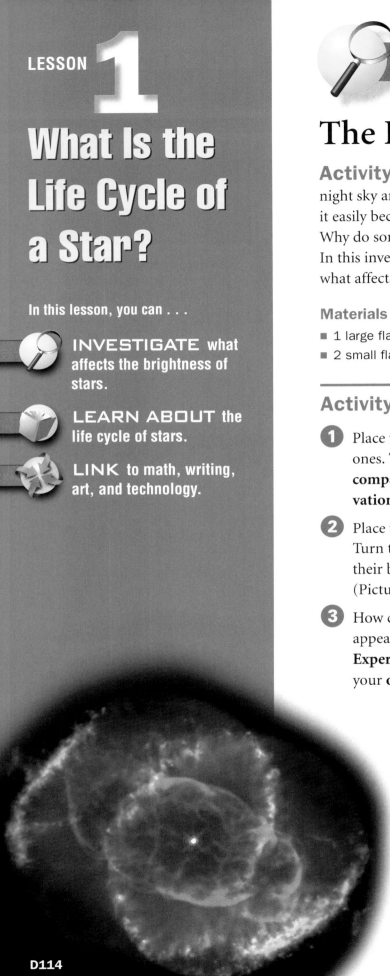

What Is the Life Cycle of a Star?

In this lesson, you can . . .

INVESTIGATE what affects the brightness of stars.

LEARN ABOUT the life cycle of stars.

LINK to math, writing, art, and technology.

INVESTIGATE

The Brightness of Stars

Activity Purpose   Have you ever looked at the night sky and seen Polaris, the North Star? You can find it easily because it appears brighter than most other stars. Why do some stars appear bright and others appear dim? In this investigation, you will **experiment** to find out what affects the brightness of stars.

Materials

- 1 large flashlight
- 2 small flashlights

Activity Procedure

1 Place the large flashlight next to one of the small ones. Turn them on. Then walk 2 m away and **compare** their brightness. **Record** your **observations**. (Picture A)

2 Place the two small flashlights next to each other. Turn them on. Again, walk 2 m away and **compare** their brightness. **Record** your **observations**. (Picture B)

3 How can you make one of the small flashlights appear dimmer than the other? **Form a hypothesis.** **Experiment** to test your hypothesis, and **record** your **observations**.

◀ The Cat's Eye Nebula is a cloud of gas and dust formed by the explosion of a star.

Picture A

Picture B

4 How can you make the brightness of the large flashlight appear equal to the brightness of one of the small flashlights? **Form a hypothesis. Experiment** to test your hypothesis, and **record** your **observations**.

Draw Conclusions

1. How did you make one of the small flashlights look dimmer than the other? How did you make the large flashlight and one small flashlight appear equally bright?

2. In your experiments, what variable did you change? How did the actual brightness of the flashlights themselves change?

3. **Scientists at Work** Scientists often **plan and conduct investigations** to test a hypothesis and **draw conclusions**. What conclusion did your investigation help you to draw about the relationship between brightness and distance?

Investigate Further How could you make one of the small flashlights look brighter than the large flashlight?

Process Skill Tip

When you **plan an investigation**, you need to think about and carefully state the question you want to answer. Then you need to make sure that the investigation really can answer the question you are asking.

The Life Cycle of Stars

The Brightness of Stars

FIND OUT

- how stars are classified
- about the life cycle of stars

VOCABULARY

fusion
main sequence
nebula
nova
supernova

Away from city lights, on a clear, dark night, you can see thousands of stars. Some are bright points of light, and others are dim specks. As you saw in the investigation, bright objects appear dimmer if they are far away. For this reason, astronomers measure two kinds of brightness, or magnitude (MAG•nuh•tood): how bright a star appears from Earth and how bright a star actually is.

How bright a star appears from Earth is its *apparent magnitude*. On the apparent-magnitude scale, the sun is the brightest star in our sky. It is so bright that no other stars can be seen in its light. But that's because it's so close. Many stars that look dim to us are actually much brighter than the sun.

The actual brightness of a star is its *absolute magnitude*. Absolute magnitude is measured as if the star were a standard distance from Earth—32.6 light-years away. So absolute magnitude isn't affected by distance. Instead, it indicates the amount of light a star actually gives off. On the absolute-magnitude scale, brighter stars are indicated by lower numbers.

In apparent magnitude, Sirius is the brightest star in the sky other than the sun. But there are stars much brighter than Sirius in absolute magnitude. They just don't look as bright, because they are much farther away.

✔ **What is the difference between a star's apparent magnitude and its absolute magnitude?**

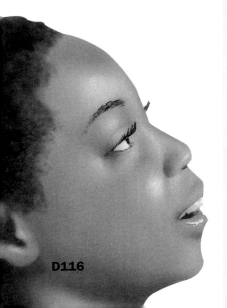

Distance affects how bright a star appears. The brighter star (top) appears dimmer because it is farther from a viewer on Earth. The dimmer star (bottom) appears brighter because it is closer.

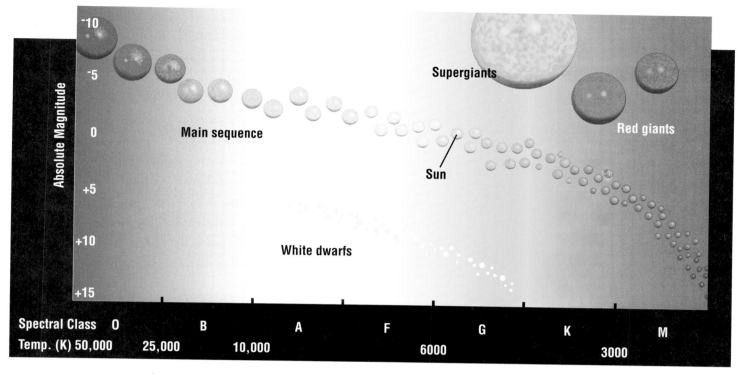

The H-R diagram shows:
- Absolute Magnitude (y-axis): -10, -5, 0, +5, +10, +15
- Spectral Class (x-axis): O, B, A, F, G, K, M
- Temp. (K): 50,000, 25,000, 10,000, 6000, 3000
- Labels: Supergiants, Red giants, Main sequence, Sun, White dwarfs

▲ In the early 1900s, the scientists Ejnar Hertzsprung and Henry Norris Russell graphed stars according to absolute magnitude and temperature. That kind of graph, shown here, is called a Hertzsprung-Russell, or H-R, diagram.

Types of Stars

Stars are huge balls of hot, glowing gases. Their energy comes from **fusion**, a process in which the nuclei of atoms are joined. In most stars, hydrogen is the fuel for fusion. The reaction gives off energy, including light and heat. Tremendous heat and pressure at the core of a star make fusion possible.

Sometimes you can estimate the temperature of a star just by looking at it. Stars can appear red, blue, or yellow. The colors indicate a star's surface temperature. The coolest stars are red. The hottest stars are blue. Yellow stars, like the sun, have surface temperatures that are between those of red and blue stars.

Astronomers classify stars by their surface temperature, color, and absolute magnitude. To do this, they use a *Hertzsprung-Russell (H-R)*

diagram like the one here. On the H-R diagram, the absolute magnitude of stars is shown from top to bottom, with the brightest stars at the top. Surface temperature is shown from left to right, with the hottest stars on the left.

Ninety percent of stars on the H-R diagram are in a band called the **main sequence**. The stars in this band vary from bright, hot blue stars shown at the upper left, to dim, cool red stars shown at the lower right. In the main sequence, the stars with the greatest mass are the hottest and brightest.

Stars outside the main sequence are different. Red giants and supergiants are cool red stars that are bright because they are so huge. White dwarfs are very hot stars, but they are dim because they are very small.

✔ **What is a main-sequence star?**

The Birth and Death of Stars

The time from the birth of a star to its death may be billions of years. People have not been on Earth long enough to observe the life cycle of any one star. But by observing many stars of different ages, scientists have developed an explanation of how stars form, how they change, and how they die. The diagram shows some of this information.

Stars form in huge, cool, dark clouds of gases and dust. Each of these clouds is called a **nebula** (NEB•yuh•luh). Gravity causes parts of nebulas to come together. The gases and dust form dense centers called *protostars*.

When a protostar has enough mass, pressure causes the temperature in its core to rise high enough (about 15 million °C, or 27 million °F) for fusion to begin. The mass of the star determines how it starts its life. It may start as a hot blue star (see high-mass star below), an average yellow star (see medium-mass star), or a cool red star (see low-mass star).

Fusion in a main-sequence star changes the hydrogen in its core to helium. After millions or billions of years, a star's hydrogen begins to run out. Then the death of the star begins.

The way a star dies also depends on its mass. When a low-mass star uses up the hydrogen in

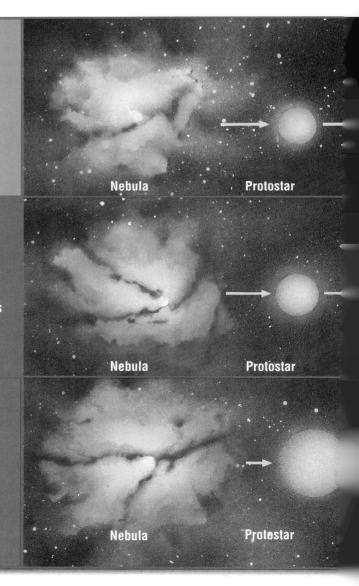

Life Cycles of Stars

LOW-MASS STARS
Small, cool stars use up the hydrogen in their cores more slowly than do larger stars. Scientists estimate that low-mass stars can last more than 30 billion years. When a star's supply of hydrogen finally runs low, fusion stops. The star becomes a white dwarf.

Nebula   Protostar

MEDIUM-MASS STARS
Stars of medium size and temperature use up the hydrogen more quickly than low-mass stars. They last about 10 billion years. When the hydrogen is used up, these stars swell into red giants. A red giant collapses after a long time. When it does, it also throws off layers of gas. The gas forms a cloud known as a planetary nebula. The star ends its life as a small, dense white dwarf.

Nebula   Protostar

HIGH-MASS STARS
The hottest, most massive stars have the shortest lives—millions of years instead of billions. Hydrogen in the core of a high-mass star is used up quickly. The star swells into a supergiant and then explodes as a supernova. If part of the core survives the blast, it collapses to become a neutron star or black hole.

Nebula   Protostar

its core, the star slowly cools and shrinks to become a white dwarf.

When a medium-mass star runs low on hydrogen, the star begins to use helium in its core as fuel. The star swells into a red giant. This will happen to our sun in about 5 billion years. Then the red giant cools and shrinks to become a white dwarf.

Sometimes a white dwarf flares brightly for a few weeks as a nova. A **nova** is a star that briefly becomes thousands of times brighter than normal.

A star with a very large mass—as much as 50 times the mass of our sun—goes out with a bang. It quickly uses up its hydrogen and becomes a supergiant. But because of its size, the core of such a massive star continues to heat up and use other materials as fuel. After that, the star explodes as a supernova. A **supernova** is one of the most violent explosions known in the universe. Its light is as bright as that from billions of stars combined.

After a supernova, the core that is left may collapse to form a small, dense neutron star. If a very massive star explodes as a supernova, the core may collapse to form an even denser black hole. A black hole is so dense that even light can't escape its gravity.

✔ **What is the relationship between mass and the length of a star's life?**

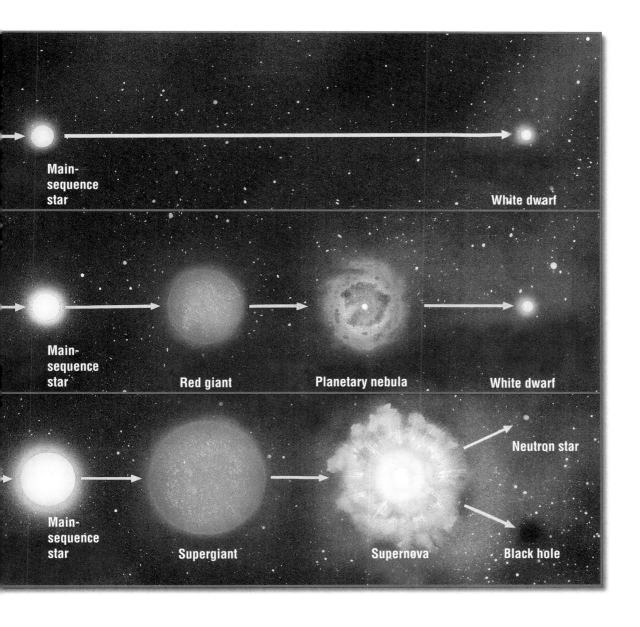

Main-sequence star   White dwarf

Main-sequence star   Red giant   Planetary nebula   White dwarf

Main-sequence star   Supergiant   Supernova   Neutron star   Black hole

Types of Starlight

Stars are not places scientists can visit. So most of what we know about stars comes from the electromagnetic radiation they give off. *Electromagnetic radiation* is energy that travels through space in waves. Light is one kind of electromagnetic radiation.

Stars give off many types of electromagnetic radiation—radio waves, infrared rays, visible light, ultraviolet waves, X rays, and gamma rays. Each type of radiation has its own wavelength. The wavelengths vary from more than 1000 m (about 3280 ft) for radio waves to a tiny fraction of a millimeter for gamma rays. Our eyes can detect radiation only in the visible range, shown on the chart.

Until recently, scientists observed stars only by the visible light they give off. Between 6000 and 8000 stars are visible with the unaided eye. With an optical telescope (a telescope that detects visible light), even more stars can be seen. But many bodies in space can't be detected by using visible light. Today scientists have tools that allow them to detect objects by using other electromagnetic radiation.

Some of these recently detected objects are dense, collapsed stars. Neutron stars can now be detected from their radio waves. Scientists have located black holes by detecting X rays. Other objects not visible to our eyes are stars hidden by nebulas. Astronomers can now detect these stars by the infrared radiation they give off.

✔ **What is visible light?**

▲ Astronomers have used X rays to find black holes. Gases can be pulled into a black hole from a nearby normal star. The force of the pull can raise the temperature of the gases to millions of degrees, causing them to give off X rays.

The starlight we can see is a very narrow part of the electromagnetic spectrum. ▼

| Gamma rays | | X rays | Ultraviolet waves | Visible light |

Summary

Stars produce light and heat through fusion. Fusion joins nuclei of atoms and produces energy in the process. A star forms in a nebula, becomes a protostar, and then remains a main-sequence star until it runs low on hydrogen. A star's mass determines how it starts its life, how long it exists, and how its life cycle ends.

Review

1. How does distance affect the brightness of stars?

2. How do main-sequence stars produce heat and light?

3. What is a supernova?

4. **Critical Thinking** Why won't our sun end its life cycle as a supernova?

5. **Test Prep** Astronomers think that the areas around black holes give off —

   A visible light **C** helium

   B nebulas **D** X rays

Sometimes nebulas can hide stars from our sight. Scientists can get a look at objects behind a nebula, and can even learn about the nebula, by looking at the radio waves. ▼

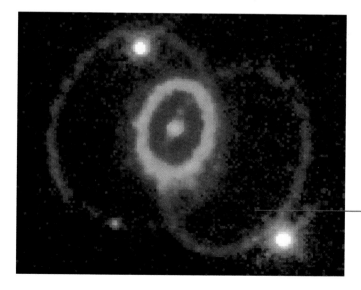

Infrared rays

Radio waves

LINKS

MATH LINK

Star Graph Use the H-R diagram on page D117 to graph the temperatures of each color of star. Show each star color on the vertical axis. Make a temperature scale on the horizontal axis.

WRITING LINK

Narrative Writing—Story You're a reporter for a newspaper on a faraway planet, and you're covering the end of the life cycle of a massive blue star. (Your spaceship protects you from radiation and explosions.) Write a story telling your classmates what you see, feel, and hear.

ART LINK

Constellations Draw a picture of the night sky, showing any constellations and bright stars you can spot. Use a star map for help. Compare your observations with those of your classmates.

TECHNOLOGY LINK

Learn more about stars by visiting this Internet site.
www.scilinks.org/harcourt

SCiLINKS™
THE WORLD'S A CLICK AWAY

What Are the Features of Galaxies?

In this lesson, you can . . .

INVESTIGATE the shapes of galaxies.

LEARN ABOUT what galaxies are.

LINK to math, writing, social studies, and technology.

Galaxies, such as the Cartwheel Galaxy, are groups of millions or billions of stars. ▼

INVESTIGATE

The Way Galaxies Look

Activity Purpose Suppose you are drawing a picture of your house or another building. Will it look the same, no matter which side you draw? Probably not. The viewpoint from which you look at something changes what you see. In this investigation you will **make a model** of one type of galaxy, or large group of stars. Then you will **observe** your model from different points of view and **compare** it with models of other types of galaxies.

Materials

- 5 sheets of white paper
- glue
- yellow marker
- 1 sheet of drawing paper

Activity Procedure

1. Choose one galaxy to model from the three that are shown in the photographs on the next page.

2. Tear the sheets of white paper into pieces about 2.5 cm square. Crumple the pieces of paper into small balls. Each ball will represent a star.

3. Arrange your paper stars to **make a model** of one of the galaxies. If you are making an elliptical galaxy, you will need glue to hold the model stars together. If you are making a spiral or barred spiral galaxy, build up the center by piling on more stars than at the edges. With the marker, color one star yellow, and place it in the outer third of your model.

4. Look at your model from above. On your sheet of drawing paper, draw what you **observe**. Now look at your model from the side. You will have to bend down until the model is at eye level. Draw what you observe. (Picture A)

Edge-On Spiral Galaxy

Face-On Spiral Galaxy

Picture A

Face-On Barred Spiral Galaxy

Edge-On Barred Spiral Galaxy

Elliptical Galaxy

5. **Compare** your model with models of other galaxy types. **Observe** the models from above and from the side. Draw what you observe.

Draw Conclusions

1. What do the models look like when viewed from above? What do they look like from the side?

2. Suppose that the yellow star in each model galaxy is the sun. How would each galaxy appear if viewed from the sun?

3. **Scientists at Work** Scientists often **compare** things to discover their similarities and differences. When you compared the models from different viewpoints, how were they different?

Investigate Further Use the models to **predict** how Earth's night sky would appear in a spiral galaxy, in a barred spiral galaxy, and in an elliptical galaxy.

Process Skill Tip

When you **compare**, you observe the properties of two or more things to find out how they are the same and how they are different.

The Features of Galaxies

Galaxies

FIND OUT

- what galaxies are
- how galaxies differ

VOCABULARY

galaxy
galactic cluster

Our sun and more than 200 billion other stars make up the Milky Way Galaxy. A **galaxy** is a large system of stars. We can't see most of our galaxy's stars from Earth because they are blocked by gases, dust, nebulas, and other stars. And some of the stars in our galaxy are simply too far away and too dim for us to see. The Milky Way is a large galaxy—more than 100,000 light-years across. If our solar system were the size of a plate, the Milky Way would be the size of the continental United States.

Until the 1920s people thought the Milky Way was the only galaxy of stars in otherwise empty space. But in 1923 the astronomer Edwin Hubble found evidence that other galaxies exist. Using the large Mount Wilson telescope in California, Hubble found that points of light in a constellation called Andromeda (an•DRAHM•uh•duh) were too far away to be in our galaxy. Andromeda is a totally separate galaxy.

Today we know that there are *billions* of galaxies! The largest are much bigger than the Milky Way. But even the smallest galaxy contains about 100,000 stars. We also know that galaxies occur in groups called **galactic clusters**.

✔ **What is a galaxy?**

The Milky Way looks like this galaxy from the edge. ▼

◄ There are no photographs of the Milky Way viewed face-on from "above," but it probably looks something like this spiral galaxy.

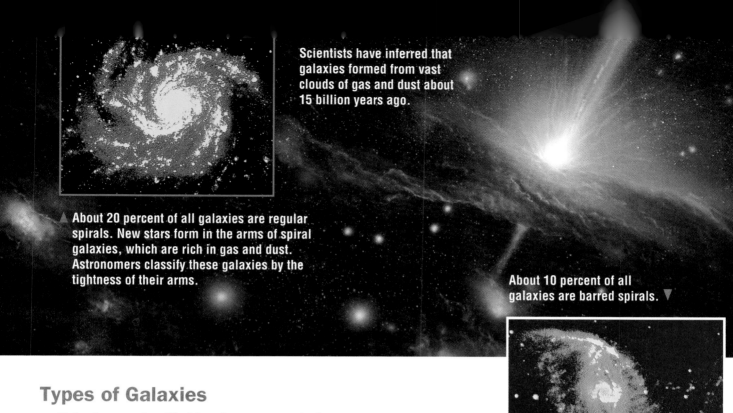

Scientists have inferred that galaxies formed from vast clouds of gas and dust about 15 billion years ago.

▲ About 20 percent of all galaxies are regular spirals. New stars form in the arms of spiral galaxies, which are rich in gas and dust. Astronomers classify these galaxies by the tightness of their arms.

About 10 percent of all galaxies are barred spirals. ▼

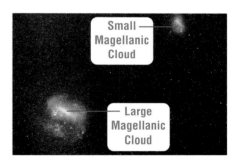

Types of Galaxies

Galaxies are classified by shape—as spirals, barred spirals, ellipticals, and irregular clusters.

A spiral galaxy has large, curved arms of stars and gases. The arms rotate around a bulging center. Gases surround the galaxy in a large spherical area. The central part of a spiral galaxy is reddish because it contains many red giants in the later stages of their life cycles. The arms are bluish because they contain many young, bright, blue stars.

Barred spiral galaxies are similar to spirals. However, the arms of barred spirals trail from two bar-shaped clusters of stars that extend from the core.

Ball-shaped and egg-shaped elliptical galaxies are the most common type. Most elliptical galaxies are much smaller than spirals, but a few are huge, with as many as 10 trillion stars. Some elliptical galaxies rotate, but they do so more slowly than spiral galaxies.

The smallest group of galaxies are irregular galaxies. They are loose collections of stars in clouds of gas and dust with no regular shape.

✔ **What are the four main shapes of galaxies?**

The Small Magellanic (maj·uh·LAN·ik) Cloud and the Large Magellanic Cloud are both irregular galaxies. They are the Milky Way's closest neighbors. About 10 percent of all galaxies are irregular. ▶

It is estimated that 60 percent of all galaxies are elliptical. There is little or no gas and dust left in elliptical galaxies, so new stars cannot form. Astronomers classify elliptical galaxies by how flat they appear. ▼

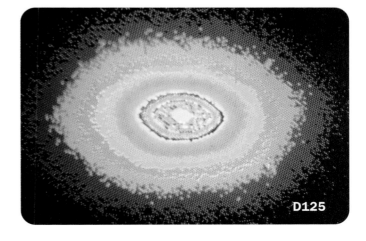

D125

BALANCED STATE If the average density of all matter in the universe is equal to 3 hydrogen atoms for every cubic meter of space, gravity will slow expansion but not totally stop it. The universe will stay pretty much as it is—not expanding greatly and not contracting greatly.

EXPANDING If the average density is less than 3 hydrogen atoms per cubic meter, the universe will keep expanding forever. Everything in the universe will continue to move farther apart.

CONTRACTING If the average density of the universe is more than 3 hydrogen atoms per cubic meter, gravity will eventually pull everything together again. Expansion will stop, and all matter in the universe will eventually collapse back in on itself. Another Big Bang could then occur. That would start the expansion-contraction cycle again.

What will be the fate of the universe? Many astronomers have concluded that the answer depends on how much matter is in the universe.

Models of the Universe

The universe is everything that exists. That includes all the galaxies and everything between them.

No one knows how big the universe is. Perhaps it never ends. Astronomers have several theories about how the universe formed and developed.

Many astronomers hypothesize that the universe started about 15 billion years ago. According to this model, a huge explosion called the Big Bang started the universe as we know it. The model states that the universe has been expanding ever since that explosion.

Astronomers know that the galaxies are all moving away from each other. But no one knows what will happen in the distant future. Will the universe continue to expand? Will it collapse in on itself? Or will it be in a balanced state that neither expands nor contracts?

✔ **What is the universe?**

Summary

A galaxy is a large system of stars. Astronomers classify galaxies by their shapes. There are spiral, barred spiral, elliptical, and irregular galaxies.

Review

1. What are galactic clusters?
2. Describe the shape of a spiral galaxy.
3. Describe the shape of an elliptical galaxy.
4. **Critical Thinking** Why would it be difficult for astronomers to discover the exact shape of the Milky Way?
5. **Test Prep** Because of a lack of gas and dust, no new stars form in —
   - **A** elliptical galaxies
   - **B** spiral galaxies
   - **C** irregular galaxies
   - **D** barred spiral galaxies

LINKS

MATH LINK

Our Sun in the Milky Way Where is our solar system located within the Milky Way? On a sheet of graph paper, draw a shape that represents the Milky Way. Make sure it is symmetrical. Include the galaxy's central hub and its four arms. Find out how far out our solar system is from the galaxy's center, and mark the solar system's position.

WRITING LINK

Narrative Writing—Story What would a trip to another galaxy be like? In a story written for your teacher, tell about leaving Earth, passing through the solar system, and traveling to planets circling a star in a nearby galaxy. Describe your spacecraft and what happens to you along the way.

SOCIAL STUDIES LINK

Constellation Stories Throughout history, groups of people around the world have seen different patterns in the stars. Choose a constellation, and find as many different stories about it as you can to share with the class.

TECHNOLOGY LINK

Visit the Harcourt Learning Site for related links, activities and resources.
www.harcourtschool.com

WELCOME TO
THE
LEARNING
SITE

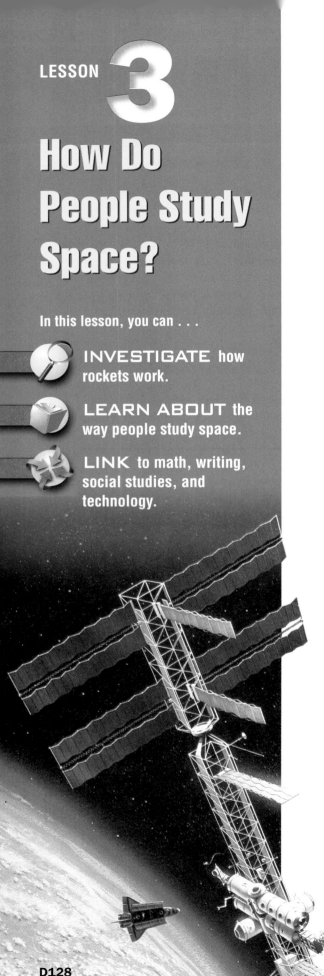

LESSON 3

How Do People Study Space?

In this lesson, you can . . .

INVESTIGATE how rockets work.

LEARN ABOUT the way people study space.

LINK to math, writing, social studies, and technology.

The space station *Freedom* will be in operation sometime during the twenty-first century. Astronauts are assembling parts of the station while in orbit around Earth.

INVESTIGATE

How Rockets Work

Activity Purpose Before a rocket lifts off, clouds of exhaust and burning gases are forced out the bottom. The downward force of the gases causes thrust that lifts the rocket off the ground. In this investigation, you will **make a model** of a rocket in which a familiar object will cause thrust.

Materials

- clay
- balloon
- string
- tape
- straws
- dowel
- paper clips
- cardboard tube
- safety goggles
- chalk
- tape measure

CAUTION

Activity Procedure

1 Think about the way a rocket works. What gives the rocket the thrust to lift off the ground and move through space? **Observe** your materials. Decide how you will produce a lifting or pushing force for your model. (Picture A)

2 Design a way to control the lifting or pushing force.

3 Next, consider the weight of your rocket. Lighter rockets can go farther. Draw a plan for your rocket. Show it to your teacher. After your teacher has approved your plan, build your model rocket. (Picture B)

Picture A

Picture B

4. **CAUTION** **Put on your safety goggles. If you are launching the rocket vertically, be sure your rocket is aimed upward and not at anyone or anything that can be harmed.** Prepare to launch your rocket outside. Using chalk, mark your launch site. Test-fire your rocket. Mark its landing site, or how far it goes. **Measure** and **record** the distance traveled.

5. **Compare** the success of your design with the success of other models. Change your design to make it work better. Test-fire your rocket again. **Record** the distance it travels.

Draw Conclusions

1. How did your rocket work on the first try? Did it travel farther after it was improved?

2. Scientists often learn from their colleagues. What did you learn from the models built by other students?

3. **Scientists at Work** Scientists often **make models** to find out how things work. In this investigation, how did making a model help you understand how rockets work?

Investigate Further What materials would make your rocket travel even farther?

Process Skill Tip

Sometimes you can **make a model** to help you learn how something works. You can't study a real rocket close up. So making a model of a rocket can help you understand how rockets work.

The Way People Study Space

FIND OUT

- who the first people in space were
- how we explore space from Earth

VOCABULARY

refracting telescope
reflecting telescope

Early Space Exploration

Since prehistoric times, people have studied the stars. They used stars to navigate. They noted the positions of stars to mark the seasons. People all over the world built observatories to watch the sky. But until the 1600s, people could observe only what was visible to the unaided eye.

After the telescope was invented in the early 1600s, people could see objects in space in greater detail. Galileo developed one of the first refracting telescopes. A **refracting telescope** uses glass lenses to gather light and magnify objects. Galileo observed mountains on the moon and "ears" on Saturn that turned out to be rings. About 60 years later, Sir Isaac Newton invented a reflecting telescope. A **reflecting telescope** uses mirrors to gather light and magnify images.

Stonehenge, in Britain, was constructed before 2000 B.C. The placement of its stones marks the position of the sun on days when the seasons change. ▼

Korea's Ch'omsongdae Observatory is the earliest observatory still standing. ▼

Astrolabes were used from the fifteenth century to the early eighteenth century. Sailors used them to find the angle between the horizon and the sun or the North Star. From this, they could calculate their latitude. ▼

2000 B.C.   A.D. 634   A.D. 1500

Using early telescopes, astronomers discovered several of the planets of the solar system and many of their moons. But during the late 1800s, astronomers and writers began to think beyond looking at space. They wondered what it would take to get there.

To travel into space, scientists had to build a vehicle that could travel at least 28,195 km/hr (about 17,500 mi/hr). That speed allows a rocket to break free of Earth's gravity. In the early 1900s, scientists began to work on the problem.

The principle of producing thrust to lift a rocket was not new. As early as the 1200s, the Chinese were shooting small rockets into the air by using burning powder. But to travel into space, a heavy rocket would need fuel that could produce tremendous thrust. It would also need to carry a supply of oxygen to burn the fuel, since space has no air.

In 1926 the American scientist Robert Goddard took an important step by successfully testing the first rocket to use liquid fuel and liquid oxygen. The tiny rocket rose just 13.6 m (about 45 ft) into the air and then crashed. But during the 1920s and 1930s, Goddard built improved rockets that contained early versions of most of the important systems used in rockets today.

Over the next few decades, scientists in the United States, Germany, and the former Soviet Union improved rocket design. Larger rockets flew higher and longer. Then, in 1957, the Soviet Union shocked the world with a successful launch that put a small satellite, *Sputnik I*, into orbit around the Earth. The space age had begun.

✔ **How did the invention of the telescope change the exploration of space?**

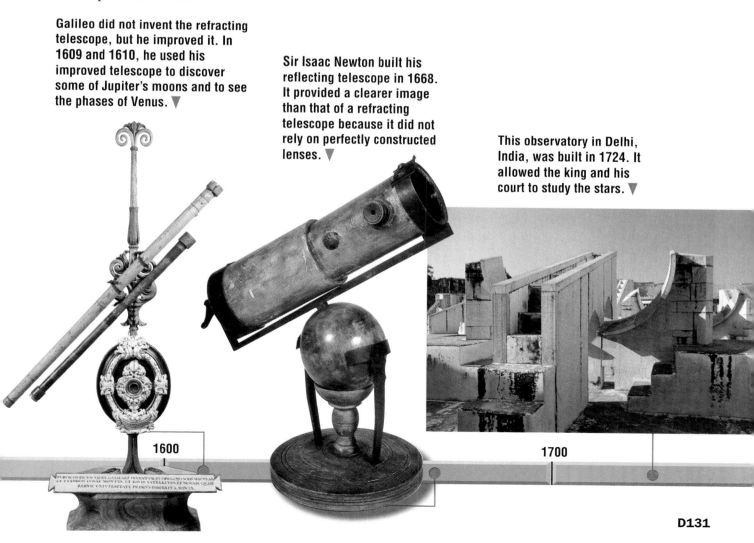

Galileo did not invent the refracting telescope, but he improved it. In 1609 and 1610, he used his improved telescope to discover some of Jupiter's moons and to see the phases of Venus. ▼

Sir Isaac Newton built his reflecting telescope in 1668. It provided a clearer image than that of a refracting telescope because it did not rely on perfectly constructed lenses. ▼

This observatory in Delhi, India, was built in 1724. It allowed the king and his court to study the stars. ▼

1600

1700

Refracting and Reflecting Telescopes

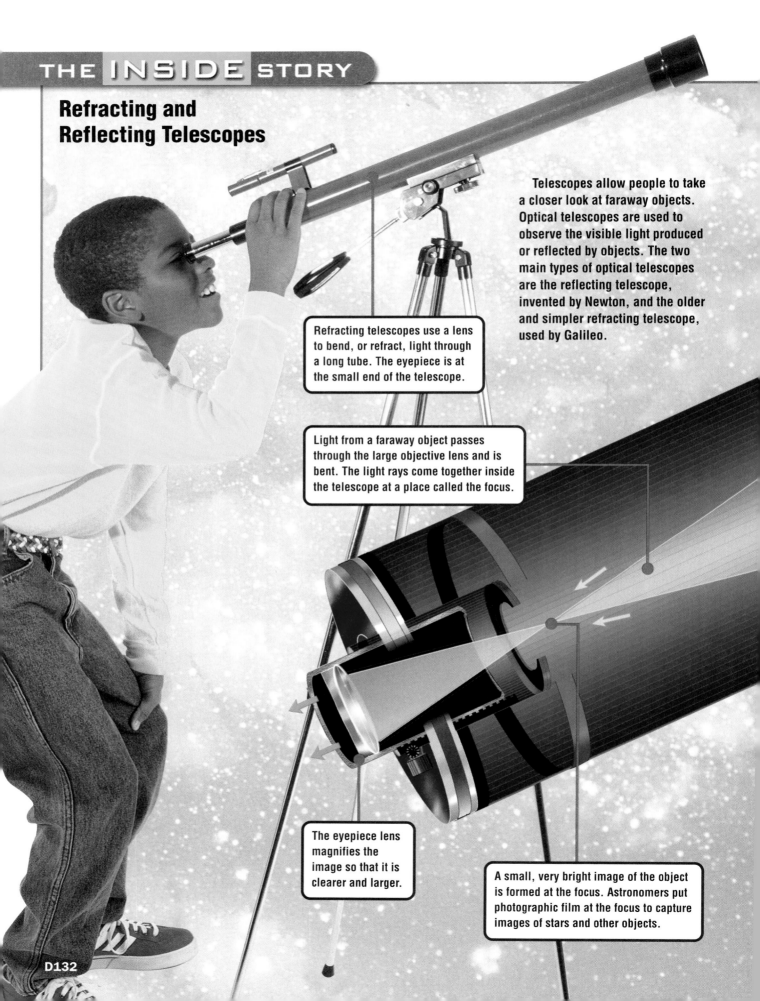

Telescopes allow people to take a closer look at faraway objects. Optical telescopes are used to observe the visible light produced or reflected by objects. The two main types of optical telescopes are the reflecting telescope, invented by Newton, and the older and simpler refracting telescope, used by Galileo.

Refracting telescopes use a lens to bend, or refract, light through a long tube. The eyepiece is at the small end of the telescope.

Light from a faraway object passes through the large objective lens and is bent. The light rays come together inside the telescope at a place called the focus.

The eyepiece lens magnifies the image so that it is clearer and larger.

A small, very bright image of the object is formed at the focus. Astronomers put photographic film at the focus to capture images of stars and other objects.

Reflecting telescopes use a curved mirror to gather and concentrate light from faraway objects. The larger the diameter of the mirror, the more light it gathers, and the dimmer the objects it can detect.

The greater the distance between the objective lens and the focus, the greater the telescope's magnification.

Sir Isaac Newton invented the Newtonian reflecting telescope in 1668. Light enters the telescope and hits the curved primary mirror. This mirror focuses light in front of it. A flat secondary mirror sends the image to an eyepiece. ▶

N. Cassegrain invented another type of reflecting telescope in 1672. The primary mirror gathers light and reflects it to a small, curved secondary mirror. That mirror sends the image through a hole in the primary mirror to an eyepiece behind it. ▶

Primary mirror   Secondary mirror

Major Crewed Space Flights	
Year	**Achievement**
1961	First person in space, Yuri Gagarin (Soviet Union, or the USSR)
1961	First American in space, Alan Shepard
1962	First American in orbit, John Glenn
1963	First woman in space, Valentina Tereshkova (USSR)
1965	First spacewalk (USSR)
1968	First crewed craft to orbit the moon (U.S.)
1969	First moon landing, *Apollo 11* with Neil Armstrong and Edwin "Buzz" Aldrin (U.S.)
1972	Last moon landing, *Apollo 17* (U.S.)
1973	First *Skylab* space station crew (U.S.)
1983	First space shuttle flight, *Columbia* (U.S.)
1986	First *Mir* space station crew (USSR)

▲ During the Apollo missions, 12 American astronauts walked on the moon between 1969 and 1972.

◀ Space shuttle crews perform experiments in space. They place new satellites in orbit and repair equipment already there. Shuttles also bring people to and from orbiting space stations.

People in Space

In April 1961 cosmonaut Yuri Gagarin of the Soviet Union became the first person in space. He made a 108-minute orbit of Earth in a small spacecraft. In May the United States sent its first astronaut, Alan Shepard, on a flight that lasted 15 minutes.

The same month that Shepard flew, President John Kennedy made an important speech. He challenged American scientists to put a person on the moon before the end of the decade. Throughout the 1960s, the U.S. space program was dedicated to reaching the moon—and to doing it first. The space race had begun.

The Mercury program used small rockets to put people into orbit and return them safely to Earth.

During the Gemini program that followed, the National Aeronautics and Space Administration (NASA) experimented with heavier loads and longer flights. Astronauts also practiced walking in space and docking with other spacecraft.

For the Apollo lunar landing program, NASA produced the most powerful rocket of its time—the Saturn V, which was 36 stories tall. In 1969, less than 10 years after Kennedy's speech, NASA accomplished its goal. On July 20, 1969, people all over the world gathered around TV sets to watch Neil Armstrong make the first footprints on the moon.

The U.S. space program now depends on the space shuttle, a reusable vehicle that goes into orbit like a rocket and then glides back to Earth like an airplane. The shuttle is being used to carry materials into orbit for a new international space station. One day it may also help build a spacecraft in orbit that could carry astronauts to Mars.

✓ **Who was the first person in space?**

Major Space Probes

Year	Achievement
1957	*Sputnik I*, first satellite in orbit (USSR)
1958	*Explorer 1*, first successful U.S. satellite
1965	*Mariner 4*, first close view of Mars (U.S.)
1966	*Luna 9*, first probe to land on the moon (USSR)
1972	*Pioneer 10*, first probe to pass asteroid belt on way to Jupiter (U.S.)
1975	*Venera 9* and *Venera 10*, first landings on Venus (USSR)
1976	*Viking 1* and *Viking 2*, first successful U.S. probes on Mars
1979	*Pioneer 11*, first close view of Saturn
1979	*Voyager 1*, first to reach Jupiter (U.S.)
1979	*Voyager 2*, first to send back pictures as it flies by Jupiter
1980	*Voyager 1*, new discoveries about Saturn's rings
1986	*Voyager 2*, first close view of Uranus
1989	*Voyager 2*, first close view of Neptune
1990	*Magellan*, first to use radar that penetrates thick clouds to map Venus' surface from orbit (U.S.)
1997	*Mars Pathfinder*, *Sojourner's* rover, first vehicle on another planet (U.S.)

▲ In 1975 two Venera probes from the Soviet Union sent back to Earth the first photos from the surface of Venus. They were the first photos taken on the surface of another planet.

Space Probes

While the United States was racing to put a person on the moon, the United States and the Soviet Union were also using space probes to explore other parts of the solar system. Probes are exploration vehicles without human crews.

The Soviet Union sent some of the earliest probes to the moon, Venus, and Mars. Its Luna probes made the first moon landings and sent back the first lunar photographs. Soviet Venera probes orbited Venus and landed on its surface, sending back photographs and information about the surface and the atmosphere.

The United States sent probes to the moon, Mercury, Venus, and Mars. Its *Mariner 4* probe provided the first close view of Mars, in 1965. From orbit, the Mariner probes gave scientists a look at the Martian surface and information about the atmosphere of Mars. During the mid-1970s, the Viking probes sent back the first photos from the surface of Mars. These probes also analyzed Martian soil.

By the early 1970s, the United States had begun to send probes to the outer planets. In 1973, *Pioneer 10* became the first probe to pass Jupiter. In the late 1970s and early 1980s, *Voyager 1* and *Voyager 2* sent back detailed photos of Jupiter and Saturn and their rings and moons. By the late 1980s, *Voyager 2* had given the U.S. the first close images of Uranus and Neptune. The Pioneer and Voyager probes are now far beyond the solar system, carrying pictures, music, and messages from Earth to any intelligent life that might someday find them.

✔ **Name the first artificial satellite to orbit Earth.**

In 1997 NASA launched the probe *Cassini* on a mission to Saturn. In 2004 *Cassini* will become the first probe to orbit Saturn. It will send back pictures of Saturn and its moons. It will also send a probe to Saturn's largest moon, Titan. ▼

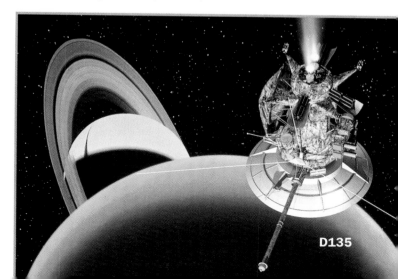

Advanced Telescopes

For hundreds of years, astronomers have used telescopes on Earth. But these telescopes have drawbacks. Earth's atmosphere distorts images. It also screens out some types of radiation, such as the gamma rays and cosmic rays that stars and other bodies in space give off.

Astronomers have put optical telescopes in orbit around the Earth to avoid the effects of the atmosphere. For example, the orbiting Hubble Space Telescope has given astronomers beautifully clear views of everything from planets in our solar system to distant galaxies. But optical telescopes cannot detect many interesting objects in space. These are objects that give off gamma rays, X rays, infrared rays, or radio waves. Many of the most advanced telescopes can detect these other types of radiation.

The Compton Gamma Ray Observatory detects gamma rays (radiation of the shortest wavelength) while orbiting Earth. It has helped astronomers learn more about pulsars and quasars (KWAY•zarz), which are strong gamma-ray sources. Quasars are small, very bright, very distant objects in space.

▲ The Very Large Array in New Mexico is a radio receiver made up of 27 separate radio telescopes. The array began working in 1980.

The Cosmic Background Explorer (COBE, pronounced KOH•bay) was put into orbit in 1989. It detects infrared radiation, or heat, given off by warm objects. COBE can detect stars hidden by nebulas.

Radio telescopes collect radio waves given off by objects in space. Radio telescopes helped astronomers discover pulsars and confirm the spiral shape of the Milky Way. The dish at Arecibo, Puerto Rico, is the world's largest radio telescope. It has a diameter of 333 m (more than 1000 ft) and can detect very faint radio waves.

✔ **Why do astronomers use telescopes that detect radiation other than visible light?**

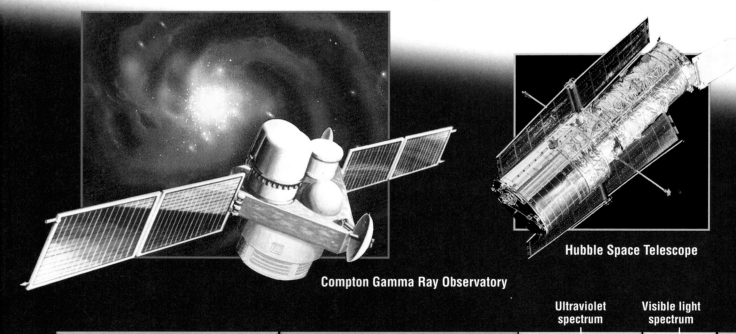

Compton Gamma Ray Observatory

Hubble Space Telescope

| Gamma ray spectrum | X ray | Ultraviolet spectrum | Visible light spectrum |

Summary

People have studied space for a long time. At first, they simply looked up at the skies. Later, telescopes helped people discover new things about space. Space missions with people and space probes without people have added to our understanding of space, with the aid of new technology.

Review

1. How does a refracting telescope work?
2. What is the main difference between a refracting telescope and a reflecting telescope?
3. Compare space probes with spacecraft that have crews.
4. **Critical Thinking** What might be one of the biggest problems with sending a person to another planet?
5. **Test Prep** Human eyes can detect only —
   - **A** X rays
   - **B** infrared rays
   - **C** visible light
   - **D** radio waves

LINKS

MATH LINK

How Long? Mars is about 61,000,000 km from Earth when the two planets are closest together. The average rocket travels at about 41,000 km/hr. If you could fly straight to Mars and back when it is closest, how long would the trip take?

WRITING LINK

Informative Writing—Report Neil Armstrong was the first person to walk on the moon. Interview someone who saw this on television in 1969. Find out where the person was and what the person saw and felt. Write a report for your classmates to share what you find out.

SOCIAL STUDIES LINK

Launch Sites NASA, the American space agency, launches rockets into space from the United States. But there are other places where rockets lift off, too. Find out what other nations have space programs and where they launch their rockets. Plot the sites on a world map.

TECHNOLOGY LINK

Find out more about what we're discovering as we look into space by watching *Extra-Solar Planets* on the **Harcourt Science Newsroom Video.**

Turner Le@rning

Cosmic Background Explorer (COBE)

Infrared Spectrum

Radio telescope

Radio Wave Spectrum

Photographs of the Source of Comets

Astronomers use an orbiting telescope to locate the place where comets form.

What theory did astronomers have about the origin of comets?

For many years some astronomers suspected that a doughnut-shaped area containing comets might surround the solar system. Scientists thought the area started just beyond Neptune and reached past Pluto. Astronomers named this area the Kuiper (KY•per) belt, after Gerard Kuiper, one of the first astronomers to hypothesize its existence. The Kuiper belt was considered the source of short-period comets—those that orbit the sun in 20 years or less.

What did powerful telescopes find?

In 1992 two astronomers using a telescope at the University of Hawaii found an object about 200 km (125 mi) wide in a circular orbit beyond Pluto. That was right in the area where the Kuiper belt was thought to be. After the 1992 discovery, nearly 30 more objects of about the same size were found in the same area.

Astronomers thought they might have found the Kuiper belt. In 1995 an image from the orbiting Hubble Space Telescope confirmed the discovery. The Hubble telescope is much more useful than many ground-based telescopes, in part because its view isn't blocked by Earth's atmosphere. Astronomers using the Hubble telescope have located more than a dozen smaller ice balls in the same area of space. They estimate that there could be millions more, and they hope to get a better view of these bodies when astronauts put a more powerful camera into the Hubble telescope.

◀ **Comet Hale-Bopp over the west wall of Zion Canyon, Utah**

Why is this discovery important?

The Kuiper belt ice balls are the first new group of objects to have been found in the solar system in 200 years. Astronomers hope to find out more about what they are made of. They also hope to study what causes the ice balls to break out of their orbits and head toward the sun.

The discovery of the Kuiper belt might also help astronomers find other solar systems. Some astronomers think the Kuiper belt forms a dusty disk around our solar system. Astronomers have seen similar disks around other stars, leading them to wonder whether planets revolve around those stars, too.

THINK ABOUT IT

1. What is the Kuiper belt?
2. How did the Hubble Space Telescope help confirm the existence of the Kuiper belt?

WEB LINK:
For Science and Technology updates, visit The Learning Site.
www.harcourtschool.com

Careers Astrophysicist

What They Do
Astrophysicists are astronomers who use physics to study the physical properties of the universe.

Education and Training
Astrophysicists must have a background in physics, chemistry, mathematics, and computer programming. An astrophysicist can begin work in the field with only a bachelor's degree but must earn a doctorate to do advanced research.

Annie Jump Cannon

ASTRONOMER

"No greater problem is presented to the human mind [than the study of the structure of the universe]. Teaching man [about] his relatively small sphere in the creation, it also encourages him by its lessons of the unity of Nature. . . ."

In her lifetime Annie Jump Cannon was probably the world's greatest expert in the classification of stars. She developed a system for classifying stars, and she used it to assign more than 250,000 stars to their places in the Henry Draper Catalog. The catalog is the largest collection of astronomical information ever assembled by one person.

Dr. Cannon's interest in astronomy began when she was a child. She would sit for hours with her mother, looking at stars from their attic window and identifying them with the help of an old astronomy book. Her parents encouraged her scientific curiosity, and at a time in the 1880s when most girls did not attend college, they agreed to send her to Wellesley.

She studied astronomy, and soon after graduation she joined the staff of the Harvard College Observatory. By then she was almost completely deaf, but that did not stop her. While working at Harvard, Cannon developed the Harvard System of Spectral Classification. She used letters and Roman numerals to rank stars—from the coolest red stars to the hottest white and blue stars. Her system is still in use today.

Cannon remained at Harvard for many years and received numerous honors. She enjoyed using her fame to encourage other women to enter science. She was also active in the political movement to give women the right to vote.

THINK ABOUT IT

1. What did Annie Jump Cannon accomplish?
2. Dr. Cannon identified about 300 variable stars—stars whose light varies in brightness over time. Why do you think she was able to discover so many?

Dr. Cannon at work, looking for and cataloging new stars

Analyzing Starlight

How do scientists learn about the distant stars?

Materials

- window facing the sun
- pan of water
- small mirror

Procedure

1. Place the pan so sunlight shines into it.

2. Put the mirror inside the pan, facing the window. Lean it against the side of the pan, with its bottom partly under water.

3. Adjust the position of the mirror until a pattern, a spectrum of colors, appears on the wall.

Draw Conclusions

How did the mirror and water work together to change the white light from the sun? What can scientists learn by studying the colors of the sun and other stars?

Building a Telescope

How does a reflecting telescope magnify objects?

Materials

- window facing the moon on a clear night
- curved shaving or makeup mirror
- small, flat mirror
- hand lens

Procedure

1. Place the curved mirror so the magnifying side faces the moon.

2. Position the flat mirror facing the curved mirror.

3. Adjust both mirrors so the moon is reflected from the curved mirror into the flat mirror.

4. Use the lens to examine the image of the moon in the flat mirror.

Draw Conclusions

What does the curved mirror do? What does the hand lens do? What would you see if you simply looked out the window and examined the moon with the hand lens?

Chapter (4) Review and Test Preparation

Vocabulary Review

Use the terms below to complete the sentences. The page numbers in ( ) tell you where to look in the chapter if you need help.

fusion (D117)

main sequence (D117)

nebula (D118)

nova (D119)

supernova (D119)

galaxy (D124)

galactic clusters (D124)

refracting telescope (D130)

reflecting telescope (D130)

1. Stars are formed from the gas and dust in a ____.

2. A large system of stars is a ____.

3. A device used to look at stars, called a ____, uses mirrors to gather light.

4. A ____ is a star that briefly becomes thousands of times brighter than normal, and a ____ is a huge explosion that happens near the end of a massive star's life cycle.

5. A device that uses glass lenses to gather light and magnify objects is called a ____.

6. The process in which nuclei join to form new elements and produce energy is ____.

7. Galaxies often occur in groups called ____.

8. The band that runs diagonally through the middle of the H-R diagram is called the ____.

Connect Concepts

Use the terms in the Word Bank to complete the concept map.

barred spiral   elliptical

galactic clusters   galaxies

irregular   spiral

universe

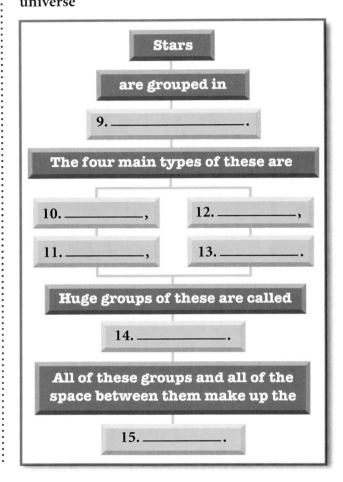

Stars

are grouped in

9. _____.

The four main types of these are

10. _____,   12. _____,

11. _____,   13. _____.

Huge groups of these are called

14. _____.

All of these groups and all of the space between them make up the

15. _____.

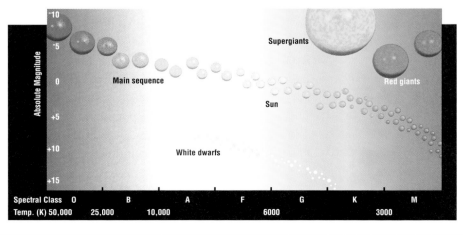

Check Understanding

Write the letter of the best choice.

16. A star's magnitude is its —
    - A distance from Earth
    - B age
    - C brightness
    - D size

17. The coolest stars are —
    - F white
    - G blue
    - H red
    - J yellow

18. Collapsed stars can form —
    - A planets
    - B black holes
    - C galaxies
    - D main-sequence stars

19. The Milky Way is —
    - F a spiral galaxy
    - G an elliptical galaxy
    - H an irregular galaxy
    - J a barred spiral galaxy

20. The first nation to send a satellite into orbit was —
    - A China
    - B the United States
    - C the Soviet Union
    - D Germany

Critical Thinking

21. Why are there no photographs of the Milky Way Galaxy from "above"?

22. How can astronomers use powerful telescopes to see parts of the universe as they appeared billions of years ago?

Process Skills Review

23. Suppose that a probe is being sent to a distant planet. You are designing an **investigation** to be conducted by the probe. What types of experiments will you set up to find out if the planet can support Earth life? What do you need to know?

24. **Compare** spiral and elliptical galaxies.

25. If you want to **make a model** of a galactic cluster, what do you need to include?

Performance Assessment

Starlight, Star Bright

Stars with higher surface temperatures usually give off more X rays. Use this information to predict which of two stars, a red star or a blue star, would give off more X rays. Write a plan for a simple investigation to test your prediction. Include what you would do and what you would use to test the prediction.

UNIT D
Unit Project Wrap Up

Here are some ideas for other projects you can do.

Make a Chart
Use a computer software program to make a chart that explains the phases of the moon.

Collect and Display
Find pictures of igneous, sedimentary, and metamorphic rocks. Label the pictures and display them with an explanation of the rock cycle.

Write a Book
Do some research to find out how people have learned about space. Write and illustrate a book to share what you learn.

Investigate Further
How can you make your project better? What other questions do you have about Earth and space? Plan ways to find answers to your questions. Use the Science Handbook on pages R2–R9 for help.

Pedro   Kiesha   Tim

★ Take It to the Top ★

Matter and Energy

PHYSICAL SCIENCE

Matter and Energy

Unit Project

Sound and Light Show
Find props, prepare a script, and give a Sound and Light show. The show should explain to your audience how sound and light waves move.

Chapter 1

Atoms, Elements, and Compounds

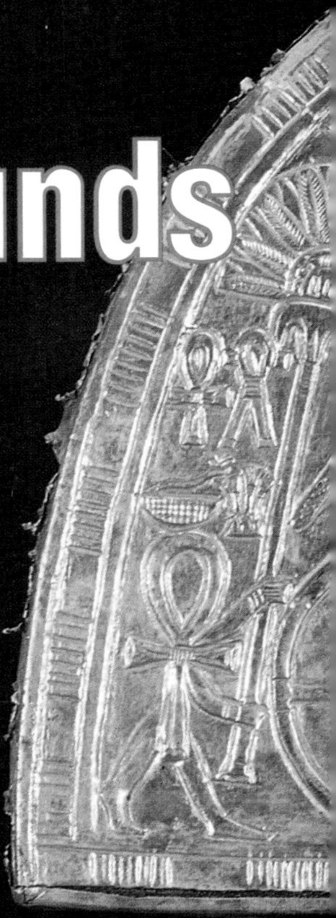

Vocabulary Preview

atom
nucleus
proton
neutron
electron
atomic number
element
metal
malleability
nonmetal
periodic table
solid
liquid
gas
compound
acid
base

Atoms are very stable. The carbon atoms that are part of the ink in this book have been around since the universe was formed. Atoms may be sturdy, but they don't stay in one place for long. By tomorrow some of the carbon atoms may have moved across the paper, onto your desk, and onto your finger.

FAST FACT

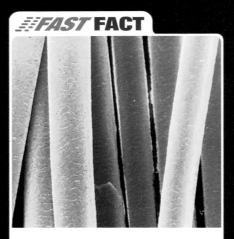

There is an expression *missed it by a hair's breadth*. It means that something came really close to something else. But when you are speaking of atoms, the width of a hair is a huge distance— more than a million atoms.

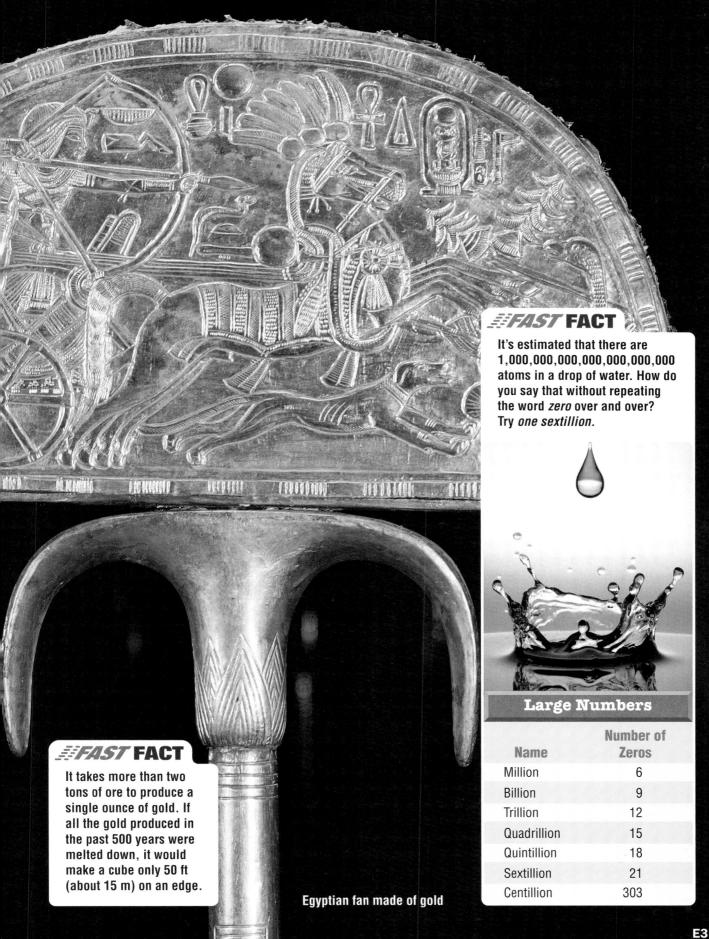

Large Numbers

Name	Number of Zeros
Million	6
Billion	9
Trillion	12
Quadrillion	15
Quintillion	18
Sextillion	21
Centillion	303

Egyptian fan made of gold

What Makes Up an Atom?

In this lesson, you can . . .

INVESTIGATE how to infer the characteristics of an object without observing the object directly.

LEARN ABOUT the structure of atoms.

LINK to math, writing, language arts, and technology.

Gold is a yellow metal that often looks smooth and feels solid. But with an atomic force microscope, the atoms that make up its structure can be seen. ▽

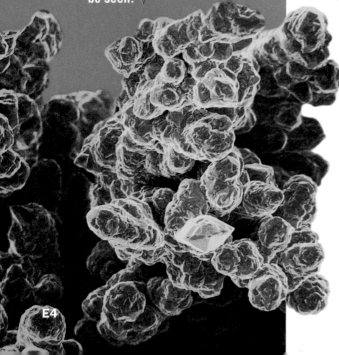

INVESTIGATE

Observing What You Can't See

Activity Purpose Even in the dark, you can probably find your way through your home without bumping into things. That's because you know the layout of your home—the things that are in it and where they're located. But how could you figure out the layout of a place without seeing it? How can you discover characteristics of objects without looking at them? In this investigation you'll discover one way to **observe** objects you cannot look at directly.

Materials
- large sheet of cardboard or poster board
- wooden blocks
- marbles

Activity Procedure

1 Work with a partner. Bend the sheet of cardboard in half lengthwise. Place it on a flat surface—the floor or a tabletop—so that you have **made a model** of a wide tunnel.

2 Take away the tunnel. Have your partner place several blocks on the flat surface. Do not look as your partner does this. There should be spaces between some of the blocks and no spaces between others. The blocks do not have to be in a pattern. Once the blocks are in place, your partner should put the tunnel back over them. (Picture A)

3 Gently roll a marble through the tunnel, and **infer** whether or not it hits a block. Repeat the process until you have **experimented** 20 times. Do not always roll the marbles in the same place. Without looking at the blocks, you are **gathering data** for a diagram of how they are arranged. (Picture B)

Picture A

Picture B

4. **Hypothesize** how the positions of the blocks in the tunnel affected the data you collected. **Interpret your data** to **infer** how the amount of blocked space in the tunnel compares to the amount of open space. Draw a picture of the positions of the blocks. Lift up the tunnel and check your inference and your picture.

5. Change roles with your partner, and repeat the experiment.

Draw Conclusions

1. How did you determine whether or not a rolled marble hit a block in the tunnel?

2. What did you **hypothesize** about how the blocks affected the data you collected?

3. **Scientists at Work** Scientists often **gather and interpret data** to **make inferences** about objects and events. How did the data you collected help you infer the positions of the blocks? How might more data have helped?

Investigate Further What other characteristics of objects could you find out using the setup from this investigation? Repeat the investigation but with other everyday objects in the tunnel. Try to identify each of the objects by the way the rolling marble acts when it hits them.

Process Skill Tip

When you **gather data,** you must be careful to record completely and accurately everything you observe. It is also helpful to collect as much data as you possibly can. This will help increase your accuracy when you need to interpret the data or communicate your results to someone else.

Atoms

FIND OUT

- what matter is made of
- what atoms are made of and what holds them together

VOCABULARY

atom
nucleus
proton
neutron
electron
atomic number

Matter Is Made of Atoms

Suppose you cut a piece of pure gold in half and then cut one of the smaller pieces in half. How many times could you keep on cutting the pieces in half? What would you end up with? For thousands of years, people tried to answer these questions. Democritus (dih•MAHK•ruh•tuhs), a philosopher who lived in Greece about 2400 years ago, suggested that there would finally be a piece that could not be divided any further. Democritus called this tiny piece an atom. An **atom** is the smallest unit of a pure substance that still has the properties of that substance.

Not until the early 1800s were scientists able to use experiments—not just ideas—to study the nature of matter. An English chemist named John Dalton was the first scientist to use experiments to support the *atomic theory*—the theory that matter is made of atoms.

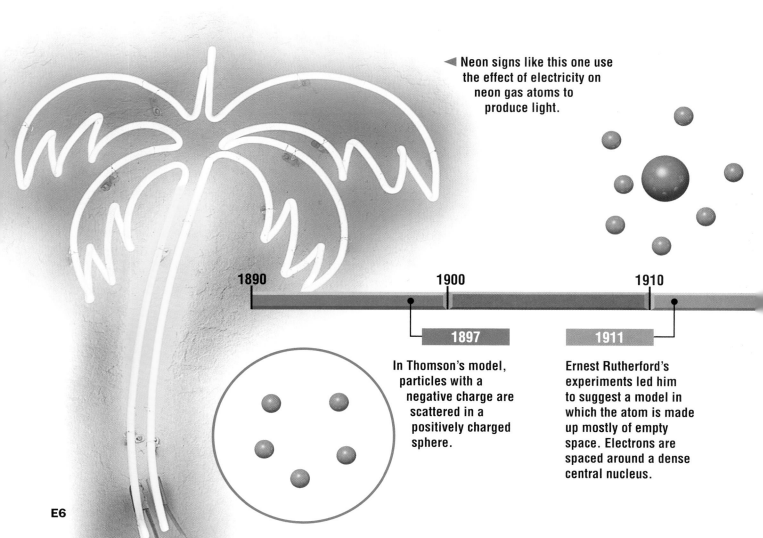

◀ Neon signs like this one use the effect of electricity on neon gas atoms to produce light.

1890 **1900** **1910**

1897

In Thomson's model, particles with a negative charge are scattered in a positively charged sphere.

1911

Ernest Rutherford's experiments led him to suggest a model in which the atom is made up mostly of empty space. Electrons are spaced around a dense central nucleus.

We now know just how tiny atoms are. A single grain of table salt may contain more than 2,000,000,000,000,000,000 (2 billion billion) atoms.

Dalton hypothesized that atoms are the smallest particles of matter and that they cannot be divided. Near the end of the 1800s, J. J. Thomson showed that atoms are made of even smaller particles. The parts of atoms are called *subatomic particles.*

Thomson made a model of an atom to explain his findings. His model was the first to include subatomic particles. The diagrams on these pages show how the structure of atoms was modeled as new information became available.

At the center of any atom is its **nucleus**. The nucleus has a positive electric charge. The nucleus is made up of at least one subatomic particle and usually several that are close together.

Every atom's nucleus contains at least one proton. A **proton** is a subatomic particle that has a positive electric charge. As you can see in the model, an atom's nucleus may also contain another kind of subatomic particle, the neutron. A **neutron** is a subatomic particle that has the same mass as a proton but no electric charge.

An **electron** is a negatively charged subatomic particle. Electrons are in constant motion around the nucleus. They have a mass much smaller than that of a proton or neutron. When electrons were first discovered to be in motion, scientists made models in which electrons orbited the nucleus. These models look something like the orbits of the planets in our solar system.

Modern models of atoms show electrons in a cloud around the nucleus. The outer edges of the cloud define the size of the atom.

✔ **What are the subatomic particles that make up an atom?**

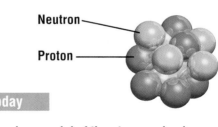

Neutron

Proton

Today

In the modern model of the atom, a cloud of electrons is around the central positive nucleus. The electron cloud is not like a rain cloud. It is the area where electrons are likely to be found.

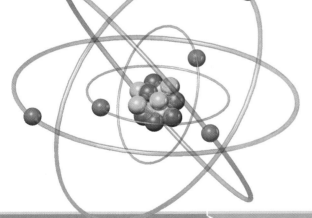

1913

The different orbits in Niels Bohr's model were a way to explain the different amounts of energy an atom's electrons can have.

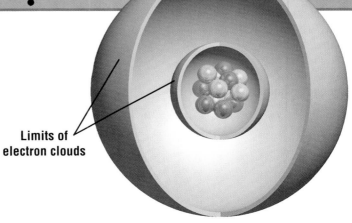

Limits of electron clouds

The Nucleus

The first evidence that an atom has a nucleus came from Ernest Rutherford's experiments in 1911. The investigation in this lesson was a simple model of Rutherford's experiment.

Rutherford fired positively charged particles at a very thin sheet of gold foil. Most of the particles traveled straight through the gold. Only a few changed direction or bounced back.

Rutherford inferred that the particles could travel straight through the gold only if they did not hit anything. Because most of the particles did not hit anything, it made sense that most of the gold was empty space. In fact, the diameter of the nucleus of an atom is about $\frac{1}{10,000}$ the diameter of an atom. If you think of the nucleus of an atom as being the size of a tennis ball, the whole atom would be a sphere with a diameter of about half a mile.

Although the nucleus takes up so little of the space in an atom, it accounts for more than 99.9 percent of the mass of the atom. A proton or neutron has nearly 2000 times the mass of an electron. Because the nucleus has a small volume and most of the mass of the atom, it is extremely dense.

The number of protons in an atom determines what kind of atom it is. For example, any atom with only one proton is a hydrogen atom. Any atom with eight protons is an oxygen atom.

The number of protons in an atom is called the **atomic number**. For example, the atomic number of hydrogen is 1 and the atomic number of oxygen is 8.

✔ **What determines the atomic number of a substance?**

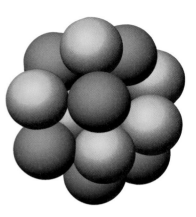

The nucleus of a carbon-12 atom contains six protons and six neutrons. Its atomic number—the number of protons—is 6. ▶

Protons   **Neutrons**

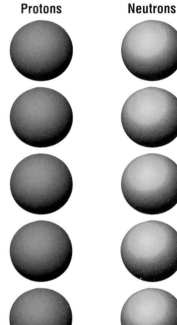

Diamonds are made of carbon atoms. The atomic number of carbon is 6, so each of the atoms in a diamond contains six protons. ▶

Isotopes

All the atoms of a substance have the same atomic number because they all have the same number of protons. But atoms of the same substance may have different masses. This difference is not due to protons, and the electrons account for hardly any of an atom's mass. The difference in mass occurs because atoms can have different numbers of neutrons.

Atoms that have the same number of protons but different numbers of neutrons are called *isotopes*. You can think of isotopes as different varieties of an element. Isotopes of the same element behave in similar ways but have slightly different structures. See the hydrogen example below.

The mass of an atom is so small that scientists don't measure it in grams. Instead, they use *atomic mass units*, or amu. Every proton has the same mass, and it is defined to be 1 amu. Neutrons have almost exactly the same mass as protons, so a neutron also has a mass of 1 amu. The *atomic mass* of a substance is equal to the total number of protons and neutrons of an atom. So, different isotopes of an element have different atomic masses.

The atomic masses of hydrogen isotopes are 1 amu, 2 amu, and 3 amu. An isotope's name is usually the name of the substance followed by the number of particles in the nucleus. For example, the isotope of hydrogen that has only a proton in the nucleus could be called hydrogen-1.

✔ **Do isotopes that have the same atomic number have the same atomic mass? Explain.**

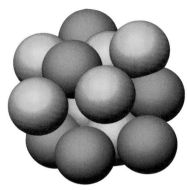

The nucleus of a carbon-13 atom contains six protons and seven neutrons. Like all carbon isotopes, its atomic number is 6. Is its atomic mass smaller or greater than the atomic mass of carbon-12?

Protons   **Neutrons**

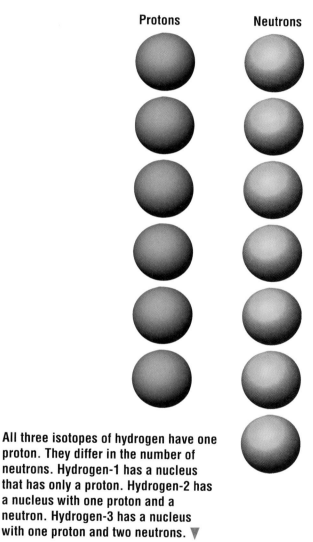

All three isotopes of hydrogen have one proton. They differ in the number of neutrons. Hydrogen-1 has a nucleus that has only a proton. Hydrogen-2 has a nucleus with one proton and a neutron. Hydrogen-3 has a nucleus with one proton and two neutrons. ▼

Hydrogen-1

Hydrogen-2

Hydrogen-3

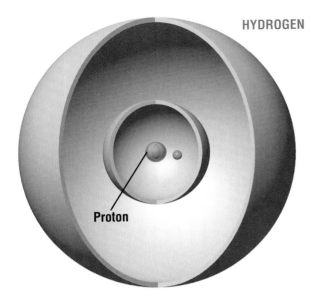

HYDROGEN

Proton

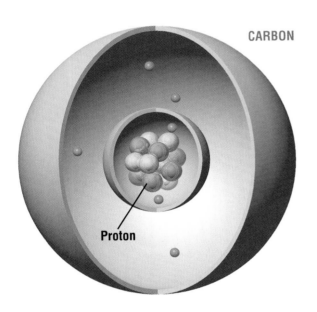

CARBON

Proton

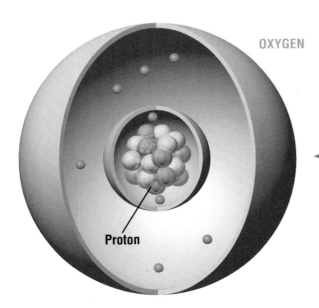

OXYGEN

Proton

Charges in Atoms

Protons have a positive electric charge. Electrons have a negative electric charge. Although their charges are opposite, a proton has the same amount of charge as an electron.

The charges of subatomic particles have a lot to do with the structure of an atom. Opposite charges attract, so the positive charge of the protons holds the negatively charged electrons in the cloud around the nucleus. Electrons closest to the nucleus are attracted more strongly than those farther away.

Opposite charges attract each other, but like charges repel each other. So why don't the protons in the nucleus repel each other? Overpowering the force of repulsion is the *strong nuclear force*. This force has an effect over only a tiny distance—a distance not much greater than the radius of a proton. The strong nuclear force has the same strength regardless of the charge of a nuclear particle. It holds the protons and neutrons together in the nucleus. Without this force, our whole universe would not hold together.

In an atom with the same number of protons and electrons, the charges balance and the atom is neutral. But sometimes one or more electrons are added to or removed from an atom. When that happens, the whole atom has an electric charge, and the atom is called an *ion*. Atoms that gain electrons become negatively charged ions. Atoms that lose electrons become positively charged ions.

✔ **A neutral atom of oxygen has eight protons. How many electrons does it have?**

◀ In a neutral atom, the number of protons equals the number of electrons. The charge of the nucleus is equal to the charge of the cloud of electrons. These diagrams show neutral atoms of hydrogen, carbon, and oxygen.

This electron micrograph reveals the atoms of graphite.

Summary

An atom is the smallest unit of a substance that still has the properties of that substance. The nucleus of an atom contains protons and neutrons and is surrounded by electrons. The atoms of different substances have different numbers of protons. Isotopes are atoms of the same substance that have different numbers of neutrons. Protons are positively charged, and electrons are negatively charged. Neutral atoms have the same number of protons and electrons.

Review

1. How are protons and neutrons alike, and how are they different?
2. Which of the subatomic particles is the smallest?
3. What are isotopes?
4. **Critical Thinking** If there is a difference between a substance's atomic number and its atomic mass, which measure must be the larger number?
5. **Test Prep** Which of the following is **NOT** a subatomic particle?
   A electron
   B ion
   C proton
   D neutron

LINKS

MATH LINK

Problem Solving Suppose an atom has an atomic number of 10 and an atomic mass of 21 amu. How many neutrons does the atom have?

WRITING LINK

Informative Writing—Report Write a short essay for your teacher about the early models of atoms. Tell how those models contributed to scientific knowledge even though they were incomplete.

LANGUAGE ARTS LINK

Origin of Words Research the origin of the word *atom*, and find out why the name is used appropriately.

TECHNOLOGY LINK

Learn more about how scientists use their knowledge of atoms to develop new technology, by watching *Atomic Laser* on the **Harcourt Science Newsroom Video.**

What Are the Properties of Elements?

In this lesson, you can . . .

INVESTIGATE the properties of elements.

LEARN ABOUT the periodic table of elements.

LINK to math, writing, health, and technology.

INVESTIGATE

Classifying Elements

Activity Purpose Just as animals and plants can be identified and classified by their characteristics, so too can nonliving materials. In this investigation you'll **observe** and describe some of the characteristics that can be used to **classify** substances.

Materials

- graphite
- sulfur
- copper wire
- thin iron nail
- magnet

Activity Procedure

1 Make a chart on which you can **record** your **observations** of each substance. Use the following headings: *Substance, Color, Shininess, Odor, Texture, Ability to Bend, Attraction to Magnets.*

2 **Observe** each substance. Use whatever methods you like to determine its characteristics. (Picture A)

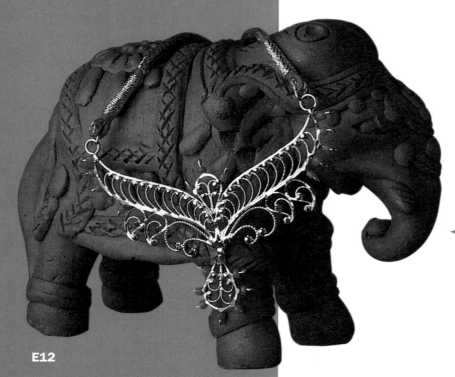

◄ Because gold can be bent and shaped into thin threads and wires, it is often used to make delicate jewelry such as this necklace.

Picture A

Picture B

3 **Record** your findings on the chart. (Picture B)

4 **Compare** the substances to find similarities and differences. **Classify** the substances into two groups based on your comparison.

5 Metals are malleable (bendable) and have luster (shininess). **Hypothesize** which of the substances you observed might be classified as metals.

Draw Conclusions

1. What characteristics did you use to **classify** the substances into two groups?

2. Which substances did you **hypothesize** might be metals? Why?

3. **Scientists at Work** Scientists **classify** substances according to their characteristics. However, not all members of a group share every characteristic. What two characteristics did you observe that differ among metals?

Investigate Further What other tests might you use to determine the properties of substances? With a partner, plan several tests that might be used to classify substances.

Process Skill Tip

When you **classify** items, look for similarities among them. But expect to find some differences among items that can be classified together.

The Elements of Matter

FIND OUT

• what an element is

• how elements are arranged on the periodic table

• why elements are grouped in different families

VOCABULARY

element
metal
malleability
nonmetal
periodic table

Elements

The substances that you tested in the investigation in this lesson are all elements. An **element** is a pure substance that's made up of only one kind of atom. It cannot be broken down into other substances by ordinary laboratory methods.

Atoms of different elements have different numbers of protons. This means that each element has a different atomic number. One property of any element is that it is the only substance that has its specific number of protons.

A total of 112 elements are known today, but some of these do not occur in nature. Instead, they are made by scientists. There are 90 elements that occur in nature, and many are familiar to you. Gold, silver, lead, sulfur, carbon, hydrogen, oxygen, and nitrogen are all elements.

Hydrogen is the most common element in the universe. The sun and other stars are made up mainly of hydrogen. Scientists hypothesize that all of the other naturally occurring elements were formed from the hydrogen in stars. In the tremendous heat of stars, hydrogen nuclei and subatomic particles join to form other elements in a process called *fusion*. In the sun, about 600 million metric tons of hydrogen undergo fusion every second.

Everything on Earth is made up of hydrogen or elements that were formed by fusion in stars. Most elements in their pure form are solids at room temperatures. Some elements—including nitrogen, oxygen, hydrogen, and neon—are gases. Only two elements—mercury and bromine—are liquids.

Even though mercury is a liquid at room temperature, it is a metal. A **metal** is an element that conducts heat and

◀ Each atom of the element boron has five protons. Any atom with five protons is a boron atom.

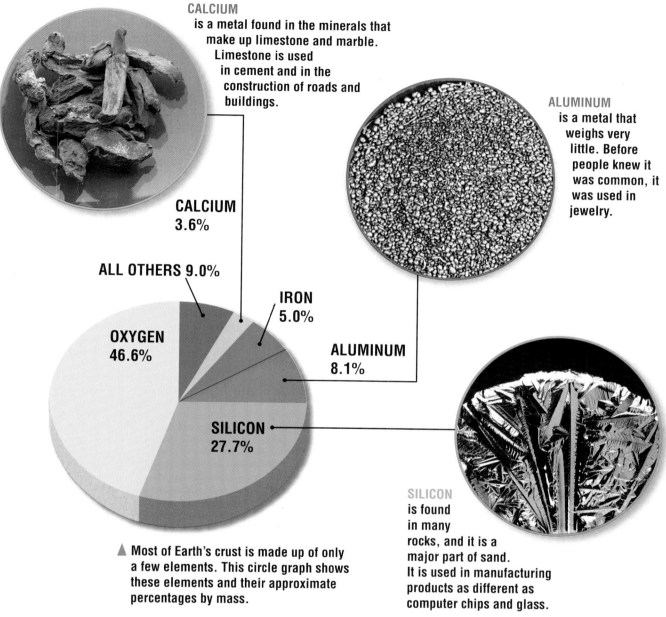

Elements in Earth's Crust

CALCIUM is a metal found in the minerals that make up limestone and marble. Limestone is used in cement and in the construction of roads and buildings.

CALCIUM 3.6%

ALL OTHERS 9.0%

IRON 5.0%

OXYGEN 46.6%

ALUMINUM 8.1%

SILICON 27.7%

ALUMINUM is a metal that weighs very little. Before people knew it was common, it was used in jewelry.

SILICON is found in many rocks, and it is a major part of sand. It is used in manufacturing products as different as computer chips and glass.

▲ Most of Earth's crust is made up of only a few elements. This circle graph shows these elements and their approximate percentages by mass.

electricity well. Most of the known elements—about 75 percent—are metals. They are shiny, and most have a gray or silver color. Iron, lead, and silver are examples. However, not all metals are silver-colored. Gold has a rich yellow color, and copper has a reddish-gold color.

Malleability (mal•ee•uh•BIL•uh•tee) is another property of metals. **Malleability** means that a metal can be bent and rolled into sheets. Elements that do not have the characteristics of metals are **nonmetals**. Nonmetals do not conduct electricity, and they aren't shiny or malleable.

✓ **What do all of the atoms of the same element have in common?**

The Periodic Table

The 112 elements that are now known are grouped in categories besides metals and non-metals. The first person to recognize a method of organizing the elements by many properties was the Russian chemist Dmitri Mendeleev (men•duh•LAY•uhf). In 1869 Mendeleev placed the elements known at the time into a table based on their atomic masses.

Mendeleev noticed that when the elements were arranged in order of increasing atomic mass, their properties fell into repeating patterns. Such patterns are called *periods*. Where there were gaps in the patterns, Mendeleev left empty spaces in his table. He predicted that elements not yet discovered would fill the holes in his table. These elements were actually found, and their properties did fit the patterns in Mendeleev's table.

Scientists later realized that the table would be more useful if it were based on atomic number—the number of an atom's protons—

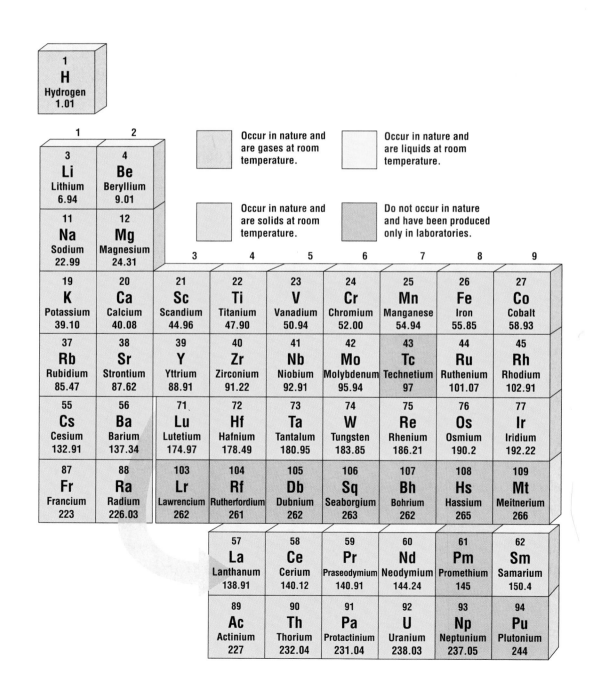

rather than on atomic mass. This led to the **periodic table**—a table of the elements arranged according to their atomic number.

Each square in the periodic table represents an element. The square contains the element's atomic number, chemical symbol (often an abbreviation of the element's name), name, and atomic mass. The colors of the squares identify the elements as being solids, liquids, or gases at normal temperatures. Color also indicates those elements that exist only when they are formed in the laboratory. Most of these elements have very high atomic numbers.

Each column of the table contains elements that have similar properties. Elements in the same column are in the same *group*, or *family*. The rows in the periodic table are called *periods*. Elements in the same period have similar arrangements of electrons in their atoms. Also, a zigzag line separates the metals and the non-metals in the table. Metals are to the left of the line, and nonmetals are to the right.

✔ **What characteristic is used to order the elements in the periodic table?**

Nonmetals

					18
					2 **He** Helium 4.00

	13	14	15	16	17	

Metals

			5 **B** Boron 10.81	6 **C** Carbon 12.01	7 **N** Nitrogen 14.01	8 **O** Oxygen 16.00	9 **F** Fluorine 19.00	10 **Ne** Neon 20.18

10	11	12	13 **Al** Aluminum 26.98	14 **Si** Silicon 28.09	15 **P** Phosphorus 30.97	16 **S** Sulfur 32.06	17 **Cl** Chlorine 35.45	18 **Ar** Argon 39.95
28 **Ni** Nickel 58.71	29 **Cu** Copper 63.55	30 **Zn** Zinc 65.38	31 **Ga** Gallium 69.72	32 **Ge** Germanium 72.59	33 **As** Arsenic 74.92	34 **Se** Selenium 78.96	35 **Br** Bromine 79.90	36 **Kr** Krypton 83.80
46 **Pd** Palladium 106.4	47 **Ag** Silver 107.87	48 **Cd** Cadmium 112.40	49 **In** Indium 114.82	50 **Sn** Tin 118.69	51 **Sb** Antimony 121.75	52 **Te** Tellurium 127.60	53 **I** Iodine 126.90	54 **Xe** Xenon 131.30
78 **Pt** Platinum 195.09	79 **Au** Gold 196.97	80 **Hg** Mercury 200.59	81 **Tl** Thallium 204.37	82 **Pb** Lead 207.2	83 **Bi** Bismuth 208.98	84 **Po** Polonium 209	85 **At** Astatine 210	86 **Rn** Radon 222
110 **Uun** Ununnillium 272	111 **Uuu** Unumunium 272	112 **Uub** Unumbium 277						

63 **Eu** Europium 151.96	64 **Gd** Gadolinium 157.25	65 **Tb** Terbium 158.93	66 **Dy** Dysprosium 162.50	67 **Ho** Holmium 164.93	68 **Er** Erbium 167.26	69 **Tm** Thulium 168.93	70 **Yb** Ytterbium 173.04
95 **Am** Americium 243	96 **Cm** Curium 247	97 **Bk** Berkelium 247	98 **Cf** Californium 251	99 **Es** Einsteinium 254	100 **Fm** Fermium 257	101 **Md** Mendelevium 258	102 **No** Nobelium 259

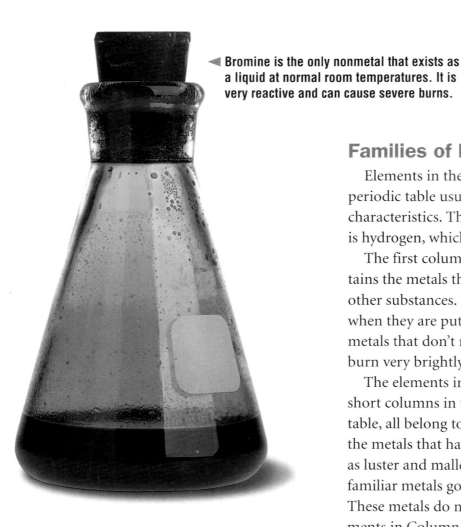

◀ Bromine is the only nonmetal that exists as a liquid at normal room temperatures. It is very reactive and can cause severe burns.

Families of Elements

Elements in the same family in the periodic table usually have similar chemical characteristics. The only exception to this rule is hydrogen, which does not fit into any family.

The first column of the periodic table contains the metals that react most strongly with other substances. In fact, these elements explode when they are put in water! Column 2 contains metals that don't react so strongly, but they burn very brightly when heated in air.

The elements in Columns 3 through 12, the short columns in the center of the periodic table, all belong to the same family. These are the metals that have the usual properties, such as luster and malleability. They include the familiar metals gold, silver, iron, and copper. These metals do not react as strongly as elements in Column 2.

Families of nonmetals include the elements in Column 17. These elements react the most strongly of all the nonmetals. They react especially strongly with the metals in the first column. The last column, column 18, contains a family called the *noble gases*. Noble gases are the least reactive family of metals or nonmetals. At one time, most scientists thought that noble gases were inert, or unable to react with any other elements. In 1962, however, scientists observed chemical reactions involving xenon. The noble gases are no longer considered inert.

✔ **How are families of elements shown on the periodic table?**

◀ Metals from Column 1 of the periodic table—for example, potassium—explode and burn when they are placed in water.

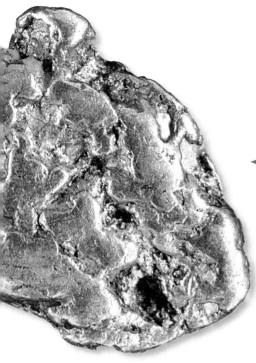

◄ Gold is sometimes found in nuggets, in which every atom is a gold atom. Although gold is unusual because it is scarce, it has the characteristics of all metals.

Summary

An element is a pure substance made of only one kind of atom. Each element has its own atomic number. Elements are arranged in the periodic table according to their atomic numbers and properties. Columns in the periodic table show families of elements. The elements in a family have similar properties.

Review

1. Where were the elements that are found in nature formed?

2. What order do the elements follow in the periodic table?

3. How are elements with similar properties displayed in the periodic table?

4. **Critical Thinking** Are any of the elements in the same family also in the same period? Explain your answer.

5. **Test Prep** At normal temperatures, what is the state of matter for most elements?

   A solid

   B liquid

   C gas

   D nonmetal

LINKS

MATH LINK

Percentages Of the 112 known elements, 90 are found in nature. To the nearest whole number, what percent of elements are found only in the laboratory?

WRITING LINK

Expressive Writing—Poem You and your friends are all made of substances that were formed in the stars. Write a short poem about "stardust" for your teacher.

HEALTH LINK

Minerals In nutrition many elements, such as iron, are called minerals. They are needed by the human body. Choose one mineral, and find out why it is needed for good health.

TECHNOLOGY LINK

Learn more about elements by visiting this Internet site.
www.scilinks.org/harcourt

SCI LINKS
THE WORLD IS A CLICK AWAY

What Are the States of Matter?

In this lesson, you can . . .

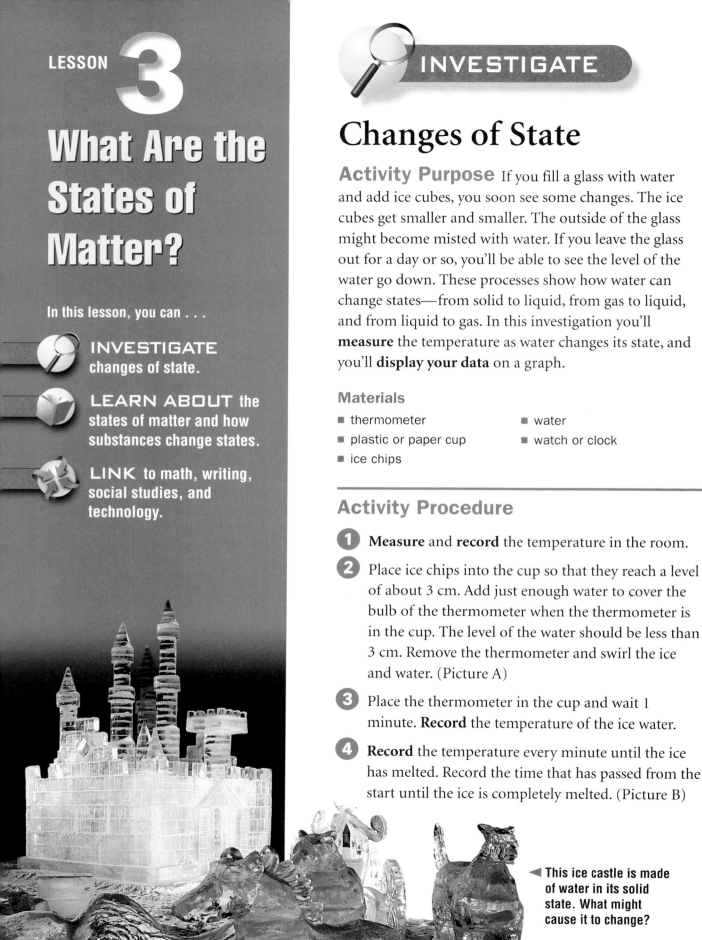

INVESTIGATE changes of state.

LEARN ABOUT the states of matter and how substances change states.

LINK to math, writing, social studies, and technology.

INVESTIGATE

Changes of State

Activity Purpose If you fill a glass with water and add ice cubes, you soon see some changes. The ice cubes get smaller and smaller. The outside of the glass might become misted with water. If you leave the glass out for a day or so, you'll be able to see the level of the water go down. These processes show how water can change states—from solid to liquid, from gas to liquid, and from liquid to gas. In this investigation you'll **measure** the temperature as water changes its state, and you'll **display your data** on a graph.

Materials

- thermometer
- plastic or paper cup
- ice chips
- water
- watch or clock

Activity Procedure

1. **Measure** and **record** the temperature in the room.

2. Place ice chips into the cup so that they reach a level of about 3 cm. Add just enough water to cover the bulb of the thermometer when the thermometer is in the cup. The level of the water should be less than 3 cm. Remove the thermometer and swirl the ice and water. (Picture A)

3. Place the thermometer in the cup and wait 1 minute. **Record** the temperature of the ice water.

4. **Record** the temperature every minute until the ice has melted. Record the time that has passed from the start until the ice is completely melted. (Picture B)

◀ This ice castle is made of water in its solid state. What might cause it to change?

Picture A

Picture B

5 Continue to **record** the temperature of the water every minute until the temperature no longer changes.

6 Draw a line graph showing the change in temperature over time. (Show temperature on the *y*-axis and time on the *x*-axis.) Mark the time at which the ice was completely melted.

Draw Conclusions

1. **Interpret the data** on your graph. What is the temperature of melting ice?

2. When you recorded the water temperature until it no longer changed, how did it **compare** to room temperature?

3. **Scientists at Work** After scientists **gather data**, they often **communicate** it in a graph so that it is easier to interpret. Use your graph and **interpret the data** it shows. When does the temperature of ice that is melting begin to change?

Investigate Further What other change of physical state does water often undergo? Design an **experiment** to **collect data** during that change of state.

Process Skill Tip

When you **gather data**, you may make observations and take measurements in an experiment. If you **communicate** the data on a graph, you and others often see patterns in the data more easily.

The Forms of Matter

FIND OUT

- about molecules
- what the states of matter are
- how matter changes between states

VOCABULARY

solid
liquid
gas

Molecules

As you've learned, an element consists of only one kind of atom. However, often atoms bond, or join, together and form larger units called *molecules*. Molecules are units formed of two or more atoms. In the air that you breathe, oxygen exists as molecules that are each formed of two bonded oxygen atoms. Carbon dioxide is a molecule formed of three atoms bonded together—one atom of carbon and two atoms of oxygen.

Molecules form when electrons in two or more atoms are attracted to the nuclei of both atoms, not just to one nucleus. This attraction holds the nuclei of the atoms together. The atoms act and move as a single particle, a molecule. Molecules are not easily separated into the individual atoms that form them.

The smallest molecules, such as oxygen molecules, are made up of two atoms. In fact, many of the elements that are gases, such as hydrogen, nitrogen, and chlorine, exist as molecules of just two atoms. Not all molecules are small, however. Cholesterol molecules, for example, are made up of 74 atoms. And very large molecules

DNA molecules are huge natural molecules. They can contain millions of atoms. ▼

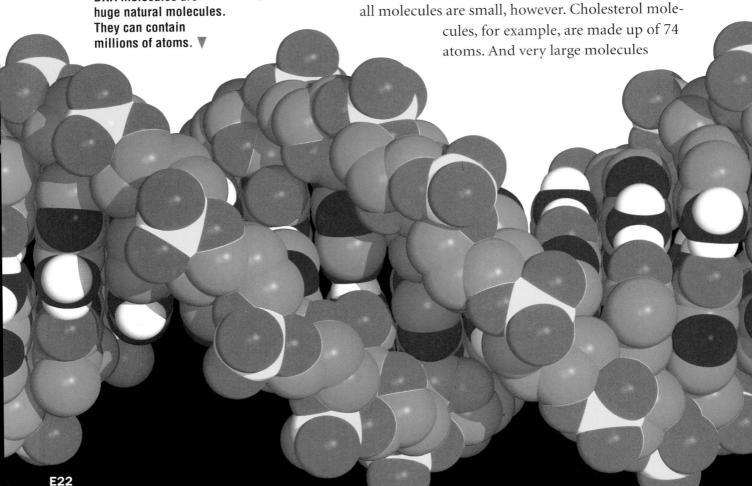

You can see water in two states—solid, as in snow or ice, and liquid, as in the flowing water of a stream. You can't see the gaseous state of water, but you can infer it from the mist in the air. This mist consists of visible droplets that have condensed from water vapor.

A water molecule is made up of two hydrogen atoms and one oxygen atom.

called *polymers* can contain hundreds or thousands of atoms. Many plastics, such as polyethylene, are polymers.

✔ **What holds the atoms of a molecule together?**

States of Matter

Matter exists in three states you know about. A substance in a **solid** state has a definite shape and volume. In a **liquid** state, a substance has a definite volume but no definite shape. It takes on the shape of whatever container it is in. As a **gas**, a substance has no definite shape or volume. It takes on the shape of its container and expands or contracts to fill the container. In all three states of matter, the atoms or molecules are constantly moving.

One substance that is familiar in all three states of matter is water. As a solid, it is ice. As a liquid, it is water. As a gas, it is water vapor.

Water is made up of water molecules. The way the molecules act together determines what state the water is in. The molecules in ice—a solid—are held tightly in place in a definite pattern. Although each atom vibrates, it does so in its fixed position. Since the atoms do not move from their positions, the solid has a definite shape.

In the liquid state, water molecules are not held in fixed positions. As in solids, the molecules are close together, but they can move freely, sliding over one another. This is why liquid water can flow or be poured. The closeness of the molecules, however, keeps them together and gives the water a definite volume. Like a solid, a liquid is very difficult to compress into a smaller volume.

Like liquid water, water vapor can also flow. Its molecules are farther apart from one another than in the liquid state. The molecules can move freely. They fill the container they are in, allowing the gas to take the shape of the container. Because of the space between the molecules, gases are easily compressed. In fact, a tank that's about 1.5 m (5 ft) tall with a diameter of about 0.3 m (1 ft) can hold enough compressed helium gas to fill almost a thousand balloons.

✔ **What are three states of matter?**

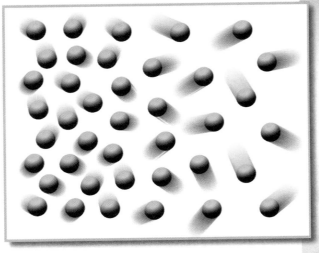

At room temperature, liquid nitrogen warms up and becomes a gas. Its molecules move faster and are farther apart. ▶

Changes of State

In solids, atoms and molecules of a substance vibrate in fixed positions. If energy is added, the speed of vibration increases. With enough energy, the atoms and molecules vibrate fast enough to shake apart and move more freely. The solid becomes a liquid. Adding energy can make the atoms and molecules move even faster, and the liquid becomes a gas.

Taking energy away from a substance has the opposite effect. A gas changes to a liquid and then to a solid. Most substances can exist in any of the three states of matter if enough energy is added or taken away. The changes between gas, liquid, and solid are called *changes of state.*

Usually, a change of state is caused by adding or taking away heat. If you take ice cubes out of the freezer, heat from the room is added to them and they melt. If you put a tray of water in the freezer, heat is taken away from it and it freezes.

If you put water in a pan on the stove, you can add heat to it. When the water boils, you'll probably see mist form. The mist seems to dissolve into the air. What you're seeing is water in its liquid state (the mist that you see) becoming water vapor in the air.

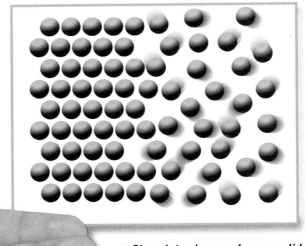

◀ Chocolate changes from a solid to a liquid as heat causes its particles to move faster. From this picture, what can you tell about the temperature at which chocolate melts?

The temperatures at which matter changes state vary from substance to substance. But every substance has two fixed temperatures at which it changes state.

The temperature at which a substance changes from a solid to a liquid is called its *melting point*. This is the same temperature at which the substance changes from a liquid to a solid, so it is sometimes called the freezing point.

The temperature at which a substance changes from a liquid to a gas is called its *boiling point*. This is the same temperature at which the substance condenses from a gas to a liquid.

Different substances have different melting points and boiling points. Substances with a strong attraction between their particles have melting points and boiling points that are high. Copper, for example, melts at 1083°C (about 1981°F) and boils at 2567°C (about 4652°F). Substances with a weak attraction between particles have low melting points and boiling points. Rubbing alcohol, for example, boils at 78.5°C (173.3°F). Its melting point is -117°C (-178.6°F).

Certain substances can change states directly from solid to gas. This is called *sublimation*. Solid carbon dioxide, or dry ice, sublimes at room temperature, changing to carbon dioxide gas without becoming a liquid first.

Adding or taking away heat isn't the only way to change the state of a substance. Changes in the pressure on a substance may also cause a change of its state. Compressing a gas causes its particles to get closer to each other—possibly close enough for the gas to become a liquid. Reducing pressure can cause a liquid to boil at well below its usual boiling point. In fact, reducing the pressure enough can make water boil at its freezing point. The bubbles that form as it boils are made of ice!

✔ **When will matter undergo a change of state?**

Melting Points and Boiling Points

Substance	Melting Point	Boiling Point
Water	0°C	100°C
Sodium chloride (table salt)	801°C	1413°C
Oxygen	-218°C	-183°C
Mercury	-39°C	357°C
Gold	1064°C	3080°C

Dry ice—solid carbon dioxide—is often used to keep substances cold because it sublimes directly from a solid to a gas. In its liquid state, the carbon dioxide would be dangerously cold and difficult to control.

Plasma

The substances you see in your everyday life are mainly solids, liquids, and gases. But those states of matter make up only a tiny fraction of the matter in the universe. Nearly all the matter in the universe, including all the stars, is in a state called *plasma*.

A plasma is a gas in which some of the electrons have been removed from the atoms or molecules. The gas has free electrons, which are negatively charged, and positively charged ions. The gas as a whole is electrically neutral, since it contains equal numbers of positive and negative charges. Unlike gases, plasmas readily conduct electricity.

The stars, including our sun, are composed of plasma because of their temperatures. Stars have such high temperatures that electrons are removed from the atoms in the gases that the stars are made of. Plasma can be made on Earth, too, by heating gases. At temperatures greater than 2000°C (about 3632°F), water vapor changes to plasma.

Natural plasmas can be seen on Earth in lightning and in the northern lights. The electric energy of lightning produces plasma in the air that it travels through. The northern lights are seen when electrons from outer space bombard layers of low-temperature plasmas in the upper atmosphere. A plasma that you can see close up is in the inner core of flames.

Fluorescent lights, neon signs, and the vapor lamps in street lights also form plasmas inside their bulbs. The electricity flowing through gases in these lamps removes electrons from some of the atoms, causing the atoms to give off light.

Lighting isn't the only practical use of plasmas. Plasmas are used to make computer chips. They are used in some types of welding to join steel. Scientists are trying to find a new power source by causing fusion—or joining—of nuclei in plasmas.

✔ **What is plasma?**

The core of a fire and the stars in the sky are both examples of plasma.

Summary

The atoms in some substances join to form molecules whose electrons are attracted to the nucleus of more than one atom. The way that particles of matter act together determines whether the state of the matter is solid, liquid, or gas. Changes of state are generally caused by heat or changes in pressure. The fourth state of matter—plasma—is a gas with free electrons and positive ions.

Review

1. What is a molecule?
2. Why do liquids flow but solids do not?
3. What change occurs when a substance is heated to its boiling point?
4. **Critical Thinking** In hydraulic machines a liquid that has filled a pipe is pushed at one end of the pipe. The liquid then pushes a machine part located at the other end of the pipe. Why isn't gas used in the pipe instead of liquid?
5. **Test Prep** Most of the matter in the universe exists as —

   A a solid   C a gas
   B a liquid   D a plasma

LINKS

MATH LINK

Volume A gas expands to fill its container. Suppose a helium gas tank is a cylinder with a radius of 7 cm and a height of 100 cm. What is the volume of the gas when the tank is full? When it's half full? (Note: The volume of a cylinder is found using the formula $V = \pi r^2 h$ where r is the radius and h is the height of the cylinder. Use $\pi = \frac{22}{7}$.)

WRITING LINK

Expressive Writing—Poem Read "Stopping by Woods on a Snowy Evening," a poem in which Robert Frost describes snow. Then write a poem of your own for your classmates that describes one of the states of water.

SOCIAL STUDIES LINK

Communities Find out how water, in each of its three states, is both helpful and harmful in a community. What do communities do to protect their environments from too much water (in different states of matter)?

TECHNOLOGY LINK

Visit the Harcourt Learning Site for related links, activities, and resources.
www.harcourtschool.com

WELCOME TO
THE LEARNING SITE

LESSON 4

What Are Some Properties of Compounds?

In this lesson, you can . . .

INVESTIGATE how to identify acids and bases.

LEARN ABOUT chemical compounds.

LINK to math, writing, art, and technology.

INVESTIGATE

Identifying Acids and Bases

Activity Purpose Some substances are classified by their properties. Acids and bases are two important groups of chemicals that are classified this way. Many products used in the home contain acids or bases. In this investigation you will experiment with several household solutions to find out which are acids and which are bases.

Materials

- safety goggles
- lab apron
- paper towels
- red litmus paper
- blue litmus paper
- droppers
- household solutions (vinegar, ammonia cleaning solution, antacid liquid, carbonated soda, powdered-detergent solution, lemon juice, milk, tea)
- wide-range indicator paper

Activity Procedure

CAUTION

1 **CAUTION** **Put on your safety goggles and your lab apron. Avoid getting any of the chemicals on your hands. Wash your hands after the experiment.** Place on a paper towel one strip of red litmus paper and one strip of blue litmus paper. Place one drop of vinegar on each strip of litmus paper. **Record** what happens. (Picture A)

2 Test the other solutions in the same way. **Record** your results. Be sure you always lay the litmus paper on a dry area of the paper towel.

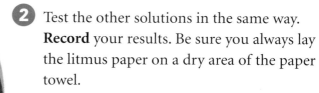

◄ The sails on this boat are made of a very light but strong human-made compound.

E28

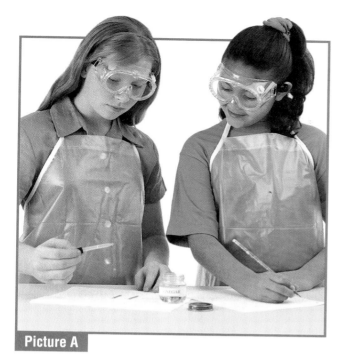

Picture A

Picture B

3 Repeat Steps 1 and 2, using wide-range indicator paper instead of litmus paper. Use the directions that came with the indicator paper to determine the pH value of each solution you test. (Picture B)

4 Now use the wide-range indicator directions to **classify** the substances you tested. Classify each as an acid, a base, or neither. **Hypothesize** what effects acids and bases have on litmus paper.

Draw Conclusions

1. How did you use the wide-range indicator directions to **classify** each substance?

2. Did you **classify** any substances as neither acid nor base? Explain.

3. **Scientists at Work** When scientists repeat experiments, they **control the variables** so that the results will be accurate. You repeated the experiment, controlling the variables when you used different indicators. What **hypothesis** did you form about the action of acids and bases on litmus paper?

Investigate Further Can you think of other solutions for which you could test the pH? **Hypothesize** whether a solution is an acid or a base before you ask your teacher if you may test it.

Process Skill Tip

When you experiment to compare substances, it is important to **control variables**. To ensure accurate comparisons, you should test each substance under exactly the same conditions.

Chemical Compounds

FIND OUT

- about compounds

- about classifying compounds as acids or bases

- about some common uses of acids and bases

VOCABULARY

compound
acid
base

Compounds

In nature, elements are not often found in their pure state. Most elements occur in combination with other elements, in compounds. A **compound** is a substance formed of the atoms of two or more elements. Water is one of the most familiar compounds. It's made up of two elements—hydrogen and oxygen—but it has very different properties from either of them. Compounds don't have the properties of the elements of which they are formed. Sugar, for example, consists of hydrogen, oxygen, and carbon. Two of these elements are gases, and the third is the element that makes up charcoal and diamonds!

A compound always has the same composition. Every molecule of water contains two hydrogen atoms and one oxygen atom. It doesn't matter whether it's in a cloud, a lake, or a water tank. Because the composition of a compound is fixed, the chemical symbols of its elements can be written as the compound's

Halite—commonly known as rock salt—is a compound formed of the elements sodium and chlorine. It occurs naturally in large crystals. ▼

Nylon is a fabric woven of a synthetic, or human-made, compound that has very large molecules. Here nylon fibers are being formed. ▼

▲ Tomatoes and pineapples contain organic compounds— that is, compounds that contain carbon. Some organic compounds are responsible for the way the fruits smell, some for the flavors, and others for the colors and structures.

chemical formula. A chemical formula doesn't just name the elements in a compound. It also shows how many atoms of each element make up one molecule of the compound.

The chemical formula for water is H_2O. The small 2 after the chemical symbol for hydrogen means that a water molecule contains two hydrogen atoms. There's no number after the chemical symbol for oxygen. That means that each water molecule has just one oxygen atom.

Water is a molecular compound—a compound made up of molecules. Atoms of hydrogen and oxygen form water molecules because some of their electrons are attracted to both a hydrogen nucleus and the oxygen nucleus. The attraction causes bonds that hold the atoms together in the molecule.

The chemical formula for table salt, or sodium chloride, is NaCl. Sodium chloride is an ionic compound.

It's made up of positive sodium ions and negative chloride ions. The attraction between the positive and negative ions results in *ionic bonds.* Those bonds hold the sodium and chlorine together to form the compound. Only a chemical reaction can separate a compound into its parts. This is true whether the compound is molecular or ionic.

Compounds are often formed in chemical reactions as well. A reaction can be fast or slow. One familiar slow chemical reaction is the formation of rust. Iron, a shiny gray metal, reacts with oxygen, a colorless gas, from the air. These elements combine to produce iron oxide, or rust, a red compound. Its chemical formula is Fe_2O_3. Each rust molecule contains two iron atoms and three oxygen atoms.

People also use iron oxides to produce iron. Hematite is an ore that has the same chemical formula as rust. It is mined and then processed to produce iron. Metals combined with oxygen are called metal oxides. These occur naturally and are mined as a source of metal.

✔ **What is a compound?**

The liquid that makes bubbles possible is another example of a common compound. ▼

Acids and Bases

Metal oxides aren't the only compounds that make up a group with similar properties. The compounds you tested in the investigation in this lesson belong to two groups: acids and bases. The compounds in each group have certain properties in common.

An **acid** is a compound that reacts easily with other substances and turns blue litmus paper red. Weak acids or acids diluted with water taste sour—but don't ever taste a chemical to test it. Many chemicals are poisonous, and strong acids are very corrosive. They can destroy skin and other body tissues on contact. However, many fruits contain weak acids. Oranges, lemons, and limes all contain citric acid. That is why they are called citrus fruits. Apples contain malic acid. Acids also react easily with the other group of compounds you investigated.

A **base** is a compound that also reacts easily with other substances but turns red litmus paper blue. You're probably familiar with a few bases. They often feel slippery, and they have a bitter taste. Soap and detergent contain bases. Many other household cleaners contain strong bases. The labels on these products include warnings against eating or drinking them or letting them come in contact with your skin. Strong bases are as destructive as strong acids.

Indicators are often used to find out if a chemical is an acid or a base. Indicators are dyes that change color in acids and bases. The litmus papers that you used in the investigation are indicators. So is red cabbage juice. Wide-range

THE INSIDE STORY

Indicators

Indicators are chemicals that help you determine whether a compound is an acid or a base. Some indicators, such as the color of hydrangea flowers, are natural. Others are made by people. But they all serve the same purpose—they show whether a compound is an acid or a base.

When the acid and the sodium hydroxide neutralize each other, the indicator turns clear. The chemical reaction produces salt (sodium chloride) and water. ▶

Lemon juice contains citric acid. It has a pH of about 2.

Hydrochloric acid is being added to a solution of sodium hydroxide, a base. An indicator has been added to the sodium hydroxide. The indicator is pink in bases and clear in neutral solutions and acids. ▶

indicators show a variety of colors to indicate the strengths of acids and bases.

The strengths of acids and bases are measured on a *pH scale*. Solutions with a pH of 7 are *neutral*. They are neither acids nor bases. Acids have a pH between 0 and 7, with the strongest acids having a pH of 0. Bases have a pH between 7 and 14, with the strongest bases having a pH of 14.

Acids and bases can be thought of as opposites. Equally strong acids and bases neutralize each other. When an acid and a base react, they form a neutral solution and a chemical called a salt. For example, both hydrochloric acid and the base sodium hydroxide are corrosive, but they react

together to form water and sodium chloride. Sodium chloride is one of the many chemicals called salts.

✔ **If you mix a weak acid and a weak base, will the mixture be stronger than either one?**

Common Acids and Bases

Solution	pH	Acid or Base
Battery acid	0	acid
Cola soft drink	2	acid
Vinegar	3	acid
Pure water	7	neutral
Milk of magnesia	10	base
Household ammonia	11	base
Caustic drain cleaner	14	base

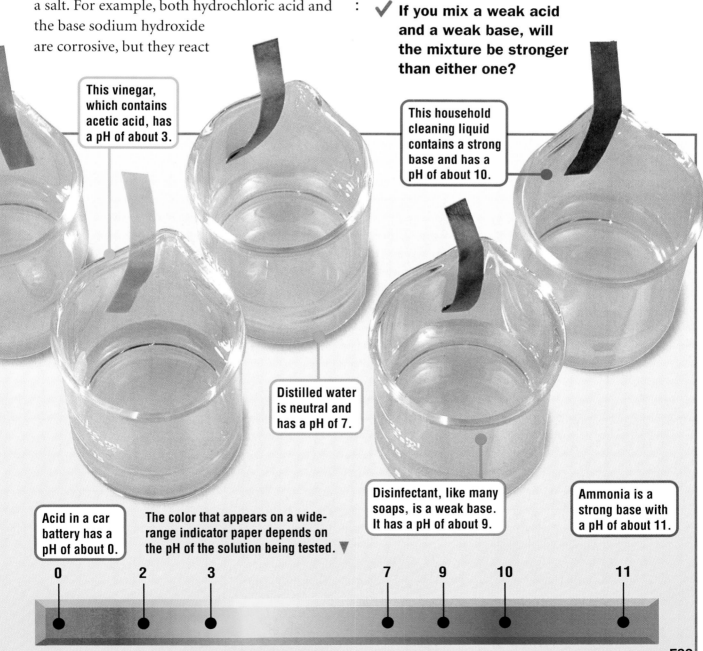

This vinegar, which contains acetic acid, has a pH of about 3.

This household cleaning liquid contains a strong base and has a pH of about 10.

Distilled water is neutral and has a pH of 7.

Disinfectant, like many soaps, is a weak base. It has a pH of about 9.

Ammonia is a strong base with a pH of about 11.

Acid in a car battery has a pH of about 0.

The color that appears on a wide-range indicator paper depends on the pH of the solution being tested. ▼

0   2   3   7   9   10   11

Uses of Acids and Bases

Acids and bases are a necessary part of everyday life. Many of the life processes of plants and animals rely on acids. For example, the human digestive system relies on hydrochloric acid produced by the stomach.

Much of the food we eat contains mild acids. Acids are found not only in citrus fruits and apples, but also in many other fruits. In addition to the natural acids found in many foods, acids are sometimes added to foods. For example, citric acid produces the sour taste in carbonated drinks, jams, and candy. It is also used to lower the pH of some canned foods. Ascorbic acid, or vitamin C, is added as a supplement to many foods. Acids are also used in the production of foods such as cheese. Even some pain relievers, such as aspirin, are acids.

Acids are also used to manufacture fertilizers and explosives. They are used in the production of dyes for cotton, wool, and silk. The acids increase the resistance of the dyes to light and to fading during washing.

Bases also play a major part in manufacturing. Besides being used in soaps and cleaners, they are an important part of cement. They are also used in paper making and petroleum refining. Both acids and bases are used in the

◀ Acids can be strong enough to cut into the surface of glass. This property of acids is used to etch designs in glass.

▲ Bases are used in paper manufacturing.

◀ Acids and bases are used in the production of some plastics.

manufacture of rayon, a fiber made from the cellulose in plants.

Acids and bases are also important in developing photographic film. Bases are used in the developing solution, the liquid that causes the negative images to appear on the film. When the film has developed long enough, dilute acid is used to neutralize the bases and prevent any further developing.

✔ **Name three uses of acids and bases in manufacturing.**

Summary

In nature, most elements occur in compounds. A compound is made up of atoms of two or more elements. Some compounds are classified as acids or bases, according to their properties. Acids and bases occur naturally in common substances. They are also important in many manufacturing processes.

Review

1. Can a compound have a molecule with a single atom? Explain.

2. What are three properties of bases?

3. What is the pH value of the strongest acids?

4. **Critical Thinking** Acid rain is caused by air pollution, which forms several kinds of acid in the water vapor in clouds. Suppose a lake were polluted by acid rain. How might you make it safe again for animals and plants to live there?

5. **Test Prep** Part of the taste of oranges and other fruits is due to —

   A bases

   B acids

   C elements

   D salts

LINKS

MATH LINK

Strength of Acids For acids, which have a pH less than 7, a decrease of 1 on the pH scale indicates an acid that is 10 times as strong. An acid with a pH of 3.5 is how many times as strong as an acid with pH 6.5?

WRITING LINK

Informative Writing—Description Many acids and bases are dangerous. Research one acid or base. Write a warning label for a bottle containing that substance.

ART LINK

Gardening Hydrangeas are plants that are sensitive to the acidity of soil. Find out why many gardeners put old coffee grounds on the soil around these plants. How might you use this information to make a garden with different colors of hydrangeas?

TECHNOLOGY LINK

Learn more about some life-saving properties of compounds by visiting the Jerome and Dorothy Lemelson Center for Invention and Innovation Internet site.
www.si.edu/harcourt/science

Smithsonian Institution®

Discovery of Particles

Parts of the Atom

By the end of the 1800s, physicists had agreed that all matter is composed of atoms and that atoms contain negatively charged particles called electrons. In 1911, aided by the newly discovered X rays, Ernest Rutherford found that electrons surround an atom's core, the nucleus. Rutherford used this knowledge to propose one of the first models of atomic structure that same year. Throughout the 1900s, physicists continued to propose models of atomic structure as they discovered more about the atom's parts.

Units of Energy

Physicists also researched how and why certain substances are radioactive. In 1900, German physicist Max Planck proposed the quantum theory. This theory suggested that all energy exists in amounts called quanta. Quantum theory changed how physicists understood the world. They could now study energy in terms of quanta. They could investigate the interactions of quanta and the effects of quanta on atoms. In 1913, Niels Bohr found that electrons follow orbits around the nucleus of an atom and that each orbit has its own energy level. Physicists found that quanta may cause the electrons to change their orbits—and thus their energy levels. Depending on the change, electrons may give off or absorb energy.

Smaller and Smaller

In the 1930s and 1940s, physicists built the first particle accelerators, machines that produce collisions between atomic particles. Particle accelerators shattered atoms and showed that the known atomic particles—protons, electrons, and neutrons—were made up of even smaller particles. In 1933, scientists discovered antimatter when they found the positron—a particle like an electron but with a positive

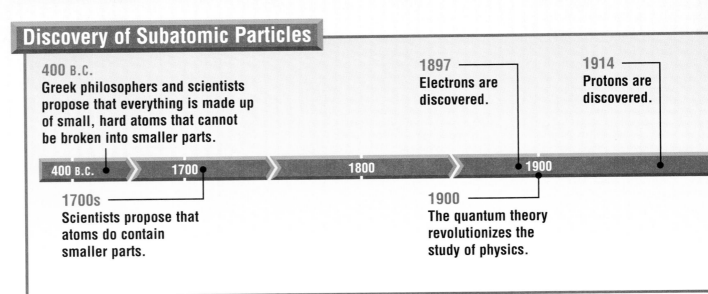

Discovery of Subatomic Particles

400 B.C.
Greek philosophers and scientists propose that everything is made up of small, hard atoms that cannot be broken into smaller parts.

1897
Electrons are discovered.

1914
Protons are discovered.

400 B.C. — 1700 — 1800 — 1900

1700s
Scientists propose that atoms do contain smaller parts.

1900
The quantum theory revolutionizes the study of physics.

charge. In 1956, physicists discovered the neutrino—a particle that may or may not have mass. By 1960, physicists had found 200 subatomic particles.

Quarks—the Smallest Yet

In 1964, physicists proposed that these subatomic particles were made up of even smaller particles called quarks. In 1991, a particle accelerator in Europe provided evidence that quarks exist. When the physicists split an atom, they saw the traces of the quarks that made up some of the subatomic particles. So far, physicists have identified six types of quarks. Physicists studying all these subatomic particles hope one day to explain their behavior in terms of one force that governs all matter.

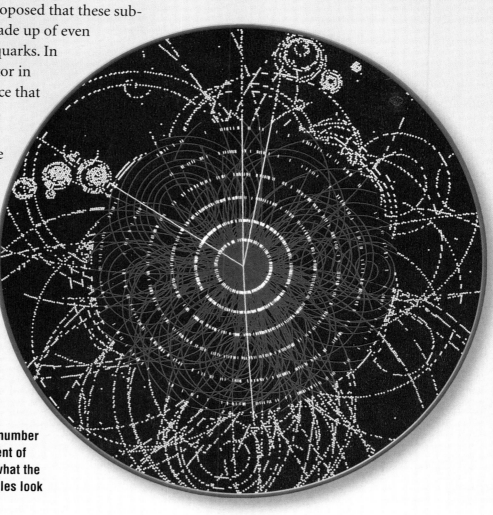

Physicists have developed a number of ways to detect the movement of subatomic particles. This is what the tracks of some of these particles look like.

THINK ABOUT IT
1. How did the introduction of quantum theory help the search for subatomic particles?
2. Why is it important to know that atoms are not the smallest particles of matter?

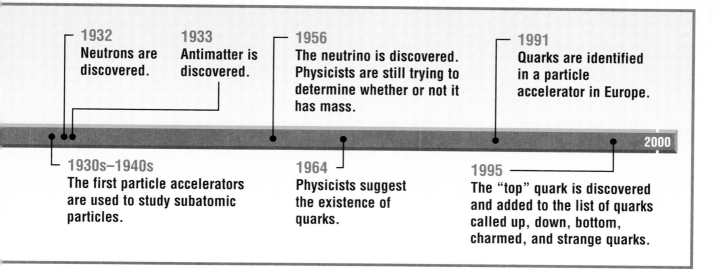

1932
Neutrons are discovered.

1933
Antimatter is discovered.

1956
The neutrino is discovered. Physicists are still trying to determine whether or not it has mass.

1991
Quarks are identified in a particle accelerator in Europe.

2000

1930s–1940s
The first particle accelerators are used to study subatomic particles.

1964
Physicists suggest the existence of quarks.

1995
The "top" quark is discovered and added to the list of quarks called up, down, bottom, charmed, and strange quarks.

Marie Curie

NUCLEAR PHYSICIST, CHEMIST

"We are now used to working with substances which manifest their presence to us only by their radioactive properties. . . . This is a particular kind of chemistry . . . which could well be called the chemistry of the imponderable."

In 1903 Marie Curie became the first woman to win the Nobel Prize. She and her husband, Pierre Curie, shared the physics prize with Antoine Henri Becquerel, for the discovery of the radioactive elements radium and polonium. In 1911 she again won the Nobel Prize, this time in chemistry. She won the second prize alone, for her work in isolating radium and discovering its chemical properties. Curie became the first person to receive two Nobel Prizes.

Born in Poland Marie Curie was originally named Marya Sklodowska. Dr. Curie was a pioneer throughout her life. She was the first woman to study at the Sorbonne, a prestigious university in Paris, earning

degrees in physics and mathematics. She later became the first woman to teach at the Sorbonne.

At the end of the nineteenth century, radiation was not well understood. Dr. Curie began to study the radioactive rays given off by natural substances. Uranium was already known. With her husband she studied pitchblende, a uranium ore, and found that it was much too radioactive to contain just uranium. By chemically separating elements from the ore, the Curies discovered radium and polonium.

During their research the Curies were exposed to extremely high doses of radiation. Although they suspected that the radiation was making them tired and sick, they had no idea how deadly it was. When Pierre died in 1906, Marie continued her research.

During World War I, she organized mobile X-ray units for the French army. In 1934 Marie Curie died of leukemia, a disease brought on by her prolonged exposure to radioactive materials.

THINK ABOUT IT

1. What were Marie Curie's greatest accomplishments?
2. How did her research harm her?

Hot or Cold?

Do Epsom salts make water colder? If so, how?

Materials

- 1/2 cup water at room temperature
- outdoor thermometer
- stopwatch (or watch with a second hand)
- 1/2 cup Epsom salts at room temperature
- spoon

Procedure

1. Put the thermometer in the water for 20 seconds. Record the temperature, and remove the thermometer.

2. Add the Epsom salts to the water and stir for about 20 seconds.

3. Measure and record the water temperature again.

Draw Conclusions

What happened to the temperature of the water after you added the Epsom salts? Did the water lose or gain energy? How do you know? It takes energy for Epsom salts to dissolve in water. Where did the Epsom salts get this energy?

Pennies and Paper Clips

How does acid affect copper?

Materials

- 1 plain steel paper clip
- about 30 copper pennies (Pennies made before 1983 contain more copper.)
- plastic container of vinegar

Procedure

1. Put the pennies in the vinegar. Drop in the paper clip so it rests on top of them. Make sure the pennies and clip are covered by the vinegar.

2. Allow the jar to sit undisturbed for 24 hours.

3. Observe the color of the pennies and the paper clip. If the color of the paper clip has not changed, rub it with steel wool or sandpaper, and start over.

Draw Conclusions

How did the color of the paper clip change? The color of the pennies? What do you think happened to change the color of the pennies and the paper clip?

Chapter 1 Review and Test Preparation

Vocabulary Review

Use the terms below to complete the sentences. The page numbers in ( ) tell you where to look in the chapter if you need help.

atom (E6)
nucleus (E7)
protons (E7)
neutrons (E7)
electrons (E7)
atomic number (E8)
element (E14)
metals (E14–15)

nonmetals (E15)
periodic table (E17)
solid (E23)
liquid (E23)
gas (E23)
compound (E30)
acid (E32)
base (E32)

1. A ____ is at the center of an atom.

2. The smallest unit of an element that still has the properties of that element is an ____.

3. A compound with a pH greater than 7 is a ____.

4. Elements are arranged by atomic number in the ____.

5. An ____ has a pH of less than 7.

6. Elements that are ____ are on the right side of the periodic table.

7. The three common states of matter are ____, ____, and ____.

8. Elements that are shiny and usually conduct heat and electricity well are ____.

9. The number of protons in the nucleus of an atom is its ____.

10. A substance made from two or more elements is a ____.

11. Three types of subatomic particles are ____, ____, and ____.

12. A pure substance made up of only one kind of atom is an ____.

Connect Concepts

Complete the concept map by filling in terms from the word bank.

electrons   compounds
molecules   atoms
neutrons   protons
matter

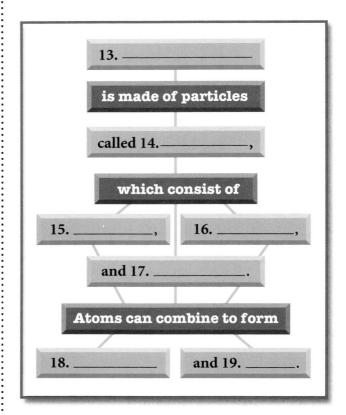

13. _____

is made of particles

called 14._____,

which consist of

15. _____,   16. _____,

and 17. _____.

Atoms can combine to form

18. _____   and 19. _____.

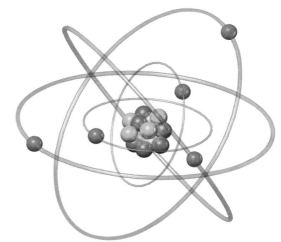

Check Understanding

Write the letter of the best choice.

20. The charge of an electron is —
  A negative
  B positive
  C neutral
  D both **A** and **B**

21. The atomic number of an element is the same as the number of its —
  F atomic mass
  G electrons
  H neutrons
  J protons

22. Most of the matter in the universe is —
  A solid
  B liquid
  C gas
  D plasma

23. An example of an acid is a substance that has a pH of —
  F 5   **H** 9
  G 7   **J** 11

Critical Thinking

24. Are all molecules compounds? Explain your answer.

25. Why isn't water included in the periodic table?

Process Skills Review

26. What can you **infer** about two substances that have the same atomic number but different atomic masses? What term would you use to **classify** the two substances?

27. How would you **control variables** to determine the melting point of salt water? How could you **communicate** your results?

28. Red cabbage juice is an indicator for acids and bases. Suppose you want to **hypothesize** how the juice indicates an acid or a base. How would you **experiment** so that you could form a hypothesis? What **data** would you **collect**?

Performance Assessment

Balloon Experiment

Design an experiment in which you determine whether temperature has an effect on the volume of a gas. Limit your materials to a balloon and anything you might find in a kitchen. Describe the variables you would control and those you would change. Tell how you would collect your data.

Chapter 2

Vocabulary Preview

physical property
texture
malleability
ductility
density
buoyancy
chemical property
combustibility
reactivity
stability
mixture
solution
suspension
colloid

Matter— Properties and Changes

Everyone knows that water can be frozen into a solid called ice and boiled into a gas called steam or water vapor. But did you realize that *everything* can exist in any of these three states? The main cause of the state is temperature.

FAST FACT

A diamond and a lump of coal have a lot in common—both are forms of carbon. If we could rearrange the atoms of a piece of coal, we could make all the diamonds we wanted.

What Are Some Physical Properties of Matter?

In this lesson, you can . . .

INVESTIGATE how to observe and measure physical properties.

LEARN ABOUT the physical properties of matter.

LINK to math, writing, art, and technology.

Observing and Measuring Physical Properties

Activity Purpose When you describe an object, you might talk about its color, shape, mass, and size. Some characteristics—color and shape, for example—can be observed. Other characteristics, such as mass and size, can be measured. In this investigation you'll **compare** objects by observing and measuring their characteristics.

Materials

- large piece of aluminum foil
- small wooden block
- balance
- ruler
- graduate
- hand lens
- water

Activity Procedure

1 Make and **record** as many **observations** of the foil and the wooden block as you can. Include such characteristics as color, hardness, texture, and whether or not the object is malleable, or can be bent and shaped. (Picture A)

2 Use a balance to **measure** the mass of each object.

3 Use a ruler to **measure** the dimensions of each object. Then **calculate** the surface area of each object by adding the areas of each of its sides. Remember, the block has six sides and the foil has two sides.

4 Find the volume of the block. The volume is the product of its length, width, and height: $V = lwh$.

◄ Although ingredients have been mixed together in pizza dough, they have not changed into different substances. When the pizza is baked, however, different substances will be formed.

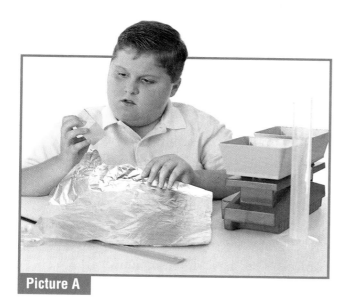

Picture A

Picture B

5 Partially fill the graduate with water. **Measure** and **record** the volume of the water.

6 Carefully roll or fold the aluminum foil as tightly as you can so that it will fit into the graduate and so that it will contain no air bubbles. It must be rolled tightly enough to go completely under the water when you place it in the graduate. Place the foil in the water and **measure** and **record** the new volume. Find a way to use your readings to **calculate** the volume of the foil. (Picture B)

7 **Calculate** the density of the two objects. Density is the mass of the object divided by the volume.

8 Make a table to **compare** your data for the two objects.

Draw Conclusions

1. What differences between the objects did you **observe**? What differences did you find when you **measured**?

2. How did you **calculate** the volume of the aluminum foil?

3. **Scientists at Work** Scientists sometimes have to use different methods to **measure** the same property of two different items. Why was it necessary to use two different methods to measure the volumes of the block and the aluminum foil?

Investigate Further How would you **classify** each object? Do you think that other objects made of either material have similar characteristics? **Plan and perform** some **experiments** to find out.

Process Skill Tip

When there are several ways to **measure** a characteristic of an object, you have a choice. Choose the method that is most convenient—as long as it works and doesn't change the object's characteristics.

Physical Properties of Matter

Physical Properties

The objects you compared in the investigation have two things in common with each other—and also with marbles, bicycles, and trees. They are made of *matter*, so they have mass and take up space. Not everything has mass and takes up space. Rainbows and sound, for example, do not. They are not made of matter.

Although marbles, bicycles, and trees are all made of matter, they are very different objects. They have different **physical properties**—properties that can be observed or measured without changing an object, or any of the materials it's made of, into something else.

Every substance has physical properties that can be used to identify it. Some of these properties, such as mass and size, can change according to how much of the substance is in an object. Other physical properties of a substance never change. These include color, smell, attraction to magnets, and melting and boiling points. Whether you're

FIND OUT

- how to recognize physical properties of matter
- which physical properties can be observed and which can be measured
- how matter goes through physical changes

VOCABULARY

physical property
texture
malleability
ductility
density
buoyancy

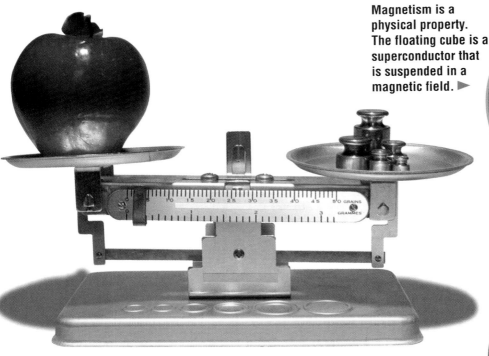

▲ Mass is a physical property that can be measured. The mass of this apple is being compared to known masses on a balance.

Magnetism is a physical property. The floating cube is a superconductor that is suspended in a magnetic field. ▶

Copper is harder than galena. That's why this penny can scratch the galena. ▶

Density of Some Common Substances

Substance	Density (g/cm³)	Buoyancy
Helium	0.00018	floats in pure water
Air	0.001	floats in pure water
Wood (white pine)	0.5	floats in pure water
Olive oil	0.9	floats in pure water
Pure water	1.0	
Diamond	3.5	sinks in pure water
Lead	11.3	sinks in pure water
Mercury	13.6	sinks in pure water

testing a tiny iron pin or a huge iron beam, the iron will be the same color, will be attracted to magnets, and will melt at the same temperature.

An observable physical property that can be used to identify a substance is its texture. **Texture** is how the surface of a substance feels. For example, the surface might be rough or smooth, waxy or powdery. Other properties that can be observed are malleability and ductility. **Malleability** is the ability of a substance to be bent, hammered into thin sheets, or otherwise shaped without breaking. As you know, many metals are malleable. **Ductility** is the ability of a substance to be pulled into thin threads without breaking. Many metals, including gold, have ductility and so can be worked into fine designs and ornaments. A substance that has the property of ductility is said to be *ductile*. The opposite of both *malleable* and *ductile* is *brittle*.

The mass and volume of a substance are physical properties that can be measured. These properties vary because they depend on the amount of the substance present.

An important physical property that can be calculated from measurements is density. **Density** is the amount of mass that fits in a given volume. The density of an object is found by dividing its mass by its volume. Even though the mass and volume of a substance may vary, the ratio of these two

measurements doesn't usually change for a solid or a liquid. The density of a gas is more variable.

The density of a substance determines another of its physical properties—its buoyancy. **Buoyancy** is the ability to float in a liquid or rise in a gas. A substance is buoyant if its density is less than that of the liquid or gas. The table on this page shows the densities of several substances and indicates whether or not they are buoyant in pure water.

✔ **What are five observable physical properties?**

Clay is malleable when it's wet. It can be shaped in many different ways, including being "thrown" on a potter's wheel.

Physical Changes

When a substance goes through a *physical change*, some of its physical properties may change, but it does not become a different substance.

A piece of paper cut into hundreds of tiny bits goes through a physical change. So does the ground when a hole is dug. The paper may be in lots of pieces, but it is still paper. None of it has disappeared or been changed into another material. The dirt that has been dug out of the hole may look different, but it has just been broken up and moved around.

In a physical change, the molecules and atomic makeup of a substance stay the same. A sandstone cliff that is exposed to the weather goes through physical changes as it gradually erodes in the wind and rain. Quartz, the main part of most sandstone, is a compound made up of silicon and oxygen atoms arranged in a specific way. As the cliff erodes, its pieces are still made up of the same silicon and oxygen atoms, arranged in the same way. The only changes that have taken place are physical—changes in the shape, size, and number of the quartz pieces.

The physical properties of a substance determine which physical changes it can undergo. For example, aluminum can be rolled into a thin, flexible foil that won't break when it is bent and shaped. Rolling, bending, and shaping are physical processes that are possible because of a physical property of aluminum—its malleability.

People make good use of the properties of substances. Copper is used for electrical wiring, for example, because it is ductile and conducts electricity well. Gold is used for jewelry, not only because it is rare and it looks good but also because it is highly malleable and ductile.

✔ **What are two physical changes that metals can undergo?**

When a balloon is filled with helium, the shape of the rubber changes but its mass does not change. The density of the helium is so low that the helium can carry the mass of the rubber, making the gas-filled balloon buoyant in air. ▶

When a pot is formed, the shape of the clay changes, but the clay does not change into other substances. ▼

Summary

The physical properties of an object are properties that can be observed or measured without changing the substances the object is made of. Some physical properties can be observed, and others can be measured. The physical properties of a substance determine its uses and the physical changes it can undergo.

Review

1. What are two physical properties that can vary even when the substance with these properties does not change?
2. What is ductility?
3. Why is the erosion of sandstone a physical change?
4. **Critical Thinking** Air has a lower density than water. If an object is buoyant in air, is it buoyant in water? Explain your answer.
5. **Test Prep** Most metals are —
   A buoyant in water
   B compounds
   C malleable
   D precious

A broken balloon has exactly the same physical properties that the full balloon has. However, because the full balloon is filled with a gas, the balloon plus the gas behave differently than the broken balloon. ▼

LINKS

MATH LINK

Density A container in the shape of a cube measures 10 cm on each side. The substance that fills the container has a mass of 1 kg. What is the density of the substance? Use the table on page E47 to determine what the substance may be.

WRITING LINK

Informative Writing—Description Write a paragraph to a friend in which you describe the physical properties of an object without naming it. Your friend can try to guess the mystery object you have described.

ART LINK

Color The pigments that are used to give paints their color sometimes exist in nature. Find out about some natural pigments. Then see if you can make paints of your own by using these pigments.

TECHNOLOGY LINK

To learn more about how scientists are developing chemicals for their physical properties, watch *Fullerenes—Amazing Molecules* on the **Harcourt Science Newsroom Videos.**

CNN
Turner
Le@rning

What Happens During a Chemical Change?

In this lesson, you can . . .

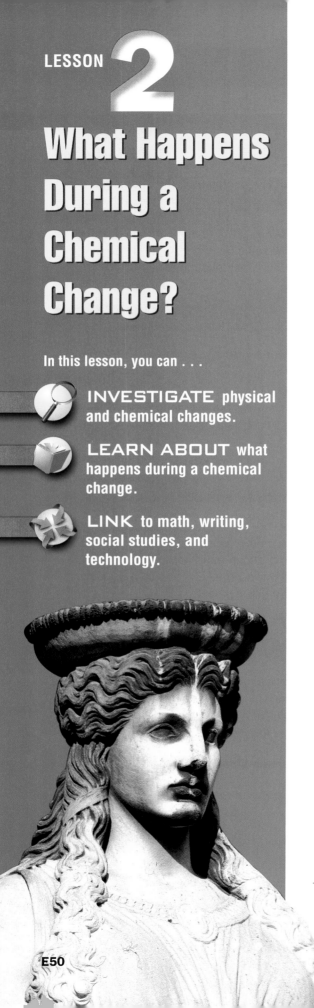

INVESTIGATE physical and chemical changes.

LEARN ABOUT what happens during a chemical change.

LINK to math, writing, social studies, and technology.

◄ This statue has gone through two different kinds of changes. Weathering has worn away the surface of the rock. And the color of the rock has changed as a result of chemicals in the air and in the rain.

INVESTIGATE

Different Kinds of Changes

Activity Purpose Some of the physical changes that you've read about can be reversed, but others can't be. Ice from the freezer can melt, changing back to the water you first poured into the ice cube tray. But a wooden plank that you've sawn in half can't be put back together. Other important kinds of changes occur that cannot be reversed. These are not physical changes, but changes that cause the substances themselves to change. In this investigation you'll **observe** and **compare** different kinds of changes.

Materials

- lab apron
- plastic knife
- apple
- paper towel
- safety goggles
- clear plastic cups
- baking soda
- water
- dropper
- vinegar

Activity Procedure

1. **CAUTION** **Put on your lab apron.** Use the plastic knife to cut the apple in half. Place the halves of the apple, cut side up, on a paper towel. Check on the apple halves several times during the activity. **Observe** any changes that take place. (Picture A)

Picture A

Picture B

2 **CAUTION** Put on your safety goggles. Put some baking soda in a cup, and add a few drops of water to it. **Observe** and **record** any changes that take place. (Picture B)

3 Repeat Step 2, but this time add a few drops of vinegar instead of water. **Record** your observations. **Interpret the data** to **compare** the results of these two **experiments** on baking soda.

Draw Conclusions

1. What change did you **observe** in the apple halves? What do you **infer** caused this change? Do you think this change can be reversed?

2. **Compare** the results of adding water to baking soda with the results of adding vinegar instead. What differences did you **observe**? Was anything new formed?

3. **Scientists at Work** Scientists use **observations** and **comparisons** to make inferences. **Interpret your data** from this investigation to **infer** which of the changes you observed were not physical changes. What did you **observe** that might be clues to a change that is not physical?

Investigate Further With a partner, write a list of other changes that occur to matter. **Compare** lists with your classmates, and **classify** your changes as physical or chemical.

Process Skill Tip

Sometimes you need to **interpret data** that is not in the form of numbers. To do this, carefully review all the observations and facts that you can, and then stop to think about how they can be explained.

E51

Chemical Reactions

Chemical Changes and Properties

FIND OUT

- how to tell a chemical change from a physical change

- about different kinds of chemical reactions

- how some chemical changes can be prevented

VOCABULARY

chemical property
combustibility
reactivity
stability

An egg that is cracked open has gone through an irreversible physical change. You can't put the egg back into the shell. If the egg is cooked in a skillet, the egg white and yolk change from liquid to solid, another irreversible change. But this kind of change is different—the egg white has changed color. This is one sign that the egg has gone through a *chemical change*. New substances have been formed, and although the same atoms are still present, they have been rearranged into a different structure.

Most chemical changes either require energy or release energy. When an egg becomes a solid, the change uses energy in the form of heat. When coal burns, forming carbon dioxide, the chemical change releases energy in two forms—heat and light.

People have found ways to use the energy released during a chemical change. Much of the energy used in

Substances formed in chemical changes often have properties that differ from those of the original substances. For example, water can be used to put out fires. But it's formed from molecules of hydrogen—an explosive gas—and oxygen—which supports burning. ▶

◄ **When a candle is burning, its wick and some of its wax go through a chemical change. The rest of the wax goes through a physical change and melts.**

everyday life comes from burning substances such as wood, oil, coal, gasoline, and natural gas. The chemical changes in the burning produce energy that is used to heat homes, generate electricity, power vehicles, and cook food.

The absorption or release of heat is one sign of a chemical change, but it can also be misleading. Changes of state, which are physical changes, also absorb or release heat. Better evidence of chemical change includes the production of light, sound, smoke, or a new color or smell. These signs can help you identify a chemical change. However, the true test is whether or not a new substance is formed.

The chemical changes that a substance can go through depend on its **chemical properties**. These properties describe the ability of a substance to react with other materials and form new substances. The ability of coal to burn, for example, is one of its chemical properties. The actual process of burning is a chemical change.

The ability to burn is called **combustibility**. Wood, paper, charcoal, and other wood products are highly combustible. Lignite, a type of coal, has such a high combustibility that it can burst into flames without being ignited. Lignite has to be stored and transported very carefully.

When a substance burns, its atoms or molecules chemically combine with molecules of oxygen. The substances produced are made up of the same atoms as the original substances, but the atoms are rearranged. The original molecules break apart, and their atoms combine with others to form new molecules and compounds. For example, methane is a combustible gas made up of carbon and hydrogen atoms. When it burns, its atoms separate and combine with oxygen atoms. Two new substances are formed—water (H_2O) and carbon dioxide (CO_2).

Methane is reactive with oxygen. **Reactivity** is the ability of a substance to go through a chemical change. The elements in the first column of the periodic table are very reactive metals. They can explode when exposed to water vapor and oxygen in the air.

Other substances—such as the noble gases, in the far right column of the periodic table—have stability. Substances with **stability** do not go through chemical changes very easily. In fact, they rarely react with other substances.

✔ **How does a chemical change differ from a physical change?**

▲ One of the signs of a chemical change is the production of a gas. When baking soda and vinegar react, carbon dioxide, a gas, is produced.

▲ When hydrochloric acid is added to a solution of a cobalt salt, the color change of the solution indicates that a chemical change is taking place.

Types of Reactions

The chemical changes you've read about in which substances burn are examples of combustion reactions. In *combustion reactions* a substance combines with oxygen. The reaction produces heat and often light. When sulfur is burned, the reaction gives off heat and light as a blue flame. The sulfur combines with oxygen to form sulfur dioxide, a colorless gas that smells like rotten eggs.

Substances don't always combine in reactions to form compounds that are more complex. In a *decomposition reaction*, a substance is broken down into simpler substances. For example, an electric current passed through water causes the water to go through a decomposition reaction that produces hydrogen and oxygen.

Ionic compounds can go through *double replacement reactions,* in which they exchange ions with each other. Reactions between acids and bases are examples of double replacement reactions. When hydrogen chloride and sodium hydroxide react, for example, the chloride ions change places with the hydroxide ions. The sodium and chloride ions combine to make sodium chloride. The hydrogen and hydroxide ions combine to make water.

✔ **How do decomposition reactions differ from combustion reactions?**

THE INSIDE STORY

Chemical changes in which the atoms of a substance lose electrons are called *oxidation reactions*. When a substance burns and combines with oxygen, its atoms lose electrons. So combustion reactions are examples of very fast oxidation reactions. Not all oxidation reactions involve combustion or oxygen.

Metallic elements often go through oxidation reactions. Rust and tarnish are results you can see of the slow oxidation of metals.

▲ When iron rusts, oxygen reacts with iron to produce iron oxide. Iron atoms lose electrons to oxygen atoms.

Types of Reactions

Combustion

Decomposition

Double Replacement

▲ When they burn, compounds made of metals from Column 2 of the periodic table produce bright colors. Fireworks provide spectacular displays of the combustion reactions of these compounds.

▲ Nitrogen dioxide (NO_2) is a brown gas. If it's heated above 140°C (284°F), it decomposes into the colorless gases nitrogen monoxide (NO) and oxygen (O_2). If those two gases cool, they form nitrogen dioxide again.

▲ Sodium chromate and silver nitrate react in a double replacement reaction. The products are sodium nitrate and silver chromate, a bright reddish-pink compound. The same color is also found in rubies, where it is caused by traces of chromium.

◄ An oxidation reaction produces the tarnish on silver. The tarnish is silver sulfide, a dark solid. It is formed when silver reacts with hydrogen sulfide in the air. The silver atoms lose electrons to sulfur atoms.

When copper reacts with oxygen, it turns green. In the oxidation reaction, copper atoms lose electrons and form either copper sulfate or copper chloride. ▼

Preventing Chemical Change

The original Declaration of Independence is stored in pure helium because helium is a noble gas. As such, it does not react with many other substances. The helium surrounding the Declaration protects it from substances such as oxygen, which might react with it and damage it. This is just one way in which knowing about reactions has helped people prevent unwanted chemical changes.

Other preservation methods are used for books and in museums. Modern books are printed on paper in which acids have been neutralized with bases. Because of that, the pages won't gradually crumble from reactions with the acids. Many museums now display objects under dim light so that chemical changes that use light energy will not take place.

Chemical changes can corrode, or wear away, metals used in industry and construction. To prevent the metals from being weakened, they are often covered with a layer of another substance. Galvanized steel, for example, has a thin coating of zinc, a metal that's more reactive than steel. By reacting itself, the zinc prevents corrosive materials from reacting with the steel. Steel is sometimes covered with a thin layer of chromium, an unreactive metal. This seals the steel against corrosive chemicals.

Chemical changes can spoil food. The reactions can involve compounds in the air or decomposers such as bacteria. Refrigerating or freezing foods removes heat energy and therefore slows down the chemical changes. Preservatives added to food prevent the growth of bacteria and the chemical reactions they might cause. Oxidation reactions can spoil foods, too. Antioxidants—chemicals that prevent oxidation—are used to keep food fresh. Some herbs, such as sage, clove, and rosemary, contain natural antioxidants and help protect foods at the same time as they enrich their flavor.

Antioxidant chemicals are also added to plastics to prevent breakdown or changes in color. They are added to oil and gasoline to prevent the corrosion of engine parts.

✔ **How does freezing prevent food from spoiling?**

◄ This painter is using a physical change—covering the fence with paint—to protect the iron. Otherwise water and oxygen would react with the iron and cause rust.

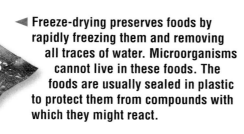

◄ Freeze-drying preserves foods by rapidly freezing them and removing all traces of water. Microorganisms cannot live in these foods. The foods are usually sealed in plastic to protect them from compounds with which they might react.

Summary

The chemical properties of a substance determine how easily it goes through a chemical change. Stable substances do not react easily, and reactive substances do. In a chemical change, atoms and molecules are rearranged to form other substances with different properties. Combustion, decomposition, and double replacement reactions are common chemical reactions. Some chemical changes are sources of energy people can use. Others are harmful and are often prevented by physical or chemical methods.

Review

1. What are four clues that a chemical change has taken place?

2. In what kind of reaction does a compound break down into simpler substances?

3. How are some metals protected from chemical change?

4. **Critical Thinking** Does removing oxygen always prevent an oxidation reaction? Explain.

5. **Test Prep** Food is protected from chemical change by —
   A painting it
   B coating it with a metal
   C freezing it
   D storing it in oxygen gas

LINKS

MATH LINK

Conservation of Mass During a chemical reaction, mass is neither made nor destroyed. If 36 g of water are formed in a reaction using 4 g of hydrogen, how much oxygen is used?

WRITING LINK

Informative Writing—Report The airship *Hindenburg* could fly because a physical property of hydrogen made it buoyant in air. But as a result of a chemical property of hydrogen, the *Hindenburg* met with disaster. Find out about the *Hindenburg*. Then write a news article about the disaster as if you were a reporter who was there for your school paper.

SOCIAL STUDIES LINK

Energy Combustion reactions are used to supply most of the electricity generated in the United States. Find out what kind of combustion reaction is used to supply electricity to your home.

TECHNOLOGY LINK

Learn more about chemical properties and molecules by visiting the National Museum of American History Internet site.
www.si.edu/harcourt/science

  Smithsonian Institution®

What Are Mixtures, and How Can They Be Changed?

In this lesson, you can . . .

INVESTIGATE how to make and separate mixtures.

LEARN ABOUT the properties of mixtures and solutions.

LINK to math, writing, social studies, and technology.

Seashells and sand are some of the ingredients of a "beach mixture." ▽

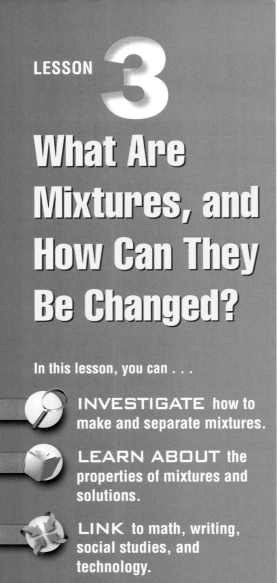

INVESTIGATE

Making and Separating Mixtures

Activity Purpose At the end of the school week, your backpack may seem to be stuffed with dozens of different things all jumbled together. But no matter how mixed up the items are, you should be able to separate them completely. Maybe you won't find your wallet right away. Maybe the cap to a pen is hidden far from the pen itself. Even so, the jumble in your backpack is the result of physical changes. The items themselves haven't changed. So in this case, you'll be able to get everything back to the way it started out. In this investigation you'll **experiment** to find physical processes that reverse some physical changes.

Materials

- cups
- water
- salt
- spoon
- fine sand
- paper towels
- iron filings
- magnet
- gravel
- sieve
- coffee filters

Activity Procedure

1 Add a spoonful of salt to a cup of warm water, and stir. **Observe** what happens to the salt. **Hypothesize** how you might return the salt to its original state by using the materials you have.

2 Add a spoonful of sand to a second cup of water, and stir. **Observe** what happens to the sand. **Hypothesize** how you might return the sand to its original state by using the materials you have. **Experiment** to test your hypothesis. (Picture A)

Picture A

Picture B

3 Mix some dry salt and iron filings together. Pour the mixture out onto a paper towel. **Hypothesize** how you might use the magnet to separate the substances. **Experiment** to test your hypothesis. (Picture B)

4 Now mix dry salt, sand, iron filings, and gravel together. Using the materials at hand, plan and conduct an **experiment** to separate the four substances.

Draw Conclusions

1. What did you **infer** about the salt mixed with water? How could you return the salt to its original state?

2. What was your **hypothesis** about separating the sand and water? Did you have to change or add to your hypothesis?

3. **Scientists at Work** Scientists often need to separate substances that are produced in reactions. They use physical methods of separation so that the substances won't be changed. What steps did you include in your **experiment** (Step 4) to separate the mixture of the four substances?

Investigate Further Repeat Step 4 of the activity, but add a spoonful or two of the dry mixture to a cup of water and stir. Plan and conduct an **experiment** to separate the substances from the wet mixture.

Process Skill Tip

When you **experiment** to test a hypothesis, make sure the experiment is carefully designed and controlled to test only what you want.

LEARN ABOUT

Matter in Mixtures

Mixtures

FIND OUT

• how mixtures are made

• how to separate mixtures

• about different kinds of mixtures and solutions

VOCABULARY

mixture
solution
suspension
colloid

A material made of only one element or compound is called a *pure substance*. Wherever and whenever a pure substance is found, its composition is exactly the same. The chemical properties and many of the physical properties of a pure substance never vary.

Most materials in nature are not pure substances. Instead, they are **mixtures**—combinations of two or more pure substances that are not chemically combined with each other. Unlike the parts of compounds, the parts of mixtures do not always have to be in the same proportions. And however well the substances in a mixture are blended, they remain separate molecules and do not form new compounds. Because of this, the chemical properties of a mixture depend on the properties of the substances it contains. If you mix sugar and water, for example, the mixture will be a sweet-tasting liquid.

Some mixtures are easy to identify because you can see their individual substances. On a beach, for example, you might see sand, pebbles, and seashells all mixed together. You can tell that this mixture isn't uniform, or the same throughout. One part of the beach may have more shells or pebbles than another.

If you look closely at a piece of granite, you'll see that it is also a mixture. It's made up of grains of quartz, feldspar, and mica. These minerals aren't chemically bonded together. If you break a piece of granite into tiny bits, each will be just one kind of mineral. And the mixture isn't uniform. One piece of granite may have more feldspar, for example, than another piece of granite.

▶ When oranges and sugar are used to make marmalade, some of their physical properties change. The chemical properties of the ingredients do not change.

The pieces of cereal that make up this granola mixture are easy to identify because none of their physical properties have changed. ▶

✔ **How does a mixture differ from a compound?**

Light oil from a spill floats on the ocean because oil has a lower density than sea water. If the spill is contained, the oil will evaporate into the air.

Separating Mixtures

Because substances do not go through chemical changes in a mixture, they can be separated from each other by physical methods. The methods work because of the physical properties of the substances in the mixture.

When the substances in a mixture have different densities, they may separate on their own. The raisins in breakfast cereal, for example, are denser than the cereal flakes. During shipping, the raisins may settle to the bottom of the box. Similarly, the oil and vinegar in salad dressing will separate so that a layer of the less dense oil floats on a layer of vinegar.

Scientists use devices to separate substances of different densities. One such device spins a container filled with a liquid mixture at very high speeds. The spinning pushes the denser parts of the mixture to the bottom. Biologists use devices like this to separate blood cells from the liquid parts of blood.

A mixture made up of a solid and a liquid can be separated by heating it. The process is called *distillation*. The liquid is changed to a gas, which can be collected and changed back to its liquid state. The solid remains a solid.

Heat can also be used to separate a mixture of two liquids. The temperature of the mixture is raised to the lower of the two boiling points of the liquids. All of one substance changes to a gas while the other substance remains a liquid.

Mixtures can be separated physically, but sometimes it's more convenient to use a chemical process. For example, air is a gas mixture. Chemical reactions can collect nitrogen from air by removing the other gases. Air is first passed through a base, which combines with carbon dioxide. The remaining mixture is passed through an acid, which combines with water vapor. Finally, the gas mixture is passed over heated copper, which combines with oxygen. The gas that's left is almost pure nitrogen.

✔ **Why can mixtures be separated by physical methods?**

Sifting separates materials by size. It's the same process—but on a larger scale—as using filter paper to separate tiny particles from a liquid. Archaeologists use sieves or screens to separate dirt from the objects they have dug from the ground. ▼

A magnet can separate iron filings from a dry mixture. This method is used in large recycling centers. A very powerful electromagnet separates all of the iron and steel from discarded metal objects.

Solutions

Substances are not always spread evenly throughout a mixture. Different parts of the mixture may have different amounts of each substance. That's what you discover from a box of breakfast cereal when most of the raisins have settled to the bottom.

In certain mixtures, however, the particles of each substance *are* mixed evenly. These mixtures are called **solutions**. Any part of a solution is identical to any other part of it. Solutions can be made up of any combination of solids, liquids, and gases.

In the most familiar kind of solution, a solid is dissolved in a liquid. An example is sugar dissolved in water. The solid that is dissolved, the sugar, is called the *solute*. The liquid in which it is dissolved, the water, is called the *solvent*.

Some liquid solutions are made from two or more liquids. Rubbing alcohol is a solution of isopropyl alcohol and water. In this solution there is more water than alcohol, so the water is considered the solvent.

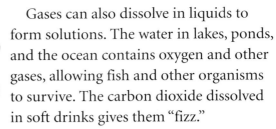

Gases can also dissolve in liquids to form solutions. The water in lakes, ponds, and the ocean contains oxygen and other gases, allowing fish and other organisms to survive. The carbon dioxide dissolved in soft drinks gives them "fizz."

Solutions aren't always liquids. A solution made of two or more gases is a gas itself. The most familiar solution of gases is air. Dry air is about 78 percent nitrogen, 21 percent oxygen, and 1 percent other gases.

Solids can also form solutions. A solid solution made up of a metal combined with another substance is called an *alloy*. Many of the materials commonly called metals are really alloys.

The chemical properties of metals do not change when they form an alloy, but the physical properties do. When people first mixed copper and tin, they discovered a material much stronger than either of the metals. This alloy— bronze—had such a great effect on civilization that the period of its first use is called the Bronze Age. Metals are mixed in different combinations to produce alloys with useful properties.

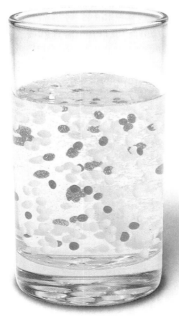

◄ The bubbles in a soft drink are carbon dioxide gas leaving the solution. Shaking or heating can speed up the release of gas from a liquid solution. That's why it isn't a good idea to open a can of soda right after it has been shaken.

Copper sulfate is a compound that exists as blue crystals. When it is mixed with water, it dissolves to form a solution. One sign of this is the uniform color throughout the mixture.

This figure of an animal is made of pewter. Pewter is an alloy that can be easily worked and highly polished. Early alloys of pewter contained lead, but now antimony is used instead. ▶

Brass is an attractive alloy with many uses. Brass that has about 70% copper is bright yellow. It is often used for decorative items around the home. ▲

Some alloys are very strong, some have low melting points, and some resist corrosion. In many cases, pure metals are not as useful as their alloys. Steel, for example, is made of iron mixed with small amounts of carbon and manganese. It has many of the properties of iron but is much, much stronger.

Gold and silver alloys are also useful. Gold is the most malleable and ductile metal. It has a beautiful luster and color and doesn't combine easily with other substances. Silver is the shiniest metal—it reflects more light than any other. Pure forms of both metals are too soft for use in most jewelry. In alloys with metals such as copper, however, gold and silver become much stronger and still have their desirable properties.

✔ Is a mixture always a solution? Is a solution always a mixture? Explain.

◀ Bronze has been used for more than 5000 years. It is a much harder material than the copper and tin that it's made of. Bronze is a solution of those two metals.

Common Alloys		
Name of Alloy	Main Substances by Percents	Properties of Alloy
Brass	70% copper 30% zinc	bright yellow, easy to work
Bronze	80% copper 20% tin	hard, resists corrosion
Pewter	90% tin 7% antimony 3% copper	silver-colored, high luster
Steel	96% iron 1% carbon 3% manganese	much stronger than iron
Stainless steel	70% iron 25% chromium 5% nickel	strong, will not corrode

Other Mixtures

Many of the mixtures you're familiar with are clear liquids. Examples are filtered fruit juices, glass cleaner, and soda water. Other mixtures, such as orange juice and chocolate milk, are not clear. If you let these liquid mixtures sit, solids will gradually settle to the bottom.

Mixtures such as orange juice and chocolate milk are called suspensions. A **suspension** is a mixture that contains particles that are large enough to be seen. The particles can be separated from the mixture by using filter paper. Water and soil form a suspension when they are mixed. The soil particles can be filtered out of the mixture or, if left alone, will slowly settle out of the mixture.

When the chocolate powder settles to the bottom of a container of milk, regular milk is left. It seems to be uniform in color and consistency, and it will pass unchanged through filter paper. But milk isn't a solution. It contains particles that are so tiny that they do not settle out of the liquid. Milk, house paint, and dish-washing liquid are all colloids. **Colloids** are suspensions that aren't easily filtered, because of the small size of their particles. Colloids differ from suspensions only in the size of their particles.

There's an easy way to tell whether or not a mixture is a colloid. When a beam of light is passed through a colloid, its path is clearly visible. You may have noticed the beams of light from car headlights in fog. You can see the path of the light because the particles in the fog—a colloid—scatter light.

✔ **What can you tell about a medicine that has directions to shake before using?**

Fog is a colloid of liquid water droplets in a gas, the air. On cold mornings water vapor in very humid air condenses into drops that are so tiny, they do not fall to the ground. ▼

Water in the Ganges River in India travels almost 2500 km (about 1550 mi) before reaching the ocean. Along the way the river picks up a lot of sediment, forming a suspension. In the ocean the sediment settles to the bottom. ▶

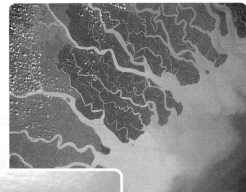

▲ Ocean water can be a mix of mixtures. Around this wreck are three kinds of mixtures—a solution of gases and compounds, a colloid of very fine undissolved particles, and a suspension. The suspension includes matter that provides food for small animals, such as the barnacles that have attached themselves to the rusty hull.

Summary

A mixture is made up of two or more substances that are not chemically combined. The substances can be separated by physical methods. A solution is a combination of gases, liquids, or solids that are spread evenly throughout. Alloys are solid solutions of metals. Suspensions and colloids are mixtures in which particles are suspended but not dissolved.

Review

1. What is the difference between a compound and a mixture?

2. What physical property of substances makes it possible to separate a mixture by spinning it at high speeds?

3. Give an example of a solid dissolved in another solid.

4. **Critical Thinking** How could you use a difference in melting points (freezing points) to separate a solution of two liquids?

5. **Test Prep** Mixtures that are not evenly mixed but cannot easily be separated by filtering are —

   A alloys

   B suspensions

   C colloids

   D solutions

LINKS

MATH LINK

Percent Solutions are sometimes described by using percents. Suppose that 500 mL of rubbing alcohol contains 350 mL of isopropyl alcohol. What percent of the solution is isopropyl alcohol?

WRITING LINK

Narrative Writing—Story A pun is a play on words, using the different meanings of words that look or sound alike. Write a "nonsense" paragraph for your teacher in which you use words such as *solution, suspension, state,* and *compound* in puns.

SOCIAL STUDIES LINK

Gold Rush In the mid-1800s, gold was discovered in several parts of the United States. The gold was in the form of small nuggets, and miners collected it by *panning.* Research one of the gold rushes of the 1800s. Find out how panning uses a difference in density to separate a mixture of gold and gravel.

TECHNOLOGY LINK

Visit the Harcourt Learning Site for related links, activities, and resources. **www.harcourtschool.com**

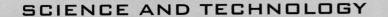
SMART PAPER

Scientists are developing a type of electronic paper that can be reused millions of times.

What is smart paper?

Smart paper is not the paper you use every day. It's an electronic display that you can write on. Like paper, it's lightweight and cheap. But, unlike paper, it can be used over and over millions of times.

How does smart paper work?

Smart paper looks like a rubbery, clear sheet on a plastic backing. The backing is actually made of silicon rubber. The paper itself is made of thousands of tiny plastic balls, each about the size of a pinpoint. The balls are white on one side and black on the other, and each one sits in its own oil-filled pit in the backing, where it can float and turn.

Before you begin to write, you give the paper an electric charge, making the balls all point in one direction. This makes the sheet a solid black, white, or gray. Then, as you write, images form as the charge from the pencil makes the plastic balls move. On a white sheet, dark letters will form everywhere the pencil touches the sheet. The display holds the image for as long as you want it.

Closeup of smart paper

The inventor of smart paper near another revolutionary breakthrough in communications—the Gutenberg Bible—the first book in the western world printed with a movable type press

Why is smart paper a good idea?

Smart paper might become a cheap alternative to today's electronic displays. In the future, the smart-paper technology might be used on laptop and handheld computers. They would be able to run with much less power than today's computers.

Smart paper could also be used as pages in electronic books. The pages of these books would be smart-paper displays assembled like the pages of any book today. The batteries and the electronics needed to control the display pages would be built into the spine of the book.

THINK ABOUT IT

1. Why might smart paper be better than regular paper?

2. What might be a drawback of smart paper?

 WEB LINK:
For Science and Technology updates, visit The Learning Site.
www.harcourtschool.com

Careers   Chemical Engineer

What They Do
Chemical engineers design and test methods and systems for the mass production of chemicals. They also develop products such as plastics, metals, detergents, foods, and medicines from these materials.

Education and Training Chemical engineers must have a background in chemistry, physics, and mathematics. They must inspect factories to correct problems in the chemical production process. Chemical engineers must have at least a bachelor's degree in chemical engineering.

James Andrew Harris
NUCLEAR CHEMIST

James Andrew Harris has had a distinguished career in nuclear chemistry. Among his achievements was helping to discover two new elements. He was part of a research team that discovered element 104, rutherfordium, in 1969. The team also discovered element 105, dubnium (which has also been called hahnium), in 1970.

Rutherfordium and Dubnium are elements that do not occur in nature. Elements are the basic building blocks of all matter. There are now 114 known elements, but only the first 92 occur naturally. Those after element 92 (uranium) are called the transuranic elements. They were all made in laboratories by producing nuclear reactions among existing elements. The transuranic elements are fairly unstable, which means that they exist for only a short time before they break down.

Harris's research group made rutherfordium by bombarding the element californium for hundreds of hours with carbon atoms. They made dubnium by bombarding californium with nitrogen ions.

James Andrew Harris grew up in Texas and earned a bachelor's degree in chemistry from Houston-Tillotson College in 1953. He joined the Lawrence Berkeley Laboratory at the University of California at

James Andrew Harris (second from the left) with his team

Berkeley in 1960, after working for several years at a smaller laboratory. A few years after participating in the discovery of the two superheavy elements, he was promoted to head of the Engineering and Technical Services Division of the Lawrence Berkeley Laboratory.

Although most of those with whom he works have Ph.D.'s, James Andrew Harris has proved that it is possible to succeed at the highest levels of scientific research with a bachelor's degree—along with hard work and determination.

THINK ABOUT IT

1. What was James Andrew Harris's greatest accomplishment?
2. What procedure did the team use to make their discoveries?

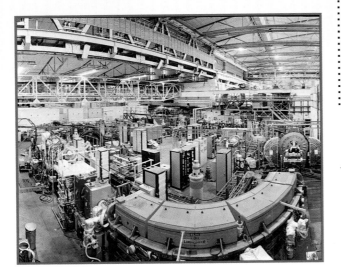

◄ **Particle accelerators are important in the production of transuranic elements.**

Floating Eggs

How can you change the density of a substance?

Materials

- plastic cup half-full of water
- 1 fresh egg in shell, uncooked
- table salt
- water
- spoon

Procedure

❶ Carefully place the egg in the cup of water, and observe whether or not it floats.

❷ Remove the egg, and stir several spoonfuls of salt into the water.

❸ Carefully replace the egg in the water, and observe whether or not it floats.

Draw Conclusions

Why did the egg sink to the bottom of the cup at first? Did the egg ever float? If so, when and why? What physical property of the water changed during this experiment?

Splitting Water

How can you break down water into its two substances?

Materials

- knife
- 2 copper wires, each about 30 cm (1 ft) long
- 2 metal paper clips
- 2 pieces of lead (actually graphite) from a mechanical pencil, each about 7.5 cm (3 in.) long
- clear plastic cup of water
- electrical or duct tape
- 9-volt battery

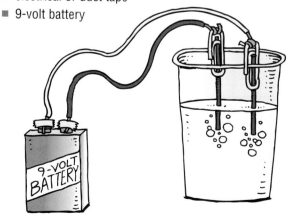

Procedure

❶ Have an adult use the knife to remove about 3.5 cm (1.5 in.) of insulation from both ends of the wires.

❷ Attach a paper clip to one end of each wire.

❸ Use the paper clips to hold the pencil lead pieces to the inside of the cup of water. Let the pieces extend into the water, as shown.

❹ Tape the other end of each wire to one of the electrodes on the battery. Don't let the wires touch each other.

Draw Conclusions

What happened after you attached the wires to the electrodes? What do you think caused this?

Chapter 2 Review and Test Preparation

Vocabulary Review

Use the terms below to complete the sentences. The page numbers in ( ) tell you where to look in the chapter if you need help.

physical property (E46)

texture (E47)

malleability (E47)

ductility (E47)

density (E47)

buoyancy (E47)

chemical property (E53)

combustibility (E53)

reactivity (E53)

stability (E53)

mixture (E60)

solution (E62)

suspension (E64)

colloid (E64)

1. The color of a substance is a ____.

2. ____ is the ability of a substance to be drawn into wires.

3. A substance with a high ____ will undergo chemical changes easily.

4. The ____ of a substance, its ability to float or rise in another substance, is determined in part by the ____.

5. The particles in a ____ are larger than those in a ____.

6. The feel of the surface of a substance is a physical property called ____.

7. The ability of a substance to be bent and shaped is called ____.

8. A characteristic such as reactivity or combustibility is a ____.

9. Substances that burn easily have a high ____.

10. A ____ is a combination of two or more pure substances that do not combine chemically.

11. A mixture in which the substances are mixed evenly throughout is a ____.

12. The property of not going through chemical changes and not reacting easily with other substances is called ____.

Connect Concepts

Complete the table with terms from the Word Bank.

oxidation   evaporation   reactivity

melting point   smell   decomposition reaction

erosion   stability

Physical Property	Chemical Property	Physical Change	Chemical Change
13. _____	15. _____	17. _____	19. _____
14. _____	16. _____	18. _____	20. _____

Check Understanding

Write the letter of the best choice.

21. Malleability and ductility are —
    A alloys
    B substances
    C physical properties
    D chemical properties

22. Marble has a greater density than water, so —
    F marble will sink in water
    G marble will change states in water
    H marble will float in water
    J marble has a high buoyancy

23. The true test of a chemical change is the formation of a new —
    A property   C substance
    B shape   D element

24. The reaction that happens when iron rusts is an example of —
    F oxidation
    G decomposition
    H combustion
    J double replacement

25. When sugar dissolves in water, water is the solvent and sugar is the —
    A suspension
    B chemical
    C colloid
    D solute

26. An alloy is a —
    F compound
    G solution
    H metal
    J base

Critical Thinking

27. A statue has been in the same location for 100 years and has been eroded gradually by the wind and rain. During the last 10 years, however, the damage seems to have become greater. What might explain this?

28. A container holds a mixture of a mystery substance and a plastic that is buoyant in oil. The container is spun very fast. Particles of the plastic are forced to the bottom. Is the mystery substance buoyant in oil? Explain.

Process Skills Review

29. How can you **measure** the volume of an irregularly shaped object?

30. How would you **experiment** to **compare** the boiling points of two substances?

31. **Interpret the data** in the table below to determine which liquids are colloids.

Comparing Liquids

Sample	Boiling Temp.	Freezing Temp.	Light Beam Visible
Liquid A	79°C	⁻3°C	not visible
Liquid B	100°C	0°C	visible
Liquid C	40°C	3°C	visible
Liquid D	140°C	23°C	not visible

Performance Assessment

Unmixing Mixtures

Pick three substances from those provided by your teacher, and make a mixture of them. Describe the properties of your mixture and explain which substance is responsible for each property. Then write the steps you would follow to separate the mixture.

Chapter 3

Energy

What is energy? *Energy* is usually defined as the "ability to do work." Whenever work is done, however, something moves or changes. So you might say that energy is the ability to make something change.

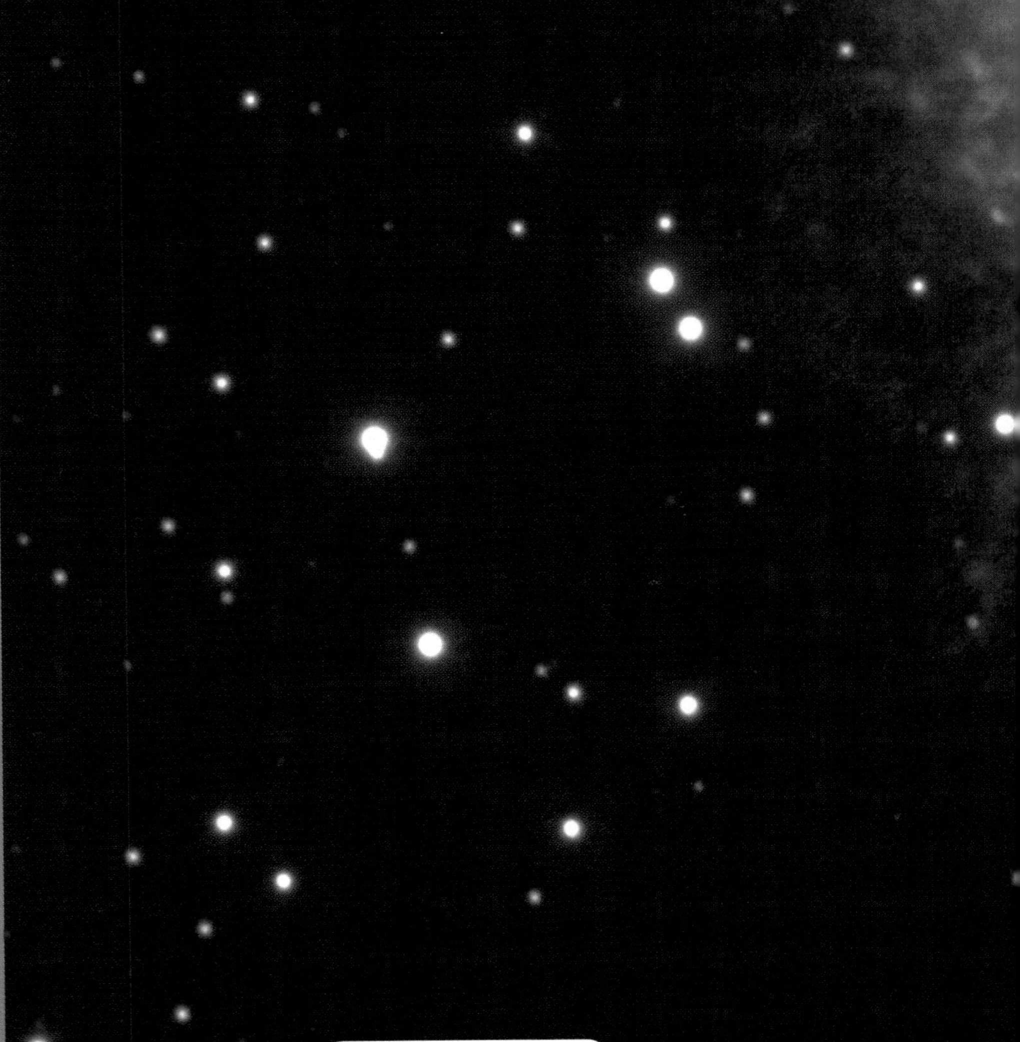

Vocabulary Preview

energy
law of conservation of energy
kinetic energy
potential energy
thermal energy
heat
conduction
convection
radiation
magnet
electricity
electric energy
circuit
electromagnet
chemical energy
nuclear energy
fission

FAST FACT

The energy that a supernova releases in a single minute is about as much as our sun would release in 9 billion years.

Crab Nebula

How Are Thermal Energy and Heat Related?

In this lesson, you can . . .

INVESTIGATE the change of potential energy to kinetic energy.

LEARN ABOUT thermal energy and its transfer.

LINK to math, writing, language arts, and technology.

Increasing the temperature of glass speeds up the movement of its particles. When there is enough thermal energy in a piece of glass, the particles can move past each other and the glass can be shaped. ▽

INVESTIGATE

Changing Energy

Activity Purpose   A ball can be still on a table, but if you nudge it over the edge, it will fall to the floor, traveling faster and faster as it falls. The nudge you give the ball is not strong enough to make it fall as fast as it does, so where does the energy come from? In this investigation you will explore the relationship between stored energy and energy of movement.

Materials
- board (about 1 m long)
- 5 books of about equal thickness
- meterstick
- cart

Activity Procedure

1 Work with a partner. Choose a smooth area of the floor for the activity. Place the board on the floor, and put a book under one end. Make sure that there is a clear space on the floor at least 1 m long extending from the lower end of the board.

2 Lay the meterstick beside the path the cart will take after it has rolled down the board.

Comparing Height and Distance Traveled

Number of Books	Height	Distance Traveled	Speed
1			
2			
3			
4			
5			

Picture A

3 **Measure** and **record** the height of the board above the floor. Hold the cart so that its back wheels are at the top of the board, and let it go. **Measure** and **record** the distance the cart travels from the lower end of the board along the floor. Also record the relative speed (slow, medium, or fast). (Picture A)

4 Repeat Step 3 using a different number of books with each trial to prop up the higher end of the board at different heights. **Compare** the measurements you **record.**

Draw Conclusions

1. From the **data** you **collected**, what can you **infer** about the relationship between the height of the books under the board and the distance the cart traveled along the floor?

2. What did you **observe** about the speed of the cart when it traveled the greatest distance and the speed of the cart when it traveled the least distance along the floor? What does this tell you about the relationship between the height of the starting position and the speed that the cart reached after it traveled down the board?

3. **Scientists at Work** When scientists want to **make comparisons** in an experiment, they make sure that the only variables that change are those that they want to change. What **variables** did you **control** in this investigation? What variables did you change?

Investigate Further Repeat the investigation with a block placed on the floor at the end of the board. **Measure** and **record** the distances that the cart pushes the block. It takes energy to push the block. What can you **infer** about the height of the starting position of the cart and the energy the cart has when it reaches the lower end of the board?

Energy

Potential Energy and Kinetic Energy

FIND OUT

- how potential energy and kinetic energy are related
- how thermal energy moves between substances

VOCABULARY

energy
law of conservation of
    energy
kinetic energy
potential energy
thermal energy
heat
conduction
convection
radiation

In the investigation you found that the higher the starting point of a moving object, the greater its speed when it reaches the ground. It takes energy to increase speed. **Energy** is the ability to cause changes in matter. An object that has energy can apply a force over a distance.

Energy is present all around us in many forms. Energy can change from one form to another. When you turn on a lamp, electric energy changes to light energy. When energy changes from one form to another, the amount of energy does not change. The **law of conservation of energy** states that the total amount of energy in a system is always the same—energy cannot be created or destroyed.

Moving objects have kinetic energy. **Kinetic energy**, or the energy of motion, has the ability to exert a force on matter that comes into contact with it. In Investigate Further, the rolling cart pushed the block at the end of the ramp. The faster an object is moving, the greater is its kinetic energy, so the greater is the force it can exert. You found that the faster the cart traveled, the farther it pushed the block.

Where does a moving object get its energy? The cart in the investigation got its energy from being lifted to the top of the ramp. This form of energy is called potential energy. **Potential energy** is energy that is due to the position or condition of an object. The potential energy in the cart when it was at the top of the ramp was due to its height above the floor. The energy used to lift it against the force of gravity was "stored" in the cart. When you released the cart, the potential energy changed to kinetic energy. The greater the elevation of the cart, the greater its potential energy. A larger amount of potential energy can be converted to a larger amount of kinetic energy.

As an object falls, its height decreases, so its potential energy also decreases. The force of gravity acting on the object causes its speed to increase, so its kinetic energy also increases. During the fall, the potential energy of the object changes to kinetic energy.

Kinetic energy can also change to potential energy. The speed of a ball that is tossed up into the air decreases as the ball gets higher. Its kinetic energy decreases. But the potential energy of the ball increases as it gets higher. At the point at which the ball stops moving, its

Chemical energy from food is stored as potential energy in the runner's body. In the race, it will be changed to kinetic energy. ▼

▲ The drops of water on the leaf have potential energy because of their height. As the water drops fall, their potential energy changes to kinetic energy.

potential energy is greatest and it has no kinetic energy. As the ball moves downward, the potential energy decreases as the kinetic energy increases.

The kinetic energy of an object depends on the mass of the object. A bowling ball that hits an object at 20 km/hr (about 12 mi/hr) can cause greater changes than a tennis ball hitting an object at the same speed. If the bowling ball has greater kinetic energy, it must have had greater potential energy, too, because energy cannot be created. So, if two objects have the same elevation, or height, the one with the greater mass has the greater potential energy.

Potential energy occurs in many forms. A battery has potential energy in the form of stored chemical energy. A compressed spring has potential energy, too. The water behind a dam has potential energy—the water at the top has potential energy due to its elevation, while the water at the bottom has potential energy due to pressure. All these kinds of potential energy can change into other forms of energy. The chemical energy in a battery changes to electric energy. As a spring expands, its energy changes to mechanical energy. The energy of the water changes to mechanical energy when the gate of the dam is opened to release the water.

✔ **How are potential energy and kinetic energy shown by a bow and arrow?**

At the top of the slope, the skateboarder's potential energy is at its greatest and he has no kinetic energy. At the bottom of the slope, the skateboarder's kinetic energy is at its greatest and he has no potential energy. At any point on his path, the sum of the skateboarder's potential and kinetic energy is the same. ▼

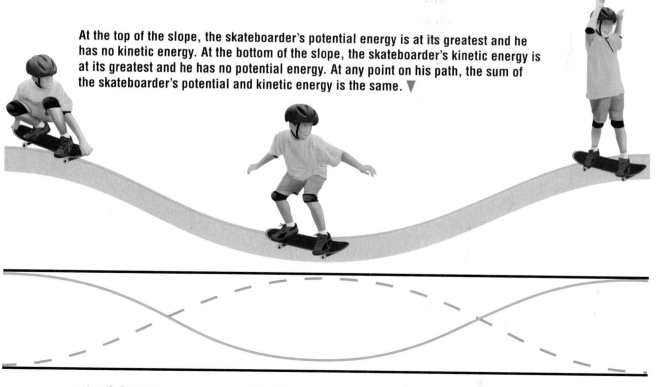

———— potential energy   — — kinetic energy

Thermal Energy and Heat

Kinetic energy is not always visible. The particles that make up a substance are always moving. These particles have kinetic energy because of their movement. The kinetic energy of the moving particles of a substance or object is called **thermal energy**. The more thermal energy an object has, the hotter it is. You have probably noticed that appliances such as computers and televisions get warmer as they run. Some of the energy used by the appliances is changed to thermal energy.

No matter how large or small the amount of water, when enough thermal energy is removed, the particles slow down and form solid ice. ▶

Temperature is a measure of thermal energy. Temperature is the average kinetic energy of the particles in an object. The faster the particles in an object are moving, the higher the temperature of the object is. When two objects have the same temperature, the average kinetic energy of their particles is the same.

Two scales are commonly used to measure temperature. On the Celsius scale, water freezes at 0°C and boils at 100°C. On the Fahrenheit scale, which is often used in the United States, water freezes at 32°F and boils at 212°F.

When objects are in contact, thermal energy moves from the object that has the higher temperature to the object that has the lower temperature. An ice cube in a glass of water melts because thermal energy from the water is transferred to the ice cube, raising its temperature. Thermal energy that is transferred is called **heat**. Heat always travels from hotter to cooler objects. When you touch an object that is colder

than your hand, it may seem as though coldness is moving from it into your hand. In fact, the feeling is caused by the heat flowing out of your hand and into the colder object.

When two objects touch, thermal energy moves between them because the particles in one object collide with, or hit, the particles in the other object. Heat resulting from the collision of particles is called **conduction**.

Conduction works best through solids, especially through materials such as metals. A stove heats food through conduction. The pots that touch the burners are usually made of metal. The metal transfers heat from the burner to the food in the pot. The pot handle is usually made of wood or plastic, which are materials that do not conduct heat very well. Metals are *conductors*, while materials such as wood and plastic are *insulators*.

Thermal energy is often transferred through fluids—liquids and gases—by a process called **convection**. When a liquid or gas is heated, it expands and its density decreases. Cooler, denser fluid moves in under the heated fluid and pushes it upward. The heated fluid moves through parts of the fluid that have a higher density, transferring thermal energy. Much of Earth's weather results from convection currents in the atmosphere.

Conduction and convection rely on matter for the transfer of thermal energy. Another method of transferring thermal energy does not. **Radiation** is the transfer of thermal energy as waves. Although radiation can travel through air, it does not need the air for the transfer of energy. Energy from the sun is transferred by radiation to Earth through space. Radiation is sometimes visible—thermal energy at temperatures above about 500°C (932°F) can change to light energy, another form of radiation.

✔ **What are the three ways heat can be transferred?**

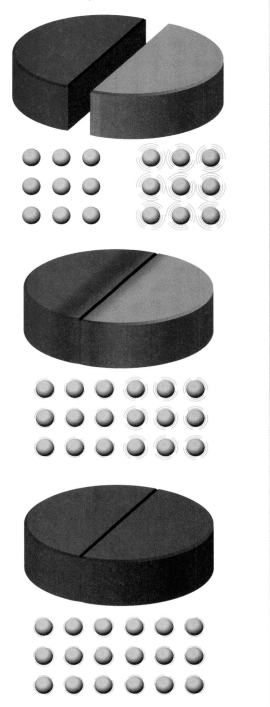

Conduction in Solids

When two objects of different temperatures are in contact, thermal energy moves from the hotter object to the cooler object. Energy from the faster-moving particles is transferred to the slower particles that they contact. The transfer of energy goes on until all the particles in both objects are moving at about the same speed. The thermal energy of each object is the same, so both objects have the same temperature. ▼

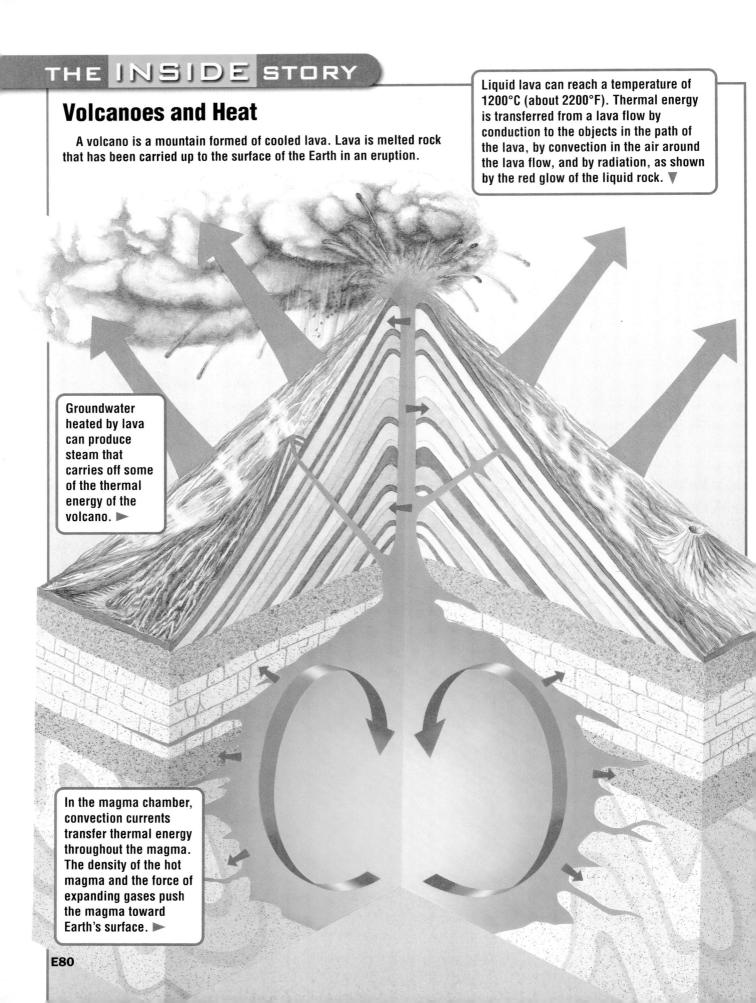

Volcanoes and Heat

A volcano is a mountain formed of cooled lava. Lava is melted rock that has been carried up to the surface of the Earth in an eruption.

Liquid lava can reach a temperature of 1200°C (about 2200°F). Thermal energy is transferred from a lava flow by conduction to the objects in the path of the lava, by convection in the air around the lava flow, and by radiation, as shown by the red glow of the liquid rock. ▼

Groundwater heated by lava can produce steam that carries off some of the thermal energy of the volcano. ▶

In the magma chamber, convection currents transfer thermal energy throughout the magma. The density of the hot magma and the force of expanding gases push the magma toward Earth's surface. ▶

Summary

Energy is the ability to cause changes in matter. Stored energy due to position or condition is called potential energy. It can change to kinetic energy—the energy of motion. The kinetic energy of moving particles of matter is thermal energy. Temperature is a measure of thermal energy. Thermal energy is transferred as heat from objects with a higher temperature to those with a lower temperature through conduction, convection, or radiation.

Review

1. What energy change takes place as a cup falls off a table?

2. What is the difference between a conductor and an insulator?

3. How does heat travel through a fluid?

4. **Critical Thinking** Suppose you put your hand into a bucket of ice water until your hand gets cold. Then you put it into a bucket of cool, but not cold, water. Will the cool water feel cool? Explain.

5. **Test Prep** A cart with a mass of 1000 kg traveling at 50 km/h has more kinetic energy than a cart with a mass of —

   A 1000 kg traveling at 25 km/h

   B 1000 kg traveling at 60 km/h

   C 1500 kg traveling at 50 km/h

   D 1500 kg traveling at 60 km/h

LINKS

MATH LINK

Equations A liter of water that has a temperature of 45°C is mixed with a liter of water that has a temperature of 25°C. Which of the following equations shows the temperature of the mixture?

a. $45° + 25° = 70°$

b. $45° - 25° = 20°$

c. $\dfrac{(45° + 25°)}{2} = 35°$

WRITING LINK

Informative Writing—Report Find out what materials are used to insulate homes. Write a paragraph for your teacher explaining why such materials are good insulators.

LANGUAGE ARTS LINK

Myths The myth of Icarus and Daedalus deals with the transfer of thermal energy. Find the story in your library, and discover the important role heat plays.

TECHNOLOGY LINK

Learn more about forms and sources of energy by visiting this Internet site.
www.scilinks.org/harcourt

How Are Magnetism and Electricity Related?

In this lesson, you can . . .

INVESTIGATE a way to generate electricity.

LEARN ABOUT how electricity and magnetism result from the movement of electrons.

LINK to math, writing, language arts, and technology.

INVESTIGATE

Making a Generator

Activity Purpose   Have you ever **observed** the meter that measures the electricity being used in your home? The constantly turning wheel in the meter shows that electricity is always being used. In this investigation you'll apply one of the basic principles that allow people to produce this important form of energy.

Materials
- bell wire with stripped ends, about 4 m
- cardboard tube
- tape
- galvanometer
- bar magnet

Activity Procedure

1 Wind the wire in a coil around the outside of the cardboard tube. Leave about 10 cm of wire free at each end. Tape the wire in place on the tube.

2 Attach the exposed ends of the wire to the galvanometer, one end to each post. (Picture A)

◀ The electric eel isn't really an eel. It's actually closely related to the catfish and the carp. The electric eel has muscle tissues in which many cells all produce a small electric charge at the same time, resulting in a shock of up to 650 volts—enough to seriously stun a person.

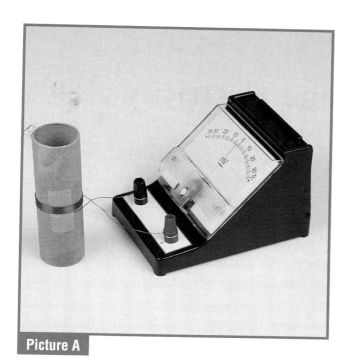

Picture A

Picture B

3 With the tube and the galvanometer in a stable position, move one pole of the bar magnet into and out of the center of the tube. **Observe** the needle of the galvanometer. (Picture B)

4 Repeat Step 3, this time moving the other pole of the bar magnet into and out of the tube.

Draw Conclusions

1. A galvanometer measures electric current in a wire. What can you **infer** from your **observations** about the action of moving a magnet through a coil of wire?

2. **Compare** the readings of the galvanometer in Steps 3 and 4.

3. **Scientists at Work** Scientists use galvanometers to **measure** both the amount of electric current traveling through a wire and the direction in which it is traveling. What can you **infer** about the electric current when you change either the direction of the magnet's movement or the pole that's moved into the tube?

Investigate Further What changes in the investigation might increase the amount of electric current produced? Design **experiments** to test your **hypotheses**.

Process Skill Tip

Sometimes you need to **measure** results with an instrument that records more than one kind of information—both quantity and direction, for example. When you use this kind of instrument, you need to observe and record each separate piece of information carefully.

Magnets and Electricity

Magnetism

FIND OUT

- why some substances are magnetic
- what electricity is
- how electricity and magnetism are related

VOCABULARY

magnet
electricity
electric energy
circuit
electromagnet

If you took apart all the appliances in your home, you'd find that many of them—including the stereo, the blender, the vacuum cleaner, and even the doorbell—contain magnets. In fact, all electric devices that have motors or loudspeakers use magnets.

You probably know some of the properties of magnets. They can *attract*, or exert a magnetic force that pulls other magnets toward them. They can also *repel*, or exert a force that pushes other magnets away from them.

The present theory of magnetism is that it results from the motion of electrons, the particles outside the nucleus of an atom. The spinning of an electron produces a tiny magnetic field—a region in which there is magnetic force.

In most substances, electrons occur in pairs that spin in opposite directions, canceling out each other's magnetic fields. Substances such as iron, cobalt, and nickel, however, have electrons that are not paired. As a result, their atoms do have magnetic fields. The atoms cluster together in microscopic groups called *domains*. A domain contains billions of atoms with their magnetic fields aligned, all contributing to the magnetic field of the domain.

In a **magnet**, all the domains of a substance are aligned in the same direction. Their magnetic fields all work together. In an object that is not a magnet, the domains point in different directions and cancel each other out. However, when a magnet is brought close, the domains in the object sometimes can align themselves. Then the object itself becomes a magnet. When the magnet is removed, the domains return to their random arrangement, and the object is no longer a magnet.

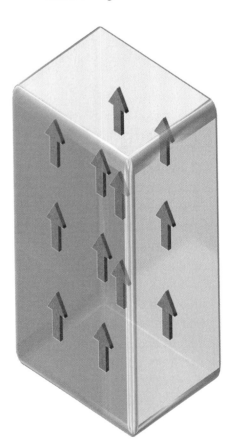

The domains in a magnet are aligned in the same direction. The domains in an unmagnetized piece of iron point in all directions in a random arrangement.

The magnetic field produced by a magnet acts only on certain magnetic materials. It passes through other materials, such as wood products or water. That is why you can use a magnet to move a pin or a tack placed on the other side of a sheet of paper. (The pin or tack becomes a magnet itself when the magnetic field causes its domains to align.)

The strength of a magnetic field decreases as the distance from the magnet increases. The magnetic field is strongest at the poles of the magnet.

Every magnet has two poles. The poles are identified as *north* and *south*. The poles of a bar magnet are at opposite ends of the bar. If the magnet is free to move, its north pole will point north and its south pole will point south. This is how a compass works. Even if a magnet is broken in half, the halves will each have a north and a south pole. In fact, each domain of a magnet has two poles. If you picture the aligned domains of the magnet, you can visualize how each half will still have north and south poles.

▲ The dial of this compass is a magnet. Its poles, at opposite sides of the dial, are attracted by the magnetic poles of Earth.

In the same way that electric charges attract or repel each other without touching, so do the poles of magnets. The north pole of one magnet is attracted to the south pole of another. Two north poles or two south poles repel each other. So, unlike poles attract and like poles repel.

✔ **How could you use a compass to find out if an object is a magnet?**

Iron filings can show the lines of force in a magnetic field. These photographs show the fields formed between unlike and like poles of two magnets. ▼

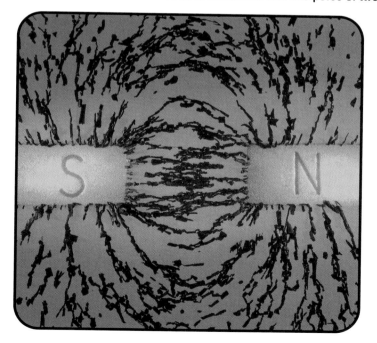

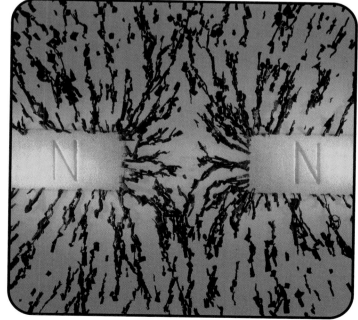

Electric Circuits

Electrons have a negative charge. This charge is responsible for **electricity**, the interaction of electric charges. If you've ever rubbed a balloon and watched it stick to a wall, you have seen an effect of static electricity. In *static electricity* the charges that are present don't flow from one place to another.

Current electricity is the flow of an electric charge. This is the electricity that runs appliances such as flashlights, washing machines, and televisions. Current electricity is the movement of energy from one place to another. It is also called **electric energy**. Electric energy can be converted to another form of energy, such as heat, light, or motion.

Unlike magnetism, electricity requires something to travel through. The material must be an electric conductor. Most materials that are good conductors of heat are also good conductors of electricity. Copper is one of the best conductors. Because it is also malleable and ductile, it is often used for electric wires. The wires are wrapped with plastic insulation so that the electric current will not travel to conductors that the wires might touch.

An electricity source—a generator or a battery—has two poles. Electric charges are separated in a battery. One pole of the battery has extra electrons and, therefore, a negative charge. The other pole has a shortage of electrons and, therefore, a positive charge. The battery has potential energy due to the position of the charged particles.

In order for current to travel, the poles of the electric energy source must be connected to each other in a **circuit**. Every electric device has two connections or wires that allow it to be connected as part of a circuit. An electric charge will flow only if a circuit is closed, or continuous. If the circuit is open, or has a break, the charge will not flow. A switch on an appliance or in a circuit can be used to break the circuit and prevent the flow of a charge.

The plastic insulation keeps the electric charge in the copper wire. ▼

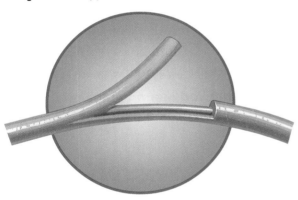

Unless both wires from the battery are connected to the light bulb, electric energy will not travel through the circuit. ▼

When both wires are connected to the bulb, the charge can flow. Electric energy reaches the bulb, where it is converted to light energy. ▼

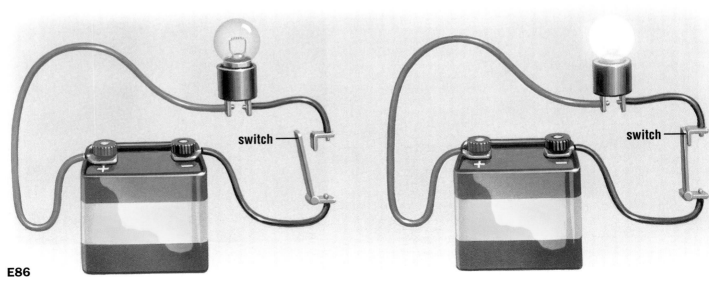

switch

switch

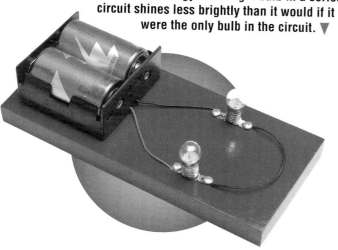

In a series circuit, the current flows through every bulb. The bulbs all use the same energy, and each gets only a fraction of the total energy. Each light bulb in a series circuit shines less brightly than it would if it were the only bulb in the circuit. ▼

In a parallel circuit, the bulbs do not share electric energy. They get as much energy as they can use. Each light bulb in a parallel circuit shines as brightly as it would if it were the only bulb in the circuit. ▼

When two or more electric devices are part of the same circuit, they can be connected in two different ways.

In a *series circuit,* the devices are connected in a row. There is a single path for the current, and it passes through each device on its way to the next device. When devices are connected in series, they cannot be switched individually. Any switch will break the entire circuit and turn off all the devices. If one of the devices breaks, it acts like a switch and also turns off all the other devices in the circuit.

In a *parallel circuit,* each device is on a separate path. The current does not pass through one device to get to another, and each device can be switched separately. The energy traveling to one device does not depend on any other device's being turned on.

✔ **What is a series circuit?**

Electromagnets

In the investigation for this lesson, you discovered that moving a magnet through a coil of wire produces an electric current in the wire. The reverse of this is also true. An electric current moving through a wire produces a magnetic field. If the wire is coiled, the magnetic field is concentrated in the center of the coil.

The more loops in the coil or the stronger the current, the stronger the magnetic field.

If a piece of iron is placed inside the coil, its magnetic domains line up with the magnetic field of the coil and strengthen it. The coil and the iron make up an **electromagnet**, a magnet run by electricity that can be turned on and off.

✔ **What advantage does an electromagnet have over a bar magnet?**

A simple electromagnet can be made with a battery, some wire, and a nail. The magnetic field produced by the current is concentrated in the iron nail in the center of the coil. ▶

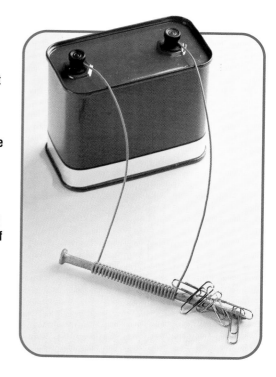

Generating Electricity

Huge amounts of electric current are generated by use of the same principle that you followed in the investigation. Most generators that provide electricity to homes and businesses are made with large coils of wire that rotate in very strong magnetic fields. Electric current is generated in the coils.

There are several common sources for the energy to turn the coils of wire. In a windmill the kinetic energy of wind is used to turn a turbine that then turns the coil. Most generators,

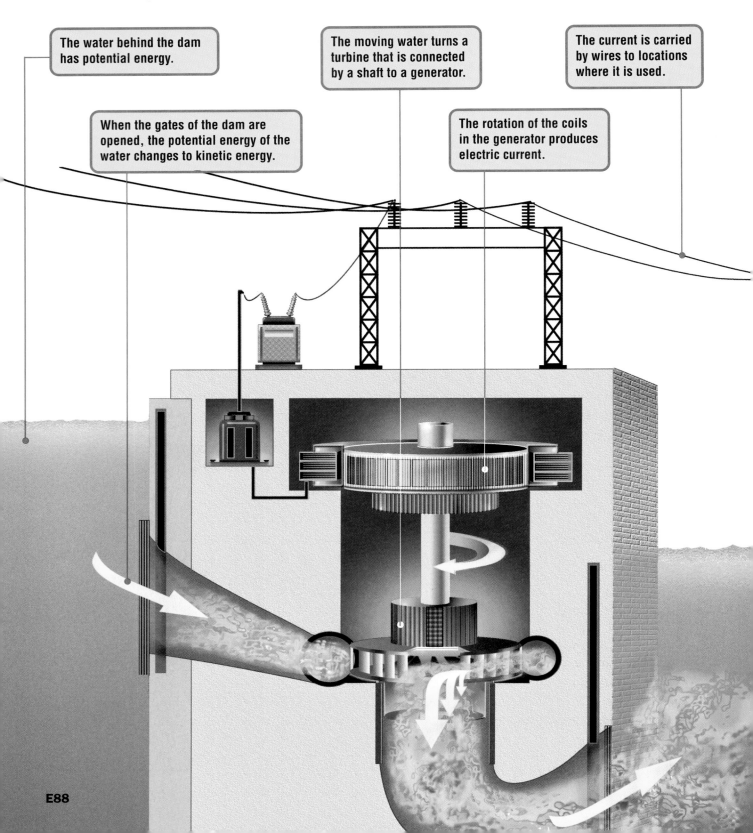

The water behind the dam has potential energy.

When the gates of the dam are opened, the potential energy of the water changes to kinetic energy.

The moving water turns a turbine that is connected by a shaft to a generator.

The rotation of the coils in the generator produces electric current.

The current is carried by wires to locations where it is used.

however, rely on the potential energy of fossil fuels. When the fuels are burned, the energy is converted to heat that is used to boil water. The pressure from the steam turns a turbine, which then turns the coils in the generator.

The diagram on the previous page shows a hydroelectric energy station. It uses the energy of moving water to turn a turbine.

✔ **Name two sources of energy for generating electricity.**

Summary

In certain substances, atoms with electrons that produce a magnetic field gather in magnetic domains. An object in which these domains are aligned is a magnet. An electromagnet is made when wire carrying an electric current is coiled around an iron core.

When a wire is moved within a magnetic field, an electric current is produced in the wire. Electricity can move only through a closed circuit. Electric devices can be connected in a series circuit or in a parallel circuit.

Review

1. What happens to the magnetic domains of a piece of iron when it is placed in a magnetic field?

2. How does a switch control an electric device?

3. What energy source does a hydroelectric plant use to generate electricity?

4. **Critical Thinking** Is the electric circuit in your home a series circuit or a parallel circuit? How do you know?

5. **Test Prep** The north poles of two magnets _____ each other.
   A align
   B repel
   C attract
   D heat up

LINKS

MATH LINK

Multiples When batteries are connected in series, the voltages of the batteries are added. Most batteries in the United States are made in voltages that are multiples of 1.5 volts. Make a chart showing the number of 1.5-volt batteries—from 1 to 10—and their total voltage when connected in series.

WRITING LINK

Informative Writing—How-to Write a paragraph or two to a friend, describing how to use a compass to find directions.

LANGUAGE ARTS LINK

Word Origins Look up the words *electron* and *electricity*. Find out their common origin, and discover why they are derived from that word.

TECHNOLOGY LINK

Learn more about the history of electric energy by visiting the National Museum of American History Internet site.
www.si.edu/harcourt/science

Smithsonian Institution®

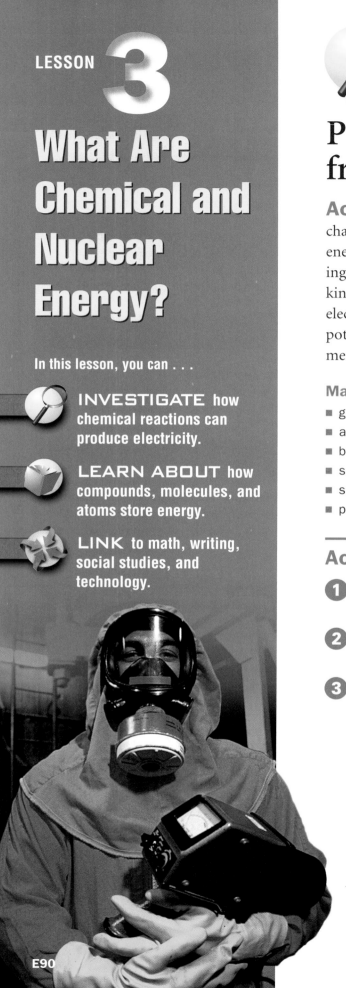

LESSON 3

What Are Chemical and Nuclear Energy?

In this lesson, you can . . .

INVESTIGATE how chemical reactions can produce electricity.

LEARN ABOUT how compounds, molecules, and atoms store energy.

LINK to math, writing, social studies, and technology.

INVESTIGATE

Producing Electricity from Chemical Energy

Activity Purpose You've read how a generator changes the energy of a moving turbine to electric energy. The turbine may be turned by the wind, by moving water, or by the pressure of steam. In each case, kinetic energy is changed into another form of energy—electricity. In this investigation you'll change a form of potential energy to electric energy and make an instrument that detects the electricity you produce.

Materials

- galvanometer
- adhesive tape
- bell wire (lacquered copper wire)
- small strip of copper
- small strip of zinc
- potato

Activity Procedure

1 Hook two lengths of bell wire to the galvanometer. (Picture A)

2 Push the strips of copper and zinc into the potato about 1 cm apart.

3 **Observe** the galvanometer as you touch one wire to the copper strip and the other to the zinc strip. (Picture B)

◀ The first nuclear energy plants were built in the mid-1900s. The science behind nuclear energy is complex. People must constantly monitor the reactions producing the energy to make sure they do not go out of control.

E90

Picture A

Picture B

4 Continue to **observe** the needle as you reverse the galvanometer wires, so that they touch different strips.

Draw Conclusions

1. What did you **observe** when you connected the galvanometer to the metal strips in the potato?

2. What can you **infer** from your **observations**?

3. **Scientists at Work** Scientists know that most pairs of different metals react together in an acid, with one metal giving up electrons to the other metal. Based on this information, what can you **hypothesize** about the metal strips and the potato? How can you explain the difference in the **observations** you made in Steps 3 and 4?

Investigate Further Try this investigation using an apple or a lemon and other pairs of metals. Test several different combinations. How can you tell if one combination produces more electricity than another?

Process Skill Tip

When you make a **hypothesis**, consider the facts that you already know as well as the **observations** that you make.

Energy from Compounds, Molecules, and Atoms

Chemical Energy

FIND OUT

- how chemical energy is stored in the bonds of molecules and compounds
- how chemical energy can be used
- how chemical and nuclear reactions can be used to produce electricity

VOCABULARY

chemical energy
nuclear energy
fission

In a chemical change, new substances, or *products*, are formed from the *reactants*, the materials that react. All chemical changes involve a change of energy. A reaction either needs energy to take place or gives off energy as it takes place. **Chemical energy** is a form of potential energy stored in the reactants. Chemical energy usually changes to heat or light energy when it is given off.

A substance has chemical energy because of its structure and composition. The molecules of the substance are held together by bonds formed by the interaction of electrons. These bonds store chemical energy.

In some reactions, the products have more chemical energy than the reactants. Energy—in the form of heat, light, or electricity—is needed to make the reaction occur. For example, electricity can be used to separate water into hydrogen and oxygen molecules. The energy from the electricity is stored as chemical energy in the bonds of these molecules.

In other reactions, the reactants have more chemical energy than the products. The extra energy—usually in the form of heat or light—is released in the reaction. For example, when hydrogen and oxygen molecules react together to form water, their stored energy is released in an explosion. In a similar way, when fossil fuels are burned, the chemical energy stored in the bonds that hold the molecules together is released as heat.

✔ **Why is chemical energy a form of potential energy?**

◄ The chemical energy of oxygen and sugar is greater than that of carbon dioxide and water. So, the reaction of photosynthesis needs energy, which is supplied as light from the sun.

Using Chemical Energy

Any fuel is a supply of chemical energy. The energy in a fuel is stored in the bonds of its molecules. When the fuel is used, a chemical change—combustion—causes the bonds to break. The chemical energy is released as heat.

Almost all the energy used in the United States comes from the burning of fossil fuels such as gasoline, coal, and natural gas. These substances contain large amounts of chemical energy. There is as much potential energy stored in a gallon of gasoline as there is in a 90,000-lb boulder 1000 ft above the ground.

Fossil fuels are compounds made up of carbon and hydrogen atoms. When the fuels are burned, the bonds between the carbon and hydrogen atoms break apart and the atoms form bonds with oxygen from the air. There is more chemical energy in the fossil fuel compounds than there is in the products of the reaction. The additional energy is given off as heat. Sometimes the heat is used directly for heating homes, cooking food, or heating water. It can also be changed into other useful forms of energy.

▲ Chemical energy in the cyclist's cells changes to mechanical energy used to push the pedals. The energy is transferred from the pedals through the chain to the rear wheel. The kinetic energy of the turning of the wheel is transferred to the whole bicycle.

◄ Some of the plant's stored chemical energy is used for growth.

When wood is burned, the plant's stored chemical energy is released as light and heat. ▼

The engine of a car changes the chemical energy of gasoline into kinetic energy. When gasoline is ignited in a car engine, the result is an explosion that moves a piston. The energy of a series of moving pistons in the engine is transferred to the wheels of the automobile.

When coal is burned at an electric energy plant, the heat that is released is used to make steam. The kinetic energy of the water molecules in steam is used to turn a turbine, which then turns a generator, producing electric energy.

The electricity carried to outlets in homes and businesses is one of the most convenient and useful forms of energy. Even so, it can travel only through wires. However, there is a supply of electricity that is portable—it can be taken anywhere and used at any time.

Batteries contain stored chemical energy. When a battery is connected to a circuit, a chemical reaction between the substances in the battery changes some of its chemical energy to electric energy. A battery will supply electricity until all its substances have been used up in chemical reactions. Batteries provide a safe way to transport energy. The energy they produce can be changed into other forms that include mechanical energy in a toy car, sound energy in a portable radio, and light energy in a flashlight.

One form of fuel that people can't live without is food. Like fossil fuels, most foods are made of hydrogen and carbon. Foods are different from fossil fuels, however, in that the process of breaking down food molecules is slow. When wood and fossil fuels are burned, the molecules are broken apart very quickly and the energy is released in the form of heat. Food molecules are broken down as the chemical energy stored in them is needed. Different kinds

Chemical energy stored in a battery is changed into electric energy when the flashlight is switched on and the circuit is closed. The electric energy is changed to light energy in the flashlight bulb. ▼

of food molecules store different amounts of chemical energy. For example, fats contain more energy than sugars and proteins do.

Food for all consumers originally comes from producers. Even animals that do not eat producers depend on other animals that *do* eat producers. Producers use light energy from the sun to carry out reactions in which carbon dioxide and water form sugar and oxygen. The energy from the light is stored as chemical energy in the bonds of sugar molecules.

When food molecules are broken down, there is less chemical energy in the products of the reaction. Energy is released. The energy is used to perform all the processes that allow an organism to live and grow.

✔ **What are some things in which chemical energy is stored?**

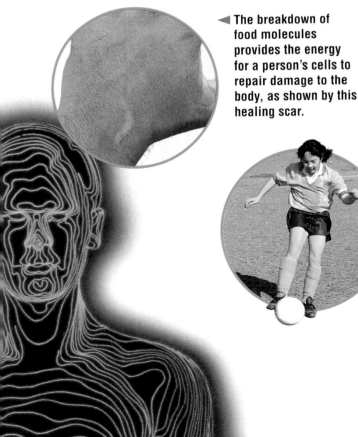

◀ The breakdown of food molecules provides the energy for a person's cells to repair damage to the body, as shown by this healing scar.

◀ The chemical energy in food is changed into kinetic energy when a soccer player kicks a ball.

◀ Chemical energy in food is changed to the heat used to maintain the body temperature of all warm-blooded animals.

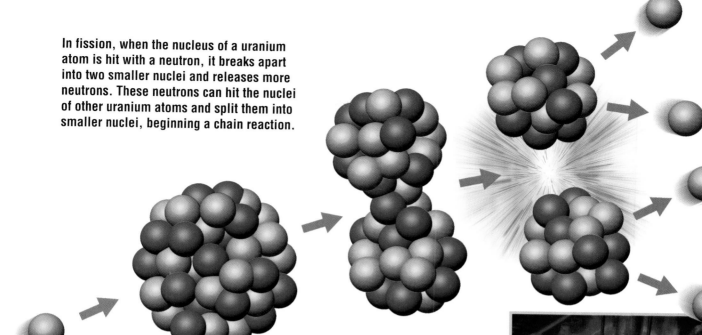

In fission, when the nucleus of a uranium atom is hit with a neutron, it breaks apart into two smaller nuclei and releases more neutrons. These neutrons can hit the nuclei of other uranium atoms and split them into smaller nuclei, beginning a chain reaction.

Nuclear Energy

Just as molecular bonds contain energy, so do the bonds holding the protons and neutrons of an atom's nucleus together. This energy is called **nuclear energy**.

Nuclear energy can be released in two ways—by nuclear *fission* and nuclear *fusion*. **Fission** occurs when a nucleus breaks into two parts, forming the nuclei of two smaller atoms. Fusion occurs when two nuclei join together to form the nucleus of a single larger atom.

Fission can take place only in very large atoms that can be broken apart easily. One of the elements used in nuclear fission reactions is an isotope, or form, of uranium called uranium-235. Its atomic number, like all uranium isotopes, is 92, and its atomic mass is 235. When a neutron is shot at a uranium-235 nucleus, the neutron is absorbed by the nucleus, which splits into two smaller nuclei. The reaction also releases two or three other neutrons and a large amount of energy. The neutrons released in the reaction may hit other uranium nuclei, and new reactions will occur. A series of reactions like this is called a *chain reaction*.

One of the effects of energy given off by fission reactions is a strange blue glow in the water surrounding the area where the reaction is occurring. ▶

A huge amount of energy is released in a chain reaction. A single kilogram of uranium can produce as much energy as 3 million kg of coal. In a nuclear energy plant, the fission reaction is controlled and used to generate electricity.

Unlike fission, fusion takes place most easily between nuclei of very small atoms. Even more energy is produced than in fission reactions. In the sun most of the energy that is released comes from fusion reactions. A great deal of research and experimentation into fusion has been done, but it still is not possible to use controlled fusion reactions to produce energy.

✔ **What is nuclear fission?**

Using Nuclear Energy

Nuclear energy is used to generate electricity. As complex as nuclear energy may seem, what it does is surprisingly simple. The energy released in atomic fission is used to heat water!

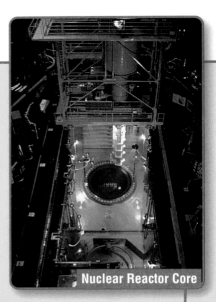
Nuclear Reactor Core

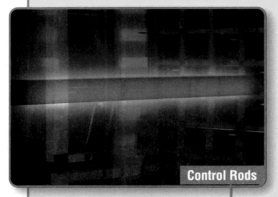
Control Rods

2 The speed of the reactions is controlled by putting in or taking out control rods. These rods are made of metals, such as cadmium, that absorb neutrons without undergoing fission. They absorb some of the neutrons and slow down the fission reaction.

1 In the core, or center, of a nuclear energy plant, uranium atoms in fuel rods are broken apart in fission reactions.

5 The steam from the heat exchanger is cooled by river water. The condensed steam, now in the form of liquid water, is then returned to the heat exchanger.

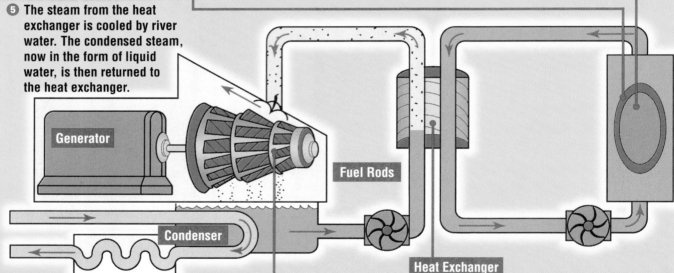
Generator · Fuel Rods · Condenser · Heat Exchanger

Turbine

4 The motion of the turbine is passed on to a generator, which changes the kinetic energy to electric energy.

3 The energy from the reaction is released as heat, which is absorbed by water under a pressure high enough to keep it from boiling. Heat from the water under pressure is transferred to water in the heat exchanger, which produces steam that turns a turbine.

Containment Building

Summary

Chemical energy is stored in the bonds of molecules and compounds. The energy is released in a chemical reaction in which the products contain less chemical energy than the reactants. Chemical energy in food, fuels, and batteries is used for many purposes. Nuclear energy, the energy that holds protons and neutrons together in the nucleus of an atom, is released in fission reactions and fusion reactions.

Review

1. Where in a substance is chemical energy stored?

2. How does energy change form in a flashlight that uses a battery?

3. What is the difference between fission and fusion?

4. **Critical Thinking** Can fission take place in the nucleus of a hydrogen atom? Explain your answer.

5. **Test Prep** Chemical energy is released when the products of a reaction contain ____ energy than the reactants.

   A less   **C** the same

   B more   **D** both more and less

The containment building surrounds the reactor. It is often dome-like. ▼

LINKS

MATH LINK

Units If 1 kg of uranium produces as much energy as 1 million kg of coal, how many kilograms of coal produce as much energy as 1 g of uranium?

WRITING LINK

Persuasive Writing—Opinion Fossil fuel energy plants and nuclear energy plants both have advantages and drawbacks. Choose one kind of energy plant, and write a booklet to convince your audience that it is the best way to produce energy in your region.

SOCIAL STUDIES LINK

The Industrial Revolution The Industrial Revolution was helped along by inventions that used chemical energy. Research how the steam engine changed industry and society. Were all the changes good? What problems did the use of the steam engine cause?

TECHNOLOGY LINK

To find out about other ways to generate electricity, watch *Alternative Energy in the Desert* on the **Harcourt Science Newsroom Video.**

Turner **Le@rning**

CHEMICAL HEAT

Scientists have developed a way to use a chemical reaction to heat food.

Why is chemical heat needed?

Except for foods like fresh fruit and vegetables, granola, or yogurt, most meals taste better hot. But how do you provide hot meals to people in deserts or forests for weeks at a time? That was a problem for food and nutrition researchers working for the U.S. military. Their solution is the Flameless Ration Heater.

How do you heat a meal without fire or electricity?

The Flameless Ration Heater contains a mixture of magnesium, iron, and salt. A soldier who wants a hot meal pours water into a plastic bag containing the heating mixture. The addition of the water starts a chemical reaction that produces heat. The temperature of the water rises to about 70°C (160°F) in about 12 minutes. That's hot enough to heat a packaged meal.

The soldier wraps the main dish of a packaged meal in the plastic bag. In ten minutes, the soldier has a hot packet containing a meal such as spaghetti, smoked sausage, burritos, or barbecued chicken. In addition to the main dish, each soldier's packet might also contain peanut butter and crackers, a cookie, candy, a fruit drink, coffee, and chewing gum.

Why is this food system useful?

Getting meals that are tasty and fresh to thousands of soldiers is difficult. The meals also have to be nutritious and easy to handle. The military's nutritionists pack the meal in foil that protects the food from oxygen and moisture. These are the main causes of food spoilage. The contents are also heated and pasteurized during packaging, to kill harmful bacteria. The taste? It's not home cooking. But most soldiers agree that hot food always makes eating better.

◀ A soldier in the field prepares a hot meal using the Flameless Ration Heater. This invention helps make life a little more comfortable for people who have no access to heating devices.

THINK ABOUT IT

1. How are the soldiers' meals heated without electricity or a flame?
2. What do you think might be some other uses for these meal packages?

WEB LINK:
For Science and Technology updates, visit The Learning Site.
www.harcourtschool.com

Albert Einstein

PHYSICIST

Albert Einstein was one of the world's greatest scientific thinkers. He was a gifted physicist who published papers that changed the way people understand some of the basic laws of the universe. Einstein's work also led to advances in using atomic energy and investigating space. Einstein won the Nobel Prize in physics in 1921.

Albert Einstein's early life was not unusual. He showed interest in science and mathematics as a young child in Germany. He graduated from high school and attended a technical college. Later he took a job as an examiner in a patent office in Switzerland, where he had become a citizen. The job enabled him to earn a living, but physics was his real interest. He worked at the patent office by day from 1902 to 1909. At night and in his spare time, he wrote a series of important papers in physics.

In his papers Dr. Einstein presented theories on the movement of atoms. He proposed the idea that light is made of photons. He introduced his theory of relativity, stating for the first time that both time and motion are relative to the observer. In one paper, he

also introduced a famous equation, $E = mc^2$. The equation showed that the amount of energy in a certain mass is equal to that mass times the square of the speed of light. In other words, mass and energy are two forms of the same thing, and one can, theoretically, be changed into the other. The equation was an important foundation for the development of nuclear energy.

By 1909 Dr. Einstein's theories had become known to the scientific community. He was offered a position teaching college physics. He continued to do research and to write. In 1921 he won the Nobel Prize for his earlier work on light energy. This work was important for the development of the solar energy panels we use today.

After the Nazis came to power in Germany in the early 1930s, Albert Einstein moved from Europe to the United States and became an American citizen. He taught at Princeton University until his death in 1955.

THINK ABOUT IT

1. What is the importance of Einstein's equation $E = mc^2$?

2. Why was it not clear at first that Einstein would become a scientist?

Producing Heat

How does electricity produce heat?

Materials
- 1 AA battery (Do NOT use a larger battery.)
- 1 strip of aluminum foil 2.5 cm × 17.5 cm (1 in. × 7 in.)

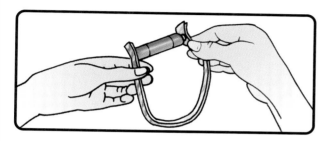

Procedure
1. Fold the foil lengthwise several times so it forms a thin strip.

2. Hold one end of the strip against one end of the battery.

3. Wait 10 seconds and feel the strip.

4. Now hold the two ends of the strip against opposite ends of the battery.

5. Wait 10 seconds and feel the strip again. **CAUTION** Do NOT hold the ends of the foil against the battery for more than 15 seconds.

Draw Conclusions
What happened when you held one end against the battery? Why? What happened when you held both ends against the battery? What kind of energy was the electric energy in the battery changed into?

Changing Forms of Energy

How can a peanut heat water?

Materials
- clean soup can half-full of room-temperature water
- indoor/outdoor thermometer
- one shelled peanut
- votive candleholder with a pointed or scalloped top edge
- wooden matches
- stirring rod or spoon

Procedure
1. Measure and record the temperature of the water.

2. Put a peanut in the candleholder, and ask an adult to light the peanut with a match.

3. Carefully and quickly balance the can of water on the candleholder, over the burning peanut.

4. When the peanut stops burning, stir the water. Measure its temperature again.

Draw Conclusions
What happened to the water temperature? What kind of energy was stored in the peanut? What chemical change released the energy in the peanut? What kind of energy was released from the peanut? Challenge question: What would happen if the bottom of the can sealed off the top of the candleholder?

Chapter ③ Review and Test Preparation

Vocabulary Review

Use the terms below to complete the sentences. The page numbers in ( ) tell you where to look in the chapter if you need help.

energy (E76)

law of conservation
of energy (E76)

kinetic energy (E76)

potential energy (E76)

thermal energy (E78)

heat (E78)

conduction (E79)

convection (E79)

radiation (E79)

magnet (E84)

electricity (E86)

electric energy (E86)

circuit (E86)

electromagnet (E87)

chemical energy (E92)

nuclear energy (E95)

fission (E95)

1. The kinetic energy of particles of matter is called ____.

2. The ____ states that energy cannot be created or destroyed.

3. ____ is the ability to cause a change in or to move matter.

4. When two substances that have different temperatures touch each other, heat moves from one to the other by ____.

5. The like poles of a ____ repel each other, and opposite poles attract each other.

6. When a book falls off a table, its ____ changes into ____.

7. Heat can be moved through liquids and gases by____.

8. Heat from the sun is transferred to Earth by ____.

9. A wire that carries electricity and is coiled around a nail makes a simple ____.

10. Breaking apart the nucleus of an atom is called ____.

11. The transfer of thermal energy is ____.

12. ____ is released during chemical reactions, and ____ is released during nuclear reactions.

13. ____, used to power light bulbs or appliances, can travel only in a closed ____.

14. In a battery, chemical energy changes to ____.

Connect Concepts

Complete the chart by filling in terms from the Word Bank.

flows through a circuit
released during fission
produced by the sun
stored in a compressed spring
produces a magnetic field

stored in fossil fuels
in a pendulum at the top of its swing
in a pendulum at the bottom of its swing
stored in the bonds of a molecule
exhibited in moving objects

Potential energy	15. _____	16. _____
Kinetic energy	17. _____	18. _____
Electric energy	19. _____	20. _____
Chemical energy	21. _____	22. _____
Nuclear energy	23. _____	24. _____

Check Understanding

Write the letter of the best choice.

25. Temperature is a measure of —
    A chemical energy
    B thermal energy
    C potential energy
    D convection

26. The north pole of a magnet will repel another —
    F north pole
    G south pole
    H magnetic field
    J electron

27. If the ends of a wire are reversed in a circuit, the current will —
    A change direction
    B be stopped
    C increase
    D decrease

28. Electricity is generated in a wire that is moving in a —
    F turbine
    G magnetic field
    H chemical reaction
    J power plant

29. All life processes of an organism use _____ stored in the organism's cells.
    A kinetic energy
    B fuel
    C chemical energy
    D nuclei

Critical Thinking

30. Why can't the sun's heat travel to Earth by conduction or convection?

31. An electromagnet holding up several pins is turned off, but the pins don't fall off the electromagnet right away. What might be the reason for this?

Process Skills Review

32. What **experiment** could you do to determine if plastic is a good heat insulator?

33. If only two of the three bulbs in a circuit are shining, what can you **infer** about the circuit?

34. What points might you use to **compare** the advantages and disadvantages of using fossil fuels to generate power?

Performance Assessment

Energetic Steps

The energy used to generate electricity from fossil fuels came from the sun. Draw a diagram showing the steps taken as energy begins in the sun and ends as electricity. Identify the form of energy at each step, and describe the process in which it is changed.

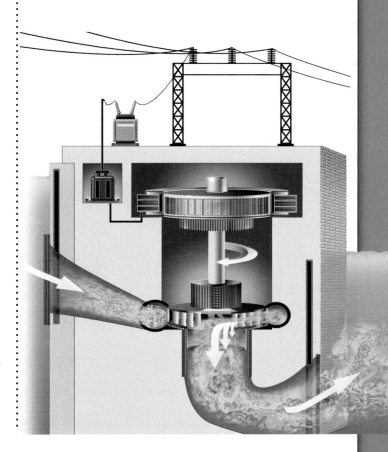

Vocabulary Preview

wave
amplitude
wavelength
transverse wave
longitudinal wave
frequency
pitch
loudness
electromagnetic waves
radiant energy
reflection
refraction
transparent
opaque
translucent

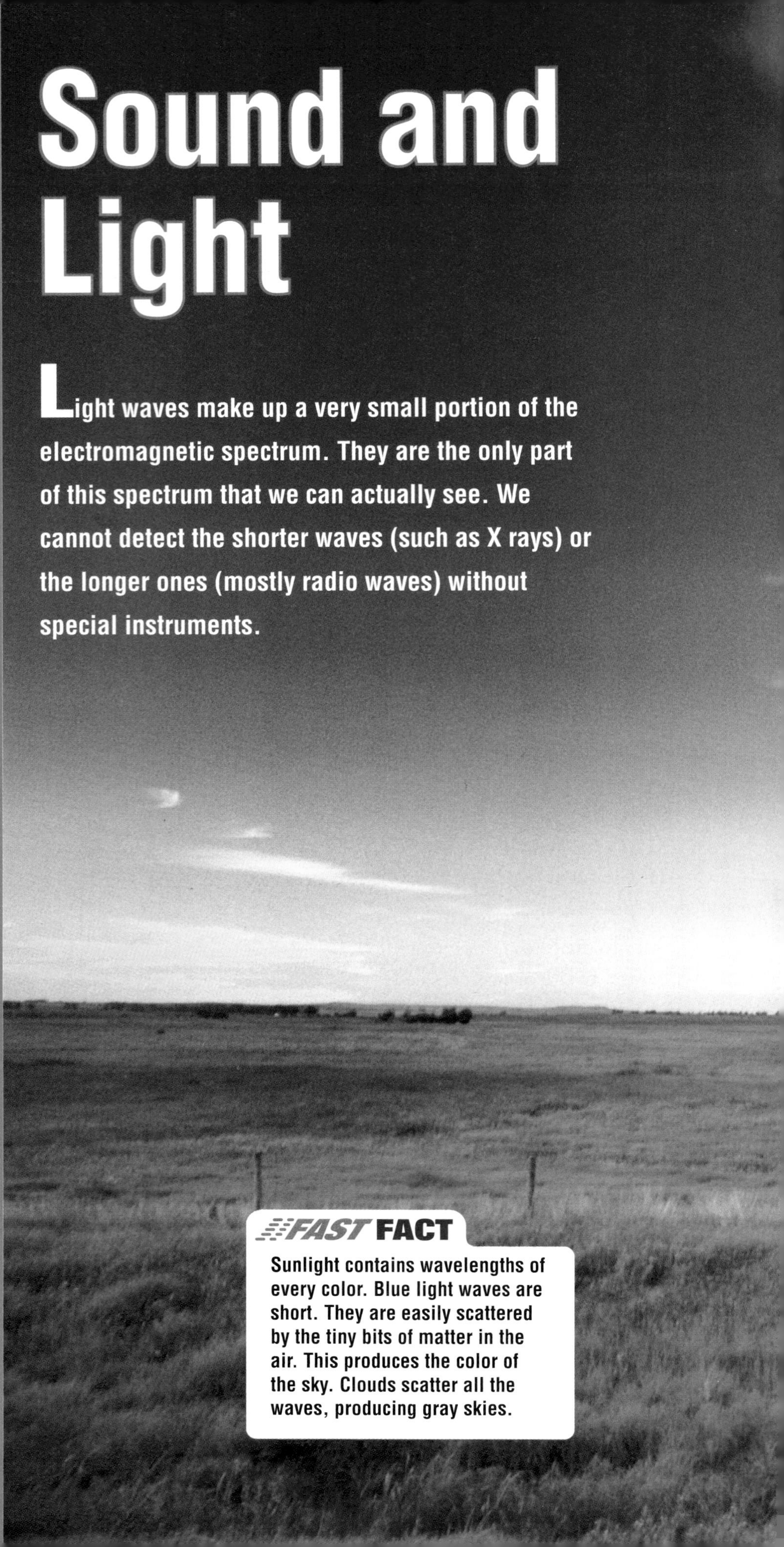

Sound and Light

Light waves make up a very small portion of the electromagnetic spectrum. They are the only part of this spectrum that we can actually see. We cannot detect the shorter waves (such as X rays) or the longer ones (mostly radio waves) without special instruments.

FAST FACT

Sunlight contains wavelengths of every color. Blue light waves are short. They are easily scattered by the tiny bits of matter in the air. This produces the color of the sky. Clouds scatter all the waves, producing gray skies.

FAST FACT

Different ears respond to different frequencies of sound. A bat cannot hear a human speaking in a normal voice, although a human can hear some of the sounds a bat makes.

Hearing Ranges

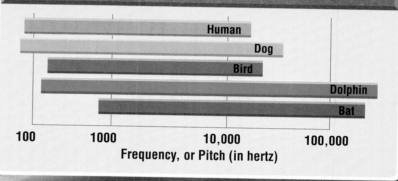

Human

Dog

Bird

Dolphin

Bat

| 100 | 1000 | 10,000 | 100,000 |

Frequency, or Pitch (in hertz)

FAST FACT

Radio telescopes must be built larger than optical telescopes because radio waves are much longer than light waves. The radio waves are captured by very large bowls that focus the waves on a receiver.

What Are Some Properties of Waves?

In this lesson, you can . . .

 INVESTIGATE how energy can travel in a wave.

 LEARN ABOUT longitudinal and transverse waves.

 LINK to math, writing, social studies, and technology.

This surfer is using a property of waves—their ability to carry energy from one point to another. ▼

INVESTIGATE

Making Waves

Activity Purpose   You have read how energy can travel long distances through wires. You've also read how, in the form of a magnetic field, energy can pass through other materials without changing them. In this investigation you'll explore how energy can travel in a wave, and you'll **observe** and **compare** two kinds of waves.

Materials
- spring toy
- piece of brightly colored yarn
- stopwatch

Activity Procedure

1 Tie the yarn around one coil of the spring toy to mark the center of the toy. Have your partner hold one end, and pull the other end to slowly stretch the spring toy along the floor to a length of about 2–4 m.

2 While your partner holds one end of the spring toy so it can't move, flip your wrist quickly to one side and back again. **Observe** the yarn and the wave. **Measure** and **record** the time the wave takes to reach your partner. (Picture A)

3 Repeat the same motion but with more energy, so that there is more sideways movement in the wave. **Measure** and **record** the time the wave takes to reach your partner.

4 Now quickly make the same motion twice. **Observe** the yarn, the two waves, and the distance between the waves as they travel along the spring toy.

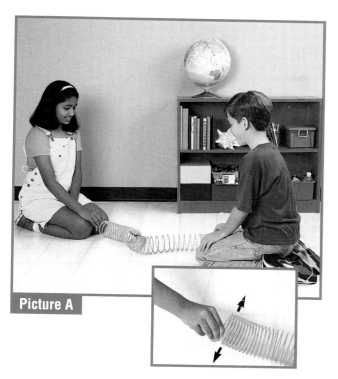

Picture A

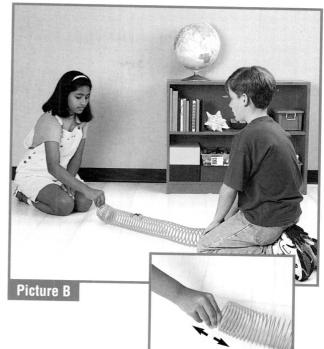

Picture B

5. Have your partner continue to hold one end of the spring toy still. In one quick motion, push your end of the spring toy forward and then pull it back. **Observe** the wave as it travels. **Measure** and **record** the time it takes to reach your partner. (Picture B)

6. Repeat the motion you made in Step 5, but make two waves. **Observe** the distance between the waves as they travel along the spring toy. **Measure** and **record** the time the second wave takes to reach your partner.

Draw Conclusions

1. **Compare** how the piece of yarn moved when you made the two different types of waves. What differences did you **observe**? What might you **infer** that a wave carries?

2. What did you **observe** about the distance between pulses in a wave? Did the distance change as the pulse traveled along the wave?

3. **Scientists at Work** Scientists use their **observations** and **measurements** to **make hypotheses. Compare** the measurements you made in Steps 2 and 3. What can you hypothesize about the speed of a wave in a spring toy?

Investigate Further Work with your partner to make the second kind of wave. This time, **observe** what happens when a wave reaches the end of the spring toy. Make a series of waves to see what happens.

How Waves Move Energy

Waves

FIND OUT

- how waves carry energy
- about two different kinds of waves
- how speed, frequency, and wavelength are related

VOCABULARY

wave
amplitude
wavelength
transverse wave
longitudinal wave
frequency

If you throw a rock into a pond, ripples will flow in circles from the point where the rock lands in the water. The ripples are waves. A **wave** is a disturbance that travels through matter or space, carrying energy from one place to another without carrying matter along with it. Almost all the information that people receive travels in the form of waves. Light and sound are both energy traveling in waves. And radio waves carry information that is received by a radio or television.

Waves that travel through water are *mechanical* waves. They need matter to travel through. The waves that you made in the investigation were also mechanical waves. They traveled through the spring toy. However, the substance moves only back and forth or up and down. It is never permanently displaced. This can be seen in the ripples in a pond. A floating object will only bob up and down as the ripples pass it. It won't move in the direction of the ripples. Waves do not transport matter; they transport only energy.

Surface waves in water are a combination of the motions of the two kinds of waves you made in the investigation. As you discovered, the wave that traveled with a sideways motion caused the attached yarn to move from side to side. The wave that traveled with a forward motion caused the attached yarn to move forward and backward. When these two movements are added together, the resulting motion is a circle.

The highest part of a water wave is called the *crest*, and the lowest part of the wave is called the *trough*. In a series of waves, the vertical distance between the crest and the trough is always the same. This is the height of the wave. In the first wave you made in the investigation, the distance the yarn traveled from side to side was the height of the

Waves at the surface of water are a combination of the movements of two other kinds of waves. Particles in the water move in almost perfect circles as a result of the interaction of the two kinds of waves. ▼

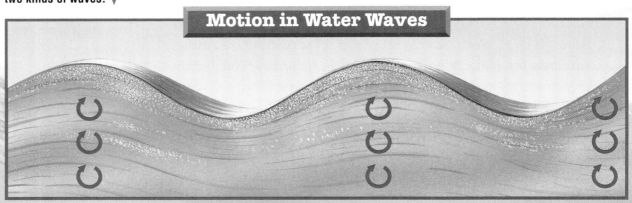

Motion in Water Waves

Katsushika Hokusai was a Japanese printmaker who lived from 1760 to 1849. Hokusai completed "The Breaking Wave off Kanagawa" about 1830, as one of a collection of views of Mount Fuji that are considered some of the finest examples of Japanese printmaking. ▶

wave. The **amplitude** of a wave is the distance that any point on the wave is moved from its resting position. It is equal to one-half of the wave height. The greater the energy of a wave, the greater its amplitude. Amplitude can be measured from the resting position to either the crest or the trough. Both measurements are the same.

The amplitude of water waves can vary greatly, from ripples with an amplitude of barely 1 mm (0.04 in.) to ocean waves with an amplitude of more than 15 m (49 ft). The height of such ocean waves is more than 30 m (about 100 ft).

Not only is the vertical distance between crest and trough always the same in a series of waves, but the horizontal distance between one crest and the next is also always the same. This

measurement is called the **wavelength**. It can be measured between any two identical points on the waves. Waves with the same wavelength don't always have the same amplitude, and waves with the same amplitude don't always have the same wavelength.

Like amplitude, wavelength can vary greatly. The wavelength of waves rolling into a beach may be several meters, while ripples may have a wavelength of only millimeters. The wavelength of light is measured in billionths of a meter, or nanometers.

✔ **What is the relationship between the height of a wave and its amplitude?**

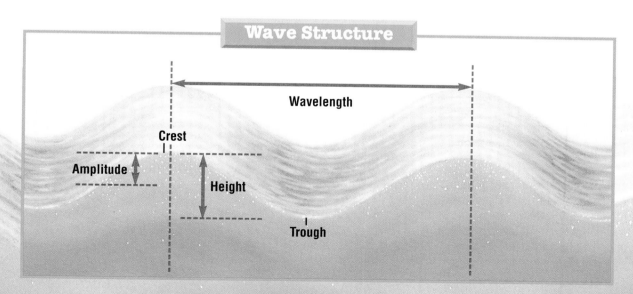

Wave Structure

Wavelength

Crest

Amplitude

Height

Trough

Different Kinds of Waves

The first kind of wave you made in the investigation was a transverse wave. The particles in a **transverse wave** vibrate at right angles to the direction of the wave. You could see this in the investigation when the attached yarn moved from side to side as the wave moved forward. The stretched strings of a musical instrument, such as a guitar, form transverse waves when they are plucked. Light also travels as a transverse wave. Unlike mechanical waves, light waves do not need a medium to travel through.

The second kind of wave you made was a longitudinal wave. The particles in a **longitudinal** (lahn•juh•TOOD•uhn•uhl) **wave** vibrate back and forth in the same direction as the wave is moving. A longitudinal wave has areas of *compression*—where the particles are closer together—and *rarefaction* (rair•uh•FAK•shuhn)—where the particles are more spread out. The coils of the spring toy you used were close together in the compressions and farther apart in the rarefactions. Sound waves, and most other waves that travel through a liquid or a gas, are longitudinal waves.

✔ **How does the vibration of particles differ between transverse and longitudinal waves?**

THE INSIDE STORY

Anatomy of a Wave

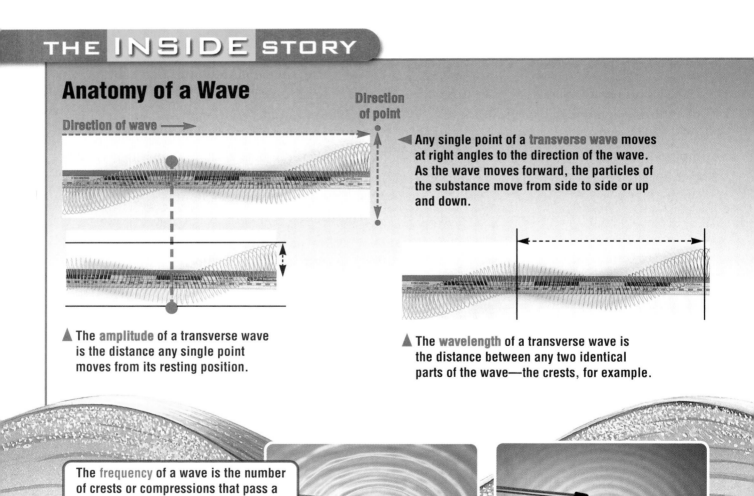

◀ Any single point of a transverse wave moves at right angles to the direction of the wave. As the wave moves forward, the particles of the substance move from side to side or up and down.

▲ The **amplitude** of a transverse wave is the distance any single point moves from its resting position.

▲ The **wavelength** of a transverse wave is the distance between any two identical parts of the wave—the crests, for example.

The **frequency** of a wave is the number of crests or compressions that pass a point in a certain amount of time. Although these water waves are traveling at the same speed, the one on the right has a higher frequency than the one on the left. ▶

Speed, Frequency, and Wavelength

The speed of a wave in a particular substance is always the same unless there are changes to the substance. Sound always travels through air at the same speed unless the temperature changes. Waves travel through water at the same speed unless the depth of the water changes. A wave's speed can be found by measuring the distance a single point in the wave—a crest or compression, for example—travels in a given time.

Although the speed of a wave doesn't change, its wavelength and frequency can change. The **frequency** of a wave is the number of vibrations it has in a given time. It can be measured by counting the number of crests or compressions that pass a point in a certain amount of time. Frequency is usually measured in units called *hertz*. One hertz is one vibration per second. So, if one crest of a wave passes a point in one second, the frequency of the wave is 1 hertz. If two crests pass a point in one second, the frequency is 2 hertz.

There is a relationship among the speed, wavelength, and frequency of a wave. The wave speed is the product of wavelength and frequency. So, if the frequency of a wave increases, the wavelength decreases. In the investigation, the faster you sent pulses along the spring toy, the smaller the distance between the pulses was.

✔ **What determines the wavelength of a wave?**

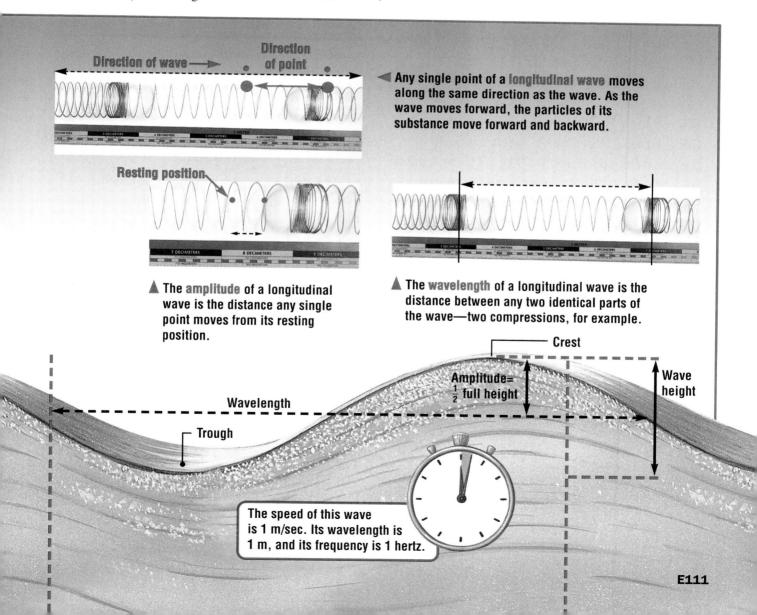

Direction of wave →
Direction of point

◄ Any single point of a longitudinal wave moves along the same direction as the wave. As the wave moves forward, the particles of its substance move forward and backward.

Resting position

▲ The amplitude of a longitudinal wave is the distance any single point moves from its resting position.

▲ The wavelength of a longitudinal wave is the distance between any two identical parts of the wave—two compressions, for example.

Crest

Amplitude= 1/2 full height

Wave height

Wavelength

Trough

The speed of this wave is 1 m/sec. Its wavelength is 1 m, and its frequency is 1 hertz.

Energy from Waves

All waves carry energy in the form of light, sound, heat, or motion. Life on Earth depends on waves that carry energy from the sun, heating the planet and allowing plants to make food.

People can use some of the energy carried in waves that occur in nature. Solar panels collect energy from sunlight, changing it to heat or electricity. Scientists are doing experiments to find inexpensive ways to use the energy of ocean waves. If ways are found, they will have several advantages. The energy scientists use will come from a renewable source. The processes won't cause pollution from combustion.

The energy in ocean waves can also destroy. Waves caused by hurricanes carry huge amounts of energy and can cause as much damage as the hurricane winds. The waves generated by undersea earthquakes carry the greatest amounts of energy. These waves, *tsunamis* (soo•NAH•meez), are sometimes called "tidal waves," although they have nothing to do with tides. A tsunami begins on the ocean floor. It has a wavelength of about 150 km (93 mi) and a speed of about 750 km per hour (470 mi per hour). The disturbance on the surface of the ocean is very slight—one wave with a height of

▲ Ocean waves produced by the powerful winds of a hurricane carry huge amounts of energy and can cause great damage.

a meter may pass every 12 minutes. By the time the tsunami reaches the shore, however, its height may reach 35 m (about 115 ft).

The energy in earthquakes themselves is carried in waves that travel through Earth. The energy travels in *seismic* waves through the ground. These are both longitudinal and transverse waves. When they reach the surface, the waves form a third wave that is very similar to the waves that travel on the surface of water. In fact, the ground sometimes ripples up and down during an earthquake.

✓ **If waves keep reaching a shoreline, why doesn't the water build up at the shore?**

This experimental "nodding duck" device rotates as the waves roll over it, changing their energy into a usable form. ▼

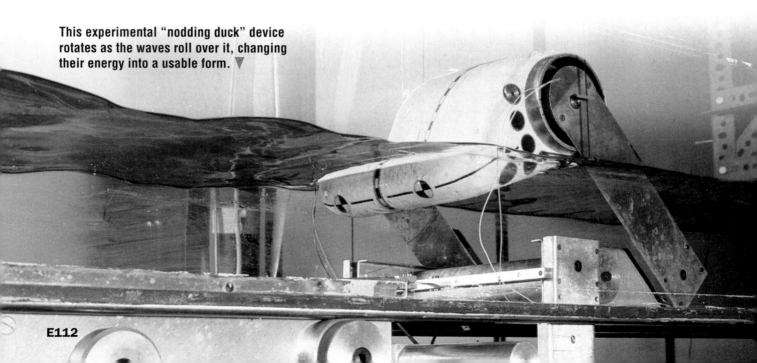

▲ In an earthquake, seismic waves that travel through Earth carry enough energy to destroy buildings.

Summary

Mechanical waves are disturbances in a substance that carry energy from one place to another without taking along the substance itself. Other waves, such as light, carry energy without needing matter to travel through. A transverse wave displaces particles at right angles to the motion of the wave, while a longitudinal wave displaces particles in the same direction as the wave. There is a relationship among the speed, wavelength, and frequency of a wave. Some energy from waves can be used, but the energy in waves can also cause great damage.

Review

1. What do waves carry from one place to another?

2. What is the difference between a transverse wave and a longitudinal wave?

3. What can you tell about the speed of two waves that have the same wavelength and frequency?

4. **Critical Thinking** Which areas of a longitudinal wave do the crest and the trough of a transverse wave correspond to?

5. **Test Prep** The height of a wave is twice the measure of its —

   A wavelength   **C** frequency

   B speed   **D** amplitude

LINKS

MATH LINK

Graphs Draw a graph of a wave that has a wavelength of 2 cm and an amplitude of 1 cm. Now draw an identical graph starting half a wavelength behind the first. The two graphs should be mirror images of each other around the x-axis. Add the y-values at several points to prove that two such waves cancel each other out.

WRITING LINK

Informative Writing—Report Most mechanical waves travel faster through solids and liquids than they do through air. Research this fact, and write a short report explaining it to a friend.

SOCIAL STUDIES LINK

Tsunamis Although they don't occur often, tsunamis are more common in some parts of the world than in others. Find out which parts of the world they generally occur in, and why.

TECHNOLOGY LINK

Visit the Harcourt Learning Site for related links, activities, and resources. **www.harcourtschool.com**

WELCOME TO THE LEARNING SITE

What Are Some Characteristics of a Sound Wave?

In this lesson, you can . . .

INVESTIGATE how to make a simple musical instrument.

LEARN ABOUT the characteristics of a sound wave.

LINK to math, writing, health, and technology.

INVESTIGATE

A Simple Musical Instrument

Activity Purpose   Sounds are made by vibrating objects, and sound energy is carried by waves. If you use a rubber band to make sounds, you can **observe** that the rubber band itself shows some of the characteristics of the waves it produces. In this investigation you'll **observe** a simple musical instrument as it produces various sounds.

Materials
- empty loose-leaf binder
- large rubber band

Activity Procedure

1 Place the rubber band around the binder so that it passes over the side that opens. (Picture A)

2 Hold the binder open, and pluck the rubber band with a finger. **Observe** the rubber band, and listen to the sound it makes. (Picture B)

3 Pluck the rubber band harder. **Observe** and **compare** what happens to the rubber band and the sound it makes. Compare this with your results in Step 2.

4 Find a way to make the rubber band produce a lower note and a higher note. **Observe** and **compare** what happens to the rubber band when it makes these notes.

◀ All sounds are produced by vibrations. If you put a few grains of salt on the top of a drum, you would see the movement of the drumhead as it makes a sound.

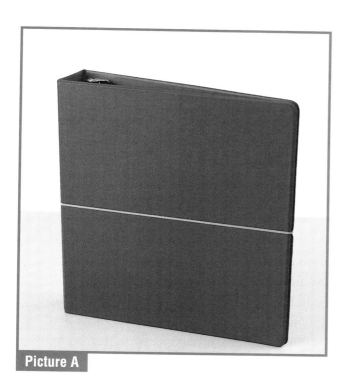

Picture A

Picture B

Draw Conclusions

1. What produced the sound when you plucked the rubber band?

2. How can you **compare** the amplitude of the wave of the rubber band with the loudness of the sound it makes?

3. **Scientists at Work** Scientists base their inferences on the results of their **experiments**. Based on your results from Step 4, what can you **infer** about a rubber band and the note it produces?

Investigate Further **Experiment** with thinner and thicker rubber bands. What can you **infer** about the thickness of the bands and the notes they produce?

Process Skill Tip

When you **experiment**, it is easier to interpret your results if you change only one variable at a time.

Sound Waves

FIND OUT

- **how sound travels through air**
- **what gives sound a different pitch or loudness**
- **how fast sound travels through various materials**

VOCABULARY

pitch
loudness

Sound

Sounds are produced by the vibrations of objects. The vibrations cause the molecules of the material around the object to vibrate. This forms a wave that travels through the material. Sound waves cannot travel through a vacuum. They need matter to travel through.

The sound of a person's voice is produced by the vibrations of the vocal cords, which cause vibrations in the air that is in the throat and mouth. A vibrating column of air also produces the sounds of instruments such as flutes and trumpets. Pianos, cellos, and guitars all rely on vibrating strings that set up vibrations in the instruments. The tightly stretched head of a drum vibrates back and forth when it's hit. A loudspeaker acts the same way. In a loudspeaker, a paper cone, pushed by an electromagnet, moves back and forth.

When the head of a drum vibrates outward, it pushes against the air molecules next to it. They push into the air molecules next to them. Those molecules, in turn, push into air molecules next to them. In this way a pulse of compressed air, or compression, travels through the air away from the drum.

The drum's vibration also consists of inward movement, away from the air molecules next to the drumhead. During this part of the vibration, air molecules are pulled into the empty space made when the drumhead moves inward. This movement produces an area where the molecules are more spread out. Air molecules next to this region are pulled in. As this process continues, a pulse of air that is less dense, called a rarefaction, travels through the air following the compression. A wave that is made up of compressions and rarefactions is called a longitudinal wave. Sound is a longitudinal wave.

Longitudinal waves such as sound are mechanical waves—they travel in matter. As with all mechanical waves, the matter itself does not travel in

The air molecules in a sound wave vibrate in the same direction as the wave. The molecules are closer together in a compression than in a rarefaction. ▼

Compression   Rarefaction

the wave. Instead, the wave is made up of energy, and it is the energy that travels. Kinetic energy is transferred from molecule to molecule in the matter, moving farther and farther away from the source of the sound.

Not all the wave's energy is passed from molecule to molecule. Some is used up in the random motion of the air molecules and is lost as thermal energy. This continues to happen as the wave travels, so the energy of the wave decreases as it travels. The sound gets quieter and quieter the farther it is from its source, until it has so little energy that the sound can no longer be heard.

When a sound wave reaches the surface of another material, some of the energy of the wave will be reflected. The harder and smoother the surface, the more energy will bounce off it, so the more sound will be reflected. This reflected sound is called an *echo*. The echo you hear if you shout in a canyon can be very clear and very much like the original sound. This happens when the sound wave bounces directly off one or two hard, flat surfaces.

When a sound wave is reflected by many surfaces, *reverberation* occurs. This is a combination of many echoes reaching a listener at slightly different times. Reverberation can make a sound richer and fuller. That's what happens when someone sings in the shower, where the sound waves can bounce off the tiled walls many times without losing much of their energy. If you observe rooms that are noisy, you'll generally see sharp angles and hard surfaces. Rooms that are quiet, on the other hand, often have a lot of soft surfaces, such as carpets and curtains.

✔ **What kind of wave is a sound wave?**

Bats use sound waves of very high frequencies to find their way and to locate prey. The sound waves produced by the bat bounce off a surface, and the bat knows the distance by being aware of the time the echo takes to return.

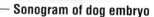
Sonogram of dog embryo

◀ Sonograms work in the same way as a bat's echolocation method. A sonogram is an image of reflected high-frequency sound waves. These waves reflect off the surfaces of the organs of the body.

◀ Sound waves produced by this tuning fork can be seen in the surface waves they produce in the water.

When the strings of a guitar are plucked, their vibrations are transferred to the wooden surface under them. This surface causes air molecules to vibrate, producing a wave of compressions and rarefactions that travels through the air. ▼

Pitch

The frequency of a sound wave is the rate at which the source of the sound is vibrating. The faster the vibration, the higher the frequency of the sound. Most people can hear sounds with frequencies between 20 hertz and 20,000 hertz. Sounds with frequencies below 20 hertz or above 20,000 hertz can't be heard by humans. However, animals such as elephants can hear sounds with lower frequencies, and animals such as dogs can hear those with higher frequencies. Whistles used to call dogs have pitches above 20,000 hertz and can't be heard by most people.

The higher the frequency of a sound, the higher its **pitch**. Pitch is the perception of the frequency of a sound as being high or low. High musical notes have high pitch and high frequency, and low musical notes have low pitch and low frequency. People hear pitches below 100 hertz as low rumbles. Pitches above 4000 hertz sound piercing and unpleasant. The highest notes an orchestra plays are just a little below 4000 hertz.

As you learned, the speed of any wave in a given material is always the same and is the product of the wavelength and frequency of the wave. So, if the frequency of a sound wave increases, the wavelength decreases.

In stringed instruments, one way to make the pitch of a note higher is to shorten the string.

When you shorten the string, you also shorten the wavelength. A guitarist uses the fingerboard of the guitar to shorten strings and change the pitch of the notes. Another way to raise the pitch of a note is to tighten the string, increasing the frequency with which it vibrates. Musicians tune their instruments by tightening or loosening the strings.

Other instruments produce sounds from a vibrating column of air. When the column is shortened, the wavelength is shortened and the pitch made higher. You may have noticed that larger instruments generally produce sounds with lower pitches than smaller instruments do. Low-pitched sounds have long wavelengths, so the column of air or the string that vibrates must be long.

✔ **What is the relationship between frequency and pitch?**

Frequency Range of Musical Instruments

Instrument	Pitch Range in Hertz
Harp	30–3136
Piano	30–4186
Bass tuba	55–311
French horn	60–698
Guitar	80–698
Clarinet	150–1568
Trumpet	170–932
Violin	200–2093
Piccolo	600–3729

The sounds from a French horn have low frequencies, so they have long wavelengths. That's why a French horn must be larger than a recorder.

The column of air in a recorder vibrates at a high frequency, so the notes the instrument produces have a high pitch.

Loudness

Just as pitch is the perception of the frequency of a sound, **loudness** is the perception of the amplitude of a sound wave. The amplitude of a sound wave is the difference in pressure between the compressions and rarefactions. Amplitude is a measure of how much energy the wave is carrying. So, the more energy a sound has, the louder it is.

Loudness is measured in a unit called the *decibel*, or dB. It was named after Alexander Graham Bell, who invented the telephone. The unit relates to the intensity of the sound wave. The higher the decibel level, the louder or more intense the sound. The threshold of hearing—the softest sound people can hear—has a loudness of 0 decibels.

The measure of loudness increases by 10 decibels each time the amplitude increases by a factor of ten. So a sound with a loudness of 20 decibels has an amplitude, or intensity, ten times greater than one of 10 decibels. The human ear, however, perceives each increase of 10 decibels as a doubling of loudness.

The loudness of sound can physically harm a person's hearing. A single burst of sound at a loudness of 140 decibels can cause immediate, permanent hearing damage. Explosions and jet engines can produce sounds this loud. Damage can also result from continuous exposure to sounds louder than 80 decibels. Construction equipment and some concerts produce sounds of this loudness.

✔ **What is the relationship between loudness and the amplitude of a sound wave?**

▲ A loud sound, such as the roar of this lion, has a greater amplitude than a quiet sound, such as the meowing of the kitten shown below.

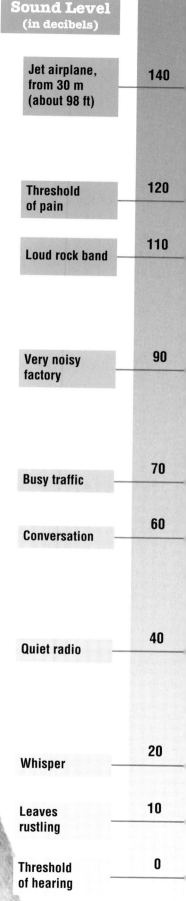

Sound Level (in decibels)

Source	Level
Jet airplane, from 30 m (about 98 ft)	140
Threshold of pain	120
Loud rock band	110
Very noisy factory	90
Busy traffic	70
Conversation	60
Quiet radio	40
Whisper	20
Leaves rustling	10
Threshold of hearing	0

The Speed of Sound

The speed of a wave through a material under given conditions is always the same. For example, all water waves travel at the same speed through water of the same depth. All sound waves travel at the same speed through air of the same temperature. The speed does not depend on the amplitude or frequency of the sound.

Sound travels faster through warm air than it does through cold air. At 20°C (68°F), the speed of sound through air is 334 m/sec (about 1115 ft/sec)—nearly 1200 km/hr (746 mi/hr). If you are close to a sound source, the speed is great enough that the sound seems to reach you instantly. However, if the sound source is a long way off, you notice the difference between the speeds of light and sound. If you are watching from a distance, you see a batter hit a baseball before you hear the crack of the bat against the ball. Light travels nearly a million times faster than sound.

Most of the sound waves you hear travel through air, but air isn't a very good conductor of sound. Sounds are much clearer when they travel through water, wood, or metal.

Sound also travels faster through materials such as water and metal than it does through air. Its speed depends on how often the

molecules in the material bump into one another, moving the sound wave along. Sound travels a little faster in air when the air is very humid, because the air molecules bump into each other more often.

Molecules in liquids and solids are closer together and bump into each other more often than molecules in gases. The speed of sound is about 4 times as great in water as it is in air. It's about 15 times as great in steel as it is in air.

✔ **Why does the speed of sound through air increase as the air temperature increases?**

▲ The Concorde carries its passengers across the Atlantic Ocean at speeds faster than the speed of sound.

Speed of Sound in Air at Different Temperatures

Temperature (°C)	Speed (m/sec)
60	366
40	355
20	343
0	331

Speed of Sound in Different Materials

Material	Speed (m/sec)
Stainless steel	5790
Pyrex® glass	5640
Gold	3240
Sea water	1531
Fresh water	1497
Plastic	540
Water vapor	494
Dry air (20°C)	343

Summary

Sound waves are longitudinal waves that travel through matter. The frequency of a sound wave is perceived as pitch, and the greater the frequency, the higher the pitch. The greater the amplitude of the sound wave, the greater its energy. Amplitude is perceived as loudness. The speed of a sound wave depends not on the frequency or amplitude of the wave, but on the material it travels through. Sound travels faster through solids and liquids than it does through gases.

Review

1. Why does the loudness of a sound wave decrease as the wave travels away from its source?

2. Why does a bass guitar have longer strings than a regular guitar?

3. Would you expect sound to travel faster through air or through copper? Explain.

4. **Critical Thinking** Why can't a sound wave travel through a vacuum?

5. **Test Prep** The compressions and rarefactions in a sound wave travel —

   A in the same direction

   B in opposite directions

   C more and more slowly

   D more and more quickly

LINKS

MATH LINK

Proportions For every increase of 10 decibels, the intensity of a sound increases by a factor of ten. How much more intense is the sound of a riveting machine with a loudness of 100 decibels than that of a whisper with a loudness of 20 decibels?

WRITING LINK

Informative Writing—How-to Due to the difference in the speeds of light and sound, you will hear a clap of thunder after you see the lightning that caused it. Sound travels through the air at the rate of about one mile every 5 seconds. Write instructions for a friend, explaining how to calculate how far away lightning is by counting the seconds between seeing the lightning and hearing the thunder.

HEALTH LINK

Noise Pollution Research noise pollution. Find out some of its causes and effects. Make a poster to present your findings to the class.

TECHNOLOGY LINK

To learn more about musical instruments and sound, watch *Theramin—Making Electronic Music* on the **Harcourt Science Newsroom Video.**

What Are the Characteristics of Light?

In this lesson, you can . . .

INVESTIGATE the reflection of light.

LEARN ABOUT how light travels as an electromagnetic wave.

LINK to math, writing, art, and technology.

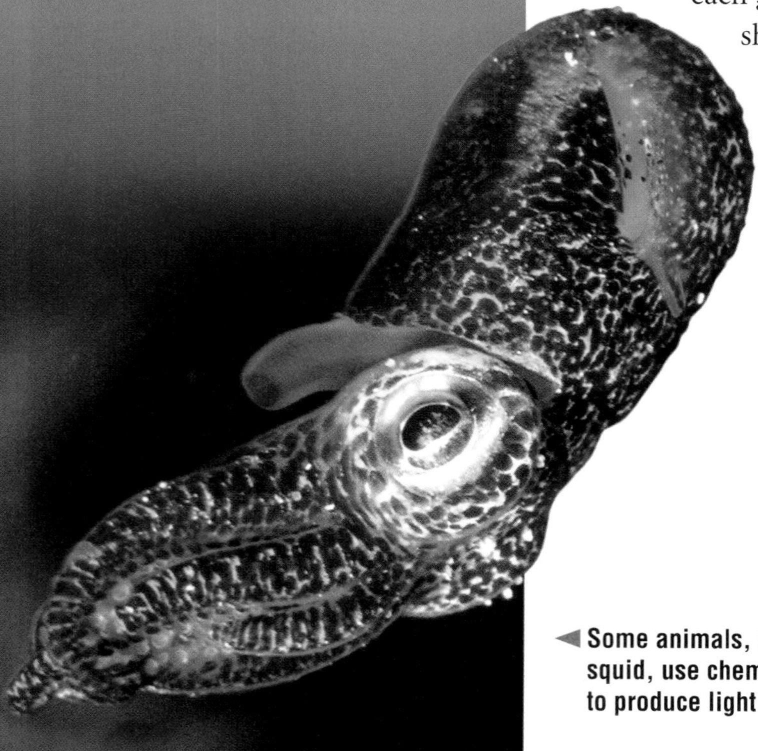

INVESTIGATE

Reflecting Light

Activity Purpose When riding in a car as the sun sets, you might have a very bright light in your eyes, even if the sun is behind you. How does the sunlight change direction to shine in your eyes? Its direction is changed when it is *reflected* off the mirrors or windows of the car in front of you. In this investigation, you will **experiment** with the reflection of light.

Materials

- flashlight
- spray bottle filled with water
- sheet of white paper
- sheet of black construction paper
- 2 small mirrors

Activity Procedure

1 Work in groups of four. One student from each group should hold the flashlight. One student should have the spray bottle. One student should have the sheet of white paper. The fourth student should have the mirrors and the black construction paper. It is easier to see the results of this experiment if the lights are turned off or dimmed.

2 The student with the flashlight should stand directly in front of the student with the sheet of white paper. The flashlight should shine on the sheet of paper. **Record** what you see. (Picture A)

◀ Some animals, such as this squid, use chemical reactions to produce light.

3 Between the flashlight and the paper, the student with the spray bottle should spray some mist. **Record** your **observations.**

4 The student with the flashlight should stand next to the student with the sheet of white paper. With both students facing forward, the flashlight should shine forward. The student with the black paper and a mirror should **experiment** to try to reflect the light onto the sheet of white paper.

Picture A

5 The student with the bottle should spray again to make the path of the light visible. **Record** your **observations** by making a drawing of what you see.

6 With the mirror in place, the student with the flashlight should move several feet to one side and then shine the light into the mirror. The student with the white paper should move until the light reflects onto the paper. The student with the bottle should spray so that all of you can **observe** the path of the light and draw a diagram of what you see. (Picture B)

Picture B

Draw Conclusions

1. What did you **observe** when you put mist in the path of the light? What can you **infer** about why this might have happened?

2. When you moved the flashlight, what did you **observe** about the direction in which the light was reflected?

3. **Scientists at Work** Scientists often **control variables** in an **experiment** to make a **hypothesis** about how variables are related. Based on the results you got, what hypothesis can you make about how a mirror changes the direction in which light travels?

Investigate Further Does the intensity of light change when it is reflected? Design an **experiment** with two mirrors to test your ideas.

Process Skill Tip

It is important to **control variables** in an experiment so that you can understand the results. For example, when the flashlight was moved, it was important to leave the mirror exactly where it was.

Light and Electromagnetic Waves

FIND OUT

- what light is
- what happens when light is reflected and refracted
- what *transparent*, *opaque*, and *translucent* mean

VOCABULARY

electromagnetic waves
radiant energy
reflection
refraction
transparent
opaque
translucent

Visible light is a tiny part of the electromagnetic spectrum. Shorter wavelengths include ultraviolet rays, X rays, and gamma rays. Longer ones include infrared waves, microwaves, and radio waves. ▼

Electromagnetic Waves

During the day, you use light that has traveled millions of miles from the sun. At night, the light you use may travel just a few feet from an electric lamp. The light from each source behaves the same and travels the same way. Light is **electromagnetic waves**, waves of vibrating electric and magnetic fields. Electromagnetic waves carry **radiant energy**.

Electromagnetic waves do not have to move through a substance to carry energy. The electromagnetic waves from the sun and other stars travel through empty space—called a vacuum—before we see them on Earth. So space is not really empty, because it is full of electromagnetic waves. In a vacuum, the speed of electromagnetic waves is 300 million m/sec (186,000 mi/sec). That means a wave of light travels 300 million meters in just one second.

All electromagnetic waves move at the same speed in a vacuum, but they can have different wavelengths and frequencies. Because they all move at the same speed, the waves with a shorter wavelength have a higher frequency. Electromagnetic waves with shorter wavelengths also carry more energy. The range of wavelengths of electromagnetic waves, called the *electromagnetic spectrum,* is shown in the diagram below and on the next page.

Visible light consists of electromagnetic waves that have wavelengths we can see with our eyes. Red light has the longest wavelength we can see. Its wavelength is about 0.000065 cm. The other colors of

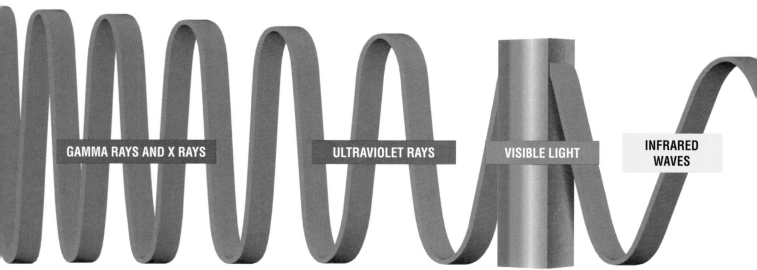

GAMMA RAYS AND X RAYS   ULTRAVIOLET RAYS   VISIBLE LIGHT   INFRARED WAVES

light in order of decreasing wavelength are orange, yellow, green, blue, and violet.

Next in the electromagnetic spectrum, with wavelengths shorter than visible violet light, are waves called *ultraviolet rays*. Because of their frequency, these electromagnetic waves carry more energy than visible light. Humans can't see ultraviolet radiation, but honeybees can. Ultraviolet radiation from the sun causes sunburns.

X rays and gamma rays have even shorter wavelengths and even more energy. Waves with such short wavelengths will travel right through most parts of your body without being absorbed. If you have ever broken an arm or a leg, your doctor probably made an X ray of the broken bone. Medical X rays are not the electromagnetic waves themselves, but pictures made by using X rays instead of visible light to expose the film. The picture of the bone appears because bones absorb X rays and prevent them from exposing areas on the film.

Some electromagnetic waves have wavelengths that are longer than visible light. Electromagnetic waves with wavelengths slightly longer than red light are called *infrared waves*. When an object gives off heat, most of the heat is in the form of infrared waves. Microwaves, which are used in microwave ovens to heat food, have even longer wavelengths. Still longer wavelengths are called radio waves. Televisions and radios use different wavelengths of radio waves.

✔ **What is visible light?**

▲ Thermograms detect infrared radiation, or heat.

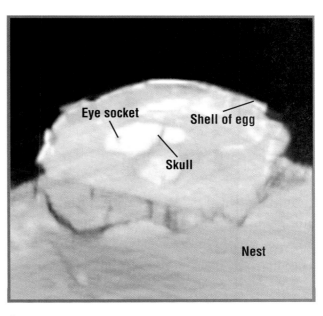

Eye socket

Shell of egg

Skull

Nest

▲ X rays can go through things that visible light cannot. So X rays can give us pictures of the insides of things. This fossil dinosaur egg in a nest has been examined with X rays.

MICROWAVES

RADIO WAVES

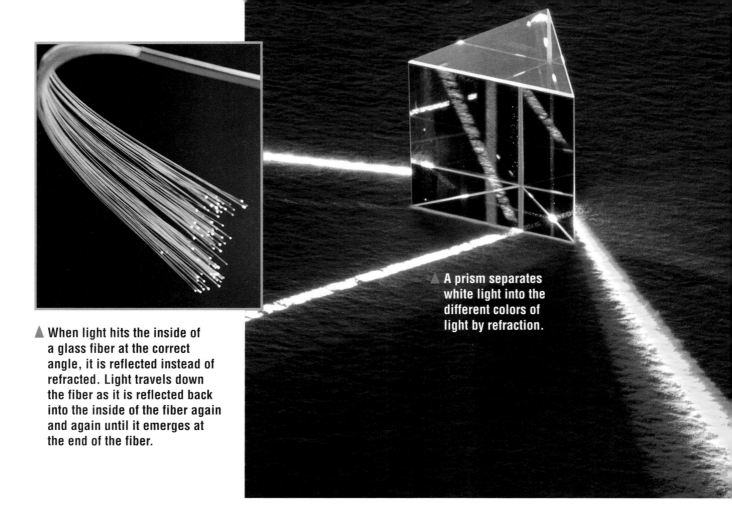

▲ When light hits the inside of a glass fiber at the correct angle, it is reflected instead of refracted. Light travels down the fiber as it is reflected back into the inside of the fiber again and again until it emerges at the end of the fiber.

▲ A prism separates white light into the different colors of light by refraction.

Reflection and Refraction

If visible light is traveling through the air all around us, why don't we see rainbows of colors filling the air? As you observed in the investigation, light is not usually visible as it travels from a light source. Instead, you see only light waves that are *reflected* off objects and into your eyes. **Reflection** is the bouncing of light waves off of a surface.

Objects have different colors because they reflect and absorb different wavelengths, or colors, of light. White light is a mixture of all the colors of light. So, an object that reflects all the colors of light, like a white T-shirt, looks white. Red socks appear red because they reflect red light and absorb the other colors. When something absorbs all of the colors of light, like a black tennis shoe, it appears black. Very few light waves are reflected off black objects.

The human eye recognizes more colors than the six that appear in the rainbow. Both you and a friend might wear red shirts that appear to be slightly different colors. The shirts are different *shades* of red because they reflect and absorb slightly different amounts of certain colors of light.

If you want proof that white light contains all of the colors of light, place a prism in some bright sunshine. When focused correctly, the prism will separate the sunlight into a rainbow of colors. When light travels through something other than a vacuum, like a glass prism, the substance it travels through is called a *medium*. The speed of light is different in different mediums. As you found out earlier, the speed of light in a vacuum is 300 million m/sec (186,000 mi/sec). The speed of light is slightly slower when it travels through air, and even slower when it travels through mediums like glass and water.

◄ **Leaves reflect mostly green light and absorb most of the other colors.**

A mirror or shiny surface behind the light source in a lighthouse reflects the light out in one direction.

When light enters a new medium, the change in speed causes it to bend. **Refraction** is the bending of a light wave when it passes from one medium to another. When light travels through a prism, it is refracted when it enters the prism and refracted again when it leaves the prism and enters the air.

When a beam of white light travels through a prism, different colors of light are bent by different amounts. This is because the amount that a wave of light is bent, or refracted, depends on its wavelength. Violet light, with the shortest wavelength, is bent the most. Red light, with the longest wavelength, is bent the least. All of the other colors of light are bent in differing amounts that fall between those of red and violet. This spreads the different colors of light out into a rainbow in order of their wavelengths.

Refraction causes many familiar phenomena.

Rainbows are made by raindrops acting as tiny prisms, and diamonds owe their multicolored sparkle to refraction. Refraction also makes a straw sticking out of a glass of water appear bent when looked at from the side. When riding in a car on a hot day, have you ever seen on the road's surface what looked like a puddle of water that disappeared as you got closer? That was a *mirage,* caused by the refraction of light when it traveled between layers of air that were at different temperatures.

✔ **What are two ways the direction of light can be changed?**

When the sun sets, we see it through a thicker layer of atmosphere than during the day. The thick atmosphere scatters almost all of the blue and violet light and scatters red, orange, and yellow light the least.

Transparent, Opaque, Translucent

Mediums, or substances that light can travel through, are **transparent**. Air, water, clear glass, and clear plastic are transparent to all wavelengths of light. You can see objects clearly through them, so they are used to make things like windows and eyeglasses. Some substances are transparent to only certain colors of light. They are sometimes described as clear because you can see objects through them, but they have a color. Apple juice is a clear liquid. You can see through apple juice well enough to read the label stuck to the back of a bottle. A cherry gelatin dessert is transparent to red light.

Substances that light can't travel through are **opaque**. Opaque objects absorb or reflect light. The light energy that they absorb turns into heat energy and makes them warmer. Wood, pottery, bricks, animals, and people are all opaque.

The windows on a greenhouse are made of transparent material so that the sunlight can pass through.

Some leaves are thin enough to be translucent.

Plants, pots, and dirt are opaque.

Some objects are not completely opaque—they let some light through. But they are not completely transparent either, because you can't see clearly through them. Substances like these are described as **translucent**. Light travels through a medium that is translucent, but the light that travels through it is so scattered that objects can't be seen clearly. Milky plastics, frosted glass, and milky stained glass are translucent.

✔ **How are transparent and translucent substances different?**

Summary

Light consists of electromagnetic waves that can be seen. Light can be reflected, refracted, or absorbed. An object's color is the result of the wavelengths of visible light that it reflects. Refraction is the bending of light due to a change of speed when the light enters a different medium. Objects that light can travel through are transparent. Objects that absorb and reflect light are opaque. Translucent objects transmit some light, but they distort or eliminate images.

Review

1. What is the speed of light?
2. Why do objects have different colors?
3. What causes a mirage?
4. **Critical Thinking** Would ultraviolet light passing through a prism be bent more or less than visible light? Explain.
5. **Test Prep** White light can be separated into a rainbow of colors by a —

   A prism
   B mirror
   C mirage
   D light separator

LINKS

MATH LINK

Light and Sound Approximately how many times as fast as sound is light?

WRITING LINK

Expressive Writing—Poem The phenomena of light have been the subjects of many poems. Write a short poem about reflection, refraction, or another effect or phenomenon of light.

ART LINK

Impressionists Impressionist artists were prominent in France in the late 1800s and early 1900s. Find out how impressionist ideas about painting were influenced by discoveries about the nature of light. Use posters to show the class how impressionists tried to paint light. Use one of the impressionist techniques to make your own painting.

TECHNOLOGY LINK

Learn more about light and reflection by experimenting with *A Reflecting Challenge* on the **Harcourt Science Explorations CD-ROM.**

SUPER DISCS

Plastic discs that are only 5 inches in diameter can store movies that are played with scanning laser beams.

How do we use technology to listen to recorded music?

The phonograph record seemed amazing when it was invented in the early 1900s. A needle running along a grooved cylinder or disc could produce music. But records have been replaced by 5-inch plastic compact discs (CDs) that produce sound using laser beams.

Now there is a new type of CD, called a digital video disc (DVD), that can hold more information and produce even better sound.

Why is a DVD better than a CD or videocassette tape?

A DVD can store the data for an entire movie and provide a better image than a videotape can. A DVD also produces sharp images when played on a computer that has a DVD-ROM player.

A DVD has a longer playing time than a CD because it can hold seven times as much information. To make the sound you hear on a CD, the CD has on it a huge number of samples, or audio "snapshots," of the piece of music. You hear these samples as continuous sound. Because it can hold much more data, a DVD has many more samples of the music. With more samples, the DVD provides a richer sound that is more like what was actually recorded.

How does a DVD work?

A DVD works much like a CD. Each DVD has rows spiraling out from the center to the edge of the disk. Each row is made up of a distinct pattern of tiny pits and flat surfaces. When you play the disc, a laser beam passes over each row as it spins. Laser light is reflected from the tiny pits and flat surfaces, forming a pattern of electronic signals. The signals are then turned into patterns of sound and images.

DVDs are different from CDs in some ways, however. A DVD uses a laser with a more tightly focused beam than the laser a CD uses. The pits of a DVD are smaller, allowing it to hold more information than a CD. What's more, the DVD pits are not only on the surface of the disc, but also just beneath its surface and on both sides of the disc rather than on just one side.

Are DVDs common now?

Some people already have DVDs and DVD players. But it will probably be several years before DVDs are as common as CDs and videotapes are now.

THINK ABOUT IT

1. How do laser beams play music on DVDs?
2. How is the DVD an advance in technology?

WEB LINK:
For Science and Technology updates, visit The Learning Site.
www.harcourtschool.com

Careers   Electronics Repair

What They Do
Electronics repair persons maintain and repair electronic equipment, including televisions, VCRs, and computers.

Education and Training Electronics repair people must be able to read and understand technical manuals. They must be able to carry out detailed maintenance procedures. Many electronics repair people take training courses at vocational schools or community colleges.

Anthony M. Johnson

PHYSICIST

When you make a phone call, there's a good chance that the work of Dr. Anthony Johnson has helped improve the quality of what you hear and the speed with which you communicate. Dr. Johnson is a professor of physics at the New Jersey Institute of Technology who has also worked in the field of communications.

Dr. Johnson says his interest in science began in his childhood, when his parents gave him a chemistry set. He started to enter school science fairs, doing projects that involved electronic and electromagnetic devices. His high school physics teacher saw his talent and encouraged his interest in science. This led him to work for a bachelor's degree and later a Ph.D. in physics.

While Anthony Johnson was in college, he worked on projects with researchers at Bell Labs who were trying to improve communication by using lasers and optical fibers. That led to a full-time job and several years of work in this area.

Dr. Johnson enjoys sharing his knowledge of and enthusiasm for physics with students in the classroom. When he isn't teaching, he loves to talk to students about the excitement of working in science.

For Dr. Johnson, encouraging young people—from kindergarten through college—to choose careers in science is an important part of his work.

THINK ABOUT IT

1. How did Dr. Johnson first become interested in science?

2. Why does Dr. Johnson enjoy teaching physics?

◄ Fiber optic cable is one of the many contributions Dr. Johnson, along with other scientists, has made to communications technology.

Changing Pitch

How can you change the pitch of a flute?

Materials

- drinking straw
- scissors
- ruler

Procedure

1 Cut one end of the straw into a point.

2 Put the pointed end into your mouth and blow gently. **CAUTION** Be careful not to cut yourself with the straw. Experiment until you make a sound.

3 Cut 5 cm (2 in.) off the unpointed end of the straw and blow again.

4 Continue making the straw shorter and blowing into it. Make a table to record how the sound changes.

Draw Conclusions

How did the sound change as the straw got shorter? People produce sound with their vocal cords. Do you think men have shorter or longer vocal cords than women? Why do you think so?

Reflection and Refraction

How can you make an object disappear—and then appear as two objects?

Materials

- 1 paper clip
- clear drinking glass with about 5 cm (2 in.) of water in it

Procedure

1 Place the paper clip under the glass.

2 Put your head near the glass. Look at the paper clip at different angles until it seems to disappear before your eyes.

3 Drop the paper clip into the glass of water.

4 Look into the glass from a slightly higher level than before. Position yourself so you see two paper clips, one floating on top of the water.

Draw Conclusions

In this experiment light rays entered the water and were reflected off the bottom of the glass. Refraction can bend light rays that pass through water. Why do you think the paper clip seemed to disappear in Step 2? Why do you think you saw two paper clips in Step 4?

Vocabulary Review

Use the terms below to complete the sentences. The page numbers in ( ) tell you where to look in the chapter if you need help.

wave (E108)
amplitude (E109)
wavelength (E109)
transverse wave (E110)
longitudinal wave (E110)
frequency (E111)
pitch (E118)
loudness (E119)

electromagnetic waves (E124)
radiant energy (E124)
reflection (E126)
refraction (E127)
transparent (E128)
opaque (E128)
translucent (E128)

1. Objects are visible due to the ____ of light.

2. The ____ of a wave is the number of crests that pass a fixed point in a given amount of time.

3. Light travels through a ____ material without being scattered.

4. The perception of the amplitude of a sound wave is ____.

5. The energy that electromagnetic waves carry is ____.

6. Particles in a ____ vibrate along the same direction as the wave.

7. The distance between successive crests of a wave is its ____.

8. The ____ of a wave is half the measure of the height of the wave.

9. Particles in a ____ vibrate at right angles to the direction of the wave.

10. The perception of the frequency of a sound wave is ____.

11. Light cannot travel through ____ substances.

12. A ____ carries energy without transporting matter.

13. Light waves and radio waves are both ____.

14. The ____ of light occurs when it passes from one medium to another.

15. Light is scattered as it passes through a ____ material.

Connect Concepts

Use the terms in the Word Bank to label the diagrams below.

wavelength   **compression**   **rarefaction**
crest   **trough**   **amplitude**
height

16. ____

17. ____

18. ____

19. ____

20. ____

21. ____

22. ____

Check Understanding

Write the letter of the best choice.

23. The greater the amplitude of a wave, the greater its —
A energy
B speed
C frequency
D wavelength

24. If a wave travels at a constant speed, the greater its wavelength, the lower its —
F energy
G speed
H frequency
J amplitude

25. The wave in a plucked guitar string is a ____ wave, and its sound is a ____ wave.
A longitudinal, transverse
B transverse, longitudinal
C sound, mechanical
D mechanical, radiant

26. Reverberation of sound is caused by —
F echoes
G pitch
H rarefaction
J loudness

27. Blue paint ____ blue light and ____ other colors of light.
A emits, absorbs
B reflects, absorbs
C absorbs, emits
D absorbs, reflects

Critical Thinking

28. Blowing across the open top of an empty glass bottle makes a sound. Will the pitch of the sound be higher or lower if the bottle is half-full of water? Explain your answer.

29. On a very sunny day, a person wearing black clothing will get hotter than a person wearing white clothing. Explain why.

Process Skills Review

30. If you **observe** that the strings of a violin are thinner than the strings of a double bass, what **hypothesis** can you make about how the thickness of a string affects the sound of an instrument?

31. Which of the following **variables** should you **control** if you are comparing the speed of sound through air of different temperatures: amplitude, humidity, frequency, time of day, measuring apparatus?

32. The waves used to transmit television signals have shorter wavelengths than those that transmit radio signals. **Compare** the amounts of energy carried by the two waves.

Performance Assessment

Octave Experiment

Design an experiment in which you use 12 strings to produce the notes in an octave. Describe the equipment you would use, and explain how you would find out if the wavelengths of successive notes differ by the same length.

Unit Project Wrap Up

Here are some ideas for wrapping up your unit project or doing other projects.

Make a Video

Videotape your Sound and Light show. Present it to other audiences.

Make Lists

Take five minutes to list matter that is around you. Make as long a list as you can. Rewrite your list, sorting the items by states of matter. Then re-sort your list by types of change possible.

Demonstrate a Change

Demonstrate a change in matter. Tell what caused the change and how it could be prevented.

Investigate Further

How can you make your project better? What other questions do you have about matter and energy? Plan ways to find answers to your questions. Use the Science Handbook on pages R2–R9 for help.

Forces and Machines

UNIT F

PHYSICAL SCIENCE

Forces and Machines

Unit Project   ## Inventor's Fair

Invent items that could help you do work. Build the inventions, and display them at an inventor's fair. Along with the items, show drawings, notes, charts, and other materials you used to develop your inventions. Then analyze ads from magazines and newspapers for other inventions. Do the ads make claims that can be tested? Test an invention and see if you can verify the claims.

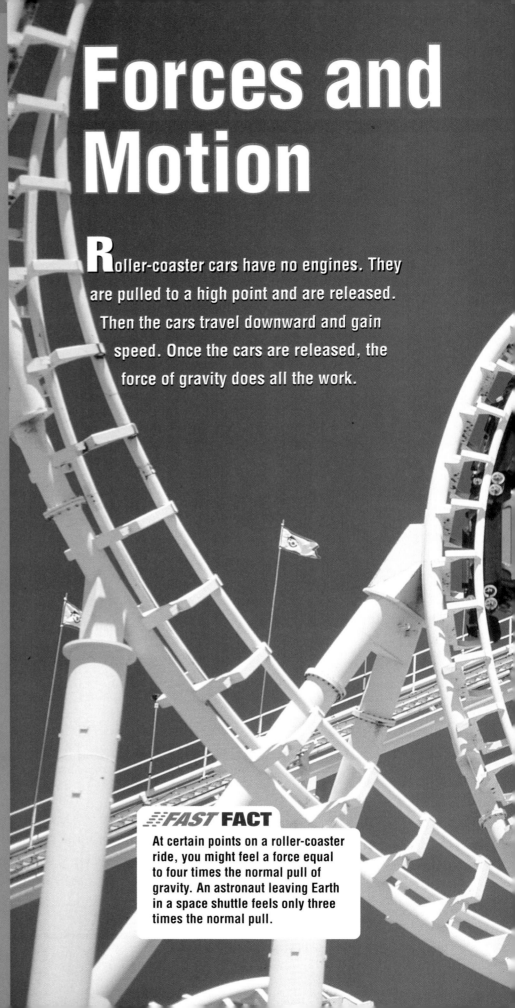

Chapter 1

Vocabulary Preview

force
gravity
newton
speed
average speed
velocity
friction
balanced forces
unbalanced forces

Forces and Motion

Roller-coaster cars have no engines. They are pulled to a high point and are released. Then the cars travel downward and gain speed. Once the cars are released, the force of gravity does all the work.

FAST FACT

At certain points on a roller-coaster ride, you might feel a force equal to four times the normal pull of gravity. An astronaut leaving Earth in a space shuttle feels only three times the normal pull.

F2

LESSON 1

What Is Gravity?

In this lesson, you can . . .

INVESTIGATE how to build and mark a spring scale.

LEARN ABOUT gravity.

LINK to math, writing, social studies, and technology.

INVESTIGATE

Building a Spring Scale

Activity Purpose Even before you get out of bed in the morning, you can feel the force of Earth's gravity. Gravity is what keeps you in your bed and what keeps your bed on the floor. In this activity you will build your own spring scale and mark it so you can **measure** the force of gravity on several objects.

Materials

- large hardcover book
- sheet of paper
- tape
- 2 large paper clips
- large elastic band
- kitchen or postage scale
- small items to weigh

Activity Procedure

1 Assemble your scale as shown. Let it hang freely for a minute. (Picture A)

2 Weigh three test items on the kitchen scale. Label each of these items with its weight to the nearest half ounce (or mass to the nearest 10 g).

3 Put a tick mark on the sheet of paper at the spot the pointer reaches when your spring scale is hanging freely. Mark this spot "0" to begin your scale.

4 One at a time, hook each of the test items to your scale. For each item, make and label a mark. (Picture B)

◄ Roller coasters use the force of gravity to provide a thrilling ride.

Picture A

Picture B

Draw Conclusions

1. You have made several marks on your scale. Ideally, the scale should show a mark for every half ounce (or 10 g). Use a ruler to help you **estimate** where these levels should be, and label them on the scale.

2. Use your scale to **measure** the force of gravity on three new objects. **Record** the weight of each object. **Compare** the weights as measured on your spring scale to their weights as measured on the kitchen scale. How accurate is your spring scale?

3. **Scientists at Work** On the moon, the force of gravity is less than it is on Earth. So a spring scale would show that an item weighs less on the moon. Scientists use a pan balance to **measure** mass. A pan balance **compares** the mass of an item to a known mass. When the two are equal, the balance is level. Explain why a pan balance on the moon would show an item's mass to be the same as on Earth.

Investigate Further Put the heaviest weight on the spring scale. Leave it on for five minutes. After you take it off, immediately reweigh one of the items you already weighed. **Hypothesize** what happened to the elastic band while the heavy weight was hanging from it. How could you test your hypothesis?

Process Skill Tip

You don't always need to use expensive instruments to **measure.** For many purposes, a homemade instrument may work just as well.

Gravity

Forces Make Things Move

A **force** is a push or a pull. Forces act on objects, and often forces affect the motion of objects.

For example, when a car moves faster, the force produced in its engine is acting on the car. As a bike rider brakes to slow down, forces in the rider's muscles are acting on the bike. Whenever an object speeds up, slows down, stops, or changes direction, a force has acted on it.

A soccer player kicking a ball applies the force of the kick to the ball in a fraction of a second. Forces can also be applied over a longer time. For example, when you ride up in an elevator, the force of the elevator's motor acts on the car the whole time the car is rising. In fact, some forces are *always* acting on us. One of these forces is gravity.

FIND OUT

- what a force is
- how the force of gravity is related to mass and distance
- how to measure gravity

VOCABULARY

force
gravity
newton

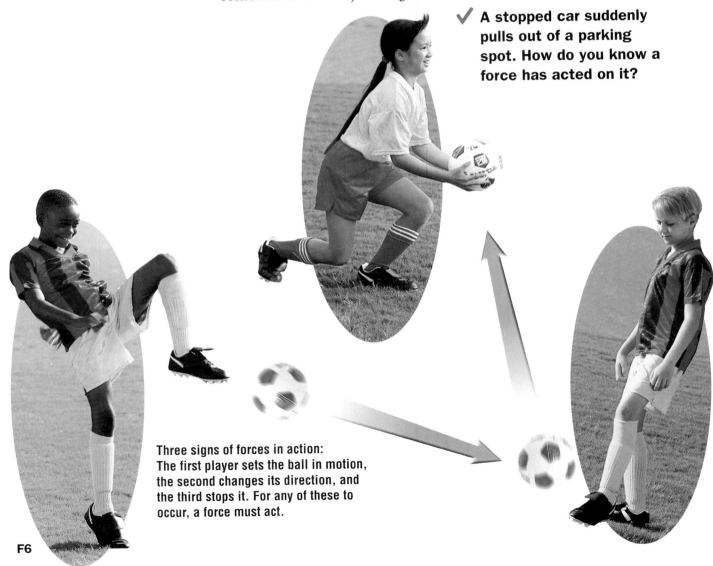

✔ **A stopped car suddenly pulls out of a parking spot. How do you know a force has acted on it?**

Three signs of forces in action: The first player sets the ball in motion, the second changes its direction, and the third stops it. For any of these to occur, a force must act.

F6

The Force of Gravity

A soccer ball moves, changes direction, or stops when a foot, a head, or a goalie's hands come into contact with it. In each case, something must touch the soccer ball to cause a force to act on it. But some forces act on objects at a distance, even without touching them.

Every piece of matter in the universe, however large or small, pulls on every other piece of matter. This force is called *gravitation*. It affects all matter in all forms or states, including liquids and gases. On Earth the gravitational force we are most aware of is the pull of Earth itself on objects at Earth's surface. This force pulls us and everything around us toward the center of Earth. Gravitation on Earth is called **gravity**.

Even the oceans and the atmosphere of Earth are kept in place by gravity. Gravity holds the oceans tightly to the surface of the planet and keeps the surface of the water fairly level. If gravity were weaker, some or all of our atmosphere might drift away into space. The moon, which has a much smaller gravitational pull,

◄ Gravity starts this amusement park ride moving toward Earth. Gravity continues to increase the ride's speed until another force slows the ride down.

could not hold on to an atmosphere like ours if it had one.

Although gravitation acts between all objects, it is a relatively weak force. The gravitational force between two tennis balls resting on a table does not bring them together. The pull between them is too weak. However, the gravitational force acting on some objects is very noticeable. The attraction between the moon and our oceans causes water in the oceans to bulge out from Earth. The oceans bulge toward the moon on one side of Earth and away from the moon on the opposite side. This causes tides on Earth wherever there are large bodies of water. At the places where the oceans bulge, high tides occur.

It may surprise you to know that the strength of the gravitational force between objects does not depend on their size. It depends on only the masses of the objects and the distance between them.

✔ **What is gravitation?**

◄ A coastline has low tide when its position on Earth is turned 90° away from ocean bulges caused by the moon's gravitational pull.

◄ As Earth rotates, a coastline that lines up with the moon has high tide.

Mass and Gravity

Mass is the amount of matter in an object. When you pick up two objects and one is heavier than the other, the heavier object has more mass. Larger objects do not necessarily have more mass than smaller ones. A basketball is larger than a bowling ball, but the bowling ball has more mass. A coin may have more mass than a balloon many times its size.

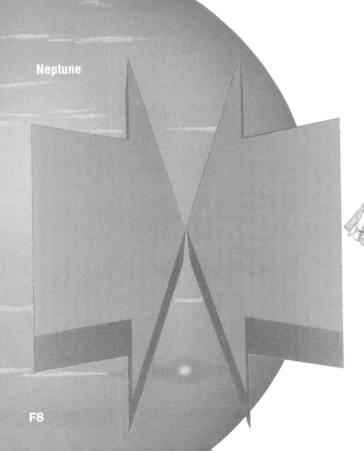

In these force diagrams, a thick arrow indicates a strong gravitational

Moon

Earth

attraction. A thin arrow indicates a weak gravitational attraction. Each space station is the same distance from the *center* of its moon or planet. Neptune has

greater mass than Earth. Earth has greater mass than the moon. So the gravitational attraction between Neptune and its space station is the strongest. The attraction between the moon and its station is the weakest.

Neptune

Mass is a property of matter that determines how much gravitational attraction there is between objects. Small objects are not massive enough to have a noticeable effect on each other's motion. For example, two bowling balls set near one another do not exert enough gravitational force to overcome forces such as friction and the pull of other objects. Therefore, they will not move together. However, objects with large masses do affect the motion of other objects.

Objects as massive as planets, moons, and even asteroids have a noticeable effect on smaller objects. When you feel tired of standing, it is because you are using force to overcome gravity. This is because the combined mass of these two objects—your mass and Earth's mass—is large. The attraction between Earth and a molecule of oxygen or nitrogen is much smaller, so Earth holds those gases more loosely in the atmosphere.

Two objects have the same gravitational pull on each other. However, gravity affects the movement of the smaller object more. In the Earth-sun system, for example, the gravitational force between Earth and the sun helps keep Earth in orbit around the sun. Earth and the sun both exert a gravitational force. However, the sun is many times as massive as Earth, so Earth's effect on the sun is hardly noticeable.

In solar systems where the masses of a star and a planet are closer in size, the planet's pull on the star *is* noticeable. The gravitational attraction between a star and a very massive planet actually makes the star wobble slightly in its path. In recent years astronomers have seen this wobble in the light from some distant stars. This is strong evidence that each of these stars may have at least one planet in orbit around it.

✔ **Why doesn't gravity cause all the objects around us to move toward each other?**

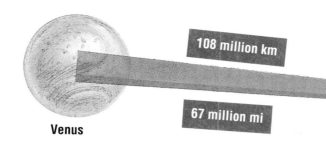

108 million km

67 million mi

Venus

Venus has about the same mass as Earth but is about 30 percent closer to the sun. So the gravitational pull between Venus and the sun is much greater than the pull between Earth and the sun.

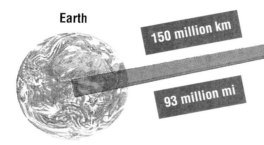

Earth

150 million km

93 million mi

Distance and Gravity

We can explain the motion of all objects in the universe, and their attraction to each other, according to the laws by which gravity works. We know that gravitational pull, besides being affected by the masses of objects, is also affected by the distance between objects. The more distant two objects are, the weaker is the gravitational force between them.

The distance factor explains the behavior of objects in everyday situations. For example, although the sun is about 330,000 times as massive as Earth, we feel Earth's gravitational pull more strongly than the sun's gravitational pull. This is because we are much closer to Earth's center than to the center of the sun. The distance to the sun's center is about 23,000 times as great as the distance to Earth's center. So its pull on us is much smaller. That's why we don't fly off of Earth and accelerate toward the sun.

The strong gravitational force due to Earth's closeness is the biggest problem in launching a spacecraft. A spacecraft must reach a speed of 40,200 km/hr (about 25,000 mi/hr) during launch to escape the force of Earth's gravity. Far beyond Earth, the spacecraft comes more and more under the influence of the sun's gravitational pull. Then the spacecraft may be guided into an orbit around the sun or another body.

When a spacecraft travels back toward Earth, the gravitational attraction between Earth's center and the spacecraft's center becomes greater. As a result, the spacecraft's acceleration toward Earth increases. In this way, the pull of Earth's gravity is used to bring the spacecraft home.

The effect of distance on gravitational attraction can be measured and observed on Earth as well as in space. The force of gravity on a person at sea level is slightly greater than the force of gravity on the same person on a high mountain. This difference occurs because the distance to the center of Earth is greater at high altitudes.

✔ **The sun is much more massive than Earth. Why aren't we pulled off of Earth and into the sun?**

At sea level on Earth, this basketball player weighs about 99 lb. On the moon, the player would weigh in at about 16 lb.

How Gravity Is Measured

Probably without realizing it, you have measured the strength of gravity many times. Every time you step on a scale, you measure the force of gravity on you. Weight is the measure of the force of gravity on an object. In the United States we usually use pounds to measure weight. The metric unit for weight is the **newton**. All forces can be measured in newtons, and weight is just one of many forces. One newton is the force needed to change the speed of, or to accelerate, 1 kg by 1 m in 1 second. At sea level, a 1-kg mass weighs about 9.8 newtons (2.2 lb).

Remember that the force of gravity (weight) and mass are not the same. Mass is the amount of matter in an object. This amount stays the same no matter where in the universe you might go. Weight is a measure of gravity and depends on the gravitational force where the object is found.

For example, gravitational attraction on the moon is only about one-sixth of what it is on Earth. If you travel to the moon, you will weigh only one-sixth of your Earth weight (although

The force of gravity on the surfaces of the moon and the planets depends on the mass and radius of each body. ▶

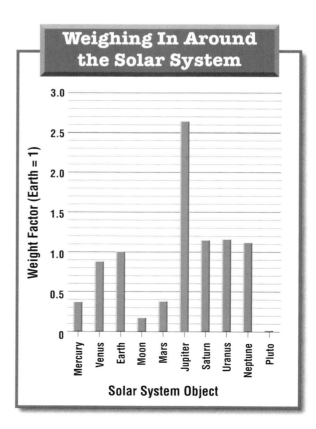

▲ Because of the reduced force of gravity on the moon, a single step can lift you much higher than it would on Earth.

Weighing In Around the Solar System

Weight Factor (Earth = 1)

3.0
2.5
2.0
1.5
1.0
0.5
0

Mercury, Venus, Earth, Moon, Mars, Jupiter, Saturn, Uranus, Neptune, Pluto

Solar System Object

your mass will not change). Gravitational attraction on Jupiter is about two and a half times what it is on Earth. If you travel to Jupiter, you will weigh about two and a half times what you weigh on Earth.

The graph on page F10 shows what fraction (or multiple) of Earth's gravity you would feel if you could stand on the surface of another planet.

✔ **At sea level, what mass has a weight of 9.8 newtons?**

Summary

Forces act on objects and often affect the motion of objects. Gravitational attraction pulls all objects toward each other. Its strength depends on the masses of the objects and on the distance between them. As mass increases, gravitational attraction also increases. As distance between objects increases, gravitational attraction weakens. Force, including the force of gravity, is measured in newtons.

Review

1. If an object speeds up, slows down, stops, or changes direction, what can you be certain of?

2. What happens to the force between two objects being pulled together by gravitational attraction?

3. Suppose two planets have the same mass but different diameters. Which planet has the stronger gravity at its surface?

4. **Critical Thinking** At the top of a skyscraper, would your weight be a little less than, a little more than, or exactly the same as it is at the bottom of the building? Explain.

5. **Test Prep** Scientists use a unit called the _____ to measure forces such as gravity.

   A newton   **C** aristotle

   B scale   **D** mass

LINKS

MATH LINK

Patterns Suppose a comet is 1 million km from the sun and is moving away from it. When it is 2 million km away, the pull of the sun's gravity is $\frac{1}{4}$ of what it was. When it is 3 million km away, the pull is $\frac{1}{9}$ of what it was. What is the pull of gravity when the comet is 4 million km from the sun?

WRITING LINK

Informative Writing—Description
A saying goes, "If you really want to learn a subject, teach it." Write a three-paragraph description of gravity to teach a third grader what it is. Write your paragraphs so you could read them to the child.

SOCIAL STUDIES LINK

Amusing History Gravity is one of the forces that puts the "thrill" in amusement park thrill rides. Do some research to discover how thrill rides have changed over the years.

TECHNOLOGY LINK

Learn more about forces by watching *Fifth Force* on the **Harcourt Science Newsroom Video.**

LESSON 2

How Can You Describe Motion?

In this lesson, you can . . .

 INVESTIGATE speed, average speed, and velocity.

 LEARN ABOUT three laws of motion.

 LINK to math, writing, physical education, and technology.

INVESTIGATE

Measuring Speed

Activity Purpose In the previous lesson, you learned how gravity can affect the motion of objects. You also learned how we measure the force of gravity. Now you will learn more about motion. In this activity you will **experiment** with measuring motion.

Materials

- ruler
- book
- marble or ball bearing
- metric tape measure or meterstick
- pencil
- stopwatch (or watch with second hand)
- compass

Activity Procedure

1 Make a ramp by propping up one end of your ruler on a book or other support that is about 8 cm high.

2 Roll a marble down the ramp. Start timing the marble as soon as it leaves the bottom of the ramp. **Measure** the distance the marble travels in 1 second. (Picture A)

3 **Record** your data in a table like the one shown on page F13. Calculate the average speed of the marble by dividing the distance the marble traveled by the elapsed time.

◀ Motion depends on your frame of reference. This astronaut probably feels motionless, but if an observer on Earth were to see him, the astronaut would appear to be moving rapidly.

Picture A

Measuring Average Speed

Time (sec)	Distance (cm)	Average Speed (cm/sec)	Velocity

④ Repeat Steps 2 and 3, but **measure** the distance the marble travels in 2 seconds, 3 seconds, and 4 seconds. Start the marble at the same height and the same place each time.

⑤ Use the compass to find the direction in which your marble rolls as it leaves the ramp. (When you include the direction of an object with its speed measurement, you get a measurement of velocity.)

Draw Conclusions

1. **Compare** the average speeds of the marble for the four time intervals. **Use numbers** to **interpret the data** by identifying the pattern in the data.

2. At what point did the marble reach its greatest speed?

3. Did the velocity of the marble change? In what way did it change?

4. **Scientists at Work** Scientists repeat **experiments** to ensure that their results are accurate. What could you do to improve the accuracy of the **measurements** you took?

Investigate Further How can you use your data to **predict** about how long the marble would roll before it stopped?

Process Skill Tip

When you **experiment**, you should repeat what you did to make certain that you get similar results the second time.

Speed and Velocity

Observing Motion

FIND OUT

• how to describe and measure motion

• how force affects motion

• three laws of motion

VOCABULARY

speed
average speed
velocity

In the investigation, you observed the motion of a controlled object and experimented with a way to measure and record motion. Motion can also be observed in everyday life. Think of the movement of a butterfly in flight, rain falling, a washer spinning, or a baseball speeding toward home plate. Motion is always observable as a change in an object's position compared to objects that are still. To describe motion scientifically, it is necessary to measure position, or distance, and time.

Exactly how fast was that fastball? To find out, first find the distance from the pitcher's mound to home plate. Then find the time it took for the baseball to move from the pitcher's hand to home plate. The relationship between the distance and the time expresses the speed of the fastball. Suppose the distance from the pitcher to the hitter is 18.4 m and the ball traveled that distance in 2 seconds. That means the ball traveled 9.2 m/sec, or about 33 km/hr.

The winner runs from the starting line to the finish line—a distance of 50 m—in 8.2 sec, running at a speed of about 6 m/sec.

Identifying Frame of Reference

At times, it can be difficult to decide which of two objects is in motion. For much of history, people believed that the sun moved across Earth's sky. And for many years, scientists assumed that Earth was motionless. In other words, they thought they could use Earth as a frame of reference for the sun's motion. When you speak of motion, a *frame of reference* is something that you do not expect to move.

Motion is observed in comparison to other objects that seem to be standing still. For example, suppose a block falls from a desk, passes the top of a drawer, the drawer handle, and then the bottom of the drawer, always changing its distance from the top of the desk, and finally lands on the floor. Or think of the wind in the branches of a tree, producing a very different kind of motion. The moving parts of a tree may be observed against the stillness of the sky. The desk and the sky in these examples are frames of reference for observing the motion of the block and the tree.

Usually, people observe and measure motion relative to positions on Earth. But sometimes it is necessary to find more distant frames of reference. Earth rotates at a speed of about 1675 km/hr (about 1041 mi/hr) at the equator. The sun is one frame of reference for Earth's rotation. By using even more-distant frames of reference, astronomers have identified other speeds. Earth goes around the sun at over 100,000 km/hr (62,000 mi/hr). The solar system orbits the center of the galaxy at about 792,000 km/hr (492,000 mi/hr).

Without frames of reference, motion cannot be observed. That is one reason we are not aware of the tremendous speeds at which we are whirling through space. It is also why it is possible to make a mistake about what object is in motion. For example, you may sense a movement backward in a train or a car, when actually a nearby vehicle has moved forward. A quick look around to check other frames of reference can tell you what has really moved.

The observation of motion depends on the observer's frame of reference. Suppose a person is walking east in a train that is heading west. An observer whose frame of reference is the train will say the person is moving east. An observer whose frame of reference is Earth will say the person is moving west.

✔ **Is this book in motion right now? Explain.**

▲ Is the skater moving, or is the background moving? Your answer might be influenced by your frame of reference. The photographer of the first photo is standing still, so the skater seems to move.

▲ The photographer of the second photo is moving along with the skater. From this frame of reference, the skater seems to be standing still while the rest of the world whooshes by.

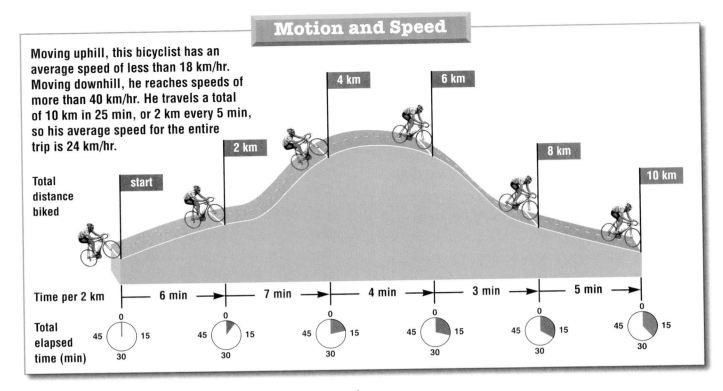

Motion and Speed

Moving uphill, this bicyclist has an average speed of less than 18 km/hr. Moving downhill, he reaches speeds of more than 40 km/hr. He travels a total of 10 km in 25 min, or 2 km every 5 min, so his average speed for the entire trip is 24 km/hr.

4 km · 6 km · 2 km · 8 km · 10 km · start

Total distance biked

Time per 2 km: 6 min → 7 min → 4 min → 3 min → 5 min →

Total elapsed time (min)

Calculating Speed

Measuring motion often requires measuring time. **Speed** is a measure of how far something moves during a period of time. It is a comparison, or ratio, of distance moved to time elapsed during the movement. Some common expressions of speed are: kilometers per hour (km/hr), miles per hour (mi/hr), and meters per second (m/sec).

The top speed a human can reach is about 65 km/hr (about 40 mi/hr). A cheetah's top speed is about 96 km/hr (about 60 mi/hr). Events that are beyond what we can sense also have speeds. Light travels at a speed of about 300,000 km/sec (186,000 mi/sec). Along the San Andreas fault in California, the continent is creeping westward at about 2 cm (less than 1 in.) per year.

Sometimes speed is a measurement of how fast an

When you hear the word *speed*, you may think of high speed. But this snail also has a measurable speed, which might be about 0.05 km/hr (about 0.03 mi/hr). ▶

object is moving in an instant of time. When the speedometer in a car reads 42 km/hr (26 mi/hr), it is showing the speed of the car at that moment in time. But the speed of a car increases and decreases as it moves. Many things—from creeping glaciers to swimming dolphins—change speed from one instant to the next.

Because of these variations, it is difficult to measure speed in an instant of time. A measurement of average speed can be more useful. **Average speed** is the measure of the total distance the object has moved divided by the total elapsed time.

For example, the drive to Chicago from Detroit is about 460 km. The trip can be made in 6 hours. What is the average speed necessary to make this trip? To find out, divide the distance, 460 km, by the time, 6 hours. The answer is about 77 km/hr.

✔ **How do we calculate average speed?**

F16

Velocity

Suppose two cars pass each other in opposite lanes of an east-west highway. Both cars are traveling at 88 km/hr, so both have the same speed. But the cars are going in different directions, so they have different velocities. **Velocity** is the speed of an object in a particular direction. One car has a velocity of 88 km/hr heading west. The other has a velocity of 88 km/hr heading east.

It is also possible that the cars could both be heading east but have different velocities because they are traveling at different speeds. One car might have a velocity of 60 km/hr heading east. The other might have a velocity of 80 km/hr heading east. Both the speed and the direction have to be the same for the velocity to be the same.

Two objects traveling at the same velocity stay in the same positions relative to each other. Suppose a car that heads north at 80 km/hr is ahead of a second car traveling at the same velocity. The second car will never overtake or fall farther behind the first car. One of the cars would have to change its speed or direction for their relative positions to change.

To remember that velocity includes direction, keep in mind that scientists sometimes use arrows to represent velocity. A velocity arrow has a length that represents the speed measurement. The direction it points to represents the direction measurement.

Velocity in circular motion is constantly changing, because the direction of the movement is constantly changing. An amusement park ride may spin in a circle, faster and faster. At last it reaches top speed and keeps going around and around at the same rate. The speed is unchanging at this point, but the velocity is constantly changing. Any time there is movement along a curve, velocity constantly changes, even if speed does not.

▲ Car A and Car B have the same speed and direction, so they have the same velocity. Car A and Car C have the same speed. Do they have the same velocity?

Any change in velocity is caused by the application of a force. When a car speeds up, slows down, or turns, it is because of an application of force. You can feel this because your body moves backward, forward, or to the side in your seat. For a moment your body resists the force of the car seat, before the force of the car seat changes the velocity of your body.

✔ **Why does your velocity constantly change when you move along a curve?**

As the car travels around the exit ramp, its speed is steady but its direction—and therefore its velocity—keeps changing. ▼

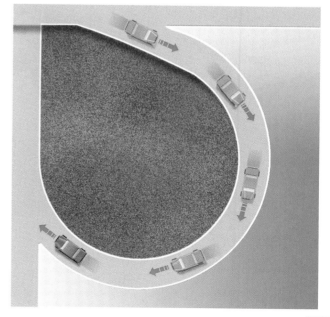

The Laws of Motion

In ancient Greece, Aristotle wrote that any moving object needs a push or a pull to keep it moving. His idea was that a constant application of force is necessary to keep an object in motion. This is incorrect. About 400 years ago, Galileo showed that a moving object would keep moving in a straight line, without a push or a pull, until something interfered with its motion.

Isaac Newton built on Galileo's work. Newton discovered laws that describe gravity, other forces, and the ways objects in motion affect each other. The laws of motion are still used to describe how planets move around the sun and how everyday objects move on Earth. However, the laws can be tested only under controlled conditions. Otherwise, there are too many other forces acting on the objects.

✔ **What did Galileo discover about motion?**

The inertia of an object is determined by the mass of the object—the amount of matter it has. The great inertia of this rock helps keep it from becoming unbalanced by forces such as wind. ▼

First Law of Motion

An object at rest tends to stay at rest, and an object in motion tends to stay in motion in a straight line until an outside force acts on it.

The first law says simply that objects do not change their velocity unless some force acts on them. A hockey puck sitting on the ice does not move until something makes it move. A puck sliding across the ice keeps going in the same direction until something acts on it. A stick may change the direction of the puck, or friction may slow it down.

On Earth, objects in motion tend to slow down and stop after we stop pushing or pulling them. They do so only because an outside force acts on them. As things rub together, they develop a force called friction that slows their velocity.

The tendency of an object to resist a change in its motion is called *inertia*. It is the property that makes it hard to get a car rolling by pushing it. It is also the property that makes it hard to stop a car once it has started rolling. The first law is sometimes called the *law of inertia*.

✔ **What property of objects makes them tend to resist a change in motion?**

When a car stops suddenly, inertia keeps the passengers moving forward. ▶

 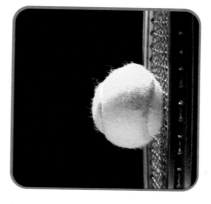 

▲ The tennis ball approaches the racket with a certain velocity. The racket delivers a force to the ball. This force changes the velocity of the ball—both its direction and its speed. The size of this change is proportional to the force applied by the racket.

Second Law of Motion

force = mass × acceleration

The second law explains how an unbalanced force changes the motion of objects. An *unbalanced force* is a force without an equal force in the opposite direction. When an unbalanced force acts on an object, it changes the velocity of the object (its speed, its direction, or both). The rate of this change in velocity is called *acceleration*. It depends on the size of the force and on the mass of the object:

- The greater the force, the greater is the acceleration, or change in velocity.
- The greater the mass, the smaller is the acceleration, or change in velocity.

The change in velocity will happen in the direction the force is applied. Suppose an unbalanced force pushes on an object that is at rest. The force will put the object into motion in the direction of the push. Or the force might push on an object that is already moving in the same direction as the push. Then the object will move faster in the same direction. An unbalanced force in the opposite direction will cause the object to slow down without changing direction or to stop.

Pushing a car from the back might get it to roll forward. Two people pushing on the back of a car can get it rolling faster. If one person pushes on a car from the back and another person pushes from the front, their two forces may cancel each other out. The car may not move because these two forces applied to the car are balanced.

The rate of change in the velocity of the car will depend on the mass of the car and the size of the forces acting on it. Pushing on a toy car and pushing on a real car with the same force produce very different changes in velocity because of the different masses of the cars.

Here is another example of how mass, force, and acceleration (change in velocity) are related. Two people at an amusement park are riding the bumper cars. One person's car is stopped. The other person drives up slowly and bumps into the first person's car. A small force is applied to the stopped car, so it moves a bit. If the driver of the moving car drives up quickly, that will apply a larger force to the stopped car. As a result, it will cause it to move much faster and farther. The acceleration of the stopped car depends on the force applied by the car in motion.

Now suppose the car in motion is a bumper car and the still car is a *real* car. Even if the bumper-car driver moves very quickly and bumps into the real car, the real car will not move much at all. It has a much greater mass and inertia than the bumper car, so its change in velocity will be much smaller.

✓ **What happens to the velocity of an object when a force acts on it?**

Third Law of Motion

For every action force, there is an equal and opposite reaction force.

The third law of motion says that forces always come in pairs. For every force there is an equal and opposite force. This means that a hand pushing on a desk (action force) produces an equal but opposite reaction force of the desk pushing on the hand. The harder the hand pushes on the desk, the harder the desk pushes on the hand. The forces of action and reaction are always equal.

If you swing your hand into the side of your desk, your hand exerts a force on the desk when you make contact. What you feel on contact results from the reaction force. It is the force that the desk exerts back on the hand that hits it.

When someone pulls a door open, the door pulls back. As a student's weight exerts force down on a chair, the chair pushes up on the student with equal force. If the chair did not, the student would fall straight through, pulled down by the force of gravity. When a skateboarder pushes backward on the ground with his toe, the ground pushes him forward with equal force. A swimmer pushes water backward with her hands and is pushed forward by the water at the same time.

The third law also applies to gravitational force. For example, when a parachuter falls toward Earth, the acceleration of the fall is due to the force of gravity. The third law states that the gravitational force exerted by the Earth on the parachuter is equal to the force exerted by the parachuter on the Earth.

Taken together, the three laws give us a way of measuring and predicting motion and the effects of forces. They hold true here on Earth and across the universe.

✔ **What is the third law of motion?**

When the first skater pushes the second, the second skater will slide forward. But the first skater will also slide backward an equal distance. ▼

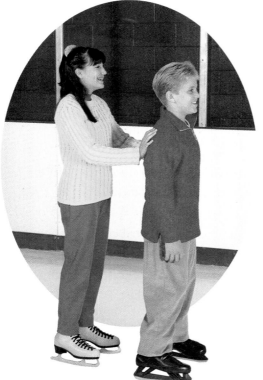

The first skater provides the force that changes the second skater's motion. The third law tells us that when the first skater pushes, an equal force pushes back on her. ▼

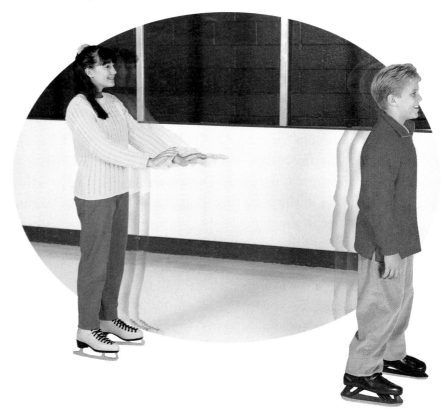

Summary

Motion is a change in the position of an object. Speed is a measure of the motion of an object over time. Velocity is a measure of speed in a particular direction. There are three basic laws describing motion.

1. An object at rest tends to stay at rest, and an object in motion tends to stay in motion unless a force acts on it.

2. An unbalanced force changes the velocity of an object. The rate of this change in velocity, or acceleration, depends on the size of the force and the mass of the object.

3. For every action force, there is an equal and opposite reaction force.

Review

1. How can you calculate the average speed of an object?

2. How does Earth's velocity change as it moves around the sun?

3. What causes the velocity of an object to change?

4. **Critical Thinking** Why is it harder to stop a heavy football player rushing with the ball than it is to stop a light player?

5. **Test Prep** The resistance of an object to a change in its motion is its —

   A gravity

   B inertia

   C speed

   D velocity

LINKS

MATH LINK

Averages Look up the world record 100-m, 400-m, and marathon track times. Calculate the average speed of the runner in each case. Do you think the runner's speed at each instant varied much from the average speed in each case? Explain.

WRITING LINK

Persuasive Writing—Opinion Write an ad or a persuasive paragraph to urge people to wear safety belts. Use the science you have learned to make your case convincing.

PHYSICAL EDUCATION LINK

Track and Field Learn more about how speed and velocity are important in track events. Do research to answer these questions: How do speed and velocity affect how far a shot is put or a javelin is thrown? How does the mass of the shot or the javelin affect the distance it is thrown?

TECHNOLOGY LINK

Learn more about motion, speed, and velocity by visiting this Internet site: **www.scilinks.org/harcourt**

LESSON 3

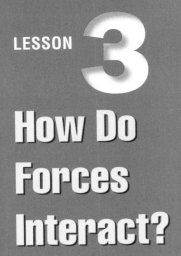

How Do Forces Interact?

In this lesson, you can . . .

 INVESTIGATE how forces act on objects to cause motion.

 LEARN ABOUT how balanced and unbalanced forces act on an object.

 LINK to math, writing, physical education, and technology.

Making It Move

Activity Purpose In Lesson 2 you studied the three laws of motion and the relationship between force and motion. In this activity you will make an object move without touching it. You will investigate forces that cannot be seen but can be inferred from their effects. And you will explore how two such forces interact to make an object move.

Materials

- plank (1 m or longer)
- pencils or lengths of dowel
- wooden cart (or skate or toy car)
- notebook paper

Activity Procedure

1 Place a pencil under the center of the plank. Place the roller cart at the center of the plank. Make a plan to cause the cart to move without touching it. Carry out your plan, and **record** what happens. (Picture A)

2 Put the cart back at the center of the plank. Make a plan to cause the cart to move from one end of the plank to the other and back without touching the cart. Carry out your plan, and **record** what happens.

3 Now place the cart on a sheet of paper. Make a plan to remove the sheet of paper without touching the cart, while making the cart roll as little as possible. Carry out your plan, and **record** what happens. (Picture B)

◄ The cowhand provides the force that keeps the lariat moving. She also provides the force that holds the lariat in. If the cowhand let go of the lariat, it would fly off in a straight path.

Picture A

Picture B

4️⃣ Place the cart at the center of the plank once again. Slowly tip the plank from one end. Estimate the angle at which the plank must be tilted before the cart starts to roll. **Hypothesize** which force or forces prevent the cart from rolling until that angle is reached. **Record** your estimate and results.

Draw Conclusions

1. **Infer** what force started the cart moving in Step 1. Tell how the force was transferred to the cart. Do the same for Step 2.

2. Look at your notes for Step 3. **Infer** what property of the cart kept it from rolling while you removed the sheet of paper.

3. **Scientists at Work** When scientists **hypothesize**, they often **design an experiment** that tests the hypothesis. What experiment could you design to test your hypothesis about the force or forces that acted in Step 4?

Investigate Further Suppose you repeat Step 4 but with the cart upside down on the plank. **Predict** whether the plank will need to be tilted to a larger angle or a smaller angle than in Step 4. **Hypothesize** what forces act on the cart in each case.

Process Skill Tip

When you **hypothesize**, you make a prediction about cause and effect. You may be able to test your prediction by **experimenting**.

How Forces Interact

Forces Act Together

FIND OUT

- how the force of friction opposes motion
- the results of balanced forces and unbalanced forces

VOCABULARY

friction
balanced forces
unbalanced forces

In the investigation you set a cart in motion by using the force of gravity. Only a force can change the motion of an object. That force must be strong enough to overcome the inertia of the object.

Whenever the motion of an object changes, more than one force is acting. For example, a runner's legs and feet provide a force that pushes back against the ground. The ground provides the reaction force that pushes the runner forward. This is described by Newton's third law of motion: for every action force, there is an equal and opposite reaction force. And still more forces—and therefore more reaction forces—act on the runner at the same time.

All forces are measured in *newtons*. At Earth's surface, gravity pulls on a 0.1-kg object with a force of about 1 newton. That means that a quarter-pound burger weighs about 1 newton. Newtons can be added and subtracted to find how forces act together.

✔ **What is the unit of measure for force?**

The force of gravity pulling down on a building is great. But the building, while standing, opposes gravity with an equal force. A demolition crew destroys the supports that provide that opposing force. This allows the force of gravity to set the building into motion, pulling it to the ground. ▶

The skier provides a relatively small force to overcome the force of friction. Once he is moving, however, the force of gravity increases his speed. ▶

Friction

The first law of motion states that an object in motion tends to stay in motion until another force acts on it. On Earth one of these interfering forces is often friction.

Friction is a force that opposes motion whenever two surfaces rub against each other. In fact, the force of friction is present only when another force, such as gravity or muscle power, acts to move an object against something else. Suppose you want to slide a heavy desk across a flat carpeted floor. Until you push on the desk, no friction is present. Once you start to push, the force of friction pushes back in the opposite direction. Until the desk starts to move, this force of friction is equal to the force you are applying to the desk.

On a carpet on a level surface, a wooden block will move only as long as it is being pushed. On a wooden floor, one push may send the block moving on its own for some distance. On ice or a highly polished surface, one push will cause the block to travel for a great distance. Of these three surfaces, the carpet produces the most friction.

Overcoming friction to put an object into motion requires energy. Once the object starts to move, the energy needed to keep it moving is less than the energy that was needed to start it moving. It is possible to reduce friction so that less energy is needed to overcome it. One way to reduce friction is to use rollers or wheels. A rolling motion causes much less friction than a sliding motion. Another way to reduce friction is by using lubricants, such as oil and grease. The microscopic particles in lubricants move over each other easily, offering very little frictional force.

Friction can be reduced, but there is no way to get rid of it entirely. In fact, friction is necessary for actions as simple as walking. As your foot pushes backward on the ground, the force of friction offers the resistance necessary to push your body forward. It is even possible and sometimes desirable to increase friction. Tire treads, shoe soles, and cleats are all designed to increase friction and to prevent slipping.

The wheels and oiled bearings on a bicycle reduce friction and allow the bike to move easily. But rubber pads that squeeze the tire rims produce friction to make the bicycle stop. Surfaces such as roads and tracks are also designed to produce some friction. These surfaces have bumps and grooves that do this.

✔ **A child slides down a slide. In what direction does the force of friction push on the child?**

▲ The tiny bumps and ridges on a sheet of paper help produce a friction force that tends to hold the pencil and paper together. The pull between this friction and the force from the writer's hand breaks off particles of graphite. These particles are left behind as writing.

Balanced Forces

Objects often have more than one force acting on them. An object sitting on a table is acted on by the force of gravity pulling the object down, and by the table pushing up against the object with equal force. The object on the table remains still because the forces are balanced. If the table suddenly breaks and does not push with a force equal to that of gravity, the velocity of the object will change suddenly. It will fall.

Balanced forces acting on an object are equal in size but opposite in direction. The result is that the two forces seem to cancel each other out. When forces on an object are balanced, either the object does not move, like the object on the table, or it continues its motion at a constant velocity.

Suppose a heavy crate slides down a steep ramp at a steady speed. An unbalanced force started the motion, but then the force stopped. The crate is not speeding up, slowing down, or changing direction, so the forces on it are balanced. The force of gravity that pulls it down the ramp is exactly matched by the force of friction that resists the motion. There is no change in the velocity of the crate. Slowing the crate down and stopping it would require an additional force, such as more friction.

Every object that is still is acted on by balanced forces. The force of every building stands against the force of gravity. When one book leans against another on a shelf, it puts a force on the second book that is balanced by the force of friction. The force of air pressure weighing down on your body is balanced by an equal force within you pressing out. If you push on an object, the object pushes equally hard back on you. If you push harder and harder, the object pushes back harder and harder, as long as it does not move. This is also true for pulling on any object. Pull on a locked door and the door pulls back on you with equal force.

Objects that move at a constant velocity are also acted on by balanced forces. The speed of a parachuter jumping from an airplane increases only for a while. Then the forces on the parachute are balanced, and the parachuter comes down under balanced forces at a constant velocity.

All objects on Earth are acted on by forces, but not all of these objects are speeding up, slowing down, or changing direction. Only an *unbalanced* force on an object causes a change in velocity.

✔ **An object is still. What can you conclude about the forces acting on it?**

When the forces exerted on the rope by the two teams are equal, the flag does not move. When one team pulls with a greater force, the forces become unbalanced and the flag moves. What would happen if one team pulled on grass while the other team pulled on ice? ▼

As the dogs start to pull on the stationary sled, the force of friction pulls in the opposite direction. As long as these forces are balanced, the sled does not move. When the force of the dogs' pulling becomes greater than the force of friction, the sled will begin to move.

Unbalanced Forces

Objects often have more than one force acting on them. The combination of all of the forces acting on an object is called the *net force*. When the forces acting on an object are balanced, the net force is zero and there is no change in the velocity of the object. Either it is still, or it moves at a constant speed and in a constant direction. But often the forces acting on an object are not balanced. **Unbalanced forces** acting on an object cause a change in velocity, making the object speed up, slow down, or change direction.

When two equal forces push in opposite directions on an object, the net force is zero. When two *unequal* forces push in opposite directions on an object, the object changes its speed in the direction of the stronger force.

In a game of tug of war, when two teams pull on the rope with the same amount of force, the net force is zero. The rope is stationary, and the velocity of the rope is zero. The rope is not moving in any direction at any speed. When one team exerts more force on the rope by pulling harder, the velocity of the rope changes in the direction of the harder pull. There is motion because the forces on the rope are unbalanced.

Suppose a car is stopped at the top of a hill, with its brakes on. The force of friction from the tires exactly balances the force of gravity.

If these forces become unbalanced, they will change the velocity of the car. In the process of the car's going down the hill, the forces will speed the car up, slow it down, or change its direction.

- *Speeding the car up:* The driver takes her foot off the brake pedal, reducing the force of friction on the tires. The forces are now unbalanced. The stronger force of gravity makes the car start to move and go faster and faster down the hill.
- *Slowing the car down:* As she nears the bottom of the hill, the driver applies the brakes. The force of friction increases. When it is equal to the force of gravity, the car moves at a steady speed. When friction becomes stronger than the force of gravity, the car starts to slow down. The forces are now unbalanced, so the velocity changes.
- *Changing the direction of the car:* The road curves. As the driver turns the wheel, the force of friction between the tires and the road increases in one direction. This unbalanced force makes the car change its direction.

✔ **In a tractor pull, two tractors pull in opposite directions. One tractor pulls with a greater force. In which direction do the tractors move?**

F27

Friction and Gravity

Two forces that we deal with regularly are gravity and friction. Often these two forces are in balance, acting against each other. In these cases an object is stationary or moves with a steady velocity. When one force is stronger, the velocity of an object changes.

The force of gravity is pulling down on this snow with a force equal to the weight of the snow. But the grains of snow and ice stick together with enough combined force to balance the force of gravity.

Eventually the force of gravity may overcome the forces holding the snow together, and an avalanche may result.

Summary

Friction is a force that opposes motion. When forces on an object are equal and act in opposite directions, they are balanced forces. They do not cause a change in the velocity of the object. When forces on an object are unbalanced, the object changes its velocity in the direction of the stronger force.

Review

1. What unit is used to measure force?
2. You slide an object to the left. In what direction does the force of friction act to resist the motion?
3. Two equal forces act on an object in opposite directions. They are the only forces acting on the object. Will the object move? How do you know?
4. **Critical Thinking** An object is not moving, even though you know the force of gravity is acting on it. What inference can you make about other forces acting on it?
5. **Test Prep** When an unbalanced force acts on an object, the object changes its —
   A velocity
   B friction
   C temperature
   D gravity

LINKS

MATH LINK

Weighing In On Earth's surface, gravity pulls on a 0.1-kg object with a force of about 1 newton. A 1-kg object weighs about 2.2 lb. Estimate the weight of an 80-lb child in newtons.

WRITING LINK

Informative Writing—Description On Earth you must fight the force of gravity every day. This is not so for astronauts in space. Suppose you are an astronaut taking your first trip in a space shuttle. Write a journal entry describing the experience of your first day of weightlessness.

PHYSICAL EDUCATION LINK

Playing with Friction Ice and snow greatly reduce the amount of friction in skating and skiing. Yet skaters and skiers need friction to change their velocity—to start out, to stop, and to change direction. Find out how athletes move their skates and skis when they need to increase friction to change their motion.

TECHNOLOGY LINK

Experiment with building a water slide by investigating *Thrills by Design* on **Harcourt Science Explorations CD-ROM.**

MAGLEV TO SPACE

Scientists are developing a way to launch rockets into space by using the force of magnetism.

What is needed to send a rocket into space?

Sending a rocket into space is difficult and expensive. Rockets have to reach a velocity of about 40,000 km/hr (about 25,000 mi/hr) to break away from Earth's gravity and get into orbit around Earth. Large amounts of expensive fuel are needed for a rocket to reach this speed. To help reduce the cost, rockets are built in stages, or sections that come apart. The first stage, or booster, launches the rocket off the ground.

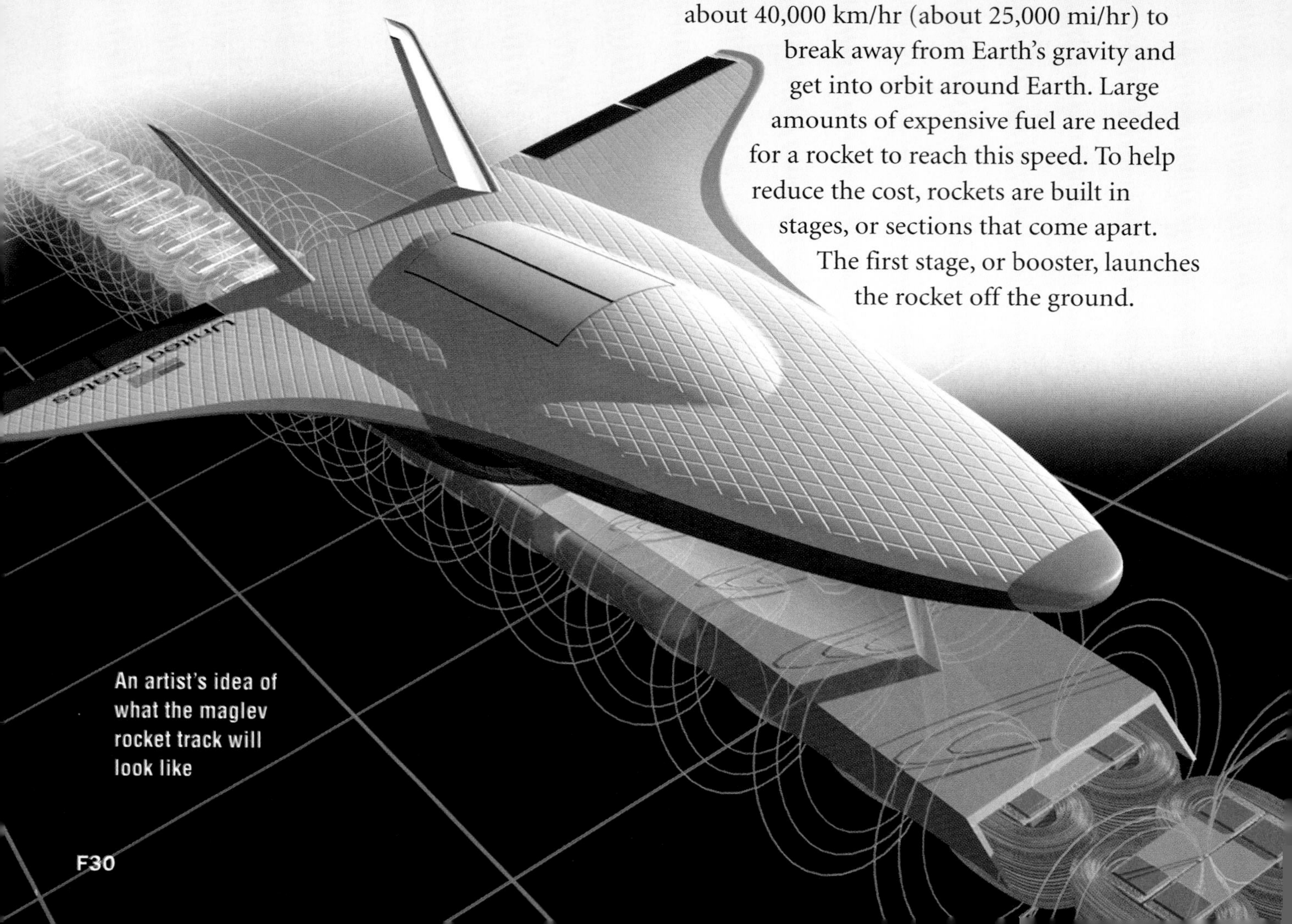

An artist's idea of what the maglev rocket track will look like

Right away the rocket begins to lighten its load as it uses the fuel in the first stage. When the fuel has been used up, the first stage drops away. This allows the second stage to boost a much lighter load into orbit.

How can a rocket be launched by using magnets?

Scientists at NASA are working on a way to make it cheaper and easier to send rockets into space. They are experimenting with the use of magnetic levitation, or maglev, technology to replace a rocket's first stage.

Engineers have been experimenting for years with the use of maglev technology in high-speed trains. Extremely powerful, or superconducting, magnets are mounted both on the track bed and underneath the train cars. These magnets repel each other, levitating, or lifting, the rail cars slightly above the tracks. A motor then shoots the train down the track, with the rails guiding it.

NASA expects to build a maglev launch-assist track (MagLifter) for rockets. A rocket carried on a maglev flatbed vehicle would be shot down a long track. As the superconducting magnets in the track repel those in the vehicle, the flatbed would shoot up a steep incline at one end, reaching a velocity of 960 km/hr (about 600 mi/hr). Once it was in the air, the single-stage rocket would separate from the flatbed. The single stage would then fire, boosting the rocket into orbit. NASA hopes to have ready for testing soon a 5,000-foot track that can be used to launch a 40,000-pound load.

Why is launching a rocket by using maglev a good idea?

The most expensive part of sending any spacecraft into orbit around Earth is the first few seconds of getting the rocket off the ground. A maglev system would be cheaper because the rocket's first stage wouldn't be needed. There would also be less maintenance because the maglev system has fewer moving parts.

Will maglev-launched rockets ever become common?

The technology is still in the experimental stage, but some scientists are hopeful. In the early 2000s, a maglev launch assist system could send satellites into orbit for hundreds rather than thousands of dollars per pound. Once the cost of launching goes down, the number of launches could increase.

THINK ABOUT IT

1. How might magnets help rockets get into space?
2. What is an advantage of using magnets to help launch a rocket?

WEB LINK:
For Science and Technology updates, visit The Learning Site.
www.harcourtschool.com

Careers — Mechanical Engineer

What They Do
Mechanical engineers plan and design tools, machines, engines, and other mechanical systems that produce, send out, or use power.

Education and Training Mechanical engineers must enjoy building things and finding out how things work. They must study mathematics, computers, and physics. Mechanical engineers need at least a bachelor's degree in mechanical engineering. Some positions in research and teaching require a master's or a doctorate degree.

Chien-Shiung Wu

PHYSICIST

Chien-Shiung Wu was one of the nation's most respected physicists. Her achievements earned her the National Medal of Science and election into the United States National Academy of Sciences. These are two of the highest honors available to a scientist working in the United States.

Dr. Wu was born in China in 1912. After she received her college degree, her family sent her to the United States to study for a doctorate in physics. When she waved good-bye to her mother and father in 1936, she didn't know that she would never see them again. World War II and political events in China kept her from returning for almost 30 years.

Chien-Shiung Wu studied physics at the University of California at Berkeley. She was a brilliant student who thought of Dr. Marie Curie, the first woman to win a Nobel Prize, as her role model. She earned her Ph.D. in physics in 1940, working long hours in the laboratory to become an expert on nuclear fission. During the 1940s and 1950s, Dr. Wu designed

experiments that helped explain the behavior of atomic particles. One experiment confirmed the existence of a type of high-speed atomic particle. Another experiment proved that a long-accepted physical law does not apply to atomic particles. For this discovery, the two male scientists for whom she had designed the experiment won the 1957 Nobel Prize for Physics. When the announcement was made, Dr. Wu was disappointed to find that she had not been included. This did not take away her enthusiasm for her work, however, and she went on to win many other honors.

During her retirement, Dr. Wu gave lectures and encouraged other women to choose careers in science.

THINK ABOUT IT

1. What kinds of forces do you think Dr. Wu studied?
2. Why did Dr. Wu admire Marie Curie?

Dr. Wu using one of the pieces of equipment that helped her make her important discoveries

Falling Coins

What are some of the effects of inertia?

Materials

- glass or plastic cup
- an index card
- quarter

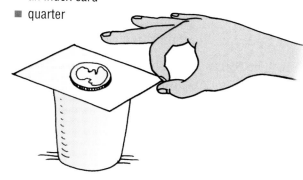

Procedure

1. Place the card on top of the glass.
2. Position the quarter in the center of the card.
3. Flick the edge of the card hard and fast with your finger. (Don't hit the quarter!)
4. Observe what happens to the quarter.

Draw Conclusions

What pulled the quarter into the cup? Why didn't the quarter shoot off the glass with the card? What would happen if the card moved out from under the quarter more slowly?

Acting and Reacting

How does Newton's third law affect motion?

Materials

- 12.5-cm (5-in.) square of heavy cardboard
- scissors
- ruler
- rubber band
- pan of water about 10 cm (4 in.) deep

Procedure

1. Cut one side of the cardboard "boat" into a point, as shown.
2. Cut a 5-cm (2-in.) square "paddle" from the other end of the boat.
3. Place the rubber band over the square end of the boat.
4. Insert the paddle between the sides of the rubber band and wind it up.
5. Place the boat on the water and let the paddle go.

Draw Conclusions

Why does the boat move? How could you make the boat move in the opposite direction? How could you make the boat go faster?

Chapter ① Review and Test Preparation

Vocabulary Review

Use the terms below to complete the sentences. The page numbers in ( ) tell you where to look in the chapter if you need help.

force (F6)   **velocity** (F17)

gravity (F7)   **friction** (F25)

newtons (F10)   **balanced forces** (F26)

speed (F16)   **unbalanced forces** (F27)

average speed (F16)

1. Divide the total distance moved by the total travel time to find the ___.

2. A push or pull is a ___.

3. Force is measured in ___.

4. ___ are equal and act in opposite directions.

5. The force of gravitation between Earth and the objects on it is ___.

6. ___ is a measure of how far something moves in a given period of time.

7. Speed in a certain direction is called ___.

8. The forces that can cause a change in the velocity of an object are ___.

9. The force that opposes motion is ___.

Connect Concepts

Complete the chart using terms from the Word Bank.

direction	size	gravity	you
force	mass	rub together	velocity
friction	Earth	inertia	unbalanced
equal	opposite	motion	speed

Laws of Motion

The First Law	The Second Law	The Third Law
An object in motion tends to remain in 10. _____ because of the property of 11. _____, until it is acted on by another 12. _____, such as the force of 13. _____, which tends to resist motion when two objects 14. _____.	When an 15. _____ force acts on an object, it changes the 16. _____ of an object (the 17. _____ of the object, its 18. _____, or both). The size of this change depends on the 19. _____ of the force and the 20. _____ of the object.	For every action force, there is an 21. _____ and 22. _____ reaction force, which means that when the force of 23. _____ pulls you toward Earth, it also pulls 24. _____ toward 25. _____.

Check Understanding

Write the letter of the best choice.

26. The strength of the force of gravitation between two objects increases as the ____ of the objects increases.
    A mass
    B weight
    C distance
    D velocity

27. The strength of the force of gravitation between two objects decreases as the ____ between the objects increases.
    F mass
    G weight
    H distance
    J velocity

28. When forces on an object are ____, there is no change in the object's velocity.
    A inertia
    B unbalanced
    C reaction forces
    D balanced

29. The third law of motion states that for every action force, there is a reaction force of equal strength in the ____ direction.
    F opposite
    G same
    H perpendicular
    J velocity

30. An object at rest tends to ____ until an unbalanced force acts on it.
    A resist friction
    B fall
    C move in a straight line
    D remain at rest

Critical Thinking

31. Suppose gravity pulls an airplane toward Earth with a force of 10,000 newtons. How strong is the force pulling Earth toward the airplane? Explain.

32. An entertainer quickly pulls out a tablecloth from under a setting of dishes. The dishes stay in place on the table. Explain what property the entertainer makes use of to perform this trick.

33. How is it possible to exert a force on an object without changing the velocity of the object?

Process Skills Review

34. What materials might you use if you wanted to **experiment** with reducing friction on a playground slide?

35. Suppose you want to **measure** and **record** the weights of your friends to help you visually estimate the average weight and the range of weights. What measurement tools will you use, and what display will you use for recording your data?

36. A soccer player kicks a ball down the field. It eventually rolls to a stop. **Hypothesize** what force acts on the ball to bring it to a stop.

Performance Assessment

Physics of Baseball

A pitcher on the mound holds a baseball and then throws it over the plate. The batter swings and sends the ball high into the air. The catcher runs for it, slides in the dirt, and reaches out his mitt. The ball drops into the catcher's mitt.

Use the concepts and terms you have learned in this chapter to describe the forces and motions at each stage in this situation. Include as much detail about gravity, friction, and velocity as possible.

2

Vocabulary Preview

work
machine
lever
fulcrum
effort arm
resistance arm
pulley
wheel and axle
inclined plane
wedge
screw
compound machine
efficiency

Machines and Work

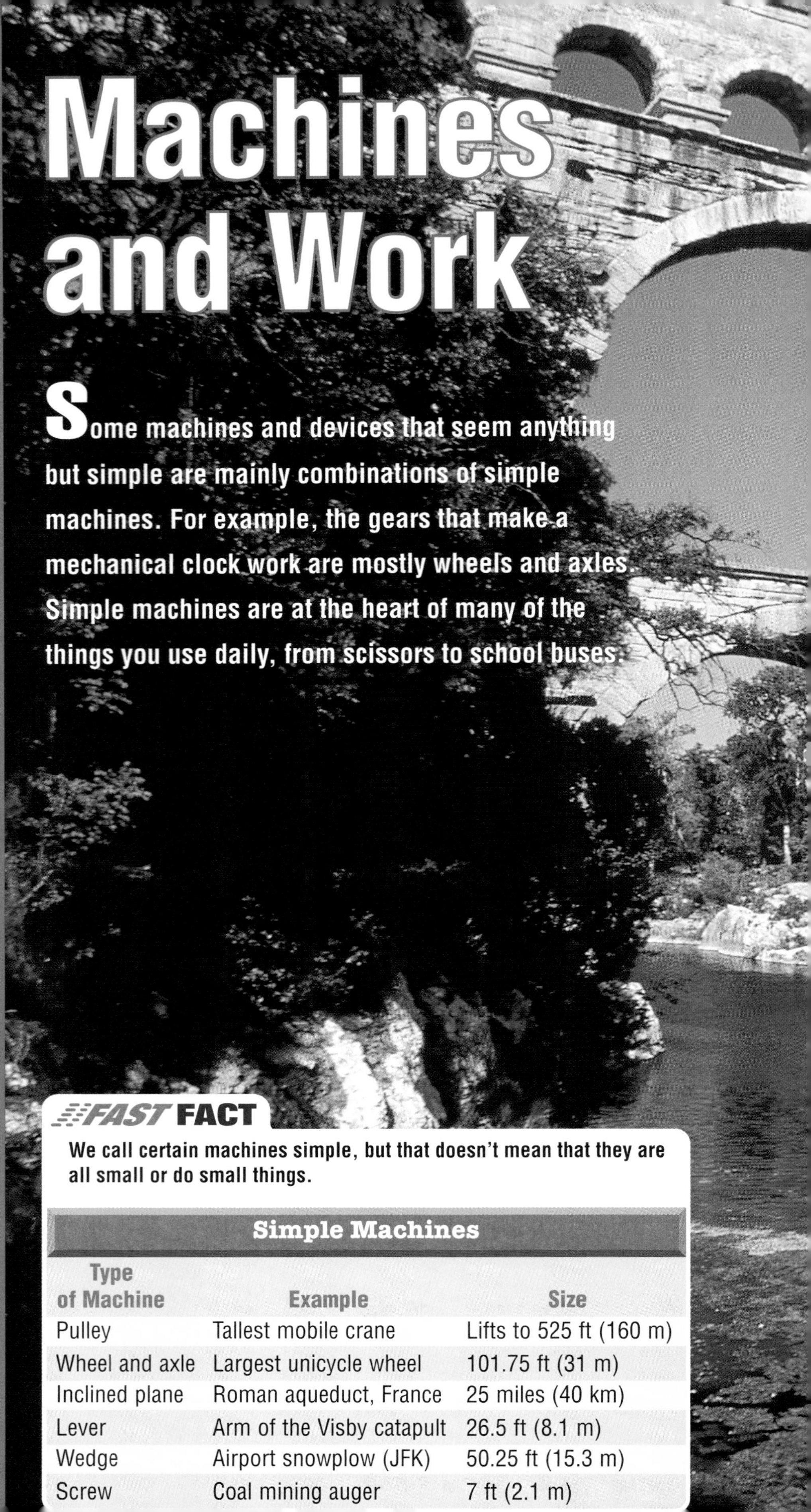

Some machines and devices that seem anything but simple are mainly combinations of simple machines. For example, the gears that make a mechanical clock work are mostly wheels and axles. Simple machines are at the heart of many of the things you use daily, from scissors to school buses.

FAST FACT

We call certain machines simple, but that doesn't mean that they are all small or do small things.

Simple Machines

Type of Machine	Example	Size
Pulley	Tallest mobile crane	Lifts to 525 ft (160 m)
Wheel and axle	Largest unicycle wheel	101.75 ft (31 m)
Inclined plane	Roman aqueduct, France	25 miles (40 km)
Lever	Arm of the Visby catapult	26.5 ft (8.1 m)
Wedge	Airport snowplow (JFK)	50.25 ft (15.3 m)
Screw	Coal mining auger	7 ft (2.1 m)

An ancient Roman aqueduct near Avignon, France.

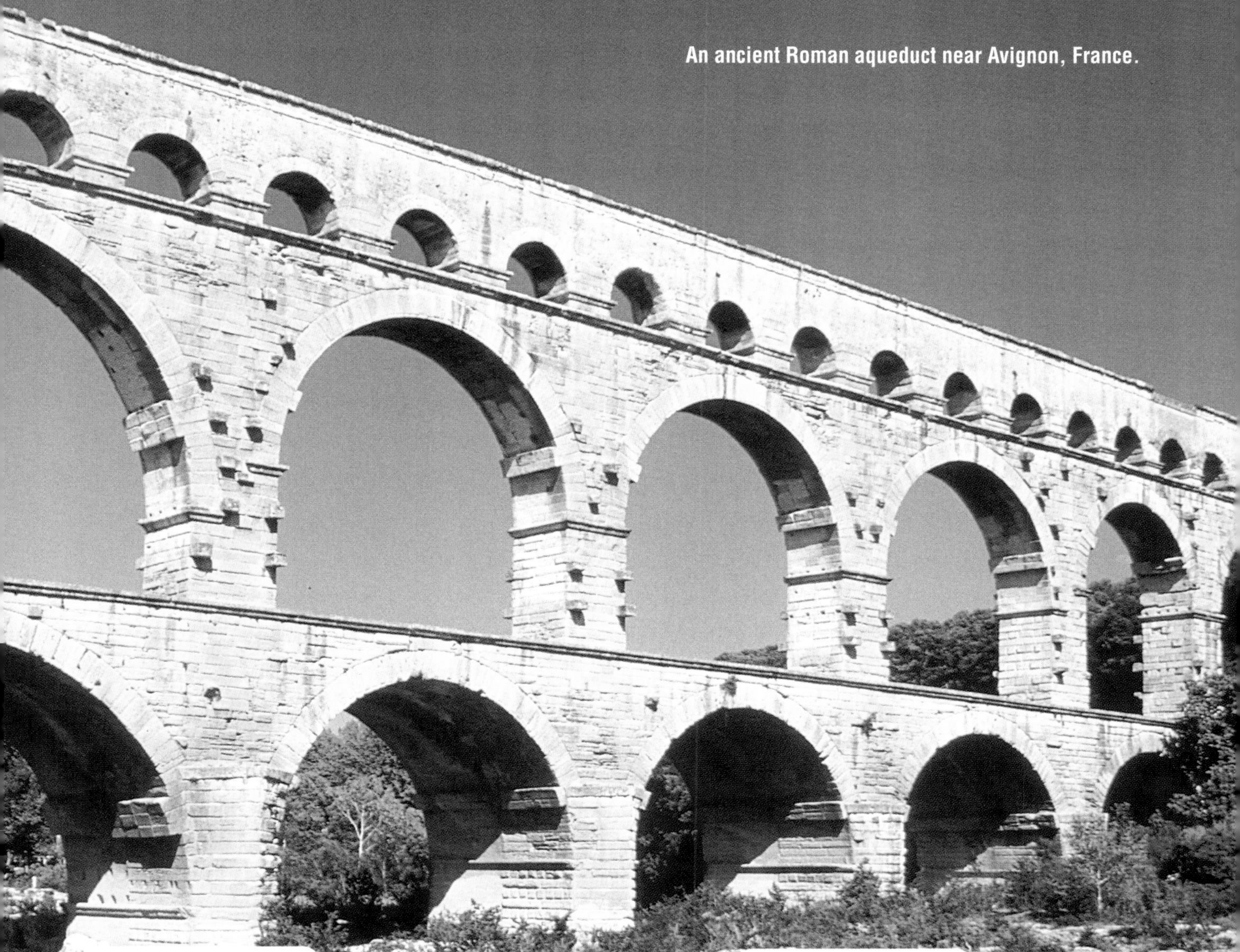

FAST FACT

The cartoonist Rube Goldberg designed complicated devices to perform uncomplicated actions. Yet most of the parts of those devices were simple machines such as pulleys and levers.

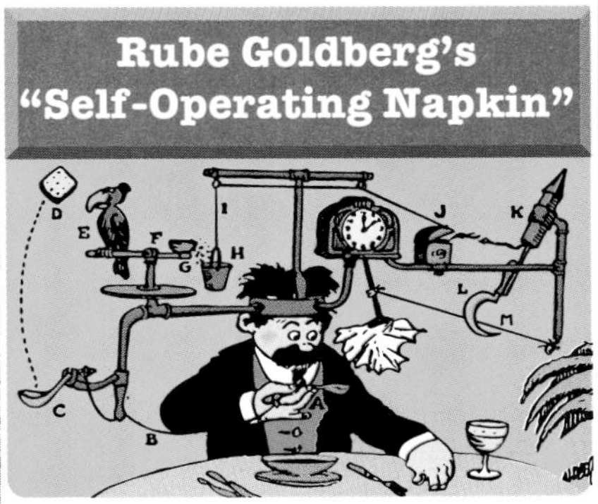

Rube Goldberg's
"Self-Operating Napkin"

Rube Goldberg ® and © Rube Goldberg, Inc. Distributed by United Media

FAST FACT

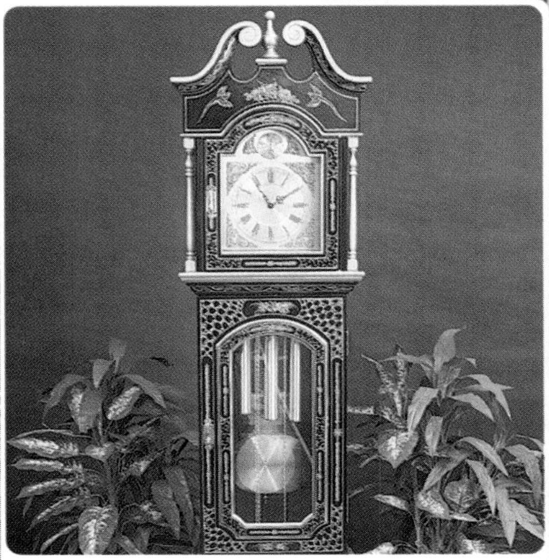

Although a pendulum is a lever, its length is used not to increase force, but to produce a swing lasting exactly one second.

How Do Levers Help You Do Work?

In this lesson, you can . . .

INVESTIGATE how levers make tasks easier.

LEARN ABOUT three types of levers and two other simple machines.

LINK to math, writing, physical education, and technology.

A fishing rod includes several simple machines. It is a lever that helps increase the speed of a cast. It also includes a wheel and axle to reel in an unlucky fish.

INVESTIGATE

Using a Lever

Activity Purpose A force does work only when it makes an object move. *Work* is the product of force times distance. In this activity you will look at the relationship between force and distance for the work put into a simple machine—a lever—and the work that comes out of the machine. You will also explore how a lever can help make tasks easier to do.

Materials

- 2 metersticks
- string
- ring stand
- ring
- metal washers
- spring scale
- large paper clip
- tape

Activity Procedure

1. Make a balance with one meterstick. Tie the string at the 50-cm mark of the meterstick, and use the string to hang the meterstick from the ring stand. (Picture A)

2. Use the spring scale to **measure** the total weight of the washers in newtons (N). Copy the table and **record** their weight in it.

Doing Work with a Lever

Position of load (cm from middle)	25 cm	25 cm	25 cm
Force of load (weight in N)			
Distance load moves (cm)			
Force × distance for load			
Position of spring scale (cm from middle)	25 cm	10 cm	40 cm
Force on spring scale (N)			
Distance spring scale moves (cm)			
Force × distance for spring scale			

3 Bend the paper clip to hang the washers 25 cm from one end of the meterstick. Use tape to help keep the paper clip in place.

4 Attach the spring scale at the same place, 25 cm from the end of the meterstick. (Picture B) Pull up on the spring scale until the balance is level. **Record** the force. Use the second meterstick to **measure** the distance that the washers and the spring scale move as you make the balance level. Record these measurements.

5 Repeat Step 4 but with the spring scale attached 10 cm from the middle of the meterstick and then 40 cm from the middle. In each case, **record** the force as well as the distances that the scale and the washers move when you make the balance level.

Picture A

Picture B

Draw Conclusions

1. Find all six products (force × distance) for the load and for the spring scale. **Compare** the products within each column of the table. Then compare the products across columns. What do you notice?

2. **Predict** how much force you would have to apply to lift the load if you hooked the spring scale at the very end of the meterstick (50 cm from the middle).

3. **Scientists at Work** Scientists **control variables** when they conduct experiments to test their hypotheses. In your investigation you controlled the position of the load and varied the position of the spring scale. **Predict** what would happen if, instead, you varied the position of the load and controlled the position of the spring scale.

Investigate Further Test your prediction in Question 3 by conducting an experiment in which you vary the position of the load and control the position of the spring scale. **Compare** your results to your prediction.

Process Skill Tip

To identify a cause and its effect, scientists try to **control variables** for all but one of the conditions in the experiment. When you are trying to find the effect of a condition, try to change only that condition.

Levers

Forces and Work

FIND OUT

- what work is

- how simple machines help make tasks easier

VOCABULARY

work

machine

lever

fulcrum

effort arm

resistance arm

pulley

wheel and axle

In the investigation you saw that you could lift a load by applying a large force over a short distance or by applying a smaller force over a greater distance. In each case, you did the same amount of work.

Applying a force and doing work are not the same thing. **Work** occurs when a force causes an object to move. To find out how much work is done, multiply the force applied to the object by the distance the object moves.

$$\text{work} = \text{force} \times \text{distance}$$

The unit of work is the joule (J).

$$1 \text{ joule (J)} = 1 \text{ newton (N)} \times 1 \text{ meter (m)}$$

This means that when a 1-newton object is moved 1 m, 1 joule of work is done. For example, picking up an apple from the ground takes about 1 joule of work.

A weight lifter who picks up a heavy object and lifts it overhead does many joules of work. Once the object is overhead, the weight lifter is applying a great force to hold it up, but no work is being done. A weight lifter who tries to lift an object and cannot is also applying a force but again is not doing any work. If an object does not move, no work is done, no matter how much force is applied. You can push against a brick wall until you are exhausted, but you do more work lifting a feather.

✔ **How can you figure out how much work is done on an object?**

If the barbell weighs 500 newtons (about 112 lb) and the weight lifter raises it 2.5 m (about 8 ft), he does 500 × 2.5, or 1250 joules of work. While he stands still with the barbell over his head, though, he applies a force, but he does no work at all.▼

Machines

When you hear the word *machine*, you probably think of something complicated, driven by electricity or gasoline. Machines like that are *compound* machines. The parts they are made of are *simple* machines. A **machine** is any device that changes the amount of force applied to an object, the direction of the force, or both.

Simple machines can make tasks easier. Suppose a mechanic wants to take an engine out of a car. The engine weighs 2000 newtons (about 450 lb), and she needs to lift it a distance of 1 m (about 3 ft). The total amount of work she needs to do is 2000 N × 1 m = 2000 J.

The 2000-newton engine is too heavy to lift directly. The mechanic cannot apply a force of 2000 newtons.

Using a set of pulleys called a *block and tackle*, the mechanic can lift the engine by applying a force of 200 newtons (about 45 lb) over a distance of 10 m (about 33 ft). Each time she pulls on the rope, the engine rises only a short distance. But she can pull the rope with a small force. She uses pulleys to trade force for distance. By applying a force of 200 newtons over a distance of 10 m, the mechanic does the same amount of work as she would lifting 2000 newtons a distance of 1 m:

2000 N × 1 m = 200 N × 10 m = 2000 J

A given amount of work can always be done in one of two ways. It can be done with a large force over a small distance or with a smaller force over a larger distance.

Simple machines can make tasks easier by changing the amount of force or the distance in the work equation. They do not reduce the amount of work to be done.

Some simple machines can increase the distance over which a force is applied. A rake is an example of a simple machine called a *lever*. When you use a rake, you move your arm a short distance. The end of the rake moves a

Pulling up on one end of the bottle opener pulls up on the edge of the bottle cap. The opener also multiplies the force but applies it over a shorter distance. ▶

A baseball bat is a simple machine. The end of the bat moves farther and faster than the batter's hands. The bat delivers more force than the batter puts into it. ▶

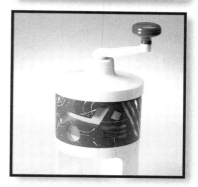

This ice-cream maker uses several simple machines. Together they deliver a great force over a short distance. ▶

longer distance, though it moves with less force than your arm does.

Some simple machines can change the direction in which a force is applied. You can use a rope over a single pulley to lift something off the ground by pulling downward to supply an upward force. The rope and pulley change the direction of the force.

On the following pages, you will learn about a number of machines. They may increase force by decreasing distance. Or they may increase distance by decreasing force. But they never change the total amount of work done.

✔ **Suppose a simple machine increases the distance over which work is done. How does it affect the force needed to do the work?**

Levers

A **lever** is a simple machine having an arm that moves around a fixed point. The fixed point is called a **fulcrum** (FUHL•krem). The **effort arm** is the part of the lever on which a person or another machine applies a force. The force applied to the lever is called the *effort force*. The part of the lever that applies a force on an object is called the **resistance arm**.

Levers can change either the direction or the amount of the force you need in order to get the work done. Some kinds of levers change the direction in which you apply a force. A lever can also increase a force. When a lever increases a force, it decreases the distance through which the force is applied. Remember that, like any other simple machine, a lever cannot reduce the amount of work.

✔ **When you press down on the end of a lever, which arm do you press on?**

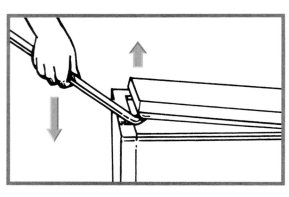

▲ A person applies a small force to the *effort arm*, moving it a large distance. The lever pivots around the *fulcrum*, which stays in place. The *resistance arm* applies a large force to the load, moving it a small distance.

◄ When a person uses a broom, the bristles move farther and with less force than the hand moving the broom. What acts as the fulcrum for this lever?

▲ The pliers are really two levers with the same fulcrum. When a person squeezes the handles of the pliers, do the jaws squeeze shut with greater force at the tips or near the pivot? Which end of the jaws moves the greater distance—the end at the tips or the end near the pivot?

Effort arm

Fulcrum

Resistance arm

An adult and a child want to ride the seesaw, a type of lever. Who should sit closer to the fulcrum in the middle of the seesaw? ►

A crowbar is a lever. The bend in the crowbar serves as the fulcrum. It separates the effort arm from the resistance arm. Because the effort arm is so much longer, when a person pushes it down, the resistance arm moves a much shorter distance.

A force of 100 newtons (about 22 lb) on a crowbar's effort arm moves it 0.5 m (about 1.6 ft), doing 100 N × 0.5 m = 50 J of work. If none of this work is lost to friction, the resistance arm also does 50 joules of work. If the resistance arm moves 0.1 m (about 0.3 ft), the force it applies must be 500 newtons (about 112 lb), doing 500 N × 0.1 m = 50 J of work.

✔ **You do 100 joules of work pushing on the effort arm of a crowbar. How much work can you expect to get out of the crowbar's resistance arm?**

▲ The load in the wheelbarrow is between the fulcrum (the wheel) and the effort force (applied by the hands lifting the wheelbarrow). The load is closer to the fulcrum, though, so the hands that lift the wheelbarrow apply less force but over a greater distance.

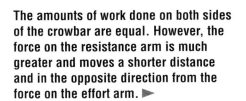

The amounts of work done on both sides of the crowbar are equal. However, the force on the resistance arm is much greater and moves a shorter distance and in the opposite direction from the force on the effort arm. ▶

Forces of a Lever		
	Effort Arm	**Resistance Arm**
Force	100 N	500 N
Distance	0.5 m	0.1 m
Work (force × distance)	100 N × 0.5 m = 50 J	500 N × 0.1 m = 50 J

Types of Levers

There are three types of levers. Each type does a different job and is defined by where the effort arm, fulcrum, and load are located. The first-class lever can give the user an advantage in force or in distance moved. Or it can simply change the direction of a force without changing the amount of force or the distance. Second-class levers always give an advantage in force, and third-class levers always give an advantage in distance.

✔ **Which type of lever should you use if you want to change the direction of a force?**

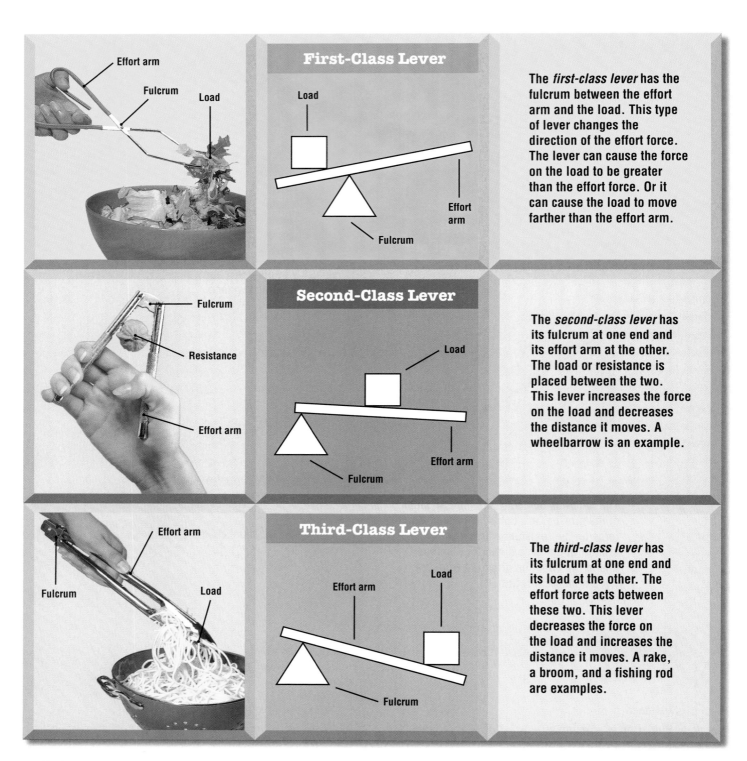

First-Class Lever

Effort arm · Fulcrum · Load

Load · Effort arm · Fulcrum

The *first-class lever* has the fulcrum between the effort arm and the load. This type of lever changes the direction of the effort force. The lever can cause the force on the load to be greater than the effort force. Or it can cause the load to move farther than the effort arm.

Second-Class Lever

Fulcrum · Resistance · Effort arm

Load · Effort arm · Fulcrum

The *second-class lever* has its fulcrum at one end and its effort arm at the other. The load or resistance is placed between the two. This lever increases the force on the load and decreases the distance it moves. A wheelbarrow is an example.

Third-Class Lever

Effort arm · Fulcrum · Load

Effort arm · Load · Fulcrum

The *third-class lever* has its fulcrum at one end and its load at the other. The effort force acts between these two. This lever decreases the force on the load and increases the distance it moves. A rake, a broom, and a fishing rod are examples.

Pulleys

A **pulley** is a wheel that has a groove along its edge. A rope or chain lies in this groove. When the rope or chain is pulled, the pulley turns.

A pulley is often considered a separate simple machine, but it is actually a form of first-class lever. The pulley pivot, at the center of the wheel, is the fulcrum. The effort and resistance arms stretch across the pulley's diameter. A pull down on the effort arm causes a pull up on the resistance arm.

A single pulley with a rope or chain simply changes the direction of a force. A downward pull on the rope results in an upward pull on the load. A change in direction is especially helpful if the load is in a place that is hard to reach.

Several pulleys along the same rope or chain can decrease the force needed to do work. A decrease in the needed force means force must be applied over a greater distance. This is how a set of pulleys, such as a block and tackle, can

◄ **What happens when you pull on the top rope of the clothesline? This use of a pulley simply changes the direction of an applied force.**

make tasks easier. A block and tackle is a machine that applies large forces to lift weight. A single block has one pulley mounted in a frame. A double block has two pulleys, and so on. Additional pulleys increase the force that can be applied to the load and decrease the distance the load travels with each pull.

It is simple to calculate how much easier a task is with a set of pulleys. Multiplying the force you input by the number of pulleys in the system gives the force on the load. Dividing how far the rope moves by the number of pulleys gives the distance the load moves.

Suppose a set of four pulleys is used to lift a piano. The pulley system has four pulleys, so the force of the pull on the rope will be multiplied by four. A downward pull of 200 newtons (45 lb) will produce a force of 4 × 200 newtons, or 800 newtons (180 lb), on the piano. But for every 1 m (about 3 ft) the rope moves, the piano will rise only 0.25 m (about 10 in.). Also, some of the force that is applied will be lost to friction. So the lifting force on the piano will be slightly less than 800 newtons.

▲ This pulley system uses one pulley. For every pull on the free end of the rope, the bucket rises. This pulley system changes the direction of the force, but not the amount of force required to lift the bucket.

✔ **Does a set of pulleys increase the force on a load or the distance the load moves?**

Water Wheel

Effort Arm

Fulcrum

Resistance Arm

◀ The fulcrum of the water wheel is the center of the wheel and axle. The effort arm is the radius of the water wheel. The resistance arm is the radius of the axle.

▲ The force of the falling water on the water wheel is multiplied as it is transferred to the axle. The axle turns more slowly but with a much larger force.

▲ When you turn the handle on a faucet, the force you apply to the outside of the handle is multiplied as it is transferred to the central stem. It would be hard to turn on the faucet if the handle were missing.

Wheel and Axle

Another form of lever is the wheel and axle. A **wheel and axle** is a simple machine in which either a wheel turns an axle or an axle turns a wheel around a central pivot. A wheel and axle can be used to increase a force or to increase the distance through which a force acts.

A familiar wheel and axle is the steering wheel of a car. Think of a point on the rim of the steering wheel and a point on the steering column (the axle the steering wheel turns on). When a driver turns the steering wheel one-quarter turn, the point on the rim travels about one-half meter. The point on the steering column travels only a few centimeters. A force applied to the rim over a large distance is transferred to the steering column, making it turn a much smaller distance. When there is a decrease in the distance that a load moves, the force on the load increases. So a steering wheel is a wheel and axle that increases the force applied to it.

A car tire is a wheel and axle that does just the opposite. It transfers force from the axle to the tire edge. The tire edge turns with less force than the axle, but it moves a greater distance. When force is transferred from an axle to a wheel, the purpose is to increase the distance—and the speed—of the work done. A Ferris wheel is another example of a wheel and axle. The seats are located out at the wheel's edge to make them move faster for a more exciting ride.

Another common use of the wheel and axle is in gears. Bicycle gears, for example, use a chain to carry force from a larger central wheel and axle, at the pedals, to a smaller wheel and axle, at the rear wheel. For every full turn the pedal gear makes, the rear wheel gear makes about two or three turns.

✓ **When you turn a screwdriver, is the result an increase in force or an increase in distance?**

Summary

Work is the product of force times distance. The unit used to measure work is the joule. Simple machines can make tasks easier by increasing a force or by increasing the distance through which a force acts. A lever is a simple machine having an arm that pivots around a fulcrum. A single pulley can change the direction of a force. A set of pulleys can increase a force. A wheel and axle can increase a force or increase distance and speed.

Review

1. A child rides a tricycle over a lawn. A warehouse worker pushes against a large crate, but he cannot move it. Who does more work?

2. Can a simple machine decrease the total amount of work?

3. Which class of lever can you push down on to lift something?

4. **Critical Thinking** Which does a doorknob increase—the force or the speed from the hand that turns it?

5. **Test Prep** You use a set of pulleys that has five loops of rope to lift a box. You pull the rope 1 m. The box moves —

   A 0.2 m

   B 1.0 m

   C 1.2 m

   D 5.0 m

LINKS

MATH LINK

Calculating Work An old-fashioned car jack is an example of a first-class lever. Suppose that pushing down a jack handle 25 cm with a force of 100 N lifts the front of a car 0.5 cm. How many newtons of force does the jack exert on the car?

WRITING LINK

Expressive Writing—Song Lyrics Could you teach a first-grader about levers? If you want to make the lesson fun and memorable, you might try putting the information into a song.

PHYSICAL EDUCATION LINK

Sports Equipment Levers are important parts of many pieces of athletic equipment. Pick a sport you like that uses a piece of equipment that includes a lever. What class of lever is involved? Does it increase force or does it increase distance? Look at as many other pieces of sports equipment as you can. Classify the levers that you find.

TECHNOLOGY LINK

Visit the Harcourt Learning Site for related links, activities, and resources. **www.harcourtschool.com**

WELCOME TO THE LEARNING SITE

How Do Inclined Planes Help You Do Work?

In this lesson, you can . . .

INVESTIGATE the use of an inclined plane.

LEARN ABOUT how the different types of inclined planes can make tasks easier.

LINK to math, writing, social studies, and technology.

Using Ramps

Activity Purpose You know something about levers, pulleys, and other similar simple machines. In this activity you will experiment with another simple machine—an inclined plane. As you do the activity, try to **compare** what you learned about levers with what you **observe** about inclined planes.

Materials
- several books
- ruler
- spring scale
- toy cart or roller skate
- 1-m plank

Activity Procedure

1 Make a stack of books about 30 cm high.

2 Attach the spring scale to the middle of the cart. Using the spring scale, slowly lift the cart to the height of the stack of books. **Measure** and **record** the least number of newtons of force you need and the total distance to lift the cart to the top of the stack. (Picture A)

Work

Lifting Method	Force (N)	Distance (m)	Work (force × distance = joules)
straight lift			
inclined plane			

◀ An icebreaker clears a path through the ice for other ships. It has a strong bow that serves as a wedge to split apart large blocks of ice.

Picture A

Picture B

3 Use the plank to make a ramp to the top of the stack. Attach the spring scale to the front of the cart, and use it to pull the cart to the top of the ramp. **Record** the least number of newtons of force you need and the total distance to roll the cart up the ramp. (Picture B)

4 **Compute** and **record** the amount of work you did in each case.

Draw Conclusions

1. **Compare** the amount of work you did using the two different methods to get the cart to the top of the book stack.

2. Which method required less force? **Hypothesize** about how you could use even less force to get the cart to the top of the book stack.

3. **Scientists at Work** If scientists performed this **experiment,** they would know that when pulling the cart up the ramp, they would lose some of the force to friction. **Hypothesize** what you could do to reduce the friction.

Investigate Further If you turned the cart over and dragged it up the ramp instead of rolling it, much more friction would work against you. **Hypothesize** which would require more force—dragging the cart up the ramp upside down or lifting it and placing it on the stack as you did in Step 2. **Experiment** to test your hypothesis.

Process Skill Tip

You **hypothesize** to describe how or why something works. When you do this, you often design experiments to test how well your hypothesis explains what really happens.

Work and Inclined Planes

Inclined Planes

FIND OUT

- how inclined planes make tasks easier
- about other simple machines related to inclined planes

VOCABULARY

inclined plane
wedge
screw

Levers, along with pulleys and wheels and axles, are types of simple machines. In the investigation you used another simple machine to make tasks easier. The ramp let you do work by applying a smaller force over a greater distance.

A ramp is a type of inclined plane. An **inclined plane** is any flat, sloping surface. Like a lever, an inclined plane is a simple machine that changes the size and direction of a force. Remember that if a machine reduces the force you must use, it increases the distance through which you must use that force. If it reduces distance, it increases force. With an inclined plane, a task such as lifting can be done with a smaller force over a greater distance.

There are many familiar examples of inclined planes that make tasks easier. A wheelchair ramp and a ramp for sliding heavy furniture up into the back of a moving van are inclined planes. So are a road up a hillside, the sloping floor of a movie theater, and even a child's slide. All of these reduce force when work is done. Like other machines, inclined planes cannot reduce the total amount of work. Work done with less force must be done over a longer distance.

✔ **Which decreases when you use an inclined plane—the force you must apply or the distance you must move?**

Which would be easier—climbing straight up the steep side of this mountain or climbing up the gentler but longer slopes and switchbacks? Both routes would require the same amount of work.

Ramps

Ramps are common examples of inclined planes. Using a ramp, a person can lift a load by applying less force over a greater distance.

Suppose you needed to move a piano onto the back of a pickup truck. You could try to get enough friends together to lift the piano straight up. Or you could get some strong boards and build a ramp. It would be hard to move the piano up a steep ramp, but it would still be easier than lifting the piano. A ramp with a long, gentle slope would make the job even easier. If the ramp were long enough, you might be able to roll the piano up the ramp all by yourself.

A ramp is also useful for slowing downward movement. For example, riding your bike down a road that slopes gently requires less braking force than riding down a road that is very steep. Riding down a steep road requires a great deal of force to stay at a safe speed. On a gently sloping road, you can maintain a safe speed using less braking force over a longer distance.

The movements of water and ice in nature also show the effects of natural ramps. Water that flows down a fairly level riverbed moves slowly. As it passes through steeper areas in the river, the water moves more quickly. Glaciers are affected in a similar way as they move over different slopes. A glacier moves more quickly down a steep mountain slope than it does through a slightly inclined valley. One of the reasons avalanches are so dangerous is that they begin on steep mountain slopes. When ice and snow break free from the mountain, they move with dangerous speed until they reach a level valley that slows them down.

✔ **What kind of simple machine is a ramp?**

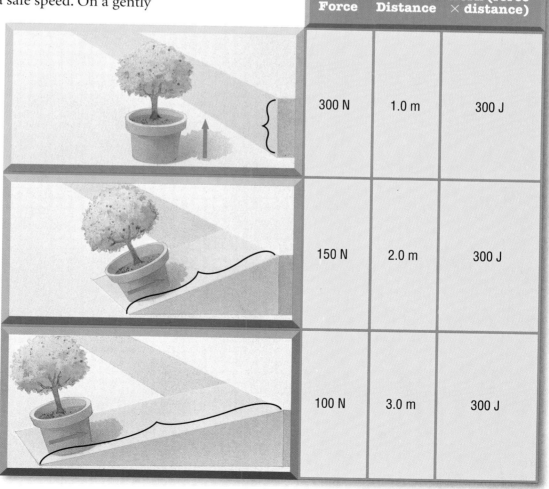

To get the plant up to the loading dock, you could lift it directly. Or you could slide it up a ramp. The first ramp lets you use less force over a greater distance to lift the plant. The second ramp makes it even easier. What happens to the amount of force needed as you move down the table? What happens to the distance moved? What happens to the total amount of work? ▶

Force	Distance	Work (force × distance)
300 N	1.0 m	300 J
150 N	2.0 m	300 J
100 N	3.0 m	300 J

▲ When the doorstop is *wedged* under the door, it applies a large amount of pressure to the floor as well as the door. The forces pressing down and up increase the force of friction, which keeps the door and wedge from moving.

Wedges

A **wedge** is a simple machine made up of one or two inclined planes. Their ends meet along a narrow edge. When a force is applied to the opposite, thick end of the wedge, the inclined planes increase the force and change its direction. You can think of a wedge as a movable inclined plane.

Most wedges are used to cut or split things, such as logs for a fireplace. A log-splitting wedge is hammered on its blunt side into the log. The sharp, thin edge where the two inclined planes meet is pushed into the wood, breaking it apart. The hammer directs a force down on the end of the wedge. The inclined planes increase this force and redirect

◄ The letter opener has a long, thin wedge along each side. When the opener is inserted into a sealed envelope, it redirects the force of a hand into pushing apart the paper fibers in the envelope flap.

it outward from their surfaces. The wedge pushes the two sides of the log farther and farther apart until finally the log splits.

The same principle is behind every sharp tool, from razor blades and needles to knives and saws. All of these are useful because they are wedges. For example, a magnified look down the edge of a knife shows two inclined planes sloping away from the sharp edge. Once that edge breaks into a substance, continued force splits the substance apart until it is cut through.

Wedges are also used to push or lift objects. A wedge serves as an efficient doorstop because it changes the small force pushing it under the door to a larger force pressing down on the floor and up on the door.

✓ **What does a wedge do to a force applied to its thick end?**

As the wood wedge is pounded into the wood, its force is increased and redirected outward. The stronger outward force acts over a shorter distance than the downward force. ▼

◄ A maul is a log-splitting wedge and a hammer all in one.

The point of a needle is a circular wedge. Starting from the tip of the needle, inclined planes move away from it on all sides. ►

Screws

Though it may not seem so at first, a screw is another form of inclined plane. A **screw** is an inclined plane wrapped around a cylinder or cone. This special type of inclined plane decreases force and increases distance. It also changes the direction of a force, making a turning force into a vertical one.

When a nut is turned onto a machine screw, the threads of the nut are forced to slide up the winding inclined plane. They must slide a long distance as they spiral up the screw, so a smaller force is needed to make the nut move.

A wood screw also acts as a long, spiraling wedge because its threads have a sharp edge. As the edge cuts into the wood, the force of the wedge spreads the wood fibers apart. The inclined plane of the thread can then slide through this opening. The screw must be turned many times before it is fully sunk into the wood.

Wood screws are better fasteners than nails because it is very hard to pull screws straight out. Any force pulling up on the screw is transferred to a much weaker twisting force. Also, the threads of the screw provide a greater surface area in contact with the wood. As a result, there is more friction between a screw and wood than there is between a nail and wood. This added friction helps keep the screw in place.

◀ The inclined plane and wedge of a wood screw let you sink a fastener into wood with a small amount of force.

One way to measure screws is to count the number of threads per inch. This is really a measure of the number of times the inclined plane spirals around one inch of screw. The greater the number of threads per inch, the gentler the slope of the inclined plane and the less force needed to turn the screw. Screws with fewer threads per inch have a steeper slope to their threads. More force is needed to tighten them.

Some devices use the threads of a screw to move something. The ancient Greek Archimedes (ar•kuh•MEE•deez) was famous for his inventions that used simple machines. One of these was a screw to raise water for irrigating fields. *Archimedes' screw* turned inside a tight cylinder. One end of the cylinder was placed under water. When the screw was turned, water would move up the threads and flow out the top of the cylinder. A similar screw is used in meat grinders to move meat to the cutting blades.

✔ **What two simple machines make up a wood screw?**

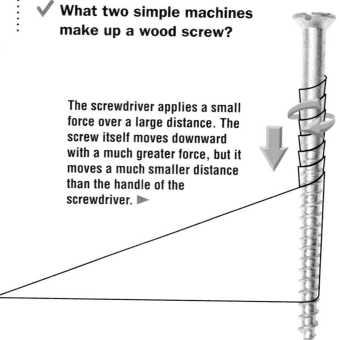

The screwdriver applies a small force over a large distance. The screw itself moves downward with a much greater force, but it moves a much smaller distance than the handle of the screwdriver. ▶

By wrapping a paper inclined plane around a cylinder, you can see the length of the threads of the screw. To tighten a nut to the top of a screw, you must slide the nut's threads along the entire slope of the inclined plane. ▶

Ancient Tools

More than 4000 years ago, the people of the Nile Valley in Egypt built mountain-sized monuments to their rulers, the pharaohs. They had no gasoline engines or electricity. Instead, humans themselves carved out stones from the Earth, moved them, and shaped them. They needed millions of stones and

lifted many of them hundreds of feet. Most researchers have concluded that the ancient Egyptians used some simple machines to make the tasks easier. Even with the help of these machines and with thousands of laborers, it took many years to complete the stone tombs.

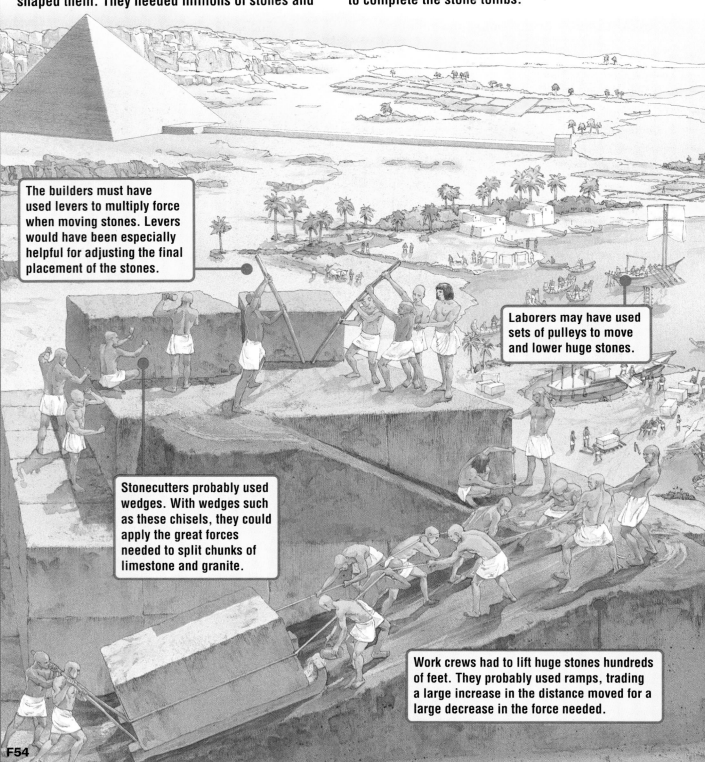

The builders must have used levers to multiply force when moving stones. Levers would have been especially helpful for adjusting the final placement of the stones.

Laborers may have used sets of pulleys to move and lower huge stones.

Stonecutters probably used wedges. With wedges such as these chisels, they could apply the great forces needed to split chunks of limestone and granite.

Work crews had to lift huge stones hundreds of feet. They probably used ramps, trading a large increase in the distance moved for a large decrease in the force needed.

Summary

An inclined plane is a simple machine that consists of a flat, sloping surface. The more gently an inclined plane is sloped, the smaller the force needed and the greater the distance over which that force must act. Wedges are simple machines that consist of one or two inclined planes that move. Wedges are often used to increase and redirect a force to split apart or cut through an object. A screw is an inclined plane that winds around a cylinder or cone. Screws can change a turning force into a vertical one.

Review

1. How does a wedge change the direction of a force?

2. How is a screw an inclined plane?

3. Why are screws better than nails for fastening wood?

4. **Critical Thinking** You have set up a ramp to slide a crate up to a door, but you still cannot push the crate up. How could you change the ramp to make it possible to move the crate?

5. **Test Prep** Inclined planes do **NOT** change the amount of ____ in this equation: work = force × distance.

   A friction

   B work

   C distance

   D force

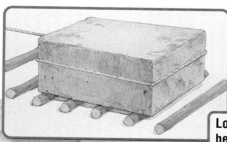

Logs could have served as wheels to help reduce the great force of friction between moving blocks and the ground.

LINKS

MATH LINK

Computing Mechanical Advantage The *mechanical advantage* of a machine is a number that tells how many times an input force is multiplied in the output force. For a ramp, mechanical advantage = length of ramp ÷ height of ramp. A 2-m ramp that raises an object 1 m has a mechanical advantage of 2 ÷ 1, or 2. Estimate the mechanical advantage of the ramp you used in the investigation.

WRITING LINK

Persuasive Writing—Business Letter Invent a new machine that makes use of ramps, screws, and wedges. Describe your invention in a letter to the president of a company that might sell your machine. Tell what your invention does and how it works.

SOCIAL STUDIES LINK

History of Science Archimedes was a Greek scientist and inventor in the third century B.C. In an encyclopedia, read more about his work on simple machines such as the lever and the screw.

TECHNOLOGY LINK

Learn more about how simple machines were used in construction by watching *Building the Pyramids* on the **Harcourt Science Newsroom Video.**

What Are Compound Machines?

In this lesson, you can . . .

INVESTIGATE how simple machines can work together.

LEARN ABOUT how friction reduces the efficiency of a machine.

LINK to math, writing, physical education, and technology.

This thrill ride is made up of several simple machines, including a large wheel and axle on which the people are riding. As the motor rotates the axle, what increases at the outer edge of the wheel—the force, or the distance and speed? ▽

INVESTIGATE

Building a Machine

Activity Purpose You've learned about several types of simple machines that can help make work easier. You use some of these machines every day, often as parts of more complex, compound machines. In this activity you will build your own compound machine. It can include as many simple machines as you think are needed to reach a simple goal—to do a certain amount of work by using the smallest possible force.

Materials

- wooden block or book
- string
- spring scale
- chair
- meterstick or tape measure
- cart or roller skate
- planks (1 m or longer)
- spools, grommets, or toy pulleys
- paper clips
- eye hooks

Activity Procedure

1. Tie a length of string around the block. Hook the spring scale to one end of the block and lift it. **Measure** and **record** the weight of the block in newtons. (Picture A)

2. **Measure** the distance from the floor to the seat of the chair. **Record** this height as a decimal part of a meter.

Picture A

Picture B

3 Make a machine to raise the block from the floor to the seat of the chair by using as little force as possible. Use any or all of the materials you have available. Test several ideas. In each case, **measure** and **record** the amount of force you must use and the distance you must move the block.

Method of Raising Block	Force (N)	Distance (m)	Work (J)

Draw Conclusions

1. **Compare** the amount of force you had to use with each machine. Which machine needed the least amount of force?

2. **Compare** your best results with the best results from other groups. **Hypothesize** how you might improve your results by making changes to your machine.

3. **Scientists at Work** When scientists design experiments, they **control variables** to observe the connection between changes in experiment conditions and changes in outcomes. How could you control variables to identify what makes the machine that requires the least amount of force to lift the block?

Investigate Further **Plan and conduct an experiment** to see if you can improve the performance of your machine by reducing the amount of force needed to lift the block. Test your hypothesis from Question 2. Which **variables** will you **control**? Which variable will you test?

Process Skill Tip

To see the effect one change can have on the outcome of an experiment, run the experiment both before and after the change. Carefully **control variables** so that the experiments are identical except for the one variable you are trying to test.

Compound Machines

Simple Machines Work Together

FIND OUT

- how simple machines work together in compound machines

- the role of friction in the use of machines

- how to increase a machine's efficiency

VOCABULARY

compound machine
efficiency

You have learned about several simple machines in the previous lessons. In the investigation you used more than one machine at a time to make work easier. In this lesson you will focus on the kind of machine you use most often—a compound machine. A **compound machine** is a device that is made up of two or more simple machines.

Almost all machines are compound machines. Even a butter knife, which seems to be a simple tool, is a compound machine. The cutting edge is a wedge—a form of an inclined plane. The entire knife is also a lever.

In some compound machines, such as the butter knife, the simple machines do different tasks. The wedge is used for cutting, and the lever is used to increase the force or the distance through which the force acts.

In other compound machines, two or more simple machines work together to do the same task. For example, a ramp can reduce the amount of force needed to lift an object. Putting wheels under the object might further reduce the force needed by reducing friction. The force could be reduced even more by using a set of pulleys (a block and tackle) to pull the object up the ramp on its wheels. The simple machines work together to greatly reduce the amount of force needed to raise an object. Some flatbed tow trucks use this same set of machines to pull cars up onto their beds.

✔ **What is a compound machine?**

The paper cutter is a compound machine. Its arm is a second-class lever, and its cutting edge is a wedge. ▶

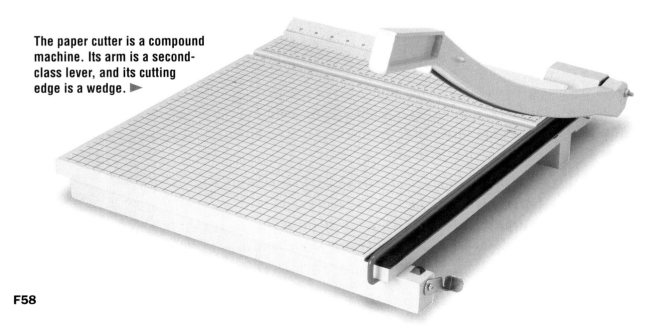

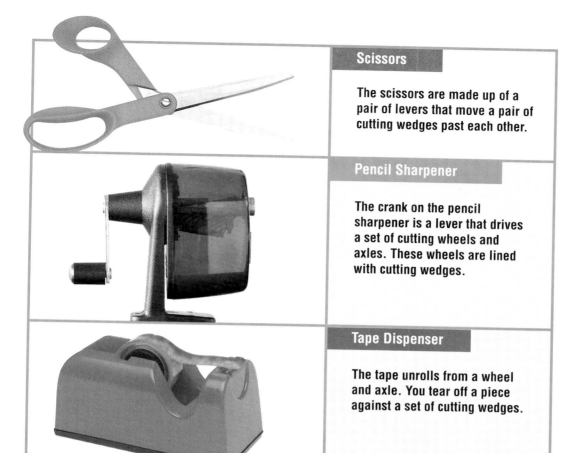

Scissors

The scissors are made up of a pair of levers that move a pair of cutting wedges past each other.

Pencil Sharpener

The crank on the pencil sharpener is a lever that drives a set of cutting wheels and axles. These wheels are lined with cutting wedges.

Tape Dispenser

The tape unrolls from a wheel and axle. You tear off a piece against a set of cutting wedges.

◄ Though they are not very complex, these everyday items are compound machines because each of them makes use of more than one simple machine.

How Machines Work

Machines do not do work by themselves. Work must go into a machine for work to come out of it. A push on one end of a crowbar puts work into a simple machine. The other end of the crowbar pushing up on the lid of a paint can represents work coming out of the same simple machine.

Compound machines such as cars and watches may have a battery, spring, or other energy source that puts work into the machine by providing a force. Other compound machines work with a force provided by a person. A bicycle is a compound machine that has a wheel and axle, levers, and screws. A person puts work into a bicycle by pushing the pedals. A wheelbarrow is a second-class lever with a wheel and axle that receives a force from a person who pushes it. A door is another second-class lever with a wheel and axle. A door receives a force from a person pushing or pulling it.

Machines do not do work by themselves, but they do make tasks easier. They do this by increasing a force put into them or by increasing the distance through which a force acts. When they increase force, they decrease distance. When they increase distance, they decrease force.

Machines can overcome other forces, such as gravity and friction. A car jack is a machine that helps overcome the force of gravity, which pulls down on a car. The wheels and axles on a skateboard help overcome friction between the board and the ground.

Machines can also move a force through a much greater distance or at a much greater speed. A tennis racket extends the lever of a player's arm so that the end of the racket can move at a higher speed than a player's hand could.

✔ **How do machines make work easier?**

A Compound Machine

One compound machine you may be familiar with is a bicycle. Most of the simple machines on a bicycle are easy to see in action. You can use the guide below and on page F61 to help you explore some of them.

◀ The handlebars serve as a wheel and axle that reduces the force the rider has to use to turn the front wheel.

▲ The brake handle is a second-class lever that increases a force applied to it. It pulls on the brake cable that goes to the brakes at the wheels.

◀ This large wheel and axle increases the distance through which the force acts, thus increasing the speed. When the gear on the rear wheel makes one turn, its edge moves about 30 cm (1 ft). When the bike wheel turns once, its outer edge moves about 200 cm (6 ft).

▲ The rider applies a force to the pedals. The pedal arms act as levers and increase the force to the gear wheel. The gear wheel, a wheel and axle, moves the chain.

The seat adjustment screw increases force. When tightened, it squeezes the metal sleeve around the seat post, keeping the post from sliding up or down. ▶

This pair of first-class levers increases the force that comes from the rider's squeeze of the brake handle. These levers act like a pair of pliers, squeezing brake pads against the wheel rim to increase friction and slow the spinning of the wheel. ▼

The chain is a series of linked wheels and axles. It transfers the force from the pedal gear to the rear gear wheel. The rear gears are smaller than the front gears, so they turn more quickly. ▶

Friction and Efficiency

Machines can increase or decrease force or the distance through which the force acts, but they can't reduce the total amount of work to be done. This means that a machine cannot produce more work than is put into it. In fact, the work done by a machine is always less than the work put into it. This is because with all machines some work is lost to the force of friction. Friction is a force that opposes motion whenever two surfaces rub together.

The ratio of the work that comes out of a machine to the work put into that machine is called the machine's efficiency (eh•FISH•uhn•see). **Efficiency** is often given as a percent. The higher the percent, the greater the machine's efficiency, and the less work the machine wastes.

A machine that produces exactly 20 J of work when 20 J of work are put into it would have an efficiency of 20 J ÷ 20 J = 1, or 100%. However, no machine is this efficient. All machines lose some work to friction, so all machines have efficiencies of less than 100%. You would be more likely to get only 16 J of work out of a machine that you put 20 J of work into. Its efficiency would be 16 J ÷ 20 J = 0.8 = 80%.

With some machines, especially simple machines such as levers, the loss of work to friction is small. As compound machines become more complex, though, the amount of work lost to friction becomes large. Each simple machine in a compound machine loses a small part of its work to friction, so a compound machine may lose a larger part of its work to friction.

Friction between the ramp and the pot uses up some of the boy's work. Lifting the pot without the ramp takes more force, but it produces less friction. ▼

◄ **The woman puts more work into the rake than she gets out of it. When she pulls the rake, it rubs through the grass and leaves. This causes friction, which opposes the rake's motion. Some of the force the woman produces goes to overcoming the friction.**

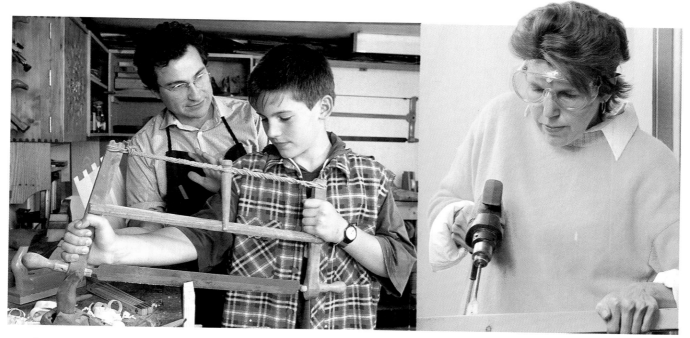

▲ A handsaw gets warm when you use it because the work lost to friction heats up the surfaces that rub together.

▲ Like most tools with electric motors, a power drill heats up as you use it. Friction at the drill's bearings produces heat as the shaft rotates at high speed. Friction between the drill bit and the wood also produces heat.

In a car engine, for example, the energy from almost one-half of every gallon of gas is used to overcome the friction of moving engine parts.

The energy that is used to overcome friction becomes heat. If you rub the palms of your hands together, you should be able to feel them get warmer. The friction of your palms rubbing together produces the heat you feel. This friction is the same force that causes falling meteors to heat up so much that they glow in the night sky as shooting stars.

To identify where the friction in a machine occurs, look for places where one part moves against another. In simple machines, friction occurs where a lever moves on its fulcrum, where a pulley spins on its pivot, and where a wheel turns on its axle. With wedges and inclined planes, friction occurs on their surfaces as objects slide over them.

Sound, light, and even smoke are other clues that energy is being lost to friction. All of these effects can occur in places where surfaces are rubbing together. Any machine that produces a loud noise is losing energy at the point where the sound is produced.

To see where friction occurs in compound machines, look for the simple machines in them. A car engine, for example, has many rotating parts, all of which are types of wheels and axles. With a wheel and axle, friction always occurs at the places where the wheel and the axle rub against other objects.

Friction must be accounted for when the amount of force or distance gained by using a machine is calculated. To lift a chair 1 m to put it on a truck might take 100 newtons of direct force. Using a 2-m ramp would take 50 newtons of force without friction. But friction occurs on all ramps, so more than 50 newtons of force are needed.

✔ **What is the term for the ratio of the work that comes out of a machine to the work put into the machine?**

Making Machines More Efficient

Engineers who design machines and mechanics who repair and maintain them try to reduce friction between the moving parts of compound machines. By reducing friction, they make the machines more efficient.

One way to reduce friction is by using lubricants (LOO•brih•kuhnts). Lubricants are substances such as oil, grease, graphite, or silicon, which allow surfaces to slide over each other easily. In an oil, the molecules slide over each other with little resistance. When oil coats two surfaces that rub together, oil molecules may stick to each surface, but they slide easily over other oil molecules, so the total friction is greatly reduced. A rusty chain on a bicycle produces a lot of friction, making the bicycle difficult to ride. A lot more effort is needed to make it move. Oiling the chain can reduce friction.

Another way to reduce friction and make machines more efficient is to use rollers and bearings. When a sphere or wheel's rounded surface touches another surface, there is only a small area where the two objects touch. This reduces the friction as the surfaces rub together. Bearings are small steel balls between two surfaces that otherwise would rub together. Instead, the surfaces rub against the bearings along a small surface. As one surface moves, the steel balls between these two surfaces roll instead of sliding. Rolling usually causes less friction than sliding.

The force of friction produced by two surfaces depends on the materials the surfaces are made of. A smooth piece of plastic produces less friction than a sheet of sandpaper when another object rubs against it. So one way of reducing friction in a machine is by choosing the machine's materials carefully. A ramp covered with steel, for example, would be more efficient than a ramp covered with soft rubber.

✔ **What are two ways to reduce friction and make a machine more efficient?**

Friction between the people and the slide slows them down. How could the efficiency of the slide be improved? ▼

Water is a good lubricant. It reduces friction to make the trip down this slide much more efficient and much faster than the trip down the slide at the left. ▼

Summary

A compound machine is a device that includes two or more simple machines. All machines actually do *less* work than is put into them because some of the work put in is lost to friction. The ratio of the work a machine does to the work put in is the machine's efficiency and is usually given as a percent. A machine is made more efficient when the friction between its moving parts is reduced. Lubricants such as oil and grease, as well as rollers, bearings, and wheels, all reduce friction.

Review

1. What two simple machines can you identify in a shovel?
2. Give an example of a machine that helps you overcome the force of gravity.
3. Give an example of a machine that helps you reduce the force of friction.
4. **Critical Thinking** A driver runs his car engine without oil. After a while, the engine parts get so hot they start to melt and the engine stops. Explain what happened.
5. **Test Prep** To calculate a machine's efficiency, ____ the work that comes out of a machine ____ the work that goes into it.
   - **A** add; to
   - **B** subtract; from
   - **C** divide; by
   - **D** multiply; by

LINKS

MATH LINK

Computing Efficiency An old-fashioned hand-cranked eggbeater is made up of several simple machines. Suppose a baker puts 30 J of work into cranking an eggbeater. The eggbeater itself, though, does only 18 J of work. What is the eggbeater's efficiency? Give your answer as a percent.

WRITING LINK

Informative Writing—Description Write for a friend a description of a time when you had to move a large or heavy object. Describe how you moved the object. Then write another paragraph telling a friend who may have to do the same kind of work how you could have made the task easier either by using more machines or by using more efficient ones.

PHYSICAL EDUCATION LINK

Friction on the Field Reducing friction or increasing it is important in sports. Identify and compare different playing surfaces or pieces of sports equipment that serve to increase or decrease friction.

TECHNOLOGY LINK

To learn more about machines and how they make our lives easier, visit this Internet site.
www.scilinks.org/harcourt

THE HISTORY OF Calculating Machines AND Computers

Ancient Adding Machines

For thousands of years, people have used machines to help them compute and calculate numbers. As early as 500 B.C., Egyptians were using the abacus to add, subtract, multiply, and divide.

Early Calculators

In 1642, Blaise Pascal invented a mechanical device that used wheels and gears to help people add and subtract. Although it was very advanced in its design and construction, the machine still needed human help at each stage of a calculation.

In 1832, Charles Babbage invented a calculator, called the difference machine, that was an early version of today's computers. Babbage wrote a program of instructions for the machine to use on cards that had holes punched in them. Lady Ada Lovelace Byron also wrote programs for this machine, which was the most complex of its time.

The Electronic Revolution

Around 1900, scientists developed the vacuum tube, through which electrons could be sent at great speeds. By the 1920s, scientists had developed a calculator that could be powered by a vacuum tube and electricity. In 1942, physicists used vacuum tubes to design the most advanced mathematical computer to date. The computer's instructions were written in binary code—a code that uses only zeros and ones for all its instructions.

Monster Machines

By 1945, ENIAC (Electronic Numerical Integrator And Computer), a room-sized computer, was completed. Programming it, however, was very difficult—cables and switches had to be moved or reset for every new task. The next

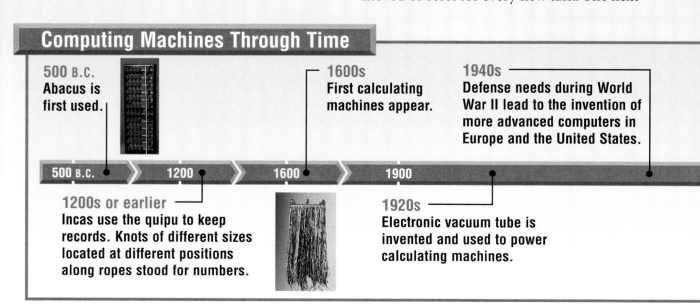

Computing Machines Through Time

500 B.C.
Abacus is first used.

1600s
First calculating machines appear.

1940s
Defense needs during World War II lead to the invention of more advanced computers in Europe and the United States.

| 500 B.C. | 1200 | 1600 | 1900 |

1200s or earlier
Incas use the quipu to keep records. Knots of different sizes located at different positions along ropes stood for numbers.

1920s
Electronic vacuum tube is invented and used to power calculating machines.

computer, EDVAC (Electronic Discrete Variable Computer), had a central processor and random-access memory— what we today know as RAM.

Semiconductors

Scientists in the 1940s and 1950s invented and perfected the semiconductor, a solid material that conducts electricity better than an insulator but not as well as a true conductor. Transistors, which are three-layer sandwiches of semiconductors, were being used in computers by 1954. Computer memory could now be held in small amounts of material. As a result, computers began to shrink as vacuum tubes were replaced by tiny but powerful transistors.

Rapid Developments

Improvements in computer technology continued at a fast and furious pace. By 1958, an electronic engineer had invented the integrated circuit—one tiny semiconductor chip containing much of the operating information a computer needs to run. Tiny computer chips led to smaller computers. The invention in the 1970s of the microprocessor led to the development of the personal computers we use today.

THINK ABOUT IT

1. Why was the invention of transistors so important to the development of computers?
2. Why do you think the abacus is still a useful tool in some places?

Microprocessors are used in products such as pocket calculators and digital watches. This microprocessor is shown compared to a penny, to give you an idea of how small microprocessors are.

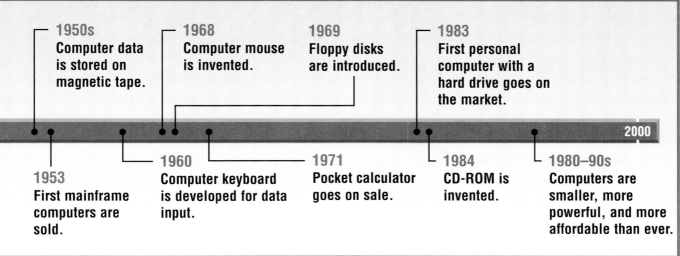

1950s
Computer data is stored on magnetic tape.

1968
Computer mouse is invented.

1969
Floppy disks are introduced.

1983
First personal computer with a hard drive goes on the market.

2000

1953
First mainframe computers are sold.

1960
Computer keyboard is developed for data input.

1971
Pocket calculator goes on sale.

1984
CD-ROM is invented.

1980–90s
Computers are smaller, more powerful, and more affordable than ever.

Grace Murray Hopper
COMPUTER SCIENTIST

"I felt that more people should be able to use the computer and that they should be able to talk to it in plain English. . ."

Grace Murray Hopper helped pave the way for modern computing. Dr. Hopper invented the first computer compiler in 1952. A compiler is software that makes it possible to write a computer program in a computer language without first writing it in binary code as a long series of numbers. Dr. Hopper also helped develop COBOL, the first computer language that allowed programmers to communicate with computers in words instead of numbers. She was the first to use the term "bug," referring to a computer program error. She came up with it when she found that a moth trapped in a computer relay was causing it to make errors.

Grace Murray Hopper's interest in machines started early. As a child, she loved to take toys and machines apart to find out how they worked. Her parents encouraged her scientific curiosity. They also encouraged her to break through the limitations often placed on women during the early 1900s. She played basketball in high school at a time when most young women didn't take part in team sports. In 1934 she also became the first woman to earn a Ph.D. in mathematics from Yale University.

After earning her Ph.D. Dr. Hopper taught until 1943. She then joined the United States Naval Reserve and developed programs for the navy during World War II. For many years after the war, she worked on important computer projects for the navy and for private business. Two of those projects were the development of the compiler and of COBOL. By the time Hopper retired from the Navy in 1986, she had reached the rank of rear admiral. She continued to give talks to young people, and she always encouraged them to be fearless in trying new things.

THINK ABOUT IT

1. How did Grace Murray Hopper's work advance the science of computing?
2. How did Dr. Hopper's parents contribute to her success?

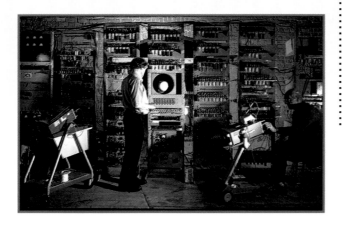

◄ **Dr. Hopper did some of her early programming on computers like these.**

Gaining Strength

How can a lever make you stronger?

Materials

- two pairs of adjustable pliers (or two wrenches that fit the nut)
- metal bolt
- nut that will screw on the bolt

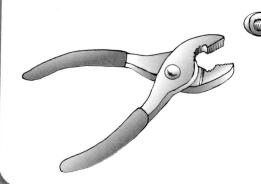

Procedure

1. Use your fingers to screw the nut on the bolt.

2. Use one pair of pliers to hold the bolt and one pair to tighten the nut.

3. Try unscrewing the nut with your fingers.

4. Now try unscrewing it with the pliers.

Draw Conclusions

Why couldn't you unscrew the nut with your fingers? Why could you unscrew it with the pliers? If you could make the handle of the pliers longer, would you need more—or less—force to unscrew the nut? Why? What other simple machine makes it easier to unscrew the nut?

Saving Force

How much can friction reduce the amount of work that is done?

Materials

- shoe box with a 2.5-cm (1-in.) square cut out of one end
- balloon
- rough surface (such as carpet)
- slick surface (such as linoleum)
- meterstick

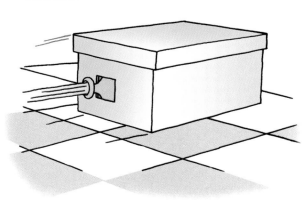

Procedure

1. Put the balloon inside the box, with the open end sticking out the hole. Put the lid on the box.

2. Blow up the balloon and hold the end closed.

3. Place the box on the rough surface and let the balloon go.

4. Measure how far the box travels.

5. Repeat Steps 1–4, blowing up the balloon the same amount. This time, place the box on the slick surface.

Draw Conclusions

On which surface did the box travel a shorter distance? Why did the box stop sooner on this surface? Compare the two distances. About how much of the available work was wasted by friction?

Chapter 2 Review and Test Preparation

Vocabulary Review

Use the terms below to complete the sentences. The page numbers in ( ) tell you where to look in the chapter if you need help.

work (F40)
machine (F41)
lever (F42)
fulcrum (F42)
effort arm (F42)
resistance arm (F42)
pulley (F45)

wheel and axle (F46)
inclined plane (F50)
wedge (F52)
screw (F53)
compound machines (F58)
efficiency (F62)

1. The ratio of work put out by a machine to the work put into it is called its ____.

2. The arm of a lever pivots around a ____.

3. A ____ changes the amount or direction of a force exerted on an object.

4. A sloping surface that allows a smaller force to be exerted is called an ____.

5. The product of force and distance is ____.

6. A simple machine with an arm that pivots about a fulcrum is a ____.

7. Force exerted on a lever is applied on the lever's ____.

8. The ____ of a lever transfers the applied force to the object being moved.

9. An inclined plane wrapped around a cylinder is a ____.

10. All ____ are made up of two or more simple machines.

11. A movable inclined plane that transfers a force so that logs can be split is a ____.

12. The steering wheel of a car is an example of a special type of lever, the ____.

13. A ____ is a grooved wheel around which a rope or chain can move.

Connect Concepts

Complete the chart, using terms from the Word Bank.

third-class levers   **machines**   **inclined planes**
screws   **wedges**   **second-class levers**
wheels and axles   **pulleys**   **levers**

14. _____ include simple machines, such as

15. _____

20. _____

first-class levers

16. _____

17. _____

18. _____

19. _____

ramps

21. _____

22. _____

Check Understanding

Write the letter of the best choice.

23. A lever in which the load is located between the fulcrum and the effort arm is a —
    A first-class lever
    B second-class lever
    C third-class lever
    D pulley

24. In any machine that increases a force, the distance the force moves is —
    F increased
    G decreased
    H doubled
    J not changed

25. However much work is put into a machine, the amount of work put out will always be —
    A less
    B greater
    C the same
    D extremely small

26. A knife is a compound machine made up of —
    F a lever and a screw
    G an inclined plane and an axle
    H a pulley and a wedge
    J a lever and a wedge

Critical Thinking

27. A person carries a heavy box along a flat street for a distance of two hundred meters but does no work. Explain why.

28. Why might it take less force to unscrew a screw from a piece of wood than it did to screw it in initially?

Process Skills Review

29. How could you **compare** two sets of pulleys to see which set makes work easier?

30. In your experiment with the pulleys, which **variables** would you **control**, and which would you change?

31. A certain lever increases the distance through which a force moves. **Predict** how the lever will change a force applied to it.

32. Make a **hypothesis** to explain why valves used to shut off water often have large wheels on them.

33. How would you plan and conduct an **experiment** to measure the efficiency of a ramp?

Performance Assessment

Cranes

Observe the photograph of a crane. Identify as many simple machines as you can in this compound machine. Explain the advantage (an increase in force or in distance) that each simple machine gives. Also identify the points at which friction may cause a decrease in the crane's efficiency, and suggest steps that might be taken to overcome the friction.

UNIT F

Unit Project Wrap Up

Here are some ideas for ways to wrap up your unit project.

Write an Instruction Manual

Write the purpose of your invention. Then give step-by-step instructions about how to use it.

Make a Diagram

Use computer software to make a diagram of your invention. Label each part.

Write a Biography

Research a famous inventor. Write a biography about him or her. Include sketches of his or her inventions.

Investigate Further

How can you make your project better? What other questions do you have about forces and machines? Plan ways to find answers to your questions. Use the Science Handbook on pages R2–R9 for help.

References

Planning an Investigation

When scientists observe something they want to study, they use a method of scientific inquiry to plan and conduct their study. They use science process skills as tools to help them gather, organize, analyze, and present their information. This plan will help you use scientific inquiry and process skills to work like a scientist.

Step 1—Observe and Ask Questions.

I wonder if a magnetized paper clip will stay magnetized if it is placed in a freezer.

- Use your senses to make observations.
- Record a question you would like to answer.

Step 2—Make a hypothesis.

My hypothesis: a magnetized paperclip will lose its magnetic strength when it is placed in a freezer.

- Choose one possible answer, or hypothesis, to your question.
- Write your hypothesis in a complete sentence.
- Think about what investigation you can do to test your hypothesis.

Step 3—Plan your test.

I'll magnetize four identical paper clips, then put two of them in the freezer. After 20 minutes, I'll test the strength of each magnet.

- Write down the steps you will follow to do your test. Decide how to conduct a fair test by controlling variables.
- Decide what equipment you will need.
- Decide how you will gather and record your data.

Step 4—Conduct your test.

I'll record the number of paper clips each one picks up.

- Follow the steps you wrote.

- Observe and measure carefully.

- Record everything that happens.

- Organize your data so that you can study it carefully.

Step 5—Draw conclusions and share results.

My hypothesis was incorrect. Freezing the paper clips didn't seem to make a difference.

- Analyze the data you gathered.

- Make charts, graphs, or tables to show your data.

- Write a conclusion. Describe the evidence you used to determine whether your test supported your hypothesis.

- Decide whether your hypothesis was true.

Investigate Further

I wonder if other conditions will affect a magnet's strength?

Using Science Tools

Using a Hand Lens

A hand lens magnifies objects, or makes them look larger than they are.

1. Hold the hand lens about 12 cm (5 in.) from your eye.
2. Bring the object toward you until it comes into focus.

Using a Thermometer

A thermometer measures the temperature of air and most liquids.

1. Place the thermometer in the liquid. Don't touch the thermometer any more than you need to. Never stir the liquid with the thermometer. If you are measuring the temperature of the air, make sure that the thermometer is not in line with a direct light source.
2. Move so that your eyes are even with the liquid in the thermometer.
3. If you are measuring a material that is not being heated or cooled, wait about two minutes for the reading to become stable. Find the scale line that meets the top of the liquid in the thermometer, and read the temperature.
4. If the material you are measuring is being heated or cooled, you will not be able to wait before taking your measurements. Measure as quickly as you can.

Caring for and Using a Microscope

A microscope is another tool that magnifies objects. A microscope can increase the detail you see by increasing the number of times an object is magnified.

Caring for a Microscope

- Always use two hands when you carry a microscope.
- Never touch any of the lenses of a microscope with your fingers.

Using a Microscope

1. Raise the eyepiece as far as you can using the coarse-adjustment knob. Place your slide on the stage.

2. Always start by using the lowest power. The lowest-power lens is usually the shortest. Start with the lens in the lowest position it can go without touching the slide.

3. Look through the eyepiece, and begin adjusting it upward with the coarse-adjustment knob. When the slide is close to being in focus, use the fine-adjustment knob.

4. When you want to use a higher-power lens, first focus the slide under low power. Then, watching carefully to make sure that the lens will not hit the slide, turn the higher-power lens into place. Use only the fine-adjustment knob when looking through the higher-power lens.

You may use a Brock microscope. This is a sturdy microscope that has only one lens.

1. Place the object to be viewed on the stage.

2. Look through the eyepiece, and begin raising the tube until the object comes into focus.

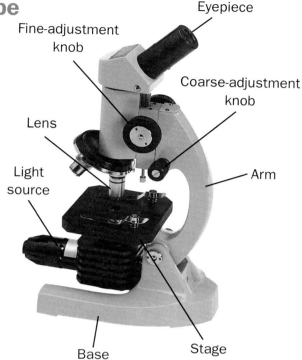

A Light Microscope

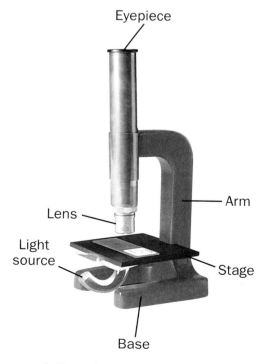

A Brock Microscope

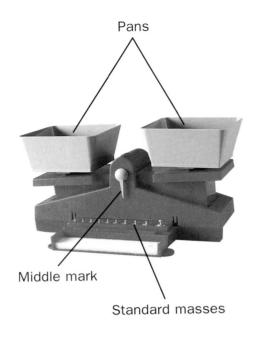

Pans

Middle mark

Standard masses

Using a Balance

Use a balance to measure an object's mass. Mass is the amount of matter an object has.

1. Look at the pointer on the base to make sure the empty pans are balanced.
2. Place the object you wish to measure in the left pan.
3. Add the standard masses to the other pan. As you add masses, you should see the pointer move. When the pointer is at the middle mark, the pans are balanced.
4. Add the numbers on the masses you used. The total is the mass in grams of the object you measured.

Using a Spring Scale

Use a spring scale to measure forces such as the pull of gravity on objects. You measure weight and other forces in units called newtons (N).

Measuring the Weight of an Object

1. Hook the spring scale to the object.
2. Lift the scale and object with a smooth motion. Do not jerk them upward.
3. Wait until any motion of the spring comes to a stop. Then read the number of newtons from the scale.

Measuring the Force to Move an Object

1. With the object resting on a table, hook the spring scale to it.
2. Pull the object smoothly across the table. Do not jerk the object.
3. As you pull, read the number of newtons you are using to pull the object.

Measuring Liquids

Use a beaker, a measuring cup, or a graduate to measure liquids accurately.

1. Pour the liquid you want to measure into a measuring container. Put your measuring container on a flat surface, with the measuring scale facing you.

2. Look at the liquid through the container. Move so that your eyes are even with the surface of the liquid in the container.

3. To read the volume of the liquid, find the scale line that is even with the surface of the liquid.

4. If the surface of the liquid is not exactly even with a line, estimate the volume of the liquid. Decide which line the liquid is closer to, and use that number.

Beaker   Graduate

Using a Ruler or Meterstick

Use a ruler or meterstick to measure distances and to find lengths of objects.

1. Place the zero mark or end of the ruler or meterstick next to one end of the distance or object you want to measure.

2. On the ruler or meterstick, find the place next to the other end of the distance or object.

3. Look at the scale on the ruler or meterstick. This will show the distance you want or the length of the object.

Using a Timing Device

Use a timing device such as a stopwatch to measure time.

1. Reset the stopwatch to zero.

2. When you are ready to begin timing, press start.

3. As soon as you are ready to stop timing, press stop.

4. The numbers on the dial or display show how many minutes, seconds, and parts of seconds have passed.

Using a Computer

A computer can help you communicate with others and can help you get information. It is a tool you can use to write reports, make graphs and charts, and do research.

Writing Reports

To write a report with a computer, use a word processing software program. After you are in the program, type your report. By using certain keys and the mouse, you can control how the words look, move words, delete or add words and copy them, check your spelling, and print your report.

Save your work to the hard disk of the computer, or to a floppy disk. You can go back to your saved work later if you want to revise it.

There are many reasons for revising your work. You may find new information to add or mistakes you want to correct. You may want to change the way you report your information because of your audience.

Computers make revising easy. You delete what you don't want, add the new parts, and then save. You can save different versions of your work if you want to.

For a science lab report, it is important to show the same kinds of information each time. With a computer, you can make a general format for a lab report, save the format, and then use it again and again.

Making Graphs and Charts

You can make a graph or chart with most word processing software programs. Or, you can use special software programs such as Data ToolKit or Graph Links. With Graph

Links you can make pictographs and circle, bar, line, and double-line graphs.

First, decide what kind of graph or chart will best communicate your data. Sometimes it's easiest to do this by sketching your ideas on paper. Then you can decide what format and categories you need for your graph or chart. Choose that format for the program. Then type your information. Most software programs include a tutor that gives you step-by-step directions for making a graph or chart.

Doing Research

Computers can help you find current information from all over the world through the Internet. The Internet connects thousands of computer sites that have been set up by schools, libraries, museums, and many other organizations.

Get permission from an adult before you log on to the Internet. Find out the rules for Internet use at school or at home. Then log on and go to a search engine, which will help you find what you need. Type in keywords, words that tell the subject of your search. If you get too much information that isn't exactly about the topic, make your keywords more specific. When you find the information you need, save it or print it.

Harcourt Science tells you about many Internet sites related to what you are studying. To find out about these sites, called Web sites, look for Technology Links in the lessons in this book.

If you need to contact other people to help in your research, you can use e-mail. Log into your e-mail program, type the address of the person you want to reach, type your message, and send it. Be sure to have adult permission before sending or receiving e-mail. Another way to use a computer for research is to access CD-ROMs. These are discs that look like music CDs. CD-ROMs can hold huge amounts of data, including words, still pictures, audio, and video. Encyclopedias, dictionaries, almanacs, and other sources of information are available on CD-ROMs. These computer discs are valuable resources for your research.

Measurement Systems

SI Measures (Metric)

Temperature
Ice melts at 0 degrees Celsius (°C)
Water freezes at 0°C
Water boils at 100°C

Length and Distance
1000 meters (m) = 1 kilometer (km)
100 centimeters (cm) = 1 m
10 millimeters (mm) = 1 cm

Force
1 newton (N) = 1 kilogram ×
    meter/second/second (kg-m/s^2)

Volume
1 cubic meter (m^3) = 1m × 1m × 1m
1 cubic centimeter (cm^3) =
    1 cm × 1 cm × 1 cm
1 liter (L) = 1000 milliliters (mL)
1 cm^3 = 1 mL

Area
1 square kilometer (km^2) = 1 km × 1 km
1 hectare = 10,000 m^2

Mass
1000 grams (g) = 1 kilogram (kg)
1000 milligrams (mg) = 1 g

Rates (Metric and Customary)
kmh or km/hr = kilometers per hour
m/s = meters per second
mph or mi/hr = miles per hour

Customary Measures

Volume of Fluids
8 fluid ounces (fl oz) = 1 cup (c)
2 c = 1 pint (pt)
2 pt = 1 quart (qt)
4 qt = 1 gallon (gal)

Temperature
Ice melts at 32 degrees Fahrenheit (°F)
Water freezes at 32°F
Water boils at 212°F

Length and Distance
12 inches (in.) = 1 foot (ft)
3 ft = 1 yard (yd)
5,280 ft = 1 mile (mi)

Weight
16 ounces (oz) = 1 pound (lb)
2,000 pounds = 1 ton (T)

Health Handbook

Good Nutrition

The Food Guide Pyramid

No one food or food group supplies all the nutrients you need. That's why it's important to eat a variety of foods from all the food groups. The Food Guide Pyramid can help you choose healthful foods in the right amounts. By choosing more foods from the groups at the bottom of the pyramid, and few foods from the group at the top, you will eat nutrient-rich foods that provide your body with energy to grow and develop.

Fats, oils, and sweets
Eat sparingly.

Meat, poultry, fish, dried beans, eggs, and nuts
2–3 servings

Milk, yogurt, and cheese **2–3 servings**

Fruits
2–4 servings

Vegetables
3–5 servings

Breads, cereals, rice, and pasta **6–11 servings**

Understanding Serving Size

The Food Guide Pyramid suggests a number of servings to eat each day from each group. But a serving isn't necessarily the amount you eat at a meal. A plate full of macaroni and cheese may contain three or four servings of pasta (macaroni) and three servings of cheese. That's about half your bread group servings and all your milk servings at one sitting! The table below can help you estimate the number of servings you are eating.

Food Group	Amount of Food in One Serving	Easy Ways to Estimate Serving Size
Bread, Cereal, Rice, and Pasta Group	$\frac{1}{2}$ cup cooked pasta, rice, or cereal 1 ounce ready-to-eat (dry) cereal 1 slice bread, $\frac{1}{2}$ bagel	ice-cream scoop large handful of plain cereal or a small handful of cereal with raisins and nuts
Vegetable Group	1 cup of raw, leafy vegetables $\frac{1}{2}$ cup other vegetables, cooked or chopped raw $\frac{3}{4}$ cup vegetable juice $\frac{1}{2}$ cup tomato sauce	about the size of a fist ice-cream scoop
Fruit Group	medium apple, pear, or orange $\frac{1}{2}$ large banana, or one medium banana $\frac{1}{2}$ cup chopped or cooked fruit $\frac{3}{4}$ cup of fruit juice	about the size of a baseball
Milk, Yogurt, and Cheese Group	$1\frac{1}{2}$ ounces of natural cheese 2 ounces of processed cheese 1 cup of milk or yogurt	about the size of two dominoes $1\frac{1}{2}$ slices of packaged cheese
Meat, Poultry, Fish, Dried Beans, Eggs, and Nuts Group	3 ounces of lean meat, chicken, or fish 2 tablespoons peanut butter $\frac{1}{2}$ cup of cooked dried beans	about the size of your palm
Fats, Oils, and Sweets Group	1 teaspoon of margarine or butter	about the size of the tip of your thumb

Preparing Foods Safely

Fight Bacteria

You probably already know to throw away food that smells bad or looks moldy. But food doesn't have to look or smell bad to make you ill. To keep your food safe and yourself from becoming ill, follow the procedures shown in the picture below. And remember—when in doubt, throw it out!

FIGHT BAC!

Keep Food Safe From Bacteria

CLEAN Wash hands and surfaces often.

SEPARATE Don't cross-contaminate.

CHILL Refrigerate promptly.

COOK Cook to proper temperatures.

TM

Food Safety Tips

Tips for Preparing Food

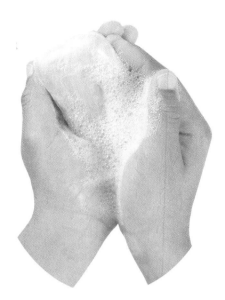

- Wash hands in hot, soapy water before preparing food. It's also a good idea to wash hands after preparing each dish.
- Defrost meat in the microwave or the refrigerator. Do NOT defrost meat on the kitchen counter.
- Keep raw meat, poultry, fish, and their juices away from other food.
- Wash cutting boards, knives, and countertops immediately after cutting up meat, poultry, or fish. Never use the same cutting board for meats and vegetables without thoroughly washing the board first.

Tips for Cooking Food

- Cook all food thoroughly, especially meat. Cooking food completely kills bacteria that can make you ill.
  - Red meats should be cooked to a temperature of 160°F. Poultry should be cooked to 180°F. When done, fish flakes easily with a fork.
  - Eggs should be cooked until the yolks are firm. Never eat food that contains raw eggs. Never eat cookie dough made with raw eggs.

Tips for Cleaning Up the Kitchen

- Wash all dishes, utensils, and countertops with hot, soapy water. Use a disinfectant soap, if possible.
- Store leftovers in small containers that will cool quickly in the refrigerator. Don't leave leftovers on the counter to cool.

Being Physically Active

Planning Your Weekly Activities

Being active every day is important for your overall health. Physical activity strengthens your body systems and helps you manage stress and maintain a healthful weight. The Activity Pyramid, like the Food Guide Pyramid, can help you choose a variety of activities in the right amounts to keep your body strong and healthy.

The Activity Pyramid

Sitting for more than thirty minutes at a time: Only Once in a While

Flexibility and Strength: Two to Three Times a Week

Light Exercise: Two to Three Times a Week

Twenty-plus minutes of continuous aerobic activity: Three to Five Times a Week

Stay active: Every Day

Guidelines for a Good Workout

There are three things you should do every time you are going to exercise—warm up, workout, and cool down.

Warm-Up When you warm up, your heart rate, respiration rate, and body temperature gradually increase and more blood begins to flow to your muscles. As your body warms up, your flexibility increases, helping you avoid muscle stiffness after exercising. People who warm up are also less prone to exercise-related injuries. Your warm-up should include five minutes of stretching, and five minutes of a low-level form of your workout exercise. For example, if you are going to run for your primary exercise, you should spend five minutes stretching, concentrating on your legs and lower back, and five minutes walking before you start running.

Workout The main part of your exercise routine should be an aerobic exercise that lasts twenty to thirty minutes. Some common aerobic exercises include walking, bicycling, jogging, swimming, cross-country skiing, jumping rope, dancing, and playing racket sports. You should choose an activity that is fun for you and that you will enjoy doing over a long period of time. You may want to mix up the types of activities you do. This helps you work different muscle groups, and provides a better overall workout.

Cool-Down When you finish your aerobic exercise, you need to give your body time to return to normal. You also need to stretch again. This portion of your workout is called a cool-down. Start your cool-down with three to five minutes of low-level activity. For example, if you have been running, you may want to jog and then walk during this time. Then do stretching exercises to prevent soreness and stiffness.

Using a Computer Safely

Good Posture at the Computer

Good posture is important when using the computer. To help prevent eyestrain, muscle fatigue, and injuries, follow the posture tips shown below. Remember to grasp your mouse lightly, keep your back straight, avoid facing a monitor toward a window, and take frequent breaks for stretching.

top of screen at or just below eye level

shoulders in line with ears and hips

neck and shoulders relaxed

arms at sides, bent as shown

wrists straight

feet flat on floor

Safety on the Internet

The Internet is a remarkable tool. You can use it for fun, education, research, and more. But like anything else, there are some downsides to the Internet. Some people compare the Internet to a real city; not all the people there are people you want to meet and not all the places you can go are places you want to be. Just like in a real city, you have to use common sense and follow safety guidelines to protect yourself. Below are some easy rules to follow to ensure that you are safe on-line.

Rules for On-Line Safety

- Talk with an adult family member to set up rules for going on-line. Decide what time of day you can go on-line, how long you can be on-line, and appropriate places you can visit. Do not access other areas or break the rules you establish.
- Don't give out personal information like your address, telephone number, or the name or location of your school.
- If you find any information on-line that makes you uncomfortable, tell an adult family member right away.
- Never agree to meet with anyone in person. If you want to get together with someone you meet on-line, check with an adult family member first. If a meeting is approved, arrange to meet in a public place and bring an adult with you.
- Don't send your picture or anything else to a person you meet on-line without first checking with an adult.
- Don't respond to any messages that are mean or make you feel uncomfortable. If you receive a message like that, tell an adult right away.

Being Safe at Home

Safety Tips for Baby-Sitters

Baby-sitting is a very important job. As a sitter you are responsible for the safety of the children in your care. Adults depend on you to make good decisions. Here are some tips to help you be a successful and safe baby-sitter.

When you accept a baby-sitting job, ask

- what time you should arrive.
- how long the adults will be away.
- what your responsibilities are.
- the amount of pay you will receive.
- what arrangements will be made for your transportation to and from the home.

When you arrive to start a job

- Arrive several minutes early so that the parents or guardians have time to give you information about caring for the children.
- Write down the place and phone number of where the parents are going and when they will be home.
- Know where emergency phone numbers are listed. The list should have numbers for the police, the fire department, and the children's doctor.
- Know where first-aid supplies are kept and if the children need any special medication. Remember: Never give the children any medication unless directed to do so by the parents or the doctor.
- Ask what and when the children should eat.
- Ask what activities the children can do.
- Ask when the children should go to bed and what their bedtime routine is.

While you are baby-sitting

- Never leave a baby alone on a changing table, sofa, or bed.
- Never leave a child alone, even for a short time.
- Check children often when they are playing and when they are sleeping.
- Never leave a child alone near a pool or in the bathtub.
- Never let a child play with a plastic bag.
- Keep dangerous items out of a child's reach.
- Know where all the doors are, and keep them locked. Do not let anyone in without permission from the parents.
- If the phone rings, take a message. Do not tell the caller that you are the baby-sitter or that the parents are out.
- If there is an injury or if a child gets sick, don't try to take care of it by yourself. Call the parents, or if they are unreachable, call the emergency numbers on the list.

◀ Never leave children playing alone.

▼ Never leave children alone near a pool or in the bathtub.

▼ Never leave a child to eat alone.

Safety in Emergencies

Fire Safety

Fires cause more deaths than any other type of disaster. But a fire doesn't have to be deadly if you prepare your home and follow some basic safety rules.

- Install smoke detectors outside sleeping areas and on any additional floors of your home. Be sure to test the smoke detectors once a month and change the batteries in each detector twice a year.

- Keep a fire extinguisher on each floor of your home. Check monthly to make sure each is properly charged.

- Work with your family to make a fire escape plan for each room of your home. Ideally, there should be two routes out of each room. Sleeping areas are most important, because most fires happen at night. Plan to use stairs only; elevators can be dangerous in a fire.

- Pick a place outside for everyone to meet. Designate one person to call the fire department or 911 from a neighbor's home.

- Practice crawling low to avoid smoke. If your clothes catch fire, follow the three steps listed below.

1. STOP

2. DROP

3. ROLL

Earthquake Safety

An earthquake is a strong shaking of the ground. The tips below can help you and your family stay safe in an earthquake.

Before an Earthquake	During an Earthquake	After an Earthquake
• Secure tall, heavy furniture, such as bookcases, to the wall. Store the heaviest items on the lowest shelves. • Check for potential fire risks. Bolt down gas appliances, and use flexible hosing and connections for both gas and water utilities. • Reinforce and anchor overhead light fixtures to help keep them from falling.	• If you are outdoors, stay outdoors and move away from buildings and utility wires. • If you are indoors, take cover under a heavy desk or table or in a doorway. Stay away from glass doors and windows and heavy objects that might fall. • If you are in a car, drive to an open area away from buildings and overpasses.	• Continue to watch for falling objects as aftershocks shake the area. • Adults should have the building checked for hidden structural problems. • Check for broken gas, electric, and water lines. If you smell gas, an adult should shut off the gas main and leave the area. Report the leak.

Thunderstorm Safety

Thunderstorms are severe storms. Lightning associated with thunderstorms can injure or kill people, cause fires, and damage property. Here are some thunderstorm safety tips.

- **If you are inside, stay there.** The best place to take cover is inside a building.
- **If you are outside, try to take shelter.** If possible, get into a closed car or truck. If you can't take shelter, get into a ditch or low area, if possible.
- **If you are outside, stay away from tall objects.** Don't stand under a lone tree, in an open field, on a beach, or on a hilltop. Find a low place to stay.
- **Stay away from water.** Lightning is attracted to water, and water conducts electricity.
- **Listen for weather bulletins and updates.** The storms that produce lightning may also produce tornadoes. Be ready to take shelter in a basement or interior hallway away from windows and doors.

First Aid

The tips on the next few pages can help you provide simple first aid to others or yourself. Always tell an adult about any injuries that occur.

For Choking . . .

If someone else is choking . . .

  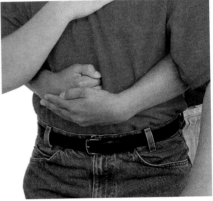

1. Recognize the Universal Choking Sign—grasping the throat with both hands. This sign means a person is choking and needs help.

2. Stand behind the choking person, and put your arms around his or her waist. Place your fist above the person's belly button.
Grab your fist with your other hand.

3. Pull your hands toward yourself, and give five quick, hard, upward thrusts on the person's stomach.

If you are choking when alone . . .

1. Make a fist, and place it above your belly button. Grab your fist with your other hand. Pull your hands up with a quick, hard thrust.

2. Or, keep your hands on your belly, lean your body over the back of a chair or over a counter, and shove your fist in and up.

For Bleeding . . .

If someone else is bleeding . . .

Wash your hands with soap, if possible.

Put on protective gloves, if available.

Wash small wounds with soap and water. Do *not* wash serious wounds.

Place a clean gauze pad or cloth over the wound. Press firmly for ten minutes. Don't lift the gauze during this time.

If you don't have gloves, have the injured person hold the gauze or cloth in place with his or her hand for ten minutes.

If after ten minutes the bleeding has stopped, bandage the wound. If the bleeding has not stopped, continue pressing on the wound and get help.

If you are bleeding . . .

- Wash your wound if it is a small cut. If it is a serious wound, do *not* wash it.
- Place a gauze pad or clean cloth over the wound, and hold it firmly in place for ten minutes. Don't lift the gauze or cloth until ten minutes has passed.
- If you have no gauze or cloth, apply pressure with your hand.
- If after ten minutes the bleeding has stopped, bandage the wound. If the bleeding has not stopped, continue pressing on the wound and get help.

Sense Organs

Eyes

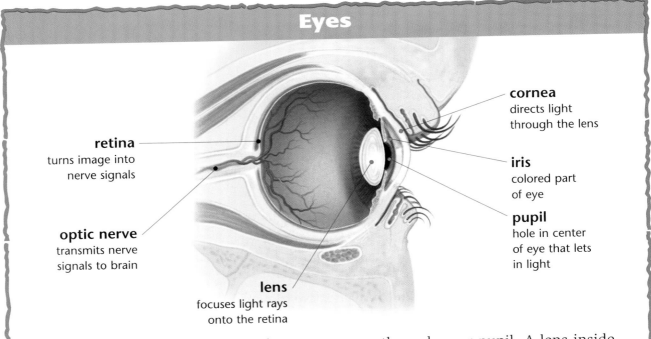

retina
turns image into nerve signals

optic nerve
transmits nerve signals to brain

cornea
directs light through the lens

iris
colored part of eye

pupil
hole in center of eye that lets in light

lens
focuses light rays onto the retina

Light rays bounce off objects and enter your eye through your pupil. A lens inside your eye focuses the light rays, and the image of the object is projected onto the retina at the back of your eye. In the retina the image is turned into nerve signals. Your brain analyzes the signals to tell you what you're seeing.

Ears

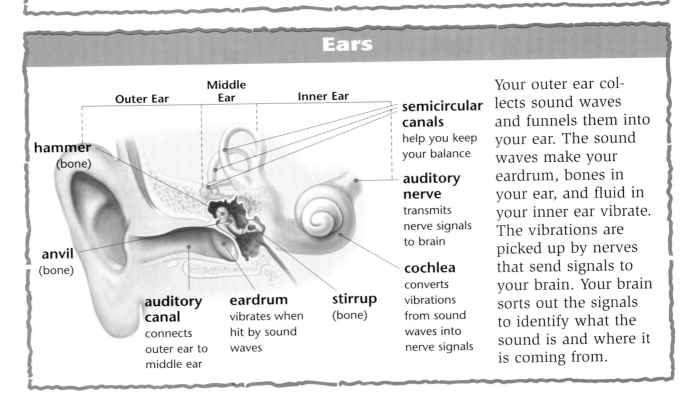

Outer Ear Middle Ear Inner Ear

hammer
(bone)

anvil
(bone)

auditory canal
connects outer ear to middle ear

eardrum
vibrates when hit by sound waves

stirrup
(bone)

semicircular canals
help you keep your balance

auditory nerve
transmits nerve signals to brain

cochlea
converts vibrations from sound waves into nerve signals

Your outer ear collects sound waves and funnels them into your ear. The sound waves make your eardrum, bones in your ear, and fluid in your inner ear vibrate. The vibrations are picked up by nerves that send signals to your brain. Your brain sorts out the signals to identify what the sound is and where it is coming from.

Nose

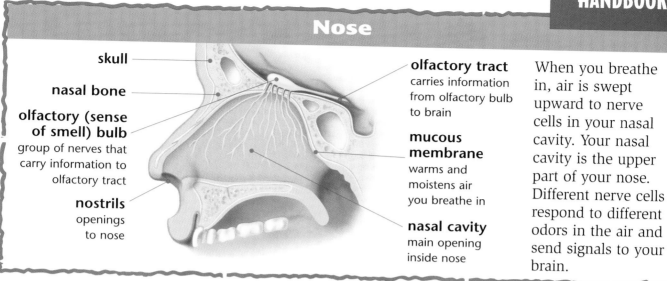

skull

nasal bone

olfactory (sense of smell) bulb
group of nerves that carry information to olfactory tract

nostrils
openings to nose

olfactory tract
carries information from olfactory bulb to brain

mucous membrane
warms and moistens air you breathe in

nasal cavity
main opening inside nose

When you breathe in, air is swept upward to nerve cells in your nasal cavity. Your nasal cavity is the upper part of your nose. Different nerve cells respond to different odors in the air and send signals to your brain.

Caring for Your Senses

Avoid sitting too close to TVs and computer monitors or holding reading materials too close for long periods of time. Close eye work can cause eye muscle strain.

Tongue

taste buds

Your tongue is covered with about 10,000 tiny nerve cells, or taste buds, that pick out tastes in the things you eat and drink. Certain taste buds respond to certain tastes and send signals to your brain.

Activity

Have four classmates stand about 15 feet (4.6 m) from your front, back, and sides. Close your eyes and have one of the four clap. Point at the clapper. Cover one ear and try four times more. Did you pick the correct clapper more often using two ears or one?

Skin

Merkel's endings
respond to medium pressure

free nerve endings
react to painful stimuli

Meissner's endings
respond to light pressure and small, fast vibration

Ruffini's endings
sense changes in temperature and pressure

Krause's endings
cold and mechanoreceptors

Pacini's endings
react to heavy pressure

Nerve cells in your skin signal your brain about stimuli (conditions around you) that affect your skin. Different kinds of nerve cells react to different stimuli, such as pressure, temperature, and pain.

Skeletal System

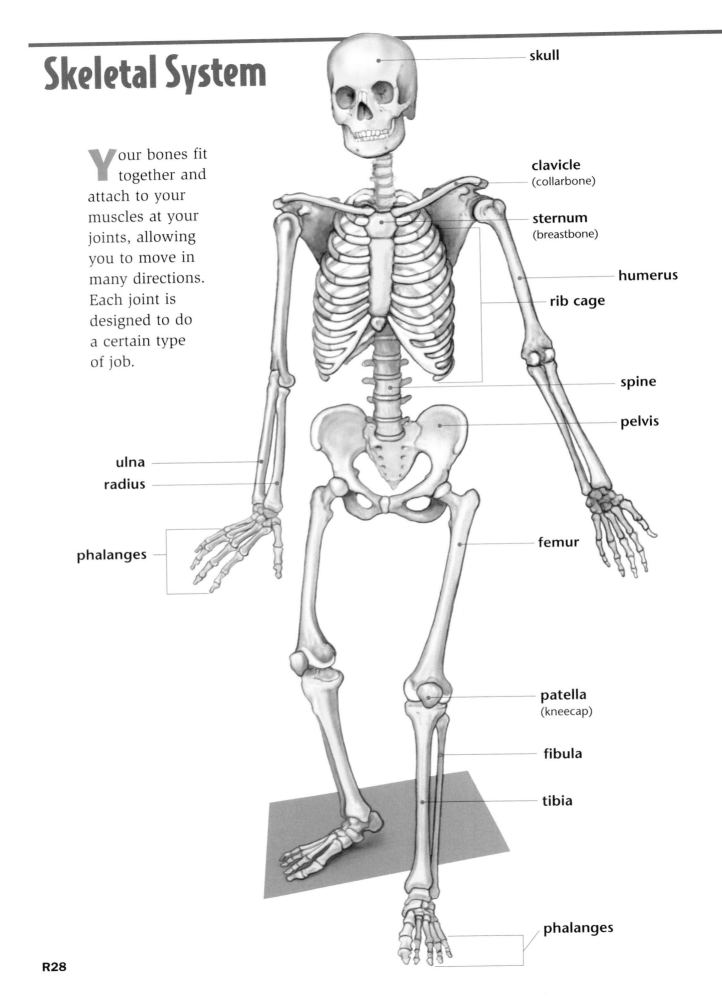

Your bones fit together and attach to your muscles at your joints, allowing you to move in many directions. Each joint is designed to do a certain type of job.

skull

clavicle
(collarbone)

sternum
(breastbone)

humerus

rib cage

spine

pelvis

ulna

radius

phalanges

femur

patella
(kneecap)

fibula

tibia

phalanges

Some Types of Joints

Ball-and-socket joints allow rotation and movement in many directions. Your hips and shoulders are ball-and-socket joints.

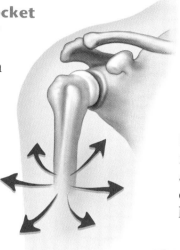

Hinge joints move only back and forth. Your elbows and fingers have hinge joints.

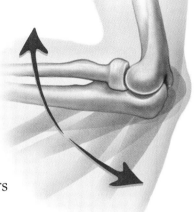

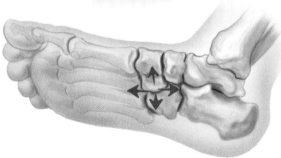

Gliding joints allow only side-to-side and back-and-forth movements. The vertebrae of your spine form gliding joints. Your wrist is a gliding joint. Your feet also contain gliding joints.

Caring for Your Skeletal System

- Move and flex your joints regularly through exercise. Strong muscles can protect your joints from injuries.

- Be sure to warm up and cool down whenever you exercise.

- You can injure a joint by using it too much at one time or without warming up or by moving it in a way it is not designed to move.

Activities

1. Curl your index finger. Point it and move it in a circle. Which joint is a hinge joint? Which joint is a gliding joint?

2. Make a model of a joint. Cut out two strips of cardboard and join them together using a round metal fastener. What type of joint does the model most nearly represent?

3. Try to run without bending your knees. Try to write without bending any of your fingers. Can you do either of these things?

Muscular System

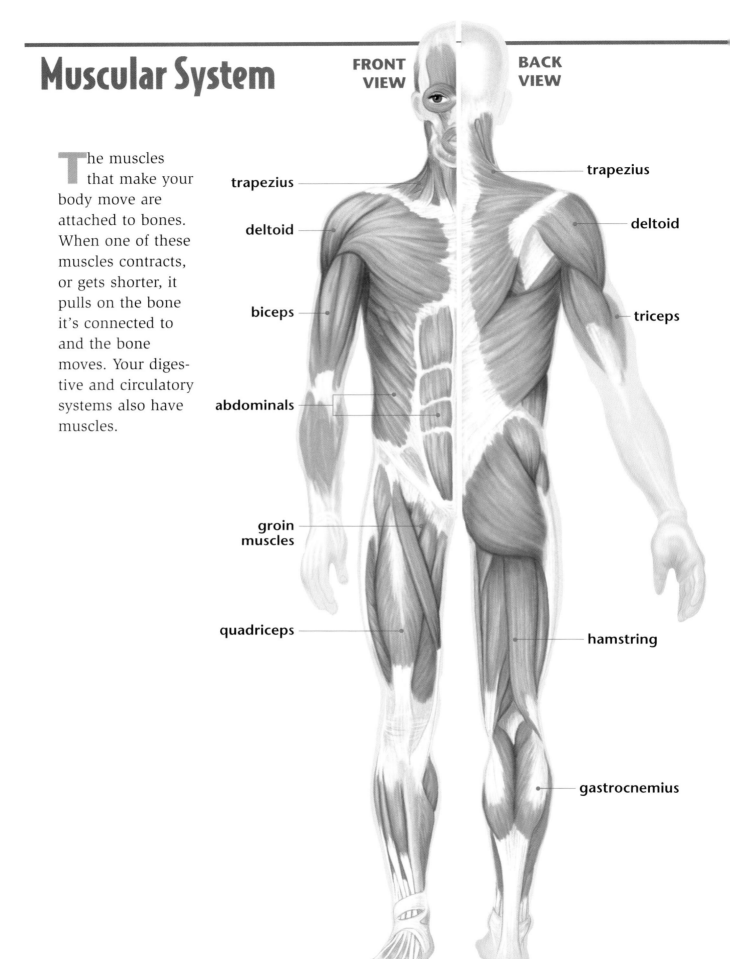

FRONT VIEW **BACK VIEW**

The muscles that make your body move are attached to bones. When one of these muscles contracts, or gets shorter, it pulls on the bone it's connected to and the bone moves. Your digestive and circulatory systems also have muscles.

trapezius

deltoid

biceps

abdominals

groin muscles

quadriceps

trapezius

deltoid

triceps

hamstring

gastrocnemius

Types of Muscle

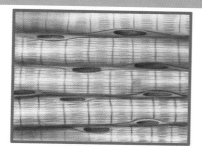

Striated Muscle Striated means striped. If you could look at your muscles without any covering of skin, you could see the thin stripes. All the muscles you use to walk and move your body are striated muscles.

Smooth Muscle Smooth muscle is part of other body systems. The walls of your esophagus, stomach, and intestines are lined with smooth muscle. These muscles squeeze and relax to move food through your digestive system.

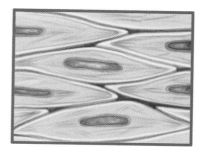

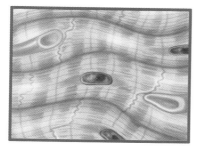

Cardiac Muscle Your heart is made of a special kind of muscle called cardiac muscle. It squeezes and relaxes every second of every day to pump blood through your body.

Caring for Your Muscular System

- An easy jog and gentle stretches before you start to play a sport loosen your tendons, ligaments, and muscles and help prevent injuries. This is called a warm-up.

- You should cool down after exercise too. Because your muscles contract during exercise, they need to be stretched when you finish.

Activities

1. With one hand, pull up on your desk. Feel the muscle on the front side of your upper arm. This is your biceps. It is a striated muscle.

2. Close your hand around a partly empty, closed tube of toothpaste. Gently squeeze starting with your little finger and ending with your index finger. Your fingers move toothpaste through the tube like smooth muscles move food through your digestive system.

3. Each second for a minute squeeze one hand into a fist and relax it. This is like the work your cardiac muscle does all the time.

Digestive System

Digestion is the process of breaking food into tiny pieces that are absorbed by your blood and carried to all parts of your body. Each part in your digestive system does a different job.

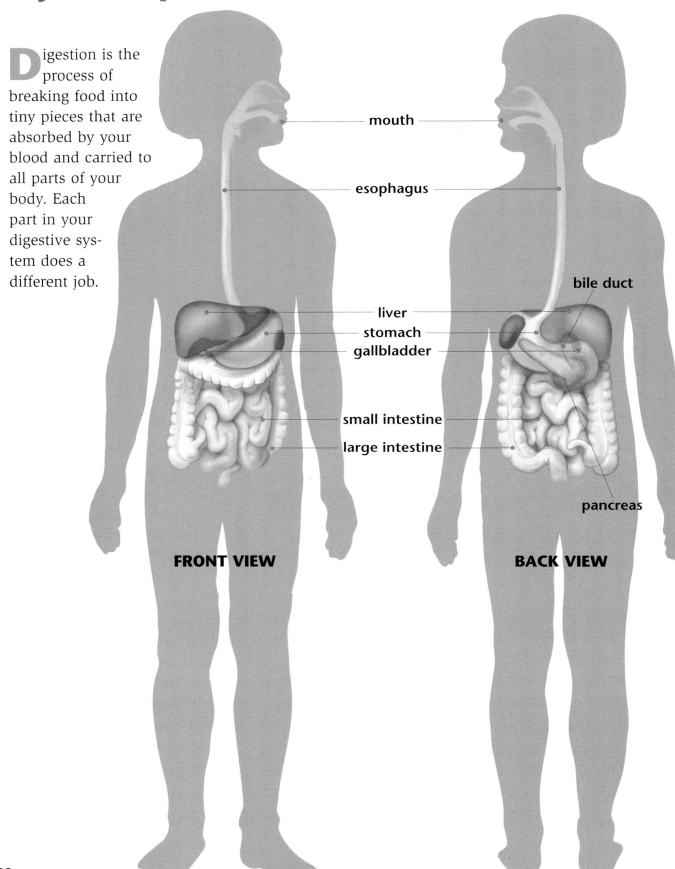

mouth

esophagus

liver

stomach

gallbladder

small intestine

large intestine

bile duct

pancreas

FRONT VIEW

BACK VIEW

Some Digestive Organs

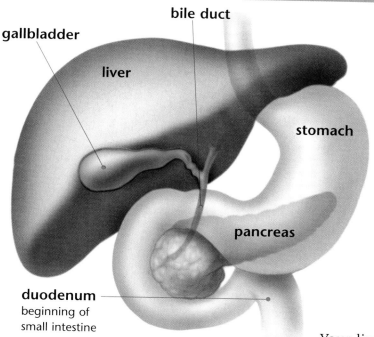

gallbladder

bile duct

liver

stomach

pancreas

duodenum
beginning of
small intestine

Liver, Gallbladder, Bile Duct, and Pancreas Your liver receives blood full of freshly digested nutrients from your small intestine. It stores some substances, such as vitamins and certain nutrients that supply your body with energy. It lets other nutrients pass through to other parts of your body. The liver also destroys poisonous waste products created during the digestion process. It breaks down chemicals such as medicines and alcohol too.

Your liver also makes bile, a fluid that breaks fats into smaller pieces. Bile is stored in your gallbladder. When it is needed, the bile flows through the bile duct into your small intestine to help with the digestive process.

Digestive juices made in your pancreas flow along a narrow tube into your small intestine, where they aid in digesting fats and proteins. Your pancreas also makes a special substance called insulin. Insulin helps your body move sugar from blood into cells.

Caring for Your Digestive System

- Drink a lot of water. Water helps food move through your digestive system.

- Don't drink alcohol. It's illegal for people your age. Drinking too much alcohol can damage your liver and pancreas.

- Keep a healthy body weight. Overweight people are more likely to have difficulty producing enough insulin.

Activities

1. **Vinegar is a kind of acid. Soak a potato chip in vinegar for 30 minutes. What happens? What process is demonstrated?**

2. **Foods with fat are harder to digest. Look at the nutrition labels on foods in your home. Which ones have the most fat per unit of weight (gram or g)?**

3. **Pretend you are a piece of food and write a story about your journey through the digestive system.**

Circulatory System

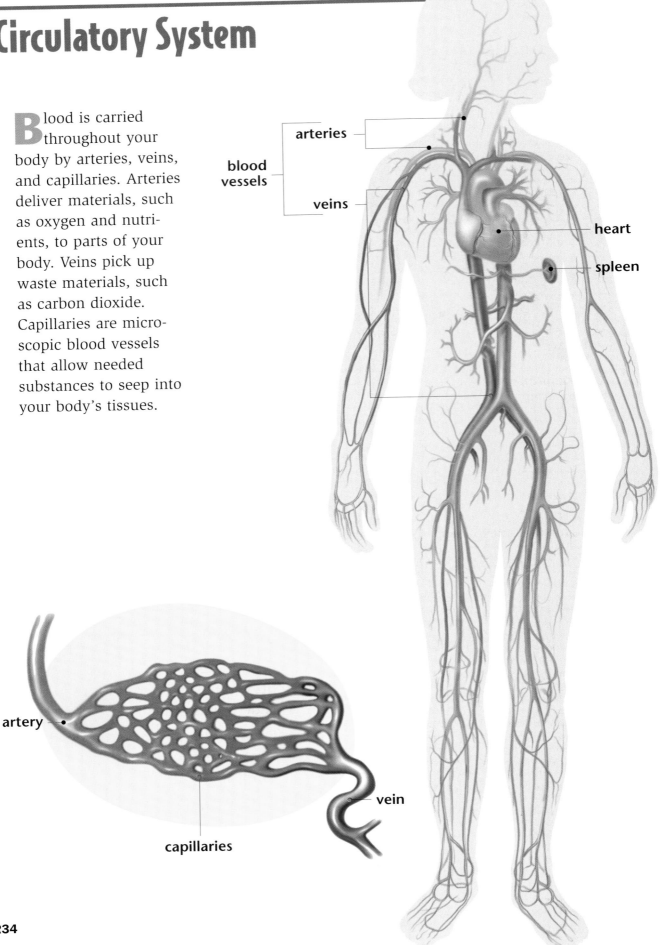

Blood is carried throughout your body by arteries, veins, and capillaries. Arteries deliver materials, such as oxygen and nutrients, to parts of your body. Veins pick up waste materials, such as carbon dioxide. Capillaries are microscopic blood vessels that allow needed substances to seep into your body's tissues.

blood vessels

arteries

veins

heart

spleen

artery

capillaries

vein

Red Blood Cells

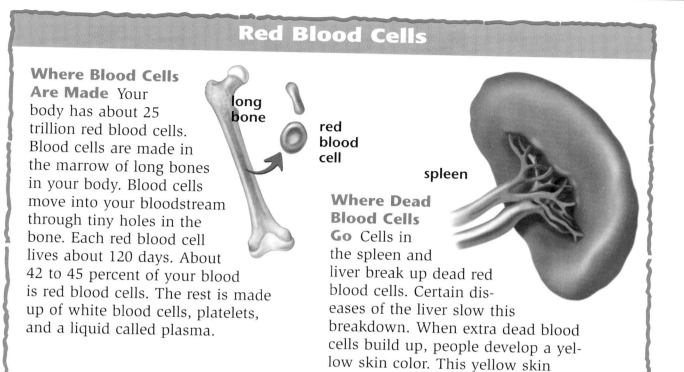

Where Blood Cells Are Made Your body has about 25 trillion red blood cells. Blood cells are made in the marrow of long bones in your body. Blood cells move into your bloodstream through tiny holes in the bone. Each red blood cell lives about 120 days. About 42 to 45 percent of your blood is red blood cells. The rest is made up of white blood cells, platelets, and a liquid called plasma.

long bone

red blood cell

spleen

Where Dead Blood Cells Go Cells in the spleen and liver break up dead red blood cells. Certain diseases of the liver slow this breakdown. When extra dead blood cells build up, people develop a yellow skin color. This yellow skin color is called jaundice.

Caring for Your Circulatory System

- Don't ever smoke. Smoking narrows blood vessels and causes high blood pressure.

- Don't use illegal drugs. Many drugs can cause liver damage.

- Follow directions for medicines carefully. Misuse of medicines can also cause liver damage.

Activities

1. Measure out 5 quarts (about 4.7 L) of water. This is about how much blood is in the average adult body.

2. Put 4 teaspoons of ground pepper into 5 teaspoons of water. Stir the mixture. The pepper represents red blood cells and the water represents plasma.

3. Take a small piece of modeling clay and roll it into a ball. Flatten the ball into a disk. Pinch the disk in the middle so that there is a dent in each side. This is the shape of a red blood cell.

Respiratory System

Your lungs are filled with air tubes, air sacs, and blood vessels. The air tubes and blood vessels in your lungs are divided until they are very small. At the ends of the tiny air tubes are air sacs called alveoli. The smallest blood vessels surround the alveoli.

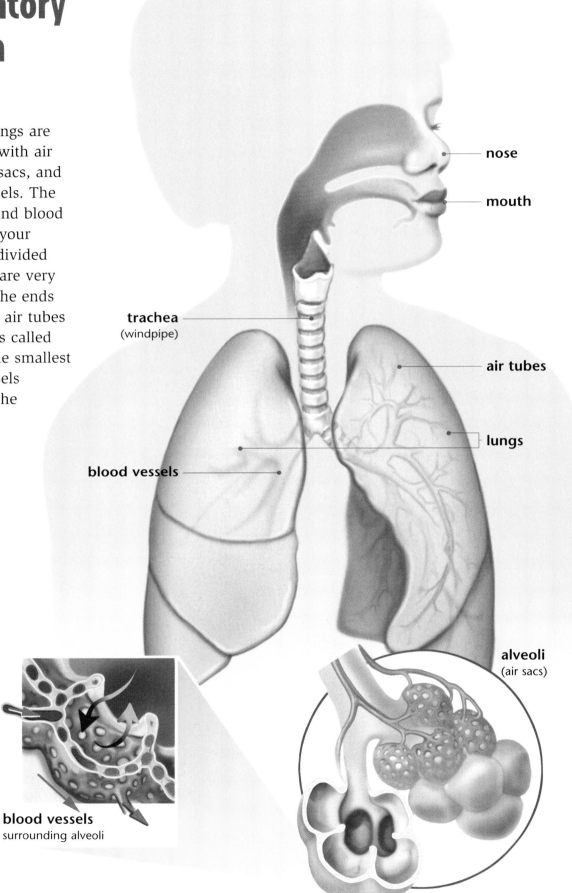

nose

mouth

trachea
(windpipe)

air tubes

lungs

blood vessels

blood vessels
surrounding alveoli

alveoli
(air sacs)

Coughing and Sneezing

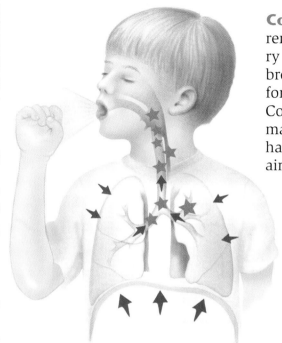

▲ **You might cough when unwanted materials reach the spots marked with stars.**

Coughing Coughing is one way your body removes unwanted material from your respiratory system. When you cough, you take a deep breath in. Then, you breathe out suddenly and forcefully through your throat and mouth. Coughing helps clear the path to the lungs. You may cough if food is stuck in your throat, if you have too much mucus in your throat, or if your airway is irritated by smoke.

Sneezing Sneezing is similar to coughing. When you sneeze, your breathing muscles contract suddenly. Air is pushed quickly out your nose and mouth. One cause of sneezing is irritation of the inside of your nose. This irritation can be from pollen, dust, dirt, or a respiratory infection.

Caring for Your Respiratory System

- Don't ever smoke. The tars in cigarettes can damage your lungs.

- Avoid smoke and air pollution. Breathing these can damage your respiratory system.

- Always cover your mouth and nose when you cough or sneeze. This helps prevent the spread of germs to other people.

Activities

1. Tear a one-quarter-inch square of notebook paper. Put it on your palm and blow it as far away as you can. When you sneeze, you can spread saliva and droplets of mucus at least that far.

2. Trace the pathway that air takes from your lungs when you sneeze or cough.

3. Cover your mouth with one hand. Put the other hand over your navel (belly button) and cough. What muscles did you use? What happened inside your throat? Wash your hand after you cough into it.

Nervous System

brain

spinal cord

nerves

Your nervous system is responsible for all of your thoughts and your body's activity. It makes your heart beat and your lungs work. It allows you to see, hear, smell, taste, and touch. It lets you learn, remember, and feel emotions. It moves all of your muscles.

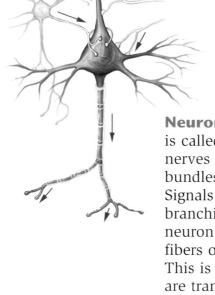

Neurons A nerve cell is called a neuron. Your nerves are made up of bundles of neurons. Signals travel along branching fibers of one neuron to branching fibers of other neurons. This is how messages are transmitted to and from your brain.

Central Nervous System

Your brain and spinal cord make up your central nervous system. Different areas of your brain control different activities.

Cerebrum The cerebrum is the top layer of your brain. It begins behind your forehead and fills the space inside the top and sides of your skull to where your neck begins. The cerebrum splits down the middle from front to back. The left and right parts are called hemispheres.

Four Lobes Each hemisphere of the cerebrum is divided into four smaller parts called lobes. The lobes are named for the skull bones that cover them.

Thinking
Speech
Movement
Touching
Hearing
Sight

cortex
analyzes information from your sense organs and is responsible for thinking abilities, such as reasoning, planning, and problem solving.

cerebellum
helps with your coordination and balance

spinal cord
bundle of nerves that relays messages between your brain and the rest of the nerves in your body

brain stem
connects brain to spinal cord and controls vital functions, such as breathing

Frontal lobes
behind your forehead. This part of the brain controls body movement.

Parietal lobes
above and just behind your ears. Parts of these lobes help you combine and understand signals from your sense organs.

Occipital lobes
behind the bulge on the back of your head. These lobes control eyesight and visual memory.

Temporal lobes
behind your temple. Parts of these lobes help you hear and understand language, and help you speak.

Caring for Your Nervous System

- Do not take any drugs unless chosen by your parents or guardian or a doctor. Some drugs can affect your brain cells.
- Eat a well-balanced diet. Your nervous system cannot work properly without certain nutrients.

Activity

Have a friend hold a ruler so that the 0-inches mark is at the bottom. Put your hand just under the ruler. Ask your friend to drop the ruler while you catch it. Note the inch mark at which you caught the ruler. Try it nine more times. What happens?

Immune System and Endocrine System

Your immune system defends your body from harmful invaders, such as organisms that cause infection. White blood cells, which are your immune system's primary infection fighters, are produced in your bone marrow, thymus, lymph nodes, and spleen.

Lymph Nodes Lymph nodes are bean-sized organs that help filter germs from your blood. The plasma in your blood moves from your capillaries into your lymph ducts and through these ducts to your lymph nodes. At the lymph nodes the plasma is cleaned and then drained back into the blood. Lymph nodes also produce plasma cells. Plasma cells produce antibodies, an essential part of your immune system.

tonsils

thymus

lymph nodes

spleen

long bone marrow

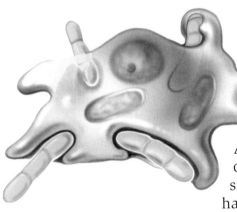

Macrophage
A macrophage is a type of white blood cell that surrounds and destroys harmful invader cells.

Caring for Your Immune System

One way to help your body fight disease is through immunization. You probably were immunized before you began school. More immunizations (boosters) may be required as you grow, if you travel to other countries, or when you are an adult.

Activity

An average disease-causing organism grows and divides into two new organisms about every thirty minutes. Calculate how many organisms there would be at the end of five hours.

Fight or Flight When you are threatened or under stress, your body prepares to fight or to run away. Your pupils dilate. Your heartbeat and breathing rates increase. Also, your adrenal glands release adrenaline into your blood to help your body keep up this reaction.

Caring for Your Endocrine System

- Doctors can sometimes give medicine to treat an endocrine system that produces too little of any chemical.

Your endocrine system works with your nervous system to help your body grow normally and work and react as it should. The endocrine system does this by releasing hormones into your bloodstream. The hormones deliver instructions to various organs and tissues.

Activity

The next time you are startled, feel your heartbeat. How is it different from normal?

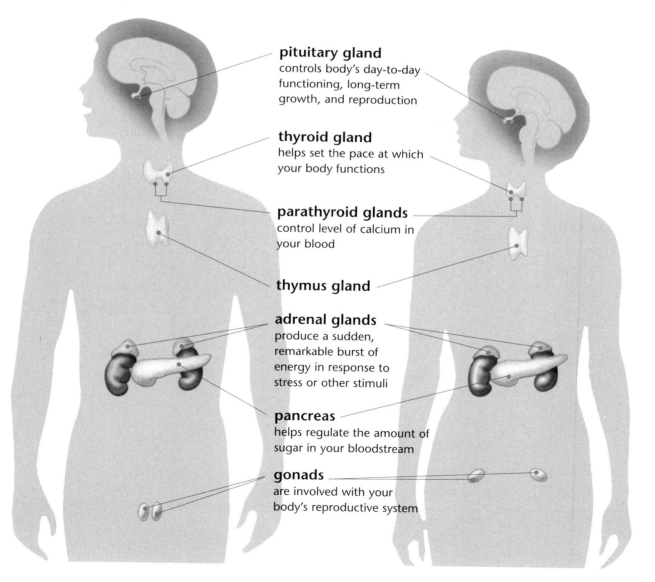

pituitary gland
controls body's day-to-day functioning, long-term growth, and reproduction

thyroid gland
helps set the pace at which your body functions

parathyroid glands
control level of calcium in your blood

thymus gland

adrenal glands
produce a sudden, remarkable burst of energy in response to stress or other stimuli

pancreas
helps regulate the amount of sugar in your bloodstream

gonads
are involved with your body's reproductive system

Glossary

This Glossary contains important science words and their definitions. Each word is respelled as it would be in a dictionary. When you see the ′ mark after a syllable, pronounce that syllable with more force than the other syllables. The page number at the end of the definition tells where to find the word in your book. The boldfaced letters in the examples in the Pronunciation Key that follows show how these letters are pronounced in the respellings after each glossary word.

PRONUNCIATION KEY

a	add, map	m	move, seem	u	up, done
ā	ace, rate	n	nice, tin	û(r)	burn, term
â(r)	care, air	ng	ring, song	yo͞o	fuse, few
ä	palm, father	o	odd, hot	v	vain, eve
b	bat, rub	ō	open, so	w	win, away
ch	check, catch	ô	order, jaw	y	yet, yearn
d	dog, rod	oi	oil, boy	z	zest, muse
e	end, pet	ou	pout, now	zh	vision, pleasure
ē	equal, tree	o͝o	took, full	ə	the schwa, an
f	fit, half	o͞o	pool, food		unstressed vowel
g	go, log	p	pit, stop		representing the sound
h	hope, hate	r	run, poor		spelled
i	it, give	s	see, pass		*a* in *above*
ī	ice, write	sh	sure, rush		*e* in *sicken*
j	joy, ledge	t	talk, sit		*i* in *possible*
k	cool, take	th	thin, both		*o* in *melon*
l	look, rule	th	this, bathe		*u* in *circus*

Other symbols:

- • separates words into syllables
- ′ indicates heavier stress on a syllable
- ′ indicates light stress on a syllable

abiotic [ā′bī•ot′ik] Relating to the nonliving parts of the environment **(C6)**

abyssal plain [ə•bis′əl plān′] The vast floor of the deep oceans **(C63)**

acid [as′id] A compound that reacts easily with other substances and turns blue litmus paper red **(E32)**

adaptation [ad′əp•tā′shən] A structure or feature of an organism that helps it meet a particular need in its natural habitat **(A45)**

air mass [âr′mas′] A large body of air that has the same characteristics throughout **(C88)**

air pressure [âr′ presh′ər] The weight of air pressing down on an area **(C92)**

amphibians [am•fib′ē•ənz] Vertebrates that can live in water or on land but must return to the water to reproduce **(B104)**

amplitude [am′plə•tōōd′] The distance that any point on a wave has moved from its resting position; equal to half the wave height **(E109)**

angiosperm [an′jē•ō•spûrm′] A vascular plant that produces flowers **(B44)**

Animalia [an′i•māl′yə] The name of the kingdom that is made up of animals **(A44)**

anther [an′thər] The part of the stamen of a flower that produces pollen grains **(B46)**

arachnid [ə•rak′nid] An arthropod with eight legs and no antennae, such as a spider, scorpion, tick, or mite **(B89)**

arthropod [är′thrə•pod′] An animal that has a jointed exoskeleton and jointed limbs **(B88)**

asexual reproduction [ā•sek′shōō•əl rē′prə•duk′shən] The form of reproduction in which a new organism is produced without the joining of a sperm cell and an egg cell **(B29)**

asteroid [as′tə•roid] A chunk of rock and metal, smaller than a planet and larger than a meteoroid, that orbits the sun **(D80)**

asthenosphere [as•then′ə•sfir′] A zone of partially melted rock in the upper mantle of the Earth **(D7)**

astronomical unit (AU) [as′trə•nom′i•kəl yōō′nit] A measurement equal to the distance between Earth and the sun, a distance of about 150 million km (93 million miles) **(D82)**

atoll [at′ôl] A ring of islands around a shallow central lagoon **(C67)**

atom [at′əm] The smallest unit of a pure substance that still has the properties of that substance **(E6)**

atomic number [ə•tom′ik num′bər] The number of protons in an atom **(E8)**

average speed [av′rij spēd′] The measure of the total distance an object has moved divided by the total time elapsed **(F16)**

axial tilt [ak′sē•əl tilt′] The angle that a planet's axis is tilted from vertical **(D95)**

axis [ak′sis] An imaginary line through the Earth's center, from the North Pole to the South Pole **(D86)**

balanced forces [bal′ənst fôrs′əz] The opposite forces acting on an object that cancel each other out **(F26)**

base [bās] A compound that reacts easily with other substances and turns red litmus paper blue **(E32)**

biotic [bī•ot′ik] Relating to the living parts of the environment **(C6)**

bird [bûrd] A warm-blooded animal that has feathers and lays eggs with hard shells **(B116)**

buoyancy [boi′ən•sē] The ability to float in a liquid or rise in a gas **(E47)**

carbon dioxide–oxygen cycle [kär′bən dī•ok′sīd′ ok′sə•jən sī′kəl] The flow of carbon dioxide and oxygen through Earth's ecosystems **(C16)**

cell membrane [sel′ mem′brān′] A thin layer that surrounds the cell and keeps it together, and controls the substances passing into and out of the cell **(A8)**

cell wall [sel′ wôl′] The stiff outer layer that protects a plant cell and gives it shape **(A8)**

cementation [sē′men•tā′shən] The gluing together of particles of sediment **(D49)**

chemical energy [kem′i•kəl en′ər•jē] A form of potential energy stored in reactants **(E92)**

chemical property [kem′i•kəl prop′ər•tē] A property that describes the ability of a substance to react with other materials and form new substances **(E53)**

chemical rock [kem′i•kəl rok′] One of a group of sedimentary rocks that is made from minerals that were dissolved in water, came out of solution, and were then deposited **(D49)**

chloroplast [klôr′ə•plast′] A kind of organelle in plant cells that contains chlorophyll, which enables the plant to make its own food **(A9)**

chromosome [krō′mə•sōm′] A structure in the cell that provides instructions for all the activities and traits of the cell and the organism **(A9)**

circuit [sûr′kit] The connection needed for current to travel between the poles of two electric energy sources **(E86)**

classification [klas′ə•fi•kā′shən] The arrangement of things in groups of similar items **(A42)**

clastic rock [klas′tik rok′] One of a group of sedimentary rocks that is made of sediments that were weathered, transported, and deposited in layers **(D49)**

cnidarian [nī•dar′ē•ən] An animal with tentacles that have the ability to sting its prey or predators **(B78)**

cold-blooded [kōld′blud′id] Relating to an animal whose body temperature changes as the temperature of the surroundings changes **(B104)**

colloid [kol′oid] A suspension that isn't easily separated, because of the small size of the particles **(E64)**

combustibility [kəm•bus′tə•bil′•ə•tē] The ability to burn **(E53)**

comet [kom′it] A ball of ice, rock, and frozen gases that orbits the sun **(D81)**

commensalism [kə•men′səl•iz′əm] A symbiotic relationship that benefits one organism and doesn't harm or help the other organism **(C50)**

community [kə•myoo′nə•tē] The populations living in the same environment at the same time **(C7)**

compound [kom′pound] A substance formed of the atoms of two or more elements **(E30)**

compound machine [kom′pound mə•shēn′] A device that is made up of two or more simple machines **(F58)**

condensation [kon′dən•sā′shən] The process by which water vapor changes from a gas to a liquid **(C15)**

conduction [kən•duk′shən] The transfer of thermal energy that results from the collision of particles **(E79)**

conifer [kon′ə•fər] A plant that grows cones that produce seeds **(B36)**

consumer [kən•sōōm′ər] An organism that eats other organisms **(C38)**

continental shelf [kon′tə•nen′təl shelf′] The gently sloping part of a continent that is under water and rings each continent **(C63)**

continental slope [kon′tə•nen′təl slōp′] The edge of a continent that drops steeply down to the deep-ocean floor **(C63)**

convection [kən•vek′shən] The transfer of thermal energy through liquids and gases **(E79)**

convergent boundary [kən•vûr′jənt boun′də•rē] A boundary where crustal plates collide with each other **(D14)**

coral reef [kôr′əl rēf′] A structure built by living creatures **(C73)**

core [kôr] The Earth's innermost layer **(D6)**

crust [krust] The Earth's outermost layer **(D6)**

cytoplasm [sī′tə•plaz′əm] A watery, jellylike substance that fills a cell and contains the other cell parts **(A8)**

decomposer [dē′kəm•pōz′ər] A type of consumer that gets its food by breaking down animal wastes and remains of dead plants and animals **(C38)**

density [den′sə•tē] The amount of mass in a given volume **(E47)**

deposition [dep′ə•zish′ən] The dropping of sediment from wind or water that slows down, or from ice that melts **(D49)**

dichotomous key [dī•kot′ə•məs kē′] A guide used to identify an organism based on its characteristics **(A56)**

dicotyledon [dī′kot•ə•lēd′ən] A seed that has two seed leaves **(B52)**

divergent boundary [di•vûr′jənt boun′də•rē] A boundary where crustal plates move away from each other **(D14)**

DNA [dē′en•ā′] A complex chemical that contains information about every part of an organism **(A10)**

dominant [dom′ə•nənt] Relating to a factor that will determine whether a trait is shown **(A26)**

ductility [duk•til′ə•tē] The ability of a substance to be pulled into thin threads without breaking **(E47)**

earthquake [ûrth′kwāk′] The sudden movement of rock along a fault which releases energy vibrations **(D22)**

echinoderm [ē•kī′nə•dûrm′] An invertebrate that has an internal skeleton and spines that are part of its skin **(B91)**

ecosystem [ek′ō•sis′təm] A community and the abiotic parts of its environment **(C7)**

efficiency [i•fish′ən•sē] The ratio of the work that comes out of a machine to the work put into that machine **(F62)**

effort arm [ef′ərt ärm′] The part of a lever on which a person or another machine applies a force **(F42)**

electric energy [i•lek′trik en′ər•jē] The movement of electrons from one place to another; current electricity **(E86)**

electricity [i•lek′tris′i•tē] The interaction of electric charges—usually classified as static electricity or current electricity **(E86)**

electromagnet [i·lek′trō·mag′nit] A device made when electric current travels through a wire coiled around a piece of iron **(E87)**

electromagnetic waves [i·lek′trō·mag·net′ik wāvz] Waves of vibrating electric and magnetic fields **(E124)**

electron [i·lek′tron′] A negatively charged sub-atomic particle **(E7)**

element [el′ə·mənt] A pure substance that is made up of only one kind of atom **(E14)**

ellipse [i·lips′] An oval-shaped path **(D87)**

embryo [em′brē·ō] The tiny plant that forms from the fertilized egg **(B53)**

endoskeleton [en′dō·skel′ə·tən] A system of connected bones or plates that lie within the body of an organism **(B70)**

energy [en′ər·jē] The ability to cause changes in matter; the ability to do work **(E76)**

environment [in·vī′rən·mənt] The surroundings in which an organism lives, which provide the specific things an organism needs **(C6)**

epicenter [ep′ə·sent′ər] The point on the Earth's surface directly above the focus of an earthquake **(D22)**

erosion [i·rō′zhən] The movement or transportation of sediment to new locations **(D49)**

estuary [es′chōō·er′ē] A place where a freshwater environment and a saltwater environment meet **(C74)**

evaporation [i·vap′ə·rā′shən] The change of water from liquid water to water vapor **(C14)**

exoskeleton [ek′sō·skel′ə·tən] A skeleton that is outside of the body of an invertebrate **(B71)**

fern [fûrn] A vascular plant that has feathery fronds and reproduces without seeds **(B34)**

fertilization [fûr′təl·ə·zā′shən] The process in which a sperm cell joins with an egg cell to produce a new organism **(B53)**

first quarter [fûrst′ kwôr′tər] The waxing phase of the moon viewed from Earth where half the moon's lit side is visible **(D102)**

fish [fish] A vertebrate adapted to living its entire life in the water **(B104)**

fission [fish′ən] The reaction that releases nuclear energy when a nucleus breaks into two parts **(E95)**

flatworm [flat′wûrm′] An animal, such as a planarian, that has a flattened body, a digestive system with only one opening, and a simple nervous system **(B80)**

focus [fō′kəs] The point in the Earth's crust where the first major movement of an earthquake fault occurs **(D22)**

force [fôrs] A push or a pull **(F6)**

forecast [fôr′kast′] A prediction of what the weather will be like in the future **(C100)**

frequency [frē′kwən·sē] The number of vibrations a wave has in a given time **(E111)**

friction [frik′shən] A force that opposes motion whenever two surfaces rub against each other **(F25)**

front [frunt] The border between two air masses that collide **(C94)**

fulcrum [fōōl′krəm] The fixed point on a lever **(F42)**

Fungi [fun′jī′] The name of the kingdom of plant-like organisms that do not make their own food but take the nutrients that they need from the environment **(A44)**

fusion [fyōō′zhən] A process in which nuclei of atoms are joined **(D117)**

galactic cluster [gə•lak′tik klus′tər] A grouping of galaxies **(D124)**

galaxy [gal′ək•sē] A large system of stars **(D124)**

gas [gas] A state of matter that has no definite shape or volume **(E23)**

gene [jēn] A section of DNA that controls specific cell activities and the characteristics of every organism **(A15)**

genus [jē′nəs] The first part of an organism's scientific name; a group of organisms that share major characteristics and are therefore closely related **(A53)**

grafting [graft′ing] A form of asexual reproduction in which parts of two plants are joined together to make a single plant **(B55)**

gravitropism [grav′i•trō′•piz•əm] A tropism in which the roots of a plant grow downward, in the direction of gravity **(B14)**

gravity [grav′ə•tē] The force that pulls everything toward the center of Earth; the force of gravitation on Earth **(F7)**

groundwater [ground′wô′tər] Water that soaks into the ground **(C15)**

gymnosperm [jim′nə•spûrm′] A seed-bearing plant whose seeds are not surrounded by a container **(B36)**

habitat [hab′ə•tat′] The part of an environment in which an organism lives **(C7)**

heat [hēt] The transfer of thermal energy **(E78)**

hurricane [hûr′ə•kān′] A large, spiraling storm system that can be as much as 600 km across **(C110)**

igneous rock [ig′nē•əs rok′] A rock formed when magma or lava cools and hardens **(D41)**

inclined plane [in′klīnd plān′] A flat, sloping surface **(F50)**

insect [in′sekt] An arthropod with six jointed legs, such as a grasshopper **(B89)**

intertidal zone [in′tər•tīd′əl zōn′] The area between the high-tide mark and the low-tide mark **(C72)**

invertebrate [in•vûr′tə•brit] An animal that does not have a backbone **(B70)**

kinetic energy [ki•net′ik en′ər•jē] The energy of motion **(E76)**

lava [lä′və] Magma that reaches the Earth's surface **(D41)**

law of conservation of energy [lô′ uv kon′ser•vā′shən uv en′ər•jē] A law that states that the total amount of energy in a system is always the same, and that energy cannot be created or destroyed **(E76)**

lever [lev′ər] A simple machine having an arm that moves about a fixed point **(F42)**

Linnaean system [lə•nē′ən sis′təm] A classification system useful for storing and finding information about living things **(A43)**

liquid [lik′wid] A state of matter that has a definite volume but no definite shape **(E23)**

lithosphere [lith′ə•sfir′] The cool, solid portion of Earth that includes all of the crust and part of the upper mantle **(D7)**

long-day plant [lông′dā′ plant′] A plant that needs short periods of darkness before it can bloom **(B16)**

longitudinal wave [lon′jə•tōōd′ən•əl wāv′] A wave in which the particles vibrate back and forth in the same direction as the wave is moving **(E110)**

loudness [loud′nis] The perception of the amplitude of a sound wave **(E119)**

machine [mə•shēn′] A device that changes the amount of a force applied to an object, the direction of a force, or both **(F41)**

magma [mag′mə] Melted rock within the Earth **(D41)**

magnet [mag′nit] An object which has all the domains pointing in the same direction and magnetic fields that work together **(E84)**

main sequence [mān′ sē′kwəns] The band on the Hertzsprung-Russell diagram where ninety percent of stars are found **(D117)**

malleability [mal′ē•ə•bil′ə•tē] The property of a metal that indicates that it can be bent and rolled into sheets **(E15)**

mammal [mam′əl] A warm-blooded vertebrate that has milk-producing glands **(B118)**

mammary gland [mam′ə•rē gland′] A milk-producing gland on a female mammal used for nursing young **(B118)**

mantle [man′təl] The layer directly beneath the Earth's crust **(D6)**

meiosis [mī•ō′sis] The process that forms reproductive cells **(A17)**

mesosphere [mes′ō•sfir′] The layer of atmosphere where air is thin and most meteors burn up **(C87)**

metal [met′əl] An element that conducts heat and electricity well **(E14)**

metamorphism [met′ə•môr′fiz′əm] The process by which any kind of rock is changed into metamorphic rock **(D56)**

meteoroid [mēt′ē•ə•roid′] A chunk of material smaller than an asteroid that orbits the sun **(D81)**

mid-ocean ridge [mid′ō′shən rij′] The place where plates of the Earth's crust along the ocean floor are being split apart and molten rock pushes up to form new ocean floor and a mountain range **(C64, D15)**

mineral [min′ər•əl] A natural, solid substance that has a definite chemical composition and physical structure **(D40)**

mitochondria [mīt′ə•kon′drē•ə] Bean-shaped organelles that break down sugar to produce energy **(A8)**

mitosis [mī•tō′sis] The process of cell division that produces new body cells with complete sets of chromosomes **(A16)**

mixture [miks′chər] A combination of two or more pure substances that are not chemically combined with each other **(E60)**

mollusk [mol′əsk] An animal with a soft body and no bones **(B86)**

Monera [mə•nir′ə] The kingdom that includes bacteria **(A44)**

monocotyledon [mon′ə•kot′ə•lēd′ən] A seed that has only one seed leaf **(B52)**

moss [môs] A very short green plant that does not have true leaves, stems, and roots **(B28)**

mutualism [myōō′chōō•əl•iz′əm] The symbiotic relationship that benefits both organisms involved **(C48)**

nebula [neb′yə•lə] A huge, cool, dark cloud of gases and dust where stars are formed **(D118)**

neutron [nōo′tron] A subatomic particle that has the same mass as a proton but no electric charge **(E7)**

newton [nōot′ən] The metric unit for forces including weight **(F10)**

niche [nich] The role of an organism in an ecosystem **(C9)**

nitrogen cycle [ni′trə•jən si′kəl] The movement of nitrogen through ecosystems **(C18)**

nonmetal [non′met′əl] An element that does not conduct electricity and is not shiny or malleable **(E15)**

nonrenewable resources [non′ri•nōo′ə•bəl rē′sôrs′ez] Resources that cannot be replaced within a human life span **(C23)**

nonvascular plant [non•vas′kyə•lər plant′] A plant that does not have tissues to transport food and water **(B10)**

nova [nō′və] A star that briefly becomes thousands of times brighter than normal **(D119)**

nuclear energy [nōo′klē•ər en′ər•jē] The energy that holds protons and neutrons together in an atom's nucleus **(E95)**

nuclear membrane [nōo′klē•ər mem′brān′] A membrane that surrounds the nucleus and controls the materials passing into and out of it **(A9)**

nucleus [nōo′klē•əs] 1 *(cell)* The control center of the cell, which directs all the cell's activities. 2 *(atom)* The center of an atom, which contains protons and neutrons. **(A9, E7)**

opaque [ō•pāk′] Not allowing light to pass through **(E128)**

orbit [ôr′bit] The path an object follows as it revolves around another object **(D87)**

ovary [ō′və•rē] The base of the pistil of a flower, containing ovules **(B47)**

parasite [par′ə•sīt′] An organism that survives by living on or in another animal and feeding on that animal **(B81)**

parasitism [par′ə•sīt′iz•əm] A symbiotic relationship in which one organism benefits and the other organism is harmed **(C47)**

periodic table [pir′ē•od′ik tā′bəl] A table of elements arranged according to their atomic number **(E17)**

petal [pet′əl] The part of the plant that is usually the largest and most visible part of a flower and helps protect the other parts of the flower **(B46)**

phase [fāz] A stage in the changing shape that the moon seems to have when it is viewed from Earth **(D102)**

phloem [flō′əm] The vessels in a vascular plant that carry food from the leaves to the other parts of the plant for use and storage **(B9)**

phototropism [fō′•tō•trō′•piz•əm] The movement of a plant toward or away from light **(B14)**

physical properties [fiz′i•kəl prop′ər•tēz] Properties that can be observed or measured without changing an object, or any part of the materials it is made of, into something else **(E46)**

pistil [pis'təl] The female reproductive part of a flower **(B46)**

pitch [pich] The level of a sound's perceived highness or lowness **(E118)**

planetary system [plan'i•ter'ē sis'təm] A system of planets revolving around a star **(D79)**

Plantae [plan'tē] The name of the kingdom that is made up of plants **(A44)**

plate tectonics [plāt' tek•ton'iks] The theory scientists use to explain the movements of plates on the Earth's surface **(D8)**

pollen [pol'ən] The powderlike male spores that develop into two male sex cells **(B37)**

pollination [pol'ə•nā'shən] The process by which pollen from the anthers of a flower lands on the stigma of a flower **(B47)**

population [pop•yə•lā'shən] Organisms of the same species living together in the same environment **(C7)**

potential energy [pō•ten'shəl en'ər•jē] The energy that exists due to the position or condition of an object **(E76)**

precipitation [pri•sip'ə•tā'shən] The liquid water that returns to Earth's surface, usually as rain or snow **(C15)**

predator [pred'ə•tər] An animal that feeds on other living animals **(C39)**

prey [prā] The animals predators eat **(C39)**

producer [prə•dōōs'ər] An organism that makes its own food **(C38)**

Protista [prə•tist'ə] The kingdom of classification in which members often have traits of both plants and animals **(A44)**

proton [prō'ton] A subatomic particle that has a positive electric charge **(E7)**

pulley [pŏŏl'ē] A wheel that has a groove along its edge **(F45)**

Punnett square [pun'ət skwer'] A checkerboard-type diagram used to find the possible combinations of factors in the offspring of two parents **(A29)**

P wave [pē' wāv'] A primary wave or "push-pull" wave of released energy in the Earth's surface that causes a back-and-forth vibration in the same direction that the wave moves **(D23)**

radiant energy [rā'dē•ənt en'ər•jē] The kind of energy carried by electromagnetic waves **(E124)**

radiation [rā'dē•ā'shən] The transfer of thermal energy as waves **(E79)**

reactivity [rē'ak•tiv'ə•tē] The ability of a substance to go through a chemical change **(E53)**

recessive [ri•ses'iv] Relating to a factor not shown when one of a pair is dominant **(A27)**

reflecting telescope [ri•flekt'ing tel'ə•skōp'] A telescope that uses mirrors to gather light and magnify images **(D130)**

reflection [ri•flek'shən] The bouncing of light waves off a surface **(E126)**

refracting telescope [ri•frakt'ing tel'ə•skōp'] A telescope that uses glass lenses to gather light and magnify objects **(D130)**

refraction [ri•frak'shən] The bending of a light wave when it passes from one medium to another **(E127)**

relative humidity [rel'ə•tiv hyōō•mid'ə•tē] A comparison of the actual amount of moisture in the air to the greatest possible amount that could be in the air at the same temperature and pressure **(C93)**

renewable resources [ri•nōō'ə•bəl rē'sôrs•əz] Resources that can be replaced within a human life span **(C22)**

reptile [rep′til] A cold-blooded animal that has a dry, protective covering of horny scales or plates, and lays eggs with leathery shells **(B115)**

resistance arm [ri•zis′təns ärm′] The part of a lever that applies a force on an object **(F42)**

reusable resources [rē•yōō′zə•bəl rē′sôrs] Resources that can be used again and again **(C22)**

revolution [rev′ə•lōō′shən] The movement of one object in an orbit around another object **(D87)**

Richter scale [rik′tər skāl′] A scale that measures the amount of energy released during an earthquake **(D24)**

rift [rift] A deep ocean valley formed where two crustal plates move apart **(D15)**

rock cycle [rok′ sī′kəl] A process by which rocks are formed from one another **(D64)**

rotation [rō•tā′shən] The turning of an object on an axis **(D86)**

roundworm [round′wûrm′] A round animal with a tubelike body with a digestive system with two openings **(B81)**

runner [run′ər] A stem that grows close to the ground and puts out roots and shoots **(B55)**

scavenger [skav′in•jər] An animal that eats the remains of animals that have died **(C39)**

screw [skrōō] An inclined plane wrapped around a cylinder or cone **(F53)**

sea-floor spreading [sē′flôr′ spred′ing] A process in which magma is slowly pushed up through cracks in a rift and then cools to form new sea floor **(D15)**

seamount [sē′mount′] A steep-sided volcanic mountain under the ocean **(C64)**

season [sē′zən] A period of the year with a certain level of temperature and type of weather **(D94)**

sedimentation [sed′ə•men•tā′shən] The process of building up layers of sediment over millions of years **(D49)**

segmented worm [seg′mənt•id wûrm′] An animal, such as the earthworm, whose body is made up of connected sections, or segments **(B82)**

sexual reproduction [sek′shōō•əl rē′prə•duk′shən] The form of reproduction by the joining of a male reproductive cell and a female reproductive cell **(A24)**

short-day plant [shôrt′dā′ plant′] A plant that needs long periods of darkness before it can bloom **(B16)**

solid [sol′id] A state of matter that has definite shape and volume **(E23)**

solution [sə•lōō′shən] A mixture in which the particles of each substance are mixed evenly **(E62)**

species [spē′shēz] The second part of an organism's scientific name that identifies one specific organism in the genus **(A53)**

speed [spēd] A measure of how far something moves during a period of time **(F16)**

sponge [spunj] A type of animal that filters the water it lives in to get food **(B76)**

spore [spôr] A structure that contains cells that can grow into a new plant without joining with other cells **(B29)**

stability [stə•bil′ə•tē] The condition where a substance does not go through chemical changes easily **(E53)**

stamen [stā′mən] The male reproductive part of a flower **(B46)**

station model [stā′shən mod′əl] An arrangement of symbols and numbers that show the weather conditions recorded at a weather station **(C100)**

stigma [stig′mə] The tip of the pistil of a flower where pollen grains land and stick **(B46)**

stratosphere [strat′ə•sfir′] The layer of the atmosphere in which ozone is present **(C87)**

style [stīl] The stemlike part of the pistil of a flower that connects the stigma to the ovary **(B47)**

supernova [sōō′pər•no′və] A supergiant star that explodes **(D119)**

surface map [sûr′fis map′] A map that includes station models and information about fronts and about centers of high pressure and low pressure **(C100)**

surface wave [sûr′fis wāv′] An energy wave from an earthquake that travels only at the surface and moves less quickly than P waves and S waves but makes the ground roll and sway **(D23)**

suspension [sə•spen′shən] A mixture that contains particles that are large enough to be seen and can be separated from the mixture by using filter paper **(E64)**

S wave [es′ wāv′] A slower kind of energy wave released by an earthquake that causes vibrations at right angles to the wave's direction of travel **(D23)**

symbiosis [sim′bī•ō′sis] A relationship between two organisms of different species that benefits one or both of the organisms **(C46)**

texture [teks′chər] An observable physical property; how the surface of a substance feels **(E47)**

thermal energy [thûr′məl en′ər•jē] The kinetic energy of moving particles of a substance or object **(E78)**

thermosphere [thûr′mō•sfir′] The upper layer of the atmosphere where temperatures are extremely high **(C87)**

third quarter [thûrd kwôr′tər] The waning phase of the moon viewed from Earth where half of the moon's lit side is visible **(D103)**

thunderstorm [thun′dər•stôrm′] A very strong storm with a lot of rain, thunder, and lightning **(C108)**

tornado [tôr•nā′dō] An intense windstorm that often forms within a severe thunderstorm **(C112)**

transform fault boundary [trans′fôrm′ fôlt′ boun′də•rē] A boundary where crustal plates grind past each other **(D14)**

translucent [trans•lōō′sənt] Relating to a substance that allows light to pass through it but scatters the light **(E129)**

transparent [trans•par′ənt] Relating to a medium or substance that light can travel through **(E128)**

transpiration [tran′spə•rā′shən] The process by which plants lose water to the air **(C15)**

transverse wave [trans′vûrs wāv′] A wave in which the particles vibrate at right angles to the direction of the wave **(E110)**

trench [trench] A place where two plates of the Earth's crust hit each other, forming a deep part of the ocean **(C64)**

tropical storm [trop′i•kəl stôrm] The stage of hurricane development when the winds of a tropical depression reach a constant speed of 63 km/hr (39 mph) **(C110)**

tropism [trō′piz′əm] The response of a plant to turn toward or away from something in its environment **(B14)**

troposphere [trō′pə•sfir′] The bottom layer of the Earth's atmosphere **(C87)**

unbalanced forces [un•bal′ənst fôrs′əz] The forces acting on an object that cause a change in velocity, making the object speed up, slow down, or change direction **(F27)**

vacuole [vak′yoo•ōl′] A storage space in a cell enclosed by a membrane **(A9)**

vascular plant [vas′kyə•lər plant′] A plant that has tissues that carry water and dissolved materials **(B8)**

velocity [və•los′ə•tē] The speed of an object in a particular direction **(F17)**

vertebrate [vûr′tə•brit] An animal that has a backbone **(B70)**

volcano [vol•kā′nō] A mountain that may form around an opening in the Earth's surface where an eruption of molten rock occurs **(D25)**

warm-blooded [wôrm•blud′id] Relating to an animal whose body stays the same temperature regardless of the temperature of its surroundings **(B116)**

water cycle [wôt′ər sī′kəl] The movement of water through Earth's ecosystems **(C15)**

wave [wāv] A disturbance that travels through matter or space, carrying energy from one place to another **(E108)**

wavelength [wāv′lenkth′] The measurement of the distance between the crests and troughs in a series of waves **(E109)**

weather balloon [weth′ər bə•loon′] A balloon released into the atmosphere that carries a package of instruments that records data about temperature, air pressure, and humidity **(C101)**

weathering [weth′ər•ing] The process of breaking rock into smaller pieces **(D48)**

weather map [weth′ər map′] A map that shows data about recent weather conditions across a large area **(C102)**

wedge [wej] A simple machine composed of one or two inclined planes **(F52)**

wheel and axle [hwēl′ and ak′səl] A simple machine that has a central pivot around which a wheel moves **(F46)**

work [wûrk] The result when a force causes an object to move **(F40)**

xylem [zī′ləm] The vessels in a vascular plant that carry water and nutrients from the roots to the leaves **(B8)**

Photo Credits

Page Placement Key: (t)-top (c)-center (b)-bottom (l)-left (r)-right (bg)-background (i)-inset

Cover and Title Pages: Dwight R. Kuhn/DRK; (bg) Maria Pape/FPG International.

Contents: Page iv Darrell Gulin/Tony Stone Images; iv (bg) Tom McHugh/Photo Researchers; v Photonica; v (bg) Kunio Owaki/The Stock Market; vi Norbert Wu/The Stock Market; vi (bg) Richard Mariscal/Bruce Coleman, Inc.; vii Earl Young/FPG Internaional; vii (bg) World Perspectives/Tony Stone Images; viii (front beaker) Jook Leung/FPG International; viii (back beakers) Michael Newman/PhotoEdit; viii (bg) Steve Barnett/Liaison International; ix Spencer Jones/FPG International; ix (bg) Phototote CD #50, Letraset USA.

Unit A: A1 (c) Tom McHugh/Photo Researchers; A1 (l) Darrell Gulin/Tony Stone Images; A2–A3 Douglas Struthers/Tony Stone Images; A3 (r) Stehling/Nature + Science; A3 (b) Mike Abbey/Visuals Unlimited; A4 Dr. Jeremy Burgess/Science Photo Library/Photo Researchers; A5 (tl) Biophoto Associates/Science Source/Photo Researchers; A5 (tc) Newcomb & Wergin/Tony Stone Images; A5 (tr) Martha J. Powell/Visuals Unlimited; A6 (l) Michael Holford; A6 (c) The Granger Collection, New York; A6–A7 (b) Phil Gates/BPS/Tony Stone Images; A7 (ti) Biophoto Associates/Science Source/Photo Researchers; A7 (r) Claude Revy, Jean/Phototake; A8 (l) Biophoto Associates/Science Source/Photo Researchers; A8 (b) Kelvin Aitken/Peter Arnold, Inc.; A8–A9 (bg) Barry L. Runk/Grant Heilman Photography; A9 (l) Robert P. Carr/Bruce Coleman, Inc.; A9 (b) Dr. Dennis Kunkel/Phototake; A10 Dr. Don Fawcett/Science Source/Photo Researchers; A11 Alfred Pasieka/Science Photo Library/Photo Researchers; A12 (l) Prof. P. Motta/Dept. of Anatomy/University "La Sapienza", Rome/Science Photo Library/Photo Researchers; A12 (r) Ken Wagner/Phototake; A14 (r) Michael Abbey/Science Source/Photo Researchers; A14 (br) Tom Davis/Tony Stone Images; A18 (r) Runk/Schoenberger/Grant Heilman Photography; A18 (l, 1–6) Carolina Biological Supply Company/Phototake; A19 (l–9) Carolina Biological Supply Company/Phototake; A19 (c) Renee Lynn/Photo Researchers; A20 (l) ZEFA Germany/The Stock Market; A20 (br) Franz Gorski/Peter Arnold, Inc.; A20 (bl) Robert Pearcy/Animals Animals; A22 Art Wolfe/Tony Stone Images; A24 (l) Brown Brothers; A25 (c) Dwight R. Kuhn; A25 (c) Robert P. Carr/Bruce Coleman, Inc.; A25 (b) David Solzberg/AGStock USA; A31 (l) Gregory K. Scott/Photo Researchers; A31 (r) M.H. Sharp/Photo Researchers; A32 (l) Jeff Foott/Bruce Coleman, Inc.; A32 (r) Masahiro Sano No Japan/The Stock Market; A33 Sanford/Agliolo/The Stock Market; A34 UPI/Corbis; A38–A39 K.G. Vock/OKAPIA/Photo Researchers; A39 (c) Cabisco/Visuals Unlimited; A39 (b) Wolfgang Baumeister/Science Photo Library/Photo Researchers; A40 (tl–tr) Hans Pfletschinger/Peter Arnold, Inc.; A40 (1) Art Wolfe/Tony Stone Images; A40 (tr), (br) Dwight R. Kuhn; A40 (cr) Robert Maier/Animals Animals; A41 (bl) Dwight R. Kuhn; A41 (br) Hans Pfletschinger/Peter Arnold, Inc.; A42 (l) Scala/Art Resource, NY; A42 (r) E.T. Archive; A43 (r) Richard Nowitz/Phototake; A44 (l) David Parker/Science Photo Library/Photo Researchers; A44 (b) Biophoto Associates/Photo Researchers; A45 (l) Hans Pfletschinger/Peter Arnold, Inc.; A45 (r) Michael Black/Bruce Coleman, Inc.; A45 (c) Fritz Prenzel/Peter Arnold, Inc.; A46 (l) Tom McHugh/Steinhart Aquarium/Photo Researchers; A46 (c) Norbert Wu/Peter Arnold, Inc.; A46 (bl) Peter Scharf/Peter Arnold, Inc.; A47 (c) Carolina Biological Supply Company/Phototake; A47 (t) Robert Brons/BPS/Tony Stone Images; A47 (tr) Manfred Kage/Peter Arnold, Inc.; A48 (c) Dwight R. Kuhn; A48 (c) S. Lowry/Univ. Ulster/Tony Stone Images; A48 (b) Andrew Syred/Tony Stone Images; A50 Kunio Owaki/The Stock Market; A53 (l) Zig Leszczynski/Animals Animals; A53 (r) Jeff Foott/Bruce Coleman, Inc.; A54 Ron Kimball Photography; A56 (l) Flip Nicklin/Minden Pictures; A56 (bg) Al Grotell; A57 Bruce Watkins/Animals Animals; A58 (c) Zoologisk Museum; A58–A59 Zoologisk Museum; A59 Telegraph Colour Library/FPG International; A60 (l) AP/Wide World Photos; A60 (r) Shahn Kermani/Gamma Liaison; A64 (l) Darrell Gulin/Tony Stone Images; A64 (r) Tom McHugh/Photo Researchers.

Unit B: B1 (c) Photonica; B1 (l) Kunio Owaki/The Stock Market; B2–B3 Tim Davis/Photo Researchers; B3 (r) Jean Pragen/Tony Stone Images; B3 (b) Ryan-Rayer/Tony Stone Images; B4 Tom McHugh/Photo Researchers; B6 (l) Rod Planck/Dembinsky Photo Associates; B6 (r) M. Elenz-Tranter/H. Armstrong Roberts; B6 (c) Dwight R. Kuhn; B7 (t) Dr. Dennis Kunkel/Phototake; B7 (c) Newcomb & Wergin/Tony Stone Images; B7 (b) Cabisco/Visuals Unlimited; B8 (l) David Sieren/Visuals Unlimited; B8–B9 (ba) John Lythgoe/Masterfile; B9 (l) Ed Reschke/Peter Arnold, Inc.; B10 (l) Kevin Schafer Photography; B10 (r) Larry West/Bruce Coleman, Inc.; B12 John Kieffer/Peter Arnold, Inc.; B14 (l) Runk/Schoenberger/Grant Heilman Photography; B14 (tr), (br) David Sieren/Visuals Unlimited; B16 (r) Ed Young/AGStock USA; B16 (bl), (br) G. R. Roberts Photo Library; B18 Andy Sacks/Tony Stone Images; B19 Matthew McVay/Stock, Boston; B20 (r) Todd Bigelow/Black Star/Harcourt; B20 (b) Phil Gates/BPS/Tony Stone Images; B22 (l), (r) G. R. Roberts Photo Library; B24–B25 Ken Clifton/Minden Pictures; B25 (l) Wally Eberhart/Visuals Unlimited; B25 (b) W. Welsser/Bruce Coleman, Inc.; B26 (l) Dr. E. R. Degginger/Photo Researchers; B26 (tl) Bill Lea/Dembinsky Photo Associates; B26 (bl) John Mielcarek/Dembinsky Photo Associates; B26 (bl) Heather Angel/Biofotos; B26 (br) Daniel J. Cox/Natural Exposures; B26 (cl) Bill Lea/Dembinsky Photo Associates; B28 (c) Ken Cole/Animals Animals; B28 (i) Dwight R. Kuhn; B29 (ti) David M. Phillips/Visuals Unlimited; B28–B29 (bg) Adam Jones/Dembinsky Photo Associates; B28 (i) Dwight R. Kuhn; B29 (ti) Ed Reschke/Peter Arnold, Inc.; B29 (bl) Jane Grushow/Grant Heilman Photography; B30 (l) Harold Taylor/Earth Scenes; B30–B31 (b) Ken Davis/Tom Stack & Associates; B32 Craig Hammell/The Stock Market; B33 (br) R. J. Erwin/Photo Researchers; B34 (tr) Tom Till/DRK; B34 (l) Milton Rand/Tom Stack & Associates; B35 (l) Walter H. Hodge/Peter Arnold, Inc.; B35 (r) Tom Till/DRK; B36 (b) Michael Fogden/DRK; B36 (tl) Norman Owen Tomalin/Bruce Coleman, Inc.; B36 (tr) John Sohlden/Visuals Unlimited; B37 Kenneth W. Fink/Photo Researchers; B38 (t) William H. Mullins/Photo Researchers; B38 (b) Heather Angel/Biofotos; B38 (tc) Ed Reschke/Peter Arnold, Inc.; B38 (l) Jim Strawser/Grant Heilman Photography; B39 (b) Tom Bean/DRK; B40 (t) Pat & Tom Leeson/Photo Researchers; B40 (b) Kotoh/Zefa/H. Armstrong Roberts; B42 Renee Lynn/Photo Researchers; B44–B45 (t) Jack Dermid/Bruce Coleman, Inc.; B44 (b) Hans Reinhard/Bruce Coleman, Inc.; B45 (c) Jerome Wexler/Photo Researchers; B45 (b) Willard Clay/Dembinsky Photo Associates; B46 Bruce Hands/Tony Stone Images; B47 (l) Bruce Coleman, Inc.; B47 (r) Steve Solum/Bruce Coleman, Inc.; B47 (c) Joy Spurr/Bruce Coleman, Inc.; B47 (b) Hans Reinhard/Bruce Coleman, Inc.; B48 (t) Randall B. Henne/Dembinsky Photo Associates; B48 (b) Merlin D. Tuttle, Bat Conservation International/Photo Researchers; B49 Jack Jeffrey/Photo Resource Hawaii; B50 Kathie Atkinson/Auscape; B52 (tl), (tr) Dr. E. R. Degginger/Color-Pic; B52 (bl) Carolina Biological Supply Company/Phototake; B52 (bc) Randall B. Henne/Dembinsky Photo Associates; B52 (tlc) John Gerlach/Tony Stone Images; B52 (blc) Dr. E.R. Degginger/Color-Pic; B54 (tr) Randall B. Henne/Dembinsky Photo Associates; B54 (bl) Davies & Starr, Inc./Tony Stone Images; B54 (bc) Joern Rynio/Tony Stone Images; B54 (br) Runk/Schoenberger/Grant Heilman Photography; B55 (tr) Kenneth W. Fink/Photo Researchers; B55 (bl) Laurie Campbell/Tony Stone Images; B55 (br) Kevin Schafer/Tony Stone Images; B56 (tl) Guy Marche/FPG International; B56 (tc) Zigy Kaluzny/Tony Stone Images; B56 (tr) Jim Strawser/Grant Heilman Photography; B56 (bl) Runk/Schoenberger/Grant Heilman Photography; B56 (bc) Darrell Gulin/Dembinsky Photo Associates; B56 (br) Eric Jacobson/FPG International; B58 (b) H. Armstrong Roberts, Inc.; B58 (t) The Granger Collection, New York; B58 (r) E.T. Archive; B59 Arthur C. Smith III/Grant Heilman Photography; B60 (t) Iowa State University; B60 (b) Rosenfeld Images LTD/Science Photo Library/Photo Researchers; B63 Stephen P. Parker/Photo Researchers; B64–B65 Skip Moody/Dembinsky Photo Associates; B65 (t) J. Krasemann/Peter Arnold, Inc.; B65 (b) Jeffrey L. Rotman/Peter Arnold, Inc.; B66 (c) Charles Krebs/The Stock Market; B66 (r) John Mitchell/Photo Researchers; B67 (b) Dr. E. R. Degginger/Photo Researchers; B67 (br) Zefa Germany/The Stock Market; B68 John Gerlach/Animals Animals; B69 (r) Fritz Polking/Dembinsky Photo Associates; B69 (b) Jane Burton/Bruce Coleman, Inc.; B70 (l) L.J. Bernard/Animals Animals; B70 (r) Alan G. Nelson/Dembinsky Photo Associates; B71 (l) Joe McDonald/Animals Animals; B71 (r) Dave B. Fleetham/Tom Stack & Associates; B71 (b) Charles V. Angelo/Photo Researchers; B72 (l) Laura Riley/Bruce Coleman, Inc.; B72 (b) Wolfgang Bayer/Bruce Coleman, Inc.; B73 Tony Mercieca/Photo Researchers; B74 Brian Parker/Tom Stack & Associates; B75 (r) Roland Birke/OKAPIA/Photo Researchers; B75 (r) David M. Dennis/Tom Stack & Associates; B78 (b) Ron Sefton/Bruce Coleman, Inc.; B77 (r) Dr. E. R. Degginger/Color-Pic; B77 (b) Fred Bavendam/Minden Pictures; B78 (b) Ron Sefton/Bruce Coleman, Inc.; B78 (tl) Auscape, J-P Ferrero/Peter Arnold, Inc.; B78 (tr) Fred Bavendam/Minden Pictures; B79 (l) Randy Morse/Tom Stack & Associates; B79 (r) Norbert Wu/Peter Arnold, Inc.; B80 (r) Ed Robinson/Tom Stack & Associates; B80 (b) Dwight R. Kuhn; B81 (b) Sinclair Stammers/Science Photo Library/Photo Researchers; B81 (r) Dwight R. Kuhn; B84 Fred Bavendam/Minden Pictures; B85 (t) Ed Reschke/Peter Arnold, Inc.; B85 (r) Andrew Martinez/Photo Researchers; B85 (br) Dr. E. R. Degginger/Photo Researchers; B85 (tr) Zig Leszczynski/Animals Animals; B86 (l) Dave Fleetham/Tom Stack & Associates; B87 (t) Chris McLaughlin/The Stock Market; B87 (b) Stephen Frink/Waterhouse Stock Photo; B88 (t) Ice Andre Martinez/Photo Researchers; B89 (t) James P. Rowan/Tony Stone Images; B89 (b) Laura Riley/Bruce Coleman, Inc.; B90 (b) Lance Nelson/The Stock Market; B90 (t) Gianni Tortoli/Photo Researchers; B90 (tr) Nurisdany & Perennou/Photo Researchers; B91 (t) Joy Spurr/Bruce Coleman, Inc.; B91 (c) Gary Milburn/Tom Stack & Associates; B91 (b) Stephen Frink/Waterhouse Stock Photo; B92 (t) Ed Reschke/Peter Arnold, Inc.; B92 (b) Stephen Frink/Waterhouse Stock Photo; B94 (t) Ed Young/AGStock USA; B95 Phil Degginger/Bruce Coleman, Inc.; B96 Marine Biological Laboratory; B96 (b) Fred Bavendam/Peter Arnold, Inc.; B99 M. H. Sharp/Photo Researchers; B100–B101 Doug Perrine/Auscape; B101 (r) Wendell Metzen/Bruce Coleman, Inc.; B102 Richard La Val/Animals Animals; B103 (tl) Patrice Ceisel/John G. Shedd Aquarium; B103 (br) Suzanne & Joseph Collins/Photo Researchers; B104 (l) Dan Guravich/Photo Researchers; B104 (r) Alfred B. Thomas/Animals Animals; B106 (t) Stephen Frink/Waterhouse Stock Photo; B106 (bl) Secret Sea Visions/Peter Arnold,Inc.; B106 (br) Nobert Wu/The Stock Market; B107 (tl) Klaus Jost/Peter Arnold, Inc.; B107 (tr) Fred Bavendam/Tony Stone Images; B107 (b) Amos Nachoum/The Stock Market; B108 (l) Kevin and Sue Hanley/Animals Animals; B108 (r) Juan Manuel Renjifo/Animals Animals; B108 (c) Steinhart Aquarium/Photo Researchers; B110 (t) Art Wolfe/Tony Stone Images; B110 (b) Michael Fogden/Bruce Coleman, Inc.; B111 Gary Meszaros/Dembinsky Photo Associates; B112 JC Carton/Bruce Coleman, Inc.; B113 (tl) Meckes/Ottawa/Photo Researchers; B113 (tr) Stephen Frink/Waterhouse Stock Photo; B88 (t) Ice Andre Martinez/Photo Researchers; B114–B115 (t) Jany Sauvanet/Photo Researchers; B114 (c) Mitsuaki Iwago/Minden Pictures; B114 (b) Roland Seitre/Peter Arnold, Inc.; B115 (t) Joe McDonald/Bruce Coleman, Inc.; B115 (b) Breck P. Kent/Animals Animals; B116 (l) Zefa Germany/The Stock Market; B116 (i) Frans Lanting/Minden Pictures; B117 Tui De Roy/Minden Pictures; B118 (l) Ed Kanze/Dembinsky Photo Associates; B118 (r) Jean-Paul Ferrero/Auscape; B118 (ri) Mitsuaki Iwago/Minden Pictures; B118 (li) Bruce E. Parer-Cook/Auscape; B119 (t) Ben Osborne/Tony Stone Images; B119 (b) Leonard Lee Rue III/Photo Researchers; B122 (t) Larry Mulvehill/Photo Researchers; B122 (b) Tom & Therisa Stack/Tom Stack & Associates; B123 (t) Doug Perrine/DRK; B123 (i) Mark A. Chappell/Animals Animals; B124 (r) Jeanne Mortimer/Caribbean Conservation Corporation; B124 (b) Soames Summerhays/Photo Researchers; B126 (l) Jane Burton/Bruce Coleman, Inc.; B128 (r) Alan G. Nelson/Dembinsky Photo Associates; B127 John Gerlach/Animals Animals; B128 (l) Kunio Owaki/The Stock Market; B128 (i) Photonica.

Unit C: C1 (c) Richard Mariscal/Bruce Coleman, Inc.; C1 (l) Norbert Wu/The Stock Market; C2–C3 Francois Gohier/Photo Researchers; C3 (r) Corbis/Jonathan Blair; C3 (b) Roy Morsch/The Stock Market; C4 David Weintraub/Photo Researchers; C6 Tom San Sant/Geosphere Project, Santa Monica/Science Photo Library/Photo Researchers; C6 (ti) Manoj Shah/Tony Stone Images; C6 (c) Barbara Gerlach/Dembinsky Photo Associates; C6 (b) Kennan Ward Photography; C7 (r) William H. Calvert/Color-Pic; C7 (c) David E. Myers/Tony Stone Images; C7 (tl) George E. Stewart/Dembinsky Photo Associates; C7 (bl) Gary Meszaros/Dembinsky Photo Associates; C8 (l) Dominique Braud/Dembinsky Photo Associates; C8 (r) Rod Planck/Dembinsky Photo Associates; C9 (b) Ed Kanze/Dembinsky Photo Associates; C9 (tl), (tr) Dr. E.R. Degginger/Color-Pic; C10 (l) Carl R. Sams, II/Dembinsky Photo Associates; C10 (ci) Wm. Munoz/Photo Researchers; C10 (ci) Vanessa Vick/Photo Researchers; C10–C11 (bg) Ken Greer/Visuals Unlimited; C12 Peter Steiner/The Stock Market; C16 (t) Barbara Gerlach/Dembinsky Photo Associates; C16 (b) Phil Degginger/Color-Pic; C18 (r) Dale O'Dell/The Stock Market; C18 (c) Stephen J. Krasemann/Photo Researchers; C22–C23 (b) Jerry L. Ferrara/Photo Researchers; C23 (l) David R. Frazier; C23 (t) J & L Weber/Peter Arnold, Inc.; C23 (l) Glennon Donahue/Tony Stone Images; C23 (ri) Dr. E.R. Degginger/Color-Pic; C24 Philip Bailey/The Stock Market; C25 (t) Adam Jones/Dembinsky Photo Associates; C25 (b) Still Pictures/Peter Arnold, Inc.; C25 (tc) Clyde H. Smith/Peter Arnold, Inc.; C25 (bc) John Bova/Photo Researchers; C26 (b) Bob Evans/Peter Arnold, Inc.; C26 (r) RAGA/The Stock Market; C26 (t) Rudolf Freund/Photo Researchers; C26 (c) Denis Waugh/Tony Stone Images; C28 Emory Kristof/NGS Image Collection; C29 The Stock Market; C30 (l) Carr Clifton/Minden Pictures; C30 (r) Sinauer Associates, 1998; C34–C35 K. H. Switak/Photo Researchers; C35 (t) David Scharf/Peter Arnold, Inc.; C35 (b) Bill Ivy/Tony Stone Images; C36 Bill Lea/Dembinsky Photo Associates; C38 (l) Terry Donnelly/Dembinsky Photo Associates; C38 (r) Stephen J. Krasemann/Peter Arnold, Inc.; C38 (c) Steve Solum/Bruce Coleman, Inc.; C39 Tom & Pat Leeson/Photo Researchers; C40 (l) Manfred Kage/Peter Arnold, Inc.; C40 (r) Dr. E. R. Degginger/Color-Pic; C40 (c) Johnny Johnson/Alaska Stock Images; C40 (cr) Norbert Wu/Peter Arnold, Inc.; C42 (t) Kennan Ward Photography; C42 (c) Larry Mishkar/Dembinsky Photo Associates; C42 (bc) Gary Meszaros/Dembinsky Photo Associates; C42 (b) Kennan Ward Photography; C45 (tr) Dwight R. Kuhn; C45 (b) Patrice Ceisel/John G. Shedd Aquarium; C44 Kennan Ward Photography; C45 (tr) Dwight R. Kuhn; C45 (b) Patrice Ceisel/John G. Shedd Aquarium; C46 (c) Dr. E. R. Degginger, FPSA/Color-Pic; C46 (r) Anthony Mercieca/Dembinsky Photo Associates; C47 (l) Walter H. Hodge/Peter Arnold, Inc.; C47 (r) Michael Abbey/Photo Researchers; C48 (t) Beverly Factor/Phototake; C48 (b) Renee Lynn/Photo Researchers; C48 (c) Nigel Dennis/Photo Researchers; C49 (t) Scott Camazine/Photo Researchers; C49 (b) D. Wilder/Tom Stack & Associates; C49 (c) Viviane Moos/The Stock Market; C50–C51 (c) Definitive Stock; C52 Tibor Bognar/The Stock Market; C53 (t), C52 (i) Nigel Cattlin/Holt Studios International/Photo Researchers; C54 (l) Larry Ditto/Photo Researchers; C54 (r) Arizona Game and Fish Department;

C57 Tom & Pat Leeson/Photo Researchers; C58–C59 Darrell Gulin/Tony Stone Images; C59 (t) The Granger Collection, New York; C59 (b) Fred McCormack/Photo Researchers; C60 Norbert Wu/Peter Arnold, Inc.; C64–C65 Marie Tharp/Oceanographic Cartographer; C65 Dr. Ken MacDonald/Science Photo Library/Photo Researchers; C66 Picture Network International; C68 Denise Tackett/Tom Stack & Associates; C69 (tl) Stuart Westmorland/Tony Stone Images; C69 (bl) Ronald Sefton/Bruce Coleman, Inc.; C70 (b) Rondi/Tani Church/Photo Researchers; C70 (r) Andrew G. Wood/Photo Researchers; C70 (l) Alex Rakosy/Dembinsky Photo Associates; C72 (l) M. H. Sharp/Photo Researchers; C72 (c) Robert C. Hermes/Photo Researchers; C74 (t) Herb Segars/Animals Animals; C73 Mike Bacon/Tom Stack & Associates; C74 (bg) Cameron Davidson/Tony Stone Images; C74 (t) John Bova/Photo Researchers; C74 (b) Dr. E. R. Degginger/Photo Researchers; C76 The Granger Collection, New York; C77 Emory Kristof/NGS Image Collection; C78 (l) W. Haxby, Lamont-Doherty Earth Observatory/Science Photo Library/Photo Researchers; C78 (r) US Geological Survey/Gov't; C81 Stuart Westmoreland/Tony Stone Images; C82–C83 John Martin/The Stock Market; C83 (r) TSADO/NOAA/NCDC/Tom Stack & Associates; C84 George Lepp/Tony Stone Images; C90 Craig Tuttle/The Stock Market; C94 Sharon Gerig/Tom Stack & Associates; C95 William Warren/Westlight; C98 Bill Tompkins/Code Red; C100 (l) Bruno P. Zehnder/Peter Arnold,Inc.; C100 (br) NASA/Media Serv. Texas; C100–C101 (bg) T Chinami/The Image Bank; C101(l) Bob Daemmrich/The Image Works; C101(c) Brownie Harris/The Stock Market; C103 (t) Phillip H. Coblentz/Tony Stone Images; C103 (b) C. Aurness/Corbis; C104 (bg), (li), (ri) Warren Faidley/International Stock Photography; C106 NASA/Science Photo Library/Photo Researchers; C112–C113 (b), C112 (tl), (bl) Larry Miller/Science Source/Photo Researchers; C114–C115 G. Jacobs, Stennis Space Center/Geosphere Project/Science Photo Library/Photo Researchers; C115 Howard Bluestein/Photo Researchers; C116 (l) Scott Camazine/Photo Researchers; C116 (r) Massachusetts Institute of Technology; C118 Larry Miller/Photo Researchers; C120 (l) Norbert Wu/The Stock Market; C120 (r) Richard Mariscal/Bruce Coleman, Inc.

Unit D: D1 (c) Earl Young/FPG International; D1 (l) World Perspectives/Tony Stone Images; D2–D3 Simon Fraser/Science Photo Library/Photo Researchers; D3 (r) Barbara Filet/Tony Stone Images; D3 (b) Colin Monteath/Auscape; D4 NASA; D10 (l) United States Department of the Interior/U.S. Geological Survey; D10 Francois Gohier/Photo Researchers; D12 RAPA/Explorer/Photo Researchers; D15 Oddur Sigurdsson/National Energy Authority; D16–D17 (b) Stephen & Donna O'Meara/Photo Researchers; D17 (t) D. Falconer/Bruce Coleman, Inc.; D20 Krafft/Photo Researchers; D23 James Sugar/Black Star; D24 Joseph Sohm/Chromosohm/Photo Researchers; D26 Calvin Larsen/Photo Researchers; D27 (r) Guido-Gozzi/Bruce Coleman, Inc.; D27 (b) Krafft-Explorer/Photo Researchers; D28 Nicholas deVore/Bruce Coleman, Inc.; D30 A.J. Copley/Visuals Unlimited; D31 (r) NASA; D31(b) Marie Tharp/Oceanographic Cartographer; D32 (t) AP Photo/Wide World Photos; D32 (b) Spencer Grant/Photo Researchers; D36–D37 David Madison/Bruce Coleman, Inc.; D37 (t) Willard Clay/Dembinsky Photo Associates; D37 (b) Rafael Macia/Photo Researchers; D38 Erich Lessing/Art Resource, NY; D40 (tl) Biophoto Associates/Photo Researchers; D40 (bl) Sinclair Stammers/Science Photo Library/Photo Researchers; D41 (l) Breck P. Kent/Earth Scenes; D41 (t) Dr. E. R. Degginger/Color-Pic; D42 (t) Breck P. Kent/Earth Scenes; D42 (b) Tom Till Photography; D43 (bl) Dr. E. R. Degginger/Color-Pic; D43 (t), (bc), (br) Breck P. Kent/Earth Scenes; D44–D45 (t) Stephen J. Krasemann/Photo Researchers; D44 (b) Bob Abraham/The Stock Market; D46 David L. Brown/Tom Stack & Associates; D48 Breck P. Kent/Earth Scenes; D49 Andrew J. Martinez/Photo Researchers; D50 (t) Breck P. Kent/Earth Scenes; D50 (bl), (br) Dr. E. R. Degginger/Color-Pic; D51 (t) Gary Moon/Tony Stone Images; D51 (bl) Mark A. Schneider/Dembinsky Photo Associates; D52 Tom Till; D53 Jerry Jacka Photography; D54 Archiv/Photo Researchers; D56 (l), (r) Dr. E. R. Degginger/Color-Pic; D56 (r) Breck P. Kent/Earth Scenes; D59 (t), (c), (b) Breck P. Kent/Earth Scenes; D60–D61 Alan Smith/Tony Stone Images; D60 Dick Keen/Envision; D62 Tom Bean/The Stock Market; D64 (tl), (bl) Alfred Pasieka/Science Photo Library/Photo Researchers; D64 (br) Dr. E. R. Degginger/Color-Pic; D65 (t) Gregory Dimijian/Photo Researchers; D65 (b) Charles Krebs/Tony Stone Images; D65 (br) Dr. E. R. Degginger/Color-Pic; D65 (cr) Ron Sanford/The Stock Market; D68 (l) Corbis; D68 (r) David Parker/Science Photo Library/Photo Researchers; D69 Gary Schultz Photography; D70 (t) Geological Society of America; D70 (b) J. Fennell/Bruce Coleman, Inc.; D73 Sinclair Stammers/Science Photo Library/Photo Researchers; D74–D75 John Thomas/Science Photo Library/Photo Researchers; D75 (r) European Space Agency/Science Photo Library/Photo Researchers; D75 (b) David A. Hardy/Science Photo Library/Photo Researchers; D76 Michael Holford Photographs; D84 NASA; D91 NASA; D92 Reinhard Siegel/Tony Stone Images; D98 (t) U.S. Geological Survey/Science Photo Library/Photo Researchers; D100 Frank Zullo/Photo Researchers; D102 NASA; D103 (tl) Telegraph Colour Library/FPG International; D104, D105 Loch Ness Productions; D106 NASA; D107 (t) Ted Soqui/Sygma Photo News; D107 (b) Arnesfeld Images/The Stock Market; D108 (t) Jonathan Blair/Woodfin Camp & Associates; D108 (b) AURA/STScI/NASA; D112–D113 Allan Morton/Dennis Milon/Science Photo Library/Photo Researchers; D113 (l) Sovfoto/Eastfoto; D113 (r) NASA; D114 J.P. Harrington and K.J. Borkowski (University of Maryland), and NASA; D120 (l) David A. Hardy/Science Photo Library/Photo Researchers; D120 (r) U.S. Naval Observatory/Science Photo Library/Photo Researchers; D121 Hubble Space Telescope; D122 Kirk Borne/STScI/NASA; D123 (t) NASA; D123 (bl) Lynette Cook/Science Photo Library/Photo Researchers; D124 (t) Royal Greenwich Observatory/Science Photo Library/Photo Researchers; D124 (b) Dr. Ian Gatley, National Optical Astronomy Observatories/Science Photo Library/Photo Researchers; D124 (l) Lynette Cook/Science Photo Library/Photo Researchers; D124 (i) Chris Butler/Science Photo Library/Photo Researchers; D125 (t) Julian Baum/Science Photo Library/Photo Researchers; D125 (b) Dr. Rudolph Schild/Science Photo Library/Photo Researchers; D125 (bc) Luke Dodd/Science Photo Library/Photo Researchers; D128 (tc), (ti) Science Photo Library/Photo Researchers; D126–D127 Chris Butler/Science Photo Library/Photo Researchers; D128 David Hardy/Science Photo Library/Photo Researchers; D130 (l) David A. Hardy/Science Photo Library/Photo Researchers; D130 (r+) Scala/Art Resource, NY; D130 (c) Rick Browne/Photo Researchers; D131 (l) Scala/Art Resource, NY; D131 (r) Glen Allison/Tony Stone Images; D131 (c) The Granger Collection, New York; D134 NASA; D135 (t) Sovfoto/Eastfoto; D135 (b) David Ducros/Science Photo Library/Photo Researchers; D136 (t) Doug Johnson/Science Photo Library/Photo Researchers; D136 (bl) NASA; D137 (t) NASA; D137 (r) John Mead/Science Photo Library/Photo Researchers; D138 Jerry Schad/Photo Researchers; D139 Felicia Martinez/PhotoEdit; D140 (t) Harvard College Observatory; D140 (b) UPI/Corbis; D143 Rick Browne/Photo Researchers; D144 (l) World Perspectives/Tony Stone Images; D144 (r) Earl Young/FPG International.

Unit E: E1 (c) Earl Young/FPG International; E1 (l) Steve Barnett/Liaison International; E2–E3 Scala/Art Resource, NY; E2 (i) Dr. Jeremy Burgess/Science Photo Library/Photo Researchers; E3 (i) Zefa Germany/The Stock Market; E4 Manfred Kage/Peter Arnold, Inc.; E6 Chris Cheadle/Tony Stone Images; E8 Chip Clark; E11 Michigan Molecular Institute; E12 Sanjay M. Marathe/Dinodia Picture Agency; E14 Dr. E. R. Degginger/Color-Pic; E15 (tl), (br) Richard Megna/Fundamental Photographs; E15 (tr) Dr. E. R. Degginger/Color-Pic; E18 (t), (b) Richard Megna/Fundamental Photographs; E19 Bancroft Library; E20 Frank Grant/International Stock Photography; E22 Prof. K. Seddon & Dr. T. Evans, Queen's University Belfast/Science Photo Library/Photo Researchers; E23 (l) Simon Fraser/Science Photo Library/Photo Researchers; E23 (r) Tom Pantages/Phototake; E24 (t) Chip Clark; E25 Charles D. Winters/Photo Researchers; E26–E27 Jan-Peter Lahall/Peter Arnold, Inc.; E28 Eric Ander/Pacific Stock; E30 (tl) Dr. E. R. Degginger/Color-Pic; E30 (tr) Dr. E. R. Degginger/Bruce Coleman, Inc.; E30 (b) George Haling Prod./Photo Researchers; E31 (l) Charles D. Winters/Photo Researchers; E32 Richard Megna/Fundamental Photographs; E33 Phil Degginger/Color-Pic; E34 (t) Christie's Images; E34 (ci) Joseph Nettis/Photo Researchers; E36 (l) Brownie Harris/The Stock Market; E37 CERN/Science Photo Library/Photo Researchers; E38 Corbis; E42–E43 (bg) Kaj R. Svensson/Science Photo Library/Photo Researchers; E43 (l) De Beers/E.T. Archive; E43 (tr) Charles D. Winters/Photo Researchers; E44 Chip Clark; E46 Spencer Grant/PhotoEdit; E46 (tr) Yoav Levy/Phototake; E46 (br) Paul Silverman/Fundamental Photographs; E47 (c) Bob Daemmrich Photography, Inc.; E47 Bob Daemmrich Photography, Inc.; E48 (b) Bob Daemmrich Photography, Inc.; E50 Don & Pat Valenti/Tony Stone Images; E52–E53 (c) Charles D. Winters/Photo Researchers; E52 (b) John Shaw/Tom Stack & Associates; E53 (bl) Charles D. Winters/Photo Researchers; E53 (br) Dr. E. R. Degginger/Color-Pic; E54 (t) Kip Peticolas/Fundamental Photographs; E54 (b) Dr. E. R. Degginger/Color-Pic; E55 (tl) Wetmore/Photo Researchers; E55 (tc) Chip Clark; E55 (tr) Richard Megna/Fundamental Photographs; E55 (bl) Kip Peticolas/Fundamental Photographs; E55 (br) Kennon Cooke/Valan Photos; E55 (i) P. A. Wilkinson/Valan Photos; E58 Chip Clark; E59 (t) Tony Freeman/Photo Researchers; E61 (b) David R. Frazier; E61 (l), E62 (t) Chip Clark; E63 (t) Christie's Images; E63 (tr) John Elk, III/Bruce Coleman, Inc.; E64 (r) World Perspectives/Tony Stone Images; E64 (c) Jeffrey L. Rotman/Peter Arnold, Inc.; E64–E65 (t) Galen Rowell/Peter Arnold, Inc.; E66–E67, E66 (c) Webb Chappell; E67 (r) Michael Newman/PhotoEdit; E68 (t) Ernest O. Lawrence Berkeley National Laboratory; E68 (b) David Parker/Science Photo Library/Photo Researchers; E72–E73 National Maritime Museum Picture Library; E74 Mark Wexler/Chihuly, Inc.; E77 (r) The Stock Market; E77 (b) Kim Taylor/Bruce Coleman, Inc.; E78 Art Wolfe/Tony Stone Images; E82 Hans Reinhard/Bruce Coleman, Inc.; E85 (t) Jon Feingersh/The Stock Market; E85 (bl), (br) Richard Megna/Fundamental Photographs; E87 (b) Richard Megna/Fundamental Photographs; E90 Patrick Robert/Sygma Photo News; E93 David Stoecklein/The Stock Market; E94 Michael Freeman/Bruce Coleman, Inc.; E94 (bc) T. Young-Wolff/PhotoEdit; E94 (br) Myrleen Ferguson/PhotoEdit; E95 U.S. Dept. of Energy/Photo Researchers; E96 (tl), (bl) Y. Arthus-Bertrand/Peter Arnold, Inc.; E96 (tr) Catherine Pouedras/Science Photo Library/Photo Researchers; E96–E97 Earl Roberge/Photo Researchers; E98 The Heater Meals Company, Cincinnati, Ohio; E99 Larry Lawfer/The Picture Cube; E100 (t) Corbis; E100 (b) UPI/Corbis; E104–E105 Charles Doswell, III/Tony Stone Images; E105 (t) A. Sahy/OSF/Animals Animals; E105 (b) Chris Cheadle/Tony Stone Images; E106 Darodems/Pacific Stock; E109 Art Resource, NY; E110 (tl), (br) Dr. E. R. Degginger/Color-Pic; E112 (t) Billy E. Barnes/PhotoEdit; E112 (b) Martin Bond/Science Photo Library/Photo Researchers; E113 Gerald French/FPG International; E114 Randy Duchaine/The Stock Market; E117 (t) Gerard Lacz/Peter Arnold, Inc.; E117 (tc) University of Florida, College of Veterinary Medicine; E117 (bc) AGE/Peter Arnold, Inc.; E118 (l) Debra Hershkowitz/Bruce Coleman, Inc.; E118 David Young-Wolff/PhotoEdit; E119 (t) Gary Randall/FPG International; E119 (b) Ron Kimball Photography; E120–E121 ZEFA, UK/The Stock Market; E122 Geo. Brown, James D. Watt/Innerspace Visions; E125 (t) NASA/Science Source/Photo Researchers; E126 (l) Andrew Brookes/Tony Stone Images; E126 (r) Gary Benson/Tony Stone Images; E127 (b) Leo De Wys, Inc./De Wys/D & J Heaton; E128 (t) Matt Meadows/Peter Arnold, Inc.; E128 (r) Mark E. Gibson; E128 (br) Alan & Linda Detrick/Photo Researchers; E130 Scott Camazine/Photo Researchers; E131 Mark Sherman/Bruce Coleman, Inc.; E132 (t) Will Wittkop; E132 (b) Chuck Savage/The Stock Market; E126 (l) Steve Barnett/Liaison International; E136 (i) Jook Leung/FPG International.

Unit F: F1 (c) Spencer Jones/FPG International; F2–F3 (l) Robert Mathena/Liaison International; F3 (r) Fred Bavendam/Peter Arnold, Inc.; F3 (b) Ken Levine/Allsport Photography USA, Inc.; F4 (b), F7 (tc) Dan Feicht/Cedar Point; F7 (bl), (br) Lee Rentz/Bruce Coleman, Inc.; F10 (b) NASA/Science Source/Photo Researchers; F12 NASA/Science Photo Library/Photo Researchers; F16 Yva Momatiuk/Photo Researchers; F17 Henley and Savage/Tony Stone Images; F18 (b) D.B. Friedrichs; F18 (t) Superstock; F19 (all) Tony Freeman/PhotoEdit; F22 Index Stock Photography; F24 (tl), (tr) Jim Zipp/Photo Researchers; F24 (bl) Paul J. Sutton/Duomo Photography; F24 (br) Duomo Photography; F25 Jan Robert Factor/Photo Researchers; F27 Geoffrey Clifford/The Stock Market; F28 (bl), (bg) Scott Warren; F30 (b) Bill Horsman/Stock, Boston; F37 UPI/Corbis; F35 Al Bello/Allsport Photography USA, Inc.; F36–F37 Phillip H. Coblentz/Tony Stone Images; F37 (l) "Self-Operating Napkin" by Rube Goldberg, © Rube Goldberg, Inc. Distributed by United Media; F38 Del Mulkey/Photo Researchers; F40, F41 (c) David Madison/Bruce Coleman, Inc.; F46 (tl) D. Logan/H. Armstrong Roberts, Inc.; F48 Gnu Images/The Stock Market; F50 (b) Jim Zuckerman/Corbis; F56 Dr. E. R. Degginger; F59 (cl) Tony Freeman/PhotoEdit; F62 (l) Michael A. Keller/The Stock Market; F63 (tl) Franz Pflugl/Tony Stone Images; F63 (b) Dan McCoy/Rainbow; F64 (br) Mark E. Gibson; F66 (c) Werner Forman Archive, Museum fur Volkerkunde, Berlin/Art Resource, NY; F67 C. Falco/Photo Researchers; F68 (t) Corbis; F68 (b) James King-Holmes/Science Photo Library/Photo Researchers; F71 (b) Mark E. Gibson; F72 (l) Phototote CD #50, Letraset USA; F72 (r) Spencer Jones/FPG International.

Health Handbook: R19 Robert E. Daemmrich/Tony Stone Images; R23 Tony Freeman/PhotoEdit.

All other photographs by Harcourt photographers listed below, © Harcourt: Weronica Ankarorn, Bartlett Digital Photography, Victoria Bowen, Eric Camden, Digital Imaging Group, Charles Hodges, Ken Karp, Ken Kinzie, Ed McDonald, Sheri O'Neal, Terry Sinclair, Annette Stahl.

ART CREDITS: Tim Alt D88, E6–7, E8, E9, E10, E14, E24, E40, E52, E79, E84, E95, E124–125; Mike Atkinson A54, A55, B70, B80, B82–83, B87, B120, B108, C16, C17, C18, C40–41, C46–47; Andrew Becket B88–89, B109, B114, B119; Paul Breeden B15; Richard Courtney B6–7, B8–9, C49; Mike Dammer A35, A61, B61, B97, C35, C55, C117, D33, D109, D141, E69, E133, F33; John Dawson B105; Eldon Doty A35, B21, B37, C79, C103, D71, L39, E9, E10, E10; Roy Flookes C66, C87, C59, C94, C95, C96–97, D41, E109, F7; Pat Foss E101, F33, F69; Dale Gustafson E86, E92–93; Nick Hall C14–15, C62–63, C64, C65, D14, D15, D16, D17, D22–23, D25, D26–27, D28, D34, E8, F9; Robert Hynes C8–9, C33, C65, C72, C73; Inklink D48, D49, D57, D78, D79, D82, D90, D103, D118–119, F51, F54–55; Olena Kassian B117; Roger Kent B34; George Ladas D23, D142, D133, E88, E103, F17, F53; Katie Lee B46–47, B52, B53; James Marffy C88, C108–109, C110–111, D6–7, D94, D118, D19, D35, D58–59, D86, D89 D94–95, D96–97; Lee-andman A52; David More A25, A26, A29; John Newman B76, B79, B86, C71, E108, E110–111; Rosie Sanders A27; Mike Saunders D80–81, D87; Bill Schmidt E77, F62; Andrew Shiff A61, B21, B61, B125, C55, C79, C117, D71, D109, D141, E39, E101, E133, F69; Wendy Smith-Griswold B28–29, B37; Tim Spransy D116, E116–117, F10; Catherine Twomey A8, A9, A10, A15, A16, A17, A30; Martin Walz D8–9, D14; Steve Weston D117, D142.